D1483162

Davis Memorial Library
Methodist College
Presented by
Fleeta Harris Gibson
Library Fund

SSSP

Springer Series in Social Psychology

Advisory Editor: Robert F. Kidd

Springer Series in Social Psychology

Advisory Editor: Robert F. Kidd

Attention and Self-Regulation:
A Control-Theory Approach to Human Behavior
Charles S. Carver/Michael F. Scheier

Gender and Nonverbal Behavior
Clara Mayo/Nancy M. Henley (Editors)

Personality, Roles, and Social Behavior
William Ickes/Eric S. Knowles (Editors)

Toward Transformation in Social Knowledge
Kenneth J. Gergen

The Ethics of Social Research:
Surveys and Experiments
Joan E. Sieber (Editor)

The Ethics of Social Research:
Fieldwork, Regulation, and Publication
Joan E. Sieber (Editor)

SSSP

Personality, Roles, and Social Behavior

Edited by
William Ickes
and
Eric S. Knowles

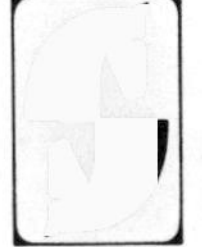

Springer-Verlag New York Heidelberg Berlin

William Ickes
Department of Psychology
University of Missouri—St. Louis
St. Louis, Missouri 63121 U.S.A.

Eric S. Knowles
Psychology and Human Development
University of Wisconsin—Green Bay
Green Bay, Wisconsin 54302 U.S.A.

Robert F. Kidd, *Advisory Editor*
Department of Psychology
Boston University
Boston, Massachusetts 02215 U.S.A.

Library of Congress Cataloging in Publication Data
Main entry under title:
Personality, roles, and social behavior.
(Springer series in social psychology)
Bibliography: p.
Includes indexes.
Contents: From individuals to group members: a dialectic for the social sciences / Eric S. Knowles —The origin and maintenance of social roles : the case of sex roles / Paul F. Secord—Roles and interaction competencies / Michael Athay and John Darley — [etc.]
1. Social psychology—Addresses, essays, lectures. 2. Social role—Addresses, essays, lectures. 3. Social interaction—Addresses, essays, lectures.
I. Ickes, William John. 1947- . II. Knowles, Eric S. III. Title. IV. Series.
HM251.P4256 302 81-18238
AACR2

Printed in the United States of America.

9 8 7 6 5 4 3 2 1

ISBN 0-387-90637-1 Springer-Verlag New York Heidelberg Berlin
ISBN 3-540-90637-1 Springer-Verlag Berlin Heidelberg New York

Foreword

Personality and Roles: Sources of Regularities in Social Behavior

For behavioral scientists, whether they identify primarily with the science of psychology or with that of sociology, there may be no challenge greater than that of discovering regularities and consistencies in social behavior. After all, it is such regularities and consistencies that lend predictability to the behavior of individuals in social contexts—in particular, to those events that constitute dyadic interactions and group processes. In the search for behavioral consistencies, two theoretical constructs have emerged as guiding principles: personality and roles.

The theoretical construct of personality seeks to understand regularities and consistencies in social behavior in terms of relatively stable traits, enduring dispositions, and other propensities (for example, needs, motives, and attitudes) that are thought to reside within individuals. Because it focuses primarily on the features of individuals, the construct of personality is fundamentally psychological in nature. By contrast, the theoretical construct of roles seeks to understand regularities and consistencies in social behavior in terms of the directive influence of coherent sets of rules and prescriptions that are provided by the interpersonal, occupational, and societal categories of which individuals are continuing members. Because it focuses primarily on features of social structures, the construct of roles is fundamentally sociological in nature.

The fact of their differing disciplinary origins provides some sense as to why psychologists more so than sociologists seem to be relatively familiar with the concept of personality, and why sociologists more so than psychologists seem to be relatively conversant with the notion of roles. But, although the differing intellectual parentages of personality and roles may constitute an explanation for the disciplinary isolation of scholars working within the traditions associated with each construct, it hardly constitutes a justification for continuing that state of affairs. Prompted by their concerns about the solitudes within which psychologists and sociologists have worked, William Ickes and Eric Knowles have invited psychologists and sociologists to contribute chapters to this volume.

A dialogue between psychologists and sociologists is the goal of the editors, who seek "to focus [their edited volume] explicitly on conceptual issues and research at the interface of a sociological and a psychological understanding of social behavior" (Preface, p. viii). Clearly, any dialogue between psychologists and sociologists about the relations among personality, roles, and social behavior is of considerable intrinsic worth. There are few, if any, among us who do not value (or, at least, profess to value) interdisciplinary communication and the cross-fertilization of theoretical perspectives and methodological orientations that it is thought to generate. However, as satisfying as the activities of that dialogue may prove to be in and of themselves, there may be benefits for the social sciences over and above the immediate satisfactions of those individuals engaged in this dialogue. Why? Because a concerted and a continuing effort by psychologists and sociologists to understand the mutual interplay of individuals and social structures has the potential to generate a hybrid social science. That hybrid of psychology and sociology may be uniquely suited to answering the question, posed originally in 1852 by the philosopher Comte (who often has been credited with providing the impetus for the creation of the social sciences): How can the individual be both the cause and the consequence of society?

If answers to this momentous question are, at long last, forthcoming, some measure of credit will be due to the editors of and the contributors to *Personality, Roles, and Social Behavior*. To a one, they have chosen to direct their efforts to concerns that appear to be central to a creative synthesis of the theoretical perspectives and the methodological orientations of psychology and sociology. And, to a one, they have provided meaningful and provocative analyses of their chosen subject matters. It very well may be that this collection of essays may tempt many psychologists and sociologists to emerge from their solitudes and join forces in the quest to understand the interplay of the individual and society.

Minneapolis, Minnesota — Mark Snyder

Preface

Since the 1930s, social psychology has been two fields: one sociological and the other psychological. The sociological tradition stems from Mead's and Cooley's emphases on self, roles, and symbolic interaction. In this tradition, social behavior is understood in terms of its meaning for the person and for the interactions in which he or she is engaged. The psychological tradition reflects the dual emphases of the brothers Allport: Floyd Allport's focus on the behavioral and attitudinal consequences of social participation, and Gordon Allport's focus on personal traits and dispositions. In this tradition, social behavior is understood as a consequence of personality and social situational determinants.

During the past 50 years, the division between these two traditions has grown too wide, to the point that it is unsettling, artificial, and unproductive. Many sociologists and personality/social psychologists are still interested in the same social psychological phenomena; however, their adherence to the conventions of their respective disciplines has made it increasingly difficult for them to talk to each other and share their insights about these common interests. Theories in the two disciplines employ different sets of constructs (and often different levels of analysis) in conceptualizing the same phenomena. Methods reveal a similar divergence, with most sociologists as firmly committed to working in the field as most psychologists are to working in the lab. And, beyond the more obvious differences in theory and method, more subtle differences in how sociologists and personality/social psychologists are trained to perceive, structure, and organize social behavior are reflected by rather striking differences in the content, style, and format of the articles written for the major journals in the two disciplines. These differences impede progress in both disciplines to the extent that each discipline is less able to learn and profit from the other.

Fortunately, however, within each tradition there are scholars who have minimized the effects of this division in their training, theoretical orientation, and research. Indeed, researchers in both fields of social psychology have increasingly formulated problems in a way that reflects a synthesis of personality, role, and situational approaches to social behavior. It is therefore somewhat disappointing to find that although many teachers and researchers are aware of and sympathetic with this emerging synthesis, few scholarly books or texts currently reflect this trend.

The present volume is intended to focus explicitly on conceptual issues and research at the interface of a sociological and a psychological understanding of social behavior. Its general purpose is to provide a forum for the views of several theorists and researchers in sociology and psychology who have actively worked at this interface in the attempt to develop more integrated approaches to the study of certain social psychological phenomena. In each of the chapters in this volume, a particular issue or area of social psychology is discussed in terms of a theoretical perspective which considers the combined influences of personality, social roles, and situational factors. The relative attention given to these three types of factors varies from chapter to chapter, however, according to the authors' interests and theoretical orientations.

We have chosen the format of an edited volume of original chapters by several different authors because we feel that it is the most realistic way of presenting the current interface between sociological and psychological approaches to social behavior. It is most realistic, we think, for at least three reasons. First, because the interface is still emerging, a consensus has not yet developed that could be summarized by a single author (or pair of authors). For this reason, it seems most reasonable to present to the reader the range of different perspectives that currently have emerged. Second, because the contributors to the present volume are among the major proponents of the synthesis of personality, role, and situational approaches to the study of social behavior, it seems desirable at this preconsensual stage to let these scholars individually present their own views, approaches, and insights. This is the best and most direct way to ensure that the positions espoused by these individuals are accurately represented. Third, by allowing the contributors to choose their own "points of application" for an integrated approach to social behavior, it becomes feasible for us to include a wide range of issues and phenomena within a single volume. We believe that consideration of these various issues and phenomena will foster an appreciation of the scope and complexity of social behavior as well as growth in the understanding and use of an integrated approach to its study.

In organizing the volume, we have attempted to order the chapters in a way that would preserve and emphasize certain continuities in theme while making salient any major differences in theory, method, phenomena of interest, and level of analysis. Accordingly, the thematic progression across the set of chapters is from general to specific, from abstract theory to concrete methods and data.

Within this progression, meaningful subgroupings are reflected. The first three chapters, for example, all address social behavior in a very general and abstract way. In the first chapter, Knowles introduces the concepts of personality and social roles and provides a historical perspective on the application of these concepts in sociology and psychology. Treating individual and group levels of analysis as dialectical elements in the social sciences, Knowles examines how the tension between these elements has influenced theoretical development and debate in the study of roles, personality, and small groups. The theoretical status of the role concept is further developed in Chapters 2 and 3. Using the case of sex roles as a specific example, Secord (Chapter 2) attempts to account for the origin and maintenance of social roles. The goal of his paper is to explain why particular role forms emerge and are maintained at the expense of others, and why, when changes in norms occur, they take the forms that they do. Athay and Darley (Chapter 3) argue strongly for a reconceptualization of the role concept "which allows for the limiting function of structural frameworks but still does not turn the actor into the automaton traditional sociologists often are accused of making him." Athay and Darley suggest that social interaction should be viewed as a process of commodity exchange in which the influences of roles and personality dispositions on social behavior are mediated by specific interpersonal skills that they call "interaction competencies."

The generality and high level of abstraction in the first three chapters are further evidenced by their internal shifts in level of analysis; in each of them, behavior is examined on at least two levels (individual, dyad, larger group, or society). In contrast, Chapters 4 and 5 are concerned almost exclusively with the dyad, focusing on individuals only to illustrate their independent contributions to the interdependent processes that characterize their interaction. Davis (Chapter 4) presents a theoretical analysis of responsiveness in dyadic interaction. Her formulation gives special emphasis to the personality, role, and situational factors that determine the quantity and quality of responsiveness which dyad members display. A complementary perspective on dyadic interaction is offered in Patterson's functional analysis of nonverbal involvement (Chapter 5). Whereas Davis's model gives primary emphasis to conversation within the dyad, Patterson's model concerns the various nonverbal behaviors by which dyad members reveal their level and mode of involvement with each other. After delineating the various functions that nonverbal behavior can serve, Patterson goes on to show how certain personality factors can be used to predict the type of involvement functions individuals are most likely to express in their nonverbal behavior.

Wegner and Giuliano's chapter (Chapter 6) must be regarded as somewhat unique in this collection. Although it resembles the other chapters in presenting a theoretical perspective that incorporates personality, role, and situational variables, it differs from the other chapters in its style (alternately serious and tongue-in-cheek), in its emphasis on social perception (as opposed to *self*-perception or to overt behavior), and in its level of analysis (it explicitly incorporates all levels). In the course of explaining how social behaviors may be partially determined by the perspectives from which social situations are viewed, Wegner and Giuliano neatly integrate the symbolic interactionist perspective of sociology with various psychological theories of social cognition.

Despite its discontinuities with the preceding chapters, Wegner and Giuliano's chapter provides a good introduction to the themes explored in subsequent ones. In particular, it sets the stage for Stryker and Serpe's discussion of identity theory, an outgrowth of symbolic interactionism (Chapter 7). With remarkable economy, Stryker and Serpe sketch the historical development of symbolic interactionism and identity theory, and then demonstrate the theory's predictive utility with an empirical research example. Their interest in the processes by which the self-concept both shapes and is shaped by the individual's interaction with others is also shared by the authors of Chapters 8 and 9. In Chapter 8, Lofland uses anecdotal, case history, and literary examples to compile a list of the different types of social ties that bind the individual to others and help define his or her unique identity. The severing of these social ties (through death, divorce, etc.) and the consequent changes in the individual's identity that result from such losses are the central concerns of Lofland's insightful analysis. The same concerns are apparent in Chapter 9, in which Chad and Paddy Gordon examine the changes in roles, goals, and self-conceptions that occur in women who have become "displaced homemakers" through the loss of their spouses. To substantiate the changes hypothesized to occur as these women acquire a new role as wage earner, the Gordons present evaluation data from an intervention program they designed to help displaced homemakers prepare for employment.

The theme of social relevance that emerges in the Gordons' chapter is also apparent in McCall's discussion of discretionary justice (Chapter 10). Both papers rely heavily on data collected in "real-world" field settings, but McCall's paper is somewhat more integrative in its attempt to determine the relative influences of personality, role, and situational variables on discretionary decision making in the criminal justice system. McCall proposes a framework for understanding discretionary justice, reviews the research that has related personality, role, and situational variables to judicial decision making, and discusses the methodological difficulties of separating these influences in field-observational research. His suggestion that laboratory studies of interpersonal processes may be particularly useful "in beginning to sort out the influences of role, personality, and situation" introduces the theme of the final chapter by Ickes (Chapter 11). Ickes gives an account of the conception, "birth," and subsequent development of an original research paradigm that combines many of the best features of laboratory and field-observational research. After reviewing the various types of studies in which the paradigm has already been applied, he discusses its potential as a basic paradigm for the study of personality, roles, and social behavior.

In any collection of papers having the range and diversity suggested by this overview, there will be corresponding diversity in style, readability, and theoretical depth. Although this diversity is often characterized as "unevenness" and regarded as a fault, we believe that there is often considerable virtue in allowing respected scholars to tell their own story in their own way. Accordingly, we have allowed our contributors a fairly wide latitude of self-expression within the rather loose constraints of a professional-level, interdisciplinary text. We hope that the result of this editorial policy is a set of clear and distinguishable voices rather than a single more "even" monotone.

We are grateful to have worked with a group of contributors who were not only willing to write for an interdisciplinary audience but were also enthusiastic about doing so. We also wish to thank Robert Kidd for convincing us that Springer-Verlag should publish the volume, and the staff of Springer-Verlag for providing the exemplary editorial and production assistance that we had been led to expect. We especially thank Connie Rentmaster for her careful proofreading and indexing.

Finally, we would like to express our appreciation to the National Science Foundation for grants (BNS 79-21443 to William Ickes and BNS 80-16202 to Eric Knowles) which facilitated the preparation of *Personality, Roles, and Social Behavior*.

William Ickes
St. Louis, Missouri

Eric S. Knowles
Green Bay, Wisconsin

Contents

Foreword v
Mark Snyder

Preface vii

1. **From Individuals to Group Members: A Dialectic for the Social Sciences** **1**
Eric S. Knowles

Gemeinschaft and Gesellschaft 1
Dialectical Trends in Role Theory 6
Dialectical Trends in Personality 10
Dialectical Trends in Group Theory 15
Conclusions 25

2. **The Origin and Maintenance of Social Roles: The Case of Sex Roles** **33**
Paul F. Secord

Social Structures and Intentional Action 33
The Case of Sex Roles 37
Conclusions 51

3. **Social Roles as Interaction Competencies** **55**
Michael Athay and John Darley

Social Action as a Process of Commodity Exchange 57
Structural Frames as Conditions of the Possibility of Face-To-Face Interaction 64
Social Roles as Sets of Interaction Competencies 77

4. **Determinants of Responsiveness in Dyadic Interaction** **85**
Deborah Davis

The Nature of Responsiveness 86
Consequences of Responsiveness 86
Personality and Situational Determinants of the Reactions to Unresponsiveness 90
Determinants of Responsiveness 91
Attention 92
Communication Accuracy 101
Response Repertoire 115
Motivation 117
Conclusions 124

5. **Personality and Nonverbal Involvement: A Functional Analysis** **141**
Miles L. Patterson

Functions of Nonverbal Behavior 144
Nonverbal Involvement and Functional Classification 150
Personality Correlates of Nonverbal Involvement 151
Functional Analysis of Normal Personality Differences 157
Summary 159

6. **The Forms of Social Awareness** **165**
Daniel M. Wegner and Toni Giuliano

Awareness of the Social World 165
The Representation of Persons in Thought 172
The Instigation of Awareness Forms 178
The Social Consequences of Awareness Forms 187
Conclusion 193

7. **Commitment, Identity Salience, and Role Behavior: Theory and Research Example** **199**
Sheldon Stryker and Richard T. Serpe

Symbolic Interaction and Identity Theory 199
Conclusion 216

8. **Loss and Human Connection: An Exploration into the Nature of the Social Bond** **219**
Lyn H. Lofland

Attachment, Grief, and Loss 219
Threads of Human Connectedness 222
Patterns of Connectedness and Directions for Research 231

9. **Changing Roles, Goals, and Self-Conceptions: Process and Results in a Program for Women's Employment** **243**
Chad Gordon and Paddy Gordon

Nature and Scope of the Problem 243
Nature of the Career Options Program at Houston Community College 247
Characteristics of the Program Participants 250
Results: Changes in Self-Conceptions and Development of Occupational Plans During the Program 257
Antecedents of Change in the Self-Conception Dimensions 272
Summary, Conclusions, and Implications 273

10. **Discretionary Justice: Influences of Social Role, Personality, and Social Situation** **285**
George J. McCall

The Phenomenon of Discretionary Justice 285
A Framework for Understanding Discretionary Justice 286
Research Paradigms for Explaining Discretionary Justice 291
Studies of Discretionary Justice 293
Concluding Thoughts on Analyzing Discretionary Justice 298

11. **A Basic Paradigm for the Study of Personality, Roles, and Social Behavior** **305**
William Ickes

Birth of a Paradigm 305
Description of the Paradigm 313
Specific Applications 319
A Preliminary Evaluation 328
Additional Applications and Extensions 335

Author Index 343

Subject Index 355

Contributors

Michael Athay, 109 East Broadway, Port Jefferson, New York 11777, U.S.A.

John Darley, Department of Psychology, Princeton University, Princeton, New Jersey 08540, U.S.A.

Deborah Davis, Department of Psychology, University of Nevada—Reno, Reno, Nevada 89557, U.S.A.

Chad Gordon, Department of Sociology, Rice University, Houston, Texas 77001, U.S.A.

Paddy Gordon, Women's Advocate, Houston Community College System, Houston, Texas 77001, U.S.A.

Toni Giuliano, Department of Psychology, University of Texas at Austin, Austin, Texas 78712, U.S.A.

William Ickes, Department of Psychology, University of Missouri—St. Louis, St. Louis, Missouri 63121, U.S.A.

Eric S. Knowles, Department of Psychology and Human Development, University of Wisconsin—Green Bay, Green Bay, Wisconsin 54302, U.S.A.

Lyn H. Lofland, Department of Sociology, University of California—Davis, Davis, California 95616, U.S.A.

George J. McCall, Department of Sociology, University of Missouri—St. Louis, St. Louis, Missouri 63121, U.S.A.

Miles L. Patterson, Department of Psychology, University of Missouri—St. Louis, St. Louis, Missouri 63121, U.S.A.

Paul F. Secord, College of Education, University of Houston, Houston, Texas 77004, U.S.A.

Richard T. Serpe, Training Program in Social Psychology, Indiana University, Bloomington, Indiana 47405, U.S.A.

Sheldon Stryker, Department of Sociology, Indiana University, Bloomington, Indiana 47405, U.S.A.

Daniel M. Wegner, Department of Psychology, Trinity University, San Antonio, Texas 78284, U.S.A.

Chapter 1

From Individuals to Group Members: A Dialectic for the Social Sciences

Eric S. Knowles

In 1887, Ferdinand Tönnies (1887/1957) published *Gemeinschaft und Gesellschaft.* This work, one of the earliest and simplest typologies of social organization, set forth a dichotomy that, if not archetypal to Western postindustrial society, certainly has become an underlying dialectic for modern social science. Tönnies conceptualized *Gemeinschaft* (translated as "Community") as a form of social organization that assumed unity; it exists when people act because they are members of a social entity, a group, a community. *Gesellschaft* (translated as "Society"), on the other hand, assumed separateness; it exists when people act because they see themselves as separate and individual actors in society. The theory of *Gemeinschaft* and *Gesellschaft* was, essentially, a description of how the assumptions of unity or individuality influence social thought, will, and action.

The dialectic between individuality and unity has had a strong influence that is still being played out in present-day social science. Both past and current developments in the social psychology of roles, personality, and social behavior participate in the tension between Gemeinschaft and Gesellschaft. This chapter examines the current status of individuality and unity, first by reviewing Tönnies' dichotomy and exposing its dialectic properties. Then, role, personality, and group theory are reviewed historically as expressions of a tension between these two perspectives. This chapter assumes that a synthesis is both desired and possible, one that simultaneously encompasses both individuality and unity. The remaining chapters in this volume point to various aspects of this dialectical process and to the issues that must be addressed in achieving a synthesis.

Gemeinschaft and Gesellschaft

How do aggregates of human beings think about and interact with each other? How do we as social scientists come to understand and analyze the forms of social organization and the forces in social interaction? Tönnies answered these questions by conceptualizing two idealized and contrasting types of social organization. Relationships, or associations as he called them, can be conceived either as organic entities whose members exist, think, and act only as elements of the whole, or as interactions between two separate, self-interested individuals who come together only to negotiate an exchange of goods or services.

> The theory of the Gesellschaft deals with the artificial construction of an aggregate of human beings which superficially resembles the Gemeinschaft insofar as the individuals live and dwell together peacefully. However, in the Gemeinschaft they remain essentially united in spite of all separating factors, whereas in the Gesellschaft they are essentially separated in spite of all uniting factors. In the Gesellschaft, as contrasted with the Gemeinschaft, we find no actions that can be derived from an a priori and necessarily existing unity; no actions, therefore, which manifest the will and the spirit of the unity even if performed by the individual; no actions which, insofar as they are performed by the individual, take place on behalf of those united with him. In the Gesellschaft such actions do not exist. On the contrary, here everybody is by himself and isolated, and there exists a condition of tension against all others. Their spheres of activity and power are sharply separated, so that everybody refuses to everyone else contact and admittance to his sphere; i.e., intrusions are regarded as hostile acts. Such a negative attitude toward one another becomes the normal and always underlying relation of these power-endowed individuals and it characterizes the Gesellschaft in the condition of rest; nobody wants to grant and produce anything for another individual, nor will he be inclined to give ungrudgingly to another individual, if it be not in exchange for a gift or labor equivalent that he considers at least equal to what he has given. (pp. 64-65)

Although, at its base, the distinction between Gemeinschaft and Gesellschaft rests with the assumption by the participants and by the social scientist analyzing them of the essential unity of the whole or the essential separateness of the parts, Tönnies goes on to spell out how this assumption is reflected in the thoughts, action, and modes of interaction between people.

The epitome of organic unity is the family. "The house constitutes the realm and, as it were, the body of kinship. Here people live together under one protecting roof. Here they share their possessions and their pleasures; they feed from the same supply, they sit at the same table . . . common fear and common honor ensure peaceful living and cooperation with greater certainty" (pp. 42-43). But the same elements of unity can be seen in associations created by location–neighborhoods or communities–and in associations created by likeness of interest or attitude–friendship. In each case the salient elements are the group and the group goals. Property is common property resulting from group effort and used by the group. Language, rules of conduct, and motives for action arise out of and preserve the social unit. For the individual members, these ties seem natural and are not open to question.

Gemeinschaft relations are not necessarily egalitarian; authority and power may be vested in some individuals more than others. The authority of the father, prince, lord, or master, however, are legitimized by the community and involve obligations of duty as well as rights of power. "In this way, through increased and diminished duties and rights, real inequalities exist and develop within the Gemeinschaft. . . .

These inequalities can be increased only to a certain limit, however, because beyond this limit the essence of the Gemeinschaft as the unity of unequal beings would be dissolved" (p. 46). "The relationship between community and feudal lords, and more especially between the community and its members, is based not on contracts, but upon understanding, like that within the family" (p. 59).

The epitome of individual separateness is the marketplace where each person comes as a separate actor to negotiate with other actors. Tönnies made the point that not only are individuals seen as identifiable and separate entities, but so are goods. Goods, services, and labor are owned and used for individual ends. In Gesellschaft, ownership is part and parcel of the separateness of individuals; "What somebody has and enjoys, he has and enjoys to the exclusion of all others" (p. 65). In the marketplace, associations are formed for the purpose of transaction, to exchange what one has for what one does not have. This exchange requires that each individual be able to identify and assign worth or value to the goods and services.

In Gesellschaft, then, interaction is seen as a negotiation and commodity exchange process. "Life is conceived and conducted as a business, that is, with the definite end or view of attaining an imaginary happiness as its ultimate purpose" (p. 144). From this view, the guiding principle of interaction is to achieve "the greatest amount of pleasure or happiness with the least amount of pain, effort, or trouble, the smallest sacrifice of goods or energy" (p. 144). Individual actors, each with hedonistic goals, come together only when each party has something to offer the other and a desire for something the other has to offer. "By means of an exchange each individual disposes of value not useful to him in order to acquire an equal value that he can use" (p. 69). "The concord of will at each exchange, inasmuch as the exchange is regarded as taking place in Gesellschaft, we call a contract. The contract is the resultant of two divergent individual wills, intersecting on one point" (p. 71).

Contracts, either social or written, become the basis of interaction. But contracts do not involve the whole individual, only those parts of the individual or possessions defined by the goods or services outlined in the contract. One individual can enter into many contracts, each covering a different sphere of activity or possession. Contracts do not even require a real individual; they can be created by corporations, associations, or other "artificial" individuals. "Gesellschaft . . . is to be understood as a multitude of natural and artificial individuals, the wills, and spheres of whom are in many relations with and to one another, and remain nevertheless independent of one another and devoid of mutual familiar relationships" (p. 76).

As Tönnies described them, Gemeinschaft and Gesellschaft were "ideal" types in the sense that they were artificial constructions that denoted opposite sets of assumptions and could be used by a social scientist to understand particular instances of interaction. Although these two forms of interaction could be defined in their "pure" form, the social phenomena to which they are applied would contain elements of each type, though often much more of one than the other. Tönnies, in his many examples, illustrated how this dichotomy would apply to various statuses and status differences. The differences between women and men, youth and old age, common people and the educated classes, rural life and city life, the family and the marketplace can be understood, in part, because the former operate more under the assumption of Gemeinschaft. Tönnies also applied the dichotomy to the historical development of society. The transitions from a family based band society, to a rural agrarian village, to a town, to a city, to a nation, to an international and cosmopolitan society involves the transition from a predominantly Gemeinschaft to a predominantly Gesellschaft form of social organization.

Ideal Types as Dialectic Forces

I chose Tönnies' ideas as the cornerstone of this chapter for two reasons. The first reason is that his dichotomy was early, simple, stark, and central to the social science theory of the last century. However, it is by no means the only discussion of ideal types that focuses on the dimension of separateness versus unity. Durkheim's (1933) discussion of the mechanical versus the organic solidarity of society illustrates the same distinction (i.e., the "mechanical" can be equated with Gemeinschaft and the "organic" with Gesellschaft). Becker (1950), Redfield (1930, 1947), Sorokin (1941), and Stark (1958) also have employed typologies paralleling Tönnies' distinction. Even Parsons' (1951) pattern variables of action orientation make use of collectivity-orientation versus self-orientation as one of the five dimensions of action.

The second reason for presenting Tönnies' distinction is that it contains threads of something more than a simple typology. It contains hints that Gemeinschaft and Gesellschaft may be seen as opposing forces in social organization, and not just as ideal types. It is this aspect of Tönnies' treatment that I wish to develop and apply in the remainder of this chapter. The dialectical nature of Gemeinschaft and Gesellschaft emerges most clearly in Tönnies' distinction between "natural will," which represents the motivation and thought of Gemeinschaft, and "rational will," which characterizes Gesellschaft. In essence, "natural will" is based unanalytically on custom and mores, while "rational will" is based on thoughts and plans about purposes and strategies. Tönnies presents the dual nature of his distinction, both as an ideal typology and as a dialectic, in the following discussion:

> As free and arbitrary products of thinking, these normal concepts are mutually exclusive; rational will and natural will are strictly separate entities. The same concepts, however, are conceived of as empirical concepts. . . . Observation and inference will easily show that no natural will can ever occur empirically without rational will by which it finds expression, and no rational will without natural will on which it is based. . . . They can coexist and mutually serve each other, but, on the other hand, to the extent that each aspires to power and control, they will necessarily contradict and oppose each other even though their separate components as expressed in norms and rules of behavior are comparable. If rational will desires to order and define everything according to end, purpose, or utility, it has to overcome the given, traditional, deeply rooted rules insofar as they cannot be applied to such purposes, or to subordinate them if possible. The more decisive rational will or purposeful thinking becomes and concentrates on the knowledge, acquisition, and application of means, the more the

> emotions and thoughts which form the individuality of natural will are in danger of withering away. And not only this, but there is also a direct antagonism, because the forms of natural will try to repress rational will and oppose its rule and domination, whereas rational will tries first to free itself from natural will and then to dissolve, destroy, or dominate it. (pp. 141-142)

The conflict present between natural and rational will also characterizes the relationship between Gemeinschaft and Gesellschaft. Tönnies presented this conflict as playing out through time (e.g., in the developmental transition from agrarian to state societies) and through class struggles (e.g., in the conflict between the proletariat and the bourgeoise). The conflict, however, can be extended to any social interaction. Just as any empirical situation contains elements of both individual separateness and organic unity, it can be seen to contain forces pushing in each direction. Even in a unified family, there are forces pushing for individual separateness, and, even in the most contractual of relationships, there are forces pushing for social union. How this conflict is played out in social interaction may prove more interesting and instructive than an analysis of how the interaction exhibits characteristics of one or the other ideal type. By understanding social interaction as a conflict between forces for unity and forces for separation, where one attempts to overcome and subjugate the other, where the other attempts to compensate or retaliate, and where eventual interaction exhibits either a continuation or a resolution of this conflict, we would come to understand the process of social interaction, not just the forms it may take.

Dialectic Forces in Social Theory

My purpose in presenting the dialectic between Gemeinschaft and Gesellschaft is not to use it to understand society and social organization, however, but to apply it to understanding the development of social theory. More specifically, the interactions I wish to look at are the interactions of social scientists attempting to define, understand, and create an explanation of social behavior. In the process of building models and theories of social behavior, social scientists have held assumptions regarding the unity or the separateness of individuals that have competed with one another and expressed a dialectic conflict. For example, role theory assumes a shared understanding of roles and role expectations, but, in several forms, assumes that separate and multifaceted individuals negotiate and perform social exchanges over carefully specified goods and services. Criticisms and modifications of role theory have been directed at both these assumptions, attempting to insert elements of individuality into role expectations and insert elements of unity into role behavior.

Theories of personality are aimed at accounting for individual differences among people. Yet, at their center, conceptions of personality have assumed a natural unity of people in the sense of Gemeinschaft. In the context of group established goals, conceptions of reality, and norms for behavior, any individual variation in performance must reflect stable predispositional differences among people. Criticisms of personality approaches have, at their base, challenged this assumption of essential unity by introducing idiographic and situation specific aspects of personality.

In the study of social groups, the conflict between Gesellschaft-like and Gemeinschaft-like forces is necessarily direct. Conceptions of groups as single unities or collections of separate individuals are definitional issues and have been confronted repeatedly. The development of the small groups movement illustrates attempts to achieve a synthesis between these two conceptions. The next sections of this chapter review the trends in the conceptualizations of role, personality, and groups from the point of view of the dialectic between Gemeinschaft and Gesellschaft.

Dialectical Trends in Role Theory

As Biddle (1979) noted, role theory is not a single, well-defined statement, but a general perspective that has evolved gradually from a variety of sources that often have been ignorant or contradictory of one another. Because of this diversity of origins, conceptions of unity and of separateness wind their ways in and around role theory in several ways. Role theory can be traced to and provides a meeting ground for two theoretical trends in sociology: the symbolic interactionism of Cooley (1902), Mead (1934), and Blumer (1969), and the structural-functionalism of Linton (1936), Parsons (1951), and Merton (1957).

The symbolic interactionist perspective on roles, well summarized by Stryker and Serpe (Chapter 7), grew out of attempts to account for how an individual becomes a member of society. The essential answer was that the self does not exist, at least initially, without the social group. It is only through interaction with others that we learn to identify, label, and value objects. One of the objects that a person learns to identify is him or herself—the "me" as seen by others (Mead, 1934). The social self develops out of interaction and is defined by the process and results of that interaction. Consequently, there are multiple selves, as many, potentially, as there are interactions. In addition to defining who we are and what we do in the context of a specific interaction, we also develop a sense of a "generalized other" that defines what people, in general, would expect and how they would evaluate our actions. Within this context, roles are particular behaviors and expectations tied to particular positional labels. Certain interactions will lead us to label ourselves as male or female, mother or daughter, clerk or customer, and will lead us to learn sets of behaviors associated with these and complementary labels. The symbolic interactionist perspective on how roles and identities are learned parallels Tönnies' view of the development from youth, imbedded in unity, to old age, embracing individualism. Roles and identities, since they arise out of interaction, require a unity, but once acquired become a more independent self and guide behavior in future interactions. From a repertoire of identities, one can call up the self that seems most appropriate to present in a particular context.

The structural-functionalist perspective grew out of attempts to represent social structure. The basic assumption was that actions are patterned into coherent and ordered systems that govern both interpersonal interaction and societal functioning. Actions are patterned, in this sense, because certain aspects of behavior seem more characteristic of the relationship or the setting than of the particular individuals involved. Thus, in an interaction between a police officer and a traffic violator, large parts of the behavior and expectations will remain the same even though the specific actors change from instance to instance.

A social system contains positions or statuses that stand in dynamic relation to one another and that prescribe and proscribe certain behaviors. These positions and groups of positions are structured to perform functions of society, such as production, social control, and socialization. In Linton's (1936) view, "A status, as distinct from the individual who may occupy it, is simply a collection of rights and duties" (p. 113). Roles are the behavioral enactment of these rights and duties by an individual. The social structure provides positional niches into which individuals fit when they perform a role. "Status and role serve to reduce the ideal patterns for social life into individual terms. They become models for organizing the attitudes and behaviour of the individual so that these will be congruous with those of other individuals participating in the expression of the pattern" (p. 113). From the structural-functionalist view, then, roles are the enactment by an individual of part of the social structure, "what the actor does in his relations with others seen in the context of its functional significance for the social system" (Parsons, 1951, p. 25).

The structural-functionalist position assumes that the social structure is known and that this knowledge is commonly shared. Davis (1948) stated this assumption as follows: "An individual carries his social position around in his head, so to speak, and puts it into action when the appropriate occasion arises. Not only does he carry it in his head but others also carry it in theirs, because social positions are matters of reciprocal expectations and must be publicly and commonly conceived by everyone in the group" (p. 88).

From these origins, role theory developed rather eclectically as a broad and now interdisciplinary perspective that deals with any patterned interaction between people. The definition of role has been extended beyond those tied to positions to include any behavior that is governed by shared expectations (Biddle, 1979). As role theory moved to the task of studying role behavior in complex everyday life, it acquired a more Gesellschaft-like perspective. As Gross, Mason, and McEachern (1958) demonstrated in their study of school superintendents, a single role is often ambiguous, complex, and incongruent. Different audiences, different situations, and different tasks often engage incompatible expectations. Faced with these imprecise or contradictory role definitions, the actor necessarily becomes more of an active agent in the process of creating the role. As Turner (1962) noted, "Roles 'exist' in varying degrees of concreteness and consistency, while the individual confidently frames his behavior as if they had unequivocal existence and clarity. The result is that in attempting from time to time to make aspects of the roles explicit he is creating and modifying roles as well as merely bringing them to light; the process is not only role-taking but role-making" (p. 22).

Goffman's (1959) dramaturgical approach separates the performance of a role and the "performed self" from the actor and the "phenomenal self." Performance, Goffman (1959) defined, is "all the activity of a given participant on a given occasion which serves to influence in any way any of the other participants" (p. 15).

Although within the symbolic interactionist tradition, Goffman's dramaturgical metaphor presents a view of the actor operating as an independent entity in the interaction, often independent or "distanced" from his or her own performance. The actor creates a front, puts on a face, and sets about the task of creating a particular definition of the situation for an audience. This individualistic perspective is made central in the social exchange approach advocated by Homans (1961) and Blau (1964). Here, the concept of role becomes an implied contract for the exchange of social goods and services in a way that closely parallels Tönnies' description of Gesellschaft relations. Athay and Darley (Chapter 3) present a new and detailed social exchange theory of role behavior, but one that is also attentive to the mutual definition of the situation and the construction of a unique interaction. As Ekeh (1974) observed, social exchange theories do not necessarily have to embrace an individualist orientation; collectivist approaches are both possible and extant (e.g., Levi-Strauss, 1969).

Although the assumption of the separateness of individuals appears strong in current American role theory, it is possible to insert more of a collectivist orientation into role considerations. Symbolic interactionism and its proposition that identities occur only out of interaction allows one avenue for asserting that the social unit is important to role definition, but only to the extent that the interaction itself, rather than the negotiation of individuals, is viewed as the creator of roles and identities. Ethnomethodological treatments of roles provide a more collectivist view. Cicourel (1970, 1974) criticized traditional conceptions of roles and status as being abstractions that did not describe (a) what procedures an actor used to recognize and generate appropriate behavior, (b) how particular norms are recognized, selected, and invoked in the context of a particular interaction, and (c) how innovation and change in the interaction alters general norms or rules. Ethnomethodology answers these questions by inserting two threads of unity into social interaction.

The first thread of unity is a deep structure of social order that is known by members of, at least, a cultural group. Paralleling Chomsky's (1965) distinction between deep and surface structures of language, Cicourel (1974) proposed that actors possessed a shared deep structure of social order that allows them to interpret the surface structure of utterances and norm invocations. "A more refined conceptual frame for understanding norms will have to specify interpretive procedures as a set of invariant properties governing fundamental conditions of all interaction so as to indicate how the actor and observer decide what serves as definitions of 'correct' or 'normal' conduct or thought .... The acquisition and use of interpretive procedures over time amounts to a cognitive organization that provides a continual sense of social structure" (p. 33). On the one hand, this suggestion parallels the structural-functionalist assumption that statuses, positions, and roles are known by all participants and carried around in the head. On the other hand, Cicourel's shared "interpretive procedures" do not concern the content of roles, but the process of interaction: "The interpretive procedures would suggest the nature of minimal conditions that all interaction presumably would have to satisfy for actor and observer to decide that the interaction is 'normal' or 'proper' and can be continued" (p. 33).

The second thread of unity is a "common scheme of reference" that is adopted by parties in an interaction. The actors adopt a "reciprocity of perspectives," whereby both parties "assume their mutual experiences of the interaction scene are the same even if they were to change places" and "disregard personal differences in how each assigns meaning to everyday activities, thus each can attend to the present scene in an identical manner for the practical matter at hand" (p. 34). In addition, the participants share or develop common meanings for words, which allows a particular word to stand for a much broader network of understanding. The assumption that actors share and act out of a common scheme of reference allows the interaction itself to become the unit of analysis.

Heine (1971) commented on the potential of role theory to bridge the gap between individual and collective levels of analysis. "The aim (and it was an ambitious one) of interaction theory from the beginning was to avoid the old opposition of individual versus group. Its solution was to be 'dialectic'; a unity of opposites was to be sought in the basic process that brought together both the principle of 'the individual' and the principle of 'the social'. . . . Interaction theory with its accompanying principles of social learning, role acquisition, and role development supplies a social psychology that permits moving beyond elementary social behavior and the tiresome controversy concerning the priority of individual or group. Role theory in itself has a splendid neutrality. It may be stated objectively, from the standpoint of society. We speak then of a role as a position to be filled, a job to be done, a function to be performed. It may also be stated subjectively–from the standpoint of the individual. We speak then of learning a role, or taking a role or performing one" (pp. 40-42).

Heine's conclusion that role theory has provided a synthesis between Gemeinschaft and Gesellschaft is premature. It is clear that assumptions of individual separation or social unity can be found within role theory, often within the same perspective or theoretical approach. The gap between individual and society, however, is not well bridged or at least the bridge is not well maintained. Too often, traversing the gap involves a shift in perspective, but not a synthesis of perspectives. It is clear in the positions and counterpositions that role theory engages the dialectic but the positions appear still separated and appear enduringly (if not tiresomely) controversial. The chapters that follow attempt to traverse this gap in several novel ways. Stryker and Serpe (Chapter 7) develop and test identity theory as a way of linking symbolic interactionism more directly to issues of social structure. Secord (Chapter 2) presents a "transformational model" of the social structure of sex roles, the basic tenet of which is that societal structures result from the intended and unintended consequences of interaction. Athay and Darley (Chapter 3) present a more detailed and more flexible social exchange theory, one that begins with the assumption that there are societal structures that govern behavior. Other chapters, such as those by Gordon and Gordon (Chapter 9), McCall (Chapter 10), and Ickes (Chapter 11), provide examples of the interplay of individual and collective influences on role behavior.

Dialectical Trends in Personality

The study of personality is multifaceted, ranging from investigations of rather limited behavioral tendencies, such as Machiavellianism (Christie & Geis, 1970) or risk taking (Knowles, 1976), to Freud's (1933) grand theory of the unconscious forces in personality development and expression. The underlying threads that identify the area of personality are probably these: (a) Personality approaches assume that the major or at least more basic determinants of behavior reside internally within the individual, rather than externally in the situation, (b) the internal determinants are predispositions for certain behaviors that influence the observed behavior in a variety of contexts and situations, and (c) the personality dispositions, once established, are relatively stable and enduring, resistant to change (Thomas, 1968).

Within the broad domain of the study of personality, I will confine my focus to that part known as the trait approach to personality. After a brief definition of this approach, I will focus on two issues that demonstrate the tension between individuality and social unity. The first issue concerns the idiographic versus nomothetic distinction that focuses attention on the interplay of individuality and commonality in the conception and investigation of personality. The second issue concerns the generality versus specificity of personality traits that focuses attention on the nature of behavioral consistency and how it is to be accounted for by personality traits.

An Overview of the Trait Approach

Gordon Allport (1937), in the most thorough, careful, and guarded analysis of this perspective, conceived of traits as inferred causes of behavioral consistency. Traits, he defined as "a generalized and focalized neuropsychic system (peculiar to the individual), with the capacity to render many stimuli functionally equivalent, and to initiate and guide consistent (equivalent) forms of adaptive and expressive behavior" (p. 295). Personality, he assumed, matured through increasing differentiation and increasing integration of behavioral tendencies. Traits reflect one level in a hierarchy of integration. With the maturation of personality, conditioned reflexes become integrated into habits. Traits, then, become "dynamic and flexible dispositions, resulting, at least in part, *from the integration of specific habits*, expressing characteristic modes of adaptation to one's surroundings. Belonging to this level are the dispositions variously called sentiments, attitudes, values, complexes, and interests" (pp. 141-142). Further up the hierarchy, coherent systems of traits become integrated into a social self, of which many are possible and which are likely to vary in different situations.

Gordon Allport (1937) implied that, in this hierarchy, the level of the trait was the most useful for the personologist because it was general enough to account for a range of behaviors across a range of situations, yet specific enough to allow for the multiple and varied content of personality. The trait approach certainly does allow for varied content. Allport and Odbert (1936), digesting the 1925 edition of Webster's *New International Dictionary*, identified 17,953 words that could be used to describe individual differences. Of these, 4,504 were classified as "names that symbolize most clearly 'real' traits of personality" (p. 25). A recent catalog of personality trait measures (Chun, Cobb, & French, 1975) identified over 3,000 different measures that have appeared in the psychological literature.

Individual versus Common Traits

Allport's definition of a trait as an intermediate level of consistency in motivation or behavior stresses its idiographic or individual nature. "Strictly speaking, no two persons ever have precisely the same trait. Though each of two men may be *aggressive* (or *aesthetic*), the style and range of the aggression (or estheticism) in each case is noticeably different. What else could be expected in view of the unique hereditary endowment, the different developmental history, and the never-repeated external influences that determine each personality? The end product of unique determination can never be anything but unique" (p. 297). Strict adherence to the idiographic assumption would require that personality only be studied on a case by case basis and that personality trait descriptions be devised for each individual as a way of organizing the consistencies in that person's behavior. White's (1966) *Lives in Progress*, his earlier (1938) "The case of Earnst," and various works in psychohistory (e.g., Erikson, 1958, 1969; Freud, 1928, 1961; Langer, 1972) suggest both the consistent themes in an individual's behavior and the insight that can be gained through the case study method.

Most research on personality and certainly most in the personality trait tradition ignores the idiographic approach, adopting instead a nomothetic assumption that people can be compared on a common dimension. Each of the 3,000 or so personality trait measures catalogued by Chun, Cobb, and French (1975) provides an instrument for assessing the level of a given trait in each person tested. For instance, Mandler and Sarason's (1952) Test Anxiety Questionnaire is a self-report scale presumed to measure "a learned anxiety drive which is a function of anxiety reactions previously learned as responses to stimuli present in the testing situation" (p. 166). People who score higher on this test are presumed to have a greater degree of the test anxiety drive or trait than people who score low. This conclusion, however, rests on assumptions of homogeneity among the population measured. First, it assumes that test anxiety is a dimension that is common to the population measured; people differ in whether they are higher or lower on this dimension, but test anxiety, as a dimension of personality, is shared by everyone. Second, it assumes that the specific items in the test (e.g., "How often do you think of ways of avoiding the test?") have the same meaning and relevance for everyone and for everyone's test anxiety trait.

As G. Allport (1937) noted, the nomothetic assumption that allows personality measures to compare individuals on a trait rests on a deeper assumption about the underlying unity or sameness of the population measured. "For all their ultimate differences, normal persons within a given culture-area, tend to develop a limited number of *roughly comparable* modes of adjustment. The original endowment of most human beings, their stages of growth, and the demands of their particular society, are sufficiently standard and comparable to lead to some basic modes of adjustment that from individual to individual are *approximately* the same. To take an example: the nature of the struggle for survival in a competitive society tends to force every individual to seek his own most suitable level of *aggression.* . . . Somewhere between the extremes of exaggerated domination and complete passivity, there lies for each normal individual a level of adaptation that fits his intimate requirements" (pp. 297-298).

The nomothetic and idiographic assumptions in personality parallel the distinction between unity and separateness or Gemeinschaft and Gesellschaft in Tönnies. As Allport noted, "At a higher level the distinction between the individual trait and the common trait is reflected in the distinction between the *person* and the *socius.* The former is the complete man, a unique biophysical product in whom cultural influences have been embedded in individual ways within a biological ground. The *socius* is the man viewed in reference to his social status. His beliefs, attitudes and traits are regarded as conforming to, or deviating from, societal standards. The frame of reference in the former case is the person himself; in the latter case, external social norms" (p. 300, footnote 13). Although examples of important research that include a strong idiographic emphasis can be found (e.g., Murray, 1938; White, 1966), most research on personality traits during the last 50 years has embraced the nomothetic assumption. The ironic conclusion, then, is that the great bulk of research studying individual differences in personality has had, as part of its base, an underlying assumption of the unity of the groups it was studying. This assumption, however, has not gone unchallenged. The strongest and most persistent attack has come from those who argue that behavior does not show the level of cross-situational consistency implied by nomothetic traits.

Generality versus Specificity of Traits

The trait approach in personality has been persistently criticized for assuming that there is more generality to behavioral dispositions than actually is there (Lehmann & Witty, 1934; Mischel, 1968). Mischel (1968) reviewed the research on common personality traits and found the predictive validity of the measures to be low and the variability of behavior from situation to situation to be high. A case in point is an early and comprehensive study by Hartshorne and May, reported in three volumes (1928, 1929; Harshorne, May, & Shuttleworth, 1930). The authors recorded the behavior of hundreds of children in a variety of experimentally created activities to see the extent to which traits such as deception, helpfulness, cooperativeness, persistence, and self-control would be revealed in behavioral consistency from situation to situation. The authors reported generally low correlations between behaviors in situations that they thought should have engaged the same trait. They concluded that the trait names reflected "groups of specific habits rather than general traits" (Hartshorne, May, & Shuttleworth, 1930, p. 1). Bolstered by evidence from studies such as this one, Mischel (1968) argued, from a social learning perspective, that responses to specific situations are not widely generalized; the fact that cross-situational correlations rarely exceed a value of +.30 results, not from methodological deficiencies, but from the fact that consistency at the level of traits does not account for more than 10% of the variability in behavior.

Authors arguing for the situational specificity of behavior have recently taken to calling their criticism an "interactionist" approach to personality (Ekehammar, 1974; Endler & Magnusson, 1976). Research from this perspective measures a number of persons in a number of situations that are thought to engage a trait such as anxiousness (Endler & Hunt, 1969) or hostility (Endler & Hunt, 1968) and reports the proportion of the variance in behavior that is attributable to situations, persons, and the interaction between persons and situations. From a variety of studies looking at variance components, Endler and Magnusson (1976) conclude that "persons and situations per se are less important sources of behavioral variance than are person-situation interactions" (p. 964). Although the interactionist attack is often levied against the trait approach (e.g., Endler & Magnusson, 1976), the empirical evidence for person-situation interactions argues against only the nomothetic assumption that there are common traits. Gordon Allport (1937), for instance, commenting on the Hartshorne and May studies, noted that "the low correlations found between the tests employed prove only that children are not consistent *in the same way*, not that they are inconsistent with *themselves*" (p. 250).

In contrast to G. Allport's (1937) idiographic approach to personality which assumes that traits are both (a) peculiar to the individual, and (b) generalize across a variety of situations, the interactionist perspective seems to assume that the causes of behavior are both (a) peculiar to the individual, and (b) situation specific. For instance, Endler and Magnusson (1976) report that "the essential four features of modern interactionism can be summarized as follows:

1. Actual behavior is a function of a continuous process or multidirectional interaction (feedback) between the individual and the situation that he or she encounters.
2. The individual is an intentional active agent in this interaction process.
3. On the person side of the interaction, cognitive factors are the essential determinants of behavior, although emotional factors do play a role.
4. On the situation side, the psychological meaning of the situation for the individual is the important determining factor." (p. 968)

This interactionist, almost symbolic interactionist, perspective eschews commonality among people and advocates the individual as the unit of analysis. However, the majority of the research embracing this perspective, at least so far, has concentrated on demonstrating the falsity of the nomothetic assumption rather than building a predictive theory of interactionism.

Dialectical Processes in Personality Theory

Reactions to the interactionist claims that personality is idiographic and situation specific have been many. Jaccard (1974) and Epstein (1979) engaged the battle in defense of the nomothetic assumption and argued that personality traits are accurate predictors (and, therefore, descriptors) of the central tendencies in behavior when that behavior is averaged over time or over a number of situations. Just as any particular item on a personality test may contain error, any particular measure of the predicted behavior may contain a good deal of random error—in the behavior or in the applicability of the situation to the trait.

Other researchers have been more tolerant of interactionist's evidence, but have sought other solutions to the conflict. Campus (1974) accepted the notion that people could be inconsistent from situation to situation. However, she assumed that such inconsistency was, in itself, a personality trait and proceeded to devise a measure of the common trait of transsituational consistency. Bem and Allen (1974) advocated a partially idiographic position; for most personality dimensions, only some of the people share a common dimension, others do not. Consistency across situations and measures would be expected only for those who shared the common trait. They found that subjects who said they were consistent in their friendliness or who exhibited consistency in responses to a questionnaire assessing conscientiousness did in fact show much higher correlations among independent measures of these traits than did subjects who indicated inconsistency. Kenrick and Springfield (1980) take the idiographic argument a step further (or a step closer to G. Allport, 1937), by arguing that individuals do show traitlike consistency, but only when the traits are defined by the individual.

In addition to these theoretical changes, the sorts of traits that researchers have been studying have shifted in recent years toward a focus on person-situation interactions and person-role interactions. Traditional personality variables, such as achievement (McClelland, Atkinson, Clark, & Lowell, 1953), anxiety (Mandler & & Sarason, 1952), or cooperativeness (Hartshorne & May, 1929), attempted to describe a consistent level of response to relevant situations. Recent personality research, however, has focused more on variables that moderate the consistency of responses to situations. For instance, Witkin's (Witkin, Dyk, Faterson, Goodenough, & Karp, 1962; Witkin & Goodenough, 1977) field dependence measure assesses the degree to which self is differentiated from the situational field. Field independent people are able to use internal standards to judge and respond to situations, whereas field dependent people are more responsive to and influenced by situational cues.

Snyder (1974, 1979) introduced the personality variable of "self-monitoring," which reflects the degree to which one is concerned about, attentive to, and skilled at presenting situationally and interpersonally appropriate behavior. The high self-monitoring individual "is particularly sensitive to expression and self-presentation of relevant others in social situations and uses these cues as guidelines for monitoring (that is, regulating and controlling) his or her own verbal and nonverbal self-presentation" (1979, p. 89). People low in this trait are neither as attentive to nor as skilled at impression management. Their behavior seems "to be controlled from within by their affective states and attitudes (they express it as they feel it) rather than molded and tailored to fit the situation" (1979, p. 89). Self-monitoring, then, may be related to situational flexibility in behavior and to role-taking ability.

Personality trait research also has begun to focus on interactions between persons and roles, particularly at the differences between those who show traditionally stereotyped versus androgynous sex roles. For instance, the Bem Sex Role Inventory (Bem, 1974) provides independent measures of masculinity and femininity for each person. The pattern of scores on these two measures allows a fourfold classification of people into those who score high on one but low on the other (traditional masculine or traditional feminine), low on both (undifferentiated), or high on both (androgynous). Androgynous individuals seem to pay less attention to sex stereotypes, interact more equally with both sexes, and display more willingness and ability to engage in behaviors traditionally associated with the opposite sex (Spence & Helmreich, 1978). This approach in the psychology of personality is moving closer to the traditional definition of personality in sociology, that is, to the view of personality as internalized roles (Heine, 1971).

These developments in theory, definition, and measures of personality traits demonstrate a recognition of and an emphasis on the more individual rather than common aspects of personality. Although measures of field dependence, self-monitoring, and androgyny still rest heavily on the nomothetic assumption, their focus is on dimensions of personality that predict consistency and inconsistency across certain kinds of situations. In this regard, they are more attentive to the interaction of persons with situations, and introduce idiographic elements into the study of personality traits. In so doing, they begin to share more common assumptions with role theory and to hold more promise of being incorporated into fuller theories that include personality, roles, and situational influences on social behavior. This promise is demonstrated, in the present volume, in the chapters by Davis (Chapter 4), Patterson (Chapter 5), McCall (Chapter 10), and Ickes (Chapter 11) where personality variables are discussed as moderators of role and social behavior. These chapters demonstrate how personality variables may be used in the study of social behavior in a way that avoids the major pitfall identified by G. Allport (1937): "The chief danger in the concept of trait is that, through habitual and careless use, it may come to stand for an assembly of separate and self-active faculties, thought to govern behavior all by themselves, without interference. We must cast out this lazy interpretation of the concept. . . . *The basic principle of behavior is its continuous flow, each successive act representing a convergent mobilization of all energy available at the moment.* No single trait—nor all traits together—determine behavior all by themselves" (pp. 312-313).

Dialectical Trends in Group Theory

"Whatever happened to the group in social psychology?" lamented Steiner (1974) in his analysis of the reasons for the decline in group research. Mullins (1973) described small group theory as the "light that flared" in the 1940s and 1950s and then faded rapidly in the 1960s, failing to achieve a clear program statement and a unified theoretical perspective that would provide direction and meaning to the research. From the perspective of the 1980s, two things are clear. The first is that Mullins' characterizations are accurate; the last three decades have seen a sharp rise and a fall in the activity and especially interest in the study of small groups (cf. Zander, 1979). The second is that questions about the nature and dynamics of social groups have a long and important history in the social sciences, even if, as

Lewin noted, "The definition of the concept 'group' has a somewhat chaotic history" (1951, p. 145).

The social psychology of groups is important precisely because it engages the difficult issues of the unity and separateness of people. The alternative positions, that a group is a single entity or a collection of separate individuals, have been strongly stated and hotly debated throughout the twentieth century. Gordon Allport (1954) noted, "Many authors, past and present, would agree that the interaction of individual minds produces a common manner of thinking, feeling, and willing, different from that of single minds in isolation, and from the mere summation of minds.... In recent years, the label 'group mind' has fallen into disuse, but ... the problem of group and the individual, of the one and the many, is still with us" (p. 31). The idea of a group mind has a long history in the social sciences. Brett (1921) traced the concept to Hegel (1807/1910) from whence it wove a path through nineteenth century social science appearing in Wundt's (1916) folk psychology and Durkheim's (1898) collective representations. In early social psychology, the most prominent and most criticized proponent of the "group mind" was William McDougall (1920).

Floyd Allport (1924) was a strong denouncer of the "group mind fallacy" and his views forcefully expressed the individualist position: "Alike in crowd excitements, collective uniformities, and organized groups, the only psychological elements discoverable are in the behavior and consciousness of the specific persons involved. All theories which partake of the group fallacy have the unfortunate consequence of diverting attention from the true locus of cause and effect, namely, the behavior mechanism of the individual. They place the group prior to this mechanism in order to study, and substitute description of social effects in place of true explanation" (p. 9). Yet, even Floyd Allport suggested that there was a legitimate arena for the study of groups, though he was not very clear about what it would entail: "Behavior, consciousness, and organic life belong strictly to individuals; but there is surely occasion for speaking of the group as a whole so long as we do not regard it as an organism or a mental entity.... While the social psychologist studies the individual in the group, the sociologist deals with the group as a whole. He [sic] discusses its formation, solidarity, continuity, and change" (p. 10).

Certainly, part of the "chaotic" history of the concept of group results from the conflict between viewing a group as a single entity and viewing it as a collection of separate actors. Empirical research on group related phenomena during the 1920s and 1930s was dominated by the individualistic perspective. Floyd Allport's (1924) views about the individual as the origin of behavior were reflected in his research on social facilitation. He (F. Allport, 1920) showed that there was some tendency for the presence of co-workers, but co-workers who did not interact, to "facilitate" speed of performance on various tasks and to decrease the differences in speed between co-workers. Travis (1925) found similar "facilitating" effects for subjects working in the presence of an audience; after extensive practice had produced high and level performance on a pursuit-rotor, many of his subjects achieved even higher scores when a small group of student spectators came in and served as an audience. Dashiell's (1935) chapter for Murchison's *Handbook of Social Psychology*, which reviewed this area of research, revealed the individualistic perspective of this approach, especially in its title: "Experimental studies of the influence of social situations on the behavior of individual human adults."

At the same time, perhaps a little later, a group-centered approach emerged in the closely related study of group productivity. In 1928, Goodwin Watson published a paper entitled, "Do groups think more efficiently than individuals," and in so doing opened an area of research that continues today. Watson observed that, on an anagram task where subjects were asked to compose many words from a collection of letters, performance was far superior for interacting groups of 3 to 10 members than it was for individuals working alone. Dashiell (1935), in particular, criticized the conclusion (insinuated in Watson's title) by noting that, since Watson compared one individual's production with the sum of the group members' production, the group's productivity was likely to reflect the "pooling" of individual performances. Nonetheless, Watson's research spurred a number of other, more sophisticated studies that looked at whether a group product differed from a pooling of individual products (e.g., Gurnee, 1937; Shaw, 1932; Thorndike, 1938). One study (Timmons, 1942) had subjects read materials about how parole decisions could be made and individually rank solutions to the problem, then either discuss and decide on the rankings as a group or study the problem individually, and, finally, rank the solutions again. If the superiority of group decisions was the result of mere pooling effects, then the individual decisions at the end of the experiment would have been the same for subjects who had discussed the issue and for subjects who had studied it alone. Discussion subjects, however, did give different answers to the problem than did individual study subjects, and answers that were "superior" since they agreed more with experts' answers. Thus, Timmons' study suggested that something had happened during the group discussion to affect the members' solutions to the problem.

These two research trends, one looking at social facilitation and the other looking at the group discussion effects, are interesting in several regards. First is their longevity. Social facilitation, traced to Triplett (1898) and spurred by F. Allport (1920) and Zajonc (1965), continues to be a strong and much debated area of research (e.g., Geen, 1980; Zajonc, 1980). The study of group discussion and decision making, begun by Watson (1928), has continued to appear in each successive decade (e.g., Burnstein & Vinokur, 1975; Gurnee, 1937; Klugman, 1944; Moscovici & Zavallone, 1969; Perlmutter & Montmollin, 1952), and culminating in the voluminous research during the last two decades on choice shifts and the polarization of opinion following group discussion (e.g., Cartwright, 1971; Myers & Lamm, 1976; Pruitt, 1971; Wallach, Kogan, & Bem, 1962). Second is the near continual debate over whether group discussion effects reflect some unique property of the group or some individual response to a social situation. Periodically, the issue of how group products differ from individual products has been presented as a group phenomenon (e.g., Osborne, 1957; Wallach, Kogan, & Bem, 1962; Watson, 1928). However, this was a weak arena for those who would advocate a group level of analysis. As happened with the study of group polarization of opinions, the issue can be rephrased in ways that are answerable, and reasonably answered, from the standpoint of the individual member.

In the late 1930s and 1940s, a different and new movement appeared in the study of groups, one usually associated with Kurt Lewin and his move from concerns with personality theory to concerns with social action (Zander, 1979). While at the Iowa Child Welfare Research Station, Lewin began to expand the analysis of individual "life space" to issues of the "social space" of groups (cf. Lewin, 1939). In several of his pre-1940 writings, Lewin had contrasted the "force field" where psychological forces originate within the individual and the "power field" where psychological forces are induced by an outside agent (e.g., Lewin, 1938). The notion that someone's desires could be imposed on another person's life space and that this could be represented as a "power field" constituted an early way that Lewin looked at the issue of interaction, but it was an explanation that preserved the individualist orientation of his personality theory.

In the 1940s Lewin explored several ways of representing the phenomena of interaction and mutual influence (cf. Lewin, 1951). In one instance, Lewin (1948, Figure XVI) represented a person in a field composed of various membership and reference groups. In another, he represented multiple memberships as cases of multiple, overlapping force fields (Lewin, 1951, Figure 51, p. 270). These, however, gave way to attempts to represent the life space of the entire group rather than of individual members. In one case (Lewin, 1951, Figure 40, p. 250), he presented the life space of the group in terms of the relations, subgroupings, and barriers between individual members. More often, though, Lewin (1951) presented the "social space" of the group without reference to the individual members. Thus, the "group" replaced the "person" in his topological representation of life space; the group operated as an entity in a psychological environment to establish goals, attempt group movement, overcome barriers, and respond to the forces acting on it.

In 1945, Lewin established the Research Center for Group Dynamics at the Massachusetts Institute of Technology to concentrate on theoretical and applied studies of group life (Lewin, 1946). Cartwright (1958) remembered that, "Those of us who assembled in Cambridge at the end of the war to embark on this new venture thought of ourselves as pioneers. We were members of an organization with no history or established tradition and with few precedents anywhere in the social sciences; we were committed to the creation of new techniques of research and the utilization of established procedures in investigating new kinds of problems; we thought that the term 'group dynamics' could be made to refer to a reasonably coherent field of knowledge" (p. 6). Part of the pioneer spirit must have come from the searching for a way to present group dynamics theory in a coherent and consistent way. Lewin's writings from this period (e.g., 1948, 1951) demonstrate a fertile mind with many insights trying different ways of presenting and conceptualizing group life.

By 1945, the underlying assumption of group dynamics was clear: groups are real and have important influences that cannot be understood entirely in terms of the individual members. The group, according to Lewin (1951), was a dynamic whole that was different than the sum of its parts—neither greater nor less, but different than the collection of individual members. As Pepitone (1981) noted, Lewin's view rested on a scientific conception of reality formulated by Cassirer (1923): The group is real because the operational manipulations of it had effects.

Lewin's forte was the ability to translate what seemed like abstract ideas into novel and dramatic empirical demonstrations. Two of the dramatic experiments that served as harbingers of the group dynamics movement were the Lewin, Lippitt, and White (1939) studies of autocratic and democratic "social climates" and Lewin's (1943a, 1947) studies of the effects of group decision on individual action. Each of these studies, and many others that followed, implied that some characteristic of the group "climate" or interaction had a directive force on the behavior of the individual members. In one of the most interesting studies coming out of the Research Center for Group Dynamics, Horowitz (1954) used the Zeigarnik effect, where interrupted tasks tend to be recalled more than completed tasks, to demonstrate that group determined goals can become individual goals. Members recalled more interrupted group tasks than completed group tasks, but recalled more interrupted group tasks when they thought that the group had voted to continue them than when they thought that the group had voted not to continue them. These studies bore the hallmark of Lewin's (1943b) approach which was to treat the group as a directive force in behavior, to understand "human beings not as isolated individuals, but in the social setting of groups" (p. 114).

Although closely identified with Lewin and the Research Center for Group Dynamics, the ascendance of the group as an explanatory concept in social psychology had wider participation. Roethlisberger and Dickson's (1939) *Management and the Worker* focused, in part, on the importance of group norms, group decision making, and social organization on the productivity of workers. Moreno's (1934) *Who Shall Survive* introduced sociometric methods as a way of studying the structure of social organization. Jennings (1943) used sociometry to study leadership in a girls' training school. Her research suggested that leadership was as much a function of the group as it was of the individual, since leaders varied from task to task, leadership was shared, and leadership behaviors continued despite turnover in the membership. Sherif's (1936) *The Psychology of Social Norms* also demonstrated the role of group created definitions and standards on individual perception and action. Concurrently with the Research Center for Group Dynamics, Bales (1950) was developing his "Interaction Process Analysis" for studying the content of group discussions. Bales' approach was often entirely group centered, analyzing the content of interaction without regard to who contributed it. Bales and Strodbeck (1951), for instance, summarized a number of group discussions in order to identify common developmental phases of interaction during problem solving.

Thus, the idea that groups could be used as units of analysis to understand social behavior was strong in various corners during the 1940s and 1950s and was demonstrating its utility in a variety of empirical studies. However, it was not this fact, in and of itself, that produced the excitement and burgeoning of the small groups area. The notion that groups were an important level of analysis in the study of social behavior had continued to be strong and active in sociology. Two things distinguished the group research of the 1940s and were more directly responsible for the creation of the small groups movement. First, the approach taken by most of the small group proponents was empirical and largely experimental. The concepts were translated into concrete operations and the demonstrations of the phenomena were, by contrast to earlier speculative treatments, quite powerful. Second, although

Lewinian theory stressed the group as the unit of analysis, much of the research went further and looked at the relations between individual behavior and group behavior. It is this second characteristic in particular that lent excitement to the small group movement.

Prior to the 1940s and 1950s, individual behavior and group behavior had been opponent explanations of social behavior. Advocates argued for one level of explanation and against the other. Although Lewin's (1948, 1951) theoretical writings continued this tradition by arguing that the group was the more meaningful level of analysis, the research that Lewin's ideas sponsored examined the intersection between individuals and groups. Lewin et al.'s (1939) studies investigated "social climate" effects on individual aggression and dependency. Horowitz (1954) studied the relation between group goals and individual goals. A great deal of research was directed at the issue of how individuals become group members. Back (1951), Festinger and Thibaut (1951), and Schachter (1951) studied the "pressures to uniformity" that meld an aggregate of opinions and standards into a single group position. Back (1951), Deutsch (1949), Festinger, Schachter, and Back (1950), and Thibaut (1950), investigating the causes and consequences of group cohesiveness, identified factors that develop separate individuals into a single group and demonstrated the effects of this development on individual and group behavior. This concern with the transformation of individuals into group members was expressed in other arenas as well. Bales (1950) and Bennis and Shepard (1956) discussed the stages of group development through which a group, early in its life, dealt with the issues of coming together and forming a single, functioning unit.

Mullins (1973) attributed the demise of the small groups movement to the lack of a clear program statement, that is, the absence of a major theoretical work that both spells out the directions that theory development and research should take and provides a framework for this development. Lewin's early death in 1947, at the height of the activity of the Research Center for Group Dynamics, prevented him from completing his theoretical development and writing such a program statement.

Whether or not Lewin's death or the absence of a program statement was the cause of the decline of the small groups movement, the course of its decline is clear. As the research programs developed during the 1950s and 1960s, they became less and less concerned with the relations between individuals and groups and tended to adopt one focus or the other. Most of the research drifted away from the group and toward the individual as the unit of analysis. For instance, Festinger's transition from "Informal social communications" (1950) in groups, to "Social comparison processes" (1954) adopted by individuals, to *A Theory of Cognitive Dissonance* (1957) and Schachter's transition from "Deviation, rejection, and communication" (1951) which studied a group's reaction to an individual, to *The Psychology of Affiliation* (1959) which studied an individual's desire to be with a group, to "Cognitive, social and physiological determinants of emotional state" (Schachter & Singer, 1962) show an increasing reliance on individual and cognitive mechanisms for explaining social behavior. For many who were part of the small groups movement, the group disappeared as a unit of analysis and as a causal agent in social behavior. A few others (e.g., Bales & Borgatta, 1955; Zander, 1971) strengthened their emphasis on the group and, in the process, gave less emphasis to the individual and the questions of how individuals become group members.

The dialectical processes operating between forces to view behavior as a product of individuals and forces to view it as a product of groups had for a brief moment threatened to come together in the small groups movement. The focus on the relations between individual behavior and group behavior and on how separate individuals become group members had provided an arena for research and theory that had the potential for accepting and integrating both levels of analysis. A large part of the excitement in the small groups movement was produced by this potential, the sense that a synthesis of individual and group levels of analysis could be achieved, a synthesis that would meld them, change them, and render them obsolete. The synthesis, however, did not emerge, due perhaps to Lewin's death, to the absence of another strong leader, or to the persistence of earlier conceptual frameworks. The decline of interest and excitement in the small groups area was coincident with and, I believe, caused by the repolarization of the theoretical approaches, away from one that tried to reconcile individual and group levels of analysis and toward ones that adopted one level of analysis to the exclusion of the other.

Recent Trends in the Cognition of Groups

Social psychology, at least the psychologist's version, has become increasingly cognitive in its orientation, stressing the origins, relations, and consequences of ideas held by individual actors. From dissonance and balance, cognitive social psychologists have moved to study attributional processes (cf. Harvey, Ickes, & Kidd, 1976; Kelley, 1972), self and self-schemas (cf. Markus, 1977), and social cognition (cf. Wegner & Vallacher, 1977). The cognitive paradigm, conceptualizing social behavior as cause and consequence of human thought, is well within the individualist tradition. Although Heider's (1958) influential monograph on social cognition, *The Psychology of Interpersonal Relations*, discussed "unit relations" and other aspects of group membership, only recently have these issues begun to receive attention within the framework of social cognition. Tajfel (1969, 1970; Tajfel, Billig, Bundy, & Flament, 1971) demonstrated the importance of perceiving groups and groupings among people. He showed that separating a collection of people into two virtually meaningless categories was sufficient to establish a positive ingroup and negative outgroup bias in reward distributions and in evaluations of the other people. Wilder (1977, 1978; Wilder & Cooper, 1981) extended this perspective to argue that the perception of groupings among an aggregate of people is an important determinant of a variety of reactions. In one study, Wilder (1977) found that the persuasiveness of six people, each advocating the same extreme position, was more a function of the number of groups advocating the position than the number of individuals. Thus, one group with six members was as persuasive as one individual, but less persuasive than two people when the subject believed these two represented different groups.

The new research on the social cognition of groups presents an interesting change and an interesting parallel to the research conducted during the 1940s and 1950s. During the height of the small groups movement, the research assumed or at least struggled with the assumption that groups were real entities. It was this assumption that had been criticized since the days of Floyd Allport (1924). The new social cognition of groups, however, need make no assumption about the external reality of groups; the focus of study is on an individual's conception of groups and groupings. By moving the question of the reality of groups from one of external reality to one of internal or subjective reality, Allport's criticism is sidestepped; the individual actor who perceives the groupings is the origin of the behavior.

As with the most exciting part of the small groups movement, the current research on the social cognition of groups is concerned with the issue of the transformation of individuals into group members. The questions now, however, are phrased in such terms as "When does a perceiver categorize people into groups or as separate individuals," "What cues does the perceiver use to form judgments of groups," and "How are reactions affected by the judgment that another person is a member of the same group, a member of an opposing group, or a separate individual?"

Structuring the Social Field

From a Lewinian framework, the social cognitive perspective has moved from considerations of the "social space" of group life back into the "life space" of an individual who attempts to understand a social field. However, both perspectives are concerned with the structure of the social field, the forces that lead to greater or lesser structure, and the effects of the structure of the social field on behavior.

Consider a social field that contains a number of people: a theatre lobby at intermission, a county council, members of the American Sociological Association, people on a bus, your acquaintances, or any other collection of people. A naive observer upon first encountering this field has two possible ways of construing the collection of people. On the one hand, this observer may consider each member as a separate, independent actor guided only by his or her individual situation and goals, or, on the other hand, the observer may consider the social field to be a single unit where the various members represent only parts of the more salient whole.

For the naive observer, the collection of people are either all independent by virtue of being separate individuals, or all related by virtue of being members of the same social field; the observer simply has no more detailed information on which to base a judgment. However, with more experience, with observation of, and information about this field, the observer may begin to discover that these people or at least some of them are neither completely independent nor completely related. Some pairs may exhibit a higher degree of dependence on one another, while other pairs exhibit lesser degrees or none at all. Dependencies will be inferred when the observer decides that the actions or states of one person are affected by the actions or states of another person (cf. Lewin, 1951). The patterns of these interdependencies will begin to define structures within the social field.

Consider a more specific example, a social field with five members in it, and assume further that the degree of dependency is judged for each of the 10 pairs of people. Table 1-1 presents such information in matrix form for a hypothetical social

Table 1-1. Hypothetical Dependencies in a Social Field of Five People

	Person				
Person	A	B	C	D	E
A	—				
B	.8	—			
C	.4	.4	—		
D	.4	.4	.6	—	
E	.2	.2	.2	.2	—

field of five persons. Persons A and B are judged to have a high degree of interdependency as might occur when they are husband and wife. Person E, on the other hand, has very low dependence on the others; he may respond to a direct question and most certainly would be influenced if another shouted "fire!" but at most times he is not affected by the others.

To the extent that people are judged to be interdependent, they may be grouped together, that is, they may be considered as a unit. But, the decision of whether or not to group people together requires the selection of some criterion (k) of how much dependency is sufficient for grouping; above this criterion, individuals will be grouped together, and, below it, they will be treated as separate units. The structure of the social field is very much affected by the level of k that is used. Figure 1-1 shows five alternative criteria that may be applied to the matrix in Table 1-1. In Figure 1-1, the strength of the dependency for each of the 10 paired relations is indicated by the height of the bar. If one adopts a very high criterion for grouping, such a dependency of $k = .9$, one is assuming that people will have to show a great deal of interdependency to be considered a group. In Figure 1-1, none of the relationships is as strong as a criterion of $k = .9$, therefore each of the people would be considered a separate and independent entity. With a criterion as low as $k = .1$, each of the paired relations would meet the criterion for grouping and the field would be treated as a single entity.

The groupings created by each criterion are presented in Figure 1-2. For instance, with a criterion of $k = .5$, persons A and B with a dependency at .8 would be considered a group as would persons C and D with a dependency at .6. None of the other relations exceeds this criterion and thus would be treated as independent. Thus, with a criterion of $k = .5$, there would be three groupings: (a) the pair created by persons A and B, (b) the pair created by persons C and D, and (c) the single person E.

When all the criteria are superimposed on the field at the same time ("All" in Figure 1-2), a topography emerges. The greater the dependency between two people, the fewer lines or boundaries there are between them. This composite figure presents both the various possibilities for grouping this social field and some indication, from the number of lines separating individuals, of the likelihood of each grouping. If this social field is going to be structured into groups, person A and person B are the most likely to be seen as a single entity, and person E is the least likely to be grouped with anyone else.

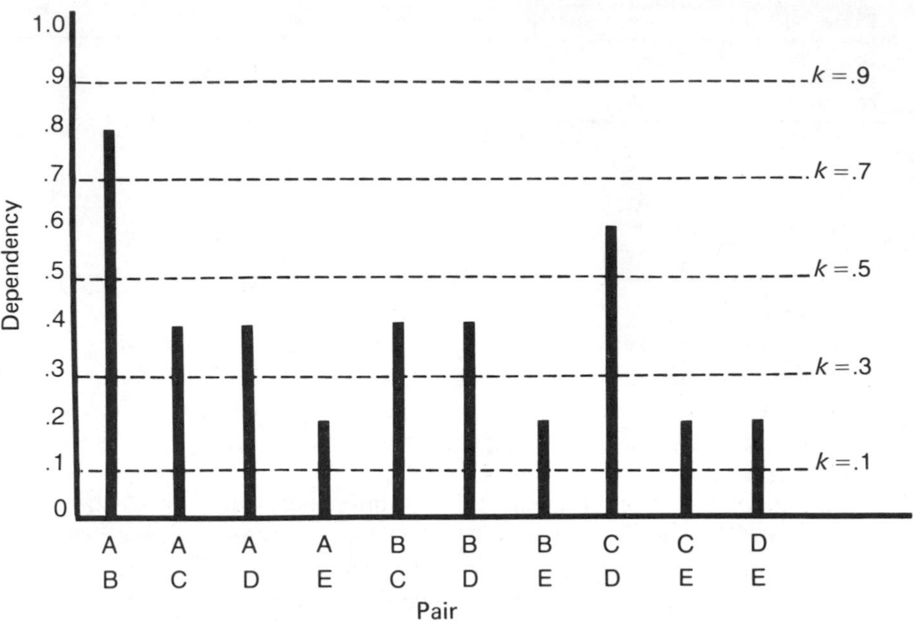

Fig. 1-1. Grouping criteria (k) applied to interdependencies in a social field. If a dependency relationship meets or exceeds the criterion, the pair is treated as a group.

This analysis of the alternatives for structuring a social field suggests that there are two separate issues underlying the question of how observers transform individuals into group members. The first issue concerns how dependencies among people are manifested and judged. Campbell (1958) provided one approach to this issue. Based on a combination of Gestalt notions and systems theory, he suggested that proximity, similarity, pregnance, common fate, and resistance to intrusion were cues that an observer used or could use to conclude that two individuals were parts of the same entity. Various studies imply that similarity and common fate may affect the strength of groupings, both for observers (e.g., Knowles, 1973; Knowles & Bassett, 1976) and for group members (Knowles & Brickner, 1981). These issues of how relations among people are manifested and judged are taken up in subsequent chapters in this volume. Lofland (Chapter 8) discusses the nature of social bonds that tie people together; Davis (Chapter 4) and Patterson (Chapter 5) examine how social bonds are established verbally and nonverbally.

The second issue suggested by this analysis of structuring the social field concerns how a particular value of k is selected as the criterion for structuring the field. Presumably, situational, personality, and role factors would lead observers to view different levels of social organization, even though the dependencies are constant. The chapter by Wegner and Giuliano (Chapter 6), in particular, discusses the factors that lead an observer and a participant to adopt a group perspective or an individual perspective toward a social field.

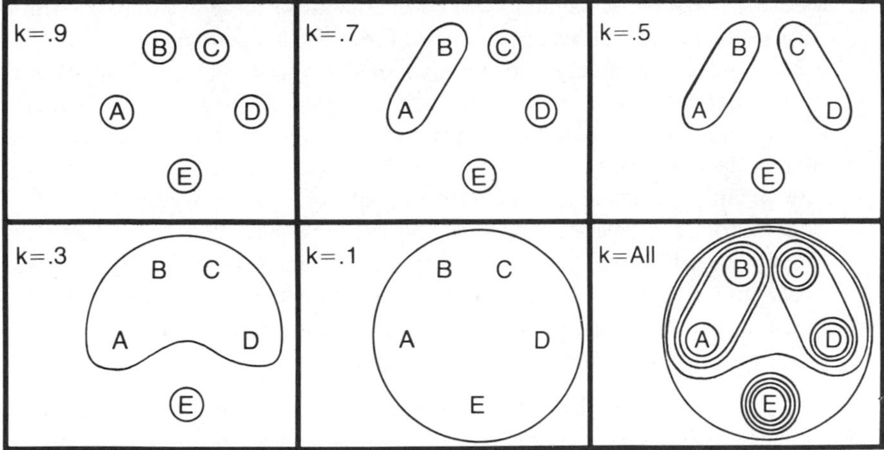

Fig. 1-2. Groupings of a social field of five persons (A, B, C, D, and E) at five dependency criteria (k).

For the observer of a social field, for the members of a social field, and for the social scientists attempting to understand a social field, the level of analysis is variable. For each, there are times, relationships, and situations where individuals are the salient units and others where associations or groups are the salient units. Social science theory has searched for the best way to represent and account for these phenomena. Although the history of the search is primarily a debate between those who adopt one perspective and those who adopt the other, the best theory would be one that accounts for both the individual and the group level of analysis. The small groups movement seemed to approach, but then miss this goal. Current work on the social cognition of groups appears to be returning to this goal; whether it will be more successful is a question of great interest, but presently unanswered.

Conclusions

Social interaction involves both separate individuals and social entities. The issue of which is primary, the group or the individual, and which serves as the locus for an explanation of social interaction has fueled debate in the areas of roles, personality, and small groups. A comprehensive theory of social interaction in any or all of these areas will have to achieve some synthesis, or at least attempt an integration of these levels of analysis. The perspective presented in this chapter leads to several hierarchically organized prescriptions for the social scientist investigating social interaction. These prescriptions begin with the most basic and simple and move to the more complex and difficult.

1. Whether you adopt a Gemeinschaft or a Gesellschaft orientation to social behavior, do not close your eyes, your theory, or your research to the operation of the opposing forces or the phenomena they produce.

2. Seek to understand when unity will be the operative force in social behavior and when separateness will be the operative force. Posing Gemeinschaft and Gesellschaft as forces in theory and in behavior that are in dialectical opposition to one another directs our attention to their interplay. Theory should be concerned not with questions of which assumption is the truer, but with questions of when and how each operates.
3. Develop an understanding and a theory of social behavior that accepts and includes both the separate individual and the organic unity of groups. A dialectical synthesis will accept both as legitimate forces and then move beyond them to deeper understanding. The task of achieving a synthesis may have to await the contributions of a social science equivalent to Einstein, but the task begins, certainly, with the assumption that a synthesis is possible.

To a great extent, explanations that assume unity and explanations that stress separateness of individuals are associated with the sociological and psychological perspectives, respectively. While this characterization may carry a kernel of truth, it is by no means invariantly accurate. As I have attempted to illustrate above, the study of roles, most typically associated with sociology, can be seen as a conceptualization dominated by assumptions of individuality, whereas the study of personality, most typically associated with psychology, can be seen as a conceptualization that rests in part on assumptions of organic unity, and both areas of study show tension between these two assumptions. Another characterization of the psychological and sociological approaches to social psychology is that each participates in its own group life without much attention to or consideration of the other discipline. This volume and the chapters that follow belie the universality of both these characterizations.

Each of the chapters that follow presents a view of social behavior at the intersection between psychology and sociology. Half of the remaining chapters are written by those trained as sociologists and half by those trained as psychologists. Each one is concerned with examining social behavior in a way that accounts for both its individual and its communal aspects. Although it is much too premature to present a unified framework for the psychosociology or sociopsychology of social behavior, each of the authors offers a suggestion, a perspective, or an example of how the sociological and psychological branches of social psychology may be brought closer together. Throughout these chapters, the reader will see attempts to come to terms with the opposition of individuality and unity, and will see approaches to social behavior that point toward a synthesis of Gemeinschaft and Gesellschaft.

Acknowledgments. The writing of this chapter was aided by a Fulbright Research Scholarship to the Department of Sociology, Göteborg University, Sweden, by a grant (BNS80-16202) from the National Science Foundation, and by a patient *Gemeinschaftlich* family.

References

Allport, F. H. The influence of the group upon association and thought. *Journal of Experimental Psychology,* 1920, *3*, 159-182.

Allport, F. H. *Social psychology.* Boston: Houghton Mifflin, 1924.

Allport, G. W. *Personality: A psychological interpretation.* New York: Holt, 1937.

Allport, G. W. The historical background of modern social psychology. In G. Lindzey (Ed.), *Handbook of social psychology* (Vol. 1). Reading, Mass.: Addison-Wesley, 1954.

Allport, G. W., & Odbert, H. S. Trait-names: A psycho-lexical study. *Psychological Monographs,* 1936, Whole No. 211.

Back, K. Influence through social communication. *Journal of Abnormal and Social Psychology,* 1951, *46*, 9-23.

Bales, R. F. *Interaction process analysis: A method for the study of small groups.* Reading, Mass.: Addison-Wesley, 1950.

Bales, R. F., & Borgatta, E. F. Size of group as a factor in the interaction profile. In A. P. Hare et al. (Eds.), *Small groups: Studies in social interaction.* New York: Knopf, 1955.

Bales, R. F., & Strodbeck, F. L. Phases in group problem solving. *Journal of Abnormal and Social Psychology,* 1951, *46*, 485-495.

Becker, H. *Through values to social interpretation.* Durham, N.C.: Duke University Press, 1950.

Bem, D. J., & Allen, A. On predicting some of the people some of the time: The search for cross-situational consistencies in behavior. *Psychological Review,* 1974, *81*, 506-520.

Bem, S. L. The measurement of psychological androgyny. *Journal of Consulting and Clinical Psychology,* 1974, *42*, 115-162.

Bennis, W. G., & Shepard, H. A. A theory of group development. *Human Relations,* 1956, *9*, 415-437.

Biddle, B. J. *Role theory: Expectations, identities, and behaviors.* New York: Academic Press, 1979.

Blau, P. M. *Exchange and power in social life.* New York: Wiley, 1964.

Blumer, H. *Symbolic interactionism.* Englewood Cliffs, N.J.: Prentice-Hall, 1969.

Brett, G. S. *A history of psychology* (Vol. 3). London: G. Allen, 1921.

Burnstein, E., & Vinokur, A. What a person thinks upon learning he has chosen differently from others: Nice evidence for the persuasive arguments explanation of choice shifts. *Journal of Experimental Social Psychology,* 1975, *11*, 412-426.

Campbell, D. T. Common fate, similarity, and other indices of the status of aggregates of persons as social entities. *Behavioral Science,* 1958, *3*, 14-25.

Campus, N. Transsituational consistency as a dimension of personality. *Journal of Personality and Social Psychology,* 1974, *29*, 593-600.

Cartwright, D. Some things learned. *Journal of Social Issues,* 1958, Suppl. No. 12.

Cartwright, D. Risk taking by individuals and groups: An assessment of research employing choice dilemmas. *Journal of Personality and Social Psychology,* 1971, *20*, 361-378.

Cassirer, E. *Substance and function* (trans. by W. C. and M. C. Swabey). Chicago and London: Open Court, 1923.

Chomsky, N. *Aspects of a theory of syntax.* Cambridge, Mass.: Massachusetts Institute of Technology Press, 1965.

Christie, R., & Geis, F. L. (Eds.). *Studies in Machiavellianism.* New York: Academic Press, 1970.

Chun, K., Cobb, S., & French, J. R. P., Jr. *Measures for psychological assessment.* Ann Arbor, Mich.: Institute for Social Research, 1975.

Cicourel, A. V. The acquisition of social structure: Toward a developmental sociology of language. In J. Douglas (Ed.), *Understanding everyday life.* New York: Aldine, 1970.

Cicourel, A. F. Interpretive procedures and normative rules in the negotiation of status and role. In A. V. Cicourel (Ed.), *Cognitive sociology.* New York: Free Press, 1974.

Cooley, C. H. *Human nature and the social order.* New York: Scribner's Sons, 1902.

Dashiell, J. F. Experimental studies of the influence of social situations on the behavior of individual human adults. In C. Murchison (Ed.), *Handbook of social psychology.* Worcester, Mass.: Clark University Press, 1935.

Davis, K. *Human society.* New York: Macmillan, 1948.

Deutsch, M. An experimental study of the effects of cooperation and competition upon group processes. *Human Relations,* 1949, *2*, 199-232.

Durkheim, E. Réprésentations individuelles et réprésentations collectives. *Rèvue de Mètaphysique,* 1898, *6*, 274-302.

Durkheim, E. *The division of labor in society* (trans. from the 1893 edition by G. Simpson). Glencoe, Ill.: The Free Press, 1933.

Ekeh, P. P. *Social exchange theory: The two traditions.* Cambridge, Mass.: Harvard University Press, 1974.

Ekehammar, B. Interactionism in personality from a historical perspective. *Psychological Bulletin,* 1974, *81*, 1026-1048.

Endler, N. S., & Hunt, J. McV. S-R inventories of hostility and comparisons of the proportions of variance from persons, responses, and situations for hostility and anxiousness. *Journal of Personality and Social Psychology,* 1968, *9*, 309-315.

Endler, N. S., & Hunt, J. McV. Generalizability of contributions from sources of variance in the S-R inventories of anxiousness. *Journal of Personality,* 1969, *37*, 1-24.

Endler, N. S., & Magnusson, D. Toward an interactional psychology of personality. *Psychological Bulletin,* 1976, *83*, 956-974.

Epstein, S. The stability of behavior: I. On predicting most of the people much of the time. *Journal of Personality and Social Psychology,* 1979, *37*, 1097-1126.

Erikson, E. H. *Young man Luther.* New York: Norton, 1958.

Erikson, E. H. *Gandhi's truth.* New York: Norton, 1969.

Festinger, L. Informal social communication. *Psychological Review,* 1950, *57*, 271-282.

Festinger, L. A theory of social comparison processes. *Human Relations,* 1954, *7*, 117-140.

Festinger, L. *A theory of cognitive dissonance.* Evanston, Ill.: Row Peterson, 1957.

Festinger, L., Schachter, S., & Back, K. *Social pressures in informal groups: A study of a housing project.* New York: Harper, 1950.

Festinger, L., & Thibaut, J. Interpersonal communication in small groups. *Journal of Abnormal and Social Psychology,* 1951, *46*, 92-99.

Freud, S. Dostoevsky and parricide. In *The complete psychological works of Sigmund Freud* (Standard ed., Vol. 21). London: Hogarth Press, 1961. (Originally published, 1928.)

Freud, S. *New introductory lectures on psychoanalysis.* New York: Norton, 1933.

Geen, R. The effects of being observed on performance. In P. B. Paulus (Ed.), *The psychology of group influence.* Hillsdale, N.J.: Erlbaum, 1980.

Goffman, E. *The presentation of self in everyday life.* Garden City, N.Y.: Doubleday Anchor Books, 1959.

Gross, N., Mason, W. S., & McEachern, A. W. *Explorations in role analysis: Studies of the school superintendent.* New York: Wiley, 1958.

Gurnee, H. A comparison of collective and individual judgments of facts. *Journal of Experimental Psychology,* 1937, *21*, 106-112.

Hartshorne, H., & May, M. A. *Studies in the nature of character* (Vol. 1). *Studies in deceit.* New York: Macmillan, 1928.

Hartshorne, H., & May, M. A. *Studies in the nature of character* (Vol. 2). *Studies in service and self-control.* New York: Macmillan, 1929.

Hartshorne, H., May, M. A., & Shuttleworth, F. K. *Studies in the nature of character* (Vol. 3). *Studies in the organization of character.* New York: Macmillan, 1930.

Harvey, J., Ickes, W., & Kidd, R. *New directions in attribution research.* Hillsdale, N.J.: Erlbaum, 1976.

Hegel, G. W. F. *The phenomenology of mind.* London: G. Allen & Unwin, 1910. (Originally published, 1807.)

Heider, F. *The psychology of interpersonal relations.* New York: Wiley, 1958.

Heine, P. J. *Personality in social theory.* Chicago: Aldine, 1971.

Homans, G. C. *Social behavior.* New York: Harcourt, Brace, & World, 1961.

Horowitz, M. The recall of interrupted group tasks: An experimental study of individual motivation in relation to group goals. *Human Relations,* 1954, 7, 3-38.

Jaccard, J. J. Predicting social behavior from personality traits. *Journal of Research in Personality,* 1974, 7, 358-367.

Jennings, H. H. *Leadership and isolation.* New York: Longmans Green, 1943.

Kelley, H. H. *Attribution in social interaction.* New York: General Learning Press, 1972.

Kenrick, D. T., & Springfield, D. O. Personality traits and the eye of the beholder: Crossing some traditional philosophical boundaries in the search for consistency in all of the people. *Psychological Review,* 1980, *87*, 88-104.

Klugman, S. F. Cooperative vs. individual efficiency in problem solving. *Journal of Educational Psychology,* 1944, *35*, 91-100.

Knowles, E. S. Boundaries around group interaction: The effect of group size and member status on boundary permeability. *Journal of Personality and Social Psychology,* 1973, *26*, 327-331.

Knowles, E. S. Searching for motivations in risk taking and gambling. In W. Eadington (Ed.), *Gambling and society: Interdisciplinary studies on the subject of gambling*. Springfield, Ill.: Charles C Thomas, 1976.

Knowles, E. S., & Bassett, R. L. Groups and crowds as social entities: The effects of activity, size and member similarity on nonmembers. *Journal of Personality and Social Psychology,* 1976, *34*, 837-845.

Knowles, E. S., & Brickner, M. A. Social cohesion affects spatial cohesion. *Personality and Social Psychology Bulletin,* 1981, *7*, 309-313.

Langer, W. C. *The mind of Adolf Hitler.* New York: Basic Books, 1972.

Lehmann, H. C., & Witty, P. A. Faculty psychology and personality traits. *American Journal of Psychology,* 1934, *44*, 490.

Levi-Strauss, C. *The elementary structures of kinship.* Boston: Beacon Press, 1969.

Lewin, K. *The conceptual representation and measurement of psychological forces.* Durham, N.C.: Duke University Press, 1938.

Lewin, K. Experiments in social space. *Harvard Educational Review,* 1939, *9*, 21-32.

Lewin, K. Forces behind food habits and methods of change. *National Research Council Bulletin,* 1943, No. 108, 35-65. (a)

Lewin, K. Psychology and process of group living. *Journal of Social Psychology,* 1943, *17*, 113-131. (b)

Lewin, K. The Research Center for Group Dynamics at Massachusetts Institute of Technology. *Sociometry,* 1946, *2*, 126-136.

Lewin, K. Group decision and social change. In T. H. Newcomb & E. L. Hartley (Eds.), *Readings in social psychology.* New York: Holt, 1947.

Lewin, K. *Resolving social conflicts.* New York: Harper, 1948.

Lewin, K. *Field theory in social science.* New York: Harper & Row, 1951.

Lewin, K., Lippitt, R., & White, R. Patterns of aggressive behavior in experimentally created "social climates." *Journal of Social Psychology,* 1939, *10*, 271-299.

Linton, R. *The study of man.* New York: Appleton-Century, 1936.

Mandler, G., & Sarason, S. B. A study of anxiety and learning. *Journal of Abnormal and Social Psychology,* 1952, *47*, 166-173.

Markus, H. Self-schemata and processing information about the self. *Journal of Personality and Social Psychology,* 1977, *35*, 63-78.

McClelland, D. C., Atkinson, J. W., Clark, R. W., & Lowell, E. L. *The achievement motive.* New York: Appleton-Century-Crofts, 1953.

McDougall, W. *The group mind.* New York: G. P. Putnam's Sons, 1920.

Mead, G. H. *Mind, self, and society.* Chicago: University of Chicago Press, 1934.

Merton, R. K. *Social theory and social structure* (rev. ed.). Glencoe, Ill.: Free Press, 1957.

Mischel, W. *Personality and assessment.* New York: Wiley, 1968.

Moreno, J. L. *Who shall survive.* Washington, D.C.: Nervous and Mental Disease Monograph, No. 58, 1934.

Moscovici, S., & Zavalloni, M. The group as a polarizer of attitudes. *Journal of Personality and Social Psychology,* 1969, *12*, 125-135.

Mullins, N. C. *Theories and theory groups in contemporary American sociology.* New York: Harper & Row, 1973.

Murray, H. A. *Explorations in personality*. New York: Oxford, 1938.

Myers, D. G., & Lamm, H. The group polarization phenomenon. *Psychological Bulletin,* 1976, *83*, 602-627.

Osborne, A. F. *Applied imagination.* New York: Scribner, 1957.

Parsons, T. *The social system.* Glencoe, Ill.: Free Press, 1951.

Pepitone, A. Some lessons from the history of social psychology. *American Psychologist*, 1981, *36*, 972-985.

Perlmutter, H. V., & de Montmollin, G. Group learning of nonsense syllables. *Journal of Abnormal and Social Psychology*, 1952, *47*, 762-769.

Pruitt, D. G. Choice shifts in group discussion: An introductory review. *Journal of Personality and Social Psychology,* 1971, *3*, 339-360.

Redfield, R. *Tepoztlan, A Mexican village.* Chicago: University of Chicago Press, 1930.

Redfield, R. The folk society. *American Journal of Sociology,* 1947, *52*, 293-308.

Roethlisberger, F. J., & Dickson, W. J. *Management and the worker.* Cambridge, Mass.: Harvard University Press, 1939.

Schachter, S. Deviation, rejection, and communication. *Journal of Abnormal and Social Psychology,* 1951, *46*, 190-207.

Schachter, S. *The psychology of affiliation.* Stanford, Calif.: Stanford University Press, 1959.

Schachter, S., & Singer, J. E. Cognitive, social, and physiological determination of emotional state. *Psychological Review,* 1962, *69*, 379-399.

Shaw, M. E. A comparison of individuals and small groups in the rational solution of complex problems. *American Journal of Psychology,* 1932, *44*, 491-504.

Sherif, M. *The psychology of social norms.* New York: Harper & Row, 1936.

Snyder, M. The self-monitoring of expressive behavior. *Journal of Personality and Social Psychology,* 1974, *30*, 526-537.

Snyder, M. Self-monitoring processes. In L. Berkowitz (Ed.), *Advances in experimental social psychology* (Vol. 12). New York: Academic Press, 1979.

Sorokin, P. A. *The crisis of our age.* New York: Dutton, 1941.

Spence, J. T., & Helmreich, R. L. Masculinity and femininity: Their psychological dimensions, correlates, and antecedents. Austin, Tex.: University of Texas Press, 1978.

Stark, W. *The sociology of knowledge: An essay in aid of a deeper understanding of the history of ideas.* New York: Free Press, 1958.

Steiner, I. D. Whatever happened to the group in social psychology. *Journal of Experimental Social Psychology,* 1974, *10*, 94-108.

Tajfel, H. Cognitive aspects of prejudice. *Journal of Social Issues,* 1969, *25*, 79-97.

Tajfel, H. Experiments in intergroup discrimination. *Scientific American,* 1970, *223*, 96-102.

Tajfel, H., Billig, M., Bundy, R., & Flament, C. Social categorization and intergroup behavior. *European Journal of Social Psychology,* 1971, *1*, 149-178.

Thibaut, J. An experimental study of the cohesiveness of under-privileged groups. *Human Relations*, 1950, *3*, 251-278.

Thomas, E. J. Role Theory, personality and the individual. In E. F. Borgatta & W. W. Lambert (Eds.), *Handbook of personality theory and research.* Chicago: Rand McNally, 1968.

Thorndike, R. L. The effect of discussion upon the correctness of group decisions, when the factor of majority influence is allowed for. *Journal of Social Psychology,* 1938, *9*, 343-362.

Timmons, W. M. Can the product of superiority of discussors be attributed to averaging or majority influences? *Journal of Social Psychology,* 1942, *15*, 23-32.

Tönnies, F. *Community and Society* (trans. from the 1887 edition by C. P. Loomis). East Lansing, Mich.: Michigan State University Press, 1957.

Travis, L. E. The effect of a small audience upon eye-hand coördination. *Journal of Abnormal and Social Psychology,* 1925, *20*, 142-146.

Triplett, N. The dynamogenic factors in pacemaking and competition. *American Journal of Psychology,* 1898, *9*, 507-533.

Turner, R. H. Role-taking: Process versus conformity. In A. Rose (Ed.), *Human behavior and social process.* Boston: Houghton Mifflin, 1962.

Wallach, M. A., Kogan, N., & Bem, D. J. Group influence on individual risk taking. *Journal of Abnormal and Social Psychology,* 1962, *65*, 75-86.

Watson, G. B. Do groups think more efficiently than individuals? *Journal of Abnormal and Social Psychology,* 1928, *23*, 328-336.

Wegner, D. M., & Vallacher, R. R. *The self in social psychology.* New York: Oxford University Press, 1977.

White, R. K. The case of Earnst. In H. A. Murray, *Explorations in personality.* New York: Oxford University Press, 1938.

White, R. K. *Lives in progress.* New York: Holt, Rinehart & Winston, 1966.

Wilder, D. A. Perception of groups, sizes of opposition, and social influence. *Journal of Experimental Social Psychology,* 1977, *13*, 253-268.

Wilder, D. A. Reduction of intergroup discrimination through individuation of the outgroup. *Journal of Personality and Social Psychology,* 1978, *36*, 1361-1374.

Wilder, D. A., & Cooper, W. E. Categorization into groups: Consequences for social perception and attribution. In J. Harvey, W. Ickes, & R. Kidd (Ed.), *New directions in attribution research* (Vol. 3). Hillsdale, N.J.: Erlbaum, 1981.

Witkin, H. A., Dyk, R. B., Faterson, H. F., Goodenough, D. R., & Karp, S. A. *Psychological differentiation.* New York: Wiley, 1962.

Witkin, H. A., & Goodenough, D. R. Field dependence and interpersonal behavior. *Psychological Bulletin,* 1977, *84*, 661-689.

Wundt, W. *Elements of folk psychology.* New York: Macmillan, 1916.

Zajonc, R. B. Social facilitation. *Science,* 1965, *149*, 269-274.

Zajonc, R. B. Compresence. In P. B. Paulus (Ed.), *The psychology of group influence.* Hillsdale, N.J.: Erlbaum, 1980.

Zander, A. F. *Motives and goals in groups.* New York: Academic Press, 1971.

Zander, A. The psychology of group processes. *Annual Review of Psychology,* 1979, *30*, 417-451.

Chapter 2

The Origin and Maintenance of Social Roles: The Case of Sex Roles

Paul F. Secord

The concept of social role has always been troublesome and a source of controversy among sociologists and social psychologists. The standard Parsonian view is that roles are structures within a social system. They are sets of normative expectations specifying the attitudes and actions that are appropriate for actors in each role category or position (Parsons, 1951; Parsons & Shils, 1951). But, along with many psychologists, those sociologists who emphasize the constructive activities of actors find this view unsatisfactory (e.g., Goffman, 1969; Turner, 1962, 1968). The difficulty centers around the problem of providing a conceptualization that simultaneously and adequately handles social structures and processes and the individual production of action. All too often what happens is that the formulation of an answer to one side of the question necessarily makes inadequate the formulation of an answer to the other side. For example, the Parsonian emphasis on the systematic, orderly, and consensual nature of societal processes tends to make the individual a mere pawn of societal forces. Speaking of Parson's system, Giddens (1979) puts the criticism aptly: "recogniseably human agents seem to elude the grasp of his scheme: the stage is set, the scripts written, the roles established, but the performers are curiously absent from the scene" (p. 253).

Social Structures and Intentional Action

The Core Problem

The core of the problem seems to be that attempts to explain the social order invoke enduring, relatively permanent structures that shape and constrain the behavior of individuals. But the postulation of structures that shape and constrain seems incompatible with the active, reflective nature of individual behavior: individuals have motives and goals that are largely personal and individual, although not without relation to society. People are not pawns all stamped in the same mold, and they are active in shaping and changing their physical and social environments. Social structures that *enable* make a better fit, but such structures are not particularly Parsonian.

For Parsons, roles are templates for given positions in a system, templates that are enforced by the role partners of the position occupant. Deviant behaviors are disapproved; conforming behaviors are encouraged and rewarded. But such a view has difficulty accounting for the individual production of action in the form of various roles that deviate from the standard, and it does not account for systematic changes that might occur in roles over time. Essentially, then, what needs to be explained is the perseverance of the dynamic balance between a weak consensus on a role and the varying individual productions of it. How do standard definitions ever arise, and how are they maintained in the face of varying individual enactments of them, and when they change, what are the forces that bring about the changes?

On the face of it, the Parsonian model does not generate problems in explaining why social roles persist over time. Since roles are normative and relate to the central values of society, they simply persist. Sanctions are applied to deviations in order to return miscreants to the proper path. But of course, given this view, change becomes impossible to explain. The prominence given to these normative properties of social role has obscured and diverted attention away from the necessity of explaining how roles originate in the first place, how they are sustained over time, and how they undergo change. A dynamic view of society requires not only that stability and persistence be explained, but also that the processes that produce change be identified.

The Transformational Model

What forces are working to preserve the social order, and what sorts of dynamics operate when the social order changes? It might appear that the answers to my questions lie in an examination of socialization processes. But socialization answers a different question: How are social roles transmitted to the next generation? My questions raise a different issue: how and why particular role forms emerge. Why, for example, do roles for young adult men and young adult women take the particular form that they do? Why these forms and not others? What are the forces and processes that create and sustain these forms? And why is it that these particular forms are supported and change prevented? When they do change, why do they change? The central importance of conformity to norms in the Parsonian scheme has lulled us into thinking that normative expectations entirely account for the persistence and continuity of social roles. But that is much too simple a view of society; in my view, the sources of role behavior are complex, and are not to be found in the role actor's passive acceptance of society's values.

The problem stated as one of dynamic balance with respect to roles is merely one instance of the more general problem of similar tensions between societal norms and individual social actions–a core problem of social science. Contemporary theorists, however, have made some progress toward resolving this central dilemma (Giddens, 1976, 1979, 1982; Bhaskar, 1975, 1979, 1982; Manicas, 1980, 1982). The conceptualization of social roles presented here owes much to this new view as represented in the thinking of these scholars. Succinctly and much too briefly, their perspective is as follows:

Social structures exist only by virtue of the activities of people. But they are nevertheless real; they are already present or given when new participants arrive on the scene. For example, marriage is a form of relationship structured by society; couples take on this preexisting form when they marry. But the structure exists only by reason of couples marrying; if all marriages were dissolved and no further marriages took place, there would be no "marital structure." Other forms of relationship might then be substituted, to be sure, but the point here is that social structures exist only through the fact that they are reproduced over and over in the social activities of people.

These statements should not be construed to mean that social structures are *intended* productions of individuals. People marry for individual reasons and for underlying motives, and not with the intention of simply reproducing the family. In their social activities, individuals in part reflect their own goals and purposes, and they monitor their behavior and direct it toward these goals (Harre & Secord, 1972). And in part their activities derive from lesser levels of awareness, which Polanyi (1966) calls "tacit knowledge" and Giddens (1979) calls "practical consciousness." Moreover, individuals interacting with one another do not necessarily produce outcomes that either or both of them intend; often the outcomes deviate markedly from what was anticipated. In a word, social activities have both intended and unintended consequences, and only rarely, if at all, is there a direct intentional connection between these individual activities and the forms that the relevant social structures take. As Bhaskar (1979) puts it, individuals do not work to sustain the structure of a capitalist economy, yet that structure depends on the activity of workers. Social structures are constituted by and in the everyday performances of actors, without which they would not exist, but they are not simply the products of intentional action.

It follows that social structures at any moment are the outcomes of preexisting forms as reproduced through the unintended and intended activities of people. As Bhaskar (1979) points out, it is this feature that provides for the possibility of social change in a way not achieved by the Parsonian scheme. In fact, this model of social structures and activities have been referred to by him as the *transformational model*, to emphasize the dynamic nature of the relation between the structures of society and the social activities of people.

Also important to note is that the actions of material objects, of people, and the structures of society are very different sorts of objects of scientific study, a difference that distinguishes social science from natural science. The three kinds of objects are real, but the structures of society are abstract or theoretical, not empirical, while the activities of people are constituted by social meanings having a material base only in the sense that people are material objects. The former are analogous to the theoretical entities of natural science, but the latter have no counterpart therein. The structures of society are real because they genuinely enable or constrain the performances of people. But—and this is important—they do not do this in an absolute fashion. Social structures may be reproduced or they may be transformed in and through the social activities of people. This is very different from the Parsonian view, which overemphasizes consensus in spite of the fact that nearly all empirical studies find role consensus to be weak. Social roles are not sharply focused: they are nearly always diffuse and blurred.

Where and how do social roles fit into the transformational model? To get roles, we must start with relationships, which are more fundamental to the transformational model. We can conceive of networks of relationships between men and women, networks that can be abstracted from their everyday interactions with one another. In a myriad of ways, those relationships derive from preexisting forms and from the balance of outcomes in interaction. Multifaceted processes of socialization ensure that the actions and attitudes of newcomers to these relationships will reflect to some extent these preexisting forms or structures. At the same time it is important to conceive of the contemporary forms that these relationships take as deriving from the mix of intentional and unintentional actions in the context of prevailing social conditions. Within this perspective, social roles would be reflected in the sets of expectations that pertain to the behavior and attitudes of interacting persons. Thus, we can see that social roles would always be relatively diffuse, and that, to the extent that they have any directive force, such force would be exerted not through "societal norms," but through the medium of social interaction.

How do social roles relate to this daily flow of interaction? Is the concept entirely superfluous, as Coulson (1972) has suggested? Not quite. Relationships are more basic, and if they are understood, the concept of social role has little explanatory force. Yet the concept can be useful in describing an empirical state of affairs that involves relationships. For such concepts, people need to be categorized on some meaningful basis, and either their modal role behaviors or modal role identities may be described. Whether or not this is meaningful depends on the attributes used in categorization. Having red hair or a crooked nose would make little sense as a role categorization, but people have attached great importance to such attributes as skin color or gender. Sometimes this kind of categorization is a pure stereotype; the descriptions of the supposed behaviors or identities are simply false. In other cases there is some truth in the description that people give. In the latter instance, what needs to be explained is how the behavior or identity is arrived at through the structures of society and through social interaction. It is in this sense that the notions of role behavior and role identity can be useful. But this is true only when the role descriptions can be linked to a complex of factors operating through the interface of individual action and social structures.

Although role identities or behaviors may readily be described through well-known empirical techniques, tracing the forces that produce particular descriptions is far from easy. Generally speaking, such analysis is only possible when changes take place in role identities or behaviors. The analysis then becomes a search for covariates of the changes. Even when individuals create role identities different from those enacted earlier by others occupying the same role positions, measurable change is not apt to be discovered if the directions of change produced by different actors are helter-skelter. Only to the extent that an appreciable number of individuals have created a set of relationships that are in tandem with each other but different from those that prevailed earlier can we say that social roles have changed. But when this happens, it follows that the change has resulted from conditions or forces that are pervasive, making their discovery possible.

In the remainder of this chapter, I will provide a sketch of how social roles might be maintained or changed as a result of the interplay between interaction and the social structure. This cannot be done for roles in general, but it can be done for a particular role. In part, such an analysis is an empirical problem, but at the same time the conceptual problems in conducting such an analysis are formidable and, ideally, a case analysis here will provide the outlines of conceptual procedures that can be applied to other roles. My choice of role is the role identities and role behaviors associated with gender.

The Case of Sex Roles

No society has a single role for males or for females; sex roles are really age-sex roles. Social expectations and behavior patterns are different for children and for adults of different ages. The focus here will be primarily on sex roles for young adults, during the period when marital selection occurs as well as the family period including the child-bearing years. During this time span adult sex roles are most distinctive and the conditions that shape and control them are most readily visible. In collaboration with Marcia Guttentag, I have already conducted and reported an extensive study of changes in relationships between men and women during several periods in history and in the contemporary United States (Guttentag and Secord, 1982). Here, I shall refer only to those features of the study that illustrate and support the conceptual analysis of sex roles being offered here.

Sex roles are associated with some very distinctive conditions that play no part in generating or maintaining other social roles or norms. These revolve around the fact that sex roles and behavior patterns concern two kinds of human beings who are biologically different from one another and who are usually present in a society in approximately equal numbers. This division into male and female introduces the possibility that biological factors might shape sex role patterns. And, as we shall see, the ratio of men to women in a population is of great importance in shaping relationships between men and women, especially in circumstances when the ratio becomes imbalanced.

Of equal importance is the prevalence of pairings between men and women. No other form of pairing among humans is so persistent and so persevering and it is this fact that makes the analysis of dyadic interaction so relevant to relationships between the sexes. Obviously this pairing is partly biological and specifically sexual, although the variety of forms that sexual behaviors take under various social conditions make clear that sexual biology is not simply and directly expressed in a narrow band of sexual behavior, or even always toward the opposite sex. Moreover, the needs of men and women for each other are not solely sexual; companionship, nurture, play, maintaining a home and family, and a great variety of other forms of expression characterize male-female transactions. In order to focus on both the structural and the dyadic properties of relationships between men and women, I shall assume no biological differences between men and women in the strength of their needs, sexual or otherwise. In the absence of strong evidence, making the assumption that men have stronger sex needs than women—or the reverse—would simply beg the questions that I am trying to answer.

A concept vital to understanding the interplay between dyadic interaction and social structures is *social power.* Within the Parsonian scheme, power remains largely unanalyzed. The presumption is that social sanctions are applied by role partners according to the accepted norms of society, or at least of the social system under study. But this leaves out the needs and characteristics of the parties to interaction, and, further, assumes that the norms are universal. In fact, norms may be used by parties to interaction in order to further their own ends. More broadly, the power position of each party in a dyad is affected by social structural conditions. In other words, we might identify two sources of social power: one that lies directly in the nature of dyadic interaction, and the other, in societal structures. I shall call these two kinds *dyadic power* and *structural power.*

Dyadic power can be analyzed within the framework of social exchange theory in terms of the resources, needs, and dependencies of each of the partners in interaction. Structural power stems from the larger society, and its most common forms are economic, political, and legal. These two kinds of power, of course, are not entirely independent of each other. One interface depends on the fact that the needs and resources of the parties to a relationship may in part be determined by structural considerations. Although the economic power of individuals might stem from their position in the larger society, their wealth or income might be a powerful resource in interacting with another party in a relationship; conversely, poverty might create dependency on the other party.

Before proceeding further, I will present a brief statement of social exchange theory with special attention to the role of dyadic power in relationships between men and women (Becker, 1976; Blau, 1964; Emerson, 1962; Homans, 1974; Kelley, 1979; Kelley & Thibaut, 1978; Thibaut & Kelley, 1959). Worth emphasizing is that social exchange theory applies with maximum force when the parties to interaction are uncommitted and when the interchanges are under the control of the parties themselves, as opposed to control by parents, parent surrogates, or community. Later, I will return to the interplay between dyadic and structural levels of analysis with respect to sex roles.

Social Exchanges and Dyadic Power

The focus of social exchange theory is on the social transactions in a relationship between two persons as these transactions take place in the context of the larger set of options that each party has in other relationships. The relationship may be initial or temporary, or it may be of long duration. As in economic exchange, interactions between a man and a woman can be viewed as exchanges wherein each party experiences certain benefits and costs. The benefits and costs are largely psychological, including not only sexual pleasures, but enjoyment of intimacy, companionship, feelings of self-worth, or whatever. Costs are also psychological, such as "spending" one's time, embarrassment or rejection, guilt or deception, and so on. These benefits and costs taken together over a period of time yield each party's outcomes.

The degree of satisfaction yielded in an exchange depends on both the resources of one's partner to benefit one, and the intensity of one's need for the resource. For example, the ability to carry on a good conversation is a resource if one has a partner who likes to participate in such conversation. A person may be beautiful or handsome, sexy, fun to be with, emotionally supportive, able to take charge of a situation, a good listener–these are common resources that most people enjoy in a partner. But clearly, whether they are resources depends on what one wants from a partner; for example, some would rather take charge of a situation themselves, or do the listening instead of the talking. Or the beauty of a woman may be a resource desired by the man she is with, but a liability if she is with a woman instead.

The extent to which resources and needs determine the level of satisfaction in the outcomes of social exchanges depends on yet another important condition that varies with prior experiences in and out of the relationship. Outcomes by themselves neither tell us about satisfactions with the series of exchanges nor whether further exchanges will take place. What is crucial is the relationship between the obtained outcome and the level of outcome that is expected. The model of economic exchange makes this clear. Whether or not a women who has just purchased something thinks that she has made a good buy depends on what she thinks the going price is. Similarly, satisfaction with the outcome in a social relationship depends on the level that is expected.

In economic exchange, the going price is the expected level. Just as this level is based on other transactions of the same kind from the past, on tentative pricings from other sellers, and even on prices that one thinks might be obtained, the level of expectation for a social transaction is based on similar transactions in the past and the alternative transactions that the party perceives as available. A desirable man may be accustomed to highly satisfying interactions with women; he expects more and would be less satisfied or even disappointed by some actions than would a less desirable man. The concept of *alternatives* is crucial; human satisfactions are always relative; their evaluation depends on what might have been experienced instead. These potential experiences may be estimated from past experiences or from optional alternatives: real, imagined, or perhaps vicariously experienced by observing other persons in life, movies, or literature. Moreover, as we shall see, it is the concept of alternative outcomes that provides a crucial link with certain features of the social structure.

From these concepts of outcomes, expectations, and alternative options follow implications about the relative satisfactions of each party, the relative dependencies of each on the other, the relative power each has over the other, and the desire to continue or discontinue the relationship.

Before continuing with this analysis of social exchange theory a common objection to it must be dealt with. This is the complaint that social exchange theory makes friendship and love appear calculating and self-serving. But social exchange theory does not require a conscious weighing of costs and benefits in a relationship –that would indeed belie the very meaning of friendship and love. Exchange theory does not even make any assumption of "equitable" exchanges between partners, because each partner's satisfactions depend on his or her own expectations and outcomes. The viewpoint taken in social exchange theory is quite different from what these critics suppose. Exchange theory assumes that the *feelings* of satisfaction, warmth, love, rejection, or bitterness are usually all that is consciously experienced, but that these feelings nevertheless result from an unconscious assessment of the balance between outcomes, expectations, and alternatives.

Although a calculus may enable prediction or explanation of the kinds of emotional reactions that will occur, it need not imply a deliberate, self-conscious calculation of benefits and costs by people in a relationship. An analogous situation may help here. Consider the case of children who have received too little attention. They are apt to engage in exhibitionism and attention-getting tactics as well as other unpleasant or inappropriate behaviors. This does not mean that they have consciously calculated the amount of attention received and compared it with some expected level; yet they react *as if* they have such knowledge and are thus responding to the lack of attention.

Social exchanges are seen in clearest outline where both participants in a relationship have maximum freedom to behave in a variety of ways, including leaving the relationship. Thus, the exchange process is most dramatically demonstrated in relationships that are tentative or new, or in an early stage. But relationships have to be open to a wide variety of possible exchanges for this to be the case, and this depends on social structural conditions.

In contrast, when a relationship between two persons is long standing and has many personal and institutional commitments, the role of exchanges is constrained in various ways, although the variety of exchanges that may be made in long-term relationships is apt to be expanded. A society that is stable, with long-standing traditions, places more constraints on the forms that relationships may take, limiting the exchanges that are open to negotiation. Another crucially important feature of enduring intimate relationships is the transformation of initial outcomes into joint outcomes (Kelley & Thibaut, 1978; Kelley, 1979). When this happens, both partners place more emphasis on their partner's outcomes; this modifies the balance of outcomes that each experiences, and is apt to reduce the contribution of alternative outcomes to the overall balance. So changes within relationships over time as well as the interlocking of exchange processes with societal structures and contexts are crucial to understanding relationships between men and women.

Attraction, Dependency, and Social Power

From the viewpoint of social exchange theory, two elements are of foremost importance in any relationship between a man and a woman: attraction of each to the other, and the dependency of each on the other. *Attraction* has to do with the level of outcomes that each experiences in transactions with the other, relative to what each party expects. *Dependency* has to do with the alternative options that each party has. Let us consider attraction first, and dependency second.

A simple principle is that the level of attraction to the other party in a relationship is a function of the level of outcomes experienced in relation to the *level that is expected*. The expected level is relatively stable and has become established as a result of the outcomes experienced in past exchanges with the same party, in similar exchanges in other relations, and of optional exchanges in alternative relationships. The more the actual outcomes exceed the expected level, the more attraction will be experienced. Put simply, a strong liking or attraction for another person results from rewarding exchanges with the person that appreciably exceed those ordinarily experienced.

The other element of social exchange theory, dependency on the relationship, and its complement, dyadic power, is central to understanding how the relationship and, ultimately, how sex roles are shaped. Staying in or leaving a relationship depends heavily on the extent to which outcomes in the relationship exceed those that are perceived to be *available in alternative* relationships. It is this fact that brings in competition and supply and demand in social relationships, and it is this fact that alters the balance of power within the relationship when sex ratios are out of balance. If the outcomes in alternative relationships are perceived by an individual to be highly satisfying (whether they actually are or not), this perception will raise the level of what is expected within the existing relationship. This makes the existing relationship less attractive, because the outcomes are then closer to the expected level. At the same time, this party is less dependent on it for satisfaction.

Commitment

So far I have been discussing tentative or early stage relationships, for alternatives loom larger in this phase, and often become more psychologically remote when a mutual commitment has taken place. Commitment is an important concept. Perhaps the most formal commitment in our society between a man and a woman is marriage, but we can conceive of commitments that are progressively weaker until they reach the point of no commitment. Commitments need not be formal. They amount to an expectation on the part of both parties that they will continue to see one another, and behave toward each other as they have in the past; in other words, the commitment has to be shared or mutually understood. At some point the commitment may be made explicit, perhaps when the couple decides to share the same residence, or to get married. But a commitment could become quite strong through mutual understanding without even being explicitly discussed.

Whether a commitment involves marriage or not, or living together or separately, such a commitment usually carries with it an agreement not to engage in intimacies outside of the relationship, and sometimes additional constraints are placed on relating to third parties. Commitment typically requires a considerable block of one's time; at the very least, much of one's recreational or spare time is shared with the other party. Along with such commitment comes an implication of emotional support and caring on the part of the other party, who becomes someone to depend on in time of need or trouble. But at the same time it implies an agreement to take the bad with the good; one puts up with the other's tantrums, quirks, or obnoxious habits. Both parties gain some benefits from the commitment. They feel more secure, they no longer need to try to impress, or to always be on their best behavior, they can relax and be more comfortable. Note particularly that a joint exclusive commitment implies a kind of sharing, a give and receive attitude on the part of both parties. Joint outcomes become salient; each considers how his or her behavior will affect the other. These various positive and negative features of commitment combine to modify outcomes for each party. For commitments to be made and maintained, each party must feel that he or she will be better off with the arrangement than without it. But again this feeling is not necessarily based on a conscious calculation; the only tangible manifestation of it may be a desire for the commitment or the lack of such desire. Where such a desire exists, both parties highly value each other, and this in turn raises the outcomes of both.

When parties to a dyad have made a mutual commitment, each party's outcomes depend more heavily than before on choices that the other party makes (mutual fate control) and on the behavior of the other party (behavior control) (Kelley & Thibaut, 1978). The outcomes of each become interdependent; formerly egoistic outcomes become transferred into what Kelley and Thibaut have called joint outcomes. For example, the welfare or happiness of the partner now contribute substantially to one's own outcomes; when the partner's outcomes are poor, one's own outcomes are also reduced, and similarly when the partner's outcomes are especially rewarding, one's own are enhanced. So, although it might have seemed that social exchange theory could not account for altruism, it in fact does so quite readily through the interdependence of outcomes and their transformation into joint outcomes. Strong commitment and resulting interdependence of outcomes for that dyad consequently nullify the possible effects of imbalance in sex ratios and the differential alternative options that they create.

Social Structure and Dyadic Relationships

If there were no biological or psychological differences between men and women, and if male-female dyads were isolated from the rest of society, there would be no role differences between men and women. This is true because biological or psychological differences are apt to affect the outcomes of dyadic interaction and thereby produce differences in role behaviors and, ultimately, in role identities. A similar consequence is produced to the extent that social structural factors affect outcomes in dyadic interaction. The variety of role patterns that might be produced by the interplay between dyadic interaction, on the one hand, and actor characteristics and social structural considerations on the other, is almost infinite, and therefore difficult to analyze. But two sets of conditions, if they existed, would be relatively easy to detect: (1) those conditions that give to one gender more dyadic power, and (2) those that provide more structural power to one gender. This would result in relationships that would be to the advantage of the more powerful gender. Because of the nature of dyadic interaction, role behaviors and identities would be shaped to suit the needs of the more powerful gender, and to the extent that that gender shares common needs, a distinctive cast would be given to role patterns. That this is clearly the case for sex roles will be demonstrated shortly.

Linkages between dyadic interaction and the social structure that affect sex roles may be stated in terms of the following propositions:

1. Social interactions between men and women are shaped by the power-dependency relationship within the dyad.
2. Biophysical differences between men and women interact with structural and other societal conditions so as to shape dyadic interactions in certain directions.
3. Gender-related features of social structures presently provide men with resources that are overwhelmingly greater than those provided women; these resources give men a great advantage in negotiating social exchanges with women, both in dyads and in the larger society.
4. Gender-related features of social structures interact with a wide range of societal conditions prevailing in any particular time and place, and the outcomes of these interactions influence dyadic interactions in various directions.
5. Gender-related features of societal structures typically place more constraints on the dyadic interactions of women than on those of men.

Consider first the proposition that the biophysical properties of men and women have influenced both dyadic interactions and the social structures that have emerged in society. We do not need to concern ourselves here with promising but inconclusive research on the relationships between hormonal processes and behavior, or with other lines of contemporary research on biological differences between the sexes, in order to draw the conclusion that there are important biophysical differences between men and women. There are several gross physical differences which no one can deny and which historically have been of enormous importance in shaping sex role differences. Females bear and suckle their young, and men are physically stronger, which has given them an advantage in hunting, warfare, and more generally, in achieving domination in any face-to-face confrontations between male and female.

It seems indisputable that these differences were important in the past in establishing women in their historical role as second-class citizens. As long as physical strength was crucial to warfare and in face-to-face encounters, the superior strength of men was bound to provide them with advantages in the economic, political, and social realm. And as long as women were confined to the home with its domestic duties and the bearing and rearing of children, their roles in the economic, political, and social world had to be severely limited. This domestic role was made especially burdensome in the absence of effective contraceptive methods. Most women bore large numbers of children, creating heavy burdens for their role as mothers. Prior to the industrial revolution, the role of homemaker was especially weighty because the home was a center of production for meeting family needs. Food and clothing were manufactured there, and most of that process was women's work.

That a woman's role was almost exclusively domestic came about not only because of biophysical differences. The superior physical strength of men gave them initial advantages in economic and political spheres. Their prowess in warfare and in endless local confrontations gave them control over resources, often including the labor of those they vanquished. And when the world was less populated, bearing large numbers of healthy children was commonly an important societal goal. Nowhere was this more apparent than in the Sparta of the classical period, where women were carefully nurtured to be breeders of strong male citizen-warriors and sturdy girls who would themselves grow up to breed more Spartan citizens (Pomeroy,

1972; Guttentag & Secord, 1982). It appears that throughout much of history, men used their superior structural powers to ensure that women were kept firmly within their domestic roles. Documentary fragments that survive from an endless variety of societies repeatedly stress the central importance of the childbearing and childrearing role of women.

Of course not all women were pressed into the domestic role of wife and mother. But these exceptions only testify further to the importance of men's superior structural power. At various times and places, women in history were also pressed into slavery, indenture, concubinage, harems, prostitution, and the role of mistresses. Even more eloquently than the domestic role, these exceptional roles testify to the exercise of power by men to shape the lives of women to their own desires.

Let us shift now to the more general notion of the role identity of women. Here the issue is the attributes that are commonly assigned to women in general. We might expect the long-term, one-down position held by women to generate beliefs about women that are commensurate with their weak power and low status positions. Let us consider what the common stereotype of women has been. While it is easy to get into a quarrel over any one of these features, several characteristics have traditionally been ascribed to women. Young women today have already changed to some extent, and are seen somewhat differently in some quarters. Perhaps the list here is better attributed to earlier generations, although many men, and women too, still have not given up these images. Women have generally been considered to be unassertive, submissive, passive, soft, and dependent; affectionate, nurturant, and domestic; devious, manipulative, emotional, and irrational. Interesting contradictions arise over sexuality. Sometimes they are believed to have more control over their sexual impulses—to have a muted sexuality—but historically they have more often been believed to be dangerously passionate and undisciplined. In contrast with women, men are believed to have a strong sex drive, to be aggressive, assertive, competitive, strong, independent, rational, and tough. Of course the perceived qualities of men and women vary from society to society, but most of these attributes are common to many societies.

Why are women perceived in this way? If they actually behave in accordance with these attributes, does this behavior stem from some inherent nature, or is it demanded by the circumstances of their dyadic and societal interactions with men? My belief is that most, or perhaps all, of these attributes are associated with the effects on women resulting from the exercise by men of the superior structural powers that men have held throughout history. Many of the attributes typically ascribed to women follow quite directly from the traditional role of mother: nurturant, domestic, soft, and affectionate. All of the remaining ones follow from the weak power position of women vis-à-vis men: unassertive, submissive, passive, dependent, devious, manipulative, irrational, and emotional. All the items in this set stem from the greater power, authority, and status that men have over women, whether as husbands, bosses, statesmen, or soldiers. Many wives are economically dependent on their husbands, and women in the work force are generally in subordinate positions. Their relationship to their husband in the traditional family is unassertive, submissive, and passive; their relationship to their boss has similar attributes.

That women are often believed to be devious and manipulative also stems from their one-down position. Women may conceal those values on which there is disagreement, may be ingratiating, may yield to pressures to conform to men's desires, and may actually shape themselves according to the image desired by men. What is seen as emotionality or irrationality in part also stems from disadvantages encountered if one tries to be direct when in a low power position. But this set of characteristics is also attributed to *every* low status, low power group, whether male or female. Similar beliefs are commonly held about racial and ethnic groups with low status and power, the lower socioeconomic classes, and servants, among others. They are a function of the disparity in status and power, and they change if that disparity changes.

Sex Roles and Imbalanced Sex Ratios

Since the position of women has been so continuous throughout history, how can we test the validity of the views expressed in the previous section? Typically, when relationships remain unchanged, it is extraordinarily difficult to provide explanations for them. The historical differences might well stem purely from differences in biology between men and women, as Tiger and Fox (1971) have argued. But in fact at some periods in history the relative dyadic powers of men and women have changed markedly, although men have almost always retained their superior structural powers. These changes have been reviewed in the book, *Too Many Women: The Sex Ratio Question*, by Marcia Guttentag and me, and they strongly support the theoretical statement that I have outlined in this paper. Here I have only enough space to cite the central argument and to refer briefly to the evidence.

A key to power and dependency in *dyadic* relationships between men and women is the sex ratio, representing the relative numbers of men and women in a population. This ratio is commonly represented as a number of men per 100 women in the population under study. For example, a ratio of 120 would mean that there are 120 men in the male cohort for each 100 women in the female cohort. Most directly relevant for our purposes are sex ratios for those cohorts of the population who are at ages when they most commonly marry. This may be calculated for single men and women in their early twenties or it may extend through the child-bearing years, to include single, divorced, and widowed individuals. But what is crucial about the ratio is that it reflects the relative marital opportunities of men and women. So a further adjustment based on the number of partners of suitable ages is essential. Common practice throughout the world is for women to marry men who are, on the average, two or three years older than themselves, so that a sex ratio that represents marital opportunities would include cohorts of men and women in which men were about two or three years older than the women, on the average. Cohorts may also be selected on the basis of income, education, or social class so as to reflect the impact on marital opportunities of marital choices commonly made on the basis of these attributes.

Sex ratios such as these are markedly affected by wars and other factors that create sex-differential mortality, by rises or falls in the birth rate, by sex-selective migration, and by parental neglect or infanticide which affects one sex differentially. Thus, there have been many periods in history where the ratios of male cohorts to their corresponding female cohorts have been either very high or very low.

How does an imbalanced sex ratio affect dyadic interaction? It works through the impact on dyadic interaction of perceived or actual outcomes in optional alternative relationships. When unattached women are in short supply, for example, men have fewer alternatives to interaction with a particular woman. She, on the other hand, has a larger number of suitable men to choose from. Similarly, if unattached men are scarce, women have fewer alternatives to forming a particular dyad or staying in it, if it is already formed. Via processes of social exchange, this circumstance provides more dyadic power to the gender that is in short supply while the gender that is in oversupply becomes more dependent on the relationship. Worth noting is the point that it is not merely the possibility of leaving the dyad and forming a new one that reduces dependency and increases power, but also that the level of expectation within the existing dyad is raised because of the availability of alternative outcomes. This makes the more powerful member of the dyad less dependent on the partner, and increases the likelihood of leaving the dyad. This is the core of the argument, but there are many subtleties that cannot be discussed in the space available here (see Guttentag and Secord, 1982, for a more extended discussion).

These shifts in *dyadic* power resulting from imbalanced sex ratios interact with gender differences in *structural* power to produce profound changes in the relationships between men and women and in the role attributes ascribed to each gender. These relationships and role identities vary with the distinctive features of different societies, although societies having high sex ratios commonly share certain effects, as do societies with low sex ratios. Before describing the interactions between dyadic and structural powers and demonstrating their consequences, I will describe elements that commonly characterize high sex ratio societies and those that characterize low sex ratio societies.

> *High sex ratios: An undersupply of women.* When sex ratios are high, there are more men than women. In such societies, young adult women would be highly valued. The manner in which they would be valued would depend upon the society. Most often, single women would be valued for their beauty and glamour, and married women as wives and mothers. Men would want to possess a wife, and would be willing to make and keep a commitment to remain with her. But in some societies, this might be carried to an extreme, and scarce women might be valued as chattels and possessions.
>
> In high sex ratio societies, women would achieve their satisfactions through traditional roles. Male and female roles would be complementary, involving a division of labor with men and women having distinctly different tasks. Women's role would be in the family, that of homemaker and mother. High sex ratios in certain cultural contexts would give women a subjective sense of power and control over their lives. This would be particularly true when they could choose among men for a marriage partner. This sense of relative power and control would *not* be expressed by

women in striving toward sexual or economic independence, but would instead be reflected within traditional institutions of the society, particularly the family. Here, women would often gain economic mobility through marriage; they would marry upward in socioeconomic class. They would not have strong career ambitions nor would they actively agitate for personal or political rights. . . .

Both men and women would stress sexual morality rather than licentiousness, especially morality for women. Men would be motivated to promote morality for women so that they could maintain exclusive possession of a woman. Virginity would be prized in potential wives. These societies would often have a double standard; males would be promiscuous, females would be expected to be chaste. In spite of various forms of illicit sexual behavior, the cultural emphasis would be on the male's commitment to a single partner for many years or for life. Occasionally, these societies would expect sexual morality and fidelity for both sexes. . . .

Low sex ratios: An oversupply of women. Women in such societies would have a subjective sense of powerlessness, and would feel personally devalued by the society. They would be more likely to be valued as mere sex objects. Unlike the high sex ratio situation, women would find it difficult to achieve economic mobility through marriage. More men and women would remain single, or if they married, would be more apt to get divorced. Illegitimate births would rise sharply. The divorce rate would be high, but the remarriage rate would be high for men only. The number of single-parent families headed by women would increase markedly.

Sexual libertarianism would be the prevailing ethos, shared by men and women alike, although, because of the surplus of women, the options would be greater for men. Sexual relationships outside of marriage would be accepted. . . . Brief liaisons would be usual. Women would more often share a man with other women. Adultery would be commonplace. At the same time, men would have opportunities to move successively from woman to woman, or to maintain multiple relationships with different women. Because of the shortage of men, these opportunities would largely be denied to women. The outstanding characteristic of times when women are in oversupply would be that men would *not* remain committed to the same woman throughout her childbearing years. The culture would not emphasize love and commitment, and a lower value would be placed on marriage and the family. Instead, transient relationships between men and women would become important. . . . We would expect various forms of feminism to be accelerated under these low sex ratio conditions. . . . (Guttentag & Secord, 1982, Chap. 1)

By and large, these features of societies with imbalanced sex ratios are confirmed in our studies, which included high sex ratio periods in classical Athens in early medieval times, in the shtetl culture of Orthodox Jews in Eastern Europe and in Colonial and early America. Contrasted with these were low sex ratio periods in classical Sparta, in the late medieval period, and in the 1970s in the United States. In high sex ratio societies, women assume the domestic role and have the role identities previously described; in low sex ratio societies marriage, the family, and women are typically denigrated, but women become more economically independent and push for other forms of independence; often women's movements arise. Spartan women were much more educated than Athenian women, and unlike them, could own and inherit property, and sometimes entered the professions. In contrast to the early medieval period during which the troubadours, love poetry, and chivalric traditions emerged, the late medieval period was characterized by the *Frauenbewegung*, or women's movements, which developed a radical feminist literature (Bucher, 1882; Guttentag & Secord, 1982). And in the late 1960s and especially in the 1970s, for the first time in its 200-year history, the United States had a low sex ratio reflecting a shortage of men as marital partners. At the time the strongest feminist movement in history was launched. Along with this has come much greater sexual freedom for women, as well as sharp rises in divorce rates, later ages for first marriages, more women remaining single, a higher ratio of illegitimate to legitimate births, and a greater ratio of divorced women to the total cohort of women in the same age brackets. These effects reflect the lessened commitment of men to an enduring relationship with women, a commitment that, in our view, has become weak because of prevailing low sex ratios.

What about structural power during the periods in question? We are assuming that it has remained relatively constant, but what are *its* effects? How does it interact with dyadic power, and what is the evidence? The key to its effects lies in the peculiar asymmetry between high and low sex ratio societies, an asymmetry that may be troublesome to the feminist-oriented reader. Such readers might well have already asked themselves why low sex ratios were not simply the opposite of high sex ratio societies. When women are scarce, men use their structural powers to insist on monogamy and induce a special morality for women which shelters and protects them and which greatly constrains their sexual activities. In this way men compensate for their weak dyadic power. When women are abundant, men have easier access to women, so they lift constraints on the sexual behavior of women, and are apt to form more than one relationship, either simultaneously or successively. And the feminist question is: "Why, when men are plentiful, don't women act exactly as men did when women were abundant and take advantage of their own scarcity by forming more than one relationship and by reducing their commitments to any one man?"

The answer lies in the fact that, in both high sex ratio and low sex ratio societies, men have held an overwhelming balance of structural power. Thus, even when dyadic power is held by women, men use their structural power to compensate for their weak dyadic power to shape women's roles in a fashion that is to male advantage: virginity and monogamy are emphasized. We can see this if we examine what it would take to produce symmetry in high and low sex ratio societies. Clearly, what we need is variations in the balance of structural power along with variations in dyadic power. This is illustrated in the fourfold matrix of Table 2-1, filled out by inventing two imaginary societies, Eros and Libertinia, which meet the condition that the structural power be held by women. First, consider the two sexually permissive societies, one familiar, and the other strange. From Table 2-1, we can see that in the familiar permissive society, men hold the dyadic power *and* the structural

Table 2-1. Societal Consequences of Gender Possession of Dyadic and Structural Power

	Gender holding structural power	
Gender holding dyadic power	Males	Females
Males (low sex ratio)	Sexually permissive society with familiar roles	Traditional society with reversed roles (Eros)
Females (high sex ratio)	Traditional society with familiar roles	Sexually permissive society with reversed roles (Libertinia)

power. In Libertinia, women hold both the dyadic power *and* the structural power. The result? In the former, men have used both powers to shape women's roles so as to maximize their own outcomes in relationships with women, but in Libertinia, women have done so. There, women have multiple relationships with men, and often exploit them. In both of these societies, the gender lacking both forms of power has the poorest outcomes in relating to the opposite sex, and Libertinia reflects (Table 2-1) a role reversal for both sexes.

Looking next at the two traditional societies, we find that structural and dyadic power are divided. In the familiar traditional society, men hold the structural power but lack dyadic power. Thus, they cannot maximize their outcomes wholly at the expense of women, but must arrive at a compromise arrangement, since women can use their dyadic power to place men in competition with one another. Because of women's power to choose among men, men are forced to make a commitment to a woman in order to have a relationship with her, and they must treat her well or run the risk of losing her to another man. But their structural power is sufficient to allow them to placc constraints on women's freedoms as well as to impose a sexual morality on them. In Eros, women hold the structural power but not the dyadic power. And they use these powers in exactly the same way that men do in a traditional society. In Eros, the men have roles like those of women in a traditional society. They stay home and raise the children, while women work in the industrial and business world, and hold most of the important positions in government. Monogamy and virginity are insisted on for men, and they are sheltered and protected. What we are suggesting, then, is that, were women instead of men to hold the structural power, the sex roles of men and women would be reversed, and the forms that these take are jointly determined by which genders hold the dyadic and the structural power. The two traditional societies are mirror images of each other, with the sex roles reversed, and the two sexually permissive societies are likewise.

The use of imaginary societies has been helpful in grasping the interplay between structural and dyadic power. But given these constructs, is there any empirical support for them? We did not expect to find and have been unable to find any society like Eros, where women hold the structural power but not the dyadic power. But we have found one society analogous to Libertinia, where women hold both the structural (mainly economic) and dyadic power. This society is the Bakweri, living in a cluster of villages in Cameroon, in West Africa, in a plantation economy (Ardener, Ardener, & Warmington, 1960). It is important to note that they were living in a state of partial social disorganization (of their original culture) because they were under a British Protectorate. They had a sex ratio of 236 men to each 100 women, with an extremely high divorce rate and great instability in relationships between men and women. The high sex ratio was created by continual migrations of Bakweri men from other areas to work on the plantations. Bakweri women were highly valued, both as wives and for casual sex. This is illustrated by the custom of requiring the husband to pay "bride-wealth" to the family of the bride in order to obtain a wife, and also by the fact that casual sex was used as a lucrative source of income by Bakweri women, both married and unmarried. Many Bakweri women earned enough through casual sex to have an independent income and some paid off their own bride-wealth in order to be free of their husband. The large number of single men who migrated to this area made this possible. Many husbands were unhappy with their wives' extramarital activities, but their wives complained of insufficient support, the most frequent divorce complaint. Wives often changed husbands if they found a man who could pay a larger bride-wealth and repay the earlier bride-wealth.

What is especially interesting about the Bakweri is the interplay between the sex ratio and dyadic and structural power. The scarcity of women gave Bakweri women a chance to gain both dyadic and structural (economic) power, which they used to achieve independence. Bakweri men often made only a marginal living. Many found it extremely difficult to come up with the substantial bride-wealth required to obtain a bride. Without structural power matching or surpassing that of their women, they were unable to impose traditional roles on them.

Let us return to the United States today. Sex ratios for cohorts of men and women of suitable ages for each other were surprisingly low in 1970 for unmarried adults (single, divorced, or widowed) in their mid-forties or younger, ranging from 72 men to 97 men per 100 women, depending on the age-cohorts examined. Of course, for unmarried women past middle age, the situation was and is much worse, ranging down to as few as 50 men per 100 women. This has meant that millions of young women have not been able to assume traditional family roles, for lack of a suitable marital partner. This shortage of men, moreover, is especially acute for the most educated women, since the established marital practice is for women to marry a man of equal or higher social status than her own, and this means that such men are even more scarce. It is this situation that creates a pool of women unable to fulfill traditional women's roles, a pool of women who constitute a recruiting ground for feminist and other movements, and who provide some of the leadership for such movements.

But the next two decades are apt to reveal substantial changes. As the current population of underage boys and girls reaches adulthood, the sex ratios will gradually move toward balance. Moreover, women have been and will continue to gain more structural power as time goes on, in both the economic and political spheres, and as legislation that discriminates against women continues to be amended or revoked. In addition, we have reached a time when physical differences in strength and in the childbearing function of women no longer places such severe constraints on the sex roles that women can assume. Briefly, physical strength is no longer a prerequisite for action in our modern, technologically advanced societies, not in industry, business, government, or even in warfare. And while bearing children remains important, effective contraceptives have enabled at least some women not to have children or to severely limit the number of children, and modern medical care has reduced the debilitating effects of having children.

Although men still hold an overwhelming advantage in structural power, the lightening of women's domestic and physical burden through modern technology and medicine and the small but important gains that they have made in economic and political spheres in the United States have already had their impact in changing the domestic roles that traditionally have been assigned to women throughout history. Predictions for the future are hazardous, but sober projections depict strong continued gains for women in the economic sphere (Smith, 1979), and there is reason to believe that political gains will also be made. If these predictions are correct, then we may anticipate that women will ultimately assume roles that are radically different from the familiar ones of history. If this happens, male roles will likewise be radically reformed, since, for both sexes, roles emerge from the interplay between dyadic interaction and social structures.

Conclusions

Returning to the larger issue of the origin and maintenance of other social roles, we may ask whether our case study of sex roles has theoretical implications for social roles in general. Although only an intensive analysis of other social roles can provide firm conclusions, certain implications stand out clearly. First, relationships and not roles are primary; roles are distillations or abstractions gleaned from stable relationships exhibited by an appreciable number of actors in a given category or class.

Second, the major contrast with the Parsonian view of social roles is the idea that, instead of being solely a reflection of internalized norms, social roles originate and are maintained by the distribution of social power among interacting participants as reflected in social structures. As Giddens (1979) has noted, the Parsonian scheme is particularly neglectful of social power. My view is that the power dimension is critical: social roles must be constantly maintained by the balance of power and, when this balance shifts, roles change as well. Although this does not give up completely the idea that social roles are internalized as norms, it substitutes the more dynamic view that these norms must be continually supported in and through role relationships, as well as the idea that, when the distribution of power among interactants shifts, roles will also change in directions appropriate to the new distribution of power.

Although it is true that in the Parsonian system the expectations held by the "role partner" have always been considered important to the role taken by an actor, little attention has been paid to the distribution of power among role partners and especially to the conditions that create such powers. Now that the power dimension has been brought to the fore, it seems almost obvious. Patients often attribute god-like qualities to surgeons; this follows from their power over the life or death of the patients. Elderly people in modern technological societies, especially when retired from active participation, have rather ineffectual role qualities attributed to them, reflecting their loss of status and power. Master-slave complexes at various times and places in history involve the attribution of role characteristics appropriate to the power positions of the participants. And the increasing salience of secular matters in modern society has subtly removed from the role of priest, minister, and rabbi qualities associated with their former legitimate authority over a wide variety of activities and limited it to a narrow sphere of spiritual matters.

The theoretical conception of social roles offered here directly suggests a research strategy. Substantial changes in particular roles should be associated with conditions that have altered either structural or dyadic powers as they bear on the particular roles. Whether the roles pertain to statuses in social organizations or in the larger society, an analysis of the bearing of dyadic and structural powers on the role changes should provide clues to those aspects of social structures, social contexts, or ongoing interactions that have altered the balance of power between role actors and their partners and thus brought about a commensurate change in the target role.

References

Ardener, E. W., Ardener, S. G., & Warmington, W. A. *Plantation and village in the Cameroons.* London: Oxford University Press, 1960.

Becker, G. S. *The economic approach to human behavior.* Chicago: University of Chicago Press, 1976.

Bhaskar, R. *A realist theory of science.* Leeds, England: Leeds Books, 1975.

Bhaskar, R. *The possibility of naturalism: A philosophical critique of the contemporary human sciences.* Brighton, Sussex: Harvester Press, 1979.

Bhaskar, R. Emergence, explanation and emancipation. In P. F. Secord (Ed.), *Consciousness, behavior, and social structure.* Beverly Hills, CA: Sage Publications, 1982 (in press).

Blau, P. M. *Exchange and power in social life.* New York: Wiley, 1964.

Bucher, C. *Die Frauenfrage im Mittelalter.* Tubingen: Verlag der H. Laupp'schen Buchhandlung, 1882.

Coulson, M. Role: A redundant concept in sociology? In J. A. Jackson (Ed.), *Role.* Sociological Studies 4. Cambridge, England: Cambridge University Press, 1972.

Emerson, R. M. Power-dependence relations. *American Sociological Review,* 1962, *27,* 31-41.

Giddens, A. *New rules of sociological method: A positive critique of interpretative sociologies.* New York: Basic Books, 1976.

Giddens, A. *Central problems in social theory: Action, structure and contradiction in social analysis.* Berkeley, CA: University of California Press, 1979.

Giddens, A. On the relation of sociology to philosophy. In P. F. Secord (Ed.), *Consciousness, behavior, and social structure.* Beverly Hills, CA: Sage Publications, 1982 (in press).

Goffman, E. *Where the action is: Three essays.* London: Allen Lane The Penguin Press, 1969.

Guttentag, M., & Secord, P. F. *Too many women: The sex ratio question.* Beverly Hills, CA: Sage Publications, 1982 (in press).

Harrè, R., & Secord, P. F. *The explanation of social behavior.* Oxford, England: Basil Blackwell, 1972.

Homans, G. C. *Social behavior: Its elementary forms* (rev. ed.). New York: Harcourt, Brace, and Jovanovich, 1974.

Kelley, H. H. *Personal relationships: Their structures and processes.* Hillsdale, N.J.: Erlbaum, 1979.

Kelley, H. H., & Thibaut, J. W. *Interpersonal relations: A theory of interdependence.* New York: Wiley, 1978.

Manicas, P. T. The concept of social structure. *Journal for the Theory of Social Behavior,* 1980, *10,* 65-82.

Manicas, P. T. A radical separation of psychology and the human sciences. In P. F. Secord (Ed.), *Consciousness, behavior, and social structure.* Beverly Hills, CA: Sage Publications, 1982 (in press).

Parsons, T. *The social system.* New York: The Free Press of Glencoe, 1951.

Parsons, T., & Shils, E. A. (Eds.). *Toward a general theory of action.* Cambridge, Mass.: Harvard University Press, 1951.

Polanyi, M. *The tacit dimension.* Garden City, New York: Doubleday, 1966.

Pomeroy, S. B. *Goddesses, whores, wives, and slaves: Women in classical antiquity.* New York: Schocken Books, 1972.

Smith, R. E. *The subtle revolution: Women at work.* Washington, D.C.: The Urban Institute, 1979.

Thibaut, J. W., & Kelley, H. H. *The social psychology of groups.* New York: Wiley, 1959.

Tiger, L., & Fox, R. *The imperial animal.* New York: Dell, 1971.

Turner, R. H. Role-taking process versus conformity. In A. Rose (Ed.), *Human behavior and social processes: An Interactionist approach.* Boston: Houghton Mifflin, 1962.

Turner, R. H. Role: Sociological aspects. In D. L. Sills (Ed.), *International Encyclopedia of the Social Sciences,* 1968, *13,* 552-557.

Chapter 3

Social Roles as Interaction Competencies

Michael Athay and John Darley

The concept of "social role" has long been experimental social psychology's favorite borrowing from the sociologists. Construed in the usual way, as the rights, obligations, and normative expectations attaching to social positions (Merton, 1957a, 1957b), roles have seemed to psychologists to be one of the few aspects of social structure susceptible to treatment in laboratory settings. During the last 10-15 years, however, the role concept has come under such heavy attack that it is by now very difficult for experimentalists to tell what, if anything, their "role variables" designate. The consequence has been a notable decline in the experimental investigation of social role phenomena, to the point where social psychologists no longer consider research on role-related topics to be anywhere near the "frontiers" of the discipline.

We think this unfortunate state of affairs is mainly the product of a failure at the level of theory formation: Familiar conceptions of social role turn out to be only tenuously related to the interpersonal actions at the face-to-face level which are the subject matter of social psychological experiments. Our objective in this chapter is to reconstruct the role concept in a way which makes it integral to the explanation of interaction at the "micro" level, but which also preserves those links with "social structure" at the "macro" level which have long motivated sociological interest in the concept. In this introduction, we will briefly describe the basis of psychologists' current suspicion of role concepts, show how these criticisms lead, not to reconstruction, but to virtual abolition of roles from the social action process, and sketch the outline of our own program of reconstruction.

Social psychologists have laudably come to recognize the importance of processes of "social cognition" in ordinary interaction. In large part, this is the result of their accepting the view of symbolic interactionist writers that the course of an interchange is determined more by participants' definitions of their setting than by normative principles of action deriving from outside the situation and enforced by larger institutional agencies. While the focus on cognitive considerations has been salutary, the tendency of interactionist writers to emphasize the freedom of individuals to define and redefine their action settings has led many social psychologists to become suspicious of the utility of positing any sort of suprasituational limitation on face-to-face interaction. And this has led to a reinforcement of a traditional reluctance to treat social structure as a factor affecting the outcomes of their experiments.

The impact of this thinking on the concept of the social role has been particularly unfortunate. This is so because the concept of a social role has long served social theorists as a convenient device for bringing considerations of macro-level social structure into the analysis of behavior at the face-to-face level. On the one hand, roles are social position categories, reflecting the larger society's articulation into structural units; on the other, a role is defined by a set of patterns of observable interpersonal behaviors.

As components of "social structure," roles must be interpreted as imposing normative limitations on interaction, limitations that it is not within the power of participants in a situation to abrogate, even through the interactionists' constructive processes of situation definition. Psychologists' too ready acceptance of the interactionist view has thus led them to weaken the role concept by giving up this limiting and controlling function. The result is to deny the concept any clear force: Where patterned behaviors cannot be identified as role determined by reference to public principles that compel performance and limit deviations, then the term "role" must be reduced to a term for any pattern of behavior whatever.

Taken to this extreme, the interactionists' stress on actors' powers of reconstruction-by-reinterpretation comes close to abolishing the role concept altogether. In the last decade and a half, a recognizable school of thought has emerged that not only accepts but makes a virtue of exactly this implication. Indeed, some of its more extreme advocates, the ethnomethodologists, extend their skepticism to embrace social position categories generally. We shall refer to writers of this general persuasion as "asocialists" in order to signal their common denial of the power of social structural categories (and attached normative principles) to control actors' efforts at constructing and reconstructing their situations (e.g., the mutual negotiation of situation definitions).

Traditionalists on the matter of social structure still abound, of course. We call them "objectivists" to signal that they believe, in exact opposition to asocialist writers, that particular courses of action are very closely determined by the role structure of the immediate situation—by factors, that is, which are considered to be wholly independent of the individual's subjective point of view and personal powers of manipulation. For objectivists, normative principles of action are fixed and rigid profiles of what to do when, imposed from without the situation and backed by all the sanctioning power of the larger community. Where asocialists deny that social structure significantly controls the details of face-to-face interaction, objectivists make actors into virtual prisoners of structural categories and normative principles.

Our principal target in this chapter is the asocialist position, but we shall argue for a conception of social structure—and in particular of social roles—that allows for the limiting function of structural frameworks but still does not turn the actor into the automaton traditional sociologists often are accused of making him. It is part of our program, in other words, to resolve this controversy by demonstrating that properly conceived role categories order interaction while leaving a wide latitude for the sort of active construction of the situation that asocialist writers have rightly identified as an essential part of social action. The dichotomization of the two positions has developed, we claim, because neither party backs its view with a general account of the structure and the functions of the interaction process itself. We believe that all social interaction at the micro level exhibits certain basic characteristics, and that once these are understood, it becomes possible to define a conception of social roles that refutes the asocialist view of action without leading to the rigidity of the objectivist alternative. It is perhaps paradoxical to say so, but our point is that the theory of social roles has ceased genuinely to be a theory of social interaction. Our project is to correct this unfortunate state of affairs by constructing a general account of the interaction process from which derives an account of the nature of social roles and of their place as basic elements in the organization of the process.

The first half of this chapter, then, will be given to analysis of social interaction. In the second half, we will argue that face-to-face interaction must be structured by some system of positional categories. We will derive a conception of social roles that fits the general characteristics we ascribe to the interaction process, and we will argue that roles so construed are the fundamental elements of every society's structure of social positions.

Social Action as a Process of Commodity Exchange

Theorists of the asocialist persuasion are generally agreed that ordinary interaction exhibits the following basic characteristics: (1) All actions, verbal and nonverbal, are in effect utterances, carrying messages (intended and unintended) about the interaction situation in both the literal and symbolic modes. (2) Appropriate understandings of the symbolic actions produced within a given interaction situation are *not* fixed by suprasituational factors of "culture" and "social structure." Actions rather count, within the immediate setting, as uninterpreted symbols. Interactants must assign significances to them, significances that are definitely fixed only for the space of their interaction. They do this through joint processes of proposing, confirming, and rejecting–processes taking the form of a kind of negotiation issuing in a working concensus as to what is taking place among them. (3) The normative arrangements governing interaction within the situation are the product of these constructive acts of interpretation. Assigning significances to symbolic actions consists largely in determining what, in the shared view of those present, counts as admissible and compulsory in their respective performances. These elements of "social organization" are not, following the sociological traditions of Marx (1977) and Durkheim (1947), imposed on the situation by larger social and historical processes. Rather, they are constructed within the situation by the collective efforts of the immediate participants–efforts that are informed, perhaps, but not ultimately limited by larger social facts. Indeed, a point is made of assigning to actors a degree of collective freedom which comes perilously close to rendering them asocial beings.

Our purpose is to demonstrate that any such strongly asocial model of social action is radically wrong–not in its contention that active construction is part of ordinary interaction, but in its use of this admirable insight to discount the role of "structural" factors. We propose to do this, moreover, by focusing our attention on exactly that domain of social life—face-to-face interactions of dyads and small groups—that has supplied most of their ammunition against the tradition. We shall argue that ordinary social action at the face-to-face level exhibits a very definite set of general features. When these features are recognized and understood, it becomes manifest that the parties to an interaction cannot possibly be free to determine the course of their affairs to the degree alleged by the asocialists. On the contrary, it is a condition of their stable interaction that the possibilities of cognition and performance available to them be sharply bounded by social structures organizing their setting.

We begin, then, with an account of the essential features of everyday social interaction. We stress that our account is intended to apply only to societies with democratic political structures and highly developed capitalistic economic systems. Although we do not have the space to elaborate here, we believe that the practices and arrangements we are about to describe are peculiar to such societies and fulfill broad social functions dictated ultimately by their economic organization.

Exchange Features of Social Interaction

Social interaction is a strongly egocentered business, with actors organizing their doings to fulfill highly personal projects of action. These projects are as various as individual interests and backgrounds. They involve such things as securing from others overt performances required for achieving specified goals; winning signs of positive affect from them; getting them to confirm some aspect of one's self-concept; and obtaining their compliance for the pure pleasure of exercising influence. The projects may be of the "occasional" sort, involving the securing of particular responses in some immediate, short-term situation; or they may be "standing" projects, involving the achievement of a particular public persona, a particular lifestyle, a set of occupational or status goals, an orderly conception of who and what one is, reconstruction of the world or a corner of it.

This egocentric orientation means that the projects of different actors normally will diverge and conflict. As the social division of labor becomes more and more advanced in modern capitalist societies, so do role differentiations become more and more elaborated. These lead to marked differences of social experience among incumbents, and so produce divergences in projects and strategies of action. Therefore, the parties to any one interaction or social relationship will tend to represent a wide range of different roles and statuses, and it is natural that there will be sharp conflicts among the requirements for achievement attaching to their various individual projects.

These conflicts and the resulting competition for social and material resources mean that an element of manipulation of others for instrumental gain inevitably enters into ordinary interaction. Each actor, in order to carry out his particular programs, is constantly in the position of requiring from others specific performances, attitudes, affective responses, etc., which they would not undertake of their own volition, or could not be counted on to undertake, of their own volition, at just the needed times and places. Each must constantly employ strategies the aim of which is to cajole, coerce, or persuade the other to perform as required, in a predictable and reliable way, even though the other's projects do not lead him, independently of their relationship, to supply those needed treatments.

Under the regime of "voluntaristic" political and legal values of a capitalist democracy, this instrumental manipulation takes the special form of attempting to bring the other to see it as serving his own egocentric interests to do what is wanted of him. Ego can *legitimately* manipulate alter ego into providing responses that ego believes are facilitative for ego's projects by proceeding in just one way: bringing alter to see it as facilitative for alter's own projects that he act as desired. Given the premise of "naturally" divergent interests and projects, this means ego must maneuver alter into adopting formulations of their joint situation and of the character of their interaction which alter likely would not come to accept on his own. Interpersonal manipulations thus amount to a form of persuasion in which the immediate object is the other's definitions of the shared situation of interaction, and the immediate goal is to convince the other of the manifest rightness of some particular construction of what is taking place, a construction the manipulator deems likely to produce responses which will be instrumentally useful from his strategic point of view.

Interpersonal manipulations of this "noncoercive" sort depend on the skillful exploitation of alter ego's normative principles of action. For the only fully reliable, fully calculable patterns of voluntary conduct on the part of another are patterns required of him by *normative* principles which he recognizes as binding. As a result, the process of manipulating others (by getting them to see it as in their interests to respond in a specified fashion) standardly takes the form of getting them to formulate the situation as one in which it is normatively required of them to perform in the desired way. Interpersonal manipulation thus consists in activating in the other normative principles of action that will lead him "naturally" to perform actions that ego believes will advance his own projects.

Goffman (1959, 1974) has described some of the techniques people commonly employ to influence each other's situation definitions under the well-known rubrics of "self-presentation" and "symbolic action." His basic insight was that the symbolic character of all behavior in social contexts makes it possible for interactants to convey interpretations of their immediate situations without having explicitly to address the issue of what is going on and what should be done by whom. This point is important because, in fact, ordinary actors do not usually make this issue an official subject of their interchanges; yet, if we are correct in our account of the form taken by interpersonal manipulation, they are constantly concerned about sending messages to each other regarding the putatively proper interpretation of the ongoing interaction.

Goffman points out that the actor influences others' situation definitions by the device of controlling information about himself (i.e., by selectively presenting strategically relevant material about his aims, background, tactics, strategies, etc., in such a way as to facilitate the other's forming a strategically useful notion of these matters); and by presenting as matters of unquestionable fact just those interpretations of the interaction that appear to him to enhance his interests. Communications carry this sort of information literally, but much more is conveyed nonliterally, by nonverbal performances as well as by speech. This is because explicitly stated formulations are open to explicit challenge and so stand always in danger of rejection. Flat statements about the situation and its participants invite alters' redefinition of the purposes of the interaction to make the validity and ulterior motives of one's formulations a central focus of activity. Not only does this inevitably sidetrack the original interaction (often to the point of serious or total disruption), it also puts at risk the formulator's attempts to manipulate everyone's definitions for his own strategic gain. Messages conveyed in a nonliteral mode, e.g., as presuppositions of literal speech or as implications "everyone recognizes" of nonverbal or verbal performances, tend to carry an implication of "that is how it is, full stop" which has a great deal of persuasive power in itself.[1]

We can summarize the points we have been making by saying that ordinary actors show a strongly instrumental orientation toward their interchanges with others, an orientation in which manipulation of the other for egocentric advantage is a dominant motivation and considerations of strategy and manipulative technique a dominant concern. This "strategic quality of ordinary interaction," to borrow Goffman's useful slogan, constitutes one of two basic features of social action as we see it.

The second feature we summarize by saying that strategic planning and instrumental manipulation are organized as a process of "commodity exchange." Actors regard their treatments of each other, the patterns of action they perform as responses to others' performances, as so many benefits to be exchanged for benefits provided in return. They regard these treatments as "commodities" in that they take them to be entities produced specifically in order to be exchanged for treatments produced by others, and not as patterns of action the role of which is to provide intrinsic satisfactions ("use-values," in the Marxian jargon from which we borrow) for the producer. Given their strategic orientation, actors seek to exchange treatments at maximal advantage to themselves, providing treatments that "cost" as little as possible to produce (in terms of "investment" of time, effort, thought, affect, self-esteem, public prestige, etc.) in exchange for treatments that have the greatest possible "value" to them (i.e., that maximally facilitate the realization of egocentric projects). They seek, in other words, to maximize "profits" in particular exchanges and over long runs of exchanges.

Under this regime, actors evaluate particular courses of action primarily as treatments to be produced for a "market" comprised by the various strategic needs of alters. Appraisals of the instrumental utility of possible actions take the form of cal-

---

[1] Jones's (1964) concept of "ingratiation" formulates one familiar and commonplace class of strategies for carrying out instrumental manipulations of others in the way we have described. The attraction-seeking behaviors he describes are designed to influence the other's cognition of the ingratiator's beliefs, skills, competencies, and other attributes relevant to the content of their interaction. They are intended to affect in particular the other's definition of that most basic component of the interaction situation, the (ingratiating) actor himself, in a way that will dispose the other to provide a favorable exercise of whatever control he can exert over the actor's outcomes.

culations of their relative "value in exchange," and come to be of overriding importance in reaching decisions to provide or withhold them, as treatments desired and bargained for by others. Processes of negotiation become a pervasive part of all social intercourse, so that interchanges standardly take on something of the structure of offer and counteroffer: Each party seeks to raise the instrumental value (i.e., the utilities for realization of his egocentric project) of the treatments he induces the other to offer him, while holding down the values (i.e., utilities for the other's egocentric projects) of the treatments he must offer in return in order to secure them. The element of competition, in other words, is endemic in the exchanges of ordinary social interaction, following our premise that divergence and conflict is normal among the egocentric projects of different individuals.

Exchange of agreements reached in the course of such negotiations commonly take the form of contractlike relationships of varying degrees of explicitness and formality. Stable interaction requires that the parties to social interchange, like the proprietors of economic goods, be able to count on each other to honor commitments to produce particular desired treatments. This is a minimal condition of confident strategic planning, hence of the sense of command over his affairs which is necessary if the actor is to carry out his programs effectively. The capacity to make and sustain contractual agreements is acquired in the course of basic socialization into the system of strategic interaction, and is a fundamental element of social competence.

Negotiation and exchange, then, provide a structure for the interpersonal manipulations of strategic social action. This is not a functional accident. We have pointed out that within the "voluntaristic" values of a democratic society, others can legitimately be manipulated only by the device of leading them to see it as in their egocentric interest to provide desired treatments. Where the ground rules are of this form, and egocentric projects provide the basic motivations for action, exchange is the most natural way for actors to go about securing what they want from each other. Where normative arrangements of this form are well developed, it is in fact *possible* for actors to secure need-satisfying treatments from others only by offering such treatments in return, for only treatment claims founded in the prospect of relations of "fair exchange" count as legitimate claims.

Negotiation and exchange likewise provide a structure for the practices of manipulating others by operating on their situation definitions. Strategic planning involves influencing the other's perceptions of his strategic interests and of the manipulative possibilities afforded by the shared situation in order to lead him to see that a particular exchange of performances on his part, for treatments one is prepared to offer in return, must be clearly advantageous for him, i.e., that the exchange is the best he can expect to do in the circumstances, is something he must accept in order to avoid serious losses, or is otherwise desirable in "cost-benefit" terms. The normative principles of action and cognition on the other's part that the actor seeks to activate to his instrumental advantage thus turns out, broadly speaking, to be principles of exchange: general accounts of what it is reasonable or desirable or tolerable to do with and for others, given that one can legitimately expect them to behave in such and so ways in return.

According to our perspective, then, actors must be conceived primarily and fundamentally as producers of "interaction commodities," as we shall call treatments of the sort we have been describing. Social action generally is to be conceived as a system of practices the function of which is to secure the production and distribution of interpersonal treatments satisfying the various social psychological needs of actors. All interaction is thus "economic" in this very broad sense of the term. Within any community of interactants, it is possible to identify determinate needs, psychological as well as material, that actors must satisfy as a condition of continually reproducing themselves as psychologically viable and socially competent members of that community. It is a commonplace of the discipline of social psychology that most such needs are satisfiable only through interchanges with other actors. We attempt to elaborate this commonplace by discovering in the need-satisfying interactions of ordinary actors the determinate structure of relations of commodity exchange.

Interaction Commodities

We can most economically specify these rather abstract remarks by now providing some concrete examples of interaction commodities. We shall propose three broad classifications of interaction commodities that seem to us potentially useful in formulating theories and experiments about instrumental interaction. We stress that these categories are mainly illustrative. A developed theory of social action of the sort we are proposing clearly must include a well worked-out taxonomy of both needs and the commodities that satisfy them, together with an account of how these vary for different types of interaction communities. For the moment, however, we aspire only to a few clarifying examples.

We call our three classifications "affective commodities," "epistemic commodities," and "facilitating commodities." The last divides into two broad subcategories. One, call them "project facilitating commodities," consists of the sort of behaviors usually treated in theories of social exchange and in social psychology experiments modeled on game-theoretic situations, viz., performances that are tailored to satisfy the requirements of another actor's ongoing projects. Many projects require that another perform some highly specific actions: writing a recommendation or providing a positive evaluation of some task performance, intervening with a party on one's behalf, or giving help on some task.

The second sort of facilitating commodities (call them "competency facilitating commodities") are treatments designed to make "spaces" in the interaction that another actor can fill with his performances. These treatments have the effect of so defining the situation that it becomes appropriate (according to communal norms) for the other to exercise some particular interaction competency. Actors who are considered "good listeners" are skilled in producing this sort of commodity. The treatments they provide—asking leading questions, signaling "genuine interest" as opposed to polite indulgence, making the "mmh" and "oh yes" noises necessary to convey appropriate attentiveness—create spaces in the interaction that the other can fill with performances exhibiting, for example, certain special conversational and/or intellectual skills: cautionary tales, personal narratives, well-told stories, incisive commentaries, and brilliant analyses indicative of the speaker's special grasp of one or another subject matter.

Both sorts of facilitating commodities are material for exchange negotiations: Actors standardly exchange treatments that are narrowly instrumental in fulfilling each other's projects, expecting assistance in careers, in specific tasks large and small, in the manipulation of third parties, and so on, whenever such assistance is given in turn. And actors standardly help each other to show specific competencies in a good light by making opportunities for those who make opportunities back–proud parents sharing their children's pictures around the office being one mundane but exemplary case in point.

Affective commodities include treatments that manifest such attitudes as hostility, approval, affirmation or disaffirmation, love and affection, and acceptance or rejection. Many performances have as their primary purpose the conveying of some such affect-laden attitude toward the other: mothers' expressions of love, reassurance, censure, etc., toward their children; colleagues' acts of encouragement or of "one-upping" criticism; expressions of sympathy and understanding between friends, etc. Even performances with narrowly utilitarian primary content usually are carried out in a way that expresses some definite affective attitude toward the receiving party.

The contents of these performances standardly become the subjects of negotiation and exchange. Appropriate affective responses–and certainly desired ones–are seldom provided gratuitously, but carry expectations of corresponding treatments in return, either immediately or over the longer term of a standing relationship. Thus, the actor who listens patiently to his friend's marital dilemma expects an affirming response when later he tells him of a self-perceived success in his job, and failure on the friend's part will earn an antagonistic response when next the tables are turned.

Epistemic commodities are an especially important type because control of their production is a principal basis of interpersonal power. Paradigmatic cases are treatments of another actor that have the effect of confirming or disconfirming some aspect(s) of his conception of himself or of the interaction situation, e.g., the appropriateness of his strategies and principles of action, and therefore the validity of the character and motives of his interaction; his view of himself; his view of his relationship with specific others. These treatments count as "epistemic" in the broad sense that they affect the viability–in his own eyes, as well as those of other interactants–of his social cognitions. Intersubjectivity, for common sense as well as for philosophers, is a minimal condition of the objective correctness of formulations of the world, including social settings of everyday action. Intersubjectivity, however, depends on the availability of confirmations and disconfirmations of a candidate view by other actors occupying different but relevant perspectives on the same situation. Objectification of a point of view–its taking on the status of "the way the world is," without reasonable doubt or question–thus presupposes that other appropriately placed actors confirm it as valid.

Production of epistemic commodities is a source of power because, in ordinary social action, the interactants who are the objects of each other's strategic manipulations also are the best placed persons to give expert judgment as to what, "in reality," is going on among them all. This special weight attaching to their confirmations and disconfirmations places each party to the immediate situation in a position of potential power with respect to his interactants. Each is dependent on the others for treatments that sustain his sense that he understands the setting and the interaction; and each is therefore in a position to demand confirmations of his own presented views in the situation (or to demand other types of interaction commodities) as a condition of his providing such desired epistemic treatments in turn.

Selective production of acts of confirmation and disconfirmation thus have the strategic effect of helping to determine the contents of others' definitions of the ongoing situation, and hence constitute a basic means of manipulating their performances for strategic gain. Production of this sort of commodity, in other words, plays a large role in the basic practice of manipulating others by influencing their conceptions of the joint situation. The fact that actors are *mutually* dependent for the securing of epistemic treatments means the manipulating will have an exchange structure: Each is in a position to bargain over his treatments, contracting to produce just the ones wanted by other actors, but only in exchange for epistemic treatments that serve his own strategies and projects. Given the fundamental role in social action of the practice of manipulating others' social cognitions, this selective production of epistemic treatments inevitably comes to figure very heavily in all relations of commodity exchange.

Confirmations and disconfirmations are not the only sort of epistemic commodities. Actors often ask each other for formulations and points of view regarding some aspect of social life. The production of formulations and the contents and qualities of these productions (considered vs. superficial, for example) routinely come to be the subject of negotiation and exchange. Advice and opinions are commodities of a similar sort, although the normative force of the first and the explicitly evaluative character of the second should be distinguished from the more fundamental matter of simply providing a sense-making conceptualization of things. In all of these cases, producing the epistemic commodities on demand has the benefit of giving their recipient a new or broader perspective on his situation, by virtue of showing him alternative ways of looking at it. "Perspectives," then, can be considered a second basic, if rather broadly defined, class of epistemic commodities.

Structural Frames as Conditions of the Possibility of Face-To-Face Interaction

We begin this second phase of our argument with a description, from the actor's point of view, of his role as operator of the commodity exchange system of interaction. Our object is to show that actors who live under this regime must come to develop an overriding concern with the *calculability* of the actions of others. They experience this concern as a preoccupation with maintaining a firm sense of control in the course of their interchanges with others. We argue that stable interaction is conditioned on actors being able to sustain this feeling of mastery over their day-today affairs, and we claim further that the feeling of mastery is in turn conditioned on their being able to feel that underlying every situation is a framework of boundaries or limits on the possibilities of its development, limits that cannot be violated by innovating constructions of its participants. We use the term "social structure" to designate this framework of social boundaries, so that our argument turns out to be the demonstration of the dependence of face-to-face interaction on suprasituational social structures that we announced in the beginning of the chapter.

The Drive to Sustain a Sense of Strategic Mastery

We begin by identifying features of social interaction that lead actors to place this high priority on preserving the sense of mastery. We do this by listing a few of the enormous number of control-threatening pitfalls to be found in even the most mundane of social relations.

Consider first the general mechanism by which actors set about securing the treatments they require to fulfill their projects of action, viz., the practice of operating on others' situation definitions in order to bring them to a perception of the relationship that will in turn lead them to see provision of treatments desired by the actor as dictated by their own strategic interests and normative principles of action. This is inevitably a tenuous business where egocentric interests diverge, and where conflict among projects and competition for the social resources to fulfill them are the "natural" state of affairs. For no matter how persuasive an actor's stories about the ultimate congruence of the treatments he wants with the other's own projects, there remains the probability that at some point their interests diverge markedly; and of course every competent operator of the commodity exchange system of action is trained to be alert to the limits of congruence, and accordingly to reserve (usually covertly) his willingness to comply. In consequence, every relationship, however well the parties feel they "understand each other," however candid their negotiations and explicit their contractual agreements of exchange, must always contain ample potential for sudden and unexpected breakdown.

The formidable social cognition problems inherent in these practices of interpersonal manipulation introduce a second element of extreme uncertainty. Actors must reconstruct each other's perceptions of their interaction, including most especially the other's perception of the actor—that notoriously difficult business of accurately "taking the perspective of the other." He must estimate the normative principles of action that the other recognizes, judge which of these principles the other could be persuaded to find applicable in the immediate circumstances, determine what specific performances those principles would lead the other to, and estimate what adjustments in the other's interpretations of the situation would lead him to apply those principles. In addition, he must at the same time evaluate all the possible outcomes of all these different factors and assess their relative utility for his strategic aims, choosing just the ones that will benefit his projects most. Clearly there is ample opportunity for error in doing such complex calculations, especially when we remember that the normal pace of action leaves little time for considered judgment or careful or systematic forming and testing of hypotheses.

But even more to the present point is the fact that actors are strongly dependent on the objects of their strategic machinations for the acts of confirmation that alone can give their social cognitions the status of objective validity. Every participant is well placed to undermine the situation definitions of the others, and each possesses the power to thwart or facilitate the other's formation of strategically effective accounts of the factors just listed. Given the natural divergence of egocentric projects, together with the manipulative character of social action, it is only reasonable to expect that the other will occasionally exercise this power against one's strategic interests.

All these considerations are complicated by the fact that most presentation of strategically relevant information is in the nonliteral mode of symbolic action, and therefore is subject to notorious variability. Every actor is thus confronted at all times with a twofold translation problem. He must read the other's self-presentations accurately in order to determine his own best strategy of presentation and to monitor its success, and he must so construct his own action patterns that their symbolic imports—the messages he *intends* them to convey—are in fact the ones read out by the other, given the other's special background and preconceptions. But of course one can never guarantee that the other will interpret one's actions as intended: The ultimate divergence of actors' perspectives and interests make it virtually inevitable that one will be "misunderstood" to one degree or another much of the time.

The exchange structure of interaction adds a final set of uncertainty-producing factors. Here the concern is with adequacy of performance as much as with cognitive adequacy. Actors are dependent on others to supply the treatments they need in order to fulfill their projects of action. But these treatments will not be forthcoming to any actor who is not competent to construct performances that are adequate to satisfy in turn the needs of his potential suppliers, i.e., of the actors who comprise his "market." But the actor's projects, and therefore his needs for treatments by others, vary enormously among individuals, and across social groupings. Actors must therefore be able to anticipate these changes and variations and to adjust their production competencies to suit the special conditions of different markets, each of which is itself in fluctuation. The consequence is a constant concern, on the part of every actor, over his capacity to meet these production demands satisfactorily, i.e., in a fashion that will permit him to realize his own projects.

Our objective in detailing this long list of difficulties is to show how structural features of the system, features that are intrinsic to social action organized on a commodity exchange basis, ensure that every strategic plan of every competent actor must be a fragile construction, forever subject to sudden breakdown in any of a great many ways—ways having to do with adequacy of cognition and communication, and with competence in the production of performances. The number and complexity of the factors that must be taken into account to ensure the success of even the simplest project-facilitating strategy are enormous. Given the ultimately tenuous hold that any actor has over another's performances, within the framework of this system, success (or failure) in any particular case must seem to him largely fortuitous. Calculability comes to be an overwhelming concern exactly because genuinely reliable, uniformly successful calculation is so nearly impossible.

Actors experience this concern as a drive to achieve a strong feeling of mastery over the events comprising their interchanges. Socialization into the commodity exchange system of action equips the actor with a profoundly compelling disposition to act in ways that he sees as preserving and extending his competence to cope effectively with the strategic demands of his interaction situations—to cope, that is, in a matter-of-course way, without stress or anxiety, without serious doubt as to his ability to bring about strategically satisfactory outcomes.

The development of this drive, we are claiming, is the natural consequence of living under a system of interaction that is inherently unplannable, inherently risky in all the ways we have described, yet one that attaches its highest values to the successful manipulation of others in order to achieve egocentric ends. The system dictates the adoption of practices that its organization makes exceedingly precarious. Under these circumstances, security comes to have a very high priority, in both cognition and action, not that people are particularly successful in achieving it. Often they feel overwhelmed by circumstance, manipulated by other actors, controlled by their interaction situations. The claim is that the issue of mastery has top priority in the actor's scheme of himself and his world, however successful or not he is in achieving it; that every actor makes it a first order of business to take whatever measures he feels are available to him to sustain his perception of command and control.

Routinization and Contextualization

Competent actors learn to employ a number of techniques for sustaining mastery. The more fundamental of these serve to *routinize* cognition and performance. In the course of acquiring the skills comprising social competence, actors develop a strong generalized propensity to establish invariances in their patterns of cognition and performance. Confronted with a new situation, their natural response is to assimilate it to some familiar situation with which they have dealt successfully in the past, applying as straightforwardly as possible the schemes that worked then.

Routinizing in cognition includes but goes well beyond the familiar sort of selectivity (psychologists often speak of disattending, or of motivated failures to notice) that is the basis of all concept formation. A particular cognitive routine will equip its author with a high degree of "readiness" (in Bruner's, 1957, sense of "perceptual readiness") to notice certain selected features of a situation, while causing him to disattend many other features, whatever their strategic importance from an "objective" outsider's point of view. But using the routine also involves a good deal of active construction. Where elements of the situation do not fit well enough to apply a routine straight-forwardly, the actor will fill gaps, posit features, draw inferences, and make assumptions until he obtains a working correspondence. Performance routines work similarly. They consist of scriptlike (Abelson, 1976) schemes of action that the actor applies with as little amendment as possible, and even automatically, wherever circumstances permit. The two sorts of routine are of course interdependent. Few actors would even recognize a distinction between cognition and performance. For the sake of a simple theory we can say that social cognition routines activate correlated performance routines, but in practice the two interpenetrate completely.

From the actor's point of view, the function of routinization and selectivity is to simplify his complex problem of coping with the social world by reducing the unfamiliar and problematic to what is thoroughly familiar and hence manageable. In the face of the complexity of strategic factors we described earlier, the actor has little choice but to select and simplify, even at the cost of misinterpretation. If he takes into account all cues that are potentially relevant to his programs, then he will never reach the point of decision in any strategic move. His attention will become absorbed in the special project of critical evaluation, and that fact will interfere with his ability to act in the rapid, smooth, natural way required by the public standards which define a "normally competent" interactant–standards that he must respect on pain of others deciding it is unsafe or unprofitable to enter exchange relations with him.[2]

Yet, if he is to preserve his sense of command over his situation, the actor must not routinize in a random or arbitrary way. It is a truism of the psychology of learning that the most manageable problems of cognition and performance are the ones most familiar from past practice. Competent actors routinize their programs of action in the attempt to reduce every situation to one that experience makes them confident they can handle in a risk-free, matter-of-course fashion.

The drive for routinization is one of two fundamental and antithetical dispositions, comprising the core of our model of the actor. The second we refer to as the disposition to "contextualize" preestablished patterns of cognition and performance to suit the particularities of each ongoing situation.[3] For while actors strive to deal with every situation by bringing it under some one of their repertoire of established routines, it is an awkward fact of social life that settings and interactants vary enormously in ways that matter for strategic success. Indeed, the same considerations that support routinization support the reasonableness of contextualization as a procedure for coping: Social life under the system of action we have described is intrinsically incalculable exactly because the array of strategic factors varies with even small changes of circumstance and setting and actor. Actors are motivated to employ routines for just the reasons that make it impossible for them to rely on routines alone.

---

[2] Like Tolman's rat, he will be "lost in thought" long after the time for action has arrived and departed. Not incidentally, the conception of the actor assumed in much recent research an attribution theory and social cognition is subject to the same criticism, and for the same basic reason that practitioners ignore the demands of interaction on the social cognition process.

[3] We describe the tension between routinization and contextualization, together with the correlative concept of an interaction competency, in much greater detail in our paper "Toward an interaction-centered theory of personality" (Athay & Darley, 1981).

Thus, the instrumental orientation and commodity exchange structure of interaction tend to enforce a need for responsiveness to idiosyncratic features of the immediate situation. The mechanism of manipulating others by operating on their situation definitions demands that the actor constantly monitor the details of others' self-presentations in order to determine the relevant features of their perspectives on the setting and on himself, and in order to appraise accurately their egocentric interests that he hopes to exploit. He must respond to even minor variations in the normative points of view which provide his basic handles on the others' performances, he must be highly responsive to the considerable situation to situation variations in the terms of advantageous exchange, and he must be attentive to nuances of self-presentation, his own and his interactants', in conducting exchange negotiations.

The lesson is that competent operation of the commodity exchange system of interaction requires of actors a highly developed facility for discriminating and responding to the specific unique features of their immediate situations.[4] The corollary of this discriminative facility is a capacity for constructing patterns of cognition and performance (out of familiar elements, to be sure) that have not been undertaken in just their present form in the past. The emphasis here is on the potentially innovative character of strategic planning. Competent actors cannot mechanically apply fixed profiles of what to do and when because the vagaries of ordinary interaction will not let them. They must constantly revise and reconstruct the programs that have worked for them in the past, and they must always be prepared to generate patterns of cognition and performance that are genuinely novel in their experience.

Clearly enough, this disposition to contextualize cognition and performance is diametrically opposed to the disposition to routinize. We claim that the two drives are equally fundamental, that in fact the tension between them ultimately explains much that is special to action as commodity exchange. Its instrumental orientation and exchange structure demand both that the actor proceed in a mechanical fashion to apply familiar programs of action and cognition; and at the same time, that he constantly reconstruct his standardized profiles to meet the ever-changing circumstances which this orientation and structure make inevitable. Every situation defini-

---

[4] Our formulation here borrows the language of a similar point about competent social action that Walter Mischel (1973) has made, and impressively documented, in advancing his well-known criticisms of the concept of a "global personality disposition." Mischel cites his own experimental work on delay of gratification and a large body of research by others to substantiate his view that ordinary actors exhibit a highly developed facility for discriminating and responding to specific details of their settings. He points out that studies of noncognitive personality dimensions (e.g., Moos, 1968, on "person-situation interaction; McGuire, 1968, on "moderator variables") regularly show (intentionally or not) that behavior is highly specific to a large number of setting variables and draws the moral that "what people do in any situation may be changed dramatically even by relatively trivial alterations in their prior experience or by slight modifications in the particular features of the immediate situation" (pp. 258-259).

tion, every plan and performance, is a more or less felicitous compromise between these ultimately quite inconsistent demands. Our point is that the contradiction is built into the system of action itself.

Interaction Competencies

In stressing the fundamental role that the routinization and contextualization tension plays in our conception of the actor, we mean to emphasize that it imposes a constraint on the formulation of all dispositions to think and act on the part of all who operate within the commodity exchange system of action. The constraint is that psychological dispositions must always be articulated in a way that expresses their character as a compromise between the two antagonistic drives. The way to satisfy this requirement, we now propose, is to construe dispositions as what we shall call "interaction competencies." We use this term to designate capacities to construct innovative patterns of performance by reconstructing familiar, practiced paradigms to meet the particular demands of varying interaction situations. The competencies are skills in the construction of cognitive schemes and performance patterns in such a fashion as to cope with situational specificities while at the same time preserving sufficient continuity with established routines to sustain the sense of command that comes only with application of familiar, matter-of-course procedures. Such a disposition concept resolves the routinization/contextualization dichotomy in the back-handed fashion of incorporating both terms in a single propensity to thought and action, producing a balance that in practice often is highly unstable.

Interaction competencies, then, are determinate skills and capacities that satisfy the general demands specified. They sort by the type of situation in which they standardly come into play, are possessed by many different actors in variable degrees, and come in different levels of generality and specificity. Competencies of the more generalized sort usually concern basic abilities without which it is impossible to operate the commodity exchange system of interaction at all. Two examples that have received some attention from social scientists are "the ability to take the perspective of the other" and "self-monitoring" abilities. Our discussions of practices of instrumental manipulation established the importance of knowing how to reconstruct accurately other points of view. Yet actors differ enormously in their capacities for adopting the perspectives of others.[5] They differ in the general capacity (often termed "empathy") for intuiting the point of view of a person not before encountered and they differ with respect to the repertoires of particular perspectives that can be used to interpret the other's point of view readily and accurately.

---

[5] "Perspective-taking" capacities have been investigated mainly by developmental psychologists. We are claiming that competence in this area of social cognition is of continuing importance throughout adult social life and must be studied, not primarily as a set of dispositions acquired in childhood, but as a necessary condition of successfully operating under the regime of interpersonal manipulation and commodity exchange. For experimental work in perspective taking in children, see Salatas and Flavell (1976) and Flavell, Botkin, Fry, Wright, and Jarris (1968).

Snyder's (1979) "self-monitoring" notion differentiates subjects with respect to the responsiveness to situational influences that they report as affecting their behaviors. Individuals he counts as "high" on the "self-monitoring" dimension are quite skillful in detecting variations in behavioral demands communicated by groups in which they are placed (Snyder and Monson, 1975). For example, when group members indicate that conformity is the appropriate orientation, the "high self-monitors" conform; when autonomy is signaled as appropriate, they conform much less; while conformity behaviors of non-self-monitors are not significantly affected by these group variations.

Snyder (1974) has also shown that high self-monitors are better at the task of simulating the expression of various emotions: When subjects were asked to read a set of lines in a way conveying anger, happiness, etc., observers were more accurate in guessing the emotion that the high self-monitors intended to convey. This ability to represent emotional reactions in a readable way is a basic strategic skill. In many social exchanges, the treatment required by the other consists of appropriate affective responses to their own emotional productions, answering sorrow with sympathy, joy with shared happiness, and so on. This skill need not be cynically construed; the emotions conveyed can be genuine. It is nonetheless necessary that they be *effectively* conveyed to the other person, and the high self-monitors also were better decoders of the intentions underlying others' attempts to convey emotions. Other research (Snyder, 1979) has tended to confirm this. Thus, a picture emerges of the high self-monitor as an individual who grasps the central social fact that achieving one's purposes requires accurate perceptions of the signals sent by others, as well as well-developed signaling capacities of one's own.

Many of the most important interaction competencies are not of this generic sort, but consist rather in highly specific skills in the production of determinate interaction commodities to satisfy quite particular sorts of social psychological needs in others. This point is the basis of our earlier assertion that the system of social action must be seen as a kind of system of production and distribution, functioning alongside the economic system that produces and distributes material commodities to satisfy material needs. The fact that members of a community have social psychological needs as well as material needs sets that community the collective task of arranging mechanisms for producing treatments to satisfy these needs. Our conception of the actor is as an instrument of social production—as that basic unit of the production system ultimately responsible, through the expenditure of personal powers of productive labor, for the transformation of the "raw materials" of symbolic action into treatments capable of satisfying the nonmaterial (as well as many of the material) needs of other actors. Within this scheme, the practices comprising "commodity exchange" count specifically as the basis of the community's organization of its distribution task.

We claim, in other words, that the basic dispositions of actors are *production* competencies: determinate skills in the production of the specific sorts of treatment of other actors that we discussed in our taxonomy of interaction commodities. An example would be skill in producing a specific sort of epistemic treatment, such as confirmations of others' judgments that exhibit the special mixture of critical evaluation and approbation required by some professional intellectuals, or the capacity to produce some specific sort of affective treatment, such as the mixture of detachment with underlying affection and approval which (sensible) people expect of the intimates to whom they appeal for advice and support.

Within any given community of interactants, each type of commodity collectively recognized as fulfilling some definite social psychological need on the part of members will be associated with some such determinate competency in its production. Following our competency notion, each such specialized capacity will take the form of a skill in reconstructing established routines of treatment in order to cope with particularities of an immediate and possibly idiosyncratic situation–skill, that is, in providing innovations to cope with the particular treatment demands of the interactants now at hand, while retaining mastery-preserving continuity with familiar patterns and strategies of scripted treatment construction.

The Argument for Structural Frames

The aim of this chapter is to refute "asocialism" by demonstrating that face-to-face interaction is possible only if actors' freedom to construct their shared situations is severely limited by supraindividual practices and arrangements of the sort commonly designated "social structure." Our argument is that social action exhibiting the features we have described in the preceding pages–egocentric motivation, instrumental orientation, organization in terms of commodity exchange, actors as collections of production competencies–can remain a viable, stable enterprise only where there are well-articulated frameworks of social position categories (roles, statuses, classes, etc.) to impose hard and fast boundaries on the possibilities of performance and cognition.

In particular we argue that the presence of structural frames is a condition of the actor's satisfying the basic drive for achieving and sustaining a sense of mastery over his activities as a producer of interaction commodities. Still more specifically, we contend that *routinization*, the basic means of maintaining mastery, is possible only if the actor is able to take for granted, in every interaction situation, the existence of an underlying framework of social relations limiting the potential for variation (the "surprise potential") in the strategically relevant circumstances and thoughts and behaviors of interactants. We use the all-purpose word "framework" in this formulation to refer to a system of interrelated social positions: classes of actor that are publicly recognized as cohesive and distinctive categories within the population of a community of interactants, and which have for the members of that community something of the givenness and independence of natural kinds, or as we shall usually say, which have the status of "social objects."[6] These public categories carry principles of action and cognition which community members consider to be binding on their incumbents, and which they therefore consider to be very highly reliable indicators (albeit at a broad level of generality) of the patterns of thought and action which incumbents will undertake under various circumstances of interaction. From the incumbent's point of view, such a positional category is a set of normative requirements governing his programs of action; from the point of view of his actors in strategic interaction, these requirements are the basis of generalizations about what he will then do.

Our analysis of social action is thus primarily an argument for the importance of social position frameworks in the processes of face-to-face interaction. Since the remainder of this chapter will be specifically about one sort of positional category, viz., social roles, we want to stress now that most of what we have to say about roles should be taken as a specification of our claims about the concept of social structure generally and its importance for social psychological analysis of action at the micro level. Our main point is that social psychologists must begin to incorporate structural categories in their theory and experimental practice, a message that is hardly fashionable among contemporary practitioners, and all of our remarks about social roles are directed toward this end.

This said, we want also to emphasize our agreement with the many social theorists who find in "role" constructs an uncommonly fruitful formulation of one basic level of social structure. This special utility of role concepts is due largely to the fact that they describe positional entities in terms that are the least removed from terms in which ordinary actors organize their social lives. Role concepts provide a fairly literal rendering of "the actor's point of view," more literal than, say, the concepts of "social class" or "income group," to name two favorite positional categories. People do think of each other more or less in terms of the roles they play, and people do group roles into larger categories more or less resembling statuses. Social psychologists have long recognized this fact, and it accounts for much of their interest in "role theory." If people ordinarily think in rolelike terms, then it should be relatively easy to operationalize role concepts by finding observable behavior patterns corresponding to their putative use.

Our defense of the place of social position frameworks in face-to-face interaction now becomes an argument for the proposition that role categories in particular are requisite for the application of the techniques of routinization on which the sense of cognitive and performance mastery rests. The heart of the matter is the dependence of routinization on the availability of public standards defining a stable background of normalcy for settings of strategic interaction. Making routines of programs of cognition and performance consists, at bottom, in restricting the scope of the features of the setting that must be made the object of critical attention. It consists in determining, by a kind of cognitive fiat, that a maximum of the situation's elements fall within the background of thoroughly normal, thoroughly expectable eventualities, and so need not figure in explicit strategic calculations. In a formula, it consists in assigning as many classes of phenomena as possible to the special cognitive category of "the safely disattendable" (to borrow from one of Goffman's, 1974, more felici-

---

[6] One method of picking out common sense role concepts having this status of "social object" within a community would be to use Rosch's (1978) technique to document what she refers to as "natural categories" of artifact and natural object: tables and chairs, animal species, automobiles, etc. Cantor and Mischel (1979) have demonstrated how this approach would be carried out for various levels of person categorization.

tous formulations)—phenomena that can be disregarded without danger to ongoing strategies and projects of action because they are so familiar and so commonplace that the actor is able to cope with them in a thoroughly matter-of-course fashion.

This sort of selective disattention is the basis of the feeling of manageability produced by routinization. The ability to classify setting features as normal, as the sort of business-as-usual that can be dealt with in practiced ways, is what makes the actor feel he is in command of his situation. An interchange will come to feel out of hand exactly when it presents features that must be attended, reflected on, and pondered for strategic imports that are not clear on their surface. Under these circumstances the actor must doubt his capacity to predict the course of events and hence his competence to produce patterns of performance that will cope adequately with whatever may be coming. In the case of strategic interaction, the unpredictable, the unfamiliar, and the inscrutable are intrinsically dangerous.

Yet for actors who are well socialized into the regime of interpersonal manipulation and commodity exchange, this determination of the "normal, hence safely disattendable" can never be a simple, unproblematic matter. Actors are trained to monitor every setting for strategy-threatening developments and so are highly predisposed to see even minor deviations as fraught with strategic significance. Indeed, systematic misdoubt is a basic mark of ordinary social competence. Disattention of the necessary sort is therefore possible for them only if authorized by principles founded in something more secure than a subjective sense of how things usually are.

The main source of such supraindividual authorizations is the principles of action attaching to role (and other social position) categories. These provide a set of official prototypes for the actor to follow in routinizing his interaction situations, prototypes that count for him as utterly reliable, as outside the scope of reasonable doubt and criticism, because they are backed by the collective power of his community. Routines conforming to the role prototypes are "safe" (i.e., their areas of disattention count as strategically safe) because incumbents are bound to the patterns of "normal" thought and action that the routines dictate with all the community's powers of sanction and social control. Here, then, we find the necessary limitations on the possibilities of action afforded by the interaction situation.

We have been describing the conditions of routinization from the point of view of the actor's problem of interpreting and predicting the thoughts and actions of other actors. But others' expectations regarding an actor's own actions are of equal importance in his strategic planning. This is so because every actor's ability to secure the treatments he needs depends on him satisfying those expectations. The treatment needs and demands of those interactants who are capable of producing the responses he requires must therefore be a principal consideration in all his calculations. The actor is able to routinize his activities only insofar as other actors' expectations regarding his productive activities remain highly stable. Every change in their demands alters his position of relative power in the exchange process, forcing him either to conform as best he can or else to seek new partners who may not be available to him. If the changes are frequent and substantial, then he is put in the position of having to redo his competencies over and over again, in ways difficult or impossible to anticipate, and often with little time for the relearning process. This sort of basic reorganization is always tremendously difficult, since the dispositions in question are basic constituents of the "self" or "personality." But even apart from this fact, it is clear that actors cannot make routines of their activities of production in the face of such irregularity. Social position frames are again the community's basic mechanism for achieving the needed stability.

We have been arguing that the actor's assignment of other actors to role categories stabilizes his expectations as to their behaviors. But the point obviously works both ways, and his own incumbency of particular social roles stabilizes their expectations of him.

We are saying, in effect, that social roles themselves are to be taken as units in a community's system for producing and distributing interaction commodities. The community articulates its social production process by establishing a framework of role categories and assigning its members (through the familiar mechanisms of social mobility and social control) to particular ones of them. Learning to fulfill the expectations attaching to any one social role thus consists in acquiring some definite set of production competencies, together with a correlated set of appropriate patterns of social cognition and strategic thinking. From the actor's point of view, the existence of such a framework means that he can legitimately expect certain production competencies on the part of others, but it also means that others can legitimately expect of him just those competencies that his role affiliations bind him to acquire and exercise.

This completes our argument against asocialist writers' contention that the organization of everyday interaction situations is created on the spot, through actors' collective procedures of situation definition and norm construction. At the deepest level, their error lies in not realizing that immediate situations of face-to-face interaction are but the observable elements of a broader system of social action that fulfills large scale social functions for the community which operates it. Once it is understood that "social action" refers to a set of interrelated mechanisms for producing and distributing interaction commodities to satisfy the needs of community members, then it becomes possible to look for features that characterize the structure of the system itself, and are therefore to be found in all particular settings. With an account of these features now in hand, we can see that so much freedom of situation construction as the asocialists allege must produce a degree of irregularity quite beyond the coping capacities of any actor.

All of this said, we believe the asocialists have a very important point to make. Indeed, we are committed to accepting much of what they have to say about the active, constructive role of participants in organizing their immediate settings. Our view of the actor as a producer of commodities to satisfy the demands of others presents him as actively constructing his patterns of action, and not as a passive medium for realizing societally dictated norms and principles. The main argument for this view rests on the necessity for contextualization in the interaction process. Actors have no choice but to be innovators, given the enormous variation in strategically significant detail which obtains from situation to situation under the regime of interpersonal manipulation and commodity exchange. Operators of this system strive to act in wholly routine, matter-of-course fashion, but as we have pointed out, the system is so structured as to guarantee that they cannot do so very much of the time, at least not without suffering the effects of gross strategic incompetence.

We are left, then, with yet another recurrence of that tension between drives for routinization and contextualization which we have identified as fundamental to the interaction process. Social roles must be so conceived as to take account of both terms in the opposition. Our solution is hardly a new one: Roles "structure" interaction in the sense of imposing normative limits on the possibilities of variation, but they do not determine particular courses of action in the sense of laying down exact prescriptions of what to do when. The limitations they impose on thought and action are exceedingly strong ones, to the point that actors normally find it very difficult to see themselves as deviating. But the boundaries are so formulated as to incorporate a high degree of indeterminacy, permitting enormously varying patterns of action to count as instantiations of the role-specified behaviors.

This point has implications concerning the nature of actors' common sense representations of role categories and the principles of action attaching to them. These representations, we contend, take the form of "concrete archetypes," as we shall call them, rather than class concepts, legalistic rules, or lawlike generalizations—the alternatives usually advanced in accounts of social norms. The archetypes are paradigms or exemplars specifying modes of cognition and performance appropriate to the exercise of the different production competencies comprising a given role category. They are made up of representations of particular concrete episodes remembered by the actor as incidents from his history of interactions and organized, in Abelson's happy formulation, into complexes resembling the scripts of scenes in plays (Abelson, 1976). Such a script will specify what each participant did in the episode and when; how each reacted to each development, and with what strategic effects; and most especially, the strategies of performance and cognition that the actor himself adopted in order to cope with those circumstances and other actors, together with the degree of success these measures brought him in his attempts to realize given projects.

Archetypal scripts organize cognition and action by specifying episodes that count for the actor as exemplary or paradigmatic. Their special utility lies in the fact that they consist of performance/cognition patterns actually carried out, with known results—patterns the actor knows he can manage because he has employed them in similar contexts, with effects he has observed and evaluated before. Thus, he equips himself with a set of model programs of thought and action of which he feels in command.

At the same time, the sort of organization imposed by archetypal concepts is not narrowly limiting, and does not preclude the actor's introducing substantial innovations in order to cope with idiosyncrasies of the situation. This is because the archetypes are representations of *concrete* historical episodes, with all their wealth of idiosyncratic detail. Applying an archetypal script consists in assimilating the situation at hand to the episodes the script describes, by looking for relations of analogy and homology among the two sets of concrete features. Indeterminacy is inevitable in this process because the concrete elements of the archetype, like all concrete elements, allow description in many different ways. Changes of "cognitive set," a product of changing projects or settings, can always turn up new perspectives on the stored information, yielding new and different lessons for the case at hand. An actor can thus confine himself well within the boundaries imposed on his thought and action by role-specified archetypes, yet find himself actively organizing the new situation in much the way the asocialists describe. The archetypes impose genuine limits. Analogy relations are not indefinitely flexible and concrete events do not allow infinite possibilities of reinterpretation, but the limits leave ample scope for varying cognition and performance strategies to take account of the special demands of any one interaction setting.

Social Roles as Sets of Interaction Competencies

We have now completed our case for the importance of social structural frames in general, and frameworks of role categories in particular, in face-to-face interaction. In our closing pages, we shall elaborate briefly the conception of social role we derive from our account of social action as a system for producing and distributing interaction commodities.

Conceived as a unit of social production, a role consists of a publicly recognized set of competencies in the production of set treatments of other persons–patterns of symbolic action satisfying needs of determinate classes of others. To "learn the role" is to acquire those production competencies; "to play the role" is to exercise the competencies by producing the specified treatments in the face of "legitimate" demands by would-be consumers.

These classes of consumer likewise comprise social roles: "audience roles" or "members of the role set" in the standard terminology of role theory; and "market" roles in ours, to signal that persons fulfilling them constitute the normal partners-in-exchange for incumbents of a given producer role. Fulfilling any given social role thus involves consumption patterns as well as productive capacities: As an incumbent of a role the actor is expected to manifest certain social psychological needs that are publicly defined as appropriate to one who exercises the particular production competencies attaching to that role, and he is expected, as consumer, to seek treatments satisfying those needs from just the actors who are incumbents of the correlated producer roles. Every role is a producer role relative to some other roles and a consumer role relative to still others.[7]

---

[7] Readers may find it helpful to think of this notion of role in terms of the more familiar (to experimental psychologists) language of "role expectations". A given social role can be specified as a publicly marked category of actors who hold and are the objects of determinate expectations of the following several sorts: expectations as to the production competencies they can be counted on to possess and exercise, expectations as to the social psychological needs (a function of their development and exercise of just those production competencies) they will normally seek to satisfy in exchange relations, expectations as to the determinate treatments they will take as satisfying these needs, expectations as to what social persons (i.e.,

role-sorted others) comprise their normal markets for and their normal suppliers of interaction commodities, and expectations as to the standards of "fair exchange" attaching to the productive activities of their own and others' roles. Within the community's shared scheme of interaction concepts, these role expectations will function something like normative profiles binding actors to perform in certain ways in certain circumstances. But following our account of common sense concepts generally, all will have the status of concrete archetypes, and so will not bind role incumbents so closely as to preclude their actively constructing innovative strategies to deal with the idiosyncrasies of their immediate situations.

This formulation suggests that role expectations themselves might be construed as a sort of interaction competency. We have presented social roles as involving expectations as to the possession and exercise of various sorts of interaction competencies, but if the latter notion is to have the far-reaching explanatory power we attribute to it, then we must take cognitive entities like expectations as competencies too. We must speak, then, of specifically cognitive competencies (competencies in social cognition) and take as especially important instances the capacity to formulate role expectations accurately and to translate them into courses of action in accordance with the shared intuitions of fellow members of the interaction community.

We want to suggest further that cognitive competencies are a sort of *production* competency. We pointed out earlier that situation definitions are the product of negotiation and exchange in the sense that the contents of each other's perspectives on the joint setting are subject to interactants' manipulative efforts. In order to secure from others the practical acceptance of formulations of the passing scene that will bring him perceived strategic benefit, the actor must be willing in return to grant other actors the validity (for the space of their interchanges, at least) of other formulations that they consider to be to their own strategic advantage. Many of the actor's social cognition processes are thus acts of producing specifically epistemic treatments to satisfy the strategic needs of others. This will be true in general of his forming and learning to apply normative principles of action, especially to role expectations. Learning the expectations attached to a social role thus involves acquiring the capacity to formulate the relevant imperatives in a fashion that preserves their continuity with the public ideal, yet which satisfies the demands of others in the immediate situation for acceptance of one or another particular account of what everyone ought to do therein. The actor must acquire the ideal itself, in the sense that he must learn to take as archetypal for that role concrete episodes that are recognizably "correct," "legitimate," and "adequate" according to the intuitions of fellow community members; he must learn to assimilate particular situations to his archetypal scripts in a way that similarly agrees with shared intuitions; and he must learn to accommodate the routines he constructs in this way to the special demands of particular others, in particular situations, for norm-formulations satisfying their strategic needs, where "accommodation" specifically includes the preservation of continuity with the routines. The last is explicitly a matter of commodity production, and given the centrality of the familiar operations of routinization and contextualization, role expectations so construed must be counted as interaction competencies. It follows that "social cognition" cannot be taken, in the fashion of so many social psychologists, as a passive process of scientist-like "coming to know." It is irrevocably part and parcel of ongoing social action of the exchange-governed, manipulative sort described throughout this chapter. Forming and

These remarks begin to make clear the sense in which roles comprise something that can intelligibly be called a social *structure* of positional categories and a *system* of social production. As our terminology suggests, these notions of "system" and "structure," implying organized relations of interdependence among a set of components, are constitutive of our conception of a social role. Doubtless there are many such interrelations, of varying degrees of functional importance, but we are now identifying producer and market relations (relations of social production) as the fundamental links among roles. In the simplest cases, a pair of roles will be related as producer and market for each other: players of one role produce determinate treatments to satisfy the needs of players of the second role, who reciprocate, as a condition of securing these treatments, by producing other treatments to satisfy the needs of the first role players. Each normally looks to the other as main providers for some range of his needs and as principal consumer of some range of his interaction commodities.

However, production relations often are not symmetrical in this way, and the alternative possibilities bring out still more clearly the system-making properties of role relationships. Role players may be producers of treatments required by other role players, but may look to incumbents of yet other roles for treatments to satisfy their own needs. Two role players will be exchange partners, but the commodities provided by the second will consist in mobilizing the resources of some "third party," to the ultimate benefit of the first. Incumbents of these "third party" roles will then be the direct suppliers of the need-satisfying treatments the first role players seek in entering exchange relations with the second role players. Here we begin to bring out a feature our account of interaction has presupposed all along, that communities organize their social production and distribution processes in terms of an extensive division of labor, call it "the division of social labor." This division of the labor of social production constitutes the most important of the system-making properties of role relations.

We have been focusing on production relations, but the role-based division of social labor extends further than this, to organize in some detail the process of distributing commodities. Social roles order distribution by ordering exchange relations among actors, and in particular, by imposing public standards of exchange value on interaction commodities. In addition to specifying the production competencies expected of an incumbent of a role, the normative principles attached to that role roughly mark out further treatments that the exercising of those competencies can be expected to "attract."

---

applying normative principles of action, role expectations included, must in consequence be taken always to involve an aspect of active production. Learning to fulfill a social role involves learning to satisfy expectations as to one's own production of interaction commodities and learning to hold expectations regarding the productive activities of others. But at the same time, learning these expectations is itself a matter of acquiring capacities in the production of a special sort of epistemic commodity, consisting in the *accommodations* of normative profiles to situation specific treatment demands.

These principles are partly an expression of market relationships: Where incumbents of a first role normally produce specified sorts of treatment to be used by incumbents of a second role, they also hold legitimate expectations as to what treatments the latter should be prepared to provide them in exchange. Wherever relations between producer and market are regular and stable, such expectations, defining "fair exchanges," will develop.

The organization of these relations in terms of social roles, publicly specified and enforced, has the effect of objectifying the expectations and formalizing their status as "legitimate" by shared communal standards. Moreover, the high degree of regularity that formalization in role categories introduces into all producer/market relationships ensures that these expectations will figure in actors' daily affairs to the point of becoming a matter-of-course part of strategic planning and performance. Because the sum of an actor's role sets embraces the whole of his activities as producer and as consumer, role-based expectations as to exchangeability will apply to virtually all the treatments he produces or must seek from his normal suppliers. As a result, the exchange values of the commodities he must deal in will be stable in the sense that (public) benchmarks are available against which to measure the adequacy of any particular set of exchanges.

Powers of exchangeability will not, of course, be rigidly determined for any of these commodities. Actors can and do negotiate departures from the role-specified standards in many particular cases. But they are not wholly at sea in evaluating the different bargains they propose to each other. Role norms are always available to cite as "objective" paradigms of what the other *ought* "in fairness" to demand and provide in exchange for what, and this social fact itself introduces enough regularity into the negotiated variations of exchange values to permit the actor a reasonable prognosis of his strategic prospects. As long as his role relations remain more or less constant, so will his position of strategic power relative to his usual partners in exchange.

This formulation of the role concept in terms of production competencies provides the basis of our claim to resolve the issue between objectivists and asocialists over the existence and status of social roles. Our notion of an interaction competency, we contend, expresses and integrates what is right in both the traditional sociologist's claim that action at the micro level must be bounded and limited by suprasituational normative principles, and the asocialists' countering claim that interaction settings are to a large extent constructed by their participants in the course of carrying out collective procedures of interpretation and negotiation.

Our argument against the asocialist is the argument that social position categories structure face-to-face interaction: The intrinsic complexities of interaction lead the actor to place the highest premium on the calculability of self and others, a disposition that is realized experientially in the form of a drive to achieve mastery over his situations. Mastery is achieved mainly by the device of applying routines of cognition and action, but routinization is possible only in the presence of limitations on the possibilities of variation in a setting, limitations that the actor safely can take utterly for granted because they have the status of social objects for him and his interactants. Systems of interrelated position categories are the means whereby communities articulate and enforce the required limitations.

Our notion of roles as bundles of interaction competencies fits into this analysis as an account of how the limits on action are realized in actors' cognitive schemes and in their behavior patterns. The routinization component of the competency concept is the basis of this account. According to our general definition, an interaction competency is an ability to contextualize established patterns of action and cognition while sustaining enough continuity with familiar types of routines to ensure a feeling of command over the situation.

We say *types* of routine because our view that an actor's routines always are comprised of archetypal scripts of concrete episodes from his personal history ensures a high degree of idiosyncrasy of detail from actor to actor. The routines attaching to a publicly defined competency thus comprise a publicly recognized type in this sense: Shared intuitions of community members must certify an individual actor's idiosyncratic routine as a genuine instance of producing the required type of interaction commodity. Acquiring the competency depends on a process of social learning leading to the development of a sense of what concrete episodes from the personal past will and will not yield performances passing the public standards for commodities subsumed by that competency; exercising the competency requires acting for maximize continuity with just those routines that gain community sanction.

The quality of compulsion attaching to normative principles is due in part to community pressure against the adoption of routines not satisfying its standards. But normative force can also be explained as a product of routinization itself. In experiential terms, acceptance of a principle carrying normative force amounts to taking the courses of action it dictates as *self-evidently* and *unquestionably* the appropriate thing to think or do in the circumstances it specifies. Reflection and criticism necessarily put the actor at a certain distance from his principles of action, establishing an attitude toward them that makes nonfulfillment a live possibility. The effectiveness of a role norm as an organizer of action will thus be impaired in the same degree as it comes regularly to be the object of critical evaluation by incumbents of the role. Routinization, we have been arguing, is the basic mechanism whereby actors come to assign to principles and patterns of action this status of being self-evident and matter of course.

Normative force is thus bound up essentially with the formation and use of interaction routines, and so, in consequence, is the power of role norms to impose limits on the possibilities of actors' constructions of their situations. The limiting mechanisms, in other words, *are* the type-satisfying routines that attach to the production competencies comprising the role. Actors can count on each other to respect broad limitations in their construction of performance strategies because they know that all parties are bound by routines appropriate to their roles as producers, consumers, and distributors of interaction commodities.

Our conception of roles as interaction competencies explain their power to fulfill the structuring and organizing function of positional categories. But we have claimed to do more than this. We have claimed that the competency notion of roles not only supports a version of the objectivists' view of roles as coercing and limiting the actor, but that it does so in a fashion that takes full account of the asocialists' insistence on the active, constructive character of ordinary action. We satisfy this claim by making the necessity of contextualization the correlative of the drive to routinize cognition and performance, and incorporating the two notions together into our concept of an "interaction competency." "Interaction competency," it will be recalled, is defined as the ability to *construct* patterns of action that meet the exigencies of particular situations while sustaining continuity with the established routines that are the basis of the sense of strategic mastery. The demands of the interaction system, together with the place of contextualization in competent interaction, ensure that the routines attached to social roles cannot become the rigid profiles of action of traditional sociology, closely determining the appropriate courses of action for all of a well-specified set of interaction situations. This fact is further guaranteed by our construal of the routines, and all common sense concepts, as concrete archetypes. Role routines so conceived are inherently indeterminate, *forcing* the actor to construct the details of his cognition and performance strategies.

This picture of the actor's condition falls far short of ascribing to him and his interactants the sort of collective freedom to make their world view which asocialist writers envision. But it is equally true that *competent* actors of the sort we describe are compelled by the structure of their interaction system to become active, constructing, innovating producers of strategies in exactly the way denied by traditional sociologists of the objectivist persuasion.

References

Abelson, R. P. Script processing in attitude formation and decision making. In J. S. Carroll & J. W. Payne (Eds.), *Cognition and social behavior.* Hillsdale, N.J.: Erlbaum, 1976.

Athay, M., & Darley, J. M. Toward an interaction-centered theory of personality. In N. Cantor & J. F. Kihlstrom (Eds.), *Personality, cognition, and social interaction.* Hillsdale, N.J.: Erlbaum, 1981.

Bruner, J. S. On perceptual readiness. *Psychological Review*, 1957, *64*, 123-152.

Cantor, N., & Mischel, W. Prototypes in person perception. In L. Berkowitz (Ed.), *Recent advances in experimental social psychology* (Vol. 12) New York: Academic Press, 1979.

Durkheim, E. *The division of labor in society.* Glencoe, Ill.: Free Press, 1947.

Flavell, J. H., Botkin, P. T., Fry, C. L., Wright, J. W., & Jarris, P. E. The development of role-taking and communication skills in children. New York: Wiley, 1968.

Goffman, E. *The presentation of self in everyday life.* Garden City, New York: Doubleday Anchor, 1959.

Goffman, E. *Frame analysis: An essay on the organization of experience.* New York: Harper & Row, 1974.

Jones, E. E. *Ingratiation*. New York: Appleton-Century-Crofts, 1964.

Marx, K. *Capital: A critique of political economy* (Vol. 1) (B. Fowkes, trans.). New York: Vintage Books, 1977.

McGuire, W. J. Personality and susceptibility to social influence. In E. F. Borgotta & W. W. Lambert (Eds.), *Handbook of personality theory and research.* Chicago: Rand McNally, 1968.

Merton, R. K. *Social theory and social structure* (rev. ed.). Glencoe, Ill.: Free Press, 1957. (a)

Merton, R. K. The role set: Problems in sociological theory. *British Journal of Sociology*, 1957, *8*, 106-120. (b)

Mischel, W. Toward a cognitive social learning reconceptualization of personality. *Psychological Review*, 1973, *80*, 252-283.

Moos, R. H. Situational analysis of a therapeutic community milieu. *Journal of Abnormal Psychology*, 1968, *73*, 49-61.

Rosch, E. Principles of categorization. In E. Rosch & B. B. Lloyd (Eds.), *Cognition and categorization*, Hillsdale, N.J.: Erlbaum, 1978.

Salatas, H., & Flavell, J. H. Perspective taking: The development of two components of knowledge. *Child Development*, 1976, *47*, 103-109.

Snyder, M. The self-monitoring of expressive behavior. *Journal of Personality and Social Psychology*, 1974, *30*, 526-537.

Snyder, M. Self monitoring processes. In L. Berkowitz (Ed.), *Advances in experimental social psychology* (Vol. 12). New York: Academic Press, 1979.

Snyder, M., & Monson, T. S. Persons, situations, and the control of social behavior. *Journal of Personality and Social Psychology*, 1975, *32*, 637-644.

Chapter 4

Determinants of Responsiveness in Dyadic Interaction

Deborah Davis

During the past ten years, psychologists have begun to devote considerable attention to the *sequential* properties of social interaction. The majority of this research has focused on description of sequential contingencies between the behaviors of interaction partners, inferences concerning the conversational control functions of the observed behaviors, and/or assessment of the degree of mutual influence between the behaviors of interaction partners. For example, the first two strategies are embodied by research designed to examine the turn taking system in dyadic conversation (e.g., Duncan & Fiske, 1977; Jaffe & Feldstein, 1970); and the third by the various research programs investigating such processes as mutual influence between mothers and infants (e.g., Thomas & Malone, 1979; Thomas & Martin, 1976), reciprocity of self-disclosure (e.g., Warner, Kenney, & Stoto, 1979), matching of paralinguistic variables such as vocal pitch and intensity or lengths of utterances and pauses (e.g., Feldstein & Welkowitz, 1978), and synchrony of body movements (e.g., Kendon, 1970; McDowall, 1978) (see Cappella, 1981, for a review of mutual influence processes for a variety of behaviors).

Unfortunately, such programs of research have not yet led to the development of systematic theoretical investigations of the process of interaction that simultaneously provide understanding of (1) the way in which interaction is regulated, (2) the impact of interaction process variables on the outcomes of interaction, (3) the influence of external variables (e.g., personality, roles) on the process of interaction, and (4) the moderating impact of external variables on the relationship between interaction process and outcomes. This chapter will present a theoretical analysis of the role of *responsiveness* in dyadic interaction that will address each of the above concerns. The regulatory functions of responsiveness, the relationship between responsiveness and interaction outcomes, and the external variables that moderate this relationship are treated in detail elsewhere (Davis & Perkowitz, 1979; Davis, Note 1). The purpose of the present chapter is to examine the *antecedents* of responsiveness. Thus, after a brief review of the nature and consequences of responsiveness, the major portion of the chapter will be devoted to consideration of personality, role, and situational determinants of responsiveness.

The Nature of Responsiveness

Each communicative behavior in interaction carries with it a set of implicit demands for response. Although the nature of these demands may vary widely (e.g., for agreement, sympathy, indignation), most basic among them are (1) that the other respond, (2) that the response address the content of one's own preceding communication, and (3) that the response be characterized by a particular degree of elaboration (e.g., monosyllabic vs. detailed commentary). Responsiveness may be thought of as the extent to which these demands are satisfied; that is, (1) the probability with which each person responds to the communicative behaviors of the other, (2) the proportion of responses that are relevant in content to (i.e., directly address) the preceding communication of the other, and (3) the proportion of responses that are of the "demanded" degree of elaboration. Several points relevant to the latter two contingencies should be emphasized.

Response Relevance

Response relevance refers to the degree to which the response is *perceived* by the recipient to address itself to the content of his/her preceding communication. The *way* in which it does so is unimportant. It may be friendly, hostile, agreeing, disagreeing, etc. Positive and negative responses may be equally relevant. However, if a response is perceived to be irrelevant, it will function as an irrelevant response from the perceiver's standpoint, regardless of whether it was either logically relevant or intended to be relevant by the speaker.

Response Elaboration

The elaboration of a response is appropriate (responsive) to the extent that it matches the demand for elaboration implicit in the preceding communication (that is, the degree of elaboration that the speaker *intended* to elicit). The nature of this demand may be inferred from the context of the communication, knowledge of the communicator, nonverbal cues such as voice inflection, the specific content of the communication, etc., but may be difficult to identify empirically. Monosyllabic (but relevant) responses are clearly unresponsive, for example, in the face of clear attempts to begin a discussion. On the other hand, detailed elaboration of the issues surrounding a particular choice will be unresponsive to a communication intended to elicit immediate action instructions (e.g., "Should I take this freeway exit or the next one?"). Responses of either excessive or insufficient elaboration will inevitably frustrate one's own goals for the interaction.

Consequences of Responsiveness

Maintenance of Interaction

Responsiveness will play an important role in the maintenance of interaction. Repeated failure to respond will have obvious deleterious effects on the flow of conversation. In addition, since irrelevant responses often communicate disinterest in the preceding communication, they may serve to discourage efforts at further communication. Waltzlawick, Beavin, and Jackson (1967), for example, have argued that irrelevant responses often constitute deliberate attempts to terminate interaction. Finally, all three components of responsiveness will affect the motivation to continue interaction. Unresponsiveness from another has a number of negative effects that will often make further interaction undesirable.

Maintenance of Focus on Conversation Topic

Most responses that directly address a preceding communication (excluding such comments as "That's boring," "Let's change the subject," etc.) will tend to promote continuing focus on the same general topic area. This is not always the case, since one may follow a relevant response with a change of subject. However, relevant responses are certainly more likely to promote such continuation than are irrelevant responses, failures to respond, or insufficiently elaborate responses. This tendency to maintain focus on a particular topic area will have important implications for control of the interaction, and for facilitation of interaction goals.

Predictability, Control, and Stress

To the extent that another is responsive, his or her behavior will be at least partially predictable and controllable. This does not imply that the content of the other's responses, or the nature of the topics they initiate, will be predictable or controllable in exact detail. However, one may expect (1) that the other will respond, (2) that the response will address the content of the preceding communication, and (3) that it will be within a certain range of elaboration. Similarly, responsiveness will allow partial control, in that one may (1) cause the other to respond, and (2) determine the general content area and range of elaboration of the response. In contrast, it is next to impossible to direct the course of interaction if the other does not respond at all, if his/her responses are typically irrelevant, or if the degree of elaboration does not correspond to one's intentions.

Since responsiveness *from* another will reduce the uncertainty associated with unpredictability, and the frustration associated with lack of control, it should also reduce stress. However, it should be noted that the effects of responsiveness *to* another are potentially quite different. Responsiveness to another provides him/her with more control of the interaction. Such abdication of control may reduce the ability to pursue one's own goals, especially if they are incompatible with those of one's partner. In addition, when one is responsive to another, the predictability of the interaction will be more dependent on one's ability to accurately guess the topics that the other will initiate. This does not imply that interaction will always be adversarial, with participants attempting to elicit responsive behavior from their partners, while withholding it themselves. In fact, there is evidence, instead, that people prefer to be responsive (Davis & Perkowitz, 1979; Davis, Note 1). The desire to avoid abdication of control, and thus responsiveness, will affect interaction most strongly in situations where one's own goals are incompatible with those of one's partner.

Facilitation of Interaction Goals

To the extent that responsiveness facilitates control over the interaction, it should also facilitate achievement of interaction goals. Response, for example, may or may not facilitate the initiator's purpose, but failure to respond will almost certainly frustrate it. Similarly, irrelevant responses and responses that are insufficiently or excessively elaborate are less likely to facilitate interaction goals (such as attempts to discuss, or gain information about, particular topics) than are relevant and appropriately elaborate responses. Thus, responsiveness from another will generally facilitate, but not guarantee, achievement of interaction goals. Responsiveness to another on the other hand, may facilitate the other's goals, but will not always facilitate one's own.

Communication Efficiency and Accuracy

Responsiveness will have substantial impact on both the efficiency and accuracy of communication. This impact has been most clearly demonstrated with respect to probability of response. For example, research on the structural organization of conversation has identified constellations of behaviors that signal when response is desired, either brief back-channel responses ("Yeah," "I see," "Mmhmm," etc.) or full assumption of the speaking turn (see Duncan & Fiske, 1977; Rosenfeld, 1978; Rosenfeld & Hanks, 1980; Sacks, Schegloff, & Jefferson, 1978). The former serve to regulate the flow of information in conversation, telling the speaker to continue, elaborate, repeat, clarify, speed up, and so forth. If such feedback is not provided at the expected junctures, or if it is prevented by features of the interaction situation, speech disruption (an index of stress) becomes more pronounced (e.g., Argyle, Lalljee, & Cook, 1968; Rosenfeld, 1967), communications become less efficient and more redundant (Erickson, 1979; Krauss & Bricker, 1967; Krauss, Garlock, Bricker, & McMahon, 1977; Krauss & Weinheimer, 1966; Kraut, Note 2), and listener comprehension is reduced (Lewis, Note 3). Similar effects would be expected as a result of failure to assume the speaking turn when signaled to do so. That is, speech may be disrupted by the consequent stress, and communications may become redundant, in repeated efforts to elicit response.

There is also reason to expect that response relevance will affect efficiency and accuracy. First, irrelevant responses may often be followed by attempts to redirect the conversation to the original topic, or to ascertain their relationship to the preceding communication. Either alternative will result in decreased efficiency. Second, irrelevant responses will often be misunderstood. Social norms dictate that responses to other communications should be relevant (e.g., Grice, 1975; Sacks et al., 1978; Weiner & Goodenough, 1977), and persons thus *expect* relevant responses from others. One's own prior utterances, therefore, provide the context (Bransford, 1979; Bransford & Johnson, 1973), antecedents (Clark & Haviland, 1977), or schemas (e.g., Taylor & Crocker, 1981), with respect to which the other's responses are processed. If they can be understood with reference to one's prior communication at all, they may be distorted to appear more relevant than they were intended by the speaker. If not, they may simply be judged incomprehensible.

The effects of relevance on comprehension have been demonstrated in two studies. Planalp and Tracy (1980) showed that increased cognitive distance between a new conversation topic and past topics was associated with less judged communicative competence on the part of the speaker, and less judged understandability of the interchange. Similarly, Holtgraves and Davis (Note 4) demonstrated that the answers of participants in a political debate were judged to be more well-organized, clearly stated, and logical, and as reflecting greater knowledge of the facts and understanding of the issues when they were responsive to the interviewers' questions than when they were unresponsive. Further, memory for unresponsive answers was less than for responsive answers.

Interpersonal Attributions

Unresponsiveness from another will result in a variety of attributions. For example, failure to respond, irrelevant responses, or inappropriately brief responses tend to lead to the inference that the other is interested neither in oneself nor what one has to say (see Rosenfeld, 1978; Davis & Perkowitz, 1979). Alternatively, one may infer that the other did not understand one's comment, did not understand the relationship between the comment and their own response, did not wish to discuss the topic, did not possess an adequate repertoire to formulate an elaborate response, had something to hide, etc. (see Holtgraves & Davis, Note 4). Most such inferences are not favorable, and will have detrimental effects on the relationship between participants.

Attraction

The various consequences of responsiveness described above will have implications for attraction. That is, unresponsive persons, who are associated with stress, frustration of interaction goals, inefficient and inaccurate communication, dislike for oneself, and other unfavorable attributions, will clearly be less attractive than responsive others.

Davis and Perkowitz (1979) reviewed substantial evidence in support of the relationship between responsiveness and attraction. In addition, the authors conducted two experiments designed to directly examine the effects of probability of response and proportion of relevant responses on attraction. Under the guise of a study of the acquaintanceship process, subjects exchanged information about themselves with another subject (confederate) by taking turns choosing and answering questions about themselves on each trial. For Experiment 1, subjects were required to answer on all trials, whereas the probability with which the confederate responded to the subject was varied. For Experiment 2, the proportion of relevant responses was varied. That is, the subject answered first, and the confederate responded to the same question on either 80% or 20% of the trials. Although the content of answers to each question was predetermined and held constant across conditions, it was assumed that an answer to the same question would be more relevant than an answer to a different question. Consistent with expectation, both probability of response and proportion of relevant responses were positively related to (1) attraction to the confederate, (2) subjects' perceptions of the confederate's attraction to themselves, and (3) the degree to which subjects felt that they and the confederate had become acquainted with one another (see also Berg & Archer, Note 5).

Personality Development

There is substantial evidence that unresponsiveness from others will make interaction uncontrollable, thus frustrating interaction goals; and that unresponsiveness tends to communicate the message that one is interested in neither the other person nor in his/her message. This suggests that the degree of responsiveness from significant others in the social environment may affect the development of locus of control and of self-esteem. For example, unresponsiveness from others will tend to frustrate attempts to control interaction; and since many of life's outcomes are derived from interaction, failure to control interaction will often imply failure to achieve other goals. Thus, a person who is confronted with unresponsive others may be more likely to develop an external locus of control than those surrounded by responsive others. Similarly, those surrounded by unresponsive others will perceive that those persons are uninterested in them and unattracted to them. Thus, such persons would be expected to develop lower self-esteem than those surrounded by responsive others.

Personality and Situational Determinants of the Reactions to Unresponsiveness

The majority of this chapter will be devoted to consideration of the situational and dispositional *antecedents* of responsiveness. However, it is important to note that such variables may also moderate the consequences of responsiveness. For example, it is known that locus of control is related to persistence in the face of failure. Unresponsiveness from another is assumed to frustrate attempts to control interaction and achieve interaction goals. Thus, it follows that externals should be more likely to cease attempts to control interactions in the face of unresponsiveness from another than should internals. Unresponsiveness is also assumed to convey lack of interest in, and attraction to, others. Several personality variables, e.g., need for approval, self-consciousness, and self-monitoring, are known to be related to concern with reactions of others to oneself. Persons who are high on such dimensions should experience unresponsiveness as more aversive, and thus react more strongly.

Situational variables will also affect reactions to unresponsiveness. For example, the situation may affect the importance of maintaining control, achievement of conversation goals, communication efficiency, etc., and thus the magnitude of the aversive consequences of unresponsiveness. Similarly, the nature of the attributions resulting from the other's unresponsiveness will vary with the situation. In some situations responsiveness will be only minimally aversive, whereas in others it will be disastrous.

Determinants of Responsiveness

Four general factors are expected to affect responsiveness in interaction: (1) attention to one's partner, (2) accuracy of understanding of one another's communications, (3) possession of response repertoires that are adequate for formulation of relevant, and appropriately elaborate responses, and (4) motivation to be responsive (Davis & Perkowitz, 1979). These four factors will affect responsiveness both directly and through their influence on one another.

Perhaps the most fundamental prerequisite for responsive interaction is attention to one's partner. Attention is necessary both in order to notice behaviors that demand response and in order to process them accurately (see reviews by Broadbent, 1968; Kahneman, 1975, for discussions of the relationship between attention and processing accuracy). Unnoticed behaviors will typically not receive response, nor will those that are inaccurately processed often elicit responses of appropriate content and degree of elaboration. The focus of attention may also affect access to one's repertoire of pertinent knowledge. Distraction, for example, is known to decrease access to task-relevant memory areas (again, see Broadbent, 1968; Kahneman, 1975). Responsiveness, then, may be either disrupted or enhanced by factors that affect attention to one's partner.

Responsiveness will also be strongly affected by the accuracy with which one's partner's communications are understood. In order to formulate a relevant response that is of the appropriate degree of elaboration, one must understand not only the literal content of the other's communication, but also the emotional content, and the implicit demand for a particular depth of response. Without this understanding, even the best intentions may result in a response that is perceived by the other as irrelevant or of inappropriate elaboration.

Given that one has understood another's communication accurately, one must yet possess a response repertoire that is adequate to the production of a response of appropriate elaboration. It is always possible to produce a relevant response (e.g., "I don't understand," "I don't know," "yes," "no") to even the most complex question. However, a response that is of the "demanded" degree of elaboration will often require substantial knowledge or experience. For example, suppose you were asked the question "What impact do you think the president's economic policies will have on inflation?" You may simply answer "Inflation will continue at its present rate," and do so without much knowledge of economics. However, suppose you were asked the same question in the midst of a group of economists, where it was clear that the questioner wanted an elaborate analysis of what would happen, and how and why. In such circumstances, your knowledge of economics, the president's policies, and current economic events would determine your ability to formulate an appropriately elaborate response.

The factors discussed so far—attention, accuracy, and response repertoire—contribute to the individual's *capacity* for responsiveness. However, the final determinant of responsiveness is motivation. One can choose whether or not to be responsive (given that the first three conditions are met), and many variables may affect that choice. Responsiveness to one's partner has several effects, noted earlier, that may or may not be desirable. That is, responsiveness tends to (1) maintain interaction, (2) maintain focus on a particular topic, (3) allow one's partner to exert more control over the interaction, (4) increase feelings of intimacy, (5) convey interest in and attraction to the other, and (6) increase the other's attraction to oneself. To the extent that any of these effects are not desired, the motivation to *be* responsive may be low.

A multitude of personality, role, and situational characteristics affect each of the four factors that influence responsiveness. Many such characteristics will be suggested below, and supporting research (where available) will be discussed.

Attention

Responsiveness may be affected by (1) the *absolute amount* of attention that is devoted to one's partner, (2) the *range of cues* in his/her behavior and communications that are attended to, and (3) the *specific categories* of cues or content that are selectively attended to. The absolute amount of attention to one's partner, and the range of cues attended to should be positively related to both the likelihood of noticing behaviors that demand response and accuracy of processing. Research on memory and attention has demonstrated that relatively well attended stimuli are processed more accurately (e.g., Broadbent, 1968; Kahneman, 1975). Further, communication may occur in many channels (e.g., verbal, facial, postural), and communication accuracy is known to increase with the number of available channels (e.g., Mehrabian and Reed, 1968), except when content is inconsistent across channels. The effects of selective attention will depend on the nature of the content or cues focused on and the context of the interaction, and will be elaborated below where relevant. The following sections will illustrate characteristics of the situation and one's interaction partners, role relationships, and personal characteristics that affect attention in any or all of the above respects.

Characteristics of the Situation

The context of interaction will affect attention in each of the three ways described above. First, situations differ with respect to demands for attention that are external to the interaction, thus affecting the *absolute amount* of attention available for one's partner. For example, one can devote more attention to one's partner when alone than when in the midst of a cocktail party. Alternatively, situations may involve preoccupation with particular concerns that distract attention from one's partner. Berkowitz (1972), for example, has shown that situations that evoke concern for the self (e.g., concern about performance) often reduce empathy for others.

Second, the situation will affect the range of cues attended to. For example, task demands, distractions, or the medium of interaction will determine which, and how many, channels of communication are available. Visual channels will be unavailable for telephone conversations and tasks that prevent face-to-face orientation, whereas audio channels will be lacking in letters or settings where the noise level prevents conversation.

Third, the context of interaction will affect the nature of demands for selective attention within the interaction. In particular, one's goals, concerns, or expectations will affect the nature of cues attended to. For example, in task oriented situations one may attend primarily to content that is task related, and pay relatively less attention to personal information or emotional reactions. In contrast, task-related conversation may be ignored when having a drink after work. Situations may also evoke particular needs or interests, and thus result in selective attention to need or interest-related content. When concerned with acceptance, for example, attention may be restricted to content that conveys information about one's partner's reaction to oneself. Finally, many situations are associated with particular expectations for the behavior of participants. These expectations may be thought of as "event," "situation," or "role" (roles are inherent in situations) schemas. As such, they would be expected to selectively direct attention to *schema relevant* aspects of others' behaviors and communications (see Taylor & Crocker, 1981; Wyer & Srull, 1980).

Reduction of either the amount of attention devoted to one's partner, or the range of cues attended to should clearly reduce responsiveness, while selective attention should, in most cases, increase responsiveness for content that is being selectively attended to and decrease responsiveness for all other content. Exceptions to the suggested effects of selective attention may occur when goals, needs, or expectations activated by the situation cause distortion in the interpretation of relevant content, for example, if fear of rejection led one to interpret others' behaviors inappropriately as hostile. To the extent that increased attention is associated with increased distortion (and thus decreased accuracy) responsiveness with respect to response relevance and elaboration would be expected to decrease.

Characteristics of Interaction Partners

Perception theorists have identified two general factors that are assumed to govern attentional processes: novelty and importance (Berlyne, 1960, 1974; Lanzetta, 1971). Many of the selective attention processes noted above may reflect the impact of importance on attentional processes. That is, goal, need, or schema relevant aspects of other's communications may be regarded as more "important" than those that are irrelevant, and thus receive more attention. Similarly, the "importance" of particular interaction partners, or of particular categories of behaviors from specific partners, may vary widely, and thus affect either the amount of attention devoted to them, or selective attention to specific content areas.

Interaction partners may be regarded as important to the extent that they possess desired resources, are in control of rewards, or are themselves inherently rewarding (e.g., physically attractive). Thus, we may attend more to others who we like or find particularly interesting, who are powerful, of high status, or on whom we are dependent.

Several theorists have discussed the effects of outcome dependence upon others on attentional processes. For example, Chance (1967) has noted that high status persons, who are presumably more likely to affect one's outcomes, receive more visual attention, and that the various channels of communication are kept open by lower status persons in order to process cues for direction, control, or reward. More generally, Berscheid, Graziano, Monson, and Dermer (1976) have argued that as one's outcome dependence upon another increases, "there should be an increased tendency for the perceiver to be attentive to the other, to collect data about the other's behavior and the context in which it occurs, and to perform an attributional analysis upon these data" (p. 979). In support of their argument, the authors found that subjects devoted more attention to others with whom they expected future interaction (and could thus affect subjects' outcomes) than those with whom they expected no future interaction (see also, Harvey, Yarkin, Lightner, & Town, 1980).

Characteristics of interaction partners may also affect the specific focus of attention. The importance of specific categories of communications may be expected to vary between partners. For example, cues reflecting reactions to task performance may receive relatively more attention when interacting with one's supervisor than with an attractive co-worker, whereas the reverse may be true for cues reflecting personal attraction.

Role Relationships

Attention is often prescribed by the role relationships within the dyad. For example, in the client-therapist relationship, it is the therapist who must attend carefully to the communicative behaviors of the client. In interactions between persons of unequal status, power, or expertise, it is often expected or required that the person of lower status or power attend carefully to the behaviors of the other, while the reverse is neither expected nor required.

Both the range and specific nature of cues attended to may also be affected by role relationships. Therapists, for example, are taught to attend to both verbal and nonverbal content in order to better understand clients' communications (e.g., Waxer, 1979). Concerns or outcome dependencies that are specific to the role relationship (e.g., teacher-student) may affect the specific nature of cues that are focused on (e.g., evaluation).

Individual Characteristics

A number of personality dimensions have been shown to be associated with either the overall amount of attention devoted to interaction partners, the specific nature of cues that are attended to in interaction, or both. Several illustrative dimensions will be discussed below, along with their potential effects on responsiveness.

Self-Consciousness

Virtually everyone is plagued from time to time with fits of self-consciousness during social interaction. Most of us are all too familiar with its disruptive effects. Preoccupied with thoughts of how we look or how we're coming across to others, we often find ourselves tongue-tied, having difficulty really listening to what is said, or being able to think of an appropriate reply.

In recent years, psychologists and sociologists have begun to devote considerable attention to the nature of self-consciousness and its consequences for social behavior (see reviews by Buss, 1980; Carver, 1979; Wicklund, 1975). Theoretical treatments of self-consciousness have in common the assumption that self-consciousness involves a shift in the focus of attention from the external environment to the self (e.g., Argyle, 1969; Buss, 1980; Carver, 1979; Duval & Wicklund, 1972; Fenigstein, Scheier, & Buss, 1975; Goffman, 1959). Further, attention may shift either to private aspects of the self, such as one's moods, feelings, attitudes, and private behaviors (private self-consciousness); or to public aspects of the self such as physical appearance, interpersonal behaviors, and reactions of others to oneself (public self-consciousness). Both private and public self-consciousness may vary dispositionally (see Buss, 1980; Fenigstein et al., 1975), and as a function of situational cues such as an evaluative audience, mirrors, cameras, and the sound of one's own tape recorded voice (see Buss, 1980; Carver, 1979; Wicklund, 1975). Dispositional public self-consciousness is assessed by such items as "I'm concerned about what other people think of me," "I usually worry about making a good impression," and "I'm self-conscious about the way I look"; and dispositional private self-consciousness by such items as "I reflect about myself a lot," "I'm alert to changes in my mood," and "I'm often the subject of my own fantasies" (Fenigstein et al., 1975).

In the context of social interaction, *public* self-consciousness should involve (1) decreased attention to one's partner's *nonevaluative* behaviors and other characteristics, and (2) increased concern with and attention to one's partner's *evaluative* behaviors. Goffman (1959), for example, has described self-consciousness as a shift in attention from what is being said to concern with the reactions of others to oneself. Similarly, Argyle (1969) has described self-consciousness as the feeling of being the observed, rather than the observer, in social interaction.

Private self-consciousness, on the other hand, should simply involve a shift in attention away from one's partner altogether. The specific focus of attention (e.g., evaluative vs. nonevaluative behaviors) should not be affected. Thus, private self-consciousness should affect the amount and range of attention devoted to one's partner, but not the specific focus, whereas public self-consciousness should affect all three factors.

Several studies have documented the relationship of public self-consciousness to concern with the reactions of others. Subjects high in public self-consciousness have been shown to be more likely to behave in ways that they expect to elicit positive evaluations from others (e.g., Froming & Carver, 1981; Hull & Levy, 1979; Santee & Maslach, in press; Scheier, 1980; Froming, Walker, & Lopyan, Note 6), to react more strongly to evaluations that are received (e.g., Fenigstein, 1979), and to report more embarrassment in awkward social situations (Froming & Brody, Note 7). Private self-consciousness, on the other hand, has been related to neither attempts to elicit positive evaluations nor reactions to evaluations received (see review by Scheier & Carver, 1981).

There is also evidence that both private and public self-consciousness reduce attention to one's partner's *nonevaluative* behaviors. Research on memory and attention (see Broadbent, 1968; Kahneman, 1975) has demonstrated that memory is better for attended than for relatively unattended stimuli. Thus, to the extent that self-consciousness reduces attention to one's partner's nonevaluative behaviors, it should also reduce one's memory for them. Several studies have supported this prediction (Kimble & Zehr, Note 8; Davis, Costella, & Droll, Note 9). In addition, in a group performance situation, Brenner (1973, Note 10) found that memory for others' performance was poorest for those group members whose performances immediately preceded and followed the subject's own, presumably those during which he or she was most self-conscious; and Diener, Lusk, DeFour, and Flax (1980) found that self-consciousness decreased memory for the environment in which a group task had been enacted.

Self-consciousness and responsiveness. The effects of self-consciousness on attention during social interaction are well documented. We are currently conducting research to directly assess the impact of self-consciousness on responsiveness. Because both private and public self-consciousness reduce attention to the nonevaluative behaviors of one's partner, both should reduce accuracy of processing, and thus responsiveness, when the content of the interaction is non–self-relevant. In contrast, when the content of the interaction is self-relevant, either evaluatively or descriptively, the opposite may be true. Public self-consciousness may increase responsiveness when the content is evaluatively relevant, unless the concern with evaluation induces distortion in the interpretation of one's partner's behaviors. On the other hand, private self-consciousness (to the extent that it involves attention to self-relevant information) may increase responsiveness when the content of another's communications is either evaluatively or descriptively relevant to oneself.

Self-Monitoring

Snyder (1974, 1976) has described the prototypic high self-monitoring person as one who "out of a concern for the situational and interpersonal appropriateness of his or her social behavior, is particularly sensitive to the expression and self presentation of relevant others in social situations, and uses these cues as guidelines for monitoring (that is, regulating and controlling) his or her own verbal and nonverbal self-presentation." The prototypic low self-monitor, on the other hand, "is not so vigilant to social information about situationally appropriate self-presentation . . . . In comparison with their high self-monitoring counterparts, the expressive behavior of low self-monitoring individuals seems . . . to be controlled from within by their affective states and attitudes . . . rather than molded and tailored to fit the situation" (Snyder, 1979, p. 89). In other words, high self-monitors are hypothesized to be both more *attentive* and more *responsive* to social information concerning appropriate behavior. Both hypotheses are well documented empirically.

Relative to low self-monitors, high self-monitors demonstrate more attention to, interest in, and involvement with others in their social environment. They are more likely to (1) seek information about others with whom they anticipate interaction (Elliott, 1979; Snyder, 1974), (2) remember more accurately information about anticipated interaction partners (Berscheid et al., 1976), (3) have rich and well-articulated images of prototypic others in a variety of behavioral domains (Snyder & Cantor, 1980), and (4) have more interpersonally oriented self-concepts, i.e., to define themselves in terms of relationships with others (Sampson, 1978) or to possess self-conceptions that reflect greater involvement with others (Ickes, Layden, & Barnes, 1978).

There is substantial evidence, as well, that high self-monitors are more responsive to situation-specific social cues, in that they (1) are more likely to offer situational explanations for their behavior (Brockner & Eckenrode, 1978; Snyder, 1976; Snyder & Tanke, 1976), (2) are more sensitive to salient reference group norms dictating either conformity or autonomy (Rarick, Soldow, & Geizer, 1976; Snyder & Monson, 1975), and (3) exhibit greater variability in behavior across situations, in such diverse behavioral domains as altruism, honesty, self-restraint (Snyder & Monson, 1975), cooperation (Danheiser & Graziano, in press), and nonverbal behaviors expressive of sociability, anxiety, and sex role identity (Lippa, 1976, 1978, Note 11; Lippa & Mash, 1981). Also indicative of the impact of situation specific cues, high self-monitors exhibit less consistency between attitudes and behavior (Bercherer & Richard, 1978; Snyder & Kendzierski, in press; Snyder & Swann, 1976; Zanna, Olson, & Fazio, in press; Zuckerman & Reis, 1978) including less change as a result of counterattitudinal behavior (Snyder & Tanke, 1976), and less consistency between mood state and behavior (Ickes, Layden, & Barnes, 1978) and between personality and expressive behavior (Lippa, 1978, Note 11; Lippa, Valdez, & Jolly, Note 12). Finally, recent evidence suggests that high self-monitors tend to gravitate to social situations that provide clear specifications for the type of individual called for whereas low self-monitors choose situations that call for behaviors consistent with their self-images (Snyder, 1981; Snyder & Gangestad, Note 13).

There is some evidence that self-monitoring directly affects the process of interaction. Ickes and Barnes (1977) videotaped pairs of subjects in a waiting room. High self-monitoring subjects were observed to more often be the first to initiate conversation, and to reinitiate conversation after periods of silence. They were also perceived by their partners as more directive and as having greater need to talk. In female dyads, the higher self-monitor engaged in more expressive behaviors than the lower, while the reverse was true for male dyads. Finally, high self-monitors perceived themselves as having been more influenced by their partner's behaviors.

Self-monitoring and responsiveness. The evidence above suggests that self-monitoring may be strongly related to responsiveness. Clearly, high self-monitors are more attentive to their partners. They should therefore be more likely to notice behaviors that demand response, and to process them more accurately. We have argued that each communicative behavior carries an implicit demand for a response from a particular content domain (a relevant response) and one of a particular degree of elaboration or depth. This "demand" may be thought of as a cue concerning appropriate behavior. As such, the high self-monitor should be more attentive to and affected by it, and thus more likely to respond with appropriate content. This speculation is consistent with the finding that high self-monitors perceive themselves as more influenced by their interaction partners (Ickes & Barnes, 1977).

The research now underway to assess the effects of self-consciousness on interaction will also examine those of self-monitoring. However, an interesting test of the relationship between self-monitoring and responsiveness was performed by Davis and Kasmer (Note 14), deriving from a modification of the original Davis and Perkowitz (1979) procedure. In the Davis and Perkowitz (1979) research, subjects were required to take turns choosing and answering one of three questions about themselves on each of twelve trials. For half of the subjects, the confederate answered first. In this condition, subjects had indicated question choice before the interaction began, and were instructed not to change it. In pilot testing, however, many subjects changed their choice of question to correspond to that of their partner, complaining that they were uncomfortable with answering different questions. Apparently, such subjects were sensitive to the implicit demand for relevant content inherent in their partners' statements. Davis and Kasmer (Note 14) repeated the Davis and Perkowitz (1979) procedure, allowing subjects to freely choose which question to answer as the interaction proceded. To the extent that high self-monitors are indeed more sensitive to the implicit demand for relevant responses to the confederate's answers, they would be expected to choose to answer the same question as the confederate more often than low self-monitors. The results confirmed this prediction.

Psychological Differentiation

Psychological differentiation refers to the degree of segregation between the self and nonself (see reviews by Karp, 1977; Witkin & Goodenough, 1977). Differences in the degree of self-nonself segregation are assumed to be associated with differences in the extent to which the self, versus the field outside, is used as a referent for behavior. The tendencies to rely on the self versus the field as referents for behavior are labeled, respectively, the field-independent and field-dependent cognitive styles.

Witkin and Goodenough (1977) have pointed out that since field-independent persons will experience their own selves as separate and distinct from others and tend to rely on themselves as primary referents for behavior, they will tend to adopt a relatively unsociable orientation. In contrast, field-dependent persons, who experience themselves as less separate from others, and who rely on others as primary referents for behavior, should exhibit a strong social orientation. The authors reviewed substantial evidence that field dependent persons exhibit greater attention to others, greater involvement with others, and more competence in social relations (see also Karp, 1977).

Several lines of evidence suggest that field dependent persons are more attentive to social information than those who are field independent. For example, field dependents show superior recall for names, faces, social words, and social aspects of a preceding experimental session (defined as reflecting attention to another person) in incidental learning situations. However, they exhibit no superior incidental recall of neutral words or task-oriented aspects of experimental sessions, nor do they achieve superior deliberate learning of names or faces (see reviews by Goldstein &

Blackman, 1978; Goodenough, 1976; Karp, 1977; Witkin, Goodenough, & Oltman, 1979; Witkin & Goodenough, 1977). The latter results suggest that the superiority of field dependents with respect to incidental learning of social material is the result of their greater attention to it, rather than their superior learning ability. Further evidence of the field dependent's tendency to focus attention on social stimuli has derived from studies of problem solving. Field dependents have been shown to maintain greater eye contact with others in situations where the other may provide useful cues for performance and to be more responsive to social cues from the experimenter (see Karp, 1977; Witkin & Goodenough, 1977).

There is also substantial evidence that field-dependent persons are more interpersonally oriented than those who are field independent. Field dependents describe themselves and are described by others as sociable, affiliation oriented, interested in people, concerned about others, helpful, having many friends, etc., whereas field independents are described as cold, distant, preferring intellectual pursuits, task-oriented, preferring solitude, etc. (see Witkin & Goodenough, 1977). The greater interpersonal involvement of field dependents is further evidenced by their preference for closer interpersonal distances and other affiliative nonverbal behaviors, their greater degree of self-disclosure to others, greater emotional involvement in films and slides depicting interaction, and finally, their greater preference for interpersonal (as opposed to impersonal) settings (see Goldstein & Blackman, 1978; Karp, 1977; Witkin & Goodenough, 1977). The field dependents' tendency to attend to others and become involved with them is further reflected in their superior social skills. Field dependents are described as friendly, warm, considerate, affectionate, polite, accepting, liking others and being liked, etc., whereas field independents are described as inconsiderate, rude, demanding, ambitious, opportunistic, manipulative, etc. (see Witkin & Goodenough, 1977).

Field dependence and responsiveness. It should not be surprising to find that field independents and dependents are also distinguished by their tendency to be responsive. The well-documented tendency of field dependents to be attentive to and interested in others may well be reflected in greater communication accuracy, greater motivation to affiliate and prolong interaction, and thus, greater responsiveness.

Introversion/Extraversion

Introverts and extraverts are distinguished in part by their tendency to be sociable. The typical extravert is "sociable, likes parties, has many friends, needs to have people to talk to, and does not like reading or studying by himself." The typical introvert, on the other hand, is "fond of books rather than people . . . reserved and distant except to intimate friends" (Eysenck & Eysenck, 1964, p. 8). Eysenck (1971) reviewed a number of studies showing that extraverts possess superior social skills, including the abilities to relate to others, to take a personal interest in them, and to anticipate their reactions. Further, extraverts tend to gravitate toward and excel in jobs that involve dealing with other people, and to show more pronounced needs to affiliate in other social situations (see also Wilson, 1977). This evidence suggests that extraverts will generally be more attentive to others. In support of this reasoning, several studies have obtained a positive relationship between eye contact and extraversion (e.g., Kendon & Cook, 1969; Mobbs, 1968; Rutter, Morley, & Graham, 1972).

Extraversion and responsiveness. The evidence cited above clearly suggests that extraverts will be more interested in others, more attentive to them, and thus presumably more responsive. Although there is no direct evidence of the relationship between extraversion and responsiveness, extraverts have been shown to talk more to strangers, exhibit shorter latencies between the other's utterances and their own, and have fewer pauses in their speech (Siegman & Pope, 1965). This is consistent with the notion that extraverts may show superior probability of response. However, previous research (Siegman, 1962) has shown that Eysenck's extraversion scale consists of both a sociability and an impulsivity factor, the latter reflecting a preference for quick action versus deliberation. To the extent that extraverts are more impulsive and less reflective (as reflected in shorter latencies), response relevance and appropriateness of elaboration may be reduced. Finally, it is important to note that although the evidence indicates that extraverts will be more interested in and attentive to the *average* person than introverts, introverts will not necessarily be less responsive to their preferred friends. When the introvert does decide to affiliate he or she may even devote more attention to that single person than would an extravert.

Selective Attention

The preceding discussion has dealt with individual differences that are associated primarily with the absolute amount of attention devoted to others. Many individual differences will be associated, in addition (or instead), with selective attention to particular content. Because much of the research dealing with selective attention is tied to issues of communication accuracy, discussion of relevant individual differences and selective attention processes will be incorporated into the section on communication accuracy.

Summary and Conclusions

The preceding sections have provided many illustrations of the way in which situational and dispositional variables may relate to attentional processes in social interaction, and of the impact that such attentional effects will have on the process of interaction. These illustrations were not intended to be exhaustive. Clearly, many other situational factors and individual differences (e.g., need for approval, need for affiliation, fear of rejection, locus of control, dominance, nurturance) will affect the amount of attention devoted to others and/or the range and nature of cues attended to. Rather, the illustrations were intended to point out that meaningful theoretical relationships between situational variables, personality, and the *process* of interaction can be examined; and hopefully to encourage research on such issues. Subsequent sections are intended to serve the same purposes.

Communication Accuracy

Communicative behaviors are accurately understood to the extent that the content encoded (expressed) by the communicator corresponds to that decoded (understood) by the receiver (e.g., Mehrabian & Reed, 1968). Encoded content may refer both to information that is deliberately conveyed (either verbally or nonverbally) and to that which is conveyed either despite intentions to the contrary or without awareness (e.g., nonverbal expression of emotion). Further, in the present context it may refer to linguistic, paralinguistic, and nonverbal cues that signal when response is demanded, and with what degree of elaboration, etc. Communication accuracy, then, will depend upon (1) characteristics of the situation, or of communication content, that affect the ease with which information is encoded and decoded, (2) individual characteristics that are associated with either skill at expressing (encoding) material in easily understandable terms, or skill in interpreting (decoding) this material, and (3) characteristics of the dyad that affect the correspondence between the encoding rules of the communicator and the decoding rules of the receiver. The impact of the latter factors should be stronger the more complex or ambiguous the content of communication (Bruner, 1967; J. Miller, 1951).

The following sections will illustrate the way in which situational, individual, and dyadic factors can affect communication accuracy. As noted earlier, responsiveness will be positively related to accuracy. The ability to recognize when response is demanded, and to formulate a response that directly addresses a preceding communication and is of appropriate elaboration, will be impaired if the communication is not accurately understood.

Characteristics of the Situation

Attention and distraction. The previous section detailed the way in which situational factors may affect attention to one's partner, and thus the accuracy with which his/her communications are *decoded.* Attention may also affect *encoding.* First, when one is distracted or preoccupied, encoding may become less precise or more haphazard. Such reduction in precision may follow from either less effort or motivation, reduced ability to access one's repertoire of relevant knowledge, or lessened sensitivity to information from or about one's partner that would allow one to take his/her frame of reference into account. Second, in most conversations failure of the listener to understand one's communications is conveyed by facial expressions, comments, requests for clarification, etc. To the extent that attention is diverted from the listener, sensitivity to such feedback will be reduced, causing the normal processes of adjustment in encoding to become impaired, and thus communication accuracy decreased.

Situational effects on expectations. The context in which interaction occurs, the ostensible purpose of the interaction, or the role relationships inherent in the interaction setting will often affect expectations concerning the content of others' behaviors, and thus interpretation of them. The relatively new field of sociolinguistics has begun to examine the way in which one's subjective definition of a situation (and attendant expectations) provide the context for the interpretation of others' behaviors (e.g., Ervin-Tripp, 1969; Hymes, 1972, 1974; Pearce, 1976; Rommetveit, 1974). Research in the area of social cognition has also addressed this issue. That is, "schemas" for events, roles, persons, etc., have been shown to guide both the search for information, and the processing and interpretation of incoming information (see reviews by Taylor & Crocker, 1981; Wyer & Srull, 1980). To the extent that schemas relevant to the situation are operative, they should selectively direct attention to the schema-relevant aspects of the other's communications, and provide the referent with respect to which they are processed.

The effects of context on interpretation of others' behaviors and communications may be manifested at least two ways. First, interpretation of others' behaviors and communications will generally be distorted in the direction of consistency with expectations. To the extent that expectations in fact coincide with the intended message, accuracy will be facilitated. If they do not, misunderstanding may result. For example, when interacting in a situation defined as task oriented, one's partner may be expected to engage primarily in task-oriented behaviors. As a result, if behaviors or comments with sexual innuendo occur they may be misperceived as task oriented. Touching, for example, may be perceived as encouragement or show of solidarity, or the statement "You're beautiful!" as a compliment on performance. Such misperceptions will result in unresponsiveness to the extent that the response addresses the (mis)perceived content, rather than the intended content, of the other's communication. Second, since one's expectations or operative schemas will provide the organizational structure with respect to which the other's communications are understood, if his/her communications cannot be related to operative expectations or schemas, they may be difficult to understand, or even uninterpretable. This kind of process has been clearly demonstrated with studies of prose comprehension. For example, Bransford and his colleagues have demonstrated that comprehension for paragraphs given a relevant context (or title) is greater than comprehension of paragraphs with no context. However, paragraphs with irrelevant contexts are understood more poorly than those with none (Bransford, 1979; Bransford & Johnson, 1973).

Channel availability and feedback. Situations differ with respect to the number of communication channels (e.g., verbal, facial, postural) that are available to the interaction partners. For example, telephone conversations provide only the verbal channels, including content and paralinguistic features such as tone, and speech disturbance. Similar constraints apply to many task-oriented settings where one must attend to tasks that prevent face-to-face orientation. In contrast, for full face-to-face interactions, a multitude of cues, such as content, tone, paralinguistic features, facial expression, gesture, and posture, are available to the participants. Verbal content is often more easily interpretable with the aid of such nonverbal cues. Indeed, a number of studies have demonstrated that communication accuracy increases with the number of available channels (e.g., Mehrabian & Ferris, 1967; Mehrabian & Weiner, 1967; Miller, Heise, & Lichten, 1951; Neely, 1956; Rosenthal, Hall,

Archer, DiMatteo, & Rogers, 1979; Sumby & Pollack, 1954), except when messages are contradictory across channels.

Accuracy is also affected by the degree to which feedback from the recipient to the communicator is possible. Feedback will permit the communicator to learn that the recipient has inaccurately decoded the message, and thus modify it. It has been shown in several studies that accuracy is affected by (1) whether feedback is available at all, (2) the amount of feedback available within a given channel (e.g., yes-no vs. commentary), and (3) the number of channels through which feedback is available (e.g., Faules, 1967; Feffer & Suchotliff, 1966; Leavitt & Mueller, 1951). It is interesting to note that responsiveness from a recipient, to the extent that it involves feedback to the communicator, should itself affect accuracy. In effect, then, responsiveness will facilitate responsiveness.

Communication Content

Mehrabian and Reed (1968) have identified a number of characteristics of communication content that affect accuracy. Accuracy has been shown to *decrease* with the ambiguity (Macy, Christie, & Luce, 1953), abstractness, and complexity of the referents (Eifermann, 1961; G. Miller, 1951; Miller et al., 1951); and to *increase* with the objectivity (Mehrabian, 1968b; Mehrabian & Reed, 1968) and organization (Abrams, 1966) of the messages, and consistency of message content between channels (Mehrabian & Ferris, 1967; Mehrabian & Weiner, 1967). Objectivity refers to the extent to which decoding is dependent upon knowledge of the context in which the communication occurs. The more necessary contextual information, the less objective the communication. Organization refers to the extent to which the communication directs the attention of the recipient to the purpose of the communication and the interrelationship between its parts, and to the predictability of the sequence of ideas.

Individual Characteristics

Encoding and decoding skills. A skillful communicator must be able to encode his/her communications articulately and in a way that reflects the abilities and perspective of the recipient. Similarly, a skillful recipient will decode messages knowledgeably and with awareness of the skills and perspective of the communicator. Skill in both encoding and decoding should thus be positively related to such characteristics as intelligence, knowledgeability, articulateness, cognitive complexity, cognitive development, and role-taking skills. Also, since communication accuracy will depend upon both verbal and nonverbal channels, characteristics that are associated with skill in employing or interpreting nonverbal cues should be positively related to accuracy. With few exceptions, the vast majority of work relating individual difference variables to encoding and decoding skills has focused upon emotional or nonverbal content rather than literal verbal content. The discussion below will also reflect this emphasis. In addition, it should be noted that this review is restricted to communications that are not deceptive or inconsistent. The definition of "accuracy" in such cases is not clear.

Psychopathology. It has been suggested repeatedly that one's degree of psychopathology will be negatively related to *encoding* skills (see reviews by Danziger, 1976; Mehrabian, 1968a; Murray, 1944). Indeed, the bizarre and inconsistent communications of schizophrenics are typical entertainment for introductory and abnormal psychology classes. However, psychiatric patients have also been shown to possess lesser *decoding* skills. Schizophrenics, for example, suffer from attentional problems that impair processing (see review by Maher, 1966), and are particularly impaired when required to process information from several channels simultaneously (e.g., McGhie, 1973; Meiselman, 1973; Rosenthal et al., 1979; Turner & Le, 1964). Rosenthal et al. (1979) have also shown that general psychiatric patients and alcoholics show inferior decoding skills, and are less able to profit from the availability of additional communication channels.

Self-monitoring. High self-monitoring individuals have been shown to be superior to low self-monitors with respect to both encoding and decoding. For example, high self-monitors are (1) better able to express and communicate a wide variety of emotions (Snyder, 1974), (2) more successful deceivers (Krauss, Geller, & Olson, Note 15), (3) better able to adopt the mannerisms of polar opposite personalities (i.e., reserved, withdrawn, introverted vs. friendly, outgoing, extraverted; Lippa, 1976), and (4) better able to control expressive behavior to facilitate expression of socially desirable dispositions while suppressing undesirable ones (Lippa, 1976, 1978). With respect to decoding skills, high self-monitors more skillfully infer the affective and emotional states of others (Krauss et al., Note 15), and are more likely to employ contextual information in order to predict (Kulik & Taylor, 1981) and explain (Geizer, Rarick, & Soldow, 1977; Jones & Baumeister, 1976; Krauss et al., Note 15) their behavior.

Self-consciousness. The effects of self-consciousness on attention, and thus decoding, were noted earlier. However, there is also some evidence suggesting that self-consciousness may affect encoding. Diener et al. (1980) had subjects enact four embarrassing tasks: acting like a chimp, fingerpainting with one's nose, making gross sounds, and sucking on a baby bottle. Behavioral "intensity," or expressiveness, was negatively related to subjects reported level of self-consciousness. To the extent that accurate encoding involves expressive competencies, self-consciousness may be detrimental.

Sex differences. A vast body of evidence has accumulated indicating that females are superior to males with respect to both encoding and decoding of nonverbal content. The superiority of females involves all nonverbal channels (e.g., face, body, voice tone, and other paralinguistics) as well as various combinations of channels (see reviews by Hall, 1978, 1979; Rosenthal & DePaulo, 1979b; Rosenthal et al., 1979), for nondeceptive communications.

Extraversion and related dimensions. A number of studies have demonstrated that extraverts exhibit superior *encoding* skills (Buck, 1975, 1977; Buck, Miller, & Caul, 1974; DePaulo & Rosenthal, 1979; Friedman, DiMatteo, & Taranta, in press;

Friedman, Riggio, & Segall, 1980). Further, a number of personality dimensions that are related to extraversion have been associated with superior encoding skills. For example, two recent studies examined five dimensions from the Jackson Personality Research Form (Jackson, 1974). Subjects who were *dominant* (influential, persuasive, forceful), *impulsive* (uninhibited, spontaneous, irrepressible), *playful* (jovial, prankish, fun-loving), *exhibitionistic* (desire to be dramatic and the center of attention), and *low in harm avoidance* (adventurous, careless, risk-taking) exhibited superior encoding skills (Friedman et al., 1980; Friedman, DiMetteo, & Taranta, in press). Further, persons with high activity levels, and high self-esteem (Buck et al., 1974), who are socially anxious (Lykken, 1957), socially adroit (Jackson, 1976) and believe that human nature is complex (DePaulo & Rosenthal, 1979), and who are high in field dependence (Harper, Wiens, & Matarazzo, 1980), and come from small towns (DePaulo & Rosenthal, 1979) are superior encoders. Finally, *self-descriptions* are related to both encoding and decoding skills. People who describe themselves as outgoing, gregarious, and physically attractive are especially skilled at both encoding and decoding, whereas those who see themselves as persuasive and influential are especially skilled encoders, but not decoders (DePaulo & Rosenthal, 1979). Further, *males* who describe themselves as self-confident, dominant, adventurous, and strongly heterosexually oriented are skilled encoders (Harper et al., 1980).

Training. It should also be noted that encoding and decoding skills may be acquired, often by specific training or occupational experience. Teachers, for example, and other public speakers or performers are trained to encode in ways that will facilitate understanding, as well as interest and attention. Others, such as psychotherapists, are trained to develop superior decoding skills.

Selective Perception and Distortion

Just as individual differences are related to various encoding and decoding skills, they are also known to be related to particular distortions in decoding. As Kihlstrom (1981) has pointed out "It should be clear that features of personality, including personal constructs, intentions, goals, motives, and emotions, can influence the interpretations given to perceptual events; and that these aspects of the individual's state are themselves features of the experiential context in which the events took place" (p. 127). He further notes that aspects of personality thus color the meaning given to an event, and to the context in which it takes place, and affect which features are available for encoding at the time of perception. Illustrations of the way in which individual differences are associated with such distortions follow below.

Self-relevance and self-schemata. Research concerning the role of the "self" in information processing has demonstrated that the self is heavily involved in the processing of information about both oneself and others (see Markus & Sentis, 1980; Markus & Smith, 1981; T. Rogers, 1981). Many have argued that the self provides the reference point, or context, with respect to which all stimuli are processed, understood, and judged. As a "cognitive prototype" (T. Rogers, 1981), or a "system of self-schemas" (Markus & Sentis, 1980), the self is assumed to operate in much the same way as other schemata. That is, it is assumed to (1) determine, and selectively direct attention to, self-relevant aspects of the environment, and (2) provide a relatively well-organized and elaborate structure (with many pertinent exemplars of behaviors, traits, physical characteristics, etc.) that provides the referent with respect to which stimuli are processed.

Since the self-structure is assumed to be more elaborate, more organized, more frequently activated, and more easily accessible than any other cognitive system, processing of self-relevant information should be more rapid and efficient. In addition, since the self-structure is assumed to selectively direct attention to self-relevant aspects of the environment, such stimuli should be noticed more and processed more deeply. Finally, since self-relevant stimuli should be noticed more and processed more deeply, discriminanda relevant to self-schemata should exert greater influence on judgments of incoming stimuli than those that are irrelevant. These processes have been well documented empirically (see reviews by Greenwald, 1981; Markus & Sentis, 1980; Markus & Smith, 1981; T. Rogers, 1981).

Several experiments varied the involvement of the self directly, by varying subjects' encoding strategies. Rogers and his colleagues (see T. Rogers, 1981) accomplished this by asking subjects to rate stimuli for degree of self-descriptiveness, versus either the degree to which they described others or their location on some other judgment dimension. Markus and her colleagues asked subjects to judge stimuli on dimensions for which they either possessed or did not possess a strong self-schema. In both lines of research, involvement of the self was associated with more rapid decision times, and greater incidental recall of task stimuli.

Other experiments have illustrated the involvement of the self by examining differences in processing of self-relevant or self-descriptive versus non–self-relevant or non–self-descriptive stimuli. This research has indicated that stimuli that are *relevant* to self-schemata (whether highly descriptive or highly nondescriptive), and those that are highly *self-descriptive,* are judged more quickly and remembered better (Markus & Sentis, 1980; T. Rogers, 1981).

The increased efficiency associated with the involvement of the self was further illustrated by Markus, Smith, and Moreland (described in Markus & Smith, 1981). Subjects were asked to perform a unitizing task (Newtson, 1973) while viewing a film that was either stereotypically masculine or gender irrelevant. Subjects who were schematic with respect to masculinity chunked the masculine film into larger segments than those who were aschematic, whereas no differences occurred for the control film. Larger chunks presumably reflect greater processing efficiency. Thus, the results provide support for the notion that self-schemas increase the efficiency with which relevant information is processed, and also point out that self-schemas can affect the processing of information about others.

The latter process has been illustrated in a series of studies by Markus and colleagues (see review by Markus & Sentis, 1980; Markus & Smith, 1981). For example, in one study independent schematics and aschematics were asked to read different versions of a story in which the central character engaged in varying amounts of independent behavior. Ratings of the central character indicated that independent schematics were more sensitive to variations in independence than were aschematics, giving more extreme evaluations of the target's independent and dependent behaviors. A conceptually similar result was obtained with judgments of foods. Subjects who were schematic with respect to body weight showed superior discrimination between "fat" and "thin" foods than did aschematics. Finally, schematics have been shown to discriminate more accurately between types of impressions others are trying to convey. Subjects who were either schematic or aschematic with respect to dominance were asked to examine a short segment of an interview in order to determine whether the interviewee was attempting to come across as either dominant and independent, or submissive and dependent. Interview segments were either videotaped with the interviewee and interviewer face-to-face, or audiotaped, where the interviewer and interviewee had been in separate rooms. Schematics showed marked superiority in the ability to discriminate between the two impression management strategies, but only in the audio condition. Presumably, the audio condition represented a much more difficult discrimination because of the reduction in available cues.

The research described above suggests that involvement of the self will often facilitate communication accuracy for content that is self-relevant. One will be more likely to notice self-relevant content and to process it deeply. In addition, content relevant to self-schemata will be processed with greater discrimination and thus greater accuracy. However, the same research suggests that the involvement of the self will produce predictable inaccuracies.

As C. Rogers (1951) noted long ago, experiences are either "(a) symbolized, perceived, and organized into some relationship to the self, (b) ignored because there is not a perceived relationship to the self-structure, or (c) denied symbolization or given a distorted symbolization because the experience is inconsistent with the structure of the self" (p. 503). The first and third alternatives have been well documented, the first by the research cited above (and much more), and the third by literature on such processes as repression, denial, and self-serving biases in attribution. The second alternative suggests avenues for future research. That is, aspects of others' communications that are not self-relevant or not understandable in terms of self-schemata may well be unnoticed, misunderstood, and not incorporated into the information that determines the interpretation given the other's communications. Understanding will thus not fully reflect or incorporate non-self-relevant information. Responsiveness would then be reduced by failure to notice or understand content that is irrelevant to the self. This process may be common in many relationships where one or both partners experience needs that are neither recognized, understood, nor responded to by the other. The unresponsive partner may simply be unable to recognize or understand communications that reflect such needs because they are foreign to his/her own self-structure.

Attitudes, beliefs, and expectations. Attitude theorists have devoted considerable attention to the propositions that people selectively attend to information that is consistent with their attitudes, and that attitude-consistent information is thus learned easier than inconsistent material. Although literature on this issue was complicated for many years by inconsistent results, recent research has indicated that selective attention and selective learning will occur in tasks that involve *incidental* learning, but not those that involve *intentional* learning (see Malpass, 1969; Zanna & Olson, in press). Further, selective learning of attitude-consistent content is more pronounced for dogmatics (Rokeach, 1960), repressors (Bell & Byrne, 1977; Byrne, 1964), internals (Rotter, 1966), and persons with high self-esteem (see Kleck & Wheaton, 1967; Zanna & Olson, in press).

Much of the research on selective learning has employed persuasive communications. Thus, selective attention in such contexts is directly relevant to current concerns. The correspondence is enhanced by the occurrence of selective attention and selective learning in incidental, but not intentional, learning tasks. Attentional processes involved in the incidental tasks are doubtless more similar to those involved in conversations. Effects of selective attention to attitude consistent material will be similar to those noted earlier. That is, to the extent that attitude-inconsistent information is not reflected in the interpretation of others' communications, accuracy will be reduced. The failure to incorporate such information and the attendant reductions in accuracy should be most prevalent for the personality types noted above.

Theorists have also devoted considerable attention to the proposition that beliefs about others are routinely used to *interpret* their behaviors and communications. These beliefs may be based on stereotypes about how certain *categories* of people think and behave, or on beliefs about *particular* people that are based on previously acquired information about or experience with them. Several areas of research have illustrated the way in which beliefs about others can direct interpretation of their behaviors and communications. For example, research in the area of attitude measurement has often assessed prejudice or other attitudes toward target groups, indirectly, by examining differences in interpretation of behaviors attributed to target versus neutral group members (see review by Kidder & Campbell, 1970). Similarly, impression formation research has illustrated how beliefs about particular individuals can affect interpretation of their communications. Consider, for example, Asch's (1952) demonstration of how the statement "I hold it that a little rebellion, now and then, is a good thing, and as necessary in the political world as storms are in the physical," is interpreted differently when attributed to Thomas Jefferson than when attributed to Lenin.

More recently, research in the area of social cognition has shown that schemas for particular persons, traits, occupations, roles, etc., direct processing of information about others, such that interpretation of their behaviors, or of information about them, is distorted in the direction of consistency with expectations derived from operative schemata (see reviews by Taylor & Crocker, 1981; Wyer, 1980; Wyer & Srull, 1980). Finally, similar processes have been explored in literature on symbolic interactionism (Mead, 1934), role theory (e.g., Cottrell, 1966), personal constructs (G. Kelley, 1969), and by several areas of research concerning the tendency of expectations to be self-fulfilling, e.g., clinical diagnosis and personality assessment, teacher expectations, experimenter bias, and labeling theories of deviance (see reviews by Jones, 1977; Darley & Fazio, 1980).

Much of the time, such stereotypes, beliefs, or schemas will facilitate accurate communication. They both help us to formulate communications in a way that will be easily understandable for others, and make it easy to understand their communications. However, to the extent that these stereotypes and beliefs are inaccurate, or to the extent that the intended message is inconsistent with expectations (however accurate) that are derived from them, they will promote misunderstanding. That is, the intended message will be distorted to appear consistent with expectations. This problem often occurs in cross-racial or cross-generation communications. The other's membership in a category that is associated with strong beliefs or expectations often interferes with the ability to interpret their behavior in a more objective, individualistic, and often more realistic fashion. The stronger and more rigid one's beliefs (Fearing, 1967) and the more inaccurate they are, the more strongly they should interfere with understanding.

The degree of attraction toward a communicator, presumably associated with expectations concerning similarity to oneself, has also been shown to be related to distortion. Kelman and Eagly (1965), for example, showed that (1) the communications of liked communicators are misperceived as more similar to one's own than they are, while the opposite is true for disliked communicators, and (2) the magnitude of distortion is positively related to extremity of attitudes toward the communicator. In a more general illustration of the distorting effects of attraction, Regan, Strauss, and Fazio (1974) demonstrated that attraction affects interpretation of behavior, such that actions that are consistent with one's attitude toward the other are attributed internally, while actions inconsistent with one's attitude are attributed externally. Similar distorting effects have been observed that serve to maintain expectations regarding physically attractive versus unattractive others (Dion, 1972; Dion, Berscheid, & Walster, 1972), racial stereotypes (Duncan, 1976), sex role stereotypes (Deaux, 1976), and prior trait attributions (Bell, Wicklund, Manko, & Larkin, 1976; Hayden & Mischel, 1976). Beliefs about oneself can also affect attributions concerning others' behavior. Stroebe, Eagly, and Stroebe (1977), for example, demonstrated that low self-esteem subjects interpreted positive evaluations from others as role play and negative ones as sincere, whereas high self-esteem subjects responded oppositely.

These effects, along with the perseverance effects noted by Ross and his colleagues (Ross, Lepper, & Hubbard, 1975; Ross, Lepper, & Steinmetz, 1977), suggest the existence of an "impression maintenance attributional bias" (Darley & Fazio, 1980) whereby the perceiver attributes expectation-consistent behavior to the dispositional characteristics of the target, and expectation-inconsistent behavior to situational factors. Such a bias would be reflected, as described above, in distortions in interpretation of others' communications toward consistency with expectations.

Authoritarianism and dogmatism. It has been suggested that both authoritarianism and dogmatism are associated with rigidity, intolerance for ambiguity, stereotyped thinking, prejudice, and avoidance of belief discrepant information (see reviews by Cherry & Byrne, 1977; Goldstein & Blackman, 1978; Kirscht & Dillehay, 1967; Vacchiano, 1977). Rigidity refers to perseveration of established behavior patterns in situations where a change in behavior would result in more efficient functioning. Intolerance for ambiguity refers to unwarranted imposition of structure when the situation is unstructured. Finally, stereotyped thinking refers in part to the inability to divorce evaluation or interpretation of behaviors or communications from attitudes or beliefs concerning their source.

There is reason to expect that each of the five characteristics associated with authoritarianism and dogmatism would decrease communication accuracy. For example, among the behaviors associated with rigidity is prolonged clinging to first impressions, even when faulty, or the relative inability to recognize change or error (see Goldstein & Blackman, 1978). Such rigid adherence to first impressions of others or their communications may prevent accurate interpretation of behaviors or communications that are inconsistent with them.

Intolerance for ambiguity can affect accuracy in at least two ways. First, the intolerance is often manifested in premature or hasty adoption of one among several possible interpretations of material. Such failure to fully consider alternative interpretations of ambiguous communications from others will often result in an erroneous choice. Second, intolerance for ambiguity has been shown to result in unwillingness to suspend judgment or to admit to indecisiveness, e.g., to say "I don't know" (see Goldstein & Blackman, 1978). In the context of social interaction, this reluctance may be manifested in failure to request clarification of ambiguous content, and thus in decreased accuracy.

The previous section described the way in which beliefs about others can influence interpretation of their communications, and thus communication accuracy. Subjects high in authoritarianism or dogmatism have been shown to hold more stereotyped conceptions of a wide variety of categories of people, to be more prejudiced, and finally, to be unable to divorce interpretation of others' behaviors from beliefs about, or attitudes toward, them (see Cherry & Byrne, 1977; Goldstein & Blackman, 1978; Vacchiano, 1977). Thus, to the extent that operative stereotypes are inaccurate, or to the extent that the behavior is inconsistent with them, accuracy of interpretation will be low. Also, the dislike and hostility associated with prejudice may lead to inappropriately negative interpretation of others' behaviors and communications, or to projection of one's own hostility to them.

Finally, as noted earlier, avoidance of belief inconsistent information may result in failure to notice communications that are inconsistent, failure to incorporate them into the total information that determines interpretation of anothers' communications, or distortion of inconsistent communications toward greater consistency. Each alternative would result in decreased accuracy.

It should be noted that while there is substantial evidence that high authoritarians and dogmatics are characterized as described above, their tendency to manifest these characteristics is strongly affected by the nature of the situation (see Cherry & Byrne, 1977; Goldstein & Blackman, 1978). It may be that communication accuracy, and thus responsiveness, will be affected only for specific content areas or categories of persons, or in particular situations that are most directly related to the dynamics of the two personality syndromes.

Emotion and repression. Transient emotional states will often guide processing of others' communicative behaviors (e.g., Bower, 1981; Pfeiffer, 1973). As Bower (1981) has noted,

> Just as the depressed person will interpret a social remark as denigrating or pitying, so the angry person will interpret it as a hostile insult and the socially anxious person will interpret it as a putdown or a rebuff. Social interactions are ambiguous, and we have to read the intentions hidden behind people's words and actions. In that reading the emotional premise from which we begin strongly influences what we perceive as others' intentions. ... The current mood activates and primes mood-congruent categories into readiness, and these are used in expectation-driven or top-down processing to classify and assimilate indeterminate experiences. (p. 140)

Consistent with this line of argument, subjects have been shown to attend more to mood consistent information, and to interpret ambiguous stimuli, as well as their own and others' behavior, in a manner consistent with their own moods (see review, Bower, 1981).

The role of emotion in interpretation of others' communicative behaviors does not end with that of transient emotional states. Pfeiffer (1973), for example, has pointed to the effects of *emotional blocks.* Certain content may produce emotional arousal that will interfere with the ability to listen to the full message, or prevent the person from ever perceiving or recognizing the nature of the content. The concept of emotional blocks is similar to psychological notions of *repression.* Contemporary treatments of repression note that information processing is selective at all stages (e.g., Erdelyi & Goldberg, 1979), and that individuals are capable of defensively biasing information processing functions so that threatening material available in both the perceptual field and memory is not represented in phenomenal awareness (Kihlstrom, 1980). Most pertinent to current concerns are the defensive functions operative at the level of interpretation. As Mandler (1975) has noted, when information is processed it undergoes a meaning analysis in which its relation with concepts already present is established. This meaning analysis may operate to avoid concepts that are associated with conflict or anxiety.

Need and motivational states. One would expect to find that various need or motivational states will guide processing of other's communicative behaviors in much the same way as emotional states; and indeed, several illustrations of such processes are available, many deriving from literature on attribution. In agreement with the view that all perceptual acts are performed in the service of making the environment stable and predictable, attribution theorists have long assumed that the need to predict and control one's environment is largely responsible for both the pervasive tendency to engage in causal analysis, and many of the distortions in the attribution process (e.g., Berscheid & Graziano, 1979; Berscheid et al., 1976; Heider, 1958; H. Kelley, 1972a, 1972b). For example, H. Kelley (1972a) argued that many of the "irrational" attribution processes, such as the tendencies to underweight situational determinants of behavior, to attribute greater dispositional influence to actions undertaken for gain than for avoidance of loss, and to engage in self-serving attributions, serve to increase the perception of control.

More recently, researchers have begun to examine the control hypothesis by direct manipulation or measurement of the need for effective control. For example, Swann, Stephenson and Pittman (1981) have shown that persons more actively seek information about others with whom they expect to interact when their perceptions of control have been threatened by recent experience of uncontrollable outcomes. Others have examined distorting effects of need for control. Miller and Norman (1975), for example, have argued that interacting individuals select or distort the meaning of available behavioral information in order to increase their attributional confidence, and thus satisfy their need for effective control. In support of this reasoning, several studies indicated that both dispositional and situationally induced need for control led subjects to draw more extreme dispositional inferences concerning interaction partners (Miller & Norman, 1975; Miller, Norman, & Wright, 1978). Similar effects were obtained by Berscheid et al. (1976), who manipulated need for control by varying the degree to which the subject was outcome dependent upon the target (see also Knight & Vallacher, 1981). Presumably, dispositional inferences are associated with greater confidence in prediction of others, and thus ability to interact effectively. Finally, the motive to maximize need satisfaction is assumed to underlie the motive to exercise control of the environment. Thus, a number of studies have indicated that subjects arrive at dispositional attributions to others that will serve to foster positive self images (e.g., Beckman, 1973; Cialdini, Braver, & Lewis, 1974), or otherwise predict need fulfillment (Berscheid et al., 1976; Berscheid, Boyce, & Darley, 1968; Darley & Berscheid, 1967; Levine, Chein, & Murphy, 1942; Pepitone, 1950; Stephan, Berscheid, & Walster, 1971).

The above data suggest that persons may avoid interpretations of others' communications that would reduce perceptions of their ability to predict and control the interaction, threaten their self-image, or threaten their ability to satisfy other needs (e.g., for approval, affiliation, love).

Dyadic Characteristics

Similarity. "In order that any two beings should establish communication, they must already have something in common" (Hocking, 1967). At the most basic level, the commonality may simply involve primitive sounds, facial expressions, or gestures for which the participants share a common definition. Such commonalities provide the basis for communication between animals, between human and animal, and often between humans who do not share a common language. However, the similarities that have been diagnosed as necessary for truly effective human communication are legion, and include such things as common (1) subjective meaning of symbols, including words, gestures, etc., (2) subjective meaning of nonverbal and paralinguistic behaviors, such as facial expression, body orientation and posture, pitch, loudness, and rate of speech (Mehrabian & Reed, 1968), (3) interpretation of one another's behaviors, so that the proper meaning will be responded to (e.g., Triandis, 1975), and (4) definition of the context within which the communication occurs, since understanding of the context will affect interpretation of meaning (e.g., Pearce, 1976; Rommetveit, 1974). Mehrabian and Reed (1968) have argued that even common *weighting* of these various factors that influence interpretation, and Zajonc (1966) that congruence between the *intent* of the communicator and the *preparatory state* (e.g., expectations) of the receiver will facilitate accuracy.

It has also been suggested that similarity in the subjective *organization* of one's stimulus world, including the concepts that are employed for categorization. the hierarchical organization of such concepts, and the degree of differentiation between and within categories of referents, will facilitate accuracy (e.g., Coombs, 1950, 1953; Meerloo, 1967; Mehrabian & Reed, 1968; Runkel, 1956; Triandis, 1959, 1960a,b). For example, if one does not employ a particular concept for differentiation between referents, the communications of others that involve relevant distinctions may be misunderstood. Similarly, if one perceives two referents as identical, communications that assume or imply difference between them may be misunderstood.

Finally, proponents of the Whorfian hypothesis of linguistic relativity argue that languages shape ideas. Since the organization and experience of one's stimulus world will be strongly affected by language, Whorf (1956) assumed that use of another acquired language would reflect the organization dictated by one's native language. It follows, then, that persons who share a native language will communicate more effectively in any language than those who do not.

The myriad similarities that have been implicated in the process of communication have led many to despair of the possibility of truly accurate communication. In agreement with Meerloo's (1967) lament that "in the same words, the souls speak different tongues," it is widely assumed that the vast differences in learning histories between the most similar of persons will interfere with even the most basic commonalities (e.g., subjective meanings of words or gestures). Even if dictionary definitions are constant, the real meaning is assumed to vary for people with different learning histories, particularly when the referents are complex or abstract. However, although perfect accuracy may often be impossible, it is clear that the greater two persons' commonality with respect to the factors elaborated above, the greater will be their potential for accurate communication, and of course, for responsiveness.

Similarity of many personal characteristics will be positively related to the commonalities associated with accurate communication. For example, people of similar cultures are more likely to share common understanding of nonverbal signals or social behaviors. People of similar cognitive structure or complexity are more comparable with respect to organization of their stimulus worlds. Many kinds of similarities will be related to vocabulary held in common (e.g., profession, interests, educational level, race). Even similarity of past experiences should be important. The importance of learning histories has already been noted. However, similarity of past experiences may be especially important for communication of feelings or experiences that are particularly difficult to define. There are some things that one can describe only by saying "You know how it is when . . . ." In such cases, only a person who has "been there" will know.

Many studies have demonstrated the relationship between similarity and communication accuracy, e.g., culture (Kent, Davis, & Shapiro, 1978; Triandis, 1964, 1975), socioeconomic class (Harms, 1961), background (Vick & Wood, 1969), cognitive structure (Menges, 1969; Padgett & Wolosin, 1980; Runkel, 1956; Shibuya, 1962; Triandis, 1959; 1960a, 1960b; Wolosin, 1975), and race (Erickson, 1979; Smith, 1973). In addition, Davis (1981; Note 16) has shown that *perceived* similarity of interests and of basic values is positively related to *expected* communication accuracy.

While the above studies of accuracy deal with communication *content,* it is interesting to note that similarity may also affect understanding of the verbal and nonverbal cues that indicate when response is desired. For example, racial differences have been shown to be associated with dissimilarities in use of behaviors that serve to regulate the flow of conversation. LaFrance and Mayo (1976) illustrated this process with the use of gaze during conversation. White tend to gaze at interaction partners while listening and avert gaze while speaking, whereas blacks exhibit the reverse tendency. Thus, when whites encounter a pause accompanied by gaze from a partner they are cued to speak, whereas blacks are cued to continue listening. Conversely, whites signal desire to relinquish the floor by initiation of gaze, and blacks by gaze aversion. These differences create problems for the operation of the turn taking system, including frequent competition for the floor, as well as many awkward silences.

Erickson (1979) documented racial differences in the use of back-channel responses (such as "Mmhmm," "Yeah"). Blacks tend to *employ* back-channel responses less frequently, and to *cue* them in a much less subtle fashion than whites. Thus, blacks often miss the cues demanding back-channel responses when interacting with whites. The lack of response is then interpreted as lack of attention, interest, or understanding, and leads the white to think the black less optimally intelligent, and to modify his/her communications to be increasingly simple or redundant. Blacks, on the other hand, become insulted by the apparent condescension on the part of the whites. Thus, a host of ill effects, including decreased communication efficiency, as well as a variety of negative attributions and decreased attraction, result from misunderstanding of the cues demanding response.

Familiarity. Similarity in subjective meaning, etc., may come naturally, along with similar personal characteristics and learning histories. However, it may also be developed with practice; either the deliberate practice such as that associated with certain family therapy (e.g., Williams, 1969) or culture training (e.g., Triandis, 1975) techniques, or the natural feedback that occurs over time in repeated interactions with other individuals or categories of individuals. As one becomes more familiar with the idiosyncratic usages of words, gestures, nonverbal signals, etc., that are associated with individuals or categories of individuals, communication accuracy will increase. One can both formulate his/her own communications so that the other can better understand them, and in addition, more accurately interpret the other's communications. As Moscovici (1967) has pointed out, repeated interaction will often result in the formation of "private languages" that facilitate communication between the participants. Finally, decreases in level of self-consciousness across repeated interactions may be associated with increased attention to one's partner, and thus increased accuracy.

Empirical support for the relationship between familiarity and communication accuracy has been obtained by Palmore, Lennard, and Hendin (1959), who showed that communication accuracy between client and therapist increased over time;

Stoddart (Note 17), who showed that communication accuracy was greater between familiar than between unfamiliar peers; and Hornstein (1967), who showed that the accuracy with which college roommates could communicate emotions to one another via meaningless content increased over the first 3 months of the academic year. Increases in communication accuracy over repeated interactions should also be reflected in increased responsiveness.

Response Repertoire

The importance of an adequate response repertoire becomes most clearly evident when another's communication "demands" an elaborate response. It is easier, for example, to be responsive when listening to a friend try to "tell you" about foreign trade than when the same friend wants you to "discuss" foreign trade. In the former case, one can simply get away with "Mmhmm," "I see," "That's interesting," "I agree," etc. In the latter, however, one must comment knowledgeably on the other's thoughts, and in addition, contribute knowledgeable thoughts of one's own in order to be responsive. In order to do so, one must possess an adequate repertoire of knowledge concerning the topic of conversation, and in addition, be able to readily access that knowledge. Further, potential responses to another are often derived from an analysis or integration of his/her communications that is independent of one's own knowledge of the subject, e.g., when a problem is posed for which all relevant facts are presented, and one is asked "What do you think this means?", or "What should I do?", etc. Thus, responsiveness will often require appropriate analytical or integrative skills. Characteristics of the situation, of individuals, and of the dyad that affect these factors will be discussed below.

Characteristics of the Situation

Characteristics of the situation will often affect both the accessibility of one's response repertoire and the ability to exercise analytical or integrative skills. As noted earlier, research on memory and attention has shown that distraction reduces access to task-relevant memory areas. Thus, in general, the inability to access one's repertoire of knowledge, or to exercise analytical or integrative skills, should become more pronounced as the amount of distraction or other cognitive processing demands that are irrelevant to the interaction increase. We have all had the experience, for example, of being unable to remember something, or to think of a response to something someone has said, when in a stressful or distracting situation, only to have it immediately pop into our head the moment we have left the situation.

A second way in which the situation may affect the capacity for response elaboration is in its effect on the topics of conversation that tend to arise. If the topics are those for which one possesses a vast repertoire of knowledge, the capacity for response elaboration will be high; if not, response elaboration will suffer. These effects are clearly dependent upon both the person and the situation.

Individual Characteristics

Individual characteristics that are associated with general knowledgeability (e.g., educational level, variety of life experience), analytical skills (e.g., intelligence, cognitive complexity or development, content-related training), or ease of retrieval (e.g., low self-consciousness, because of its relationship to distraction), will be positively related to the capacity for response elaboration. The effects of many such characteristics, however, will be dependent on the topic of conversation. Particular areas of expertise or particular analytical skills will often be of use only when related topics of conversation arise.

It should be noted that *transient* states of the individual, such as arousal, stress, anxiety, inebriation, or various drug-induced states, may affect both processing of another's communications and access to one's own response repertoire. Such transient states will affect responsiveness, in part through their effects on memory. One may initially notice that the other has said something, and even process it accurately. However, it is often the case that by the time the opportunity to respond has arisen one has forgotten what the other said. Alternatively, one may remember what the other said, and formulate a suitable reply, only to forget one or both as one begins to speak.

Access to *particular areas* of memory will also be affected by transient states of the individual. For example, material congruent with one's mood is more readily recalled, as is material that has been more recently activated in memory. The latter two transient states are among a larger list of determinants of the "availability" of information in memory, including the frequency of activation and concreteness or vividness of the information, the degree to which it is connected to, and thus accessible through, other areas of memory, the extent to which the cognitive structures that guide the retrieval attempt match the attributes that were encoded as features of the information in memory, and the extent to which the person's state (mood, arousal, hypnosis, drug-induced, etc.) at the time of encoding matches that at the time of attempted retrieval (see Bower, 1981; Collins & Loftus, 1975; Kihlstrom, 1980; Tversky & Kahneman, 1973; Wyer & Carlston, 1979).

Access to particular areas of memory may also be affected by more stable individual characteristics. Work on repression (e.g., Erdelyi & Goldberg, 1979; Kihlstrom, 1980; Mandler, 1975) suggests that access to particular areas will be affected by the degree to which the content is threatening or unpleasant. Individuals may both *encode* threatening or unpleasant information in ways that render it minimally accessible, and *limit memory search* processes to avoid its retrieval. Thus, the availability of one's response repertoire (as well as the motivation to be responsive) may be reduced for such topic areas. Personality or other individual differences will be related to specific content areas that are perceived as threatening, and thus to the accessibility of information in those areas of memory. Such individual differences may also affect the availability of specific content areas through their influence on such variables as (1) the frequency with which relevant information or concepts are activated, (2) the vividness with which they are encoded, (3) concepts, strategies, etc., employed for encoding and retrieval, and (4) characteristic mood, arousal, and emotional states that would affect retrieval pathways, in other words, through their influence on any of the known determinants of availability.

Dyadic Characteristics

Dyadic characteristics will affect the capacity for response elaboration in at least two ways. First, in the course of repeated interactions with others, one develops an increasing repertoire of factual knowledge about them. This repertoire will be particularly useful for formulation of elaborate responses when the other is talking about him/herself. Thus, familiarity between interaction partners will facilitate response elaboration, particularly when the content is self-relevant. Second, dyadic factors will affect the degree to which the topics that one person initiates correspond to those for which the other possesses adequate knowledge and analytical skills. Role relationships (e.g., doctor-patient, teacher-student) often affect the topics that arise or the demands for response elaboration such that adequate repertoires will be available. In addition, similarity of many characteristics will facilitate this correspondence (e.g., profession, past experiences, current concerns, interests).

The effects of similarity on *expectations* concerning responsiveness were investigated by Davis (Note 16). Subjects rated hypothetical stimulus persons who were either similar or dissimilar with respect to four attitude categories: (1) interests, (2) values, (3) politics, and (4) matters of fact (e.g., "Is the pill or IUD more free of side effects?"). Subjects responded to questions designed to assess expectations concerning understanding (e.g., "Would this person be likely to understand what you say the way you mean it, or to misinterpret you?" "Is this person likely to use words the same way you do?"), response repertoire (e.g., "Is this a person with whom you could have many interesting conversations?" "Would you have much in common to talk about?" "If you initiated a conversation on a topic you were interested in, would this person be able to respond in a way that would invite further conversation on the subject?"), and response relevance (e.g., "If you initiated a conversation on something that interested you, would that person be more likely to change the subject, or to continue the discussion along the lines you began?"). Both similarity of interests and of values strongly affected expectations in all three categories, whereas similarity of political opinions and opinions about matters of fact had no significant effects. Presumably, the commonalities necessary for accurate communication, and the correspondence between the topics initiated by one person and the response repertoire of the other, are more strongly associated with similarity of interests and values.

Motivation

Motivation to *be* responsive will be affected by the degree to which one's interaction goals are facilitated versus impaired by responsiveness. Among the potential effects of responsiveness *to* another are (1) maintenance of interaction, (2) maintenance of focus on a particular topic, (3) allowing one's partners increased control over the interaction, (4) increased acquaintance and/or intimacy, (5) appearing to like or be interested in the other, and (6) increasing the other's attraction to oneself. To the extent that these effects are consistent with one's interaction goals, the motivation to be responsive will be high. On the other hand, if one desires to terminate interaction, change the subject, appear to dislike or be uninterested in the other, avoid intimacy, maintain greater control over the interaction, etc.; the motivation to be responsive will be low. Individual characteristics and characteristics of the situation or one's partner that will affect the motive to be responsive are discussed below.

Characteristics of the Situation

Characteristics of the situation may affect the desirability of each of the potential effects of responsiveness. For example, the situation may influence the degree to which maintenance of interaction is desirable in at least four ways. First, the motives or goals of the participants may vary such that continued interaction will either facilitate or impair them. When watching an exciting movie, for example, or trying to complete a task requiring concentration, one may not wish to prolong conversation. On the other hand, when trying to sell a car, or seduce a date, one will wish to prolong interaction, at least until one's goal is accomplished. Second, the situation may involve rules or expectations that dictate continuation or termination of interaction, e.g., don't talk in class, be polite to one's guests, etc. Third, physical characteristics of the setting or other features of the situation may affect the desire to remain, independent of the interaction. When standing shivering in the cold, the desire to remain, and thus to continue interaction, will surely be less than when reclining leisurely in front of a warm fire. Finally, other factors such as time constraints and other commitments may dictate how long one can remain in the situation, and thus in interaction.

The desire to maintain focus on a particular topic will be affected in much the same ways as described above. The motives, moods, and goals of the participants will affect the nature of the topics each desires to focus on. When in a good mood, for example, one may not wish to encourage conversation on morbid topics. Similarly, implicit or explicit rules or expectations will affect the nature of topics deemed appropriate. For instance, when at dinner with one's parents it may be undesirable to respond to a friend's comments on experience with psychedelic drugs in a way that would invite further conversation. In contrast, the motivation to be responsive would be higher when at a party among permissive friends. Finally, limitations on the amount of time available may narrow the range of permissible topics to those most relevant to the primary goals of the interaction.

The situation may also affect the degree to which one is willing to abdicate control of the interaction to one's partner. That is, the more important specific goals become, the more important it becomes to control the interaction in a way that will facilitate them, and thus the less willing one becomes to abdicate control. In such circumstances, responsiveness to one's partner would be reduced for goal irrelevant content.

Finally, the situation may affect the necessity or desirability of impression management or intimacy. In many circumstances, impression management is central to the accomplishment of one's goals, e.g., job interviews, first meetings with in-laws, or persuasion and sales. In others, even with the same person, it is less important. For example, the young man who has taken his girlfriend to the drive-in in hopes of stealing his first kiss may be especially attentive and responsive in order to enhance his chances of success. When driving her to an orchestra rehearsal, where the chances of a kiss are small, he may take less care to appear interested in her or to make her interested in him. Rosenfeld (1966) illustrated the importance of the motive to seek approval as a determinant of responsiveness by recording various verbal and nonverbal behaviors of subjects instructed to either seek or avoid approval from a naive interlocutor. Approval seekers used more back-channel responses than approval avoiders. Further, the use of such responses was correlated with approval actually received from naive partners.

Characteristics of Interaction Partners

The motivation to maintain interaction, to increase intimacy, to appear to like and be interested in the other, and to be liked by him/her should be highest either when interaction with the other is expected to be rewarding, or when the other's positive regard is expected to lead to other rewards. Rewards may involve simple pleasure with the other's company or with looking at him/her, interesting conversation, enjoyable joint activities, acquisition of information, facilitation of noninteraction goals (e.g., getting promoted), and much more. Thus, the motivation to be responsive should be relatively high with partners who are liked, physically attractive, interesting conversationalists, potential playmates, in possession of desired information or other resources, in control of one's outcomes, of high status, etc. It is interesting to note that people who are of extremely high status, popularity, attractiveness, etc., often respond to discussions concerning responsiveness with comments like "That's interesting, but are people really unresponsive all that often?" Apparently, a more responsive social environment is among the many privileges accorded those possessing characteristics that bestow social power (see Weiner & Goodenough, 1977; Donaldson, 1979).

Characteristics of one's partner may also affect the desire to focus on a particular topic. For example, one may be quite embarrassed to discuss sex with parents, but be quite willing to discuss it in great detail, and with considerable relish, with close friends. The motivation to focus on a particular topic may also be affected by the reason for interaction with another. If the purpose of the interaction is to gain information on a particular topic, the motivation to be responsive may be low when other topics are brought up.

Role relationships. Responsiveness is often required by the role relationship between interaction partners. Therapists, for example, are trained to be responsive in order to facilitate client progress. Public servants and information givers are required to respond to requests for service; teachers are required to interact with students, and are encouraged to appear interested in them. Finally, salesmen or other public persuaders (e.g., politicians, preachers) try to appear to be interested in and attracted to their targets and to make the targets like them, in order to be more persuasive, and do so in part by being responsive.

Individual Characteristics

Affiliation and intimacy. Several of the personality characteristics that were discussed in earlier sections were linked to the tendency to affiliate and become involved with others, e.g., self-monitoring, field dependence, extraversion, and need affiliation. Since responsiveness is assumed to promote interaction, intimacy, and attraction, persons who possess such characteristics should be relatively highly motivated to be responsive.

Concern with impression management. Responsiveness may be viewed as an impression management device; it will tend to increase attraction toward oneself, and to produce the impression that one is interested in and attracted to the other. Thus, characteristics that are associated with concern with impression management should be positively related to the motivation to be responsive. Persons who are high in self-consciousness, self-monitoring, and need for approval (see review by Strickland, 1977) have been shown to behave in ways that they expect to elicit positive evaluations from others. Thus, they should also be more motivated to be responsive.

Need for control. Since responsiveness to another will involve some abdication of control over the interaction to one's partner, characteristics that are associated with the need to control (e.g., dominance) should be negatively related to the motivation to be responsive. Unresponsiveness may also be used as a method for restoration of power, or as a technique for inducing compliance (e.g., "I won't speak to you until . . .").

Beliefs and expectations: Hypothesis testing. Earlier sections illustrated the ways in which beliefs and expectations concerning others may influence selective attention processes, as well as interpretation of their communications and behaviors. There is also reason to expect that such beliefs and expectations may influence the motive to be responsive. That is, they may lead one to be selectively responsive to content that is consistent and/or relevant. If so, selective responsiveness may contribute to the processes responsible for the tendency for expectations to be self-fulfilling (e.g., Darley & Fazio, 1980; Jones, 1977).

Snyder and colleagues (see Snyder, 1981; Snyder & Gangestad, 1981, for reviews) have demonstrated in a series of studies that people tend to test hypotheses about others by asking questions that generally elicit confirmatory evidence. That is, they ask questions that would typically be asked of a person *already known* to possess the hypothesized trait, and as a result, tend to receive evidence consistent with their hypothesis. In the context of more naturalistic interactions, such hypothesis testing activities may be manifested in greater responsiveness to hypothesis relevant or consistent content, i.e., more back-channel responses, more elaborations on, or questions about, the other's comments, less tendency to change the subject, etc. Such responsiveness would tend to maintain focus on hypothesis-relevant content, encourage initiation of similar topic areas, and ultimately to elicit evidence confirming the hypothesis. In other words, selective responsiveness may be as effective and pervasive a strategy for hypothesis confirmation as selective questioning.

The hypotheses that one chooses to test may derive from a multitude of sources, such as information from others, stereotypic beliefs, or schemas. However, it is interesting to note that individuals' self-schemas will often provide the hypotheses that are selected. Using Snyder's hypothesis-testing paradigm, Fong and Markus (Note 18) demonstrated that introvert and extravert schematics chose to ask questions relevant to their respective self-schemas, whereas aschematics asked primarily neutral questions. This suggests that persons may be selectively responsive to content relevant to their self-schemas. To the extent that such selective responsiveness tends to elicit information suggesting that others are *similar* to oneself (confirming the hypotheses derived from one's self-schemas), it may contribute to the processes responsible for the tendency to overestimate the degree of others' similarity to oneself (i.e., the false consensus bias; e.g. Ross, 1977).

Interaction rhythms. Chapple (1970) has pointed to the "circadian" interaction rhythms that characterize humans and other animals. He suggests that each person has a total amount of interaction to be expended during the day. Deviations from this optimal level will produce strong compensatory pressures: too much interaction will enhance the need for isolation, and too little the need for affiliation. It follows from Chapple's analysis that the motive to interact (and thus to be responsive) at a given point in time will be a function of the combination of the dispositional preference for amount of daily interaction and the amount of interaction that has immediately preceded the point in time in question. Persons who prefer smaller amounts of interaction will be motivated to interact and be responsive for smaller proportions of the day, and will become less motivated to interact after smaller amounts of preceding interaction than those who prefer greater amounts of interaction. In addition, regardless of dispositional preferences, the more a person has interacted in the immediate past, the less he or she will be motivated to interact at present.

Schutz (1960) has argued that relationships that are characterized by similarity with respect to preferences for amount of daily interaction, or "interchange compatibility," will be more harmonious. When one person desires more interaction than another, the first will be frustrated by lack of response, while the second will be drained by constant demand. However, even when dispositional needs for interaction are equivalent, conflict may arise from differences in daily demands for interaction that are external to the relationship (e.g., occupation, family, friends). Consider the housewife, who after a day alone at home, greets her husband enthusiastically with tales of the day's events and television wisdom, only to be frustrated by his monosyllabic responses and lack of attention. The husband, in contrast, after a day of intense conferences at the office, conversations over lunch, etc., is irritated by his wife's demands for interaction, wishing only to be left alone in compensation for the excess interaction at the office.

Chapple (1939, 1940, 1970) has also pointed to another feature of interaction rhythms that may affect responsiveness, that is, dispositional preferences for the speaker versus listener roles. A person who prefers the listener role may be unmotivated to engage in elaborate responses when they are demanded. In contrast, one who prefers the speaker role, impatient to begin his/her turn, may be unwilling to devote sufficient attention to the other's communications to process them accurately. Chapple demonstrated that conversations between persons who both prefer the speaker role are characterized by competition for the floor (e.g., multiple interruptions, overlapped speech), whereas those between persons who prefer the listener role are characterized by a lot of silence.

Finally, persons may differ with respect to preferences for both density and speed of conversation within a given period of interaction. Some persons prefer constant conversation, with never a moment's silence, whereas others prefer periodic silences and pauses for contemplation. Similarly, some prefer slower speech and somewhat longer response latencies, whereas others prefer rapid speech and short response latencies. Incompatibility with respect to preferences for either speed or density may produce problems. When two persons are incompatible with respect to density preferences, the one who prefers greater density can become frustrated by lack of response, while the other becomes exhausted by the constant demand. The same problem will characterize interactions between persons with different speed preferences. In addition, rapid conversation involves demands for faster processing of others' communications, as well as faster formulation of one's own responses. These demands may prove onerous for a person who prefers slower speeds. Opposite problems may arise for the person who prefers faster conversation speeds. It is sometimes difficult to avoid jumping in and finishing a slow speaker's sentences, or to continue to attend to their slow moving conversation.

Sex. Research on sex differences has shown that men tend to adopt self-presentation and interaction strategies that are characterized by assertion of status and dominance and maintenance of interpersonal distance, whereas the self-presentation and interaction strategies of females are characterized by preference for affiliation and minimization of status differences. For example, males engage in less eye contact, less self-disclosure, greater interpersonal distances, more competition and aggression, and more touching for assertion of status than females (see reviews by Deaux, 1977; Henley, 1977; Rosenthal & DePaulo, 1979a). Since responsiveness to another will facilitate affiliation but reduce control over the interaction, it follows that males should be less responsive than females, especially in situations that make sex roles salient.

This assumption has been well supported. For example, in same-sex conversations, females use more acknowledgments (e.g., "Mmhmm," "I see," "That's interesting") and more elaborations on the other's statements than males. Males, on the other hand, tend to argue and pursue their own thoughts more (e.g., Bernard, 1972; Dittman, 1972; Hirschman, Note 19, Note 20; Crosby, Note 21). Females are also more attentive, both visually (see review by Harper, Wiens, & Matarazzo, 1978) and posturally (Mehrabian, 1972) in both same and mixed sex interactions.

The male's relative unresponsiveness is most apparent in mixed-sex interactions. Men tend to talk more, listen less (Henley & Thorne, 1975; LaFrance & Mayo, 1978), and exhibit unresponsive behaviors that will maintain control of the interaction. For example, in mixed-sex interactions, males tend to interrupt more than females, and women allow interruption more than men; whereas in same-sex dyads their behavior is equivalent (e.g., Argyle, Lalljee, & Cook, 1968; Henley, 1975; Natale, Entin, & Jaffe, 1979; Zimmerman & West, 1975). Zimmerman and West (1975) noted that when a female tried to develop a topic in her turns at talk, the male made minimum responses that, along with more frequent interruptions by males, functioned as a mechanism by which the males controlled the conversation. Bernard (1972) supplied the tennis metaphor that women serve balls that men never return. He also noted that in group interactions women have a harder time getting the floor than men, and are more likely to lose it to successful interruption. Finally, Chester (1971) argued that it is almost impossible for a woman to control a conversation when men are present. He suggests that women are likely to sit silently, listening to men, whereas men almost never listen silently to women. They ask women questions in order to ultimately control the conversation (see also review by Baird, 1976). J. Davis (1978) has demonstrated this unilateral influence process with respect to the intimacy level of topics of conversation. The disclosures of females are more affected by those of their male partners than those of males are by the disclosures of their female partner.

Lack of motivation to be responsive between men and women may also derive from differences in preferred conversation topics. Women tend to prefer more social topics (people, personal lives, needs of household members, social life, husband), and men more business topics (politics, legal matters, taxes, sports, wages, work) (see review by Henley & Thorne, 1975).

Androgyny. Recent research concerning sex roles and dyadic interaction suggests that effective interaction may require both masculine and feminine skills (e.g., Ickes & Barnes, 1978; Ickes, Schermer, & Steeno, 1979). Androgynous persons (Bem, 1974, 1979) are assumed to possess both the instrumental skills (emphasizing achievement, autonomy, and striving for control) associated with masculinity, and the expressive skills (emphasizing communion, commonality, desire to relate effectively, and active expression of feelings) associated with femininity. Androgynous individuals should therefore possess both skills requisite for satisfying interaction, whereas sex-typed individuals should possess only one, and undifferentiated individuals neither. Several studies have examined unstructured interaction between individuals varying in sex role orientation. The findings across studies indicate that interactions between two sex-typed persons are less satisfying than those where at least one person is androgynous. The former tend to interact less, exhibit less involvement in the interaction (as indicated by gaze, smiling, laughing, gesturing, etc.), and report less attraction to one another (see Ickes & Barnes, 1978; Ickes et al., 1979). Perhaps as the number of androgynous persons within our culture increases, the sex differences noted above will become less pronounced.

Conclusions

Study of the sequential properties of social interaction will come of age when interaction process variables are identified that provide meaningful theoretical understanding of (1) the role of interaction process variables in the regulation of interaction, (2) the relationship of such variables to interaction outcomes, (3) the effects of external variables (personality, interaction goals, situations, etc.) on interaction process variables, and finally (4) the way in which external variables moderate the relationship between interaction process variables and interaction outcomes. The analysis presented in this chapter of the role of responsiveness in dyadic interaction provides the first systematic illustration of this approach to the study of social interaction.

The review presented in this chapter focused on the wide variety of situational and dispositional determinants of responsiveness. It provides a vivid demonstration of the way in which a vast array of knowledge from most areas of psychology, as well as from other disciplines, may be brought to bear on the investigation of a single interaction process variable. It is my hope that this demonstration will inspire similar analyses with respect to other interaction processes, and encourage meaningful theoretical explorations of interaction as a dependent variable.

Acknowledgments. I would like to thank the editors of this volume, Carl Backman, Gerald Ginsburg, Anthony Greenwald, Robert Krauss, and Thomas Ostrom for their comments on previous drafts of this manuscript. I would also like to thank Gordon Bower for his enlightening suggestions concerning the effects of mood on responsiveness.

Reference Notes

1. Davis, D. *Antecedents and consequences of responsiveness in dyadic interaction.* Manuscript in preparation, University of Nevada, 1981.
2. Kraut, R. E., Schechter, E., & Thompson, A. *Listener responsiveness, deception, and the structure of conversation.* Paper presented at the American Psychological Association Convention, Montreal, 1980.
3. Lewis, S. H. *Listener responsiveness and comprehension in conversation.* Paper presented at the American Psychological Association Convention, Montreal, 1980.
4. Holtgraves, T., & Davis, D. *Debator responsiveness: Impressions of candidates and memory for their answers*. Unpublished manuscript, University of Nevada, 1981.
5. Berg, J. H., & Archer, R. L. *Nature of disclosure reciprocity: Three forms of reciprocation.* Paper presented at the American Psychological Association Convention, Montreal, 1980.
6. Froming, W. J., Walker, G. R., & Lopyan, K. J. *Public and private self-awareness: When personal attitudes conflict with societal expectations.* Unpublished manuscript, University of Florida, 1981.

7. Froming, W. J., & Brodey, L. R. *Public self-consciousness, social anxiety and audience familiarity.* Unpublished manuscript, University of Florida, 1981.
8. Kimble, C. E., & Zehr, H. D. *Self-consciousness, information load, self-presentation and memory in a social situation.* Paper presented at the Midwestern Psychological Association Convention, St. Louis, Missouri, 1980.
9. Davis, D., Costella, H., & Droll, D. *Self-consciousness, social perception and social interaction.* Unpublished research, University of Nevada, 1981.
10. Brenner, M. W. *Memory and interpersonal relations.* Unpublished doctoral dissertation. University of Michigan, 1976.
11. Lippa, R. *Self-presentation and the expressive display of personality.* Paper presented at the American Psychological Association Convention, Toronto, 1978.
12. Lippa, R., Valdez, E., & Jolly, A. *Self-monitoring and the consistency of masculinity and femininity cues.* Paper presented at the American Psychological Association Convention, New York, 1979.
13. Snyder, M., & Gangestad, S. *Self-monitoring and the choice to enter situations.* Unpublished manuscript, University of Minnesota, 1981.
14. Davis, D., & Kasmer, J. *Personality determinants of responsiveness in dyadic interaction: The role of self-consciousness and self-monitoring.* Unpublished research, University of Nevada, 1982.
15. Krauss, R. M., Geller, V., & Olson, C. *Modalities and cues in perceiving deception.* Paper presented at the American Psychological Association Convention, Washington, D.C., 1976.
16. Davis, D. *Similarity and interaction.* Paper presented at the American Psychological Association Convention, Toronto, Canada, 1978.
17. Stoddart, R. M. *The effects of listener's familiarity on preschool children's communicative skills.* Paper presented at the Southeastern Conference on Human Development, Atlanta, April, 1978.
18. Fong, G., & Markus, H. *The influence of self-schemas in seeking information about others.* Paper presented at the American Psychological Association Convention, Montreal, 1980.
19. Hirschman, L. *Female-male differences in conversational interaction.* Paper presented at the Linguistic Society of America, 1973.
20. Hirschman, L. *Analysis of supportive and assertive behavior in conversations.* Paper presented at the Linguistic Society of America, 1974.
21. Crosby, F. *The effect of mode of interaction, sex, and acquaintance on conversation management.* Doctoral dissertation, Boston University, 1976.

References

Abrams, A. G. The relation of listening and reading comprehension to skill in message structuralization. *Journal of Communication,* 1966, *16*, 116-125.

Argyle, M. *Social interaction.* New York: Atherton, 1969.

Argyle, M., Lalljee, M., & Cook, M. The effects of visibility on interaction in a dyad. *Human Relations,* 1968, *21*, 3-18.

Asch, S. *Social psychology.* Englewood Cliffs, N.J.: Prentice-Hall, 1952.

Baird, J. E. Sex differences in group communication: A review of relevant research. *Quarterly Journal of Speech,* 1976, *62*, 179-192.

Beckman, L. Teachers' and observers' perceptions of causality for a child's performance. *Journal of Educational Psychology,* 1973, *65*, 198-204.

Bell, P. A., & Byrne, D. Repression-sensitization. In H. London & J. E. Exner, Jr. (Eds.), *Dimensions of personality.* New York: Wiley, 1977.

Bell, L. G., Wicklund, R. A., Manko, G., & Larkin, L. When unexpected behavior is attributed to the environment. *Journal of Research in Personality*, 1976, *10*, 316-327.

Bem, S. L. The measurement of psychological androgyny. *Journal of Consulting and Clinical Psychology,* 1974, *42*, 155-162.

Bem, S. L. Beyond androgyny: Some presumptuous prescriptions for a liberated sexual identity. In J. Sherman & F. Denmark (Eds.), *The future of women: Issues in psychology.* New York: Psychological Dimensions, 1979.

Bercherer, R. C., & Richard, L. M. Self-monitoring and consumer behavior. *Journal of Consumer Research,* 1978, *5*, 159-162.

Berelson, B., Lazarsfield, P., & McPhee, W. N. Political perception. In E. E. Maccoby, T. M. Newcomb, & E. L. Hartley (Eds.), *Readings in social psychology.* New York: Holt, Rinehart, & Winston, 1958.

Berkowitz, L. Social norms, feelings, and other factors affecting helping and altruism. In L. Berkowitz (Ed.), *Advances in experimental social psychology* (Vol. 6), New York: Academic Press, 1972.

Berlyne, D. *Conflict, arousal, and curiosity.* New York: Academic Press, 1960.

Berlyne, D. Attention. In E. Carterette & M. Friedman (Eds.), *Handbook of perception* (Vol. 1). New York: Academic Press, 1974.

Bernard, J. *The sex game.* New York: Atheneum, 1972.

Berscheid, E., Boyce, D., & Darley, J. Effect of forced association on voluntary choice to associate. *Journal of Personality and Social Psychology,* 1968, *8*, 13-19.

Berscheid, E., & Graziano, W. The initiation of social relationships and interpersonal attraction. In R. L. Burgess & T. L. Huston (Eds.), *Social exchange in developing relationships.* New York: Academic Press, 1979.

Berscheid, E., Graziano, W., Monson, T., & Dermer, M. Outcome dependency: Attention, attribution and attraction. *Journal of Personality and Social Psychology,* 1976, *34*, 978-989.

Bower, G. H. Mood and memory. *American Psychologist*, 1981, *36*, 129-148.

Bransford, J. D. *Human cognition: Learning, understanding and remembering.* Belmont, California: Wadsworth, 1979.

Bransford, J. D., & Johnson, M. K. Consideration of some problems of comprehension. In W. G. Chase (Ed.), *Visual information processing.* New York: Academic Press, 1973.

Brenner, M. The next-in-line effect. *Journal of Verbal Learning and Verbal Behavior,* 1973, *12*, 320-323.

Broadbent, D. E. *Decision and stress.* New York: Academic Press, 1968.

Brockner, J., & Eckenrode, J. Self-monitoring and the actor-observer bias. *Representative Research in Social Psychology,* 1978, *9*, 81-88.

Bruner, J. S. Personality dynamics and the process of perceiving. In F. W. Matson & A. Montagu (Eds.), *The human dialogue: Perspectives on communication.* New York: The Free Press, 1967.

Buck, R. W. Nonverbal communication of affect in children. *Journal of Personality and Social Psychology,* 1975, *31*, 644-653.

Buck, R. W. Nonverbal communication of affect in preschool children: Relationships with personality and skin conductance. *Journal of Personality and Social Psychology,* 1977, *35*, 225-236.

Buck, R. W. Individual differences in nonverbal sending accuracy and electrodermal responding. The externalizing-internalizing dimension. In R. Rosenthal (Ed.), *Skill in nonverbal communication: Individual differences.* Cambridge, Mass.: Oelgeschlager, Gunn & Hain, 1979.

Buck, R. W., Miller, R. E., & Caul, W. F. Sex, personality and physiological variables in the communication of emotion via facial expression. *Journal of Personality and Social Psychology,* 1974, *30*, 587-596.

Buss, A. H. *Self-consciousness and social anxiety.* San Francisco: Freeman, 1980.

Byrne, D. Repression-sensitization as a dimension of personality. In B. A. Maher (Ed.), *Progress in experimental personality research* (Vol. 1). New York: Academic Press, 1964.

Cappella, J. N. Mutual influence in expressive behavior: Adult-adult and infant-adult dyadic interaction. *Psychological Bulletin,* 1981, *89*, 101-132.

Carver, C. S. A cybernetic model of self-attention processes. *Journal of Personality and Social Psychology,* 1979, *37*, 1251-1281.

Chance, M. R. A. Attention structure as the basis of primate rank orders. *Man,* 1967, *2*, 503-518.

Chapple, E. D. Quantitative analysis of the interaction of individuals. *Proceedings of the National Academy of Science,* 1939, *25*, 58-67.

Chapple, E. D. Measuring human relations: An introduction to the study of the interaction of individuals. *General Psychological Monographs,* 1940, *23*, 3-147.

Chapple, E. D. *Culture and biological man: Explorations in behavioral anthropology.* New York: Holt, Rinehart, & Winston, 1970.

Cherry, F., & Byrne, D. Authoritarianism. In T. Blass (Ed.), *Personality variables in social behavior.* Hillsdale, N.J.: Erlbaum, 1977.

Chester, P. Marriage and psychotherapy. In the Radical Therapist Collective (Eds.), produced by Jerome Agel, *The Radical Therapist.* New York: Ballatine, 1971.

Cialdini, R. B., Braver, S. L., & Lewis, S. K. Attributional bias and the easily persuaded other. *Journal of Personality and Social Psychology,* 1974, *30*, 631-637.

Clark, H. H., & Haviland, S. E. Comprehension and the given-new contract. In R. O. Freedle (Ed.), *Discourse production and comprehension* (Vol. 1). *Discourse Processes: Advances in research and theory.* Norwood, N.J.: Ablex, 1977.

Collins, A. M., & Loftus, E. F. A spreading activation theory of semantic processing. *Psychological Review,* 1975, *82*, 407-428.

Coombs, C. H. Psychological scaling without a unit of measurement. *Psychological Review,* 1950, *57,* 145-158.

Coombs, C. H. Theory and methods of social measurement. In L. Festinger & D. Katz (Eds.), *Research methods in the behavioral sciences.* New York: Holt, Rinehart, & Winston, 1953.

Cottrell, L. S., Jr. The analysis of situational fields in social psychology. In A. P. Hare, E. F. Borgatta, & R. F. Bales (Eds.), *Small groups: Studies in social interaction* (rev. ed.). New York: Knopf, 1966.

Danheiser, P. R., & Graziano, W. G. Self-monitoring and cooperation as a self-presentational strategy. *Journal of Personality and Social Psychology,* in press.

Danziger, K. *Interpersonal communication.* New York: Pergamon Press, 1976.

Darley, J., & Berscheid, E. Increased liking as a result of the anticipation of personal contact. *Human Relations,* 1967, *20,* 29-40.

Darley, J. M., & Fazio, R. H. Expectancy confirmation processes arising in the social interaction sequence. *American Psychologist,* 1980, *35,* 867-881.

Davis, D. Implications for interaction versus effectance as mediators of the similarity-attraction relationship. *Journal of Experimental Social Psychology,* 1981, *17,* 96-117.

Davis, D., & Perkowitz, W. T. Consequences of responsiveness in dyadic interaction: Effects of probability of response and proportion of content-related responses on interpersonal attraction. *Journal of Personality and Social Psychology,* 1979, *37,* 534-551.

Davis, J. D. When boy meets girl: Sex roles and the negotiation of intimacy in an acquaintance exercise. *Journal of Personality and Social Psychology,* 1978, *36,* 684-692.

Deaux, K. Sex: A perspective on the attribution process. In J. H. Harvey, W. J. Ickes, & R. F. Kidd (Eds.), *New directions in attribution research* (Vol. 1). Hillsdale, N.J.: Erlbaum, 1976.

Deaux, K. Sex differences. In T. Blass (Ed.), *Personality variables in social behavior.* Hillsdale, N.J.: Erlbaum, 1977.

DePaulo, B. M., & Rosenthal, R. Ambivalence, discrepancy, and deception in nonverbal communication. In R. Rosenthal (Ed.), *Skill in nonverbal communication: Individual differences.* Cambridge, Mass.: Oelgeschlager, Gunn & Hain, 1979.

Diener, E., Lusk, R., DeFour, D., & Flax, R. Deindividuation: Effects of group size, density, number of observers, and group member similarity on self-consciousness and disinhibited behavior. *Journal of Personality and Social Psychology,* 1980, *39,* 449-459.

Dion, K. K. Physical attractiveness and evaluations of children's transgressions. *Journal of Personality and Social Psychology,* 1972, *24,* 207-213.

Dion, K. K., Berscheid, E., & Walster, E. What is beautiful is good. *Journal of Personality and Social Psychology,* 1972, *24,* 285-290.

Dittman, A. T. Developmental factors in conversational behavior. *Journal of Communication,* 1972, *22,* 404-423.

Donaldson, S. K. One kind of speech act: How do we know when we're conversing? *Semiotica,* 1979, *28-¾,* 259-299.

Duncan, B. L. Differential social perception and attribution of intergroup violence: Testing the lower limits of stereotyping of blacks. *Journal of Personality and Social Psychology,* 1976, *34*, 590-598.

Duncan, S., & Fiske, D. W. *Face-to-face interaction.* Hillsdale, N.J.: Erlbaum, 1977.

Duval, S., & Wicklund, R. A. *A theory of objective self-awareness.* New York: Academic Press, 1972.

Eifermann, R. Negation: A linguistic variable. *Acta Psychologica*, 1961, *18*, 258-273.

Elliott, G. C. Some effects of deception and level of self-monitoring on planning and reacting to a self-presentation. *Journal of Personality and Social Psychology*, 1979, *37*, 1282-1292.

Erdelyi, M. H., & Goldberg, B. Let's not sweep repression under the rug: Toward a cognitive psychology of repression. In J. F. Kihlstrom & F. J. Evans (Eds.), *Functional disorders of memory.* Hillsdale, N.J.: Erlbaum, 1979.

Erickson, F. Talking down: Some cultural sources of miscommunication in interracial interviews. In A. Wolfgang (Ed.), *Nonverbal behavior: Applications and Cultural Implications.* New York: Academic Press, 1979.

Ervin-Tripp, S. M. Sociolinguistics. In L. Berkowitz (Ed.), *Advances in experimental social psychology* (Vol. 4). New York: Academic Press, 1969.

Eysenck, H. J. *Readings in extraversion-introversion II: Fields of application.* London: Staples, 1971.

Eysenck, H. J., & Eysenck, S. B. G. *Manual of the Eysenck Personality Inventory.* London: University of London Press, 1964.

Eysenck, H. J., & Eysenck, S. B. G. *Manual of the EPI* (French ed.). Paris: Centre for Applied Psychology, 1971.

Faules, D. The relation of communicator skill to the ability to elicit and interpret feedback under four conditions. *Journal of Communication,* 1967, *17*, 362-371.

Fearing, F. Toward a psychological theory of human communication. In F. W. Matson & A. Montagu (Eds.), *The human dialogue: Perspectives on communication.* New York: The Free Press, 1967.

Feffer, M., & Suchotliff, L. Decentering implications of social interactions. *Journal of Personality and Social Psychology,* 1966, *4*, 415-422.

Feldstein, S., & Welkowitz, J. A chronography of conversation: In defense of an objective approach. In A. W. Siegman & S. Feldstein (Eds.), *Nonverbal behavior and communication*. Hillsdale, N.J.: Erlbaum, 1978.

Fenigstein, A. Self-consciousness, self-attention, and social interaction. *Journal of Personality and Social Psychology,* 1979, *37*, 75-86.

Fenigstein, A., Scheier, M. F., & Buss, A. H. Public and private self-consciousness: Assessment and theory. *Journal of Consulting and Clinical Psychology,* 1975, *43*, 522-527.

Friedman, H. S., DiMatteo, M. R., & Taranta, A. A study of the relationship between individual differences in nonverbal expressiveness, and factors of personality and social interaction. *Journal of Research in Personality,* in press.

Friedman, H. S., Riggio, R. E., & Segall, D. O. Personality and the enactment of emotion. *Journal of Nonverbal Behavior,* 1980, *5*, 35-48.

Froming, W. J., & Carver, C. S. Divergent influences of private and public self-consciousness in a compliance paradigm. *Journal of Research in Personality,* 1981, *15,* 159-171.

Geizer, R. S., Rarick, D. L., & Soldow, G. F. Deception and judgment accuracy: A study in person perception. *Personality and Social Psychology Bulletin,* 1977, *3,* 446-449.

Goffman, E. *The presentation of self in everyday life.* Garden City, N.Y.: Doubleday Anchor, 1959.

Goldstein, K. M., & Blackman, S. *Cognitive style: Five approaches and relevant research.* New York: Wiley, 1978.

Goodenough, D. R. The role of individual differences in field dependence as a factor in learning and memory. *Psychological Bulletin,* 1976, *83,* 675-694.

Greenwald, A. G. Self and memory. In G. H. Bower (Ed.), *Psychology of learning and motivation* (Vol. 15). New York: Academic Press, 1981.

Grice, H. P. Logic and conversation. In P. Cole & J. L. Morgan (Eds.), *Syntax and semantics* (Vol. 3), *Speech Acts.* New York: Academic Press, 1975.

Hall, J. A. Gender effects in decoding nonverbal cues. *Psychological Bulletin,* 1978, *85,* 845-857.

Hall, J. A. Gender, gender roles, and nonverbal communication skills. In R. Rosenthal (Ed.), *Skill in nonverbal communication: Individual differences.* Cambridge, Mass.: Oelgeschlager, Gunn & Hain, 1979.

Harms, L. S. Listener comprehension of speakers of three status groups. *Language and Speech,* 1961, *4,* 109-122.

Harper, R. G., Wiens, A. N., & Matarazzo, J. D. *Nonverbal communication: The state of the art.* New York: Wiley, 1978.

Harper, R. G., Wiens, A. N., & Matarazzo, J. D. The relationship between encoding-decoding of visual nonverbal emotional cues. *Semiotica,* 1979, *28 1/2,* 171-192.

Harvey, J. H., Yarkin, K. L., Lightner, J. M., & Town, J. P. Unsolicited interpretation and recall of interpersonal events. *Journal of Personality and Social Psychology,* 1980, *38,* 551-558.

Hayden, T., & Mischel, W. Maintaining trait consistency in the resolution of behavioral inconsistency: The wolf in sheep's clothing? *Journal of Personality,* 1976, *44,* 109-132.

Heider, F. *The psychology of interpersonal relations.* New York: Wiley, 1958.

Henley, N. M. Power, sex, and nonverbal communication. In B. Thorne & N. M. Henley (Eds.), *Language and sex: Differences and dominance.* Rowley, Mass.: Newbury House, 1975.

Henley, N. M. *Body politics.* Englewood Cliffs, N.J.: Prentice-Hall, 1977.

Henley, N., & Thorne, B. Sex and topics of conversation. In B. Thorne & N. Henley (Eds.), *Language and sex: Differences and dominance.* Rowley, Mass.: Newbury House, 1975.

Hocking, W. E. Knowledge of other minds. In F. W. Matson & A. Montagu (Eds.), *The human dialogue: perspectives on communication.* New York: The Free Press, 1967.

Hornstein, M. Accuracy of emotional communication and interpersonal compatibility. *Journal of Personality,* 1967, *35*, 20-30.

Hull, J. G., & Levy, A. S. The organizational functions of the self: An alternative to the Duval and Wicklund model of self-awareness. *Journal of Personality and Social Psychology,* 1979, *37*, 756-768.

Hymes, D. Models of the interaction of language and social setting. In J. J. Gumperez & G. D. Hymes (Eds.), *Directions in sociolinguistics: The ethnography of communication.* New York: Holt, Rinehart & Winston, 1972.

Hymes, D. *Foundations of sociolinguistics: An ethnographic approach.* Philadelphia: University of Pennsylvania Press, 1974.

Ickes, W. J., & Barnes, R. D. The role of sex and self-monitoring in unstructured dyadic interactions. *Journal of Personality and Social Psychology,* 1977, *35*, 315-330.

Ickes, W. J., & Barnes, R. D. Boys and girls together–and alienated: On enacting stereotyped sex roles in mixed-sex dyads. *Journal of Personality and Social Psychology,* 1978, *36*, 669-683.

Ickes, W. J., Layden, M. A., & Barnes, R. D. Objective self-awareness and individuation: An empirical link. *Journal of Personality,* 1978, *46*, 146-161.

Ickes, W. B., Schermer, B., & Steeno, J. Sex and sex-role influences in same-sex dyads. *Social Psychology Quarterly,* 1979, *42*, 373-385.

Jackson, D. N. *Personality research form manual.* New York: Research Psychologists Press, 1976.

Jaffe, J., & Feldstein, S. *Rhythms of dialogue.* New York: Academic Press, 1970.

Jones, E. E., & Baumeister, R. The self-monitor looks at the ingratiator. *Journal of Personality,* 1976, *44*, 654-674.

Jones, R. A. *Self-fulfilling prophecies: Social, psychological, and physiological effects of expectancies.* Hillsdale, N.J.: Erlbaum, 1977.

Kahneman, D. *Attention and effort.* Englewood Cliffs, N.J.: Prentice-Hall, 1975.

Karp, S. A. Psychological differentiation. In T. Blass (Ed.), *Personality variables in social behavior.* Hillsdale, N.J.: Erlbaum, 1977.

Kelley, G. A. Ontological acceleration. In B. Maher (Ed.), *Clinical psychology and personality: The selected papers of George Kelley.* New York: Wiley, 1969.

Kelley, H. H. Attribution in social interaction. In E. E. Jones, D. E. Kanouse, H. H. Kelley, R. E. Nisbett, S. Valins, & B. Weiner (Eds.), *Attribution: Perceiving the causes of behavior.* New York: General Learning Press, 1972. (a)

Kelley, H. H. Causal schemata in the attribution process. In E. E. Jones, D. E. Kanouse, H. H. Kelley, R. E. Nisbett, S. Valins, & B. Weiner (Eds.), *Attribution: Perceiving the causes of behavior.* New York: General Learning Press, 1972. (b)

Kelman, H. C., & Eagly, A. H. Attitude toward the communicator, perception of communication content, and attitude change. *Journal of Personality and Social Psychology,* 1965, *1*, 63-78.

Kendon, A. Movement coordination in social interaction: Some examples described. *Acta Psychologica,* 1970, *9*, 180-182.

Kendon, A., & Cook, M. The consistency of gaze patterns in social interaction. *British Journal of Psychology,* 1969, *60*, 481-494.

Kent, G. G., Davis, J. D., & Shapiro, D. A. Resources required in the reconstruction of conversation. *Journal of Personality and Social Psychology,* 1978, *36*, 13-22.

Kidder, K. L., & Campbell, D. T. The indirect testing of social attitudes. In G. F. Summers (Ed.), *Attitude measurement.* Chicago: Rand McNally, 1970.

Kihlstrom, J. F. On personality and memory. In N. Cantor & J. F. Kihlstrom (Eds.), *Personality, cognition, and social interaction.* Hillsdale, N.J.: Erlbaum, 1981.

Kirscht, J. P., & Dillehay, R. C. *Dimensions of authoritarianism: A review of research and theory.* Lexington, Ky.: University of Kentucky Press, 1967.

Kleck, R. E., & Wheaton, J. Dogmatism and responses to opinion-consistent and opinion-inconsistent information. *Journal of Personality and Social Psychology,* 1967, *5*, 249-252.

Knight, J. A., & Vallacher, R. R. Interpersonal engagement in social perception: The consequences of getting into the action. *Journal of Personality and Social Psychology,* 1981, *40*, 990-999.

Krauss, R., & Bricker, P. Effects of transmission delay and access delay on the efficiency of verbal communication. *Journal of the Acoustical Society of America,* 1967, *41*, 286-292.

Krauss, R., Garlock, L., Bricker, P., & McMahon, L. The role of audible and visible back-channel responses in interpersonal communication. *Journal of Personality and Social Psychology,* 1977, *35*, 523-529.

Krauss, R., & Weinheimer, S. Concurrent feedback, confirmation, and the encoding of referents in verbal interaction. *Journal of Personality and Social Psychology,* 1966, *4*, 324-346.

Kulik, J. A., & Taylor, S. E. Self-monitoring and the use of consensus information. *Journal of Personality,* 1981, *49*, 75-84.

LaFrance, M., & Mayo, C. Racial differences in gaze behavior during conversation: Two systematic observational studies. *Journal of Personality and Social Psychology,* 1976, *33*, 547-552.

LaFrance, M., & Mayo, C. *Moving bodies: Nonverbal communication in social relationships.* Monterey, Calif.: Brooks/Cole, 1978.

Lanzetta, J. T. The motivational properties of uncertainty. In H. I. Day, D. E. Berlyne, & D. E. Hunt (Eds.), *Intrinsic motivation: New directions in education.* Toronto: Holt, Rinehart & Winston of Canada, 1971.

Leavitt, H. J., & Mueller, R. A. H. Some effects of feedback on communication. *Human Relations,* 1951, *4*, 401-410.

Levine, R., Chein, L., & Murphy, G. The relation of the intensity of a need to the amount of perceptual distortion: A preliminary report. *Journal of Psychology,* 1942, *13*, 283-293.

Lippa, R. Expressive control and the leakage of dispositional introversion-extraversion during role-played teaching. *Journal of Personality,* 1976, *44*, 541-559.

Lippa, R. Expressive control, expressive consistency, and the correspondence between expressive behavior and personality. *Journal of Personality,* 1978, *46*, 438-461.

Lippa, R., & Mash, M. The effects of self-monitoring and self-reported consistency on the consistency of personality judgments made by strangers and intimates. *Journal of Research in Personality,* 1981, *15*, 172-181.

Lykken, D. T. A study of anxiety in the sociopathic personality. *Journal of Abnormal and Social Psychology,* 1957, *55*, 6-10.

Macy, J., Jr., Christie, L. S., & Luce, R. D. Coding noise in a task-oriented group. *Journal of Abnormal and Social Psychology,* 1953, *28*, 401-409.

Maher, B. A. *Principles of psychopathology: An experimental approach.* New York: McGraw-Hill, 1966.

Malpass, R. S. Effects of attitude on learning and memory: The influence of instruction-induced sets. *Journal of Experimental Social Psychology,* 1969, *5*, 441-453.

Mandler, G. *Mind and emotion.* New York: Wiley, 1975.

Markus, H., & Sentis, K. The self in social information processing. In J. Suls (Ed.), *Social psychological perspectives on the self.* Hillsdale, N.J.: Erlbaum, 1980.

Markus, H., & Smith, J. The influence of self-schemas on the perception of others. In N. Cantor & J. Kihlstrom (Eds.), *Personality, cognition, and social interaction.* Hillsdale, N.J.: Erlbaum, 1981.

McDowall, J. J. Interactional synchrony: A reappraisal. *Journal of Personality and Social Psychology,* 1978, *36*, 963-975.

McGhie, A. Psychological studies of schizophrenia. In B. Maher (Ed.), *Contemporary abnormal psychology.* Harmondsworth, England: Penguin, 1973.

Mead, G. H. *Mind, self, and society.* Chicago: University of Chicago Press, 1934.

Meerloo, T. A. M. Conversation and communication. In F. W. Matson & A. Montagu (Eds.), *The human dialogue: perspectives on communication.* New York: The Free Press, 1967.

Mehrabian, A. *An analysis of personality theories.* Englewood Cliffs, N.J.: Prentice-Hall, 1968. (a)

Mehrabian, A. The effect of context on judgments of speaker attitude. *Journal of Personality,* 1968, *36*, 21-32. (b)

Mehrabian, A. *Nonverbal communication.* Chicago: Aldine-Atherton, 1972.

Mehrabian, A., & Ferris, S. R. Inference of attitudes from nonverbal communication in two channels. *Journal of Consulting Psychology,* 1967, *31*, 248-252.

Mehrabian, A., & Reed, H. Some determinants of communication accuracy. *Psychological Bulletin,* 1968, *70*, 365-381.

Mehrabian, A., & Wiener, M. Decoding of inconsistent information. *Journal of Personality and Social Psychology,* 1967, *6*, 109-114.

Meiselman, K. C. Broadening dual modality cue utilization in chronic and nonparanoid schizophrenics. *Journal of Consulting and Clinical Psychology,* 1973, *41*, 447-453.

Menges, R. J. Student-instructor cognitive compatibility in the large lecture class. *Journal of Personality,* 1969, *37*, 444-459.

Miller, D. T., & Norman, S. A. Actor-observer differences in perceptions of effective control. *Journal of Personality and Social Psychology,* 1975, *31*, 503-515.

Miller, D. T., Norman, S. A., & Wright, E. Distortion in person perception as a function of need for effective control. *Journal of Personality and Social Psychology,* 1978, *36*, 598-607.

Miller, G. A. *Language and communication.* New York: McGraw-Hill, 1951.

Miller, G. A., Heise, G. A., & Lichten, W. The intelligibility of speech as a function of the context of the test materials. *Journal of Experimental Psychology,* 1951, *41*, 329-335.

Miller, J. G. Unconscious processes in perception. In R. R. Blake & G. U. Ramsey (Eds.), *Perception: An approach to personality*. New York: Ronald Press, 1951.

Mobbs, N. A. Eye contact in relation to social introversion/extraversion. *British Journal of Social and Clinical Psychology*, 1968, 7, 305-306.

Moscovici, S. Communication processes and the properties of language. In L. Berkowitz (Ed.), *Advances in Experimental Social Psychology* (Vól. 3). New York: Academic Press, 1967.

Murray, E. Studies in personal and social integration. *Speech Monographs,* 1944, *11*, 9-27.

Natale, M., Entin, E., & Jaffe, J. Vocal interruptions in dyadic communication as a function of speech and social anxiety. *Journal of Personality and Social Psychology,* 1979, *37*, 865-878.

Neely, K. K. Effect of visual factors on the intelligibility of speech. *Journal of the Acoustical Society of America,* 1956, *28*, 1275-1277.

Newtson, D. Attribution and the unit of perception of ongoing behavior. *Journal of Personality and Social Psychology,* 1973, *28*, 28-38.

Padgett, V. R., & Wolosin, R. J. Cognitive similarity in dyadic communication. *Journal of Personality and Social Psychology*, 1980, *39*, 654-659.

Palmore, E., Lennard, H. L., & Hendin, H. Similarities of therapist and patient verbal behavior in psychotherapy. *Sociometry*, 1959, *22*, 12-22.

Pearce, W. B. The coordinated management of meaning: A rules-based theory of interpersonal communication. In G. R. Miller (Ed.), *Explorations in interpersonal communications.* Beverly Hills, Calif.: Sage, 1976.

Pepitone, A. Motivational effects in social perception. *Human Relations,* 1950, *3*, 57-76.

Pfeiffer, J. W. Conditions which hinder communication. In J. W. Pfeiffer & J. E. Jones, *The 1973 annual handbook for group facilitators.* Iowa City: University Associates, 1973.

Planalp, S., & Tracy, K. Not to change the subject but . . .: A cognitive approach to the management of conversation. In D. Nimmo (Ed.), *Communication Yearbook 4.* New Brunswick, N.J.: Transactions, 1980.

Rarick, D. L., Soldow, G. F., & Geizer, R. S. Self-monitoring as a mediator of conformity. *Central States Speech Journal,* 1976, *27*, 267-271.

Regan, D. T., Strauss, E., & Fazio, R. Liking and the attribution process. *Journal of Experimental Social Psychology*, 1974, *30*, 385-397.

Rogers, C. R. *Client-centered therapy*. Boston: Houghton Mifflin, 1951.

Rogers, T. B. A model of self as an aspect of the human information processing system. In N. Cantor & J. Kihlstrom (Eds.), *Personality, cognition, and social interaction*. Hillsdale, N.J.: Erlbaum, 1981.

Rokeach, M. *The open and closed mind.* New York: Basic Books, 1960.

Rommetveit, R. *On message structure: A framework for the study of language and communication.* London: Wiley, 1974.

Rosenfeld, H. M. Approval-seeking and approval inducing functions of verbal and nonverbal responses in the dyad. *Journal of Personality and Social Psychology,* 1966, *6*, 597-605.

Rosenfeld, H. M. Nonverbal reciprocation of approval: An experimental analysis. *Journal of Experimental Social Psychology,* 1967, *3*, 102-111.

Rosenfeld, H. M. Conversational control functions of nonverbal behavior. In A. W. Siegman & S. Feldstein (Eds.), *Nonverbal behavior and communication.* Hillsdale, N.J.: Erlbaum, 1978.

Rosenfeld, H., & Hanks, M. The nonverbal context of verbal listener responses. In M. Key (Ed.), *The relationship of verbal and nonverbal behavior.* The Hague: Mouton, 1980.

Rosenthal, R., & DePaulo, B. M. Sex differences in accommodation in nonverbal communication. In R. Rosenthal (Ed.), *Skill in nonverbal communication: Individual differences.* Cambridge, Mass.: Oelgeschlager, Gunn & Hain, 1979. (a)

Rosenthal, R., & DePaulo, B. M. Sex differences in eavesdropping on nonverbal cues. *Journal of Personality and Social Psychology,* 1979, *37*, 273-285. (b)

Rosenthal, R., Hall, J. A., Archer, D., DiMatteo, M. R., & Rogers, P. L. Measuring sensitivity to nonverbal communication: The PONS text. In A. Wolfgang (Ed.), *Nonverbal behavior: Applications and cultural implications.* New York: Academic Press, 1979.

Ross, L. The intuitive psychologist and his shortcomings: Distortions in the attribution process. In L. Berkowitz (Ed.), *Advances in experimental social psychology* (Vol. 10). New York: Academic Press, 1977.

Ross, L., Lepper, M., & Hubbard, M. Perseverance in self-deception and social perception: Biased attributional processes in the debriefing paradigm. *Journal of Personality and Social Psychology,* 1975, *32*, 880-892.

Ross, L., Lepper, M. R., Strack, F., & Steinmetz, J. Social exploration and social expectation: Effects of real and hypothetical explorations on subjective likelihood. *Journal of Personality and Social Psychology,* 1977, *35*, 817-829.

Rotter, J. B. Generalized expectancies for internal versus external control of reinforcement. *Psychological Monographs,* 1966, *80* (Whole No. 609).

Runkel, P. J. Cognitive similarity in facilitating communication. *Sociometry,* 1956, *19*, 178-191.

Rutter, D. R., Morley, I. E., & Graham, J. C. Visual interaction in a group of introverts and extraverts. *European Journal of Social Psychology,* 1972, *2*, 371-384.

Sacks, H., Schegloff, E. A., & Jefferson, G. A simplest systematics for the organization of turn taking for conversation. In J. Schenkein (Ed.), *Studies in the organization of conversational interaction.* New York: Academic Press, 1978.

Sampson, E. E. Personality and the location of identity. *Journal of Personality,* 1978, *46*, 552-568.

Santee, R. T., & Maslach, C. To agree or not to agree: Personal dissent amid social pressure to conform. *Journal of Personality and Social Psychology,* in press.

Scheier, M. F. The effects of public and private self-consciousness on the public expression of personal beliefs. *Journal of Personality and Social Psychology,* 1980, *39*, 514-521.

Scheier, M. F., & Carver, C. S. Private and public aspects of the self. In L. Wheeler (Ed.), *Review of Personality and Social Psychology* (Vol. 2). Beverly Hills, Calif.: Sage, 1981.

Schutz, W. C. *FIRO: A three-dimensional theory of interpersonal behavior.* New York: Holt, Rinehart & Winston, 1960.

Shibuya, Y. A. A study in the relationship between cognitive similarity and communication effectiveness. *Japanese Journal of Psychological Research,* 1962, *4*, 173-177.

Siegman, A. W. A cross cultural investigation of the relationship between introversion-extraversion, social attitudes and anti-social behavior. *British Journal of Clinical and Social Psychology,* 1962, *2*, 196-208.

Siegman, A. W., & Pope, B. Personality variables associated with productivity and verbal fluency in the initial interview. *Proceedings of the 73rd Annual Convention of the American Psychological Association,* 1965, 273-274.

Smith, A. L. *Transracial communication.* Englewood Cliffs, N.J.: Prentice-Hall, 1973.

Snyder, M. The self-monitoring of expressive behavior. *Journal of Personality and Social Psychology,* 1974, *30*, 526-537.

Snyder, M. Attribution and behavior: Social perception and social causation. In J. H. Harvey, W. J. Ickes, & R. F. Kidd (Eds.), *New directions in attribution research* (Vol. 1). Hillsdale, N.J.: Erlbaum, 1976.

Snyder, M. Self-monitoring processes. In L. Berkowitz (Ed.), *Advances in experimental social psychology* (Vol. 12). New York: Academic Press, 1979.

Snyder, M. On the influence of individuals on situations. In N. Cantor & J. Kihlstrom (Eds.), *Personality, cognition, and social interaction.* Hillsdale, N.J.: Erlbaum, 1981.

Snyder, M. Seek and ye shall find: Testing hypotheses about other people. In E. T. Higgins, C. P. Herman, & M. P. Zanna (Eds.), *Social cognition: The Ontario Symposium on Personality and Social Psychology.* Hillsdale, N.J.: Erlbaum, 1981.

Snyder, M., & Cantor, N. Thinking about ourselves and others: Self-monitoring and social knowledge. *Journal of Personality and Social Psychology,* 1980, *39*, 222-234.

Snyder, M., & Gangestad, S. Hypothesis testing processes. In J. H. Harvey, W. J. Ickes, & R. F. Kidd (Eds.), *New directions in attribution research* (Vol. 3). Hillsdale, N.J.: Erlbaum, 1981.

Snyder, M., & Kendzierski, D. Acting on one's attitudes: Procedures for linking attitudes and behavior. *Journal of Experimental Social Psychology,* in press.

Snyder, M., & Monson, T. C. Persons, situations, and the control of social behavior. *Journal of Personality and Social Psychology,* 1975, *32*, 637-644.

Snyder, M., & Swann, W. B., Jr. When actions reflect attitudes: The politics of impression management. *Journal of Personality and Social Psychology,* 1976, *34*, 1034-1042.

Snyder, M., & Tanke, E. D. Behavior and attitude: Some people are more consistent than others. *Journal of Personality,* 1976, *44*, 510-517.

Stephan, W., Berscheid, E., & Walster, E. Sexual arousal and heterosexual perception. *Journal of Personality and Social Psychology,* 1971, *20,* 93-101.

Strickland, B. R. Approval motivation. In T. Blass (Ed.), *Personality variables in social behavior.* Hillsdale, N.J.: Erlbaum, 1977.

Stroebe, W., Eagly, A., & Stroebe, M. Friendly or just polite? The effects of self-esteem on attributions. *European Journal of Social Psychology,* 1977, *7,* 265-274.

Sumby, W. H., & Pollack, I. Visual contribution to speech intelligibility in noise. *Journal of the Acoustical Society of America,* 1954, *26,* 212-215.

Swann, W. B, Jr., Stephenson, B., & Pittman, T. S. Curiosity and control: On the determinants of the search for social knowledge. *Journal of Personality and Social Psychology,* 1981, *40,* 635-642.

Taylor, S. E., & Crocker, J. Schematic bases of social information processing. In E. T. Higgins, C. A. Herman, & M. P. Zanna (Eds.), *Social cognition: The Ontario symposium on personality and social psychology.* Hillsdale, N.J.: Erlbaum, 1981.

Thomas, E. A. C., & Malone, T. W. On the dynamics of two-person interactions. *Psychological Review,* 1979, *86,* 331-360.

Thomas, E. A. C., & Martin, J. A. Analysis of parent-infant interaction. *Psychological Review,* 1976, *83,* 141-156.

Triandis, H. C. Cognitive similarity and interpersonal communication in industry. *Journal of Applied Psychology,* 1959, *43,* 321-326.

Triandis, H. C. Cognitive similarity and communication in a dyad. *Human Relations,* 1960, *13,* 175-183. (a)

Triandis, H. C. Some determinants of interpersonal communication. *Human Relations,* 1960, *13,* 279-287. (b)

Triandis, H. C. Cultural influences upon cognitive processes. In L. Berkowitz (Ed.), *Advances in experimental social psychology* (Vol. 1). New York: Academic Press, 1964.

Triandis, H. C. Culture training, cognitive complexity, and interpersonal attitudes. In R. Brislin, S. Bochner, & W. Lonner (Eds.), *Cultural perspectives on learning.* New York: Halsted/Wiley, 1975.

Turner, J., & Le, B. Schizophrenics as judges of vocal expressions of emotional meaning. In J. R. Davitz (Ed.), *The communication of emotional meaning.* New York: McGraw-Hill, 1964.

Tversky, A., & Kahneman, D. Availability: A heuristic for judging frequency and probability. *Cognitive Psychology,* 1973, *5,* 207-232.

Vacchiano, R. B. Dogmatism. In T. Blass (Ed.), *Personality variables in social behavior.* Hillsdale, N.J.: Erlbaum, 1977.

Vick, C. F., & Wood, R. V. Similarity of past experience and the communication of meaning. *Speech Monographs,* 1969, *36,* 159-162.

Warner, R. M., Kenney, D. A., & Stoto, M. A new round robin analysis of variance for social interaction data. *Journal of Personality and Social Psychology,* 1979, *37,* 1742-1757.

Watzlawick, P., Beavin, J. H., & Jackson, D. D. *Pragmatics of human communication: A study of interaction patterns, pathologies and paradoxes*. New York: Norton, 1967.

Waxer, P. Therapist training in nonverbal behavior: towards a curriculum. In A. Wolfgang (Ed.), *Nonverbal behavior: Application and cultural implications.* New York: Academic Press, 1979.

Weiner, S. L., & Goodenough, D. R. A move toward a psychology of conversation. In R. O. Freedle (Ed.), *Discourse Production and Comprehension* (Vol. 1). *Discourse Processes: Advances in Research and Theory.* Norwood, N.J.: Ablex, 1977.

Whorf, B. L. *Language, thought and reality: Selected writings of Benjamin Lee Whorf* (J. B. Carroll, Ed.). Cambridge, Mass.: MIT Press, 1956.

Wicklund, R. A. Objective self-awareness. In L. Berkowitz (Ed.), *Advances in experimental social psychology* (Vol. 8). New York: Academic Press, 1975.

Williams, J. R. Feedback techniques in marriage counseling. In B. N. Ard & C. C. Ard (Eds.), *Handbook of marriage counseling.* Palo Alto, Calif.: Science & Bevior Books, 1969.

Wilson, G. Introversion/extraversion. In T. Blass (Ed.), *Personality variables in social behavior.* Hillsdale, N.J.: Erlbaum, 1977.

Witkin, H. A., & Goodenough, D. R. Field dependence and interpersonal behavior. *Psychological Bulletin,* 1977, *84*, 661-690.

Witkin, H. A., Goodenough, D. R., & Oltman, P. K. Psychological differentiation: Current status. *Journal of Personality and Social Psychology,* 1979, *37*, 1127-1145.

Wolosin, R. J. Cognitive similarity and group laughter. *Journal of Personality and Social Psychology,* 1975, *32*, 503-509.

Wyer, R. S., Jr. The acquisition and use of social knowledge: Basic postulates and representative research. *Personality and Social Psychology Bulletin,* 1980, *6*, 558-573.

Wyer, R. S., Jr., & Carlston, D. E. *Social cognition, inference, and attribution.* Hillsdale, N.J.: Erlbaum, 1979.

Wyer, R. S., Jr., & Srull, T. K. The processing of social stimulus information. In R. Hastie, T. Ostrom, E. Ebbesen, R. Wyer, D. Hamilton, & D. Carlston (Eds.), *Person memory: The cognitive bases of social perception.* Hillsdale, N.J.: Erlbaum, 1980.

Zajonc, R. B. *Social psychology: An experimental approach.* Belmont, Calif.: Wadsworth, 1966.

Zanna, M. P., & Olson, J. M. Individual differences in attitudinal relations. In M. P. Zanna, C. P. Herman, & E. T. Higgins (Eds.). *Variability and consistency of social behavior: The Ontario symposium* (Vol. 2). Hillsdale, N.J.: Erlbaum, in press.

Zanna, M. P., Olson, J. M., & Fazio, R. H. Attitude-behavior consistency: An individual difference perspective. *Journal of Personality and Social Psychology,* in press.

Zimmerman, D. H., & West, L. Sex roles, interruptions and silences in conversation. In B. Thorne & N. Henley (Eds.), *Language and sex: Differences and dominance.* Rowley, Mass.: Newbury House, 1975.

Zuckerman, M., & Reis, H. T. A comparison of three models for predicting altruistic behavior. *Journal of Personality and Social Psychology,* 1978, *36*, 498-500.

Chapter 5

Personality and Nonverbal Involvement: A Functional Analysis

Miles L. Patterson

Systematic research into the nonverbal components of social behavior has been common only in the last 15 to 20 years. From hindsight the relatively late development of this area seems puzzling. This is especially the case in the light of judgments by researchers such as Mehrabian (1972, chap. 6) and Birdwhistell (1970, p. 158) that the majority of the meaning conveyed in a social interaction is determined by the nonverbal cues. It is not my intention to discuss the reasons for the relatively recent development of this research area. Instead, I will attempt to analyze some of the consistencies in nonverbal social behavior apparent in the extensive research over the last two decades.

There are clearly differing perspectives from which one can pursue an analysis of nonverbal social behavior. One contrast, reflecting the theme of this book, would involve a role or situational approach versus a personality approach. Representative of the former approach would be Goffman's (1961, 1963, 1967, 1972) descriptive analysis of social behavior as guided by the rules of the situation or "frame." From this perspective, the individuality of the actor is deemphasized, and in its place the unique nature of the frame and its relationship to the social structure is stressed (Gonos, 1977). A similar orientation from ecological psychology stresses the influence of behavior settings in contributing to the homogeneity of social behavior across individuals (Barker, 1968). Alternately, a role analysis would focus on both an individual's position in a social network and the relationships to others in that network. All these approaches share a common emphasis on the rules or norms of the situation as forces guiding social behavior. In contrast, a personality approach attempts to identify differing individual characteristics as causes, or at least correlates, of social behavior. Because a great deal of research on nonverbal social behavior has developed from a personality perspective, this chapter will focus on that research. Nevertheless, it is clear that generalizations about the influence of personality will often have to be tempered with a recognition of role and situational influences.

In setting the background and providing a structure for discussing the influence of personality on nonverbal behavior, I would like to describe three important changes in this area of research: (1) a greater focus on the processes that underlie patterns of nonverbal behavior; (2) an increased appreciation and use of multiple nonverbal measures; and (3) a growing sensitivity to the functions served by nonverbal behavior. This last point, emphasizing a functional perspective, will provide the organizing theme for this chapter's discussion.

With respect to the first point, I sense a change in the type of research questions pursued. Much of the early research was highly descriptive and, frankly, fairly shallow. Studies were often limited to the mere description of differences in the use of distance, eye contact, or facial expressions as a function of one or more demographic characteristics. Too infrequently was there a focus on potential causal factors determining behavior patterns observed. Perhaps, such an emphasis on descriptive studies in the early research is typical in the evolution of research strategies in any area of inquiry. Ideally, later studies should focus more on the underlying processes or mediators contributing to distinct results. This seems to have been the case with at least some of the research on nonverbal social behavior.

For example, a popular paradigm for studying the role of space in social settings involves the use of spatial invasions or intrusions. Felipe and Sommer's (1966) classic study and our extension of it (Patterson, Mullens, & Romano, 1971) described the distance and arrangements under which close approaches by an intruder might produce reactions in a naive subject. Very close (6-12 in.) adjacent seating choices precipitated flight from the setting by approximately 50% of the subjects in the Felipe and Sommer study. At slightly greater, but still close, adjacent positions, subjects initiated behavioral adjustments (e.g., turning away or blocking with an arm) apparently designed to lessen the close presence of the intruder (Patterson et al., 1971). Many studies followed which described differences in response to spatial invasion as a function of sex, age, or race of the intruder or subject. However, more recently Fisher and Byrne (1975) have identified differences in attribution following invasions, while Middlemist, Knowles, and Matter (1976) have found evidence for increased physiological arousal under conditions of close spatial invasion. Thus, these latter two studies have moved from mere description to focusing on the processes potentially mediating individuals' reactions to invasion. Arousal and attribution processes have become central components in more recent theoretical formulations regarding nonverbal behavior (Ellsworth & Langer, 1976; Patterson, 1976, 1977a; Worchel & Teddlie, 1976). Such changes in purpose and strategy of research and theory are indicative of the kind of increased sophistication needed to provide a more comprehensive understanding of patterns of nonverbal behavior.

A second trend is indicated by the increased frequency of studies measuring a variety of nonverbal behaviors. At first glance, this may appear to be a cosmetic change only, reflecting some sort of "more is better" value. I believe, however, that measurement and analysis of multiple dimensions is critical to any comprehensive understanding of nonverbal social behavior. It is tempting to isolate our focus of interest to a single specific behavior, whether it is distance, touch, gestures, facial expressiveness, or any other behavior. However, such a focus provides a very limited, and occasionally misleading, picture of an interactive sequence. For example, theoretical discussions of intimacy (Argyle & Dean, 1965; Patterson, 1976) immediacy (Mehrabian, 1969), and proxemics (Hall, 1968) all assume that fluid, dynamic relationships exist within specific sets of nonverbal behavior. In other words, changes in any component behavior may precipitate changes in one or more related behaviors. Thus, research in which only one behavioral indicator is arbitrarily sampled from a larger set frequently provides a very incomplete understanding of some social interchange.

Obviously, it is impossible to analyze everything that occurs in an interaction, and the present discussion does not prescribe such a strategy. However, it is usually possible to define a small set of behaviors that take precedence over other behaviors with respect to a specific research problem. Such a multivariate approach is facilitated by the availability of moderately priced videotape systems which produce permanent records of interactions. From these videotape records, detailed observations of several different behaviors might be scored at the researcher's convenience. Alternately, one or two judges can rate several behaviors in a live interaction, when such observations are appropriately scheduled. For example, I have used a tape-recorded cuing procedure that directs a rater's attention to different behaviors of one or more parties on a time-sampling procedure (Patterson, 1977). With enough replications, the observations from a single rater can provide a fairly stable picture of the pattern evolving from several behaviors of one or more people.

A particularly interesting consequence of monitoring several behaviors is the opportunity to examine sequential relationships among behaviors. Instead of merely describing the course of change in one behavior over time, a researcher might examine the sequential dependencies or probabilities among the behaviors of interest. Procedures such as path analysis (Heise, 1969) or one of the available probabilistic analyses (Bakeman & Dabbs, 1976) provide a framework for describing or testing specific sequential relationships among behaviors. The multivariate approach advocated here is more demanding, in terms of both the initial time demands and research expense, but it is clearly more comprehensive and, in the long run, probably a more economical way to conduct research.

A third trend, related to the first one, is the growing appreciation of diverse functions served by nonverbal behavior. That is, by attending more to the mediational processes affecting patterns of nonverbal behavior, researchers are forced to think in terms of the functions related to those processes. Analyzing and describing nonverbal behavior in terms of its functions may prove to be very useful for classifying patterns of nonverbal behavior. In fact, I would like to propose such a classification of the functions of nonverbal behavior as a framework for the discussion of personality differences. The functional organization presented here builds on other similar classification (e.g., Argyle, 1972), but also proposes a number of new distinctions.

Functions of Nonverbal Behavior

Providing Information

Perhaps the most basic function of nonverbal behavior might be broadly described as an informational one. From a receiver's or decoder's perspective, most of the actor's or encoder's behavior can be seen as potentially informative in some way. Specifically, the decoder might use a particular behavioral pattern to infer something about the encoder's characteristic disposition, his/her more fleeting reactions, or to specify the meaning of the verbal exchange.

Many researchers make a distinction between informative behavior that is *communicative* and that which is *indicative*. One perspective, that might be described as the holistic systems approach, defines communication as any verbal or nonverbal behavior occurring in the presence of another person (Watzlawick & Beavin, 1967). According to this orientation, communication, as a system, cannot be conveniently segmented into encoder and decoder elements. Focusing on one person in an interaction or on a limited number of behaviors does violence to the whole communication process by breaking down the basic interpersonal and multichannel relationships in that process. That is, in an interaction both parties are simultaneously engaged in behavior (communication), often at different levels. Consequently, designating one person as the encoder and one as the decoder, each only occasionally "communicating," misrepresents a complicated interdependent system.

A distinctly contrasting position holds that communication must be defined by the behavior of the sender or encoder in a particular exchange, independent of its particular meaning to the receiver or decoder. Specifically, there has to be evidence the sender is actually encoding some message, that the communicative behaviors are based on a common code, and that those communicative behaviors could be essentially substitutable for their corresponding verbal forms (Wiener, Devoe, Rubinow, & Geller, 1972). For example, if you were asked a difficult question for which you had no easy obvious answer, you might pause to search for the desired, but unavailable information, and simply say, "I don't know." Alternatively, you could similarly pause (indicating that you are attempting to encode an answer) and then shrug your shoulders while turning the hands outward in a palms-up direction. There is a generally understood code, at least in Western culture, that such a movement means "I don't know." Thus, the nonverbal movement is directly substitutable for the verbal message. However, such a restrictive classification for communication would result in relatively few behaviors being described as communicative. Of course, that does not mean that the vast majority of nonverbal behaviors falling outside of the communication category are unimportant in social exchange—merely that we should not designate them as communication.

A final perspective on communication focuses on the intention (Ekman & Friesen, 1969) or goal-directedness (McKay, 1972) of behavior in defining communication. This orientation, like the previous one, focuses on the activity of the encoder. Specifically, is there some intention or purpose underlying a particular behavior pattern? If the behavior is intentional, and there is at least some code for translating it, then that behavior should be classified as communicative. Behavior not grounded in some specific intention may still *indicate* a person's feelings or reactions, but from this perspective it would not be an attempt to *communicate* those feelings or reactions. Although an actor's intention is often difficult to assess, it is probably an evaluation commonly made by observers. My own belief is that a distinction based on intention or goal-directedness has considerable utility.

If one accepts this intention or goal directed criterion as the basis for identifying communicative behaviors, then some clear examples of indicative behavior can be given. In general, indicative behaviors would include those unintentional or non-goal-directed reactions related to some internal state or enduring disposition. Such reactions are generally more spontaneous and more likely to be out of awareness than are behaviors identified as communicative. Facial expression may be the most important behavioral component in indicative behavior. It is clear that facial expressiveness can, but does not always, reliably represent internal affective reactions to observers (Ekman & Friesen, 1975). Although this discussion, and, in fact, most of the research deals with facial expressiveness, other muscular and postural cues may be important. Further, it might be noted, on the receiving or decoding side, that general categories of facial expressiveness can be accurately identified by observers (Ekman, 1978). Among the emotion categories in which accuracy of identification is very high are happiness, sadness, surprise, anger, disgust, and fear. In fact, it appears that across cultures such emotional states are both similarly expressed or encoded and similarly interpreted or decoded (Ekman, 1978). Other expressive cues are also important in indicating something about an actor. For example, fidgeting, postural shifts, or scratching might indicate discomfort or anxiety.

A second aspect of indication concerns the effects that facial cues and other bodily movements have on informing the encoder of his/her own experience of emotion. Here there is considerable disagreement over the research evidence and its interpretation. On one side, some researchers (Laird, 1974; Leventhal, 1974) have resurrected and modified James's (1884/1968) view that emotional experience is the consequence of feedback from facial and bodily cues. That is, a person reacts expressively first, and that particular pattern of feedback resulting from these reactions "informs" the individual that he/she is happy, sad, or angry. Thus, the subjective experience of emotion develops from the bodily reaction. However, Buck's (1980) critical review of this research and Tourangeau and Ellsworth's (1979) recent data argue against a causal link between facial expressiveness and reported emotional states. It seems likely that changes in facial expression per se are not the primary determinants of the experience of emotion, but it is probably too early to discount their potential influence entirely.

Regulation of Interaction

A second function of nonverbal behavior relates to its role in the *regulation of interaction.* The behavioral framework for comfortable conversations appears to be determined substantially by the "standing features" (Argyle & Kendon, 1967) of an interaction, which include distance, body orientation, and posture. These behaviors usually remain relatively stable over the course of an interaction, but are important in setting potential limits for involvement in an interaction. Hall (1966, 1968) discusses some of the limitations that interpersonal distance, alone, places on social involvement with others. For example, within the zone that Hall describes as intimate (0-18 in.), tactile and olfactory cues may predominate while visual information is often distorted due to the very short focal distance. Within the close phase (0-6 in.) of intimate distance, activities such as love making, wrestling, comforting, or protecting are possible. As distance increases from the intimate zone through the personal zone (1.5-4 ft.) to the social-consultative zone (4-10 ft.), interactions become more formal and more dominated by visual information. At distances falling within the public zone (beyond 10 ft.), common casual interactions are infrequent. In the public zone, formal speeches or lectures are the typical form of social exchange.

Although the standing or fixed features of an interaction broadly set limits on the form of an exchange, other more subtle cues apparently regulate momentary conversational changes. For example, Duncan (1972) described six different speaker cues that were predictive of the listener's taking over the speaker's role: (1) a change in the pitch of the voice; (2) the termination of a gesture or relaxation of a tensed hand; (3) termination of a grammatical clause; (4) drawl on the final or stressed syllable of a terminal clause; (5) the occurrence of verbalizations such as "but uh," "or something," or "you know", and (6) decreased pitch or loudness in combination with the verbalizations in (5). In addition, Kendon (1967) had found that the likelihood of a smooth change in conversational turns was increased when the speaker ended his turn with an extended look at the listener, compared to the absence of such a gaze. In general, it appears that a listener directs more gaze toward a speaker than a speaker does toward a listener. Listener behavior may similarly affect the speaker's activity. For example, verbal reactions such as "mm-hmm," "uh huh", or "yeah," or nonverbal reactions such as nodding one's head or smiling signal listener agreement and/or willingness to let the speaker continue. Lack of an adequate reaction, e.g., failing to nod the head or smile, where it is appropriate can lead to disruptions in the speaker's turn or modification of the substance of the speaker's comment (Rosenfeld, 1978).

Expression of Intimacy

A third function of nonverbal behavior may be described as the expression of intimacy. The term "intimacy" was used by Argyle and Dean (1965) to describe the cumulative effect of behaviors such as distance, touch, eye contact, body lean, smiling, and verbal intimacy on the affective intensity of an interaction. Similar constructs include those of "proxemics" (Hall, 1963) and "immediacy" (Mehrabian, 1969). In general, common to all of these constructs is the assumption that increased intensity (usually positively valenced, e.g., liking or love) is manifested by closer approaches, increased touching, higher levels of gaze, forward lean, more frequent smiling, and more personal disclosure in conversations. Further, Argyle and Dean (1965) proposed that a comfortable or appropriate level of intimacy is definable in any given interaction. If that level of intimacy is disturbed by one or the other party in an interaction, behavioral adjustments will be initiated to return the intimacy to the appropriate level. For example, a too close approach by one person in an interaction may result in the other turning away and decreasing his/her gaze. Adjustments of this type that serve to restore the intimacy equilibrium have been described as *compensatory* reactions. However it is also clear that contrasting adjustments involving the *reciprocation* or enhancement of increased intimacy may also occur (Breed, 1972; Chapman, 1975; Jourard & Friedman, 1970; Whitcher & Fisher, 1979). For example, increased intimacy in the form of a close approach, smiling, or touch between lovers or good friends is often reciprocated in some fashion.

One theoretical explanation for these opposing patterns is developed in an arousal model of intimacy exchange (Patterson, 1976). Specifically, the model proposes that a sufficiently noticeable change in intimacy by one person in an interaction precipitates an arousal change in the other person. That arousal change becomes affectively experienced positively or negatively on the basis of situational cues (cf. Schachter & Singer, 1962), past experience, or other factors such as the relationship between the interactants. The valence of these feeling states, in turn, mediates the differential adjustments to the initial intimacy change. Negative feeling states such as fear or anxiety facilitate compensatory adjustments, whereas positive feeling states such as liking or love facilitate reciprocal adjustments. My own current judgment is that the mediating cognitive process proposed in the model may be focusing too heavily on the individual's attributions regarding his own feelings. Instead, these evaluative cognitions may be focused more on the intentions of the other person, or on the constraints of the situation. In either case, it is likely that the attribution process and related arousal change are common to different patterns of intimacy adjustment.

Social Control

A fourth function of nonverbal behavior might be described as social control. This function describes those situations in which one's behavior is managed in order to achieve a particular effect. It is difficult to address the question of awareness of one's behavioral management attempts for any given occurrence. It is clear that some management is consciously purposive, while at other times there may be little awareness of the function served by a behavioral routine. In the latter circumstances, the behavioral change may be the product of conditioning with no current awareness available to the individual. Perhaps the most insightful source for describing and analyzing the management of social behavior is the work of Erving Goffman (1959, 1967, 1972). Goffman analyzes social behavior in terms of performances or routines that are acted out in front of audiences. Because these audiences are often explicitly or implicitly concerned with evaluating the actor, the actor constructs or manages the performance to create a favorable impression. This might involve either simply exaggerating or intensifying a particular behavior pattern, or actually fabricating a front to mask a completely opposing underlying disposition. Verbal reactions, facial expression, postural changes, paralinguistic cues, and other behaviors may all contribute to a multidimensional performance.

Social control may also be manifested in the use of nonverbal behavior to establish or reinforce status differences. For example, touch is more likely to be initiated by a higher status person in an interaction. Henley (1973) observed that when age and social class were equated, males touched females more than females touched males. Henley's interpretation of this difference was that men are generally granted higher status than women in our society. Social control might also describe situations of attempted deception (Ekman & Friesen, 1974) or those involving persuasion (Mehrabian & Williams, 1969). Again, common to all these differing instances of social control is a managed presentation in contrast to the spontaneous response indicative of expressive release.

Task Service

The final category, a task-service function, identifies bases for nonverbal behavior which are essentially impersonal. That is, the particular patterns of nonverbal behavior do not reflect anything about a personal relationship. Heslin (1974) describes this type of function with respect to the use of touch. Examples of relationships in which touch is appropriate are those of physician-patient, golf professional-student, fireman-fire victim, and barber/hairdresser-customer (Heslin, 1974). Although close approaches, touch, or sustained gaze are common in these and some other professional relationships, such behavior is merely the means to an end of treating, teaching, or otherwise serving the needs of an individual. It should be noted that in such professional or service exchanges, the high involvement is often unidirectional, i.e., no analogous response is expected, or for that matter, even appropriate from the patient or customer. Such profession-service relationships are very interesting because they demonstrate the considerable influence that role and situational norms have on the initiation of nonverbal behavior. Other occasions of variable involvement may be required for the completion of some impersonal exchange, e.g., touching someone's hand in returning change. In addition, this category might include those adjustments necessary because of some sensory handicap, e.g., a person with a hearing loss may have to sit closer to others and try to gaze more directly at them in order to understand the conversation better.

It seems likely that the clarity of the expectancies about the professional-service relationships will affect one's comfort in such exchanges. The nonverbal intimacy in the form of touch or gaze from a stranger, which may be quite inappropriate and uncomfortable outside of the professional relationship, becomes tolerated, when the role expectancies are clarified. Of course, repeated instances of such intimate professional exchanges will often serve to both stabilize future expectancies and desensitize individuals to the initial discomfort.

Evaluation of a Functional Approach

There are several distinct issues that might be considered in evaluating the utility of a classification of functions. On the plus side, independent of the merits or weaknesses of this particular classification, a functional analysis pursues the issue of the reason for some particular behavior pattern and/or the purpose(s) which it serves. Even if the "Why?" question cannot be adequately answered, it is still likely to be asked. Discussions that are primarily descriptive do not provide an insight into questions of causality.

A second apparent advantage is that a functional analysis can engage a multivariate perspective in attempting to describe and understand patterns of nonverbal behavior. Such a holistic or integrating approach seems preferable to the common technique of arbitrarily discussing a single behavior in isolation.

A third advantage is that a taxonomy built on functions or purposes provides a framework for connecting information about patterns of nonverbal behavior across a variety of important psychological and social processes. For example, the intimacy function may be particularly relevant for attraction, liking or disliking, and impression formation, whereas the social control function is potentially related to various types of influence processes such as persuasion, social dominance, aggression, or leadership. Because a functional approach attempts to classify by focusing on the purposes of the relevant behaviors, rather than by discriminating on the basis of formal characteristics (e.g., type of behavior, characteristics of the interactants or setting), this approach has a substantive orientation rather than a structural one.

So much for the laudatory, self-serving comments in support of the functional approach. What are its disadvantages? First, it should be noted that inferences about functions are often shaky and based on minimal evidence. Even if we are able to inquire about the intentions or purposes of actors, they may not themselves be aware of them or may be biased in their reports. Fortunately, if a pattern of nonverbal behavior is consistent, over time within actors or across different actors, we can often make a prudent evaluation of the functional significance of the behavioral pattern. This is basically the technique that Goffman and Hall use in classifying and analyzing social behavior.

A second limitation of this particular functional approach is that there is no common a priori set of characteristics underlying the classification judgment. Awareness and intentionality may be important in distinguishing between the informational function and in identifying social control, but such concerns are less critical for the remaining functions. Some distinctions might be proposed on the basis of scope or duration of the relevant behaviors. Many behaviors serving informational or interaction regulating functions could be described as molecular units, e.g., isolated gestures, a specific facial expression, or a head nod. In contrast, intimacy, social control, and task-service functions may be represented by molar units or patterns, e.g., sitting close, sustaining gaze over a period of time, or in holding another person's hand.

A third concern, related to the second, is that most behavioral sequences serve more than one function. A given behavioral pattern cannot only serve different functions at different points in time, but that pattern can serve multiple functions at the same time. For example, a particular behavioral performance such as an angry stare initiated by a superior toward a subordinate may be communicative but it may also be a means of exerting social control. Serving multiple functions is not necessarily a negative characteristic, especially if it reflects reality, but it is, at least, a complicating one.

Of course, other classifications of functions of nonverbal behavior may be less vulnerable to the concerns expressed here, while still possessing the advantages described. Futher, even if the present classification proves useful, it is likely to require revision as more research on the functions of nonverbal behavior accumulates.

Nonverbal Involvement and Functional Classification

Up to this point I have discussed my view of some trends in research and have outlined a functional framework for analyzing nonverbal behavior. In doing so, I have offered a number of examples of different types of nonverbal behavior, but I have avoided trying to define or limit the network of nonverbal behavior appropriate to this discussion. Before initiating a discussion of personality, it is appropriate to limit the focus of this analysis to a group of behaviors which might be described as involvement behaviors, behaviors that define the degree of involvement manifested between individuals in a social setting. Many nonverbal behaviors have a potential for signifying or affecting a relationship, whether individuals are interacting or merely sharing a common presence, i.e., the focused versus unfocused categories of interaction (Goffman, 1963). Within this group of involvement behaviors, I would include interpersonal distance, gaze, touch, body orientation, lean, facial expressiveness, talking duration, interruptions, postural openness, relational gestures, head nods, and paralinguistic cues. In general, increased in the intensity or frequency of these various behaviors signal greater involvement with others in a social setting. Does this leave anything for a noninvolvement category? Well, it does but the list is somewhat more restrictive. For example, most leg and foot movements, grooming behaviors, self-manipulations (scratching, fiddling with one's keys or rings), nonrelational gestures (pointing, emblematic movements) most postural adjustments, and artifactual clues (clothing, glasses) should typically fall outside the involvement category.

In general, the involvement behaviors can be seen as having relatively direct potential for influencing the interaction process, whereas such influence potential is distinctly less for noninvolvement behaviors. I want to be clear in emphasizing that noninvolvement behaviors can carry considerable meaning in a social setting, especially to an astute observer. However, they are typically less important for the interactional process than are the involvement behaviors.

It is important to note that the involvement classification is essentially independent of the functional categories proposed earlier. This approach to defining a focal set of behaviors avoids the trap of identifying the behaviors in terms of their possible function in a given situation. Unfortunately, I have contributed to that very problem in my own recent work on intimacy exchange. Following the tradition established by Argyle and Dean (1965), I have referred to behaviors such as distance, gaze, touch, lean, and smiling as intimacy behaviors or intimacy cues (Patterson, 1976, 1978). Although these dimensions are identified as intimacy behaviors, it is readily admitted that such behaviors can serve other functions (Argyle & Dean, 1965; Patterson, 1976). Such conceptual confusion might be avoided by the kind of distinction proposed here. That is, separate the identification of a set of socially relevant behaviors from the possible functions served by them. The role of these functions and their relationship to the process of nonverbal exchange is discussed in detail in a recent theoretical paper (Patterson, 1981).

A personality orientation toward describing and analyzing social behavior involves an emphasis on type, characteristic, or trait differences among individuals. That is, according to a personality perspective, individual differences in social behavior may be ascribed to predisposing, stable differences in personality. Some caution is appropriate in appreciating that personality per se cannot invariably predict behavior, but the opposing orientation advocating situationism–situations, not personality, determine behavior (Mischel, 1968)—is also open to criticism. A compromise between the two extremes seems to offer a more defensible, representative orientation. That compromise perspective might be described as an interactionist orientation of personality and situational determinants (Endler & Magnusson, 1976). The direct effect of situations and the interactive effect of situation × personality must be recognized. However, in reflecting the prominent position of the personality orientation in research on nonverbal social behavior, the current focus will be limited primarily to an analysis of personality correlates of nonverbal involvement. Nevertheless, there will be occasions in which generalizations about personality will have to be qualified by role and situational constraints.

Personality Correlates of Nonverbal Involvement

It should not be surprising that a great deal of research on nonverbal involvement has been initiated from a personality orientation. Even the layperson's use of various personality descriptors provides ample opportunity for inferences about involvement behaviors. For example, it is easy to visualize the "pushy" acquaintance as standing too close, talking too much, occasionally interrupting, and possibly initiating unwarranted touch. In contrast, the shy or reserved person might be expected to remain aloof (physically distant), initiate little gaze, and talk infrequently.

Before discussing the specific relationships between personality characteristics and nonverbal behavior, it may be useful to examine the intraindividual stability of the involvement behaviors. If patterns of nonverbal behavior can be related to specific personality characteristics, detecting such relationships would seem possible only to the extent that the relevant behaviors manifest temporal stability. In other words, we are likely to find relationships between personality and the involvement behaviors only when there is consistency in the way people use nonverbal behaviors. Fortunately, this consistency does seem to be the rule, at least for those behaviors on which we have such information. In two separate studies examining the stability of approach distances in interview settings, the correlations between the first and second approaches were approximately $r = .90$ (Daniell & Lewis, 1972; Patterson, 1973). The stability of approach distances was manifested for intervals from 20 minutes to 2 weeks with the same interviewer. When different interviewers were employed, the stability coefficients still averaged approximately $r = .80$ (Daniell

& Lewis, 1972). Data on gazing behaviors also indicate high levels of stability, both within a given interaction (Kendon & Cook, 1969; Libby, 1970) and across interactions (Daniell & Lewis, 1972; Patterson, 1973). Finally, there is evidence that the degree of forward lean and body orientation in seated interactions is relatively stable over time (Patterson, 1973). These findings on intraindividual stability over time indicate that people apparently do use at least some of their involvement behaviors in a consistent manner over time. This does not mean, however, that situational influences such as the type of setting or activity or varying role relationships will not modify a common pattern of nonverbal involvement.

Because people do seem to manifest stability on nonverbal involvement over time, it is appropriate to examine the predictive utility of personality with respect to nonverbal involvement. First, the rather extreme and pervasive differences between groups of people will be examined as predictors of nonverbal involvement. Included here would be comparisons between abnormal or deviant groups and normal groups. The remaining coverage will focus on more limited and specific comparisons within a normal range of personality differences.

Normal-Abnormal Differences

There is considerable evidence that psychiatric patients, particularly those diagnosed as schizophrenic or depressive, generally show less social involvement with others than do normal subjects. Noninvolvement or even avoidance among psychiatric patients is manifested by larger interpersonal distances (Horowitz, Duff, & Stratton, 1964; Sommer, 1959), nonconfronting body orientations (Sommer, 1959), and distinctly lower levels of gaze directed at others (Rutter & Stephenson, 1972; Waxer, 1974). The dynamics underlying these differences were examined in a study by Williams (1974) on gaze patterns between normals and schizophrenic patients. Williams sought to determine if the lower level of gaze initiated by such patients was a part of general pattern of avoidance of a wide range of environmental stimuli or was specific to the avoidance of people only. The study involved observing gaze patterns in schizophrenic and control subjects in a waiting room. The control subjects were a mix of nonschizophrenic patients and a small number of hospital employees. The salient gaze targets were either a television program or the confederate. The proportions of television watching and occasional confederate-directed glances were comparable across the two groups of subjects during the first part of the waiting period when the confederate was silent. However, once the confederate tried to initiate a conversation about impersonal, innocuous topics, substantial differences appeared in the gaze patterns of the schizophrenic and control subjects. While confederate-directed gaze increased in both groups, the increase for the controls was noticeably greater. Conversely, the decrease in television watching in response to the confederate's comments was much less for the schizophrenic subjects. These findings are obviously consistent with the suggestion that the schizophrenic's gaze aversion is specific to other people and not indicative of a broader stimulus avoidance pattern.

More recent work by Rutter (1976, 1977, 1978) suggests that the duration and timing of gaze by schizophrenics is really comparable to that of normals. Speifically, Rutter suggests that gaze avoidance may be more a product of focusing conversations on their problems, which are personally embarrassing, than of stable individual styles. Thus, the schizophrenics may be acting just as normals would if the normals had to discuss personally embarrassing issues. This interpretation does not seem to explain the differences found in the Williams (1974) study, but it may identify a potential confound occasionally present when comparing the behavior of normal and schizophrenic subjects, i.e., the degree of potential embarrassment in typical conversations between the two groups.

Interpersonal avoidance behaviors may also be typical of a very different kind of group–violent and aggressive individuals. In separate studies, two with adult male prisoners (Kinzel, 1970; Roger & Schalekamp, 1976) and another with underachieving male adolescents (Newman & Pollack, 1973), larger approach distances were found for the aggressive than the nonaggressive subgroups. The differences were particularly striking in Kinzel's study with prisoners. In that study, the male experimenter sequentially approached each prisoner from eight different directions until the subject told him to stop. The average area required by the aggressive prisoners was over 4 times that required by the nonaggressive prisoners. This difference was clearly not just the product of some casual preference. Kinzel reported that several of the violent prisoners reported perceiving the experimenter "rushing" or "looming" at them as he walked closer. Others clenched their fists, experienced goose pimples, or had to turn around to view the experimenter when he appoached from behind. The violent group was also characterized by disproportionately larger rear buffer zones. Kinzel interpreted the larger approach distances from behind as being a product of concern about homosexual attack, expecially given this realistic fear in the prison context. However, a more general explanation may be that anyone who is habitually violent may have a good reason, in terms of self-defense, to fear others who approach from behind. The results from the Roger and Schalekamp (1976) study, conducted on black South African prisoners, also showed large differences between violent and nonviolent prisoners. In that study the total area required was 2-4 times as great as the Kinzel experiment. However, the rear buffer zones were not disproportionately larger, as they were in the Kinzel study.

How can these contrasting patterns between normal and abnormal populations be evaluated in functional terms? At the risk of some oversimplification it might be suggested that the relatively lower levels of involvement manifested in the abnormal populations might reflect the combined influence of the social control and intimacy functions. For the psychiatric groups, such as schizophrenics and depressives, social withdrawal is a common element in their clinical descriptions (Rutter & Stephenson, 1972). If Rutter's (1978) suggestion that psychiatric patients' patterns of social avoidance are simply the product of reasonable embarrassment about their problems, then their decreased spatial and visual involvement may be seen as means of managing and controlling the potential embarrassment. In terms of intimacy regulation, the decreased nonverbal involvement may be seen as a means of compensating for the high intimacy produced by talking about personal problems. For the aggressive groups, the strong preference for increased distancing can similarly be viewed as an attempt to control their social environment. In this case the motive would probably be one of self-protection. It is reasonable to assume that aggressive or violent individuals might develop greater sensitivity to close approaches, especially when such approaches occasionally result in violent exchanges. In addition, it is possible that, for whatever reason, aggressive individuals differ initially from normals in having much less tolerance for common levels of interpersonal involvement. If that were the case, frequent violation of that preferred involvement may be stressful and precipitate aggressive reactions. Thus, it is possible that a preference for minimal social involvement is a contributing cause, rather than an effect of aggressive tendencies.

Differences within Normal Populations

The remaining discussion focuses on the influence of more limited personality differences within normal populations. I will give primary emphasis to those personality dimensions that demonstrate convergence across several involvment behaviors and that are grounded in a definable theoretical framework. Thus, I will *not* attempt a comprehensive review of all of the studies linking some personality dimension to one or more involvement behaviors.

Social approach-avoidance. At least one group of personality characteristics, including the dimensions of affiliation, introversion-extraversion, and social anxiety, seems to offer some hope for predicting nonverbal involvement. Although these three dimensions are nominally distinct, there is empirical evidence that they are highly related. Specifically, a factor analytic study of these dimensions showed that a majority of items from scales of affiliation, introversion-extraversion, and social anxiety loaded on a common social approach-avoidance factor (Patterson & Strauss, 1972). Consequently, the discrete findings described below may reflect a pattern relating a more general social approach-avoidance dimension to nonverbal involvement.

Individuals scoring higher on affiliation scales apparently prefer closer seating arrangements than do low scorers (Clore, 1969; Mehrabian & Diamond, 1971). In addition, there is also some evidence that high affiliative females look more at others (Exline, 1963), although Ellsworth and Ludwig (1972) suggest that such an effect may depend on the subject's expectations of approval. The relationship between nonverbal involvement and extraversion parallels that described of affiliation. Specifically, extraverts choose closer seating distances than introverts (Cook, 1970; Patterson & Holmes, 1966; Pedersen, 1973) and engage in higher levels of eye contact (Kendon & Cook, 1969; Mobbs, 1968). In summarizing the research on vocal cues and personality, Siegman (1978) reported that extraversion has been consistently related to a louder speaking voice and a faster tempo of speech. Also, extraversion is correlated with a high amount of speaking (Campbell & Rushton, 1978). In a similar manner, increased levels of social anxiety have been marginally related to more distant approaches (Patterson, 1973, 1977b) and to decreased talking and gaze (Daly, 1978) in interview settings. Although much of the evidence relating these three personality dimensions to nonverbal involvement indicates only weak to moderate relationships, the convergence among these dimensions suggests a more common underlying pattern.

There are, of course, numerous other possibilities for examining personality correlates of nonverbal involvement. In general, much of the research on personality correlates has shown either relatively weak relationships to nonverbal behavior or relationships that cannot be replicated. Another limitation of much of the personality research is the lack of a solid theoretical framework for interpreting the relationships that are found. The remaining dimensions considered here are those which develop out of theoretical frameworks and have relevance for a variety of involvement behaviors.

Internal-external locus of control. Rotter (1966) drew a contrast between internals, individuals who perceive themselves as generally being subject to forces outside of themselves. Duke and Nowicki (1972) applied this personality dimension to the regulation of interpersonal distance. The basic assumption of the Duke and Nowicki model is that the combined effect of internal-external control and situational expectancies influences the degree of preferred closeness to others. Specifically, internals and externals are predicted to act similarly in situations in which clear expectancies are present for the reactions of others, e.g., interacting with friends or relatives. However, in settings for which specific expectancies are not available (e.g., interacting with strangers) externals will be more reserved and distant than internals. In extending Duke and Nowicki's model to other behaviors, a general prediction can be offered that externals, compared to internals, will prefer lower levels of involvement because of the lack of control they feel when interacting with strangers. Results from two studies reported by Duke and Nowicki (1972) supported these predicted differences in distancing by internals and externals. One recent study reports results directly contrasting those of Duke and Nowicki. In that study, externals talked more and looked at one another more than internals (Rajecki, Ickes, & Tanford, 1981). A higher level of nonverbal involvement by internals in uncertain situations was also reported in a study of leadership seating choices. Specifically, internal control subjects were more likely to choose leadership seating positions than external control subjects (Hiers & Heckel, 1977). In another study, internal control subjects found the same group setting less crowded than did external control subjects (Schopler & Walton, 1975). Finally, there is evidence that internal locus of control subjects are more assertive in the manner (paralinguistic level) than in the context (verbal level) of their conversations, whereas the opposite pattern holds for external locus of control subjects (Bugenthal, Henker, & Whalen, 1976). Because the paralinguistic channel may be more influential in transmitting one's intention or motivation than the verbal channel, internals may be more effective in managing assertiveness or power.

As the situational or role expectancies become more structured, a generalized locus of control expectancy should have less impact on the initiation of nonverbal involvement. In other words, the interaction of locus of control and role expectancies may better predict nonverbal involvement than either dimension in isolation.

Field dependence. The dimension of field dependence is one which has substantial relevance for a wide variety of social behaviors. The field dependence-independence dimension contrasts individuals whose cognitive styles reflect reliance either on external referents (field dependent) or on internal referents (field independent). Another way of describing this contrast is in terms of the field-independent person's clear differentiation of his/her own self from others versus the field-dependent person's less differentiated self-other distinction. In terms of social behavior, this dimension implies greater automomy in social relations for the field-independent person, and a greater reliance on others for the field-dependent person (Witkin & Goodenough, 1977).

Given these general differences we might expect that field-dependent persons would prefer greater involvement with others than field-independent persons. In fact, three different unpublished dissertations cited by Witkin and Goodenough (1977) showed such a contrast in the subjects' use of interpersonal distance. In two studies, field-dependent subjects stood closer to the person with whom they interacted than did field independent subjects (Holley, 1972; Justice, 1969). In the third study, field-dependent subjects emitted more dependency behaviors such as palms-up gesturing, lip and tongue activity, and mouth touching when seated at 5 ft. than at 2 ft. (Green, 1973). In contrast, field-independent subjects did not increase their use of the dependency behaviors at the greater distance.

Gazing behavior also shows increased reliance on others by field-dependent people. Some findings showing that field-dependent subjects look at others more than field-independent subjects, apparently for informational purposes (Konstadt & Forman, 1965; Nevill, 1974). However, Kendon and Cook (1969) found that field-independent subjects looked more at the other while speaking than did field-dependent subjects. It might be that the salience of field dependence-independence for gazing behaviors is qualified by the ambiguity of either the situation or the other's reaction. Specifically, as that ambiguity increases the field-dependent person's reliance on others for social comparison information similarly increases, whereas the field-independent person's behavior remains unaffected.

A final interesting result related the degree of facial expressiveness to field dependence-independence. Field-dependent subjects were found to be less expressive than field-independent subjects (Shennum, 1976). The author speculated that field-dependent persons are more likely to be the products of settings where strict adherence to family and social authority is stressed, while the field independents are more likely to come from settings calling for autonomous functioning. Further, those parents who stress authority and conformity may be more likely to restrict expressiveness, whereas such demands may be less frequent in the field-independent's family. Whatever the dynamics, this result appears to be inconsistent with the studies on distance and gaze which show greater involvement for the field-dependent subjects. However, if field dependents are engaged in monitoring others' behavior, they may be less expressive facially with their own behavior. In addition, in this study, expressiveness was monitored in reaction to the presentation of pictorial stimuli, i.e., expressiveness was not assessed in an interpersonal context. Consequently, this result may not be as germane for involvement as the earlier studies were.

Self-monitoring. A final dimension, self-monitoring, was introduced by Snyder (1974) in an attempt to assess the degree to which individuals manage their behavior for both effective self-presentation and adjustment to others in social settings.

More specifically, those scoring high on self-monitoring should endorse items reflecting concern with the social appropriateness of their self-presentation, sensitivity to changing situational cues, and an ability to modify self-presentations to fit differing purposes. Such a dimension should have considerable relevance for managing one's level of nonverbal involvement. In fact, Lippa (1976) found that high self-monitoring subjects were generally better able to control their expressive behavior by facilitating the expression of more desirable characteristics (e.g., introversion-extraversion or masculinity-femininity), while inhibiting the expression of less desirable characteristics (e.g., anxiety). In dyadic interactions, self-monitoring was also found to affect interaction styles (Ickes & Barnes, 1977). In particular, high self-monitoring, compared to low self-monitoring, subjects were more likely to talk first, intitate later conversational sequences, feel more self-conscious about their behavior, and use their partner's behavior as a guide for their own actions.

The description of the self-monitoring dimension and the results just cited do not suggest a simple relationship between self-monitoring and nonverbal involvement. Rather, an increased level of self-monitoring should be related to both an increased awareness to social cues and an ability to manage one's nonverbal involvement. The high self-monitoring individual's concern with social appropriateness may result in high levels of nonverbal involvement in one setting and low levels in another. Finally, although self-monitoring may offer considerable promise for identifying individual style differences in social interaction, a recent factor analytic study of the self-monitoring scale suggests that the scale is not unidimensional (Gabrenya & Arkin, 1980). It is interesting to note that one, and possibly two, of the factors identified by Gabrenya and Arkin appear to be comparable to the social approach-avoidance dimension discussed earlier.

Functional Analysis of Normal Personality Differences

The selective review of normal personality influences focused on four personality dimensions as promising predictors of nonverbal involvement: (1) social approach-avoidance, (2) internal-external locus of control, (3) field dependence-independence, and (4) self-monitoring. This section discusses each dimension in terms of the functional analysis presented earlier.

The social approach-avoidance dimension, as described in this chapter, seems to encompass the related dimensions of introversion-extraversion, social anxiety, and affiliation. In general, there is a consistent preference of approach types (extraverted, high affiliative, low socially anxious) for closer approaches, increased gaze, and increased talking in social interactions as contrasted with the opposite pattern for avoidance types (introverted, low affiliative, high socially anxious). Perhaps the strongest functional basis related to these contrasts between social approach and social avoidant types is the management of intimacy exchange. It is possible that these contrasting patterns of nonverbal involvement may be linked to arousal level differences which Eysenck (1967) describes as typical of introverts and extraverts. Specifically, introverts, or the social avoidant types in this classification, are generally more easily aroused by a variety of stimulus situations than are extroverts or social approach types. In terms of social settings, Eysenck (1967) suggests that the introvert's decreased interest in stimulating social activities may serve to maintain arousal at more comfortable levels. In contrast, to attain an optimal arousal level, extraverts may have to seek out increased social stimulation. If such contrasting interactive strategies are representative of social approach and social avoidant individuals, then their application to patterns of nonverbal involvement is a direct one. Because increased nonverbal involvement has been related to increased arousal (Patterson, 1976), the lesser involvement of social avoidant types and greater involvement of social approach types may similarly serve to maintain arousal at optimal levels.

Although the internal-external locus of control and self-monitoring dimensions are theoretically independent, their influence on nonverbal involvement might be analyzed in terms of a similar function—social control. With respect to the locus of control dimension, Duke and Nowicki's (1972) theorizing is based on the importance of expectancies in mediating distancing preferences. When specific expectancies about distancing, or more generally nonverbal involvement, are not available, then the individual's own generalized expectancy relative to locus of control may predominate. In the case of externals, who perceive themselves as having less control over their life circumstances than internals, greater separation from strangers is preferred. Thus, when the focal concern is the management of an appropriate degree of involvement with strangers, externals seem to prefer lessened involvement than internals. This contrast may be the joint product of different elements of social control operating for internals and externals. For internals greater involvement may facilitate their controlling or influencing others more easily. For externals, decreased involvement may be a defensive tactic designed to lessen their vulnerability to control by strangers. When the setting is less clearly social in nature or extremely ambiguous, the involvement patterns just described might even be reversed. This may account for the Rajecki et al.'s (1981) findings that externals looked at one another more and talked more than internals did in an ambiguous social situation. Thus, when greater structure or information is required in a social setting, externals may be motivated by the informational function to initiate greater involvement than internals. Although this last point is quite speculative, it might be expected that the different functionally based motives of internals and externals, elicited by different types of activities, could lead to more variable patterns of nonverbal involvement.

Although the persuasion, power, or more direct influence aspects of social control may be most relevant for internal-external control, the self-presentation component of social control may be closely related to self-monitoring. In fact, Snyder's (1974) own description of that dimension emphasizes the high self-monitoring individual's concern with self-presentation. This may frequently result in the high self-monitoring person demonstrating greater nonverbal involvement in social settings (e.g., Ickes & Barnes, 1977). In addition, increased nonverbal involvement by those scoring highly on self-monitoring may relate to an increased awareness of or ability to control their expressive behavior. Thus, for high self-monitoring people, the informational function may be served by increased nonverbal involvement.

Finally, the contrasting patterns apparent between the field dependent and field independent individuals suggests that the influence of intimacy and informational functions may be primary. If one attends to explicitly social activities, then the preference for increased nonverbal involvement by field dependents may be most parsimoniously viewed in terms of the intimacy function. That is, in general, field dependents have a stronger interpersonal orientation and are more interested in relating to others than are field independents (Witkin & Goodenough, 1977). In settings that are less social in nature, such as work or recreational activities having a specific task focus, field dependents are likely to seek greater involvement with others for informational reasons. That is, the resulting social comparison motive in field dependents may elicit greater nonverbal involvement.

Summary

This chapter started with a discussion of developing trends in research on nonverbal social behavior. One of those trends—the analysis of functions served by nonverbal behavior-provided an organizing theme for the chapter. The classification of functions of nonverbal behavior proposed here provides a structure within which personality differences may be analyzed. Specifically, personality differences in nonverbal involvement were examined with respect to the functions of (1) providing information, (2) regulating interaction, (3) expressing intimacy, (4) social control, and (5) meeting task-service requirements. Besides the clear contrast between normal and psychiatric groups, the personality dimensions of (1) social approach-avoidance, (2) internal-external locus of control, (3) field dependence-independence, and (4) self-monitoring seemed to offer the greatest promise of predicting differences in nonverbal involvement. The functions judged to be of most importance in explaining these personality differences were those of expressing intimacy and social control.

There are clearly different functional classifications one might propose for analyzing nonverbal behaviors relevant for social interaction. For the researcher interested in personality and nonverbal behavior this perspective may be particularly useful. Specifically, an examination of the salience of different nonverbal involvement functions for distinct personality types may provide a promising direction for future research.

Acknowledgment. Preparation of this chapter was supported by a National Institutes of Health Grant USPH 5 RO1 MH 32386-02 awarded to the author.

References

Argyle, M. Non-verbal communication in human social interaction. In R. A. Hinde (Ed.), *Non-verbal communication.* Cambridge: Cambridge University Press, 1972.

Argyle, M., & Dean, J. Eye-contact, distance, and affiliation. *Sociometry*, 1965, *28*, 289-304.

Argyle, M., & Kendon, A. The experimental analysis of social performance. In L. Berkowitz (Ed.), *Advances in experimental social psychology* (Vol. 3). New York: Academic Press, 1967.

Bakeman, R., & Dabbs, J. M., Jr. Social interaction observed: Some approaches to the analyses of behavior streams. *Personality and Social Psychology*, 1976, *4*, 335-345.

Barker, R. G. *Ecological psychology: Concepts and methods for studying the environment of human behavior.* Stanford, Calif.: Stanford University Press, 1968

Birdwhistell, R. L. *Kinesics and context.* Philadelphia: University of Pennsylvania Press, 1970.

Breed, G. The effect of intimacy: Reciprocity or retreat? *British Journal of Social and Clinical Psychology*, 1972, *11*, 135-142.

Buck, R. Nonverbal behavior and the theory of emotion: The facial feedback hypothesis. *Journal of Personality and Social Psychology*, 1980, *38*, 811-824.

Bugenthal, D. B., Henker, B., & Whalen, C. K. Attributional antecedents of verbal and vocal assertiveness. *Journal of Personality and Social Psychology*, 1976, *34*, 405-411.

Campbell, A., & Rushton, F. P. Bodily communication and personality. *British Journal of Social and Clinical Psychology*, 1978, *17*, 31-36.

Chapman, A. J. Eye contact, physical proximity and laughter: A re-examination of the equilibrium model of social intimacy. *Social Behavior and Personality*, 1975, *3*, 143-155.

Clore, G. Attraction and interpersonal behavior. Paper presented at the annual meeting of the Southwestern Psychological Association, Austin, 1969.

Cook, M. Experiments of orientation and proxemics. *Human Relations*, 1970, *23*, 61-76.

Daly, S. Behavioral correlates of social anxiety. *British Journal of Social and Clinical Psychology*, 1978, *17*, 117-120.

Daniell, R. F., & Lewis, P. Stability of eye contact and physical distance across a series of structure interviews. *Journal of Consulting and Clinical Psychology*, 1972, *39*, 172.

Duke, M. P., & Nowicki, S. A new measure and social-learning model for interpersonal distance. *Journal of Experimental Research in Personality*, 1972, *6*, 119-132.

Duncan, S., Jr. Some signals and rules for taking speaking turns in conversations. *Journal of Personality and Social Psychology*, 1972, *23*, 283-292.

Ekman, P. Facial expression. In A. W. Siegman & S. Feldstein (Eds.), *Nonverbal behavior and communication.* Hillsdale, N.J.: Erlbaum, 1978.

Ekman, P., & Friesen, W. V. The repertoire of nonverbal behavior: Categories, origins, usage and codings. *Semiotica*, 1969, *1*, 49-97.

Ekman, P., & Friesen, W. V. Detecting deception from the body or face. *Journal of Personality and Social Psychology*, 1974, *29*, 288-298.

Ekman, P., & Friesen, W. V. *Unmasking the face.* Englewood Cliffs, N.J. Prentice-Hall, 1975.

Ellsworth, P. C., & Langer, E. J. Staring and approach: An interpretation of the stare as a nonspecific activator. *Journal of Personality and Social Psychology,* 1976, *33* 117-122.

Ellsworth, P. C., & Ludwig, L. M. Visual behavior in social interaction. *Journal of Communication,* 1972, *4*, 375-403.

Endler, N. S., & Magnusson, D. Toward an interactional psychology of personality. *Psychological Bulletin,* 1976, *83*, 956-974.

Exline, R. V. Explorations in the process of person perception: Visual interaction in relation to competition, sex, and need for affiliation. *Journal of Personality,* 1963, *31*, 1-20.

Eysenck, H. J. *The biological basis of personality.* Springfield, Ill.: Charles C Thomas, 1967.

Felipe, N. J., & Sommer, R. Invasion of personal space. *Social Problems,* 1966, *14*, 206-214.

Fisher, J. D., & Byrne, D. Too close for comfort: Sex differences in response to invasions of personal space. *Journal of Personality and Social Psychology,* 1975, *32*, 15-21.

Gabrenya, W. K., Jr., & Arkin, R. M. Self-monitoring scale: Factor structure and correlates. *Personality and Social Psychology Bulletin,* 1980, *6*, 13-22.

Goffman, E. *The presentation of self in everyday life.* Garden City, N.Y.: Anchor, 1959.

Goffman, E. *Encounters.* New York: Bobbs-Merrill, 1961.

Goffman, E. *Behavior in public places.* New York: Free Press, 1963.

Goffman, E. *Interaction ritual.* Garden City, N.Y.: Anchor, 1967.

Goffman, E. *Relations in public.* New York: Harper Colophon, 1972.

Gonos, G. "Situation" versus "frame": The "interactionist" and the "structuralist" analysis of everyday life. *American Sociological Review,* 1977, *42*, 854-867.

Green, L. R. Effects of field independence, physical proximity and evaluative feedback on affective reactions and compliance in dyadic interaction (Doctoral dissertation, Yale University, 1973). *Dissertation Abstracts International,* 1973, *34*, 2284B-2285B. (University Microfilms No. 73-26, 285)

Hall, E. T. A system for the notation of proxemic behavior. *American Anthropologist,* 1963, *65*, 1003-1026.

Hall, E. T. *The hidden dimension.* New York: Doubleday, 1966.

Hall, E. T. Proxemics. *Current Anthropology,* 1968, *9*, 83-108.

Heise, D. R. Problems in path analysis and causal inference. In E. F. Borgatta (Ed.), *Sociological methodology.* San Francisco: Jossey-Bass, 1969.

Henley, N. M. Status and sex: Some touching observations: *Bulletin of the Psychonomic Society,* 1973, *2*, 91-93.

Heslin, R. *Steps toward a taxonomy of touching.* Paper presented at the annual meeting of the Midwestern Psychological Association, Chicago, May 1974.

Hiers, J. M., & Heckel, R. V. Seating choice, leadership, and locus of control. *Journal of Social Psychology,* 1977, *103*, 313-314.

Holley, M. Field-dependence-independence, sophistication-of-body-concept, and social distance selection (Doctoral dissertation, New York University, 1972).

Dissertation Abstracts International, 1972, *33,* 296B. (University Microfilms, No. 72-20, 635)

Horowitz, M. J., Duff, D. F., & Stratton, L. O. Body-buffer zone. *Archives of General Psychiatry,* 1964, *11,* 651-656.

Ickes, W., & Barnes, R. D. The role of sex and self-monitoring in unstructured dyadic settings. *Journal of Personality and Social Psychology,* 1977, *35,* 315-330.

James, W. What is an emotion? In M. Arnold (Ed.), *The nature of emotion,* Baltimore, Md.: Penguin, 1968. (Originally published, 1884.)

Jourard, S. M., & Friedman, R. Experimenter-subject "distance" and self-disclosure. *Journal of Personality and Social Psychology,* 1970, *15,* 278-282.

Justice, M. T. Field dependency, intimacy of topic and interperson distance (Doctoral dissertation, University of Florida, 1969). *Dissertation Abstracts International,* 1970, *31,* 395B-396B. (University Microfilms No. 70-12, 243)

Kendon, A. Some functions of gaze direction in social interaction. *Acta Psychologica,* 1967, *26,* 22-63.

Kendon, A., & Cook, M. The consistency of gaze patterns in social interaction. *British Journal of Psychology,* 1969, *60,* 481-494.

Kinzel, A. Body-buffer zone in violent prisoners. *American Journal of Psychiatry,* 1970, *127,* 57-64.

Konstadt, N., & Forman, E. Field dependence and external directedness. *Journal of Personality and Social Psychology,* 1965, *1,* 490-493.

Laird, J. D. Self attribution of emotion: The effects of expressive behavior on the quality of emotional experience. *Journal of Personality and Social Psychology,* 1974, *29,* 475-486.

Leventhal, H. Emotions: A basic problem for social psychology, In C. Nemeth (Ed.), *Social psychology: Classic and contemporary integrations.* Chicago: Rand McNally, 1974.

Libby, W. L. Eye contact and direction of looking as stable individual differences. *Journal of Experimental Research in Personality,* 1970, *4,* 303-312.

Lippa, R. Expressive control and the leakage of dispositional introversion-extraversion during role-played teaching. *Journal of Personality,* 1976, *44,* 541-559.

McKay, D. M. Formal analysis of communicative processes. In R. A. Hinde (Ed.), *Non-verbal communication.* Cambridge: Cambridge University Press, 1972.

Mehrabian, A. Some referents and measures of nonverbal behavior. *Behavior Research Methods and Instrumentation,* 1969, *1,* 203-207.

Mehrabian, A. *Nonverbal communication.* Chicago: Aldine-Atherton, 1972.

Mehrabian, A., & Diamond, S. G. Seating arrangement and conversation. *Sociometry,* 1971, *34,* 281-289.

Mehrabian, A., & Williams, M. Nonverbal concomitants of perceived and intended persuasiveness. *Journal of Personality and Social Psychology,* 1969, *13,* 37-58.

Middlemist, R. D., Knowles, E. S., & Matter, C. F. Personal space invasion in the lavatory: Suggestive evidence for arousal. *Journal of Personality and Social Psychology,* 1976, *33,* 541-546.

Mischel, W. *Personality and assessment.* New York: Wiley, 1968.

Mobbs, N. A. Eye contact in relation to social introversion-extraversion. *British Journal of Social Clinical Psychology,* 1968, 7, 305-306.

Nevill, D. Experimental manipulation of dependency motivation and its effects on eye contact and measures of field dependency. *Journal of Personality and Social Psychology,* 1974, *29*, 72-79.

Newnam, R. C., & Pollack, D. Proxemics in deviant adolescents. *Journal of Consulting and Clinical Psychology,* 1973, *40*, 6-8.

Patterson, M. L. Stability of nonverbal immediacy behaviors. *Journal of Experimental Social Psychology,* 1973, *9*, 97-109.

Patterson, M. L. An arousal model of interpersonal intimacy. *Psychological Review,* 1976, *83*, 235-245.

Patterson, M. L. An intimacy-arousal model of crowding. In P. Suedfeld, J. A. Russell, L. M. Ward, F. Szigeti, & G. Davis (Eds.), *The behavioral basis of design* Book 2). Stroudsburg, Pa.: Dowden, Hitchinson, & Ross, 1977. (a)

Patterson, M. L. Interpersonal distance, affect, and equilibrium theory. *Journal of Social Psychology,* 1977, *101*, 205-214. (b)

Patterson, M. L. Tape-recorded cuing for time-sampled observations of nonverbal behavior. *Environmental Psychology and Nonverbal Behavior,* 1977, *2*, 26-29. (c)

Patterson, M. L. Arousal change and cognitive labeling: Pursuing the mediators of intimacy exchange. *Environmental Psychology and Nonverbal Behavior,* 1978, *3*, 17-22.

Patterson, M. L. *A multi-stage functional model of nonverbal exchange.* Unpublished manuscript, 1981.

Patterson, M. L., & Holmes, D. S. Social interaction correlates of the MPI extraversion-introversion scale. Paper presented at the annual meeting of the American Psychological Association, New York, 1966.

Patterson, M. L., Mullens, S., & Romano, J. Compensatory reactions to spatial intrusion. *Sociometry,* 1971, *34*, 114-126.

Patterson, M. L., & Strauss, M. E. An examination of the discriminant validity of the social-avoidance and distress scale. *Journal of Consulting and Clinical Psychology,* 1972, *39*, 169.

Pederson, D. M. Correlates of behavioral personal space. *Psychological Reports,* 1973, *32*, 828-830.

Rajecki, D. W., Ickes, W., & Tanford, S. Locus of control and reactions to strangers. *Personality and Social Psychology Bulletin,* 1981, 7, 282-289.

Roger, D. B., & Schalekamp, E. E. Body-buffer zone and violence: A cross-cultural study. *Journal of Social Psychology,* 1976, *98*, 153-158.

Rosenfeld, H. M. Conversational control functions of nonverbal behavior. In A. W. Siegman & S. Feldstein (Eds.), *Nonverbal behavioral and communication,* Hillsdale, N. J.: Erlbaum, 1978.

Rotter, J. Generalized expectancies for internal versus external control of reinforcement. *Psychology Monographs,* 1966, *80*(1, Whole No. 609).

Rutter, D. R. Visual interaction in recently admitted and chronic long-stay schizophrenic patients. *British Journal of Social and Clinical Psychology,* 1976, *15*, 295-303.

Rutter, D. R. Visual interaction and speech patterning in remitted and acute schizophrenic patients. *British Journal of Social and Clinical Psychology*, 1977, *16*, 357-361.

Rutter, D. R. Visual interaction in schizophrenic patients: The timing of looks. *British Journal of Social and Clinical Psychology*, 1978, *17*, 281-282.

Rutter, D. R., & Stephenson, G. M. Visual interaction in a group of schizophrenic and depressive patients. *British Journal of Social and Clinical Psychology*, 1972, *11*, 57-65.

Schachter, S., & Singer, J. E. Cognitive, social and physiological determinants of emotional state. *Psychological Review*, 1962, *69*, 379-399.

Schopler, J., & Walton, M. The effects of expected structure, expected enjoyment, and participants' internality-externality upon feelings of being crowded. Unpublished manuscript, 1975. Cited in R. G. Harper, A. N. Wiens, & J. D. Matarazzo (Eds.), *Nonverbal communication: The state of the art*. New York: Wiley, 1978.

Shennum, W. A. Field-dependence and facial expressions. *Perceptual and Motor Skills*, 1976, *43*, 179-184.

Siegman, A. W. The telltale voice: Nonverbal messages of verbal communication. In A. W. Siegman & S. Feldstein (Eds.), *Nonverbal behavior and communication*. Hillsdale, N.J.: Erlbaum, 1978.

Snyder, M. Self-monitoring of expressive behavior. *Journal of Personality and Social Psychology*, 1974, *30*, 526-537.

Sommer, R. Studies in personal space. *Sociometry*, 1959, *22*, 247-260.

Tourangeau, R., & Ellsworth, P. C. The role of facial response in the experience of emotion. *Journal of Personality and Social Psychology*, 1979, *37*, 1519-1531.

Watzlawick, P., & Beavin, J. Some formal aspects of communication. *American Behavioral Scientist*, 1967, *19*, 4-8.

Waxer, P. Nonverbal cues for depression. *Journal of Abnormal Psychology*, 1974, *56*, 319-322.

Whitcher, S. J., & Fisher, J. D. Multi-dimensional reaction to therapeutic touch in a hospital setting, *Journal of Personality and Social Psychology*, 1979, *37*, 87-96

Wiener, M., Devoe, S. Rubinow, S., & Geller, J. Nonverbal behavior and nonverbal communication. *Psychological Review*, 1972, *79*, 185-214.

Williams, E. An analysis of gaze in schizophrenics. *British Journal of Social and Clinical Psychology*, 1974, *13*, 1-8.

Witkin, H. A., & Goodenough, D. R. Field dependence and interpersonal behavior. *Psychological Bulletin*, 1977, *84*, 661-689.

Worchel, S., & Teddlie, C. The experience of crowding: A two-factor theory. *Journal of Personality and Social Psychology*, 1976, *34*, 30-40.

Chapter 6

The Forms of Social Awareness

Daniel M. Wegner and Toni Giuliano

The theme of this chapter can be expressed in two simple observations. The first is that a person can think about different things. The second is that even in thinking about one thing, the person may do so from different perspectives. Because these observations can be made with remarkable frequency in daily life, their importance is often cloaked in what Heider (1958) called the "veil of obviousness." We hope to open the veil a bit for these deceptively commonplace ideas by introducing a systematic way of understanding their profound influence on social behavior. This analysis begins with an exploration of what it means to think about different things from different perspectives in the course of social encounters. We then define several forms of social awareness–states of mind in which the person is consciously aware of a specific range of social experience from a specific point of view. After identifying some personal and situational antecedents of these forms, we turn finally to an outline of the crucial behavioral effects that can be traced to their variations.

Awareness of the Social World

When one is engaged in a social interaction, the array of things one might conceivably be thinking about seems almost limitless. On being stopped for a traffic violation by a police officer, for example, one might think about seeming irrelevancies ("Precious few bluejays out today"), or more likely, one would concentrate on the officer ("Those mirrored sunglasses are such a cliche"), oneself ("Does this mean I'm a criminal?"), the two together ("We're holding up traffic"), or yet other topics relevant to the episode. At the same time, the possible points of view one might entertain are many. Thinking about this interaction could be accomplished from one's own perspective ("Now I'll never get to the rodeo on time"), from the officer's ("My excuses must sound pretty common"), or even from the point of view of those outside the interaction ("The folks down at the insurance agency will love my larger premium checks"). Mercifully, however, it is also true that one cannot possibly think about all these things, or use all these perspectives, at the same time. The many different ways of understanding the meaning of a social encounter can only occur to the person in a temporal succession.

Our analysis of social awareness is predicated on this idea, and on the additional realization that certain ways of understanding interactions may predominate for a person under certain circumstances. A form of social awareness, in this light, is a particular configuration of perception, interpretation, and memory that allows for a rather limited way of knowing the social environment. Although most people can adopt each of the possible awareness forms at different times, there are a number of instigating factors that can incline a person toward only a single form in a particular episode. It is easy to see in the case of the traffic violation, for instance, that one might spend a large part of the interaction thinking about the officer from one's own point of view ("This cop has the mind of a mossy rock"). Locked in this particular way of seeing the episode, one would naturally have a limited way of understanding what had occurred, and so would find only a restricted range of behavioral options appropriate as well.

The Tacit-Focal Distinction

As a first step in categorizing the social awareness forms available to the individual, it is useful to draw a general distinction between two ways in which social entities—self, individual others, or groups—may be represented in a person's thoughts. This distinction draws on one offered by the philosopher Polanyi (1966, 1969), and is a useful way of formalizing the difference between "topics of thought" and "perspectives on these topics" that we have emphasized to this point. Quite simply, when a social entity is a topic of a person's thought, we can speak of the person's *focal awareness* of the entity. When a social entity provides a perspective on a topic of thought, or otherwise serves as a cue or guide to that topic, we can speak of the person's *tacit awareness* of that entity. These two kinds of awareness have very different properties, and yet are highly interdependent as they operate to give the person access to the social world. Our initial description of these forms follows the extension of Polanyi's reasoning developed by Wegner (1982).

Focal awareness. When a person becomes focally aware of experience, a number of interesting things happen. At perhaps the most basic level, the target of focal awareness becomes "something." It is *constituted* as a unitary portion of experience and so can be seen as something different from other things. When we notice the ballerina who careens into the shrubbery during *Swan Lake*, for example, she suddenly becomes something, an item of experience that is clearly separate from everything else in the theater. And when our attention shifts to the starring dancer, to the dance troupe as a whole, or for that matter, to the time left before intermission, the clumsy ballerina recedes into the blurred background of our thoughts. Although she may be constituted once again when memories of her performance become focal, she is really nothing at all to us when our focal awareness dwells on other targets. In short, the extent to which an item of experience is constituted as a separate and bounded unit, be it a physical object, an event, a social entity, or yet something else, is dependent on the extent to which it is given focal awareness.

The second natural consequence of focal awareness is that the target is *comprehended.* The constituted object is made meaningful, in that it can be compared with other things, categorized, labeled, imaged, described, and otherwise understood. Something as meaning-laden as a hungry wolf licking one's hand, after all, will remain meaningless without one's focal awareness of the experience. Since there are degrees to which experience is given focal awareness, it is not surprising to find recent research suggesting that greater comprehension occurs with greater focal awareness. Langer's (1978) work on "mindfulness," for instance, finds greater attention to a situation leading (through increased comprehension) to more rational behavior. Taylor and Fiske's (1978) studies of attention indicate that increased focal awareness of a person results in an enhanced appreciation for the person's causal agency. And Pennebaker's (1980) research on symptom reporting reveals that attending to bodily sensations increases the likelihood that they will be comprehended as symptoms.

The third aspect of focal awareness we wish to emphasize is that it increases the likelihood that the target will be *evaluated.* Insofar as evaluation is the prime dimension of comprehension (Wegner & Vallacher, 1977), targets held in focal awareness are evaluated more intensely. Research by Tesser (1978) has shown that people who express a minimally positive or negative attitude toward some target regularly become more extreme in their evaluations of the target when they spend some time thinking about it more carefully. Wicklund (1975) has reviewed evidence in favor of a similar effect for self-awareness; when one becomes focally aware of oneself, the intensity of self-evaluation is increased. This feature of focal awareness specifies, quite simply, that villains we attend to become more dastardly, heroes we focalize become more admirable, delicacies we think about become more tempting, and poorly written sentences we read carefully become more annoying.

The reasoning thus far leads us to the conclusion that focal awareness is necessary for knowing the social world. It contributes directly to the constitution of distinguishable units of experience, to the clarity of comprehension of those units, and to the intensity of evaluation to which they are subject. Even so, we cannot help but wonder how these functions are guided and specified. We see people, not noses, strolling down the street; what guides us to constitute experience in units this particular way? We see taller and shorter people, not greener and bluer ones; what specifies that we comprehend them in this way? We prefer the smiling pedestrian, not the scowling one; why do we evaluate them so? Obviously, there is more to our minds than focal awareness alone. Polanyi (1966, 1969) has called this missing system "tacit knowledge" and has given some initial directions for understanding how it makes the human mind complete.

Tacit awareness. The idea that we can know things tacitly can be illustrated with a variety of common examples. When one examines an otherwise invisible organism with the aid of a microscope, for instance, it seems improper to say that one is looking *at* the microscope. Rather, one looks *through* the microscope. Though the microscope itself is not in focal awareness, it contributes in a crucial way to one's focal awareness of the organism. Similarly, when one converses on the telephone, it would seem strange to say "I'm talking to the phone." The telephone system linking oneself and another party serves as a conduit through which one's focal awareness is directed, and through which an otherwise unattainable conversation can be carried on. And when one leaves the microscope in the lab and the phone in the office to spend some leisure hours fishing, one ends up becoming focally aware of the movements of a hook some yards beneath the water, again through a system—the pole and line—that need not be concentrated on at all. Of course, one could be focally aware of any of these objects. But paying close attention to a microscope leaves the microbe unobserved, listening to the phone leaves one's conversation partner unheeded, and concentrating on the pole makes one fail to notice the tugging of the fish. It is only when one is tacitly aware of these tools that one can become focally aware of the targets they afford.

William James once remarked that "the relation of knowing is the most mysterious thing in the world" (1890, p. 216). We believe Polanyi (1969) provided an important clue to this mystery when he pointed out that the person is tacitly aware of the sensation and interpretation systems of the body and mind. When we look *at* the microscope, for example, we are no longer tacitly aware of it, but we remain tacitly aware of our eyes, of the nerve structures that underlie their operation, and of the mental processes and structures by which the microscope is focally known. And, just as the microscope in tacit awareness allows us to constitute, comprehend, and even evaluate a microbe in focal awareness that we would otherwise never see, our minds in tacit awareness afford us the possibility of focal awareness of things in general. James' "relation of knowing," in this light, can be expressed as the relationship between tacit and focal awareness. In short, tacit awareness supplies the dimensions and metrics by which targets of focal awareness are known.

In a general sense, we are tacitly aware of anything that guides our focal awareness to something else. Wegner (1982) has used this idea to suggest that it is reasonable to speak of tacit awareness of social entities, and to use this language to systematize what we might call "perspectives," "interests," or "viewpoints" in everyday terms. Suppose, for instance, that we encounter a small girl standing on a sidewalk. We might at first become focally aware of her (as we did with the ballerina) and so constitute her ("here's something"), comprehend her ("a small child"), and evaluate her ("she's filthy"). But at some point we might also note that she is gazing down at the sidewalk. We follow her line of sight and discover a dropped ice cream cone. This very act of moving our focal awareness to coincide with hers makes us, however briefly, tacitly aware of her. For this instant, we may see her situation in focal awareness, with our machinery of constitution, comprehension, and evaluation guided entirely by tacit awareness of her. The melting cone becomes an ugly blot on our consciousness as we think about it from her point of view, and in this instant we may want very much to buy her a new one. Whether we do this hinges entirely on whether we remain in this form of awareness. We could, for example, focalize the child again ("not only filthy but clumsy"), or simply revert to tacit awareness of ourselves ("better not step in the mess"). There are a variety of different awareness forms we could assume in any such encounter, and it is to an enumeration of these that we turn next.

The Forms of Social Awareness

Each distinguishable form of social awareness can be specified in terms of two features: what is tacit and what is focal. In this sense, a form of social awareness is a kind of shorthand for representing a person's perspective and the person's topic of thought at once. To introduce these forms, we begin with the *primary* social awareness forms to show how each of the major social entities–self, other, and group–can be portrayed in either tacit or focal awareness. Then, several of the most commonly experienced *combined* forms will be presented.

Primary awareness forms. Several forms of social awareness represent recurrent themes both in social life and in the writings of social psychologists. These primary forms, which include both tacit and focal awareness of the self, a specific other, and a group, are presented in Table 6-1. As shown in the table, there is a unique combination of entities occupying tacit and focal awareness for each awareness form.

Tacit self awareness is the first and most basic awareness form. In this form the self serves as a window through which the world may be viewed. In looking outward this way, it is one's own situation that absorbs one's attention, and that is therefore the target of focal awareness. Examples of this state in its pure form occur when a person is working alone on a task that demands almost complete attention, e.g., a draftsman working on a final floor plan, a musician learning a new piece, or a student tackling a difficult calculus problem. Because tacit self awareness involves attention directed outward to tasks or the environment, this form resembles what James (1890) called the "self as knower," what Schutz (1932/1967) called the "natural attitude," what Mead (1934) called the "I," what those in the Lewinian tradition defined as "task orientation" (Lewis, 1944), and what Duval and Wicklund (1972) term "subjective self awareness." Because taking one's own perspective is an inevitable first step in becoming aware of anything else, tacit self awareness serves as the starting point for all other forms of awareness. This aspect of social aware-

Table 6-1. Primary Forms of Social Awareness

Awareness form	Position of social entity: Tacit	Position of social entity: Focal
Tacit self awareness	Self	Self's situation
Focal self awarenes	Self	Self
Tacit other awareness	Self, other	Other's situation
Focal other awareness	Self	Other
Tacit group awareness	Self, group	Group's situation
Focal group awareness	Self	Group

ness is represented by the appearance of an initial tacit "self" in each of the tabled awareness forms.

The self remains tacit, for instance, even when one thinks directly about oneself in focal self awareness. But instead of viewing just any aspect of the world, in focal self awareness one reflects on oneself, a particular entity in that world. This reflective capacity has been identified previously in the history of social psychology as the "self as known" (James, 1890), the "social self" (Cooley, 1902), the "self-regarding sentiment" (McDougall, 1908), the "me" (Mead, 1934), and most recently, "objective self awareness" (Duval & Wicklund, 1972). The body of research generated by Duval and Wicklund's conceptualization of this awareness form suggests many examples of its occurrence in everyday life. When one's attention is drawn to oneself by exposure to one's mirror or video image, for instance, one focuses on self from one's own tacit perspective; this is the primary form of focal self awareness.

Tacit other awareness, the next tabled form, corresponds in important ways with "role-taking" (Flavell, Botkin, Fry, Wright, & Jarvis, 1968; Mead, 1934), "sympathy" (Cooley, 1902), and "empathy" (Stotland, 1969). In this form of awareness, tacit awareness of a specific other is appended to tacit awareness of self; thus, one may focalize aspects of the other's situation from the other's perspective. When our hands sweat as we watch our best friend give an important talk before a crowd, or when we get teary eyed at the movies as our favorite actress discovers that her lover fell down a well, we are putting ourselves in another's place to see how the world appears from his or her point of view. By contrast, in focal other awareness, one looks at someone through one's own (tacit self) perspective. We would, for example, stare and perhaps giggle at a business executive in a cafeteria who is blissfully ignorant of the display of food on his shirt, instead of trying to understand the other things he has to think about. This state, in which another person serves as the object of one's own focus, is reminiscent of Schutz's (1932/1967) "objectification," Jones and Thibaut's (1958) "value maintenance set," and Taylor and Fiske's (1978) "person salience."

The final two primary awareness forms extend the operation of tacit and focal awareness to a group, an aggregate of individuals perceived as a unitary social entity. Cooley's (1902) identification of the "we-feeling" was an early recognition of the state of mind one assumes in becoming aware of one's own group. That one's own and other groups might be seen as units was later suggested by Campbell (1958), Heider (1958), and others. And the distinction between groups seen as subjects and objects, one paralleling exactly our distinction between tacit and focal group awareness, has been made by Holzner (1978). In our view, regardless of whether one is a group member or not, a group can be the focus of one's attention (focal group awareness), or the guiding representation through which its situation is focalized (tacit group awareness). For example, a fan watching the halftime show at a football game could assume focal group awareness of the band, and so comment on its overall qualities. This awareness form would preclude for the moment focal awareness of any other entity, including the individuals in the band; therefore, the fan would not be likely to remark that John was out of step or Susie looked good in her tuba. Likewise, when the football coach is tacitly aware of his team in the second half and yells "Go, team!" or "We only need forty points to win," he does so with the interests of the group in mind.

Combined awareness forms. Although the primary awareness forms provide a basic system of cognitive representation, these elements can be combined to yield an even wider range of ways to understand the social environment. For the primary awareness forms, the contents of tacit and focal awareness are summarized in Table 6-1. In expanding this system we move to a notation in which each combined form is specified by noting both the contents of tacit awareness and focal awareness (e.g., tacit other/focal self). Before we consider how awareness forms can be combined, however, certain defining characteristics should be noted. First, recall that all forms of social awareness begin with tacit self awareness. Second, tacit awareness of any number of ordered social entities may follow. Finally, the eventual focal target must either be a single social entity, or the situation of the most recent entity in tacit awareness. With these rules, the combinations of tacit and focal social entities can produce an endless array of potential awareness forms. We must caution, however, that the capacity of the human mind for tacit extension is limited. On entering a situation that leaves one thinking about what Lulu thinks about what Frieda thinks about what Elsie thinks about Duard, for example, it is likely one's judgments will be less than sensible. For this reason, we believe only a restricted set of potential combinations require description.

Among the most common types of combined forms of awareness are those that involve the self in a focal position. There are certain times when, apart from the primary form of focal self awareness in which self is also tacit, one may come to view oneself from the perspective of other entities. Similar in many respects to concerns for self-presentation or impression management (see Wegner, 1982), these combined forms predominate when one considers oneself from the perspective of another person (tacit other/focal self) or group (tacit group/focal self). One may wonder in tacit other/focal self awareness, for instance, what one's potential employer is thinking about the Mickey Mouse watch one is wearing. In tacit group/focal self awareness as a member of a basketball team, in turn, one might be concerned with how the team views one's two point season contribution. Being similarly capable of adopting tacit group/focal self awareness for a group to which one does not belong, one might also realize how valuable one's contribution might seem to each opposing team.

Combined awareness forms can also exist without the self in a focal position. In tacit other/focal group awareness, for example, one focalizes a group from the perspective of a person held in tacit awareness. This might be the state of mind of a teacher who takes a week leave of absence and tries to discern what the substitute will think of the class. Conversely, in tacit group/focal other awareness, the teacher might be concerned about how the class will view the substitute. This awareness of how one entity views another might also occur in perceiving the interaction between two individuals or two groups; seeing how one's mother views one's date, for instance, might be symbolized as tacit other (mom)/focal other (date) awareness; seeing how one's carload of high school compatriots is viewed on the town's main drag by a carload of opposite-sexed cruisers could be accomplished in tacit group (them)/focal group (us) awareness. The ingroup/outgroup dichotomy familiar to social psychologists (see Brewer, 1979; Wilder & Cooper, 1981) would be likely when members of two groups each adopted tacit group (us)/focal group (them) awareness.

Finally, there can exist combined awareness forms in which one is aware of the same entity in tacit and focal awareness. Like the primary awareness form that has this feature—focal self awareness—the combined forms of this type seem to represent a kind of reflective awareness. In tacit other/focal other awareness, then, we see people as they see themselves, understanding their self-satisfactions and self-criticisms in a very personal way. We might note in passing that it seems particularly easy to become aware of adolescents in this way. Perhaps because of their especially telling symptoms of self-consciousness, we find equally contagious their exuberance over a passed exam and their mortification over the most recent facial blemish. In tacit group/focal group awareness, in turn, we are attuned to the manner in which a group views itself. Seeing the downcast looks on all the players of a losing hockey team, for instance, may lead us to recognize the group's self-evaluation more than the individual self-evaluations of any of the players.

In presenting these many examples of awareness forms in everyday life, we have tried to show how these forms of awareness can provide a rich representation of the social world. Although we realize that a system capable of such complexity carries the danger of becoming too unwieldy for proper scientific analysis, we wish to emphasize that this apparent complexity is effectively reduced in two ways. First, it is reduced on a practical level when we consider how these forms are actually used. As we see it, awareness forms are never simultaneously evoked, nor are all awareness forms necessarily available to the individual in any situation. Rather, the person typically adopts only a few forms of awareness in the confines of a particular episode, and even then may emphasize one at the expense of others. Complexity is reduced in a second way on the theoretical level. Each of the combined awareness forms, after all, can be understood in terms of the six primary forms, and all of these in turn can be summarized in terms of the simple distinction between tacit and focal awareness. Because this basic distinction is the key to our system, we now turn to a more detailed analysis of the different understandings of people that the partition entails.

The Representation of Persons in Thought

What does it mean to know a person or a group? We believe that radically different answers to this question are appropriate depending on whether one knows the social entity in tacit awareness or focal awareness. In tacit awareness, one knows an entity in what seems to be a very indirect way; the entity serves only as a template through which aspects of its situation may be interpreted and focalized. In focal awareness, one knows an entity more directly; it serves as an object of thought whose features and characteristics are identifiable. In both cases, however, it is sensible to argue that an observer who becomes aware of an entity uses some sort of mental representation of the entity in the enterprise of perceiving, storing, and retrieving information.

To distinguish between the kinds of representations that must be necessary to accommodate different forms of awareness, we will discuss in this section first the *transparent representation* of an entity held in tacit awareness, and then the *opaque representation* of an entity held in focal awareness. Each of these representations is a knowledge structure that has functions and properties consistent with its associated form of awareness. In turning to this language of "representation," it also becomes clear that knowledge of social entities exists in some interconnected network despite flux in the observer's social awareness. Changing our awareness of a person, for example, does not make us suddenly believe we are thinking about someone else. In the last part of this section, we will offer some ideas about how these different representations are linked into a unified body of social knowledge.

Transparent Representation

Imagine a couple who have each been given a pair of magic glasses—magic, in that each pair only shows things from the point of view of its owner. One evening, the couple exchanges glasses, and the male finds his way out of the living room and into the kitchen while seeing only his partner's view of the living room where she sits. The female, in turn, could sit comfortably in a chair and watch large items of furniture loom into view, a door appear and swing aside, and a low-hanging lamp in the kitchen grow larger and then bounce sharply away from a point just above the field of vision. The message of this example is that, while such glasses are not yet available, we each have transparent representations of others that can have a similar enlightening impact on our understanding.

General properties. A transparent representation of an entity is a store of knowledge about how the entity's environment should be focalized. It contributes in an important way to the constitution of focal targets, for example, by alerting us to those targets that are likely to be selected by the entity; so, when we observe someone shopping for a gift to be given to a female, our transparent representation of the shopper leads us to attend primarily to appropriate female gifts (Zadny & Gerard, 1974). Similarly, a transparent representation guides our comprehension of the environment by leading us to understand and thus remember the events and objects that would be meaningful to the represented entity. Thus, when we read a story about an island from the perspective of a shipwrecked person, we understand and remember a very different set of story ideas than when we read it from the perspective of a florist who wants an out-of-the-way place to raise flowers (Pichert & Anderson, 1977). Indeed, a transparent representation even guides comprehension of information that is stored in our own memories. Asked to recall a story from one perspective, when we previously read it using another, we may be able to recall facts and ideas relevant to the new perspective that we otherwise would have been unable to report (Anderson & Pichert, 1978).

The influence of a transparent representation that may be most significant in social interaction, however, is its power to change our evaluation of the environment. With a transparent representation, we assign valences to objects and events in accord with the perceived preferences of the represented entity. In this way, we become especially sensitive to the entity's future. After all, in assigning labels of "good" and "bad" to the environment in accord with the entity, we are expressing the entity's goals (good things to be approached, bad things to be avoided), plans (good means for goal attainment), and problems (bad things to be made good). The transparent representation of a used car buyer, for instance, makes observers emphasize the goal of finding a low-priced car, whereas such representation of the seller makes observers more appreciative of high prices (Birnbaum & Stegner, 1979). So, while we would identify as general properties of transparent representations their guiding influences on constitution, comprehension, and evaluation, we wish to stress their evaluative impact.

Memory for goals. We believe that this evaluative impact of transparent representations is most clearly manifested in their tendency to enhance memory for an entity's goals. An excellent illustration of this point was provided in early research by Lewis (1944) and Lewis and Franklin (1944). These investigators were interested in the Zeigarnik effect–the tendency of a person to remember unachieved goals better than achieved goals. In an initial study, precisely this effect was found; when subjects worked alone on 18 different tasks, half of which they finished and half of which were interrupted, they later recalled more of the incomplete tasks. When these researchers arranged for an antagonistic experimenter to complete in the subject's presence those tasks the subject did not finish, this effect was again observed. However, subjects in a third group were exposed to an experimental situation we believe would induce tacit group awareness, and hence, transparent representation of the group rather than the self; each of these subjects worked with a cooperative partner who finished the tasks the subject had left undone. With the *group's* goals accomplished, subjects recalled complete and incomplete tasks equally. These findings show that transparent representations may have a substantial influence on goal memory.

Recent research points to a similar conclusion. In a study using a technique developed by Bower (1978), we induced the transparent representation of different social entities in a story by having subjects see different versions of the story's first paragraph (Wegner & Giuliano, 1981). This initial introduction of a "point of view" featured an entity (i.e., one girl, a pair of girls including the first, or a third girl) setting off for a shopping mall, and was followed by a standard 537-word story about all three girls spending the afternoon shopping. We found that subjects were more likely later to recognize the goals expressed in the story that were those of their transparently represented entity. So, for example, if the story began with the group (Janet and Susie), subjects were more inclined later to remember the group's common goals (e.g., Janet and Susie both wanted to get salads for lunch). This finding is consistent with a growing body of research on story comprehension that points to the fundamental role of goal understanding in the comprehension of action. In fact, Bower (1978) has found that observers who read a story in which the main character's goals are obscure will judge the story to be incoherent and recall it poorly. Without goal information, a transparent representation is impoverished.

The feature of transparent representation we wish to emphasize, in sum, is that it functions to facilitate the processing of information about an entity's goals. Goal information is sought, stored, and retrieved most readily when transparent representation is activated. Such information is relatively unavailable, however, given opaque representation of an entity.

Opaque Representation

Imagine now that our couple agrees to try some "new, improved" magic glasses, ones through which each can only see the other. The male again wanders from the living room, this time able to look only at the female; the female again sits in a chair, now able to see the male at all times. Wary of the lamp, the male removes his glasses as he enters the kitchen. He notes that the room is already occupied by a bear, and then explodes into a frenzy of arm waving, eye rolling, and cabinet climbing. Because the female can only see him, and not the bear, she understandably concludes that he has gone mad. This example shows that an observer's interpretation of a person may be developed in a very special, limited way when an opaque representation, like these magic glasses, is brought to bear.

General properties. An opaque representation of an entity is a store of knowledge about how the entity should be focalized. Its most basic function is constituting the entity as a distinct unit of experience. In service of this goal, any differences between the entity and other experience are exaggerated, while differences among various properties, aspects, or subparts of the entity itself are underestimated. This feature of opaque representation is perhaps most evident in the perception of groups. In the typical ingroup/outgroup situation, for example, an ingroup member would be most likely to focalize the outgroup; hence, the difference between the outgroup and the general population is exaggerated (Wilder & Cooper, 1981), and the differences among outgroup members are minimized (Quattrone & Jones, 1980). This press toward seeing the focal entity as a distinct unit is evident in the perception of an individual as well. Ickes, Layden, and Barnes (1978), for example, found that self-focused attention made individuals more likely to describe themselves in "individuated" terms, while Vallacher (1978) found that increased attention to others led observers to make more fine discriminations among them.

Opaque representations lead us to comprehend entities by characterizing them. We look for their most permanent, unique, and characteristic qualities, and search for these primarily by considering the entity's past. An entity's future, after all, is but an uncertain construction, and most goals that an entity may profess are not especially unique (Worchel & Andreoli, 1978) or permanent. Trying to find the one person who wants a hot dog in a ballpark, for example, would often lead to the selection of several hundred fans, and the composition of this crowd would even tend to differ from one moment to the next. It is for this reason that opaque representation of an entity guides us to become naive "trait" theorists, searching for the enduring dispositions of the entity by generalizing from instances of behavior and appearance in the past. With greater focalization of an entity, then, we become more likely to believe that the entity possesses some previously observed characteristic (Strack, Erber, & Wicklund, 1980).

When our tacit perspective sets us to evaluate an entity in some way, our opaque representation of the entity supplies a structure for perceiving the entity as good or bad. The evaluation of an entity regularly becomes more extreme with greater focal awareness of the entity (Eisen & McArthur, 1979; McArthur & Solomon, 1978; Taylor, Fiske, Etcoff, & Ruderman, 1978) because opaque representation is a knowledge structure within which such extremity is fostered. Now, the development and maintenance of any extreme position is no simple matter. A person who wanted, for example, to hold the strong belief that sneezing causes instant death would be forced to ignore observed facts, invent unobserved supportive information, reinterpret neutral information in the right way, and so on. An opaque representation of an entity is saddled with precisely these kinds of tasks; in this sense, it can be said that opaque representations are the source of the well-known halo effect in person perception. The tendency to see an entity as all good or all bad, and the accompanying thought structures that distort understanding in service of producing such extremity are necessarily components of opaque representation.

Memory for characteristics. The contemporary study of the perception of persons and groups is, in large part, the study of opaque representation. In such research, psychologists typically present observers with a stimulus person or group, ask the observers to describe or evaluate the stimulus in some way, and then concentrate on the properties of this description or evaluation. Under these conditions, the entity being perceived is of course an object of sustained focal awareness, and the properties of social perception discerned in this fashion are those of opaque representation. Although this broad background suggests many potentially interesting features of opaque representation, we believe that one such feature, memory for characteristics, deserves emphasis because of the strong contrast it suggests between opaque representation and transparent representation.

Our point is that opaque representations, unlike transparent representations, are particularly inclined to promote memory for an entity's characteristics. Because characteristics do not include goals or other temporary states, but do include the lasting and distinctive qualities of persons such as traits and physical features, it is possible to draw a clear distinction between the influences of the different kinds of representation on memory. The "shopping spree" story comprehension study by Wegner and Giuliano (1981) yielded findings highly relevant to this distinction. As mentioned earlier, subjects in this study were assigned to one of three different conditions, each designed to induce transparent representation of a particular social entity. What we failed to mention earlier was that these variations were also planned as subtle manipulations of opaque representation. We reasoned that just as taking one side in a dispute necessarily entails opposing the other, taking the perspective of one entity in this story would increase the likelihood that other entities would be focalized. Since this effect would be particularly discernible in the case of only two entities, we paid special attention to the conditions in which transparent representation of one entity in the story (i.e., either Ellen or the group comprised of Janet and Susie) would leave only one other entity to be remembered (i.e., the group or Ellen). In these conditions, subjects' memory for the characteristics of the complementary entity was enhanced. So, for instance, subjects who took the tacit perspective of Ellen were later more likely to recognize those common characteristics of Janet and Susie that were expressed in the story (e.g., Janet and Susie both had long hair and both were cheerleaders, etc.).

This study indicates that in understanding a simple story, we do not only look for a character's goals. Although we do this for at least one main character, such transparent representation leads us to adopt opaque representations of other entities, and so to remember their characteristics. To a large extent, this is also how we understand the characters in our own life stories.

The Structure and Interaction of Representations

In the attempt to draw the distinction between the transparent and opaque representation of an entity as clearly as possible, we have avoided until now discussion of the connection between these representations. Certainly, however, there must be a profound connection; even though transparent and opaque representations may move us to understand an entity in very different ways, there is still no question in our minds that it is the same entity. This connection can be traced to two sources. First, transparent and opaque representations are linked because they operate from the same knowledge base. Second, transparent and opaque representations of an entity may inform each other from time to time, allowing certain kinds of information to be transferred between them.

The idea that the two representations of an entity may function from the same knowledge base is evident when we consider perceptions of action. Suppose we are told, for instance, that Flo ate a turnip. This is not preinterpreted information about Flo's goals or characteristics such as the information subjects were presented in our shopping spree study. It is merely a record of action. From this same knowledge base, a transparent representation of Flo might lead us to interpret the act as an expression of her goal ("Flo wanted a turnip"), whereas an opaque representation of her would guide us to interpret the act as a manifestation of her character ("Flo is a turnip-eater"). Just as the perpetrator of an act is likely to emphasize intention in explaining it, whereas an observer of the act is more inclined to stress the permanent traits of the actor that may have caused it (Jones & Nisbett, 1971; Passer, Kelley, & Michela, 1978), transparent and opaque representations activate these different ways of interpreting an entity's behavior. So, to the extent that the same behavioral knowledge base is available as input to both kinds of representation ("Flo ate that turnip, no matter why"), the representations are connected at a very fundamental level.

The second source of connection between the two representations is evident when we consider their use in ongoing interaction. Suppose, for instance, that one comprehends a person in focal awareness, and guided by the rules of opaque representation, one interprets and stores the person's behavior—holding up a filling station—as a characteristic. The person is thought of as a thief. Now, suppose one meets the person again, this time under conditions conducive to transparent representation (e.g., one is appointed the person's attorney). It seems that the opaque representation might inform the transparent representation about this person. The label of "thief" might be used to generate inferences about the person's goals quite directly (e.g., thieves want money, so the person wanted money), or it might provide access to the original action description (e.g., the person held up a filling station), and so to potential goal inferences.

In many cases, however, the transfer of information from one representation to the other is difficult or impossible because the two representations organize the information in incompatible ways. Several different instances of a person's behavior, for example, might all be organized in an opaque representation in terms of their relevance to a single characteristic; falling out of a car, tripping on a carpet, and slipping on a diving board might all be seen as instances of a person's clumsiness. These individual instances might only be retrievable to the degree that the "clumsy" characteristic is itself available. If the observer now turns to tacit awareness of this person and is asked to discern, say, what the person might like to do on a summer vacation, the opaque representation could be useless as a way of finding an answer. Although the diving board incident provides a hint that the person might want to go swimming, this behavioral information is inaccessible for representation as a summer vacation goal because it is organized with, and only accessible via, the characteristic of clumsiness. Unless we mention clumsiness in our question about the vacation goal, the answer will not be retrieved. As Hoffman, Mischel, and Mazze (1981) have shown, the characteristic- and goal-based organizations of behavioral information that arise as a result of different awareness forms can lead to variation in memory for instances of behavior. It is for this reason that transparent and opaque representations of an entity may lead somewhat independent existences, each fairly uninformed of information held in the other.

Although we have stopped far short of developing a detailed structural model of the cognitive representation of social entities, our brief discussion in this section suggests the form such a model might take. We hold that transparent and opaque representations are very different ways of organizing information in memory. In opaque representation, information is linked together in terms of characteristics of the entity, and these characteristics may in turn be linked in a network resembling an "implicit personality theory" structure. In transparent representation, information is linked together by virtue of its association with goals of the entity, and these goals may in turn be linked in a network resembling a "script" (cf. Schank & Abelson, 1977), or more generally, an "implicit situation theory" (cf. Wegner & Vallacher, 1977). These different organizations of information afford the person the possibility of understanding the entity differently in focal and tacit awareness.

The Instigation of Awareness Forms

Awareness forms and their associated representations of social entities do not, like sugar plums, merely dance in the person's head. Rather, their occurrence and change can be traced to a set of personal and situational instigators that are fairly well circumscribed. In this section, we outline the operation of three broad categories of instigation.

Attentional Instigation

The nature of our perceptual engagement with the environment can promote different forms of social awareness in two major ways. First, certain targets of focal awareness may be more salient or attention-seizing than others; *target salience* may lead us to hold a target in focal awareness and adopt the tacit perspective most suitable for understanding it. Second, certain targets of focal awareness may only be salient in a transitional sense; their *cue value* quickly leads our attention elsewhere, leaving us tacitly aware of them and in search of their focal target.

Target salience. When something in our environment draws our attention, it becomes at least temporarily the target of our focal awareness. Focal awareness of self, other, or group would result, then, when such an entity is a salient target. Tacit awareness of one of these entities could often occur, in turn, when something in its situation is a salient target. These rules relating attention and awareness forms have been implicit in much of our discussion to this point, and so should be relatively straightforward. The situational and personal factors that underlie target salience, however, deserve some additional consideration.

As a rule, situational stimuli are salient and draw our attention to the extent that they are distinctive. It is not uncommon, for example, to turn our attention to the lone female on a Little League team, or to the single drummer who turns left as the band turns right. Distinctiveness seems to be a key factor in the Gestalt principles of attention (Koffka, 1935), such that objects or persons made distinct through brightness, movement, complexity, novelty, and the like, have been found to attract attention (see Duval & Hensley, 1976; Taylor & Fiske, 1978; Wegner & Schaefer, 1978). Each of these different qualities of stimulation functions to make the target figural against the ground of other experience.

In the course of research on such salience, a variety of situational manipulations have been used. Seeing oneself in a mirror, hearing one's own tape-recorded voice, or being reminded of one's uniqueness are some of the ways the self has been made salient in inducing focal self awareness (Duval & Wicklund, 1972; Wicklund, 1975). Similarly, the simultaneous placement of two or more people in front of a mirror has produced focal group awareness in these individuals (Giuliano & Wegner, 1981; Pennebaker, McElrea, & Skelton, 1979). Focal and tacit other awareness can be induced through situational manipulations of salience as well. Using videotape and special camera angles, researchers have made a person salient by showing observers only the person's face, and have made the person's situation salient by showing observers a tape made from a point above and behind the person's shoulder (Storms, 1973; Taylor & Fiske, 1978).

The salience of a target can also be measured as it is reflected in the perceiver's state of mind. Since thoughts about a salient target are likely to be readily available (Pryor & Kriss, 1977; Tversky & Kahneman, 1973), one way to measure what is salient for people is to tap directly into what they are thinking about. This can be accomplished through thought sampling, a method developed to study the stream of consciousness (Klinger, 1978). When people report their most available ongoing thoughts, it is likely that the target of their focal awareness—whatever is most salient—will be revealed. One approach to thought sampling has been to present subjects with a series of incomplete sentences and to have them fill in what they believe are appropriate pronouns (Davis & Brock, 1975; Wegner & Giuliano, 1980). Since in no case is one pronoun more "right" than another, frequent use of a particular type of pronoun can be taken as an indicator of the salience of the particular entity to which it applies. This means, then, that a person who chooses to use a majority of first person singular pronouns (i.e., I, me, my) in completing sentences is apt to be focally aware of the self, whereas a person using more first person plural pronouns (i.e., we, us, our) is focally aware of a group comprised of self and others (Giuliano & Wegner, 1981). Although the thought sampling techniques presented here are useful for determining focal targets, they offer no information about tacit awareness. It is possible, however, given more complex verbal productions than pronouns, that tacit perspectives might be able to be tapped as well.

As our thoughts are constantly changing, these thought sampling techniques measure "states," and are most useful as current, momentary indicators of salience. In some cases, however, the salience of a target may be considered a "trait" rather than a "state" of the perceiver. People may have propensities to focus on certain things, and they can report those things they typically think about in the same way they can report what is currently in their thoughts. Personality psychologists have taken advantage of this self-report capability and have developed certain personality measures that are useful for determining individual differences in salience. Individual differences in public and private self-consciousness (Fenigstein, Scheier, & Buss, 1975), for example, suggest that for individuals high in either of these traits, the self will be salient, and there will be a tendency to engage in focal self awareness. Unfortunately, since it has not yet been determined whether there are reliable individual differences that result in salience of other entities or situations, we are limited in exploring further the relationship between social awareness and attention-related personality variables.

The final point we wish to make about target salience is that in focusing on whatever target is salient, the perceiver may encounter an interpretive dilemma. Although a target may be salient to a particular tacit perspective, it may not be as clearly interpretable from that point of view as it would be from another. While we often revert to our own tacit perspective under these circumstances, this can be inappropriate at times when the target is noticeable yet meaningless to the tacit self. For clarity, we may search for a tacit perspective that will help us understand the salient target (cf. Schachter, 1959). Before calling for help as a wild man runs toward us with arms flapping, for instance, we might look to the friend walking with us to see if he is offering a similarly embarrassing greeting. Looking through a tacit entity at an ambiguous target provides us with a different and often informative way of interpreting the target. For this reason, as we note next, target salience is regularly accompanied by the cue value of targets as a determinant of our awareness form.

Cue value. When something in our environment does not draw attention to itself, but rather directs our attention to something else, it serves as a cue for focal awareness. If this cue is provided by a social entity, we shift from focal to tacit awareness of it, and subsequently focalize whatever the entity is leading our attention toward.

As an illustration of this, suppose that Wally is sitting on the couch with three friends. If all three simultaneously jump up and dart toward the window, we can expect Wally not to remain seated staring at them for long, but soon to be looking right along with them. With only the vaguest idea of what the proper target of focal awareness might be, Wally moves to seek that target. In general, we can define a social entity's propensity to guide a person's focal awareness in this way as the entity's cue value for the person.

A social entity is likely to have high cue value when what is focal for that entity is potentially of interest or relevance to the perceiver's tacit self, for it is under such circumstances that becoming tacitly aware of another entity might prove useful. When the social entity being focalized is an individual, there are four classes of behavioral evidence the entity might display that would contribute to its cue value. A person may attract our attention to something in his or her focus through verbalization ("Watch out!"), through nonverbal gestures signifying orientation (staring, sniffing, etc.), through facial or bodily emotional expression (moaning, laughing, etc.), or through target-directed action (pointing, throwing a spear, rolling a bowling ball, etc.). The cue value of the individual is enhanced with more obvious display of such behaviors because the individual's focal target is seen as more important to the perceiver's tacit self. The more urgent a verbalization, the more intent an orientation, the more extreme an emotional expression, or the more vigorous an action, the greater the likelihood the perceiver will move focal awareness away from the behaving individual and toward the seemingly important new target. At a crowded social gathering, after all, one is more likely to search for the focal target of someone yelling "Fire!" than of someone mumbling into a basket of fruit.

The four kinds of behavioral evidence are also likely to increase the cue value of a group we are focalizing, but there are additional features of groups that can affect their cue value (cf. Wilder & Cooper, 1981). Suppose we see a group of people, all of whom are running and pointing in different directions. Because of the confusion, no matter how urgent or threatening we perceive the situation to be, we may never take the appropriate tacit perspective to understand their agitation. For a group to have high cue value, its behavioral evidence of the appropriate focal target must show some degree of unanimity. This unanimity not only increases the likelihood a group of persons will be seen as a single social entity and not as individuals, it also increases the chance that a group with a common target will convey its message. Beyond unanimity, we can also note that the larger the group focalizing a single target, the greater the group's cue value. Milgram, Bickman, and Berkowitz (1969) made this point in a study by arranging for crowds of different sizes to gaze upward from a city sidewalk. Passers-by more often looked up in the presence of larger groups.

The cue value of a social entity acts as a sort of "shield" by which our focal awareness is deflected. But in the very act of moving to the cued target, we become aware of the entity in a tacit fashion. The question of whether we remain tacitly aware of the social entity for some time thereafter, or move immediately back to our own tacit perspective, is then determined by the relative clarity and usefulness of the different perspectives. If the cued target has immediate and profound meaning for us (a falling piano), we revert to tacit self awareness and comprehend it for ourselves. However, if the cued target has greater meaning for the entity that led us to perceive it initially (a piano falling toward them), we may continue in tacit awareness of that entity and may even respond to the entity's situation in a way that would satisfy the entity's goals (take instrumental action to move the entity).

Just as for some people there is a tendency for certain targets to be salient in focal awareness, for some people there is a tendency for the cue value of some entities to be greater than that of others. Reliable individual differences in empathy, for example, suggest people differ in the extent they can and will adopt a tacit other or tacit group perspective (Mehrabian & Epstein, 1972). Those high in empathy may be more sensitive to the cue value of others in general, as well as being more likely to remain in tacit awareness once a perspective is adopted. In a similar way, although the dimensions of private and public self-consciousness (Fenigstein et al., 1975) both imply the same focus of attention, the self, it could be that the distinction between them lies in the cues that lead to this focus. For persons high in public self-consciousness, it may be the cues provided by others or groups (such as audiences) that direct attention toward the self; for persons high in private self-consciousness, the cues directing attention toward the self may be provided by the tacit self alone.

Affective Instigation

We begin the journey to different forms of social awareness in what phenomenologists (e.g., Schutz, 1932/1967) call the "natural attitude"—tacit self awareness. For this reason, the goals, interests, standards, and evaluative tendencies of the tacit self are paramount in the determination of the particular awareness form we may next assume. This important instigational influence can be conceptualized in terms of two general kinds of effects. First, *evaluation effects* on social awareness occur when the individual adopts an awareness form as a result of the way a social entity is evaluated in focal awareness. Second, *mood effects* are observed when the individual adopts an awareness form as a result of his or her own mood. In both cases, a person may exhibit more or less affinity for a particular awareness form through variations in affective instigation.

Evaluation effects. In the state of tacit self awareness, we encounter various social entities and focalize them in turn, discerning their characteristics and judging them to be good or bad for us. We may base our evaluative judgments on characteristics as important as the entity's competence or morality (Vallacher, 1980), or on characteristics as seemingly insignificant as the entity's favorite cheese. We may even base our evaluation on simple familiarity, without benefit of knowing the entity's specific characteristics at all (Zajonc, 1980). But the evaluation we reach is crucial, for it then determines the form of awareness we are most likely to adopt with respect to the entity, and so defines the ways we will understand the entity in the future.

The negative evaluation of an entity in focal awareness leads to a continued propensity to hold the entity in focal awareness. Graziano, Brothen, and Berscheid (1980) made this point quite clearly in finding that subjects were more likely to turn on a video monitor to view a person who had been negative toward them than to watch a person who had been positive. The point was made in another way in earlier research showing that observers are more likely to make precise and discriminating characterizations of people they dislike than of people they like (e.g., Irwin, Tripodi, & Bieri, 1967). In essence, what this means is that we are inclined to hold enemies "frozen" in focal awareness, and so to see them rather inflexibly as problems to be dealt with each time they impinge on our consciousness. This is not to say, however, that we spend large portions of our time each day seeking out and focalizing negative entities. As a rule, the realization that some entity is negative leads us to avoid the entity. This strategy of avoidance ensures that in the long run we will only infrequently hold the entity in *any* form of awareness.

The positive evaluation of an entity in focal awareness introduces a tendency to hold the entity in tacit awareness. So, while there is a general inclination to focalize any entity that has potential importance to the tacit self (Berscheid & Graziano, 1979), this inclination can often be set aside when the entity is seen as positive in value for the self. In essence, this transition represents an extension and refinement of the tacit self's own goals. Beginning with the simple goal of keeping the positive focal entity present, the tacit self engages tacit awareness of the entity and thereby encounters new goals to be attained. This transition is commonly known as "identification." When it happens, we come to see the world from the entity's perspective, and for this reason, may find ourselves in a self-perpetuating system. Tacit awareness of liked others or groups makes it unlikely that we will process their behavior in a way that would detract from our initial positive evaluation of them (Regan, Straus, & Fazio, 1974).

Now, under certain conditions, the positive evaluation of an entity in focal awareness may have yet another effect on our subsequent awareness form. If there is a way to become tacitly aware of a group that is comprised of both the entity and ourselves, we may do so. Although this may be decidedly difficult for us in the case of admired movie stars, heroes and heroines we learn to adore at a distance, or other unrequited loves, in those instances in which some grouping principle is available, our natural next step is to see the valued entity and ourselves as *us*. A good example of this is shown in studies of football fans by Cialdini, Borden, Thorne, Walker, and Freeman (1976). These researchers found that while fans of a losing team were likely to say that *they* lost, fans of a winning team tended to say that *we* won. Fans of losers saw them negatively, and so focalized the team. Fans of winners, however, saw them positively, and so took the opportunity to include themselves and the team in a larger group—"our side."

Finally, we should note that these differential effects of positive and negative evaluation have some intriguing consequences for one's awareness of oneself. On committing some error that leaves one's self-evaluation negative, the tendency to focus on negative entities that cannot be avoided should ensure that focal self awareness is prolonged. The joke that bombs before an audience, for example, can leave one feeling self-conscious into the wee hours of the night. On attaining some success that renders one's self-evaluation positive, in turn, tendencies toward focal self awareness would be relatively short-lived and one would more often revert to tacit self awareness. The joke that makes the audience giggle provides a moment for self-congratulation that lasts only until the giggling stops. This evaluative asymmetry in the duration of self-focus has been documented by Wicklund (1975), and is also reflected in the finding that low self-esteem persons tend toward greater chronic self-consciousness (Brockner, 1979).

Mood effects. A somewhat more subtle form of affective instigation involves the impact of the perceiver's current mood on social awareness. As a way of understanding such instigation, it is useful first to note that as a general rule the target of focal awareness tends to "absorb" the affective tone of the perceiver's mood. Either by searching for negative items in memory and experience, or by interpreting neutral items in a negative way, a person in a bad mood or depressive state ultimately focuses on negative targets (Beck, 1976); a person in a good mood focuses on positive targets by the same token (Isen, Shalker, Clark, & Karp, 1978). This effect extends into focal awareness of persons in an interesting way. Enzle and Harvey (1978) found that observers in a good mood who focalize a person interpret the person's good behavior as a reflection of his or her personal characteristics; paralleling this, grumpy observers are more likely to see a focal target's bad behavior as a sign of his or her personal characteristics. Had observers in this study been tacitly aware of these persons, we would have expected a quite different effect. In focalizing a person's situation, the mood absorption rule would suggest that a sullen observer would see bad behavior as a characteristic of the situation, and that a light-hearted observer would see good behavior as situationally induced.

Because of the connection between one's mood and one's evaluation of focal targets, tacit awareness of others can be a tricky business. There is something highly disturbing, for example, about being in a bad mood and having a well-meaning friend drop by to talk about sunshine, flowers, and baby ducks. The friend's view of things seems especially foreign. And on the day we feel on top of the world, a chat with a gloomy neighbor about her collection of cancer-causing agents is similarly hard to bear. When we are experiencing a strong mood state, we typically find it easier to attain tacit awareness of entities exhibiting the same state because their evaluation of focal targets often coincides with ours. Bower (1978) has shown this in a story comprehension study; subjects who, through posthypnotic induction, shared the mood of a particular story character were more likely to adopt that character's point of view in remembering the story.

Symbolic Instigation

There are names for awareness forms in everyday language. Just as a person may label states of mind such as emotions or mood, talk about them with others, and understand what others mean when they convey their own moods in return, the person can symbolize, communicate, and understand the social awareness forms of self and others. This symbolizing capacity provides a means by which awareness forms may be instigated. At the most basic level, awareness forms may be instigated by *direct solicitation*; everyday requests to "look at this" or to "take my point of view" can produce particular forms of awareness. At more complex levels, awareness forms may be instigated by broader, more encompassing symbols that call for the adoption of norms, roles, or scripts; requests to follow a norm, adopt a role, or play out an interaction script suggest not only a range of appropriate behavior but a set of appropriate awareness forms as well.

Direct solicitation. States of mind are not entirely in our control. Although we may want very much to dispel a negative mood state, for example, and may engage in a variety of strategic activities to further this end, there is still a certain "automatic" quality to the mood that can resist our control attempts (cf. Clark & Isen, 1981). In the same way, attempts to change our own forms of social awareness may be thwarted by the "automatic" imposition of the awareness form that is most naturally instigated by our perceptual and affective systems. When these perceptual and affective forces are weak, however, and when we are at the same time in a position to attain the goals of the tacit self by choosing to engage a form of awareness, we may be responsive to direct requests for such change.

The assumption that people are responsive to the solicitation of awareness forms underlies much previous research. The studies following the Stotland (1969) tradition of empathy research, for example, have regularly used instructional sets calling for empathy, and so for tacit other awareness. In such instructions, both the appropriate tacit stance (the other's) and the appropriate focal target (the other's situation) are described in detail. In everyday interaction, there exists a similar though much abbreviated parlance that serves the same purpose. A person who is failing to empathize with another, for instance, may be told that he or she is being "judgmental," and may be asked to "take my perspective," "step into my shoes," or "think how I must feel." Each of the other forms of awareness similarly has common language labels that are used to symbolize it, and so to call it forth or send it away. Tacit group awareness is called for when the cheerleader asks the crowd "Where's your pep?"; focal group awareness is summoned when a citizen points to the group of youths down on the corner, saying "Just look at those hoodlums"; focal self awareness is warded off when the piano teacher tells the nervous young performer to "Forget about the audience–pretend you're playing alone at home." Every persuasion attempt, every appeal to join a cause, every admonition to attend or to think in one way or another asks us to change our state of social awareness. The direct solicitation of awareness forms is an integral part of symbolic interaction in daily life.

To some appreciable extent, then, such calls must work. We can control our forms of awareness through some sort of metacognitive system that allows us to respond to symbolic communication about them. And, given this socially derived symbolic system for thinking about our awareness forms, it is also likely that we may engage in some conscious control of awareness forms without external solicitation. Although it is difficult to judge what proportion of the variation in an individual's awareness forms might be accounted for by such self-regulation, it is easy to think of examples in which conscious control can produce social awareness changes. On finding oneself becoming too extreme in derogating some unfortunate person or group, for instance, one may want to balance this extremity by spending a moment thinking about "What if it were me?" One may even consciously manipulate certain perceptual or affective instigators as a means of modifying a form of awareness ("Turn down the house lights so I can't see the audience").

Whether we change awareness forms in response to solicitation from others or in response to our own self-control concerns, however, it is clear that we can do so only because we have a commonsense language in which these states of mind can be symbolized (cf. Wegner & Vallacher, 1981). Direct solicitations of awareness forms may occur by means of symbols that are easily translated into the scientific language of social awareness (e.g., "focus," "perspective," etc.), or may occur by symbols that are far more obscure (e.g., "Where's your pep?"). But the fact that we can symbolize and communicate about these things affords us some opportunity of controlling them both in others and in ourselves.

Norms, roles, and scripts. Social psychologists have traditionally found the concepts of norm and role to be useful in summarizing ranges of social behavior; a norm summarizes a set of behaviors all people or all group members are likely to enact in a given setting, whereas a role summarizes a set of behaviors a person is likely to enact in a particular social position in a group (e.g., Thibaut & Kelley, 1959). The more recent terminology of "scripts" serves a similar function; a script summarizes the sequence of behaviors that comprise a complex action or interaction of some duration (Schank & Abelson, 1977). The common feature of these three social psychological concepts, then, is that they each suggest a way in which the wide array of potential social behaviors may be restricted to a certain subset. We believe that behavior is often guided and restricted by norms, roles, and scripts through a process of symbolic instigation of awareness forms.

People use terms or phrases that can be classified as norms ("help the needy"), roles ("wife"), or scripts ("going to a restaurant") with great regularity in ordinary discourse. These social psychological concepts are part of the common language by which laypersons symbolize and communicate about the social world. We believe that just as a person may learn to adopt a form of social awareness in response to direct solicitation ("look here!"), people come to know that symbols of norms, roles, and scripts entail certain associated awareness forms. After years of watching people in action, the translation of these broad symbols into their more direct counterparts becomes a simple matter. So, on being asked to follow a norm such as "wipe your feet before coming inside," one may fairly automatically adopt tacit other/focal self awareness to see if one's feet are suitably wiped for the norm-giver. On being asked to adopt the role of judge for a beauty contest, one is likely to understand the necessity of focalizing each contestant in turn. And on being asked to "buy a carton of milk," one will typically begin with tacit self awareness in search of the store, move to tacit other awareness of the clerk as one assembles payment, and so on, engaging in a sequence of awareness forms in line with the milk-buying script. Without at least an elementary knowledge of the awareness forms associated with a norm, role, or script, one cannot respond to such a symbol at all. For this reason, the process of training people to respond to these complex symbols often involves much direct solicitation of appropriate awareness forms.

As a final note, we should point out that not all norms, roles, or scripts act as symbolic instigators of awareness forms. Obviously, this is true in cases when a person does not know the forms of awareness associated with a symbol. But it is also true in cases when a person's awareness form is already determined by attentional and affective factors, without any reference to a symbol. A young human playing what we might call the role of "child," for example, probably does not do so because he or she is asked to adhere to this symbolic representation. Rather, attentional and affective factors inherent in the child's environment come together to determine the child's forms of awareness. To some degree, this must also be true of an adult playing the role of "parent." It is only when a person makes the choice to adopt a symbol of this sort that we can say the person's awareness form is a result of symbolic instigation.

The Social Consequences of Awareness Forms

The most dangerous feature of any cognitive analysis of human behavior is that it has the capacity to gather sufficient momentum to break all but the most superficial ties with the behaviors and relationships of daily life. In fashioning the present analysis, we have been deeply concerned with counteracting this tendency by showing how the awareness forms are implicated in everyday behavior. One way of exploring this connection has been reported by Wegner (1982). In that analysis, evidence was assembled indicating that the awareness forms serve as important antecedents of a variety of justice-related behaviors. Tacit self awareness was found to portend self-interest; tacit other awareness was identified as a cause of need-based allocation to others; focal awareness of self and other were shown to predict concern for equity in distribution to each; and the forms of group awareness were found to predict equal allocation among group members. In this final section, we hope to show the usefulness of a social awareness analysis to realms of social behavior beyond those linked to justice. We examine first the implications of social awareness for behaviors associated with interpersonal influence, and then move to a consideration of how social awareness may be used to understand the intricacies of intimate relationships.

Influence

One of the major tenets of social psychology is that people can be influenced by others to behave in ways they otherwise would not. At the most rudimentary level, influence may occur when one person's behavior has a physical impact on that of another, e.g., Person A decks Person B with a rabbit punch. But such physical influence is not commonly studied by social psychologists, nor does it comprise a large portion of the instances of everyday influence. Rather, the important forms of influence involve behavior change that is mediated by the behavior-production systems of the influenced person. The nature of this mediation becomes clear when it is recognized that one person may influence the social awareness form engaged by another, and so guide the other to a fixed range of behavioral options. Quite simply, we are influenced by others when they lead us to adopt a form of awareness we otherwise would not adopt.

Influence properties of awareness forms. What forms of awareness might an influencing agent find useful in a person to be influenced? Perhaps the most obvious answer to this question is tacit awareness of the agent. A person in this form of awareness would be concerned with perceiving and judging the world as the agent does, interested in focalizing things of importance to the agent, and motivated to attain the agent's goals and solve the agent's problems. Certainly, a few dozen people tacitly aware of oneself would make splendid items to have around the house. When such individuals became focally aware of themselves or their group, an additional benefit of their tacit awareness of oneself would be revealed. These people would perceive and evaluate themselves and their group in accord with one's interests, and so regulate themselves to keep one happy. To the degree that one wants others to emulate, serve, and conform to oneself, the establishment of tacit awareness of oneself in them seems to be a powerful tool.

An influencing agent might find the development of tacit group awareness in others useful for similar reasons. If another can be made tacitly aware of a group comprised of self and the influencing agent, then group goals will be foremost in the other's mind. These goals may not suit the agent exactly, but they are likely to be more acceptable than the other's goals alone. When a couple is selecting a package of cold cuts at the grocery, for example, he with salami in mind and she thinking bologna, both might be able to agree that pimento loaf is best for the group. If the female finds the male reaching for salami, her interests as an influence agent could at least be partially served if she were to initiate tacit group awareness, with its accompanying pimento loaf, in his mind. To the degree that group goals correspond with the individual goals of the influencing agent, tacit group awareness in others can provide the agent with goal attainment.

The influencing agent could also wield some power, however, merely by taking advantage of a person's tacit self awareness. When an agent has enough knowledge of a person's tacit self to predict with some certainty what the person would do in confronting a particular focal target, the agent may find it useful to alert the person to a specific focus. The back-seat driver who wishes to avoid a wreck needs only to point out the approaching hazard to the front-seat driver, trusting that such redirection of this person's focal awareness will have the intended effect regardless of the person's current tacit stance. A reliance on the person's tacit self is commonly a part of yet other awareness manipulations that may provide a basis for influence. The influencing agent may find it effective to arrange for the person to focus on the self in focal self awareness, or for the person to become focally aware of a group in which he or she is a member. In these cases, the person being influenced may come to evaluate the self or the self's group with reference to some tacit perspective—one with which the influencing agent is sympathetic. Any self-regulation or group-regulation that ensues could be just what the influencing agent had in mind. Finally, we might note that the agent may often find that a necessary first step to any of these awareness changes in a person is the establishment of the person's focal awareness of the agent. In short, one often must gain another's attention to have an impact on the other's state of mind.

There may be yet other awareness forms that can serve as avenues to influence. We have presented here some of the most clear and frequent illustrations of influence mediated by the influence target's form of social awareness. In so doing, we have spoken of influence as though it were always a calculated strategy on the part of the influencing agent. We should emphasize at this point that the use of awareness forms in the enterprise of social influence is perhaps more often an unplanned, natural occurrence. Influence agents may lead people to adopt new tacit perspectives and new focal targets without intending to do so or even realizing what has happened once the influence episode is complete. Behavioral contagion in crowds, loyal adherence to the wishes of a beloved leader, and many other instances of influence, after all, may occur without any special planning by an influence agent.

Influence by instigation. A person influences another by instigating an awareness form in the other. Such instigation may take place by way of one or more of the three major forms of awareness instigation: attentional, affective, or symbolic. With attentional instigation, an influencing agent may take advantage of the perceptual proclivities of others, making others focally aware of certain targets by enhancing target salience or making them tacitly aware of certain entities by increasing entity cue value. With affective instigation, the influencing agent can introduce or draw on existing evaluative or emotional tendencies in others, leading them toward particular tacit and focal stances. With symbolic instigation, the influencing agent can ask others for particular awareness forms, using others' propensities to regulate themselves in accord with social feedback and self-evaluation to motivate changes. The symbolic instigational function of norms, roles, and scripts makes this path to influence responsible for the induction of the complex sequences and patterns of awareness that integrate social interaction. In short, the varieties of instigation suggest a broad spectrum of means by which individuals influence each other's awareness, and thus influence each other's behavior.

The social awareness analysis of influence provides a unifying system within which many social influence processes and tactics can find representation. The apparent enigma of the young child who treats his parents to frequent temper tantrums, for example, can be interpreted in terms of the child's influence on his parents' awareness; we would argue that gaining his parents' focal awareness by these means often allows the child to cue the parents to tacit awareness of him. He gets his way through manipulations of parental awareness. Many influence processes identified by social psychologists are open to similar analysis. The tactic of ingratiation (Jones, 1964), for example, may be interpreted as an influence agent's attempt to establish a positive evaluation of himself or herself in the focal awareness of another person; through evaluative instigation, the other then tends to become tacitly aware of the agent, and so allows the agent to reap the benefits of this sympathetic awareness. The tactic of threat (Deutsch, 1973) or coercion (French & Raven, 1959), in turn, may be understood as the combination of affective and symbolic instigation by an influencing agent. With threat, the agent becomes the target of negative evaluation, and thus is focalized frequently by the person being influenced. The agent's threatening communication also suggests through symbolic instigation that the person would do well to adopt the agent's tacit perspective, behave in the agent's interest, and monitor the agent's satisfaction by focalizing self from this perspective as well. The threatened person thus finds it necessary to alternate among several forms of awareness—tacit awareness of the agent to find out what the agent wants, and focal awareness of self and of the agent to monitor the agent's satisfaction and continuing threat potential.

These examples of ingratiation and threat bring to light what may be an important general rule. Like ingratiation, there are a number of influence tactics (e.g., information control or the exercise of legitimate power) that have regularly been found to instill private acceptance of influence; like threat or coercion, there are other influence procedures (e.g., the offering of reward or the promise of embarrassment) that seem only to yield public compliance to influence. We believe that those influence tactics that result in private acceptance are ones that operate by instigating only a single form of awareness in the person. Those influence tactics that promote public compliance, in contrast, commonly involve an alternation among two or more awareness forms. One of these is the one the influencing agent wants the person to adopt, whereas the others are usually monitoring awareness forms in which the person focalizes the agent, focalizes the self from the agent's point of view, or otherwise inspects the influence setting in service of determining the degree to which the first awareness form must be engaged. It is this additional awareness of the influence episode that allows the person to revert to the perspective of the tacit self once the influencing agent's instigational tactics are no longer in force.

In concluding our remarks about awareness and influence, it is interesting to reflect briefly on the awareness forms that might be taken by an influencing agent. Cooley (1902) observed in this regard that the best leaders are those who are most sensitive to the perspectives of their followers. The leader who becomes tacitly aware of his or her followers, after all, is in the best position to understand the attentional, affective, and symbolic instigators that might move their awareness in the preferred direction.

Intimacy

The study of intimate relationships has recently become a topic of special interest to social psychologists. Its appeal lies both in the fact that such relationships are common and important facets of everyday life, and in the realization that intimate relations harbor a diverse and complex set of social behaviors unobserved in other forms of interpersonal contact. In this section, we present an overview of the ways in which social awareness forms are implicated in the bonds of intimacy, first by considering how an intimate relationship develops, and then by reviewing some problematic turns that this development may take.

Development of intimacy. As two strangers become acquaintances, then friends, and eventually intimates, they change the way they think about themselves, each other, and their dyadic group. These changes are reflected in the different forms of awareness that are predominant for such individuals in the earlier and later stages of the relationship. Although each growing relationship may chart a unique course of development as a result of its own special circumstances, we believe there is a fairly standard progression by which awareness patterns may unfold. This progression begins with the usual awareness form by which the lone person tends to apprehend the world–tacit self awareness.

When two people meet, they focalize each other to form what becomes a first impression. Although they each may engage in some focal self awareness, they do this with minimal information about the other's perspective, and so think primarily about how they appear to themselves ("Is my hair something I can be proud of?"). Interspersed with these brief glimpses of self, each is also developing an evaluation of the other in focal other awareness. An initial negative evaluation will of course serve to terminate the relationship at this point, whereas a positive evaluation can serve to continue the development of the progression. Since a positive evaluation of someone in focal other awareness often instigates tacit awareness of that person, two mutually attracted people will change their awareness forms to accommodate each other. Rather than seeing only the other's characteristics in focal awareness ("He's tall, dark, and chubby"), each also moves in tacit other awareness to thoughts about the other's goals, needs, and interests ("He'd probably love to visit a cozy little out-of-the-way fudge warehouse"). Taking the other's perspective naturally entails seeing oneself from the other's stance, so considerable adjustment of one's presented self is attempted. This is managed through frequent self-regulation in accord with the interests of the other, and is the stage that is often fondly recalled by couples who have moved further in the relationship ("I remember when you said you loved my hog calls").

As the couple spends increasing amounts of time together, they share not only themselves, but their activities, interests, and goals. The partner's satisfactions and dissatisfactions become associated with one's own, and the distinctions between self and partner are blurred (cf. Levinger, 1979). As an appreciation of this "oneness" supplants thoughts of "you" and "me," group awareness–both tacit and focal–emerges as the predominant form of understanding in both partners. A transparent representation of the group arises as both partners' principle way of understanding the world; the goals that come to mind are frequently group goals ("Let's go to Disneyworld!"), and the situation evaluations that seem appropriate are often group-determined ("We don't like porridge, thank you"). A detailed opaque representation of the group develops as well; characteristics of the group are readily ascertained ("Here we are–late again"), and evaluations of the group are similarly available ("We certainly make a fine-looking couple"). This "mutuality of being" (Davis, 1973) overtakes the perception of oneself and one's partner as individuals to such a degree that many of the ground rules of social exchange within the group are suspended (cf. Clark & Mills, 1979; Derlega, Wilson, & Chaikin, 1976; Morton, 1978). Between acquaintances, a shared quarter, ride, or secret is customarily returned in short order; between intimates, however, who owes what to whom is of little concern.

Although the earlier stages of a relationship are more often characterized by tacit and focal awareness of self and other as separate social entities, and later stages by tacit and focal group awareness, any of these awareness forms may still be assumed at any point. Of course, relationships of long duration are likely to ensure that each partner is strongly group aware much of the time. But it is likely that more flexible forms of intimacy occur when partners maintain at least some sense of individuality. Throughout a relationship, it is important on at least some occasions to be focally self aware (to make sure one is doing what is right for oneself), focally other aware (to understand the other as an individual), tacitly other aware (to make sure the goals one assumes for the group are good for the other), and focally aware of the self through the tacit other (to make sure one is good for the other). Problems may arise when any of these awareness forms are unused, for it is then that the partners are less than fully aware of their intimate world.

Problems of intimacy. Difficulties in a relationship may arise at any point, from before the initial encounter to after a stable intimate connection has been established. The relationship can be broken at the outset, of course, if the two people do not evaluate each other positively in focal awareness. If they do evaluate each other as worthy of pursuit, and move toward taking each other's tacit perspective, problems may yet arise when they see themselves from the other's point of view ("He likes me only for my pudding"), or when they discern that the other's goals may be incompatible with their own ("He wants to spend all his time collecting hubcaps"). This incompatibility in early stages can effectively prevent the establishment and maintenance of group goals, and so can interfere with each partner's level of group awareness. As a rule, breaking up is not very hard to do at this point.

In some cases, a relationship may continue to develop into quasi-intimate stages despite atypical awareness patterns. Two people who are extremely interested in each other (and not very self-confident), for example, may develop a stable pattern of doing things to please and satisfy each other. In mutual states of tacit other awareness, they become so sensitive to the other's needs that they fail to consider their own, and so fail to provide their partner with much information concerning them. At the extreme, individuals in this sort of relationship are concerned only with making each other happy, and yet provide each other with minimal prompting on how to do so. The result is a vacuous and unsatisfying relationship for both. The relationship dissolves into a politeness contest reminiscent of the homelife of television couples like Ozzie and Harriet.

A more common quasi-intimate pattern emerges when initial evaluations are asymmetric. The person who evaluates the other more positively in focal awareness will be more inclined to take the other's tacit view, and thereby adopt the other's goals. This relationship often reaches a stable state in which both persons take the tacit stance of the dominant (more liked) partner, evaluating both the situation and the less dominant partner from that point of view. In the stereotyped relationship of the working male and the houseworking female, for example, the wife's role is often seen as a matter of pleasing her husband. Her satisfaction is derived from aiding in the attainment of her husband's goals at home, exulting in his achievements at work, and being what he wants her to be. This kind of quasi-intimate relationship is not limited to such heterosexual homemakers; it may arise in any dyad in which one partner's tacit perspective is frequently adopted by both. And, though it may not represent the most flexible and equal pairing, it still can be stable and satisfying to both partners as long as the initial asymmetric evaluation is maintained.

Even intimate relationships that have developed in a typical fashion are not free from troubles. Group awareness is the most distinctive feature of intimacy, but at the same time it can be the most limiting. It may lead, for instance, to a profound incapacity to recognize the other apart from the relationship. One may often (and wrongly) assume that what is best for the group is best for the other ("I thought we wanted it this way"). In a study by Stephenson (1981), for example, subjects who were group aware did more poorly on a task that required taking the perspective of a fellow group member than did subjects who were self aware. In conceptualizing the world from the group perspective, it is difficult to see the other as an individual and to understand the other's unique point of view.

For the same reason, a person immersed in group awareness may lose a sense of separate identity for self. Without the input from tacit and focal self awareness, the characteristics, goals, and interests of the self fade into those of the group; the self and group become indistinguishable. Although a relationship of this type may be satisfying for the group, the realization of this loss of personal identity may even be enough in some cases to lead a partner to abandon the group ("I need to find myself"). The tendency to fuse self with group can be particularly devastating when the group dissipates. The empty feeling that comes on losing an intimate is a consequence of losing much of one's world view as well. If there is an ideal intimate relationship, then, it may be one in which the intimates have the capacity to take a group perspective in every situation, yet maintain a reserve of self and other awareness to protect their individual identities.

Conclusion

The study of social awareness forms is an attempt to bridge the gap between two very different kinds of theorizing in social psychology. One sort of theory, largely attributable to proponents of social cognition, is responsible for the specification of the cognitive structures and processes whereby the individual apprehends the social world. The other sort of theory, more often developed by those interested in the explanation of social behavior, involves the examination of social stimulus conditions under which particular social behaviors are likely to arise. A social awareness analysis brings these approaches together by drawing on parallel lines of thought that are implicit in each. The lines of thought can both be identified in terms of the notion of "states of mind."

The idea of a "state of mind" can be found in social cognitive psychology when it is recognized that knowledge structures, schemas, cognitive processes, precepts, and the like are activated in a temporal sequence. Although social cognitive psychologists have been remarkably adept at specifying the form of many of these cognitive structures, they have often failed to appreciate the fact that these structures are used by an individual in what artificial intelligence analysts call "real time." People cannot think of everything at once. The social awareness framework emphasizes this feature of thought by suggesting that people encounter the social world in a sequence of limited and specifiable forms of awareness. Although the awareness forms certainly do not include all the possible mental configurations that might be susceptible to temporal variation, they do encompass a significant subset that have captured the attention of theorists over the years. In outlining the forms and some of their consequences here, we have provided a template for understanding the flow of social consciousness as a succession of states of mind.

The idea of a "state of mind" is also regularly applicable to much of the work on social behavior. As a rule, studies in this theoretical tradition expose people to some social event or stimulus that is implicitly assumed to set up a state of mind in each person. So, for example, events or stimuli are arranged to make the person feel guilty, develop an expectancy, be uncomfortable, attend to something, feel empathic, or the like. The impact of the stimulus, as mediated by the assumed state of mind, is examined in the person's response to yet another stimulus; the investigator checks to see if the guilty person will help someone, if the expectant person will perform differently, and so on. Although social behavior theorists might balk at the representation of their approach in terms of states of mind, it is difficult to find a more appropriate term for underlying mediators ranging from guilt and expectancy to mood, attention, empathy, and beyond. With the social awareness approach, we have selected a specific subset of such mediators for explicit inclusion in a unified system of states of mind. Because each awareness form can be traced to particular instigational factors, and can then be seen as the cause of a particular range of social behavior, these forms are entirely compatible with the social behavior tradition.

In essence, the social awareness framework offers a system of social cognition within which the basic elements of social behavior can find ready representation. The forms of social awareness comprise one important way in which the bristling array of social stimulation is filtered, stabilized, and translated through cognition into coherent sequences of social behavior.

Acknowledgments. The preparation of this chapter was facilitated by National Science Foundation grant BNS 78-26380. We wish to thank Richard L. Archer, John S. Carroll, Margaret S. Clark, Blair Stephenson, William B. Swann, Jr., Robin R. Vallacher, Robert A. Wicklund, and the editors of this volume for their helpful comments on an earlier draft.

References

Anderson, R. C., & Pichert, J. W. Recall of previously unrecallable information following a shift in perspective. *Journal of Verbal Learning and Verbal Behavior*, 1978, *17*, 1-12.

Beck, A. *Cognitive therapy and emotional disorders.* New York: International Universities Press, 1976.

Berscheid, E., & Graziano, W. The initiation of social relationships and interpersonal attraction. In R. L. Burgess & T. L. Huston (Eds.), *Social exchange in developing relationships.* New York: Academic Press, 1979.

Birnbaum, M. H., & Stegner, S. G. Source credibility in social judgment: Bias, expertise, and the judge's point of view. *Journal of Personality and Social Psychology*, 1979, *37*, 48-74.

Bower, G. H. Experiments in story comprehension and recall. *Discourse Processes*, 1978, *1*, 211-231.

Brewer, M. B. Ingroup bias in the minimal intergroup situation: A cognitive-motivational analysis. *Psychological Bulletin*, 1979, *86*, 307-324.

Brockner, J. Self-esteem, self-consciousness, and task performance: Replications, extensions, and possible explanations. *Journal of Personality and Social Psychology*, 1979, *37*, 447-461.

Campbell, D. T. Common fate, similarity, and other indices of the status of aggregates of persons as social entities. *Behavioral Science*, 1958, *3*, 14-25.

Cialdini, R. B., Borden, R., Thorne, A., Walker, M., & Freeman, S. Basking in reflected glory: Three football field studies. *Journal of Personality and Social Psychology*, 1976, *34*, 366-375.

Clark, M. S., & Isen, A. M. Toward understanding the relationship between feeling states and social behavior. In A. Hastorf & A. M. Isen (Eds.), *Cognitive social psychology.* New York: Elsevier North-Holland, 1981.

Clark, M. S., & Mills, J. Interpersonal attraction in exchange and communal relaships. *Journal of Personality and Social Psychology*, 1979, *37*, 12-24.

Cooley, C. H. *Human nature and the social order.* New York: Scribners, 1902.

Davis, D., & Brock, T. C. Use of first person pronouns as a function of objective self awareness and prior feedback. *Journal of Experimental Social Psychology*, 1975, *11*, 381-388.

Davis, M. S. *Intimate relations.* New York: Free Press, 1973.

Derlega, V. J., Wilson, M., & Chaikin, A. L. Friendship and disclosure reciprocity. *Journal of Personality and Social Psychology*, 1976, *34*, 578-582.

Deutsch, M. *The resolution of conflict: Constructive and destructive processes.* New Haven, Conn.: Yale University Press, 1973.

Duval, S., & Hensley, V. Extensions of objective self awareness theory: The focus of attention–causal attribution hypothesis. In J. H. Harvey, W. J. Ickes, & R. F. Kidd (Eds.), *New directions in attribution research* (Vol. 1). Hillsdale, N.J.: Erlbaum, 1976.

Duval, S., & Wicklund, R. A. *A theory of objective self awareness.* New York: Academic Press, 1972.

Eisen, S. V., & McArthur, L. Z. Evaluating and sentencing a defendant as a function of his salience and the perceiver's set. *Personality and Social Psychology Bulletin*, 1979, *5*, 48-52.

Enzle, M. E., & Harvey, M. D. *Perceiver mood state, action outcomes, and causal attributions.* Paper presented at the MacEachran Conference, University of Alberta, Edmonton, 1978.

Fenigstein, A., Scheier, M. F., & Buss, A. Public and private self-consciousness: Assessment and theory. *Journal of Consulting and Clinical Psychology*, 1975, *43*, 522-527.

Flavell, J. H., Botkin, P., Fry, C., Wright, J., & Jarvis, P. *The development of role-taking and communication skills in children.* New York: Wiley, 1968.

French, J. R. P., & Raven, B. The bases of social power. In D. Cartwright (Ed.), *Studies in social power*. Ann Arbor, Mich.: University of Michigan Press, 1959.

Giuliano, T., & Wegner, D. M. Justice and social awareness. Presented at symposium: *Justice as a pervasive theme in social behavior.* American Psychological Association, Los Angeles, August, 1981.

Graziano, W. G., Brothen, T., & Berscheid, E. Attention, attraction, and individual differences in reaction to criticism. *Journal of Personality and Social Psychology*, 1980, *38*, 193-202.

Heider, F. *The psychology of interpersonal relations.* New York: Wiley, 1958.

Hoffman, C., Mischel, W., & Mazze, K. The role of purpose in the organization of information about behavior: Trait-based versus goal-based categories in person cognition. *Journal of Personality and Social Psychology*, 1981, *40*, 211-225.

Holzner, B. The construction of social actors: An essay on social identities. In T. Luckman (Ed.), *Phenomenology and sociology.* New York: Penguin, 1978.

Ickes, W., Layden, M. A., & Barnes, R. D. Objective self-awareness and individuation: An empirical link. *Journal of Personality*, 1978, *46*, 146-161.

Irwin, M., Tripodi, T., & Bieri, J. Affective stimulus value and cognitive complexity. *Journal of Personality and Social Psychology*, 1967, *5*, 444-448.

Isen, A. M., Shalker, T., Clark, M., & Karp, L. Affect, accessibility of material in memory, and behavior: A cognitive loop? *Journal of Personality and Social Psychology*, 1978, *36*, 1-12.

James, W. *Principles of psychology.* New York: Holt, 1890.

Jones, E. E. *Ingratiation.* New York: Appleton-Century-Crofts, 1964.

Jones, E. E., & Nisbett, R. E. *The actor and the observer: Divergent perceptions of the causes of behavior.* Morristown, N.J.: General Learning Press, 1971.

Jones, E. E., & Thibaut, J. W. Interaction goals as bases of inference in interpersonal perception. In R. Tagiuri & L. Petrullo (Eds.), *Person perception and interpersonal behavior.* Stanford, Calif.: Stanford University Press, 1958.

Klinger, E. Modes of normal conscious flow. In K. S. Pope & J. L. Singer (Eds.), *The stream of consciousness.* New York: Plenum, 1978.

Koffka, K. *Principles of gestalt psychology.* New York: Harcourt, Brace, 1935.

Langer, E. J. Rethinking the role of thought in social interaction. In J. H. Harvey, W. J. Ickes, & R. F. Kidd (Eds.), *New directions in attribution research* (Vol. 2). Hillsdale, N.J.: Erlbaum, 1978.

Levinger, G. A social exchange view on the dissolution of pair relationships. In R. L. Burgess & T. L. Huston (Eds.), *Social exchange in developing relationships.* New York: Academic Press, 1979.

Lewis, H. B. An experimental study of the role of the ego in work. I. The role of the ego in cooperative work. *Journal of Experimental Psychology*, 1944, *34*, 113-126.

Lewis, H. B., & Franklin, M. An experimental study of the role of the ego in work. II. The significance of task-orientation in work. *Journal of Experimental Psychology*, 1944, *34*, 195-215.

McArthur, L. Z., & Solomon, L. K. Perceptions of an aggressive encounter as a function of the victim's salience and the perceiver's arousal. *Journal of Personality and Social Psychology*, 1978, *36*, 1278-1290.

McDougall, W. *An introduction to social psychology.* London: Methuen, 1908.

Mead, G. H. *Mind, self and society.* Chicago: University of Chicago Press, 1934.

Mehrabian, A., & Epstein, N. A measure of emotional empathy. *Journal of Personality*, 1972, *40*, 525-543.

Milgram, S., Bickman, L., & Berkowitz, L. Note on the drawing power of crowds of different sizes. *Journal of Personality and Social Psychology*, 1969, *13*, 79-82.

Morton, T. L. Intimacy and reciprocity of exchange: A comparison of spouses and strangers. *Journal of Personality and Social Psychology*, 1978, *36*, 72-81.

Passer, M. W., Kelley, H. H., & Michela, J. L. Multidimensional scaling of the causes for negative interpersonal behavior. *Journal of Personality and Social Psychology*, 1978, *36*, 951-962.

Pennebaker, J. W. Self-perception of emotion and internal sensation. In D. M. Wegner & R. R. Vallacher (Eds.), *The self in social psychology.* New York: Oxford University Press, 1980.

Pennebaker, J. W., McElrea, C. E., & Skelton, J. A. Levels of selfhood: From me to us. Presented at symposium: *The self in social psychology.* American Psychological Association, New York, September, 1979.

Pichert, J. W., & Anderson, R. C. Taking different perspectives on a story. *Journal of Educational Psychology*, 1977, *69*, 309-315.

Polanyi, M. *The tacit dimension.* Garden City, N.Y.: Doubleday, 1966.

Polanyi, M. *Knowing and being.* Chicago: University of Chicago Press, 1969.

Pryor, J. B., & Kriss, M. The cognitive dynamics of salience in the attribution process. *Journal of Personality and Social Psychology*, 1977, *35*, 49-55.

Quattrone, G. A., & Jones, E. E. The perception of variability within ingroups and outgroups: Implications for the law of small numbers. *Journal of Personality and Social Psychology*, 1980, *38*, 141-152.

Regan, D. T., Straus, E., & Fazio, R. Liking and the attribution process. *Journal of Experimental Social Psychology*, 1974, *10*, 385-197.

Schachter, S. *The psychology of affiliation.* Stanford, Calif.: Stanford University Press, 1959.

Schank, R. C., & Abelson, R. *Scripts, plans, goals, and understanding.* Hillsdale, N.J.: Erlbaum, 1977.

Schutz, A. *The phenomenology of the social world.* Evanston, Ill.: Northwestern University Press, 1967. (Originally published, 1932.)

Stephenson, B. The relationship between self-awareness and perspective taking. Unpublished doctoral dissertation, University of Texas at Austin, 1981.

Storms, M. D. Videotape and the attribution process: Reversing actors' and observers' points of view. *Journal of Personality and Social Psychology*, 1973, *27*, 165-175.

Stotland, E. Exploratory studies of empathy. In L. Berkowitz (Ed.), *Advances in experimental social psychology* (Vol. 4). New York: Academic Press, 1969.

Strack, F., Erber, R., & Wicklund, R. A. Effects of salience and time pressure on ratings of social causality. Unpublished manuscript, University of Mannheim, 1980.

Taylor, S. E., & Fiske, S. T. Salience, attention, and attribution: Top of the head phenomena. In L. Berkowitz (Ed.), *Advances in experimental social psychology* (Vol. 11). New York: Academic Press, 1978.

Taylor, S. E., Fiske, S. T., Etcoff, N. L., & Ruderman, A. J. Categorical and contextual bases of person memory and stereotyping. *Journal of Personality and Social Psychology*, 1978, *36*, 778-793.

Tesser, A. Self-generated attitude change. In L. Berkowitz (Ed.), *Advances in experimental social psychology* (Vol. 11). New York: Academic Press, 1978.

Thibaut, J. W., & Kelley, H. H. *The social psychology of groups.* New York: Wiley, 1959.

Tversky, A. & Kahneman, D. Availability: A heuristic for judging frequency and probability. *Cognitive Psychology*, 1973, *5*, 207-232.

Vallacher, R. R. Objective self awareness and the perception of others. *Personality and Social Psychology Bulletin*, 1978, *4*, 63-67.

Vallacher, R. R. An introduction to self theory. In D. M. Wegner & R. R. Vallacher (Eds.), *The self in social psychology.* New York: Oxford University Press, 1980.

Wegner, D. M. Justice and the awareness of social entities. In J. Greenberg & R. L. Cohen (Eds.), *Equity and justice in social behavior.* New York: Academic Press, 1982.

Wegner, D. M., & Giuliano, T. Arousal-induced attention to self. *Journal of Personality and Social Psychology*, 1980, *38*, 719-726.

Wegner, D. M., & Giuliano, T. Social awareness in story comprehension. Unpublished manuscript, Trinity University, 1981.

Wegner, D. M., & Schaefer, D. The concentration of responsibility: An objective self awareness analysis of group size effects in helping situations. *Journal of Personality and Social Psychology*, 1978, *36*, 147-155.

Wegner, D. M., & Vallacher, R. R. *Implicit psychology.* New York: Oxford University Press, 1977.

Wegner, D. M., & Vallacher, R. R. Common-sense psychology. In J. P. Forgas (Ed.), *Social cognition: Perspectives on everyday understanding.* London: Academic Press, 1981.

Wicklund, R. A. Objective self awareness. In L. Berkowitz (Ed.), *Advances in experimental social psychology* (Vol. 8). New York: Academic Press, 1975.

Wilder, D. A., & Cooper, W. E. Categorization into groups: Consequences for social perception and attribution. In J. H. Harvey, W. J. Ickes, & R. F. Kidd (Eds.), *New directions in attribution research* (Vol. 3). Hillsdale, N.J.: Erlbaum, 1981.

Worchel, S., & Andreoli, V. Facilitation of social interaction through deindividuation of the target. *Journal of Personality and Social Psychology*, 1978, *36*, 549-556.

Zadny, T., & Gerard, H. B. Attributed intentions and informational selectivity. *Journal of Experimental Social Psychology*, 1974, *10*, 34-52.

Zajonc, R. B. Feeling and thinking: Preferences need no inferences. *American Psychologist*, 1980, *35*, 151-175.

Chapter 7

Commitment, Identity Salience, and Role Behavior: Theory and Research Example

Sheldon Stryker and Richard T. Serpe

The generic, indeed the defining, task of social psychology is to investigate the interrelationships among society, the social person, and social behavior. Every theoretical perspective or framework in social psychology approaches this immense task by narrowing it, by selecting particular dimensions of society, persons, and behavior as especially worthy of attention. While the ultimate goal for social psychology may be a single, unified theoretical framework sufficiently comprehensive to incorporate "all" the "important" aspects, etc., of the defining conceptual variables of social psychology,[1] that goal is not in sight. In the meantime, and before the millenium, all social psychological perspectives or frameworks are partial, selective in their approaches to the world they hope to explicate. That assertion is true of symbolic interactionism, the theoretical framework out of which the theory examined in this chapter develops, although perhaps less so than for most contemporary frameworks in social psychology.

Symbolic Interaction and Identity Theory

Symbolic interactionism directs the social psychologist to that aspect of the social person termed the "self" as the key conceptual variable in the explanation of social behavior. As an intrapersonal, potentially transsituational phenomenon, self is the basis for a sociological conception of personality or (at least) that aspect of personality that is sociologically most relevant. The theory also instructs the student of social behavior to regard the self as the product of society. Thus, it points to the positions that underlie structured relationships among persons and to the social roles

---

[1] It is probably meaningless to presume even an ultimate development of this kind of theoretical statement. Theory is, after all, built to answer questions; and concepts develop in the course of seeking answers to these questions. Since the questions that can be posed and the ways of conceptualizing relevant phenomena are for practical purposes limited only by the creativity of the human minds at work, it is not likely that a "completed" framework can ever be achieved.

that accompany these positions as the significant sources of relevant variation in the self. The most general and fundamental theoretical propositions of symbolic interactionism assert that structured role relationships impact on self and through self on social behavior, and that there is reciprocity in the direction of impact.

This fundamental theoretical proposition is a reassertion, albeit with slightly greater specificity, of the defining problem of social psychology: the explanation of social behavior insofar as that behavior is the consequence of characteristics of the society in which it takes place and of the persons who are involved. However, it too lacks desirable—and for purposes of research, requisite—specificity. So general as to be almost banal, the fundamental theoretical proposition deriving from the symbolic interactionist framework itself requires translation into more precise or particularized terms to be useful either as a hypothesis to guide research in social psychology or as a meaningful summary of such research.

The necessary specification has been the concern of identity theory, which is in part a refinement and in part an extension of the traditional symbolic interactionist perspective (Meltzer, Petras, & Reynolds, 1975; Stryker, 1980; Stryker, 1981). Ideally, an exhaustive catalog of the dimensions of the central conceptual terms in the perspective's fundamental proposition could be produced and used to develop theory in the form of hypothesized relationships among the particular dimensions of social structure, self, and social behavior contained in that catalog. That exhaustive catalog, however, does not exist. In its absence, identity theory proceeds by doing with respect to the structure of role relationships and to self just what symbolic interactionism does with respect to the full range of possible social psychological variables: it focuses on particularized translations of these concepts that appear to be especially promising or strategic from the point of view of theory development and theory-guided research. Its focus is on the concept of *commitment*, a particularization of the larger concept of structure of role relationships, which in turn is a particularization of the still larger concept of society. Its focus as well is on the concept of *identity salience*, which is a particularization of the larger concept of the self, which in its turn is a particularization of the still larger concept of personality or the social person. It uses these concepts—commitment and identity salience—to build a tentative explanation of certain forms of social behavior.

As the foregoing suggests, the goal of the specification process that has been illustrated is to permit the formulation of theory precise enough to be tested in empirical research. Assuming that the outcome of such research does not negate hypotheses derived from the theory or provide evidence indicating the greater likelihood of some alternative explanation for its findings, such research can provide confidence in the validity of the theoretical statements from which the research proceeded. To the degree that hypotheses derived from these theoretical statements are found to be empirically tenable, the more general theoretical assertions (such as what we have called symbolic interactionism's fundamental proposition) become more substantial.

This chapter will present identity theory as developed by Stryker (1968, 1980). It does so by first presenting enough about symbolic interactionism, its history, major assumptions, and thrusts, to motivate the discussion of the evolution of identity theory. Then, it elaborates the theory by defining and illustrating its principal variables, exemplifying its hypothesized linkages among these variables, and suggesting its scope and limitations. Next, the chapter provides an example of research that grows out of the theory and is intended as a test of some of its derived hypotheses. The research was designed to deal primarily with the relationships among commitment, identity salience, and role-related behaviors. While the research from which our chosen example is drawn concerns four roles—religious, work, spouse, and parent—the example used largely concerns religion. Specifically, we model the dependent variable of time spent engaging in religious activities as a function of commitment and identity salience (as well as other control and ancillary variables), building the model from hypotheses provided by identity theory. Subsequently, we investigate the "fit" of the data obtained in a survey research to the proposed model. The chapter concludes with a brief reconsideration of identity theory in the light of the empirical results provided through this analysis.

Symbolic Interactionism

Identity theory grows out of symbolic interactionism. The latter represents the still evolving product of a long development that can be conveniently traced to the Scottish Moral Philosophers, whose work in the eighteenth century established a basis for the empirical study of man and society (Bryson, 1945). This label refers collectively to Adam Smith, David Hume, Adam Ferguson, Francis Hutchinson, and others who tended to share a set of ideas about humans, their society, and the relations between the two. Viewing society as a network of interpersonal communication, they saw human nature as the outgrowth of that communication. Human behavior, they argued, had to be understood as the consequence of communication, imitation, sympathy, habit, and custom. Sympathy was the means by which persons put themselves in the place of others, and came to see the world as did these others; and sympathy made possible the communication that shaped and reshaped who and what the individual human being is. In these ways, the Scottish Moral Philosophers presaged the contemporary symbolic interactionist vision of the basic nature of society (as a system of interpersonal communication and interaction) and of the basic nature of the individual (as the product of society).

These underlying ideas about the nature of society and of the person are reflected in the thinking of the American pragmatic philosophers: William James, John Dewey, and George H. Mead. Although James' (1890) view of humans as having a variety of types of self, and his argument that the human being has as many "social selves" as there are persons who react to that human being, take on peculiar importance in current theorizing,[2] Mead is more important than any other thinker in the development of the symbolic interactionist framework. Mead (1934) argued that social psychological analysis must begin with ongoing social interaction—the social

[2] It is importantly the leads coming out of this idea that suggested the conception of the self as composed of multiple identities—a conception that is the basis for identity theory.

process—for it is from the social process that mind, self, and society derive. Mind emerges when persons initiate activities that relate them to their physical and social environment. Mind (or the activity of thinking) is instrumental; it occurs in the context of solving problems. Thus, Mead, as did Dewey (1896), argued that persons do not simply respond to stimuli that exist independent of their ongoing activity. Things become stimuli—objects—only as they take on meaning for persons engaged in problem solving; and the meaning of an object is the way it can be expected to function in the course of problem solving activity.

Not only do "things" acquire meanings through ongoing activity, so do people. As coparticipants in social (cooperative problem solving) acts, persons communicate using vocal and other gestures which come to be significant symbols, i.e., to have the same meanings for coparticipants in the sense of indicating the same future phases of the activity to each of them. We come to know who others are—to invest them with the meanings that define them for us and that anticipate their future behavior—by interacting with them through significant symbols. Anticipating their responses, we adjust our own responses to these anticipations. We come to have minds, to think, through being part of a social process in which significant symbols emerge. These symbols provide the meaning of the objects, other people and things, that constitute our social and physical environment.

The "self" develops through the same social process. In other words, we come to know who and what we are through interaction with others. We become objects to ourselves by attaching to ourselves symbols that emerge from our interaction with others, symbols having meanings growing out of that interaction. As any other symbols, self symbols have action implications: they tell us (as well as others) how we can be expected to behave in our ongoing activity. Moreover, the self can become a stimulus that affects the course of that activity.

The meanings that Mead emphasized—the symbols that attach to objects in the physical environment, to other persons, to ourselves—are emergents from behavior, but they function in minded activities. In that sense, while they are not private, they are part of subjective experience. In Mead's view, one cannot understand or predict human behaviors without comprehending both the facts of objective and of subjective experiences.

Since humans are members of society, their relationships with others typically occur in the context of socially organized systems of activities. Selves arise out of interaction of persons in organized groups; thus, the prior (to particular selves) existence of organized society is presupposed. But, according to Mead, as society shapes the self, so the self shapes society. In contemporary language, social interaction is constructed; society continuously is being created and recreated.

To this analysis by Mead, symbolic interactionism wedded the thinking of (in particular) three sociologists: Charles H. Cooley, William I. Thomas, and Robert A. Park. For Cooley (1902), society and individual are simply two sides of the same coin. Thus, there is no individual apart from society—personality develops from social life and from communication among those sharing that social life. Thomas (1937) emphasized the importance of both objective and subjective aspects of human experience in accounting for social behavior. Situations—circumstances calling for some adjustive response on the part of persons or groups—constitute the objective facts. The adjustive responses, however, are not only a function of the characteristics of situations; rather, intervening between situations and responses are definitions of the situations. Thomas provided a powerful rationale for arguing the significance of the subjective in social life, and also provided symbolic interactionism's prime methodological rule, through his dictum: "if men define situations as real, they are real in their consequences" (Thomas & Thomas, 1928). Park (1955) offered a vision of society as composed of smaller units of communities and groups, and of these communities and groups as structures of positions (e.g., the family group is a structure of the related positions of father, mother, child, etc.) to which patterned behavior or roles are attached. He saw the self as emerging from the multiple roles played by the person in the various communities and groups of which he or she is a member. Indeed Park, along with Simmel (1950), may be taken as the progenitor of the sociological view that conceptualizes personality as reflecting or even being constituted by the roles people play.

Although there are many contributors to a developing symbolic interactionism who link the past that has been described to the present (Stryker, 1980, 1981), there is no need to review them. We can note that various strands from the thinking of the Scottish Moral Philosophers, the American pragmatic philosophers, and early sociologists such as Cooley, Thomas, and Park were brought together in a theoretical framework to which the label symbolic interactionism has been given. We can then move directly to a summary statement of the framework as of the very recent past.[3]

Symbolic interactionism has been characterized as building on a set of assumptions and a predilection (Stryker, 1959). The framework assumes, it has been suggested, that humans must be studied on their own level and that reductionist efforts to infer principles of human behavior from the study of nonhuman forms is misguided.[4] Further, it assumes that the most fruitful approach to the study of human social behavior is through an analysis of society; this assumption follows from Mead's argument, reviewed earlier. It assumes that the human infant enters social life as neither a social or antisocial creature but rather as an asocial being with the

---

[3] The term "symbolic interactionism" is Herbert Blumer's (in Schmitt, 1937) invention, and the framework is sometimes identified with him. The term is more generally appropriate, however; indeed, the statement of symbolic interactionism presented here is very different from Blumer's, particularly with respect to its emphasis on social structure and the related emphasis on the importance of social roles in constraining selves and interaction.

[4] This assumption reflects the emphasis within the framework on symbolic communication, especially through language. Although recent research suggests, at least to some, that the assumption by early symbolic interactionists of qualitative difference between humans and other animals with respect to symbolization may be something of an exaggeration, the assumption as stated is justified by the highly developed symbolic capacities of human beings.

potentialities for human development.[5] It also assumes that the human being is an active agent of behavior rather than simply a passive respondent to external stimuli. The argument for this assumption is contained in our prior discussion of the nature of objects and the ways objects become stimuli by acquiring meaning. The predilection is to stay close to the world of everyday behavior both in the development of the framework and in the application of its ideas.[6]

An efficient way to summarize the symbolic interactionist framework out of which identity theory evolves is to offer a synoptic statement that has appeared elsewhere. According to that statement (Stryker, 1980, pp. 53-55), which arbitrarily begins with the impact of society on person:

1. Behavior depends on a named or classified world. The names or class terms attached to aspects of the environment, both physical and social, carry meaning in the form of shared behavioral expectations that grow out of social interaction. From interaction with others, one learns how to classify objects one comes into contact with and in that process also learns how one is expected to behave with reference to those objects.
2. Among the class terms learned in interaction are the symbols that are used to designate "positions," the relatively stable, morphological components of social structure. It is these positions which carry the shared behavioral expectations that are conventionally labeled "roles."
3. Persons who act in the context of organized patterns of behavior, i.e., in the context of social structure, name one another in the sense of recognizing one another as occupants of positions. When they name one another they invoke expectations with regard to each other's behavior.
4. Persons acting in the context of organized behavior apply names to themselves as well. These reflexively applied positional designations, which become part of the "self," create in persons expectations with respect to their own behavior.
5. When entering interactive situations, persons define the situation by applying names to it, to the other participants in the interaction, to themselves, and to particular features of the situation, and use the resulting definitions to organize their own behavior in the situation.
6. Social behavior is not, however, given by these definitions, though early definitions may constrain the possibilities for alternative definitions to emerge from interaction. Behavior is the product of a role-making process, initiated by expectations invoked in the process of defining situ-

[5] The grounding for this assumption has not been presented. Its polemic use has been to argue against views, e.g., Freudian theory, that seem to derive human nature from biology and against related views that seem to beg the issues of learning and socialization by assuming that humans are born with characteristic human social qualities. Its justification lies in the almost infinite ways that humans can and do develop.

[6] Again, this notion has not been adequately prefaced in this chapter. The predilection arises from pragmatic philosophy as well as the problem-solving orientation of the Scottish Moral Philosophers from which symbolic interactionist thinking emerged.

ations but developing through a tentative, sometimes extremely subtle, probing interchange among actors that can reshape the form and content of the interaction.

7. The degree to which roles are "made" rather than simply "played," as well as the constituent elements entering the construction of roles, will depend on the larger social structures in which interactive situations are embedded. Some structures are "open," others relatively "closed" with respect to novelty in roles and in role enactments or performances. All structures impose some limits on the kinds of definitions which may be called into play and thus the possibilities for interaction.
8. To the degree that roles are made rather than only played as given, changes can occur in the character of definitions, in the names and the class terms utilized in those definitions, and in the possibilities for interaction. Such changes can in turn lead to changes in the larger social structures within which interactions take place.

Identity Theory

Identity theory builds on these assumptions, definitions, and propositions of symbolic interactionism. It has developed in the attempt to deal with a set of empirical issues (Stryker, 1968), and it has developed by refining basic conceptions of symbolic interactionism with an eye toward making tractable the measurement of variables implied by these conceptions.

The empirical issues with which identity theory is concerned revolve around choices made in situations in which alternative courses of action are available and reasonable to the person. Social roles are frequently or even typically ambiguous in the performance expectations that define them. Nor are situations frequently or typically "pure" with respect to the positions and roles that are more-or-less appropriate to them, again making role performances problematic. And while positions and roles may be conceptualized as relatively discrete from other positions and roles, they are not discrete when they are (as they must be) embodied in concrete persons. Thus, role performances are often problematic, and it is this fact which poses the issues to which identity theory is addressed. In particular, there are issues to which the theory addresses itself having to do with (1) both behavioral consistency and inconsistency as persons move from situation to situation; (2) the greater or lesser resistance to change that is exhibited by persons as they respond to changes in the structure of their interpersonal relations and to changes in larger social circumstances; (3) the explanation of alternatives selected when persons are faced with conflicting role expectations; and (4) the allocation of (at least relatively) scarce resources for interpersonal interactions.

To deal with such issues conceptually and theoretically, identity theory returns to the root idea of symbolic interactionism: the reciprocity of society and self. It takes more seriously than does traditional symbolic interactionism, however, a vision of society as a multifaceted mosaic of interdependent but highly differentiated parts —groups, institutions, strata—whose relationships run the gamut from cooperation to conflict.[7] If one adopts an image of society as complexly differentiated but nevertheless organized, it follows from the premise that self reflects society that the self must also be complexly differentiated and organized. This insight in good part undergirds the development of identity theory.

The theory also capitalizes on William James' (1890) argument that people have as many selves as there are others who react to them, although it modifies the argument to refer to classes or categories of others rather than to individuals per se. Despite its longevity in the literature of symbolic interactionism, this idea lay relatively fallow until recently while theorists concentrated on a conception of self that emphasized its global character. A conception of self in global, undifferentiated terms is consistent with an image of society as a relatively undifferentiated, cooperative whole, and inconsistent with an emphasis on multiple selves. Conversely, a complexly differentiated and organized society requires a parallel view of the self and is compatible with James' idea of persons having multiple selves.

To meet both the theoretical needs generated by a changed image of society and to deal with the kinds of empirical issues noted above, identity theory introduces the concepts of identity, identity salience, and commitment.

Identities are reflexively applied cognitions in the form of answers to the question "Whom am I?" These answers are phrased in terms of the positions in organized structures of social relationships to which one belongs and the social roles that attach to these positions. They refer to more-or-less discrete "parts" of the self—internalized positional designations that represent the person's participation in structured role relationships. Thus, there is an intimate relationship between role and identity, emphasized in the term "role-identity," used by Burke (1980) and McCall and Simmons (1978) to refer to what we call "identity." Given our definition, it is clear that persons may have as many identities as the number of distinct sets of structured relationships in which they are involved. Thus, a person may hold the identities of doctor, mother, churchgoer, friend, skier, etc., all of which collectively make up her self.

Identity salience represents one of the ways, and a theoretically most important way, that the identities making up the self can be organized. Identities, that is, are conceived as being organized into a salience hierarchy. This hierarchical organization of identities is defined by the probabilities of each of the various identities within it being brought into play in a given situation. Alternatively, it is defined by the probabilities each of the identities have of being invoked across a variety of situations. The location of an identity in this hierarchy is, by definition, its salience. Implied in this conceptualization and definition is the general proposition that an identity's location in a salience hierarchy will affect its threshold for being invoked

[7] Historically, symbolic interactionists tend not to have a very sophisticated image of society, perhaps reflecting Mead's philosophy which looked to the evolution of a single universe of discourse uniting all mankind and thus a single, undifferentiated society. In part, this limited perspective reflects the preoccupation of persons using the framework with face-to-face interaction, and their concentration on social process, both of which concerns would lead them away from a focus on relatively stable social structure.

in situations and thus the likelihood that behavior called for by the identity will ensue. Whether or not that behavior will, in fact, occur will clearly depend on the way that salience of an identity interacts with (1) defining characteristics of situations (such as the degree to which the situation permits alternative identities to be expressed behaviorally), and (2) other self characteristics (such as self-esteem or satisfaction). It is worth emphasizing that, from the viewpoint of identity theory, the organization of identities in a salience hierarchy is a specification of the sociological conceptualization of personality as a structure reflecting the roles persons play. It is intrapersonal (although, if the theory is correct, *not* independent of social relationships) and it is, by hypothesis if not definition, transsituational. While presumably affected by features of situations per se, it is a product of prior interactions which has an independent effect on behavior in those situations.

Commitment is defined as the degree to which the person's relationships to specified sets of others depends on his or her being a particular kind of person, i.e., occupying a particular position in an organized structure of relationships and playing a particular role. By this usage, a man is committed to the role of "husband" in the degree that the number of persons and the importance to him of those persons requires his being in the position of husband and playing that role. Similarly, a woman is committed to her position and role as physician in the degree that she has important social relationships premised on her being a physician. Just as the concept of identity salience represents a specification of the larger concept of self that can offer greater precision and analytic power in discussions of society-person linkages, the commitment concept represents a specification of the broad notion of society that offers the same advantages. It provides a useful way of conceiving "society's" relevance for social behavior, doing so by pointing to social networks—the number of others to whom one relates by occupancy of a given position, the importance to one of those others, the multiplexity of linkages, and so on—as the relevant considerations.

These concepts permit a restatement of symbolic interactionism's fundamental proposition: society impacts on self, and through self on social behavior. The restatement, promising greater explanatory power than its predecessor, is: commitment affects identity salience which in turn affects role-related behavioral choices. This new, still very general, theoretical premise leads to a reasonably large number of testable hypotheses that bear rather close logical relationship to one another and so can be said to constitute a theory in a technical sense. While we will not in our research example be concerned with testing very many of them, we offer a representative set of hypotheses both to illustrate the theory and to further suggest its research potential:

1. The greater the commitment premised on an identity, the more salient will be that identity.
2. The greater the commitment premised on an identity, the more salient will be that identity, and the more positive will be the evaluation of that identity.
3. The greater the commitment premised on an identity, the more salient will be that identity, and the more general self-esteem will be based on that identity.
4. The more a given network of relationships is premised on a particular identity,

as against other identities that may also enter that network, the more salient will be that identity.

5. The larger the number of persons included in a network of relationships premised on a given identity for whom related identities are highly salient, the more salient will be that identity.
6. The more salient an identity, the more likely will be role performances consistent with the expectations attached to that identity.
7. The more salient an identity, the more likely a given situation will be perceived as an opportunity to perform the role underlying the identity.
8. The more salient an identity, the more likely opportunities to perform the role underlying the identity will be sought out.
9. The greater the commitment, the more salient will be the identity, and the greater will be the impact of role performance on role-specific self-esteem and on general self-esteem.
10. The greater the commitment, the more salient will be the identity, and the more likely will role performances reflect generally shared values and norms.

Before moving to an example of research examining identity theory, we must return to the note with which this chapter began: every extant theoretical framework in social psychology is partial and selective in its focus. Identity theory is even more selective than its parent, symbolic interactionism. The behavior it seeks to explain is role-related behavior, and not all social behavior is role-related. It focuses more particularly on choice behavior, and not all social behavior involves choices. Choice presumes a social structure that provides options. It may be true in some larger sense (since every social arrangement is created by human beings) that all social life involves options, but it is clear that prisons as a practical matter afford their inmates fewer of these than do other organized social contexts. Indeed, it may be said that the meaning of social structures lies precisely in the ways in which they limit or constrain choices—who is brought into contact, what possible role relationships can emerge, what resources can be used in these relationships, etc.

Moreover, the pragmatic philosophy that undergirds identity theory argues that mind emerges in response to problematic situations met in the course of social conduct. Thus, the cognitive activity and the emergent self to which identity theory gives overriding import occur in the degree that situations are problematic, which is simply another way of saying in the degree that humans are faced with choice.

Although problematic situations and choice peculiarly represent the human condition, not all social situations involve these, at least in the same degree. The degree of their presence represents a boundary condition for identity theory.

A Research Example

Having reviewed identity theory by outlining its history and course of development and by suggesting a set of hypotheses drawn from the theory articulating expected relationships among commitment, identity salience, and role performance, we are now ready to discuss a research effort examining the theory. Only a segment of that research can be presented here. The segment chosen for presentation takes the time spent in religious role activities as its concern, viewing such allocation of time to a role as a function of (in particular) commitment and identity salience.

The sample and measurement. The data are from the 1978 Indianapolis Area Project of Indiana University's Department of Sociology, a survey research directed by the senior author. The data were collected in the spring and summer of 1978 in the Indianapolis Standard Metropolitan Statistical Area (SMSA). Nonwhites were excluded from the sample because it was not possible to control through the study's design the race of the interviewers relative to the race of the respondents, and because of our belief that the interview's focus on identity raised the probability of cross-race bias. Age limits of 18-65 were set because we wished to maximize the numbers of respondents who occupied particular major structural positions (parent, spouse, worker, religion).

An area probability sample was drawn from the Indianapolis SMSA after census blocks with high black populations (utilizing the 1970 census) were systematically excluded from the population to be sampled. The sample was contacted and interviewed following a standardized questionnaire. The data collected on the 300 respondents in this study represent a response rate of 56%. This response rate, while absolutely low, is close to the level found in most current survey research. It may reflect, as well, the "overstudied" character of the research site, Indianapolis, and sample requirements that emphasized active and busy persons. Comparison of sample characteristics with census-provided population characteristics reveals no great response rate-related bias.

The content of the questionnaire focused on the three major classes of theoretical variables previously discussed: commitment, identity and role performance. In addition, several other social psychological constructs (self-esteem, satisfaction, etc.) were measured, and standard background information was obtained.

For the analysis presented here, we chose to focus on social behavior or role performance in the context of the religious role. This role was chosen rather than any of the other three available roles (parent, spouse, worker), singularly or in combination, because of its straightforward and clear appropriateness for examining identity theory. The religious role is not overly complicated by statistical interactions with the presence or absence of other roles.

Further, perhaps more than the other roles studied in the larger research effort, religious role performance–in particular, time spent in role–is realistically subject to choice, and so meets an important boundary condition of identity theory. Three major independent variables were selected for use in an analytic model, derived from identity theory, of religious role performance. The first variable is "religious commitment." Commitment, defined theoretically as relations to others formed as a function of occupancy of a particular position, was operationalized by a six-item scale with a Cronbach's alpha reliability coefficient of .73. The commitment scale consists of the following items:

1. Of all the people known through religion, how many are important to you, that is, you would really miss them if you did not see them?
2. Think of those people who are important to you. About how many would you

lose contact with if you did not do the religious activities you do?
3. How many people do you know on a first name basis through your religious activities?
4. Of the people you know through your religious activities, how many are close friends?
5. The fifth item is constructed from ratings of the importance of organizations the respondent participates in and the people the respondent knows through religious activities who also participate in the organizations.[8]
6. The sixth item is constructed from ratings of the importance of specific activities (other than religious, such as hobbies and recreation) the respondent engages in and whether or not the respondent participates in these activities with people known through religious activities.[9]

The commitment variable thus represents a measurement of the extensiveness and the intensity of relations with others in everyday life which are a function of participation in religious activities. The larger the number of and the more important these relations, the greater the commitment to the religious role.

The second variable is the "salience of the religious identity in relation to the salience of other identities," or the "location of religious role identity in the identity salience hierarchy." The salience of the religious identity was operationalized by a two-item scale with an alpha reliability coefficient of .75. For each item, the respondent was asked to rank religion in relation to the other roles in the study (parent, spouse, worker). The two items were:

1. Think about meeting people for the first time. You want to tell them about yourself so that they'll really know you, but you can only tell them one thing about yourself. Of the following (doing the work you do, being a husband or wife, being a parent, doing the religious activities you do, something else), which would you tell them (first, next, next)?
2. Suppose it were a weekend and you had a choice to do the following things (go to a religious service or activity, go on an outing with/visit your children, catch up on work, spend time with your husband or wife, none of these). Which would you most likely do? Next? Next?

The higher the ranking of the religious role in relation to other roles, the higher the identity salience of the religious role.

The third variable is "religious satisfaction," operationalized by a three-item scale with an alpha reliability coefficient of .66. The three items which make up

---

[8] Item 5 is a composite of eight items dealing with organizational memberships of the respondent. For up to four organizations to which the respondents belonged, they were asked to rate the importance to them of the organization, and whether or not they also knew through religious activities persons in each organization. The item was built by multiplying the importance rating by whether (=1) or not (=0) persons known through religion were in that organization, and then summing across organizations. The higher the score on item 5, the greater the importance of the relationships with others in these organizations with respect to the religious role.

[9] Item 6 was built in the same way as item 5, and was based on 14 items referring to everyday life activities (hobbies, sport activities, dining out, etc.).

this scale were presented in Likert scale form, with response categories ranging from strongly agree to strongly disagree:

1. In my religious activities, I am very satisfied.
2. I have met or am meeting my goals in my religious activities.
3. I can depend on feeling rewarded for what I do in my religious activities.

The higher the score on this scale, the greater the religious satisfaction.

In addition to the three main independent variables presented above, the analysis controlled for age and income of the respondent and the presence of other roles. The presence of other roles (see the discussion preceding Hypothesis 7, below, for the theoretical rationale justifying including other roles in the analysis) was controlled for by entering into the analysis a dummy variable for each role: parent, spouse and worker. Thus, if a respondent also occupied other positions, the effect of these roles was included in the analysis as the presence or absence of a specific role.

The dependent variable chosen for this analysis was "time spent in the religious role." Time in role was measured by an item asking the respondent, "How many hours in an average week do you spend in doing things related to religious activities?" The responses to this question provided us with a measure that can be viewed as behavioral, representing performance within the religious role. In addition, the time-in-role measure permitted a reasonable test of the theoretical position under examination: one would expect that the higher the commitment to a specific role, the larger the number of hours the person will spend in that role. Similarly, it is reasonable from the theory to expect that the higher the identity salience, the larger the number of hours devoted to a role. Time in role, then, is a measure of one aspect of role performance that theoretically should reflect commitment and identity salience. The responses to our time-in-role question were in the form of exact number of hours. The resulting distribution was skewed, and a natural log transformation has been used.

As indicated above, we have added role satisfaction to our repertoire of independent variables. Although such satisfaction is not directly implicated in identity theory, we conceive of it as an index of the intrinsic value placed by the person on a particular role and think it may be important as a determinant of time allocated to that role, either independently or in interaction with commitment and identity salience.

The model. Identity theory can be used to state more specifically our expectations about the impact of commitment, identity salience, satisfaction, and the presence of other roles. The theory posits a set of relationships between the independent and dependent variables in this study which can be examined using ordinary least squares regression techniques to estimate a path model for these relationships (see Alwin and Hauser, 1975, for a straightforward discussion of the techniques and procedures used).

Commitment is viewed within identity theory as central to the development of identity salience (Stryker, 1968, pp. 560-562) and thus plays a primary causal role in the development of the relationships specified by the theory. That is, commitment as a variable should be predictive of identity salience and should relate to other variables which are theoretically linked to identity and self. From this, we posit the following:

Hypothesis 1. The higher the commitment, the higher the identity salience.
Hypothesis 2. The higher the commitment, the higher the time spent in role.

Identity salience is presented by the theory as a variable that contributes to the explanation of the relations between the self and specific role performances (Stryker, 1968, pp. 561-562). That is, we expect a direct link between the salience of an identity tied to a specific role and the performance of activities associated with that role. The character and intensity of a role performance is theoretically a function of the location of the pertinent role identity within a salience hierarchy. Therefore:

Hypothesis 3. The higher the identity salience, the higher the time spent in role.

We would expect role performance to also be affected by the intrinsic value received from or placed on the performance of specific role activities, and so have introduced religious satisfaction as a variable in this analysis. The logic of our theoretical argument links satisfaction to commitment. That is, if commitment is high, satisfaction with the interpersonal ties linked to a role should be high. Unfortunately, our interview instrument failed to include satisfaction questions linked to interpersonal relations, but dealt rather with the consequences of performances in the role for the individual without reference to these. Nevertheless, we predict the following relationships:

Hypothesis 4. The higher the commitment, the higher the religious satisfaction.
Hypothesis 5. The higher the identity salience, the higher the religious satisfaction.
Hypothesis 6. The higher the religious satisfaction, the higher the time spent in role.

The concept of an identity salience hierarchy suggests that specific role identities are arranged in a hierarchical fashion and that the probability of one identity being invoked over another identity is a function of the situation and the location of the identities within the hierarchy (Stryker, 1968, p. 563). The concept of identity salience thus assumes that if a position is occupied, the identity associated with its role must be placed within the hierarchy, and that the salience of any identity is affected by the salience of other identities. We do not measure the specific salience of other identities relative to the religious identity within this analysis, but whether persons occupy other positions will indirectly affect the salience of the religious identity. Time is a finite commodity; consequently, occupancy of any given position necessarily intrudes in some degree on the time available for role performances attached to any other position. Therefore, other positions have been entered into the analysis as dummy variables which indicate whether or not the position is occupied. We predict:

Hypothesis 7. The presence of other roles (parental, spousal, worker) will be inversely related to the salience of the religious identity.

The inclusion of age and income in the analysis is based on the assumption that social structures constrain the development of social relationships (Stryker, 1980), and that opportunities for and the circumstances of such relationships are not distributed randomly in a population. It is, of course, in terms of such structural principles as age and income that relationships with given kinds of other persons are formed or not formed, endure or fail to endure. Thus, we can expect that age and income will relate to variables in our model of greater theoretical interest, aid in the attempt to understand the relationships among these variables of greater theoretical interest, and contribute to the overall explanatory power of our model.

The results. The means, standard deviations and zero-order correlations of the variables in our model are presented in Table 7-1. The number of persons from the total sample of 300 analyzed here is 164, the number of respondents within the sample who indicated they were active in the religious area (measured by attendance at religious activities). The analysis uses pairwise deletion of cases when information for a case on a variable is missing, a technique allowing the use of all available data for each respondent. The lowest number of respondents used in the analysis at any time given the pairwise deletion procedure was 164. There were 63 males and 101 females in this subsample. Males and females were examined separately in this preliminary analyses, and no differences were found; consequently, sex was not included in the final analysis.

Table 7-2 presents the standardized regression coefficients, the unstandardized regression coefficients, and associated standard errors for each pair of variables linked in the model. Figure 7-1 represents the path model specified by the significant path coefficients resulting from ordinary least squares regression procedures. Overall, this model is strongly supported, evidenced by the R^2 = .489 for the ultimate dependent variable, time spent in role. That is, almost half of the variance in time spent in religious role behaviors is accounted for by the variables incorporated into the model in Figure 7-1. In general, this represents a good fit of the theory and the data. A closer look at specific relationships provides strong support for the relationships hypothesized by the theory.

The expectations proposed in Hypotheses 1, 2, 3, 5, and 6 above, which specified the relationships between the theoretically significant independent variables and the dependent variable, all received strong support. These results suggest that there is a strong relationship between commitment and identity salience and that role performance is strongly affected by the strength of both the commitment and the identity salience variables. The hypothesized relationships between identity salience and satisfaction, as well as the hypothesized relationship between satisfaction and time in role were also supported at statistically significant, although somewhat weaker, levels. Hypothesis 4, linking satisfaction to commitment, received no support. These relationships suggest that the theoretically predicted links between commitment, identity salience, and role performance are very strong, and that commitment and identity salience account for much of the variance in role performance. Satisfaction was included in this analysis on the assumption that intrinsic value received or placed on a specific role performance also has a significant direct effect on that role performance, and this was found to be the case.

Table 7-1. Zero-Order Correlations, Means, and Standard Deviations Among the Variables

	2	3	4	5	6	7	8	9	SD	$\overline{X}$
1. Age	.10	.22***	.07	-.12*	.22**	.03	.11	.14*	41.57	12.35
2. Income		.24***	.34***	.10	.17*	-.23**	.08	.11*	9.30	2.50
3. Parental role			.44***	.02	.08	-.32***	-.17**	-.02	.81	.39
4. Spousal role				-.04	.05	-.25***	-.03	.16**	.76	.42
5. Worker role					.00	.36***	-.20**	-.13	.75	.43
6. Religious commitment						.40***	.16*	.51***	14.95	7.02
7. Religious role salience							.29***	.49***	5.49	2.08
8. Religious satisfaction								.32***	2.82	.70
9. Time in role									.71	.83

*$p < .05$.
**$p < .01$.
***$p < .001$.

Table 7-2. Regression Coefficients for the Path Model

Dependent variable	Predictor variable	Standardized regression coefficients	Regression coefficients	Standard error
Religious commitment ($R^2 = .037$)	Age	.200**	.114	.047
	Income	.158*	.435	.239
	Parental role	.006	.111	1.645
	Spousal role	-.019	-.317	1.545
	Worker role	.009	.137	1.321
Religious role salience ($R^2 = .465$)	Religious commitment	.467****	.139	.019
	Age	-.031	-.005	.010
	Income	-.167***	-.137	.054
	Parental role	-.256****	-.136	.371
	Spousal role	-.122*	-.599	.349
	Worker role	-.349****	-1.680	.298
Religious satisfaction ($R^2 = .154$)	Religious role salience	.233**	.777	.035
	Religious commitment	.026	.003	.009
	Age	.106	.006	.005
	Income	.138	.038	.024
	Parental role	-.196**	-.349	.164
	Spousal role	.112	.185	.148
	Worker role	-.113	-.181	.139
Time spent in role ($R^2 = .489$)	Religious commitment	.364****	.135	.034
	Religious role salience	.337****	.043	.009
	Religious satisfaction	.191***	.230	.078
	Age	.041	.003	.004
	Income	-.235****	-.078	.022
	Parental role	.007	.015	.156
	Spousal role	.309****	.612	.140
	Worker role	.068	.132	.131

*$p < .10$.
**$p < .05$.
***$p < .01$.
****$p < .001$.

Hypothesis 7, which specified that there would be an inverse relationship between the presence of other roles and the salience of the religious identity, was also supported. The paths from the parental role and the worker role to salience are strong, while the path from the spousal role is somewhat weaker. This finding reinforces our conception of identities as ordered hierarchically, with the consequence that the salience of one identity will have reciprocal effects on the salience of others.

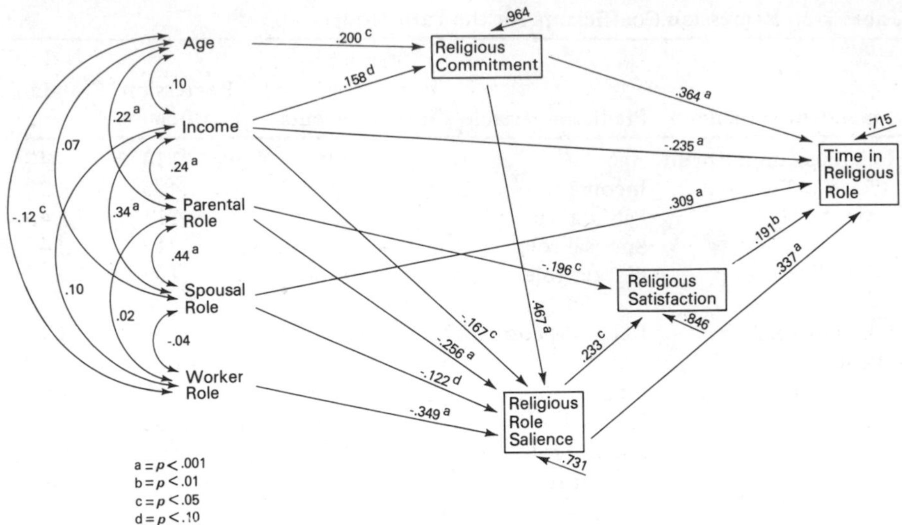

Fig. 7-1. Path model specified by significant path coefficients.

The inclusion of age and income result in some interesting findings and specifications of the model. As indicated by the rationale for their inclusion, there is an age and income structure that must affect the social psychological constructs investigated in this model. Specifically, age and income have direct effects on religious commitment. That is, the older the person, the more religious commitment increases; and the higher the income of the individual, the higher the religious commitment. Since commitment is a function of the number, type, and quality of relations with others, it makes sense that it will increase with both age (experience) and income (resources). Income was also found to have a negative effect on both identity salience and time in role: the higher the income, the lower the salience of the religious identity and the less the time spent in the religious role. People who are higher in the income structure, while they have a greater religious commitment, spend less time in religious activities and the salience of their religious identities relative to identities based on other roles is lower.

There were two significant findings not predicted by the theory and for which we have no clear theoretical or even any speculative explanation: the strong positive relationship between the spousal role and time spent in the religious role, and the weaker but significant negative effect of the parental role on religious satisfaction.

Conclusion

Identity theory, positing the centrality of commitment and identity salience to the process by which role performances are shaped, is in turn premised on the importance of the relationships between role variables and person variables in the explanation of social behavior. The utility of a framework built on this premise is thus strongly argued by the research findings just reported, which provide clear support for identity theory.

The empirical results presented contain no real surprises, certainly none that would call for radical revision of identity theory. The specific hypotheses generated from the theory indicated that commitment should be directly and positive related to identity salience, and that both commitment and identity salience should be directly and positively related to time spent in role (our role performance variable). The support for these hypotheses is unequivocal, and it is these hypotheses that are critical to the theory.

The model examined contained an indicator of the intrinsic value to the person of a role area in the form of a measure of religious satisfaction. We hypothesized that commitment and identity salience would have direct effects on satisfaction, and expected that satisfaction would have a direct effect on our role performance variable. The results indicated the existence of the hypothesized link between identity salience and satisfaction and between satisfaction and hours in role, but failed to show a link between commitment and satisfaction. This negative result could easily be a function of our failure to measure satisfaction in terms strictly relevant to the theory; it is thus premature to seek an appropriate modification of the theory.

The concept of an identity salience hierarchy receives support from the finding of inverse relationships between occupany of other roles and the salience of the religious identity. This finding provides further bolstering, then, for a conception of self that stresses its differentation and organization.

The framework on which identity theory draws sees social structure as entering the determination of social behavior by affecting interpersonal opportunities. This view is also reinforced by our empirical results. Income and age are important in the specification of commitment and identity salience; in addition, income has a significant direct effect on time in role. These findings suggest that attempts to understand the relationships of social psychological constructs among themselves and to behavior will profit by further explication of the ties of such constructs and behavior to the larger social structure that frames social action.

A social psychology that posits relationships among society, self, and social action must seek evidence for theoretically argued relationships. We began this chapter with a review of symbolic interactionism that emphasized the importance of the self, and offered in identity theory a contemporary development from symbolic interactionism that builds on a reinterpretation of the concept of self. We then operationalized concepts specified by identity theory and presented data collected to test our theory. We examined the theory by presenting a model designed to formalize it, and then evaluated hypotheses contained in that model. The result is empirical support, strong but by no means conclusive, for the assertion that the theory works, at least within the limits of the data, the operationalizations, and the analysis offered.

It is clear that further study is necessary, not only to model other kinds of roles, identities, and role performance than those examined here, but to model the relations between the roles and identities (religious, parent, spouse, worker, etc.), and to explore the possibility of reciprocal effects among our variables. The analysis reported was limited to exploring one role and identity in the presence of other roles and identities, i.e., it could not specify relationships among these. Both the concept of commitment and the concept of identity salience imply reciprocal relationships among roles and among identities, as well as between roles and identities.

It is not our intent to assert, via the use of path analysis, that there is no "looping" or "reciprocal causation" between any of the variables presented in the analysis, but rather to suggest that the relationships hypothesized by identity theory should be more thoroughly researched. Other than the potential reciprocity of commitment and identity salience, it is also possible that behavioral products of the process we have postulated feed back on the other variables in the model. For reasons implied in Mead's analysis, we believe the major causal direction is that incorporated into our model. Future research, some of which will treat the data set drawn on here, will examine such interactions both within and between specific situations. The product, on the evidence produced by the work reported here, should provide better understanding of the processes that shape social behavior.

References

Alwin, D., & Hauser, R. M. The decomposition of effects in path analysis. *American Sociological Review,* 1975, *40*, 37-47.

Bryson, G. *Man and society: The Scottish inquiry of the eighteenth century.* Princeton, N.J.: Princeton University Press, 1945.

Burke, P. J. The self: Measurement requirements from an interactionist perspective. *Social Psychology Quarterly,* 1980, *43*, 18-29.

Cooley, C. H. *Human nature and the social order.* New York: Scribners, 1902.

Dewey, J. The reflex arc in psychology. *Psychological Review,* 1896, *3*, 357-370.

James, W. *Principles of psychology* (2 vols.). New York: Holt, 1890.

McCall, G. J., & Simmons, J. T. *Identities and interaction* (rev. ed.). New York: Free Press, 1978.

Mead, G. H. *Mind, self and society.* Chicago: University of Chicago Press, 1934.

Meltzer, B. M., Petras, J. W., & Reynolds, L. T. *Symbolic interactionism: genesis, varieties and criticism.* London: Routledge & Kegan Paul, 1975.

Park, R. A. *Society.* New York: Free Press, 1955.

Schmitt, E. P. (Ed.). *Man and society.* New York: Prentice-Hall, 1937.

Simmel, G. *The Sociology of Georg Simmel.* (Kurt H. Wolff, Ed.). New York: Free Press, 1950.

Stryker, S. Symbolic interaction as an approach to family research. *Marriage and Family Living,* 1959, *31*, 111-119.

Stryker, S. Identity salience and role performance. *Journal of Marriage and the Family,* 1968, *30*, 558-564.

Stryker, S. *Symbolic interactionism: a social structural version.* Palo Alto, Calif.: Benjamin/Cummings, 1980.

Stryker, S. Symbolic interactionism: Themes and variations. In M. Rosenberg & R. Turner (Eds.), *Social Psychology: Sociological Perspectives.* New York: Basic Books, 1981.

Thomas, W. I. *Primitive behavior.* New York: McGraw-Hill, 1937.

Thomas, W. I., & Thomas, D. S. *The child in America.* New York: Knopf, 1928.

Chapter 8

Loss and Human Connection: An Exploration into the Nature of the Social Bond

Lyn H. Lofland

In Western culture, the involuntary severance (through death, desertion, or geographical separation, for example) of a relationship defined by actor as "significant" or "meaningful" is generally conceived of as a "loss" experience. In this essay, I want to pursue the question: What is lost? Stated more positively, I want to ask what it is that humans *do* for one another? What links self to other, personality to society? I want to make, that is, a modest foray into those matters that psychologists typically pursue with such concepts as "attachment," "affect," and "separation anxiety," and that sociologists pursue in their inquiries into the nature of the social bond.

To place the question of concern here–what is lost?–in its appropriate context, it will be useful, in the first section of this chapter, briefly to review the literature from sociology and psychology dealing with the closely related matters of attachment and grief. Having thus, hopefully, posed the question more fully, the second section will attempt a provisional answer to it by describing seven "threads of connectedness" between humans, seven "ways" in which self and other are linked. Finally, I will suggest some hypothetical and empirical "patterns" of connection and the possible utility of these patterns for our continuing attempts to understand more deeply the meaning and variability of both attachment and grief and the insight they provide us into the social animal that is ourself.

Attachment, Grief, and Loss

Human are social animals. This rather simple, even simplistic, statement covers a multitude of complexities. Lift it up and we see such matters as these: that the human animal is slow to mature and thus stands in a relationship of need to older members of the species for a considerable period of time; that "humanness"–the capacities and characteristics of the species–is a social creation, forged from the biological clay by the group; that all human behavior is necessarily social; and that attachments–emotional linkages–to other humans occur. It is this latter "fact," as part of the complex of "socialness," that is of concern here. Humans do not simply live in proximity of one another. They link themselves to one another. They tie. They bond. They bind. (Cf. Ainsworth and Wittig, 1969; Bowlby, 1969, 1973a, 1980; Cohen, 1974; Henderson, 1977; Weiss, 1973, 1975.) John Bowlby (1973b) has postulated that this attachment behavior is a hallmark of the species and a key to its survival.

> Man is a large, ground-living primate and, like other species of the sort, has probably always lived, until recent centuries, in small stable bands from a dozen to a hundred or so strong, comprising members of both sexes and all ages. Observation of other such species, for example, baboons, shows that each band usually moves as a unit and that the only animals at all likely to be found alone are adult males. Furthermore, when a band moves off, it does so in formation. Females and young tend to be near the center and near also to the mature males; whilst the young males are likely to be around their periphery. By adopting this formation, the band is well placed to withstand attack. When that happens, the young males, acting as scouts, give the alarm and withdraw closer to the center, females hastily gather young and move away from the point of alarm, mature males edge toward it. Thus, a marauding predator, hyena or leopard, ever waiting in the wings, is balked of his prey. Should an animal for any reason be isolated from the band, however, the outcome will be very different. Unless it is a strong, mature male able to put up a fight, the predator pounces and all is soon over.
>
> To be isolated from your band, therefore, and especially when young, to be isolated from your particular caretaker is fraught with the greatest danger. Can we wonder then that each animal is equipped with an instinctive disposition to avoid isolation and to maintain proximity? For any animal not so equipped would live but briefly. By contrast, animals well endowed in this regard would become parents of, and pass on their characteristics to, the next generation. Protection from predators seems, therefore, more than likely to be the function performed by attachment behavior not only in man but in other species as well. (pp. 46-47)

Attachment behavior may or may not be as "primal" as Bowlby suggests, and it may or may not be a contributor to human survival. It most certainly is a contributor to human pain. For the dark side of attachment is grief.

> It was when [Mary] came to the door, to walk through it, to leave this room and leave this shape of existence forever, that realization poured upon and overwhelmed her . . . . The realization came without shape or definability . . . but came with such force, such monstrous piercing weight, in all her heart and soul and mind and body but above all in the womb, where it arrived and dwelt like a cold and prodigious spreading stone, that she groaned almost inaudibly, almost a mere silent breath, an Ohhhhhhh, and doubled deeply over, hands to her belly, and her knee joints melted.
>
> Mary . . . rocked quietly back and forward and from side to side, groaning quietly, from the depths of her body, not like a human creature but a fatally hurt animal; sounds low, almost crooned, not strident, but shape-

less and orderless, the sisters, except in their quietude, to those transcendent, idiot, bellowing screams which deliver children. (Agee, 1956, p. 230)

James Agee's eloquent, if fictional, evocation in *A Death in the Family*, of the pain of severed attachment (in this instance, a marital attachment) is echoed over and over again in the extensive first-person, clinical, and scholarly literature on the grief experience in the contemporary United States and Great Britain. (See, for example, Averill, 1968; Beck, 1965; Becker, 1933; Caine, 1974; Charmaz, 1980, pp. 280-319; Clayton, Desmarais, & Winokur, 1968; Eliot, 1932-1933; Fulton, 1970; Glick, Weiss, & Parkes, 1974; Harvey & Bahr, 1980; Hurston, 1977-1978; Kohn & Kohn, 1978; Kutscher, 1969; Lewis, 1961; Lindemann, 1944; Lopata, 1973, 1979; Marris, 1958; Parkes, 1970, 1972; Peppers and Knapp, 1980; Pine et al., 1976; Schoenberg et al., 1970, 1974, 1975; Thomas, 1957; Wallace, 1973; Waller, 1967; Weiss, 1975.)

It is generally assumed by scholars of bereavement that the emotional experience described in this literature is a human universal. In fact, there is very little evidence either to support or refute such an assumption. We know a great deal about mourning, both historically and cross-culturally [that is, about how people *behave* when they are presumed grieving (see, for example, Bendann, 1930; Davey, 1889; Goody, 1962; Habenstein & Lamers, 1974; Jackson, 1977; Kalish, 1980; Mandelbaum, 1959; Morley, 1971; Rosenblatt, Walsh, & Jackson, 1976; Stannard, 1975, 1977)], but we do not have the comparable rich clinical, interview, and first-person accounts of *feelings* on other populations that have been accumulated on contemporary Americans and the English. Since all humans form attachments, there is actually good reason to suppose that all humans experience some form and degree of pain when those attachments are severed. But there is also very good reason to suppose that the shape, length, and intensity of the experience is profoundly altered by the cultural milieu.

Nearly 25 years ago, in his classic "Bereavement and Mental Health" (1957/1976), Edmund Volkart provided a glimpse into the array of insights that might be achieved through the adoption of a more comparative perspective on grief. Unfortunately, few have followed in his lead (but see Anderson, 1965; Charmaz, 1980, pp. 280-319; Kalish, 1980; Kalish & Reynolds, 1976; Levy, 1973; Lifton, 1967; Rosenblatt, Walsh, & Jackson, 1976; Yamamoto, 1970). There has been some concern with variations in the grief experience occasioned by variations in the context of the death (e.g., Charmaz, 1980, pp. 280-319; Sheskin, 1979; Sheskin & Wallace, 1976) or by variations in the kin or other relational link between deceased and survivor (Charmaz, 1980, pp. 280-319; Peppers & Knapp, 1980; Sanders, 1979-1980). But even in that relatively small portion of the literature which grants the *influence* of sociocultural forces, grief itself is granted a presocial, psychic, or biological status. The revolutionarly and exciting work of such people as Arlie Hochschild (1975, 1979; see also Kemper, 1978), which takes emotion out of the realm of the "organismic" and brings it into the realm of the thoroughly social, has yet to deal seriously with grief.

For my purposes, however, the question of cultural variability may, for the moment, be set aside. What is crucial for what follows is the unquestioned fact that when some modern Westerners undergo the rupturing of a relationship they define as significant, they report experiencing a discomforting combination of physical and psychic symptoms, typically labeled, grief.[1] I want to ask: For these persons, what is the cause of the pain? The simple answer, the breaking of an attachment, is satisfactory at one level. But I wish to delve more deeply. I wish to inquire into the nature of the attachment itself. I want to ask, with *what* do we attach ourselves to others? What, more specifically, are the ties that bind?

I should caution that the current endeavor is quite limited in that its goal is simply the dissection of a specific phenomenon and the identification of its component parts. Thus, beyond recognizing the mutuality of our concerns, I shall make no conscious attempt to link my efforts to those of my fellow scholars who have worked or are working on such closely related but considerably broader topics as loneliness (Fromm-Reichman, 1959; Lopata, 1969; Weiss, 1973), stress and life crises (Janis, 1971; Monat & Lazarus, 1977; Moos, 1976), varying objects of attachment and forms of loss (Benoliel, 1971; Burnside, 1970; Charmaz, 1981a, 1981b; Levinson, 1972), and the interrelations of loss and change (Marris, 1974) and of grief and disease (Lynch, 1977; Parkes, 1970, 1972).

Threads of Human Connectedness

In this section, I will propose seven "threads of connectedness": seven kinds of ways that humans bond themselves to one another. The materials from which this formulation emerges are of four types: (1) intensive interviews with persons who had experienced an involuntary[2] relational loss; (2) published first-person accounts of a grief experience; (3) published case and interview data from scholarly investigations of the grief experience; and (4) unpublished letters of condolence, funeral memoralizations, and personal anecdotes. Of these diverse materials, I continually asked the questions: What are these people saying about what it is that is missed? What do they say the "lost" person did for them? What is it they think they have lost?

Although the formulation that follows cannot be said to be built upon prior efforts to categorize types of relationships or types of interpersonal loss, it is nonetheless thoroughly informed by them. In 1967, for example, Warren Breed,

[1] Enumerations of the diverse but consistently reported "symptoms" of grief may be found in Charmaz, 1980; Clayton et al., 1968; Glick, Weiss, & Parkes, 1974; Hoyt, 1980-1981; Lindemann, 1944; Marris, 1958; Parkes, 1970, 1972; Stern, 1965.

[2] I here emphasize *involuntary* severance on the presumption that situations of *voluntary* severance are likely to tell us more about frustrated expectations than about relational components. However, in his study of broken marriages, Robert Weiss (1975) found considerable evidence of "grieving" among the *instigators* of the separation/divorce. Clearly, a relationship, however unsatisfactory, is still a relationship, involving "connections," and is thus relevant to the matters under consideration here. Nonetheless, I shall restrict my inquiry to instances of involuntary severance on the strategic grounds of "cleanliness."

noting that "loss" is a recurrent notion in the psychological and psychoanalytic literature on suicide causation, asks (as I do) "What is lost?" and answers: position, person, mutuality (Breed, 1967). Robert Weiss (1969) has proposed five categories of relational functions, each of which, he postulated, was for the most part provided by a different relationship: intimacy, social integration, opportunity for nurturant behavior, reassurance of worth, and assistance–with guidance added as a possible sixth function (see also Lopata, 1969).

But it is Samuel Wallace's (1973) ruminations about the meanings of his interview data on the bereavement experience of widows of suicides which most clearly herald the route taken herein:

> The loss occasioned but not limited to a death is not simply the loss of an *object*; a *relationship*, a *status*, a *way of being* are also lost when someone goes out of our lives. The "object" or person lost also takes with him or her that part of our self that they alone maintained–our self which was a son, our self which was a mother, our self which was a spouse. The loss of object and relationship also loses us a status, a position in the social universe. No longer are we married, have children, or are known as the lost one's friends. And within whatever status is lost lies an equally lost way of being.
>
> Bereavement, then, is social loss, of person, relationship, status, and way of being. The experience may be said to *vary* with our life's involvement with the person, relationship, status and way of being which is lost. (p. 231 [italics added])

Let us now examine each of the seven "connections" in turn. They are, as will be clear, both logically and empirically interrelated. But that interrelationship is not invariant and the separation performed here is, I believe, both analytically useful and empirically justified.

Role Partner

Much of the descriptive and analytic literature on loss and grief seems to touch on the role partner "thread of connectedness"–unsurprisingly, since it is one of the easiest to see and conceptualize, both for the actor and observer. Clearly, certain roles–certain organized and recurrent ways of being and acting–require for their realization, an "other." If the other is lost, so is the opportunity for playing the role. One cannot "be" daughter without mother, father without child, lover without lover, helper without helped, employee without employer, even enemy without enemy (see Lifton, 1973, pp. 45-46). It is primarily to this kind of loss that widows in Helena Lopata's study refer when they report that they are "lonely for the husband as [among other things] . . . a partner or companion in activities; an escort in couple-companionate interaction; 'someone' with whom to talk; 'someone' around whom work and time are organized . . ." (Lopata, 1973, p. 68; see also 1979, pp. 117-118). Similarly, a young male informant speaks of missing his deceased grandmother as a "playmate" and a young widow writes, in her diary, a letter to her dead husband about what their sons are missing.

> At times Keith is so frustrated; he misses you, Dwight, and needs you. He needs you as only an eight-year-old boy can need a father. I love him and try to show my love but that doesn't take your place. He needs that father and son shoulder-to-shoulder companionship and approval of work well done. But you knew he would need you! And Gary needs you; he needs you to help with all of his many building projects. He wants to build and create rockets, boats, hot rods.[3] (Beck, 1965, pp. 53-54)

Of course, most role partners, *qua* partners, are replaceable. The line of activity can be reactivated as part of one's continuing repertoire, although the speed or ease of replacement will vary according to the role itself and across time and space. And, when a single other serves as a partner in multiple roles, as in C. S. Lewis' (1961) description of his dead wife,

> She was my daughter and my mother, my pupil and my teacher, my subject and my sovereign; and always, holding all these in solution, my trusty comrade, friend, shipmate, fellow-soldier. (p. 39)

replacement, even substituting multiple others for the one, may become highly problematic. But until replacement occurs, the individual is in a condition of loss.

Mundane Assistance

People help one another. When the help is desired (it may not be, of course), the absence of the helper engenders a loss. The death of a neighbor may mean that one now has no one to look after pets and plants when one is away. The death of a work acquaintance may mean that one no longer has a ready source of job advice (personal communication). The death of a teenaged son may leave many household tasks undone, as this extract from the summary of an interview with a bereaved mother makes clear.

> She says that the entire family did not fully appreciate just how much he did in the way of helping tasks until he died. He was the kind of boy, she says, who did things without being asked—cleaning his room, emptying the trash, pruning the roses, mowing the lawn. On this past Christmas day, her two other children got up about 6:00 a.m. She asked them why, since they hadn't gotten up that early the year before. "Oh, yes, we did," they said, "but [the teenaged son] wouldn't let us come downstairs until 7:30."[4]

Or, the death of a husband may eliminate a buffer in one's relations with others.

> anytime the children do something wrong that goes against me, I start to think about him. They fly up against me, they never did when their father was here. They say things to hurt me, you know, and that's when I think

---

[3] One sees here a first example of the frequent empirical compounding of "ties"—in this instance, the tie of "role partner" between son and father is compounded by "mundane assistance" (see below).

[4] Quotations not otherwise referenced are from my interviews.

> about him. He would never have allowed them to talk to me that way. . . . (Wallace, 1973, p. 166)

It is important to recognize that removal of a helper may necessitate more than simply "picking up the slack" or finding substitute sources of aid. It may, as often in the illness or death of a spouse, necessitate learning a whole new set of skills, and as such, require the jettisoning of old "selves" or aspects of selves– yet another loss.

> A year ago, he was the boss, he managed this house completely, even the kids he controlled with the strictest discipline. I had to learn how to pay bills, I had never even written a check and I had to balance the checkbook, and oh, that was so hard to learn, everything that he used to do. Everything I did I used to ask him about first. I needed his advice, I depended on him so. He always knew the answers to everything. Then when he got sick, I had nobody, no one to take his place. *I had to learn how to live all over, to be a different person*. (Wallace, 1973, p. 39 [italics added]; see also Lopata, 1969, p. 253; Weiss, 1975, p. 97)

In fact, the literature on the experience of widowhood–as well as what little is available on widowers–suggests that a large element of the trauma engendered by the loss of a spouse in contemporary Western societies has to do with the loss of mundane assistance. People find themselves burdened with other aspects of the loss at the same time that they have to cope with such new matters as earning a living, balancing a checkbook, cooking, driving a car, making household repairs, cleaning house, and washing clothes. This has led some observers–quite independent of any feminist inclinations–to call for a reduction in sex-role specialization in the marital relationship (see, for example, Caine, 1974; Wedemyer, 1974).

Linkages to Others

The considerable social isolation of men and women following the deaths of their spouses or the breakup of their marriages is reported frequently in the literature on "loneliness." As Lopata notes,

> Many wives enjoy company parties, golf, couple-companionate dinners, and such events, and will not engage in them after the husband dies or have them no longer available *since it was his presence which formed the connecting link in the first place.* (Lopata, 1969, p. 253 [italics added]; see also Lopata, 1979, p. 118; Weiss, 1975, pp. 52, 58)

But it is clearly not only in the multiple bondedness of a marital relationship that persons can serve this linking function for one another. Friends and acquaintances often involve one another in their larger individual friendship and acquaintance networks–person A meets and relates to persons C, D, and E primarily through the arrangements of person B. One informant told me of feeling absolutely devastated when a close friend moved to another city, importantly because, rather to her surprise, she discovered that she had "no friends of my own"–only acquaintances through the now absent friend. Of course, the secondary linkage that B has provided between A and C, D, and E may eventually become primary. But when it does not, then loss of B occasions the simultaneous loss of C, D, and E, as well.

The Creation and Maintenance of Self

John Donne's caution not to "send to ask for whom the bell tolls, it tolls for thee" seems, even at this remove, both poetic metaphor—capturing a truth of the human condition—and empirical generalization—reflecting the phenomenological experience of many who suffer relational loss. At the level of poetic metaphor, Donne speaks to the profound interpenetration of self and the larger society through the dialectic of history, of culture, of socialization. At the level of empirical generalization, Donne also speaks to that fusion—to the experience, documented again and again, that in the loss of a single other, part or all of self is lost as well.

> When the loss has been sudden, large, and forced upon the attention, words implying mutilation and outrage tend to be used. One widow described her feelings on viewing the corpse of her husband: "It's as if my inside had been torn out and left a horrible wound there." A comparison is sometimes made to amputation: widows say that their husband has been "cut off," "as if half of myself was missing." In less violent terms, the loss of self is often referred to as a "gap"—"it's a great emptiness," "an unhappy void." (Parkes, 1972, p. 97).

At both levels, Donne's poetry forecasts a long tradition in social psychology which understands the self and its components importantly as the ongoing creation of the significant others who surround the actor.[5] From within that tradition, reports of self loss are not viewed merely as description through analogy but as literal depiction. That aspect of self (or those multiple aspects) that was significantly and uniquely generated and/or sustained in interaction with the other is, quite literally, lost when the other is lost.

If one's desirability, for example, is proffered and affirmed only in interaction with a single other human, the death of that human is the death of that part of self. A widow remembers:

---

[5] I am here separating out "role" from self—a separation that, to a degree, does violence to the conventions of social psychology. While the literature certainly understands role and self as distinct concepts, it also reflects an appreciation for their problematic but empirically frequent interpenetration (see, for example, Goffman, 1961; Turner, 1962, 1968, 1976, 1978; Zurcher, 1977, 1979). The separation is justified here, I believe, not because it reflects the most sophisticated understanding of these matters (as noted above, all the "connections" are logically and empirically interrelated), but because the separation is to be found in people's accounts. In my reading of the data, people are simply not talking about the same things when they speak of the loss of someone as role partner and when they speak of loss of self through loss of other. On the creation and maintenance of self, see, among others, Cooley (1902, 1909), Lemert (1951), Lifton (1961), J. Lofland (1969), Mead (1934), Murphy (1958), and Sullivan (1953).

> Here I am so big and fat and sometimes I'd be reading and would look up and he'd be sitting there looking at me—and I'd say, "What are you thinking about?" And he would say, "Oh, I was just thinking how pretty you are." (Lopata, 1969, p. 252)

Another widow reports,

> I think he found me as a very strong person. And being able to handle almost anything. And I think I probably saw in him someone who needed me very much. Which my first husband obviously did not. . . . When someone needs you, you . . . just automatically respond to them. . . . And I needed to be needed. (Wallace, 1973, p. 27; see also Thomas, 1957, Chap. 4; McCabe, 1970)

Similarly, a woman writes of a recently deceased friend:

> But the main thing that welded me to her so strongly was that she thought so much of me. She didn't flatter; she just never seemed to suspect that I wasn't as witty or wise or talented or nice as she thought I was, so I tried never to let on. In our 13 years of friendship, there was nothing she thought I couldn't do, and there was, in turn, nothing I wouldn't have done for her. (Barthel, 1972, p. 56)

Even when there are multiple others in the actor's milieu who help to maintain some aspect of self, a particular individual may be viewed as pivotal, as especially crucial to the actor's conception of self. Speaking of a man, now deceased, who had been important to him in his boyhood, a male informant muses over what this person had meant to him.

> He believed in me. He gave of his self to me, in the sense that he gave me responsibility, trusted me with responsibility for his very body [during epileptic seizures], his very physical existence which I was very honored to have someone trust me that way. That was probably the most responsibility I'd ever been given. Let's say the most meaningful responsibility.

James Thurber, in a letter to a friend, expresses a comparable judgment about Harold Ross, long-time editor of *The New Yorker.*

> I'm going to do a piece about Ross, but it will take time. He was the principal figure in my career, and I don't know what I would have amounted to without his magazine in which ninety percent of my stuff has appeared. He was also a great part of my life and I realize how much I loved him and depended on him. *There was no appreciation quite the same as his, because it was all tied up with him and his life. What* [E. B.] *White and I did was a part of the guy, and we realize how much of our work was done with him in mind.* (Bernstein, 1975, pp. 419-420 [italics added])

It might be argued, of course, that self maintenance is not threatened by the death or other loss of a significant other because memory allows continued—if entirely internal—interaction. To some degree, and for some period of time, this may be true. But the author, C. S. Lewis, writing about his "grief" over the death of his wife, suggests that the continued evocation of the other through memory has serious limitations.

> Slowly, quietly, like snow-flakes—like the small flakes that come when it is going to snow all night—little flakes of me, my impressions, my selections, are settling down on the image of her. The real shape will be quite hidden in the end. Ten minutes—ten seconds—of the real H. would correct all of this. And yet, even if those ten seconds were allowed me, one second later the little flakes would begin to fall again. The rough, sharp, cleaning tang of her otherness is gone. (Lewis, 1961, p. 19)

Support for Comforting Myths

For many humans, living comfortably in a world beset by the possibility of sudden death, catastrophic illness, unforeseen financial difficulties—all the hazards of existence—would seem to be made possible by the embrace of myth, of comforting stories about possibilities, situations, eventualities, self, others. These are stories that the individual knows, quite rationally, to be impossible, but which are clung to nonetheless. Like aspects of self, the reality of which seem to reside in the eyes of others, some of these myths appear to depend for their continued viability on the presence, or at least existence, of other persons. If these persons disappear, so do the myths and all the comfort and protection they afford. A particularly articulate informant, who shared with me some entries in her private journal, writes of just such a loss.

> Bob, like Ann, was so intertwined with so many memories of Rocklane [her home town] and my growing up there, that he and the town are, in some sense, synonymous. Not that he was always there while I was growing up. I was 10 to 11 or 12 before I ever met him, and he was gone for a period between about 8th grade and second year high school. But the time he was there, he was so crucial, that especially during my adolescent years, I cannot think of Rocklane without a memory of him crowding in. When my folks moved, I felt a tie to the home town cut, but it was not until Bob's death that I felt the real sense of the break. He was dead. The years of my adolescence were really gone. The hometown of my childhood was passed and could never be regained, because the person who had been so much a part of that time and that town was dead. *For the first time, really for the first time, I understood that I was growing older and that what was passed was forever, irremediably passed. It could never come again.* Of course, we always know this in our heads. I mean, one can't be alive without knowing it. But only with Bob's death did the full realization of this "fact of life" hit me with full force. I would never be 16 again, Rocklane would never again be for me the place it had been at 16. The people who peopled my memories of those years were gone; their older versions might still be around, but they were gone. The past was passed. It could not be reclaimed. [italics added]

The comfort from the myths seems not to reside in their sharpness or detail. Rather, they sit in the mind, shadowy, rather unsubstantial, off to the side, obliquely and intermittently viewed. Only when the myth is destroyed must its content be fully recognized.

> You tell me, "she goes on." But my heart and body are crying out, come back, come back. Be a circle, touching my circle on the plane of Nature. But I know this is impossible. I know that the thing I want is exactly the thing I can never get. The old life, the jokes, the drinks, the arguments, the love-making, the tiny, heartbreaking commonplace. *On any view whatever, to say, "H. is dead," is to say, "All that is gone." It is a part of the past. And the past is the past and that is what time means. . . .*" (Lewis, 1961, pp. 22-23 [italics added] ; see also Beck, 1965, p. 7; Orbach, 1959)

It should be noted that the keystone of the myth may reside less in the person than in the relationship itself, as in the following interview extract in which a woman informant speaks of her separation from her husband.

> I had an almost mystical sense that no matter what I did, no matter how I behaved, no matter what, he'd be there, sticking to me, my assurance not only that I could "hold a man," but that somebody cared for me. Rather like a child feels with very loving parents. We'd had a lot of fights and threatened each other with divorce many times, but it was all unreal. He was my secure future, my "Linus blanket" which told me that the things that happened to other people, the terrible painful things, couldn't happen to me. (see also, Caine, 1974, p. 135; Weiss, 1975, p. 49)

Reality Maintenance

Peter Berger and Hansfried Kellner in "Marriage and the Construction of Reality" (1964) have written persuasively of the reality validating character of marital and other intimate relationships.

> Every individual requires the ongoing validation of his world, including crucially the validation of his identity and place in this world, by those few who are his truly significant others. . . . Again, in the broad sense, all the actions of the significant others and even their simple presence serve this sustaining function. In everyday life, however, the principal method employed is speech. In this sense, it is proper to view the individual's relationship with his significant others as an ongoing conversation. As the latter occurs, it validates over and over again the fundamental definitions of reality once entered into, not, of course, so much by explicit articulation, but precisely by taking the definitions silently for granted and conversing about all conceivable matters on this taken-for-granted basis. . . . In a very fundamental sense it can be said that one converses one's way through life.
>
> If one concedes these points, one can now state a general sociological proposition: the plausibility and stability of the world, as socially defined, is dependent upon the strength and continuity of significant relations in which conversation about this world can be continually carried on. Or, to put it a little differently: the reality of the world is sustained through conversation with significant others. (1964, pp. 4-5)

Certainly, the scholarly and popular literature on grief would appear to confirm these observations (see references on p. 221 above). Colin Parkes has noted, for example, how the death of a husband alters the character of the world inhabited by the wife. "Even when words remain appropriate, their meaning changes—'the family' is no longer the same object it was, neither is 'home' or 'marriage'; even 'old age' now has a new meaning" (1972, p. 93). First-person accounts of the grief experience, as another example, typically contain references to feeling "odd," "strange," "peculiar," "out of touch with reality," "weird"—in fact, an "altered sensorium" is considered part of the normal symptomatology of grief (see references cited in Footnote 1).

But reality maintenance would appear to connect more than just intimates. As Berger and Kellner argue,

> This validation [of common-sense reality] . . . requires ongoing interaction with others who co-inhabit this same socially constructed world. In a broad sense, all the other co-inhabitants of the world serve a validating function. Every morning the newspaper boy validates the widest co-ordinates of my world and the mailman bears tangible validation of my own location within these co-ordinates. (1964, p. 4)

In this sense, the death or other loss of any noticed other in one's world threatens, however mildly, the validity of common-sense reality, and mass death may, as Robert Lifton (1967) has argued, destroy the survivor's very faith in the "connectedness of the world"—a possibility we will look at more closely in the concluding section.

The Maintenance of Possible Futures

Finally, the materials here under analysis suggest that persons are connected to one another through the parts they play in one another's futures. To "lose" certain persons is to lose certain futures, certain quite realistic possibilities for action, the very possibility of which provides comfort and/or pleasure to the actor. C. S. Lewis, for example, found pain in the realization that

> Never, in any place or time, will she [his decreased wife] have her son on her knees, or bathe him, or tell him a story, or plan for his future, or see her grandchild. (1961, p. 24)

A widow spoke of watching

> this older couple—I think this gets to me quicker than anything—is to see an older couple walking along the street, you know, and I say to myself, "I'll never be there." (Wallace, 1973, p. 114)

And a woman whose son had been killed in an accident told me that her sense of loss seemed to revolve primarily around a sense of potential not realized. She felt that her son was on his way to manhood, that he was in the process of becoming an interesting person, not just a son, but someone of whom she could feel proud, whom she could enjoy, with whom she could be friends. It was this potential that had been stripped away. She had been cheated— deprived—of the person her son was in the process of becoming.

The future that is destroyed by the loss of the other may be broadly and generally conceived, as the foregoing interview extracts suggest. But very circumscribed and/or detailed scenarios may also be cherished and relinquished with pain—a "scene" that will bring a relationship right again, for example.

> When I heard, in a letter when I was in college, that he had died, I was very angry that no one had told me because I had felt this strong need to put things right between us. To come to an understanding. I don't know what kind of understanding. To have corrected any misunderstanding that might have been there. To tell him how much I appreciated all that he had cared for me. Which I never got to tell him. That's what hurt the most of all, that I feared that he felt that I did not appreciate what I thought he had done; that I had rejected him because I could not, did not want to, do his [organizational] trip anymore. That was a rejection of him. I feared that he did not make that distinction. And I never got the opportunity to make that distinction.

Or, a "place" in which a relationship is to be played out. A woman, separated from her husband, describes one such, now forfeited, location.

> Do you know what [the southern part of a state] is like? Well, up towards . . . we wanted to buy some land and build an A-frame and it's, like, really hilly and forested and we had an area picked out where we wanted to buy some land there and we drew up this house that we wanted to build and there was room in it for two kids. . . . We called it the gingerbread house.

In sum, then, I am postulating that the "ties that bind," the "threads of connectedness" are of seven sorts. We are linked to others by the *roles* we play, by the *help* we receive, by the wider *network* of others made available to us, by the *selves* others create and sustain, by the comforting *myths* they allow us, by the *reality* they validate for us and by the *futures* they make possible. I make no claim that this listing is exhaustive, nor even that it is the most felicitous that could be conceived. I have, however, found it useful in thinking about varying patterns of connectedness and the possible relationship between such patterns and the grief experience. To those matters, let us now turn.

Patterns of Connectedness and Directions for Research

In the foregoing, I have attempted to conceptualize differing links or ties between humans; I have not attempted to describe any clusters of such ties as they might be found distributed among varying relationships. I have not done so because it is precisely the clustering or patterning that is problematic; it is this that I would hope we will seek to "discover"—the threads of connectedness having only provided a set of conceptual tools (although empirically derived) for the empirical task. In this section I would like first, simply by way of illustration, to look at some hypothetical (but plausible) patterns of connectedness, and second, to suggest some directions for future inquiry.

Table 8-1 illustrates four different ways that a person (A) might distribute his or her "connections"—each of the seven variations in linking symbols between Person A and Person B, Person A and Person C, and so forth, standing for one of the seven links. Thus, in the first pattern, we conceive of a person who, in a network of others, manages to encompass all seven ties, but with a minimum of multiple bonding to any one person. That is, Person A in this pattern is tied to Person B as role partner and for mundane assistance, to Person C as a link to others, to Person D through reality and future maintenance and to Person E as a creator and maintainer of self and as a supporter of comforting myths. Pattern 2 imagines a person, also with a minimum of multiple bonding, but in this instance, lacking the full range of possible linkages. Here Person A is tied to B as a role partner, to C as a link

Table 8-1. Patterns of Connectedness[a]

1. Full range of connections, spread among multiple others

- - - - - - - - - - - - A++++++++++++B	A: : : : : : : : : : : : :C A#############E ★★★★★★★★★★★★★	============ A. . . . . .D

2. Limited connections, spread among multiple others

A- - - - - - - - - - - - -B	A: : : : : : : : : : : : :C #############	A. . . . . .D

3. All connections to a single other, multiples of such others

★★★★★★★★★★★★★ - - - - - - - - - - - - : : : : : : : : : : : : A++++++++++++B ============ . . . . #############	★★★★★★★★★★★★★ - - - - - - - - - - - - : : : : : : : : : : : : A++++++++++++C ============ . . . . #############	★★★★★★★★★★★★★ - - - - - - - - - - - - : : : : : : : : : : : : A++++++++++++D ============ . . . . #############

4. All connections linked to a single other

★★★★★★★★★★★★★ - - - - - - - - - - - - : : : : : : : : : : : : A++++++++++++B ============ . . . . #############

[a] _ _ _ _ _, role partner; +++++, mundane assistance; : : : : :, linkages to others; #####, creation and maintenance of self; ★★★★★, support for comforting myths; = = = = =, reality maintenance; . . . . ., maintenance of possible futures.

to others, and as a creator and maintainer of self and to D through future maintenance; the other possible connections are simply missing. Pattern 3 postulates someone who is maximally multiply bonded to multiple others, while Pattern 4 illustrates maximal multiple bonding, but to a single other. The reader can imagine many other possible patterns and can complicate the picture enormously simply by varying, more than has been done here, the number of others to whom any given actor is linked.

There are additional "complications" which, in this brief essay, I will not address. For example, some linkages can themselves be compounded or intensified in a single relationship, as in many intimacies involving multiple role partnerships. Or, as another matter, I have throughout assumed the status of adult among relational participants. When it is a child, especially a very young child, who is at the receiving end of a set of connections, one would expect the "power" of any single tie to be intensified.

The point, of course, as indicated, is not the elaboration of hypothetical patterns, but the discovery of empirical ones. Nonetheless, appreciation of the possible existence of variant patterns can guide the inquiry into their occurrence. We might ask, as one line of inquiry, whether there is *historical and cultural variation* in the *range, dominance and idealization* of extant patterns. And, assuming such variation to be discovered, we might ask further whether or in what way it relates to possible differences in the emotional experience of grief, to observed differences in mourning practices and to other social psychological and/or structural diversities among human groups.

For example, might it be that "death demographics" are importantly linked to the dominant pattern or patterns or even range of patterns to be found in a given social order during a given period? That is, might it be that what appears to be, by modern standards, relative emotional coolness in the face of the death of presumed intimates among historic Westerners is best understood as a quite reasonable "spread" of connections (e.g., a preponderance of Patterns 1 and 2 over 3 and 4) under conditions of high mortality rates?[6] When the demographer E. A. Wrigley reports that

> It was entirely in accord with the usage of that time [early 1600's in England], that the children's father, William, should have remarried so soon after the death of his first wife. Remarriages within a period of weeks rather than months were not uncommon. (1969, p. 83)

are we observing not an historically different social psychology, nor even a greater (in contrast to contemporary) acceptance of death, but a different structural patterning of connectedness?

---

[6]This suggestion is, at least, implicitly present in the writings of many of the demographers, historians, sociologists, and anthropologists who have considered the issue of mortality and social structure. See, for example, Ariès (1962, 1974), Blauner (1966), Goldscheider (1971, 1976), Jackson (1977), Marshall (1980, pp. 30-37), and Stannard (1975, 1979).

As another example, might observed cultural differences in mourning practices be linked to a group's typical patterning of linkages? Edmund Volkart postulated exactly such a connection nearly 25 years ago, although he limited his discussion by using only the language of "roles."

> In his study of the Ifaluk people, [M. E.] Spiro was puzzled by some features of bereavement behavior there. When a family member died, the immediate survivors displayed considerable pain and distress, which behavior was in accordance with local custom. However, as soon as the funeral was over, the bereaved were able to laugh, smile and behave in general as if they had suffered no loss or injury at all. Their "grief" seemed to disappear as if by magic, and this too was approved by custom. . . . In terms of the thesis being developed here, the bereavement behavior of the Ifaluk suggests that their family system is such as to develop selves that are initially less vulnerable in bereavement than are the selves we are accustomed to. . . . Another way of stating this is that in self-other relations among the Ifaluk, the other is not valued by the self as a unique and necessary personality. Functionally speaking, not only are the roles of others dispersed, but the roles themselves are more important psychologically than are the particular persons who play the role vis-à-vis the self. Multiple and interchangeable personnel performing the same functions for the individual provides the individual with many psychological anchors in his social environment; the death of any one person leaves the others and thus diminishes the loss.[7] (1976, pp. 247-249; for further discussions on cultural variation, see Anderson, 1965; Devereux, 1942; Levy, 1973; Plath, 1968; Yamamoto, 1970)

Taking the lead from Volkart, is it possible that there exists a dominance of and/or preference for some variant on Pattern 3 (which might be termed "the multiple intimates pattern") among contemporary Americans? (A perfectly rational preference, by the way, given current mortality conditions. See L. Lofland, 1978.) And if so, might its discovery illuminate such other apparent extant patterns as, for example, Robert Weiss' finding that

> It is not possible for an individual to compensate for the absence of one relational provision by increased acquisition of others; to put it another way, relational provisions cannot be substituted for one another. Thus, someone whose life is without emotional attachment cannot compensate for this deficit by throwing himself into his work or entering into more active relations with friends or devoting himself to his children. (1973, p. 227; see also 1969)

That is, might it be that Americans cannot substitute one "relational provision for another" because they believe that the only meaningful relationships—the only

---

[7]We must bear in mind that in descriptions of bereavement behavior such as this one, we do not know whether we are viewing mourning alone or mourning and grieving in combination. If the former, we learn much about cultural form but little or nothing about emotional states. (See p. 223.)

relationships that provide "emotional attachment" are intimate ones? Might a discovered preference for a "multiple intimates" pattern help us to understand Richard Sennett's assertions about the contemporary American penchant for privatism, intimacy, and "community" and the consequent lack of appreciation for those more impersonal but urbane relationships which are the essence of effective political activity? (1970, 1977; see also Tinder, 1980).

I have suggested that inquiry into historical and cultural variation in patterns of connectedness might be fruitful. Let me suggest further that inquiries into *experiential variation* might prove equally so. That is, if we hold constant time and cultural space, we might inquire into the particular experience of death itself—into the threads or multiples of threads broken—and the relationship between that experience and its emotional accompaniment.

One such variant in the experience of death provides the focus of a goodly portion of the scholarly and first-person literature on grief—what might be called *devastating loss.* It is in reference to devastating loss that the literature, quite properly, speaks of survivors, for the language of its accompanying grief is the language of personal disaster.

Devastating loss may occur when there is a death involving a *solitary multibonded relationship.* If we imagine a continuum of connectedness based on numbers of persons involved, we can visualize at one end an actor who is linked in diverse ways (some multiple bonding, some single bonding, etc.) to a very large number of others. At the other end is a person who has literally placed all his or her eggs in one basket—all the linkages are to a single other person (Pattern 4, above). Now, this latter situation is probably empirically very infrequent, possibly nonexistent. Even if others are linked to us in no other ways, they are, as Berger and Kellner (1964) have pointed out, at least contributing to the validation of our commonsense reality. Nonetheless, close approximations of this extreme situation are anything but rare.

> Everything I did revolved around him. He was my whole world. [When he died] my heart was gone. My reason to live, everything.

And death involving such a relationship (or its approximation) is devastating because in one fell swoop all (or almost all) of the actor's "connections" are severed.

As numerous commentators have suggested, it may be that the very intense grief experience reported so frequently by widows and widowers in the contemporary United States and Britain (see references cited on p. 221) has importantly to do with a tendency for marital relationships to become solitary and multibonded. *A* significant other becomes *the most* significant other—permeating every corner of our lives.

> At first I was very afraid of going to places where H. and I had been happy—our favorite pub, our favorite wood. But I decided to do it at once—like sending a pilot up again as soon as possible after he's had a crash. Unexpectedly, it makes no difference. Her absence is no more emphatic in those places than anywhere else. It's not local at all. I suppose that if one were forbidden all salt, one wouldn't notice it much more in any one food than

in another. Eating in general would be different every day, at every meal. It is like that. *The act of living is different all through. Her absence is like the sky, spread over everything.* (Lewis, 1961, p. 13 [italics added])

Another sort of devastating loss results not from the removal of a single person in whom all connections are encompassed but from the simultaneous removal of all connections, that is, in circumstances of *mass death*. Of course, once again, we are dealing with a continuum. The extreme case where every single known other in the actor's world is removed, is empirically rare. But, tragically, close approximations are less so.[8] Robert Lifton's studies of the survivors of Hiroshima provides one of the most detailed records of this particular death experience (1967, 1976)—an experience that in its intensity and profundity seems almost to defy our capacity to understand it. In his attempts to convey the survivor's experience, Lifton's language often moves toward the mystical. But he forecasts the argument presented herein when he writes that Hiroshima occasioned in its survivors

> a vast breakdown of faith in the larger human matrix supporting each individual life and, therefore, a loss of faith (or trust) in the structure of existence (1976, p. 203; see also Wallace, 1957)

I suggested at the beginning of this chapter that my intent was to make a modest foray into that area of inquiry which sociologists would identify as involving the nature of the social bond. Typically in such sociological inquiries, analysis proceeds at a considerably more abstract level than I have employed here—at the level of varying forms of social organization, say, or the structural components of social systems. Robert Nisbet, for example, in his book, *The Social Bond*, identifies "social interaction," "social aggregates," "social authority," "social roles," "social status," "social norms," and "social entropy" as the elements of that bond (1970, pp. 49-56; see also Nisbet and Perrin, 1977, pp. 38-45). While I have no specific argument with this formulation or others like it, it and they do seem to me to have strayed rather far from the classic and, I believe, more fruitful orientations of such representatives of nineteenth century concerns with the social bond as Durkheim and Tönnies. Durkheim's discussion of mechanical and organic solidarity (1947) and Tönnies' discourse on *Gemeinschaft* and *Gesellschaft* (1940) are more than attempts to describe changing social structure under conditions of industrialization and urbanization. They are, profoundly, also attempts to describe the changing *affective* tie between actors and others, between selves and societies. They are, that is, not merely forays into social organization, but explorations into social psychology as well. Despite this precedent, the foregoing pages have, regretfully, dealt more with social psychology than with social organization, just as typical work on the social

[8] Just how painful or personally disruptive various sorts of disasters may be is a matter of some debate (see, for example, Erikson, 1976; Janis, 1971; Quarantelli, 1980). Thinking about these matters in terms of experiential variations in the severed connections might begin to resolve some of the conflict, or at least clarify some of the issues. For a revisionist view of the long-term effects of the holocaust, see Weinfeld et al. (1979).

bond deals more with social organization than with social psychology. Such an admission, however, by no means subverts the very desired and classic goal, shared by large numbers of social scientists, of dealing, eventually, with both simultaneously, and of doing so in a way that slanders neither.

I happen to believe, and I think others working in the areas of attachment, connection, grief, and loss would concur, that these areas provide one plausible route to the achievement of that goal. Certainly we have a long way to go. As the reader has discovered, we are far from understanding even experiential variations in patterns of connection and loss, much less the historical and cultural structuring of connection and loss, and even less the relation between such patterning and structuring and the organization of social orders. To strive for such an understanding, however, as I hope I have made clear, is well worth the effort. Such an understanding should bring us closer to grasping that very social and socially connected animal that is ourself and that matrix of connectedness that is our social order and our home.

Acknowledgments. I owe a great debt of gratitude to many informants, friends, and colleagues—all of whom must remain anonymous—who have shared so freely of personal mementos, anecdotes, memories, and musings about matters that for many of them are still sources of pain. I am grateful as well for the generosity of colleagues who read earlier drafts of this paper and who provided support and comments and/or criticisms. I wish publicly to thank Kathy Charmaz, Gary Hamilton, William Ickes, Eric Knowles, John Lofland, and Victor Marshall. I must admit, however, to having resisted dealing with a number of their more telling and well-taken criticisms. I trust this resistance will in no way threaten any of our "threads of connection."

References

Agee, J. *A Death in the Family.* New York: Avon Books, 1956.

Ainsworth, M. D., & Wittig, B. Attachment and exploratory behavior of one-year-olds in a strange situation. In B. Foss (Ed.), *Determinants of infant behavior* (Vol. 4). London: Methuen, 1969.

Anderson, B. G. Bereavement as a subject of cross-cultural inquiry: An American sample. *Anthropological Quarterly,* 1965, *38*, 181-200.

Ariès, P. *Centuries of childhood.* New York: Knopf, 1962.

Ariès, P. *Western attitudes toward death from the middle ages to the present.* Baltimore, Md.: Johns Hopkins University Press, 1975.

Averill, J. R. Grief: Its nature and significance. *Psychological Bulletin,* 1968, *70*, 721-748.

Barthel, J. I promise you, it will be all right. The dilemma of a friend's dying. *Life,* March 17, 1972.

Beck, F. *The diary of a widow.* Boston: Beacon Press, 1965.

Becker, H. The sorrow of bereavement. *Journal of Abnormal and Social Psychology,* 1933, *27*, 391-410.

Bendann, E. *Death customs: An analytical study of burial rites.* New York: Knopf, 1930.

Benoliel, J. Q. Assessments of loss and grief. *Journal of Thanatology,* 1971, *1*, 182-194.

Berger, P., & Kellner, H. Marriage and the construction of reality. *Diogenes*, 1964, *46*, 1-24.

Bernstein, B. *Thurber: A biography*. New York: Dodd Mead, 1975.

Blauner, R. Death and social structure. *Psychiatry*, 1966, *24*, 378-394.

Bowlby, J. *Attachment and loss* (Vol. 1). *Attachment*. New York: Basic Books, 1969.

Bowlby, J. *Attachment and loss* (Vol. 2). *Separation: Anxiety and Anger*. New York: Basic Books, 1973. (a)

Bowlby, J. Affectional bonds: Their nature and origin. In R. S. Weiss (Ed.), *Loneliness: The experience of emotional and social isolation*. Cambridge, Mass.: MIT Press, 1973. (b)

Bowlby, J. *Attachment and loss* (Vol. 3). *Loss: Sadness and depression*. New York: Basic Books, 1980.

Breed, W. Suicide and loss in social interaction. In E. S. Shneidman (Ed.), *Essays in self destruction*. New York: Science House, 1967.

Burnside, I. M. Loss: A constant theme in group work with the aged. *Hospital and Community Psychiatry*, 1970, *21*, 21-25.

Caine, L. *Widow*. New York: William Morrow, 1974.

Charmaz, K. C. *The social reality of death*. Reading, Mass.: Addison-Wesley, 1980.

Charmaz, K. C. *Chronic illness and identity*. Unpublished manuscript, 1981. (a) (An earlier version of this paper presented at the meetings of the Pacific Sociological Association, Sacramento, California, 1977.)

Charmaz, K. C. *Time and the situated self*. Unpublished manuscript, 1981. (b) (An earlier version of this paper presented at the meetings of the Pacific Sociological Association, Spokane, Washington, 1978.)

Clayton, P., Desmarais, L., & Winokur, G. A study of normal bereavement. *American Journal of Psychiatry*, 1968, *125*, 64-74.

Cohen, L. J. The operational definition of human attachment. *Psychological Bulletin*, 1974, *81*, 207-217.

Cooley, C. H. *Human nature and the social order*. New York: Scribner, 1902.

Cooley, C. H. *Social organization*. New York: Scribner, 1909.

Davey, R. *A history of mourning*. London: Jay's, 1889.

Devereux, G. Social structure and the economy of affective bonds. *The Psychoanalytic Review*, 1942, *29*, 303-314.

Durkheim, E. *The Division of Labor in Society* (G. Simpson, trans.). Glencoe, Ill.: The Free Press, 1947.

Eliot, T. D. A step toward the social psychology of bereavement. *Journal of Abnormal and social psychology*, 1932-1933, *27*, 380-390.

Erikson, K. T. *Everything in its path: Destruction of community in the Buffalo Creek flood*. New York: Simon and Shuster, 1976.

Fulton, R. Death, grief and social recuperation. *Omega*, 1970, *1*, 23-28.

Fromm-Reichman, F. Loneliness. *Psychiatry*, 1959, *22*, 1-15.

Glick, I. O., Weiss, R. S., & Parkes, C. M. *The first year of bereavement*. New York: Wiley, 1974.

Goffman, E. *Encounters*, Indianapolis, Ind.: Bobbs-Merrill, 1961.

Goldscheider, C. *Population, modernization and social structure.* Boston: Little, Brown, 1971.

Goldscheider, C. The mortality revolution. In E. Shneidman (Ed.), *Death: Current perspectives,* Palo Alto, Calif.: Mayfield, 1976.

Goody, J. *Death, property and the ancestors: A study of the mortuary customs of the Lodagaa of West Africa.* Stanford, Calif.: Stanford University Press, 1962.

Habenstein, R. W., & Lamers, W. M. *Funeral customs the world over.* Milwaukee, Wisc.: Bulfin Printers, 1974.

Harvey, C. D. H., & Bahr, H. M. *The sunshine widows.* Lexington, Mass.: Lexington Books, 1980.

Henderson, S. The social network, support and neurosis: The function of attachments in adult life. *British Journal of Psychiatry,* 1977, *131*, 185-191.

Hochschild, A. R. The sociology of feeling and emotion: Selected possibilities. In M. Millman & R. M. Kanter (Eds.). *Another voice: Feminist perspectives on social life and social science.* Garden City, N.Y.: Doubleday Anchor, 1975.

Hochschild, A. R. Emotion work, feeling rules and social structure. *American Journal of Sociology,* 1979, *85*, 551-575.

Hoyt, M. F. Clinical notes regarding the experience of "presences" in mourning. *Omega,* 1980-1981, *11*, 105-111.

Hurston, R. O. The grief cycle in the management of affect. *Case Analysis,* 1977-1978, *1*, 39-64.

Jackson, C. O. (Ed.). *Passing: The vision of death in America.* Westport, Conn.: Greenwood Press, 1977.

Janis, I. L. *Stress and frustration.* New York: Harcourt Brace Jovanovich, 1971.

Kalish, R. A. (Ed.). *Death and dying: Views from many other cultures.* Farmingdale, N.Y.: Baywood, 1980.

Kalish, R. A., & Reynolds, D. K. *Death and ethnicity.* Los Angeles: University of Southern California Press, 1976.

Kemper, T. D. *A social interactional theory of emotion.* New York: Wiley, 1978.

Kohn, J. B., & Kohn, W. K. *The widower.* Boston: Beacon Press, 1978.

Kutscher, A. H. (Ed.). *Death and bereavement.* Springfield, Ill.: Charles C Thomas, 1969.

Lemert, E. M. *Social pathology.* New York: McGraw-Hill, 1951.

Levinson, H. Easing the pain of person loss. *Harvard Business Review,* September-October, 1972, pp. 80-88.

Levy, R. I. *Tahitians: Mind and experience in the Society Islands.* Chicago: University of Chicago Press, 1973.

Lewis, C. S. *A grief observed.* New York: Seabury Press, 1961.

Lifton, R. J. *Thought reform and the psychology of totalism: A study of "brainwashing" in China.* New York: Norton, 1961.

Lifton, R. J. *Death in life: Survivors of Hiroshima.* New York: Vintage, 1967.

Lifton, R. J. *Home from the war.* New York: Simon & Schuster, 1973.

Lifton, R. J. Psychological effects of the atomic bomb in Hiroshima: The theme of death. In R. Fulton (Ed.), *Death and Identity* (rev. ed.). Bowie, Md.: Charles Press Publishers, 1976. (Originally published, 1963)

Lindemann, E. Symptomatology and management of acute grief. *American Journal of Psychiatry*, 1944, *101*, 141-148.

Lofland, J. *Deviance and identity*. Englewood Cliffs, N.J.: Prentice-Hall, 1969.

Lofland, L. H. *The craft of dying*. Beverly Hills, Calif.: Sage, 1978.

Lopata, H. Z. Loneliness: Forms and components. *Social Problems*, 1969, *17*, 248-261.

Lopata, H. Z. *Widowhood in an American city*. Cambridge, Mass.: Schenkman, 1973.

Lopata, H. Z. *Women as widows: Support systems*. New York: Elsevier, 1979.

Lynch, J. J. *The broken heart: The medical consequences of loneliness*. New York: Basic Books, 1977.

McCabe, C. A sprig of rosemary. *San Francisco Chronicle*, May 5, 1970.

Mandelbaum, D. G. Social uses of funeral rites. In H. Feifel (Ed.), *The meaning of death*. New York: McGraw-Hill, 1959.

Marris, P. *Widows and their families*. London: Routledge & Kegan Paul, 1958.

Marris, P. *Loss and change*. New York: Pantheon, 1974.

Marshall, V. W. *Last chapters: A sociology of aging and dying*. Monterey, Calif.: Brooks/Cole, 1980.

Mead, G. H. *Mind, self and society*. Chicago: University of Chicago Press, 1934.

Monat, A., & Lazarus, R. S. (Eds.). *Stress and coping: An anthology*. New York: Columbia University Press, 1977.

Moos, R. H. (Ed.). *Human adaptation: Coping with life crises*. Lexington, Mass.: Heath, 1976.

Morley, J. *Death, heaven and the Victorians*. Pittsburgh, Pa.: University of Pittsburgh Press, 1971.

Murphy, G. *Human potentialities*. New York: Basic Books, 1958.

Nisbet, R. A. *The social bond: An introduction to the study of society*. New York: Knopf, 1970.

Nisbet, R. A., & Perrin, R. G. *The social bond: An introduction to the study of society* (2nd ed.). New York: Knopf, 1977.

Orbach, C. E. The multiple meanings of the loss of a child. *American Journal of Psychotherapy*, 1959, *13*, 906-915.

Parkes, C. M. "Seeking" and "finding" a lost object: Evidence from recent studies of the reaction to bereavement. *Social Science and Medicine*, 1970, *4*, 187-201.

Parkes, C. M. *Bereavement: Studies of grief in adult life*. New York: International Universities Press, 1972.

Peppers, L. G., & Knapp, R. J. *Motherhood and mourning: Perinatal death*. New York: Praeger, 1980.

Pine, V. R., et al. (Eds.). *Acute grief and the funeral*. Springfield, Ill.: Charles C Thomas, 1976.

Plath, D. W. Maintaining relations with kin: Social ties after death in Japan. In H. K. Geiger (Ed.), *Comparative perspectives on marriage and the family*. Boston: Little, Brown, 1968.

Quarantelli, E. L. An assessment of conflicting views on the consequences of disasters for mental health. Columbus, Ohio: Disaster Research Center, Ohio State University, 1980.

Rosenblatt, P. C., Walsh, P., & Jackson, D. A. *Grief and mourning in cross-cultural perspective.* HRAF Press, 1976.

Sanders, C. M. A comparison of adult bereavement in the death of a spouse, child and parent. *Omega,* 1979-1980, *10*, 303-322.

Sennett, R. *The uses of disorder: Personal identity and city life.* New York: Vintage, 1970.

Sennett, R. *The fall of public man.* New York: Knopf, 1977.

Sheskin, A. *Cryonics: A sociology of death and bereavement.* New York: Irvington, 1979.

Sheskin, A., & Wallace, S. Differing bereavements: Suicide, natural and accidental death. *Omega,* 1976, *7*, 229-242.

Schoenberg, B., et al. (Eds.). *Loss and grief: Psychological management in medical practice.* New York and London: Columbia University Press, 1970.

Schoenberg, B., et al. (Eds.). *Anticipatory grief.* New York and London: Columbia University Press, 1974.

Schoenberg, B., et al. (Eds.). *Bereavement: Its psychosocial aspects.* New York and London: Columbia University Press, 1975.

Stannard, D. E. (Ed.). *Death in America.* Philadelphia: University of Pennsylvania Press, 1975.

Stannard, D. E. *The Puritan way of death.* Oxford: Oxford University Press, 1977.

Stern, K., Williams, G., & Prados, M. Grief reactions in later life. In R. Fulton (Ed.), *Death and identity.* New York: Wiley, 1965.

Sullivan, H. S. *The interpersonal theory of psychiatry.* New York: Norton, 1953.

Thomas, C. *Leftover life to kill.* Boston: Little, Brown, 1957.

Tinder, G. *Community: Reflections on a tragic ideal.* Baton Rouge, La.: Louisiana State University Press, 1980.

Tönnies, F. *Fundamental concepts of sociology* (C. F. Loomis, trans. and supplementer). New York: American Book, 1940.

Turner, R. H. Role taking: Process versus conformity. In A. M. Rose (Ed.), *Human behavior and social processes.* Boston: Houghton Mifflin, 1962.

Turner, R. H. Role: Sociological aspects. *International encyclopedia of the social sciences* (Vols. 13-14). New York: Macmillan and The Free Press, 1968.

Turner, R. H. The real self: From institution to impulse. *American Journal of Sociology,* 1976, *81*, 989-1016.

Turner, R. H. The role and the person. *American Journal of Sociology,* 1978, *84*, 1-23.

Volkart, E. H. (with collaboration of S. T. Michael). Bereavement and mental health. In R. Fulton (Ed.), *Death and identity* (rev. ed.). Bowie, Md.: Charles Press, 1976. (Originally published, 1957.)

Waller, W. *The old love and the new: Divorce and readjustment.* Carbondale & Edwardsville: Southern Illinois University Press, 1967. (Originally published, 1930)

Wallace, A. F. C. Mazeway disintegration: The individual's perception of sociocultural disorganization. *Human organization,* 1957, *16*, 23-27.

Wallace, S. E. *After suicide.* New York: Wiley, 1973.

Wedemeyer, D. Widowers: They face unique problems which widows do not. *Sacramento Bee*, November 16, 1974.

Weinfeld, M., Sigal, J. J., & Eaton, W. *Long-term effects of the holocaust: A cautionary note.* Unpublished manuscript, 1979.

Weiss, R. S. The fund of sociability. *Trans-action* (now, Society), July/August, 1969, 36-43.

Weiss, R. S. *Loneliness: The experience of emotional and social isolation.* Cambridge, Mass.: MIT Press, 1973.

Weiss, R. S. *Marital separation.* New York: Basic Books, 1975.

Wrigley, E. A. *Population and history.* New York: McGraw-Hill, 1969.

Yamamoto, J. Cultural factors in loneliness, death and separation. *Medical Times*, 1970, *98*, 177-183.

Zurcher, L. A. *The mutable self.* Beverly Hills, Calif.: Sage, 1977.

Zurcher, L. A. Role selection: The influence of internalized vocabularies of motive. *Symbolic Interaction*, 1979, *2*, 45-62.

Chapter 9

Changing Roles, Goals, and Self-Conceptions: Process and Results in a Program for Women's Employment

Chad Gordon and Paddy Gordon

Nature and Scope of the Problem

Displaced homemakers experience a relatively new form of role loss. This loss can result from divorce, desertion, separation, or the disability or death of a spouse on whom the displaced homemaker previously had been dependent. Alternatively, the loss may be due to economic necessity. From whichever source, the loss of the homemaker role involves reduction of the financial and emotional security that derived from previously relatively well-defined roles as wife and mother. Such loss forces the displaced homemaker into a job market that is accurately characterized in terms of both agism and sexism, and also may involve the burden of racism. Although some men may face the circumstance of suddenly losing a relationship that had provided economic as well as emotional support, men face much less discrimination even as they move into their middle years. For this reason, the present chapter will restrict the phrase "displaced homemaker" to women.

The term "displaced homemaker" was coined in 1974 by Tish Sommers, a California feminist and advocate for older women, to capture the situation of women who were "caught in the middle" after being "forcibly exiled" from the apparently secure dependency of their wife and mother roles due to the rapidly increasing divorce rate and due to the effects of inflation on lower- and middle-income families (Shields, 1981, p. ix). Sommers observed that these women either found themselves to be completely inexperienced at occupational roles outside the home, or, because their work experience was many years in the past, they were functionally obsolete. They generally face discrimination in employment both because they are older than typical new applicants coming into business personnel offices and because as women they tend to seek employment in service fields where opportunities are not good even for highly qualified and recently trained applicants. Displaced homemakers may come from any socioeconomic level, but their current circumstance may render them ineligible for social security because they are too young or because they were divorced from husbands to whom they had been married less than 10 years. They may have lost rights as beneficiaries under their husbands' health plans after divorce. Moreover, they may be unacceptable to private health insurance plans because of their age, and may not qualify for any form of public assistance program because of what few resources they may have gathered from their divorce or inheritance arrangements.

Frequently shattered by the experience of divorce, desertion, or widowhood, these women, regardless of their age, may experience very low self-esteem and self-confidence, thus adding depression and sensed inadequacy to their objective problems in securing training or employment. Sommers' conceptualization of the displaced homemaker, the first to appear, has provided working definitions for those who have been organizing in efforts to benefit these women. In addition, it has, with relatively little change, been written into the state and federal laws resulting from these organizing efforts:

> By definition, according to Sommers, a displaced homemaker is an individual who has, for a substantial number of years, provided unpaid service to her family, has been dependent on her spouse for income but loses that income through death, divorce, separation, desertion or disablement of her husband. (Shields, 1981, p. ix)

National Scope of the Displaced Homemaker Problem

In 1975, Tish Sommers and her organization, the Alliance for Displaced Homemakers (ADH), developed the "unofficial" estimate that approximately 3-6 million women in the country closely matched the definition of a displaced homemaker. An additional 15 million more women were estimated to be potential displaced homemakers based on the increasing rates of divorce and desertion. In 1978, the Department of Labor drew upon the data from its own Survey of Income and Education (March, 1976) and more recent material from its Womens' Bureau to produce an "official" estimate of approximately 4 million displaced homemakers, including 3 million who were between the ages of 40 and 64 (Shields, 1981, p. ix). The problems of the older (40- to 64-year-old) women are especially severe for at least two reasons: first, age-based discrimination affects women earlier than it does men (Bernard, 1975; L. Rubin, 1979; Sales, 1978; Sontag, 1972) and, second, the years that the older displaced homemakers have invested in home management and activities in voluntary organizations are rarely valued positively, even when they can objectively be seen to have been excellent preparation for various kinds of jobs. In fact, older workers are frequently superior to younger ones with regard to their motivation, stability, loyalty, and relatively lower rates of accidents and absenteeism (Guilfoy, 1980, p. 3). For other important connections between work and age, see Saranson (1977).

Between 1974 and 1978, the idea of defining displaced homemakers as a category of persons sufficiently vulnerable and disadvantaged and also sufficiently worthy to receive governmental aid and support achieved considerable attention. It provided the basis for initial legislation in California, and for a wide range of other state programs. It then gave rise to an embryonic national effort. Although the national financial commitment was not great in relation to the number of women at risk ($5 million in relation to at least 4 million displaced homemakers comes to only a little over $1 per person), the national funding effort did establish a number of ongoing projects concerned with the general area of displaced homemaker activity (cf. Eliason, 1979; Ekstrom, 1979; Berman, 1980; Guilfoy, 1980).

Hypotheses About Displaced Homemakers

The literature on displaced homemakers has been almost exclusively applied in character, and has not contained much in the way of explicit theorizing. However, a symbolic interactionist approach to role theory, and especially to the issue of involuntary role loss is obviously relevant to formulating hypotheses with which to approach analysis of new empirical data from a displaced homemaker program. The basic ideas regarding the relationship between self, role, and immediate social situation are drawn from the classic and contemporary perspectives on symbolic interactionism (cf. Gordon & Gergen, 1968; Kaplan, 1979; Manis & Meltzer, 1978; McCall & Simmons, 1978). The conceptual approach to the analysis of roles is that of Ralph Turner (1962, 1968, 1976). The particular approach to analysis of the typical stages of the life cycle and to the study of transitions between them can be found in C. Gordon's work 1971a, 1971b, and 1976), which builds on the work of Erik Erikson (1950, 1959) and many other life cycle theorists. The thrust of these ideas is that values form the organizing center of roles, whereas self-conceptions link the person to both values and roles.

The theoretical and empirical issues surrounding the questions of whether and to what degree personality changes during adulthood are represented in an immense literature. There are advocates of stability (cf. Block, 1981; Costa & McCrae, 1980) as well as change (cf. Brim & Kagan, 1980; Levinson, 1978), but the issues remain largely unresolved (Z. Rubin, 1981). We hope this chapter will provide some additional valuable evidence.

Ideas specific to the circumstance of leaving any important role come from A. Blau (1973), George (1980), Glaser and Strauss (1971), and Rosow (1976). Perspectives concerning marital separation have been integrated by Weiss (1975). Finally, Lopata (1973) has done especially important work on the effects of role loss on widows' self-conceptions.

The questions of how self-conceptions relate to roles and role changes have been dealt with in many papers (C. Gordon, 1968a, 1968b, 1969, 1976; Gordon, Gaitz, & Scott, 1975). In the present context, we will extrapolate to the situation of displaced homemakers the conceptualization of *role loss* in old age as formulated by Irving Rosow (1973). Rosow asserts that progressive loss of roles produces both negative self-evaluations and the experience of severe personal stress. Both these effects may be eased or ameliorated by particular personality capabilities on the one hand, and by valued group support on the other. That these effects accurately characterize the situation of displaced homemakers can be seen by substituting that category for "the aged" in Rosow's theoretical formulation:

> The most crucial single rule by far involves the progressive loss of roles and functions of the aged, for this change represents a critical introduction of stress. Role loss generates the pressures and sets the conditions for the

> emerging crisis, and taken together, these delineate the social context of the aging self. What does this involve?
>
> First, *the loss of roles excludes the aged from significant social participation and devalues them.* It deprives them of vital functions that underlie their sense of worth, their self-conceptions and self-esteem. In a word, they are depreciated and become marginal, alienated from the larger society. Whatever their ability, they are judged invidiously, as if they have little of value to contribute to the world's work and affairs. In a society that rewards men mainly according to their economic utility, the aged are arbitrarily stigmatized as having little marginal utility of any kind, either economic or social. On the contrary, they tend to be tolerated, patronized, ignored, rejected, or viewed as a liability. They are first excluded from the mainstream of social existence, and because of this nonparticipation, they are then penalized and denied the rewards that earlier came to them routinely. (Rosow, 1973, p. 82)
>
> Finally, *role loss deprives people of their social identity*. This is almost axiomatic, for sociologists define the social self as the totality of a person's social roles. These roles identify and describe him as a social being and are central to his very self-conceptions. The process of role loss steadily eats away at these crucial elements of social personality and converts what *is* to what *was* – or transforms the present into the past. In psychological terms, this is a direct, sustained attack on the ego. If the social self consists of roles, then role loss erodes self-conceptions and sacrifices social identity. (Rosow, 1973, p. 83; emphasis in original)

Sociologists who are now beginning to observe displaced homemakers are noting this same configuration of damaged self-conceptions and felt stress. In the specific case of displaced homemakers, Ruth Jacobs has described them as the "victims of personal loss and social change":

> Whatever self-confidence they have is eroded when they experience rejection by employers. Already traumatized by divorce, many desire nurturant and familiar teaching or social service jobs, which are in short supply. They have little interest or training for more plentiful technical and business jobs.
>
> Widows also become displaced upon the loss of spouses. Widowhood is the frequent fate of mid-life American women because, sadly, males die on the average eight years younger than females and males marry, or remarry after divorce, substantially younger women than themselves. Inflation quickly erodes widow's inheritances and many widows have no inheritance, only debts. (Jacobs, 1980, pp. 2-3)

In addition to the generally similar effects of the role displacement on self-conceptions and subjectively experienced stress, Jacobs sees another common element in the fundamental need of displaced homemakers for paid work:

> As the first displaced homemaker program director, Milo Smith of Oakland, California, told us, "There is nothing like that first paycheck to restore self-confidence." Although displaced homemakers have suffered emotional trauma, they are not the only Americans to have private griefs.

> Research results back up the folklore that work is healing; it also pays the rent and gets you out with people. Displaced homemakers can benefit, as many other Americans, from mental health and other life-style rehabilitation services. Yet, they have as a first priority the need for vocational counselling and training leading to paid employment so that they may become independent and have the security, self-esteem, dignity and social respect that comes with that independence. If they are forced to work at menial work that may not last, they will be anxious. If they have skills, job security and rewards, they may well be able to handle other stresses. To pay taxes, rather than being recipients of charity, is what displaced homemakers want and deserve. (Jacobs, 1980, p. 7)

By using the general hypotheses of a symbolic interactionist approach to role loss in conjunction with the displaced homemaker information supplied by Jacobs, we have produced a set of four hypotheses that will guide the presentation and analysis of data to follow:

1. Displaced homemakers typically will be found to have a number of important self-conceptions that are negative, especially on dimensions that have closest reference to the self-directed application of skills and capacities (i.e., competence and self-determination, rather than unity or moral worth; C. Gordon, 1968a, 1968b).
2. Displaced homemakers typically will experience confusion and uncertainty about their occupational futures.
3. A successful program for displaced homemakers will help these women improve their self-conceptions, gain a realistic familiarity with the existing employment market, clarify their employment and lifestyle values, and develop the necessary job-getting skills. In addition, the program staff should actively assist the participants in getting work or in getting into the desired work training program.
4. Those program participants who improve most in their self-conceptions will also be those who gain most in effectively coping with their economic situations.

Nature of the Career Options Program at Houston Community College[1]

During the spring semester of 1980, Houston Community College (under a grant from the Texas Education Agency) offered a Career Options Program designed to assist displaced homemakers in reentering the workforce. The program was organized as a series of discussion and support group sessions, with each group of from 7 to 14 women meeting for approximately 6 hours per day for a full month. The participants who took part in the first four groups form the data base for the present program evaluation and theoretical research, a total of 38 women who agreed to share information about their lives with us through the means of questionnaires, interviews, staff ratings, and long discussions about their plans and activities.

[1] This program was under the direction of Dean Donald L. Clark. The project administrator was Carol Creswell, and the program itself was designed and facilitated by Paddy Gordon and Patricia Lubar.

Goals and Objectives of the Program

The goal of each 4-week program was to facilitate the successful reentry of displaced homemakers into the labor force. The participants were assisted in defining their career goals and developing realistic individual educational and employment plans that could be acted on, at least in part, before the completion of the program. Special emphasis was placed on the exploration of nontraditional career opportunities.

Methods and Procedures

The group process was the heart of the method used by the staff, who facilitated the sharing of experiences and feelings. Although the staff encouraged the participants to discuss their fears and expectations regarding possible career and educational decisions within the context of the group, it was understood that all final decisions would be made by the individual with the support of the staff and group.

The staff stressed that the career and educational decisions should be realistic. Unfortunately, much of the literature on careers for displaced homemakers is highly unrealistic in relation to a sophisticated job market such as Houston, so the facilitators were forced to develop many of their own exercises and materials. For example, the placement specialist conducted a series of mock interviews, using videotaping for subsequent evaluation by the individual and group. Field trips were taken to the business section of the Houston Public Library so that the participants could learn how to do effective research on companies that might be potential employers. Resumé writing and skills of personal presentation were also developed, both in the group context and privately.

Five Component Parts of the Program

The workshop experience can be viewed in terms of five component parts: (1) initial explorations and assessment, (2) preparation for job search, (3) assisted entry into the Houston job market, (4) life improvement skills training, and (5) support group sessions. Each will be outlined in turn.

1. Initial explorations and assessment. Eight subcomponents provided information that served as a baseline for the evaluation and assistance in the clarification of occupational goals:

a. Self-conception assessment of the participants' self-perceived strengths and weaknesses, interests, and values.
b. Review of major social trends affecting women's education and employment, including the changing roles of women in modern America, and women in education and occupational careers in the Houston of the 1980s.
c. Field trips to visit vocational and technical classes at Houston Community College System to familiarize the participants with educational opportunities in the vocational and technical area.
d. Career goal setting: Administration of questionnaires regarding the participants' occupational preferences and special job requirements.

e. Effective communication skills to increase competence in all areas of the participants' communicative lives.
f. Coping strategies pertaining to time management, stress management, the legal rights of women in Texas, financial management, and the use of community and college resources.
g. Individualized educational and career counseling.
h. Guidelines for making specific educational and career choices in Houston.

2. Preparation for job search. This second component was designed to assist the participants in preparing to enter the Houston job market by providing them with experience in the following areas:
a. Effective interviewing skills.
b. Resumé writing.
c. Personal presentation and grooming skills.
d. Coping with possible rejection in employment interviews.
e. Selecting from among the available employment alternatives.
f. Using the business section of the Houston Public Library (field trip).
g. Learning how to survive the first month on the job.
h. Learning how to maximize job satisfaction.
i. Learning about the working rights of women.

3. Assisted entry into the Houston job market. The third component was designed to maximize the participants' reentry into the job market. In this phase:
a. Paddy Gordon (who has had wide professional experience in job placement work in the private sector) actively solicited specific job openings for the participant.
b. The women then participated in these prearranged interviews and in other interviews.

4. Life improvement skills training. The fourth component of the program was offered by the college as a service to Career Options. Through manipulative, experiential activities performed on an individual basis, the participant was made aware of the elements necessary to complete tasks successfully, and learned the value of becoming committed to high quality performance.

5. Support group sessions. The final component of the workshop consisted of the establishment of support groups, offering the participants continuing support to counteract feelings of isolation and to build confidence and self-esteem as they pursued their occupational and educational goals.

Characteristics of the Program Participants[2]

Demographic and Social Characteristics

Our evaluation and analysis use the data from the first four cycles of the program. This group was composed of 38 women, ranging in age from 18 to 55, with a mean age of 39. Six of the women were Mexican-Americans, 9 were Black, and 23 were Anglos. Half were married and living with their husbands; 6 were separated. Among the 13 single women, 5 had always been single, whereas 8 were divorced. Twenty-eight of the women had at least one child at home, and 5 had four or more children for whom they were responsible. Almost all the women currently living with their husbands were either planning for divorce or considering it.

Education is obviously of great importance in determining occupational futures, and here the women in the study were quite diverse: 5 had less than a high school education, 4 had obtained a G.E.D. or high school equivalency degree, and 7 had completed high school. The largest group (17 women) had gone on to complete some college or vocational training, but only three of these had completed a bachelor's degree, and only two others had some graduate education, with only one of these having completed a master's degree. Thus, 42% had completed only high school or less, 45% had some college, and an additional 14% had finished college or taken some advanced work.

Past work experience. All the women except one had worked at some previous point in their lives, although none was employed upon entering the Career Options Program. Their previous jobs included household service (2 women), food service (4), retail sales (5), general office work (18), administration or teaching (7), and middle-level management (1). The women's specific past jobs were coded according to the Duncan Socioeconomic Status Index (Reiss, 1961, Chap. 6 and Appendix B), which assigns socioeconomic status (SES) scores to occupational titles based on the age-adjusted education and income averages for all persons in that occupation. This status index has been used in many research applications, and has been shown to possess satisfactory reliability and validity (cf. Blau & Duncan, 1967; Duncan, 1967; Duncan, Featherman, & Duncan, 1972).

The Duncan SES scores that were assigned to the 37 women who had given information on past occupations had a mean of 43.4 and a standard deviation of 15.3 points on a scale that theoretically could range from 2 to 96. Since these women were still relatively young, and since most had raised one or more children, it is not surprising that the length of time on their previous jobs was not great: only 38% had worked for 6 years or longer. Their highest salaries on these past occupations also were not large, ranging from a low of $1-2/hour (3 women), through a modal group at $2-3/hour (15 women), up to a group of 7 women who had made over $6/hour.

---

[2] An additional 22 persons participated in other workshop groups in the Career Options Program, but they were already employed people who were interested in changing careers. Their groups met only one night a week, and contained some men. For all these reasons, the 22 are not included here.

Husbands' work situations. Of the 29 women who provided information about their husband's occupational situations, 8 described their husbands as major professional, 6 as middle-management, 4 as administrators or teachers, 7 as employed in sales occupations, 2 in food service, and 2 in unskilled jobs. When the occupations of the husbands were coded according to the Duncan Socioeconomic Status Index, they yielded a mean of 58.1 (much higher than the women's mean of 43.3). The status scores of the men's occupations were more variable than those of the women.

Comparison of participants' previous occupations and husbands' occupations to national employment patterns. An examination of the women's past occupations reveals that the participants in the Career Options Program previously had been in jobs that were substantially concentrated in the white collar range, much more so than is the case with women's employment nationally (84% as compared with 66% of the 40.9 million American working women; U.S. Department of Labor, 1980a, Table A-22). The jobs reported for the husbands were even more highly concentrated in the white collar category (86% as against 42% for men nationally). It should be noted, however, that the participants were concentrated in the clerical category (49%), whereas their husbands were found only in the sales, managerial, and professional classifications.

None of the women previously had worked in blue collar occupations (as against 14% of women nationally), and only a very few husbands (7%) were currently working in blue collar occupations (as against 45% nationally). Neither the husbands nor the wives had farm occupations, but 16% of the women were classified as service workers, primarily in other than household work, a pattern similar to the national one (19%). The husbands also were fairly similar to the national pattern regarding service work (7% as contrasted with 9% nationally).

These overall comparisons make it clear that most of the participants in the Career Options Program had previously held lower-middle-class jobs (84%), with concentrations of previous work experiences in the area of general office work, teaching at elementary or secondary level, or retail sales. A much smaller group (16%) previously had been employed in lower-working-class jobs, as service workers. The status of the husbands was substantially higher, concentrated in the middle- to upper-middle-class managerial and professional or technical ranks). It should be remembered, however, that many of these women's work experiences had occurred a substantial number of years in the past. For this reason, these experiences were not necessarily transferable to the participants' current search for the type of jobs that would seem at least adequate (if not especially "meaningful") from their present viewpoint.

Comparison of Study Group to the Depiction of Displaced Homemakers

Consideration of the above demographic characteristics leads us to the conclusion that our study group was only moderately similar to the depiction of the displaced homemaker provided by Jacobs (1980) and Shields (1981). The women in our study were, for the most part, younger, better educated, and had more recent and higher status occupational experience; furthermore, none was forced out of the home by widowhood. (This same pattern is being found in "displaced homemaker" programs around the state.) In addition, less than half of the participants expressed any feelings of really being *forced* to leave a *desired* homemaker role. Rather, most felt that they *wanted* to take on an occupational role, either for the benefits it might offer in the world beyond the narrow confines of the home, or as a way of reducing their dependence on a man for economic support.

The fact that these women were found to differ substantially from the orienting view of the displaced homemaker alerts us to the probability that our first hypothesis may not hold precisely, because it presupposed a significant degree of unwanted role displacement. However, we are still dealing with cases of role *change* (even though in most cases it is of a voluntary character), and thus we will still expect the other three hypotheses to be supported.

Motivations for Participation in the Career Options Program

Each of the women was asked, as a part of the intake questionnaire and then again in an early exercise entitled "My Goals," to list the objectives they sought through participation in the Career Options Program. A wide range of goals was mentioned by the participants, but these motivations were classifiable under 5 headings (the percentages given below add up to more than 100 because each woman was free to mention any number of goals). The *desire for economic enhancement* topped the list of expressed motivations (87%), followed closely by the *search for self-fulfillment* 76%), and for *group experiences* (74%). The desire for *increased social status* (47%) and the desire for *escape from an unpleasant home situation* (42%) were much less frequently expressed, although they still were important to just under half of the women.

Staff Ratings of the Participants' Personal Characteristics and Interpersonal Styles

At the outset of the program, Paddy Gordon made ratings of the personal characteristics and interpersonal styles of the program participants. Five-point rating scales were used to represent the admittedly subjective social evaluations of the participants on 11 personal and interpersonal dimensions. The 11 dimensions were grouped in terms of the results of a subsequent factor analysis of the raw ratings. The first three factors (in descending order of matrix variance explained) and their component ratings that loaded over +.40 were *mental set* (decisiveness, motivation, and attitude), *physical presentation* (appearance, taste, organization), and *interactive style* (participation and verbal ability). Additional ratings dealt with *self-sufficiency, flexibility,* and *employability*.

Characteristics of Possible Jobs as Rated According to Participant Preferences

These preference ratings of specific job features help us understand the qualitative character of possible jobs that the participants felt attracted to at the start of the program. Calculation of mean preference ratings from the 5-point scale data revealed that there were three distinct sets of preferences. Receiving mean ratings at or above the "somewhat high" point were five job characteristics that deal with applying skills to the job and obtaining direct rewards for that application: "use my skills," "salary," "security," "advancement" and "appreciation." A second group was rated of medium importance; items in this group involve specific features of the job itself: "opportunity to help people," "use my creativity," "work with people," "freedom from supervision," and "exercise my leadership." Finally, the lowest rated characteristics (between somewhat low and medium) were two that seem far removed from the housewife role these women seek to leave: "provide adventure," and "glamor/status." In total, these ratings of desired job characteristics convey a feeling of sought-for stability and reward for the application of skills and abilities, coupled with the impression that the move from the limiting housewife role into the work world is seen as quite enough of a jolt without the additional components of "adventure" and "glamor/status."

The one major difference between the present study's results and those obtained by Rosenberg from a large sample of college students in the late 1950s is that the college students ranked the value of salary much lower than the application of their skills, whereas the women rated salary in second position, even higher than security. Of course, there are very substantial differences between the economic and social circumstances facing these women as compared with those facing college students in the relatively noninflationary 1950s. Yet we can conclude from these data that the women in our study were definitely oriented toward seeking both salary and security in future jobs, and were not looking only for "self-expression" or other such emotional values as are often attributed to women entering the job market.

Social circumstances of a desired future job. The respondents also indicated their preferences about a future job in terms of four adjective pairs describing the social circumstances of a possible job scene: individual vs. social, competitive vs. cooperative, self-structure vs. prestructured, and relaxed vs. pressured. In each case, the respondent could indicate two degrees of positivity toward one of the adjectives or could indicate two degrees of negativity toward one of the adjectives, or could indicate a preference for neither. The resulting scores showed that the program participants preferred to find jobs that were cooperative and social over those that were individual and competitive. They also sought a relaxed rather than pressured environment, and a self-structured rather than a prestructured set of circumstances.

Participants' Self-Conceptions at the Start of the Program

A 31-scale semantic differential called the Self-Conception Profile was developed by the authors as a way of assessing the participants' self-conceptions at the start of the program and again at the end of the program, thus serving as a vehicle for ascertaining changes in self-conceptions over the course of the program. This Self-Conception Profile (shown in Figure 9-1) is based on earlier work in self-conception methodologies (C. Gordon, 1968a, 1969), and particularly on the idea that specific

Fig. 9-1. Self-conception Profile for "Jane Keller." (Copyright© 1979 by Person-Conceptions Analysis, Houston, Texas).

These pairs of opposite words are useful in describing people. Please place a single check on each line to indicate which word of each pair fits you best and the degree to which it fits you.

	Extremely	Quite	Slightly	In Between	Slightly	Quite	Extremely	
1. Calm	___	✓	___	___	___	___	___	Emotional
2. Friendly	___	✓	___	___	___	___	___	Unfriendly
3. Bad	___	___	___	___	___	✓	___	Good
4. Young	___	___	___	✓	___	___	___	Old
5. Unattractive	___	___	___	___	✓	___	___	Attractive
6. Happy	___	___	✓	___	___	___	___	Unhappy
7. Dependent	___	___	✓	___	___	___	___	Independent
8. Strong	___	___	___	✓	___	___	___	Weak
9. Passive	___	___	___	___	✓	___	___	Active
10. Interested in enjoyment	___	✓	___	___	___	___	___	Interested in achievement
11. Shy	___	___	✓	___	___	___	___	Outgoing
12. Optimistic	___	✓	___	___	___	___	___	Pessimistic

	1	2	3	4	5	6	7	
13. Important			✓					Unimportant
14. Submissive				✓				Dominant
15. High in self-confidence						✓		Low in self confidence
16. Unpopular					✓			Popular
17. Creative					✓			Uncreative
18. Unlucky					✓			Lucky
19. Heavy in weight			✓					Light in weight
20. Tall					✓			Short
21. Assertive					✓			Unassertive
22. Incompetent						✓		Competent
23. Healthy	✓							Unhealthy
24. Responsible	✓							Irresponsible
25. Unambitious					✓			Ambitious
26. Cautious			✓					Adventurous
27. Verbal		✓						Non-verbal

Fig. 9-1 (*continued*)

	Extremely	Quite	Slightly	In Between	Slightly	Quite	Extremely	
28. Secure	___	___	✓	___	___	___	___	Insecure
29. Powerless	___	___	___	✓	___	___	___	Powerful
30. Well-educated	___	___	✓	___	___	___	___	Uneducated
31. Tense	___	___	___	___	✓	___	___	Relaxed

aspects of self-conception may be more closely and meaningfully related to different forms of role change and subsequent outcomes than would some more holistically conceived evaluative dimension, usually labeled "self-esteem" (C. Gordon, 1968b; Rosenberg, 1979, Chaps. 1, 2, 12; Rosenberg, 1981).

The sample Self-Conception Profile presented represents the initial self-ratings of a 37-year-old woman whom we shall call "Jane Keller." Her initial profile indicated that she conceived of herself to be quite calm, friendly, good, interested in enjoyment, optimistic, verbal, and competent. She rated herself as extremely healthy and responsible, but also quite low in self-confidence. It should be noted that adjective pairs are presented in the Self-Conception Profile so that the "positive" ends of the pairs are randomly distributed between the left and right sides of the page in order to minimize the problems of response-set.

Time 1 self-esteem. Because of the theoretical importance of self-esteem, we constructed such a measure from the component elements of the Self-Conception Profile. Numerical scores ranging from 1 to 7 were assigned to each respondent's answers to the profile elements, with the score of 1 indicating an extremely negative response and a score of 7 indicating an extremely positive response on an adjective dimension. One modification was made: we deleted adjective pair 10 (interested in enjoyment vs. interested in achievement) because this pair did not reflect the "positive" and "negative" distinction that characterized the others, having been included for its own theoretical interest. Thus, the resulting self-esteem scale score is the sum of the participant's responses to the remaining 30 dimensions of the Self-Conception Profile. Only 34 of the 38 respondents gave full self-ratings at both the outset and the conclusion of the study; therefore, only the data for these 34 respondents were used in the reported analysis.

The scores on the self-esteem scale at the outset of the program ranged from a low of 110 to a high of 185, with a mean 145.9 and a standard deviation 16.6. These obtained scores fell in the middle- to upper-middle range of the theoretically possible values, indicating that (as is typical of "normal" study groups) the participants described themselves in at least moderately favorable terms. As a further point of reference, the Time 1 (T1) self-esteem measure was found to relate appreciably only with education among the background variables (+.35); however, Anglos tended to score lower (142) than did Blacks (150) and Mexican-Americans (156). This pattern of minority group members scoring higher in self-esteem than Anglos has been found in other settings (C. Gordon, 1963, 1972; Rosenberg & Simmons, 1972).

Results: Changes in Self-Conceptions and Development of Occupational Plans During the Program

Self-Conception Scoring Patterns At Time 1 and Time 2

Figure 9-2 shows the mean score for each of the 30 dimensions of the Self-Conception Profile, both at Times 1 and 2. The dimensions are labeled for the "positive" side of the original adjective pair (see Figure 9-1). The data analyses were guided by the hypotheses put forth in the first section of this chapter.

Hypothesis 1 proposed that displaced homemakers typically will be found to have a number of important self-conceptions that are negative, especially on dimensions that have closest reference to the self-directed application of skills and capacities. Consideration of the data in Figure 9-2 reveals that while the rough center of balance of the mean scores at Time 1 is at approximately 5 on the 7-point scale ("slightly" positive), 9 of the 30 dimensions show mean ratings substantially below 5: young, happy, independent, dominant, confident, adventurous, secure, powerful, and relaxed. This set of dimensions deals quite directly with the questions of autonomous action, the security necessary for it, and feelings of self-satisfaction with rewarding results. In contrast, the dimensions on which the women in the study group rated themselves substantially higher than the midpoint were concerned primarily with social skills and a responsible approach to future action: friendly, competent, healthy, responsible, and ambitious.

These patterns of mean scores confirm the prediction in Hypothesis 1 concerning self-conceived success at actually independent actions. Yet the hypothesis is

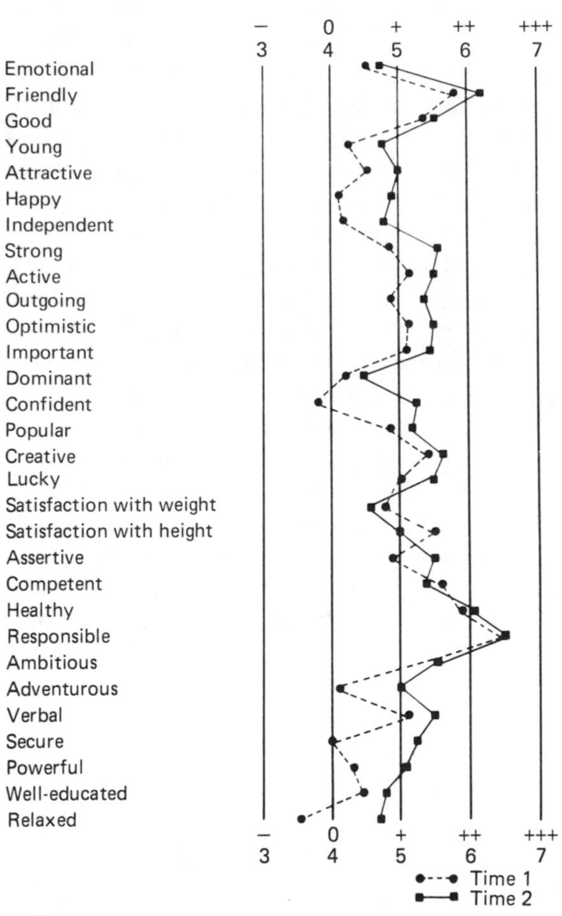

Fig. 9-2. Self-Conception mean self-ratings at Time 1 and Time 2 ($N = 34$).

apparently too broad concerning the issue of competence. These women *do* feel that they are competent (5.1 out of 7). They feel they have competencies that *may* in the future be utilized in direct action, even though they have not yet used these competencies in the job market. Thus, their more negative ratings appear to reflect the feeling that they have not yet *proved* their capacities for autonomous actions, even though they feel that they *possess* such capacities.

Self-Conceptions at the End of the Career Options Program

Hypothesis 3 proposed that a successful displaced homemakers program would result in improved self-conceptions among its participants. Inspection of the Time 2 data in Figure 9-2 shows that the Time 2 mean ratings are more favorable than the corresponding Time 1 ratings on 24 of the 30 dimensions. These 24 dimensions are listed below, along with a designation of the level of significance obtained from one-tailed, single-sample t tests for changes. We recognize, of course, that these t tests are not strictly valid, since we do not have a true sample from a specified population, and are not attempting to estimate statistical probabilities or predict population parameters. Still, since the sample size is the same (34) for all the comparisons between Time 1 and Time 2 scores, the usual "level of significance" can be used as a rough measure of the magnitude of the observed differences. (As with all such presentations in this chapter, we will use one asterisk to designate the .05 level, two for the .01 level, and three for the .001 level.)

The fact that 24 out of 30 evaluative dimensions show at least some change in the positive direction supports Hypothesis 3: participation in the Career Options Program does seem to be associated with increasing favorability of self-conceptions along a large number of especially important dimensions closely connected with vigorous and effective action. It is possible, of course, that the demand characteristics of the program and testing situations produced much or all of this "positive" effect. If so, few later correlations would be expected. However, it will be shown below that the self-conception measures derived from the Self-Conception Profile do in fact stand in a wide range of substantial and interesting relations with other solidly operationalized variables.

Self-Conception Dimensions Showing Greater Positivity over the Program	
***Confident	*Creative
***Secure	*Assertive
***Powerful	Friendly
***Relaxed	Good
**Young	Outgoing
**Strong	Important
**Adventurous	Dominant
*Attractive	Popular
*Happy	Lucky
*Idependent	Healthy
*Active	Verbal
*Optimistic	Well-educated

Change in self-esteem. An obvious implication of Hypothesis 1 is that global self-esteem would be expected to increase over the course of the Career Options Program. Inspection of the frequency distribution for the Time 2 self-esteem variable shows a low score of 130 and a high score of 181, with a mean of 157.0 and a standard deviation of 15.5 points. This Time 2 mean is more than 11 points higher than the Time 1 self-esteem mean, and the results of single-tailed t test for correlated means yielded a significance value of $p < .001$. Thus, the derived hypothesis of increased self-esteem over the course of the program is strongly supported.

It is interesting to note that the "self-esteem change" score is related negatively to its starting point, self-esteem at T1 (- .48) and positively to T2 (+ .44). This "crisscross" pattern could, of course, be due to the artifact of regression toward the mean (Campbell & Stanley, 1963, p. 41). If this were the case, self-esteem change would be strongly related to any other variables. However, self-esteem change is related, for example, to four antecedent variables: staff ratings of motivation (+.36) and flexibility (+.44), the participant's desire for a job that is social in character (+.43), and the participant's ethnic group (Blacks increased an average of 3.4 self-esteem points, Mexican-Americans averaged *minus* .2 points, and Anglos increased by an average of 16.4 points). Perhaps this last relationship indicates that the minority group members did not come to perceive as big a change in their employment prospects as did the Anglos, possibly because they became even more aware of employment discrimination barriers, especially for those who do not speak English well. Another plausible explanation in this case, however, may be the effect of statistical regression.

Factor analysis of the T1 Self-Conception Profile. We have attempted to go beyond the use of a single evaluative dimension such as the self-esteem score discussed above, and yet produce a manageable set of variables to use in analyzing the formation of the participants' occupational aspirations and actions. In order to do so, we subjected 26 scales within the Self-Conception Profile (after removing those that did not fit in strictly with a "positive" and "negative" logic–calm vs. emotional, interested in enjoyment vs. interested in achievement, satisfaction with weight, satisfaction with height, and tense vs. relaxed) to a principal components factor analysis with varimax rotation. We elected to sum only the highest-loading scales for a given extracted factor, using only those scales that actually give the factor its major meaning. By this procedure, we obtained four factors which together explained 74% of the variance in the matrix of 26 self-ratings, and provided very meaningful clusters for use in the analyses to follow. The order of the four factors and the factor loadings of their component elements are indicated in Table 9-1.

Sociability is the title chosen for the first factor, which individually accounted for 39% of the variance. It is defined by a set of dynamic social characteristics (beginning with "outgoing" and "popular") that imply a positive reception by one's partners in interaction.

Self-Confidence is our name for the second largest factor, which accounted for 13% of the variance. This dimension closely parallels earlier writings on unity as an important "systemic sense of self" that is less global than self-esteem but more

Table 9-1. Factor Structure of Time 1 Self-Conception Profile, with Factor Loadings

1. Sociability		2. Self-confidence	
Outgoing	.88	Confident	.59
Popular	.66	Lucky	.59
Assertive	.58	Young	.56
Verbal	.57	Secure	.55
Adventurous	.52	Happy	.54
Friendly	.43	Optimistic	.52
3. Vigor		**4. Autonomy**	
Strong	.85	Independent	.64
Dominant	.54	Powerful	.57
Secure	.39	Competent	.48
Verbal	.34	Attractive	.46
Active	.33		

abstract than the kind of self-conception ratings included in the profile (C. Gordon, 1968a, 1968b). Self-confidence reflects feelings of secure optimism regarding past accomplishments, present circumstances, and future outcomes.

Vigor is our label for the third factor, which accounted for 11% of the variance. Calling up imagery of the all-American pragmatist, vigor connotes strong verbal attempts to actively dominate encounters.

Autonomy is the title for the fourth factor, which accounted for 10% of the variance. It represents the combination of competence and self-determination, producing a capacity for autonomous action involving both freely chosen goals and freedom of control by others (C. Gordon, 1968c).

We are aware that our additive procedure does not produce true orthogonality (zero-correlation) between the factor–surrogate variables to the degree to which the constituent dimensions originally intercorrelated, and to the degree to which the same dimension appears on two or more factor-surrogates. This problem is not great, however, and can be handled by entering all four self-conception factors into regression equations simultaneously, so that the effect of each on a particular dependent variable is assessed separately.

In order to reduce even further the number of variables that are necessary for a multiple regression analysis of occupational goals and actions, it is possible to express the amount of change in a given T1 factor as a proportion of the starting point. These proportionate scores are calculated for any given variable by using the formula (T2 - T1)/T1 , with the result being multiplied by 100 to produce a variable that is actually the percentage change in the factor from Time 1 to Time 2. The use of this approach to calculate percentage changes in each of the four factor-surrogate dimensions of self-conception produced the distributions represented in Table 9-2, which are ordered in terms of the amount of mean change over the course of the program.

As these data indicate, the sociability percentage change dimension, although showing the least amount of change over the course of the program, still revealed

Table 9-2. Mean Percentage Change in the Self-Conception Factors from T1 to T2.

Self-conception percentage change dimension	Lowest obtained score	Highest obtained score	Standard deviation	Mean change
Self-confidence % change	-35	+79	22.8	+16.6
Vigor % change	-14	+92	22.6	+14.1
Autonomy % change	-26	+100	22.3	+11.6
Sociability % change	-15	+63	17.9	+8.9

an average improvement of almost 9%. The dimension showing the greatest amount of change, self-confidence, revealed a 16.6% average gain.

Development of Occupational Goals and Actions

It will be remembered that the women came to the Career Options Program with only quite limited (and in many cases quite vague or contradictory) plans for their occupational futures. Over the course of the sessions within the program, they were assisted by the staff members in clarifying their occupational goals, specifying their values and preferences, and in making realistic assessments of their relevant skills and abilities. At the end of the program, each participant was asked to indicate what plans she had regarding specific occupational objectives or regarding further formal education or technical training.

Clarity of plans. When the participants' plans were assessed by the project staff members regarding their number, clarity, and possibility of being turned into successful action, it was found that 63% had expressed a single, clear, and actionable plan. An additional 26% had a single plan, but one which was less clear and directly actionable. The remaining 11% had not yet formulated any concrete plan that could lead to a successful outcome. Thus, at the simplest level of testing the validity of Hypothesis 3 (i.e., whether or not the Career Options Program was successful in moving its participants from having no very clear idea of what they might become toward having a single, clear, and actionable plan), the fact that 63% had done so completely and that another 26% had only slightly more vague plans constitutes initial evidence that the program was successful in attaining this most basic objective.

Possible determinants of plan development. That some aspects of self-conception are likely to be relevant in determining the development of plans is suggested by the finding that while global self-esteem at Time 1 only correlated -.16 with the plan/no-plan dichotomy, the *change* in self-esteem correlated +.47 with it. Breaking down global self-esteem into the various factor-derived self-conception variables, we found relationships with presence of clear plans to be as shown in Table 9-3. These data indicate that the self-confidence dimension had no correlation with development of plans at Time 1, but stands in the strongest relation of the four dimensions at Time 2. In other words, the more a participant comes to believe that she has her life fairly well under control, the more likely she is to formulate a clear actionable plan for the future.

Table 9-3. Correlations with Presence of Clear Occupational Plans

Dimension	Time 1	Time 2	Change measure	Percentage change measure
Sociability	-.06	.13	.24	.23
Self-confidence	.00	.43	.40	.48
Vigor	-.07	.34	.48	.46
Autonomy	-.31	-.03	.38	.36

Furthermore, we have here the first instance of a pattern that underlies much of our data: there is a negative relationship between a self-conception dimension at Time 1 and a given aspect of occupational plans or actions, but the relationship is seen to be fairly strongly positive by the end of the program, especially when the self-conception dimension is measured as a change score or as a proportionate change score.

When the proportionate change measures are entered into a multiple regression equation set up to predict to development of actionable plans (dichotomized as a criterial variable into the simple presence vs. absence of a plan), first step beta weights produced a multiple correlation coefficient of .50. In this analysis, one of the self-conceptions dimensions (sociability percentage change) drops out completely in the presence of the other three. Moreover, when the set of predictor variables is expanded to include such relatively powerful zero-order predictors as interactive skill rating (–.411), education (.342), and the mental set rating (.263), the three remaining self-conception factors still maintain positive and appreciable (if not overwhelming) predictive strengths: autonomy, .164; self-confidence, .193; and vigor, .320. The self-conceptions together produced a multiple correlation of .50; adding in the other variables raised this value to .69.

In other words, apart from other important factors, those respondents who felt that they had become more autonomous, more self-confident, and especially more vigorous in personal encounters (such as job interviews) were most likely to develop specific, clear, and actionable occupational plans. This finding constitutes the first of a number of empirical supports for Hypothesis 4: those program participants who improved most in self-conceptions also were those who gained the most in coping with their economic situation. Further, these data indicate that improvement on the dimensions of vigor, self-confidence, and autonomy is more closely connected to making clear occupational plans than is change on the sociability dimension.

Type of economic plan developed. The participants' stated plans as they came to the end of the program were coded regarding their qualitative character. All stated at least some kind of economic plan; none intended to stay at home. A rather low 47% reported that they intended to apply for a traditional "pink collar" or "woman's job." By contrast, 32% reported planning to get further technical training, and 21% said that they planned to apply for a nontraditional job. These latter figures seem quite high given the fact that only about 14% of employed women now hold jobs in the blue collar occupations, and only about 7% are in the upper managerial occupations (U.S. Department of Labor, 1980a, p. 38). These findings further support the assertion that the Career Options Program opened up its participants' minds regarding potential occupational futures.

When asked what type of technical training they would like to get, 11 of the 18 women choosing training as a plan chose high-level business training. Visualizing themselves in high-level business careers indicated a substantial alteration in self-conceptions among women who had previously operated primarily in terms of their roles as wives and mothers. Along the same lines, those who indicated the plan of applying for a traditional job further specified their aspirations as (in descending order of frequency): administration, general office work, middle management and high-level sales, retail sales, major professional, and food service.

Socioeconomic status of planned job. The same form of status coding that had been applied to the women's previous jobs and to their husbands' jobs was used to assign status scores to their planned jobs, those jobs that the women said they planned to enter either directly or after completion of further training. The resulting set of scores had a mean of 55.4 and a standard deviation of 15.3 points. As is generally the case with occupational aspirations, these status scores clustered somewhat toward the upper end, but had sufficient range and variance to permit analysis through the technique of multiple regression.

The results of the regression analysis indicated that only two of the self-conception change dimensions were appreciably related to the SES level of the participants' occupational plans, and that these self-conceptions worked in opposite directions: autonomy percentage change had a beta weight of .173, whereas self-confidence percentage change yielded a value of -.168. Together, the four self-conception change dimensions produced a multiple correlation of .20, and while this is not a very impressive figure (representing only 4% of variance in the dependent variable), the "mental set" rating (of motivation, decisiveness, and attitude) of the participant by the staff has a much stronger effect (+.330), as does the number of dependents (-.289). One factor sets up the perception of needful desire; the other frees the person to formulate the distant goal. The distant goal may thus express the feeling that the participant is not yet where she wants to be, but now has the capacity to choose a course of conduct substantially different from before (the very definition of autonomy).

Change in socioeconomic status from previous circumstances. We have available two measures of potential status change for our participants because we can ascertain the gap between the status score assigned to their planned occupations and two sets of scores relating to their past situations: the status of their own previous work, and the status of their husbands' jobs. The first of these change variables, "difference between previous and planned job status" was formed by subtracting the status score of a woman's previous work experience from that of her planned occupation. This change variable has a mean of +12.7 points and a median of 15.7 points, indicating that the women do plan (on the average) to enter occupations that are substantially higher in status than those in which they last worked. Not all of the women showed increases, however. In total, 19% of the women were scored as decreasing in status from past job to plan, 1% as staying the same, whereas 80% of the women sought status increases from past job to planned job.

When the occupational target of the participants is measured in terms of "difference between previous and planned job status," the autonomy and self-confidence change dimensions operate in the same opposite-direction way as in the previous analysis, but the relationships are approximately double in magnitude (+.363 and -.360, respectively). The pattern is the same, but stronger: the less satisfied with current circumstances and the more autonomous, the greater the relative reach toward higher socioeconomic status.

In addition, the proportionate change in vigor now approaches an appreciable level (+.174); it as though making a substantial change will require strong efforts. On the other hand, the sociability change variable is still essentially unrelated to the difference between previous and planned job status. Again, it can be seen that the four self-conception dimensions operate in diverse ways.

The structural variables operated in strong fashion to aid in predicting the difference between previous and planned job status. The lower the previous job, the greater the gap between it and the planned job (-.447). Education works in an independent and almost as powerful a fashion (-.326), and the number of one's dependents is perceived as an important barrier to status increase (-.340). The few Black women, starting from a lower previous job base, are reaching farther up.

Two of the staff ratings were also positive predictors: positive scores on physical appearance (+.253) and, especially, the mental set rating (+.380) were associated with larger gaps between past job and planned job.

When change in socioeconomic status is considered in reference to the job of the husband, other interesting relationships are revealed. In many regards, it is the job of the husband that best characterized the status of the wives, because often the women's own "previous job" had been many years in the past. Although only 29 of the women had husbands (current or former) and provided descriptions of their jobs, the new variable "difference between the husband's job status and the planned job status" gives us another important insight into the process by which the program participants made judgments concerning possible economic futures for themselves. The linkage of the participants' starting status with that of their husbands is not complete, however, since the 14 separated or divorced women had been apart from their husbands quite some time.

Expressed as distance away from their husband's occupational status, the wives on average planned occupations that would produce a slight status *decrease* (the mean difference was -1.7 points, with a median of 0.0 points). Almost half the women (48%) planned lower status jobs, with the largest decrease registering -40 points. One woman planned a job of the same status as that of her husband, and the remaining 48% chose higher-status jobs, with the largest increase being a jump of 32 points. Considering the fairly high status of their husbands' jobs and the difficulty of women even conceiving of themselves in such highly paid and prestigious occupations (let alone getting the necessary training and actually getting hired), it is not surprising that this group of wives planned occupations near but not necessarily above those of their husbands. In addition, there is the statistical ceiling effect involved in trying to top scores that are already quite high in the theoretically obtainable range.

A small degree of predictability (multiple r = .23) was obtained for this second SES difference score variable when a regression equation was set up involving the four self-conception factors and the other important factors, but the explained variance is largely due to the presence of the "husband's job status" variable: In general, the lower the husband's status, the more the wife's planned occupation exceeded his status, and vice versa. The four self-conception variables displayed relatively little explanatory power in this instance.

Action taken as a result of the Career Options Program. The staff of the program attempted to keep in touch with all the participants after the formal workshop sessions were over, in order to ascertain the degree of progress being made toward attainment of the participants' planned goals and also to provide direct help and information about possible jobs or training opportunities. Specific information was obtained concerning each woman's accomplishments as of approximately 1, 3, 4, and 7 months after the end of her particular program workshop. Table 9-4 provides a breakdown of the number of participants who achieved each possible outcome.

The data of Table 9-4 once again support Hypothesis 3: the Career Options Program was extremely successful in helping its participants either to apply for a job and be hired, or to apply for a training program and be accepted. In temporal sequence, by the end of the first month after the close of the program, 58% of the participants had either gotten jobs or gotten into a training program. By the end of 3 months this figure had gone up to 71%, and up to 74% by the end of 4 months. Finally, by the end of 7 months, 82% of the program participants had successfully gotten a job or job training.

Only two women had taken no action toward either a job or job training: one broke her leg in an accident during the last week of the program and was in a cast for many months; the other decided that her conception of being a "good Christian woman" required that she stay at home until her teenage children were off and on their own. At that time, however, she may decide to enter the job market. At the end of the program, "Jane Keller" planned to apply for a secretarial job with a view

Table 9-4. Cumulative Number of Participants in Each Program Outcome (N=38)

	Information collection period (months after)			
Outcome category	1	3	4	7
In job training	9	10	9	7
Applied but not hired	4	4	3	–
Offered job but refused it	3	–	–	–
Applied and was hired	5	6	7	11
Applied for one job, but was hired for a better one	8	11	12	13
No action taken	5	3	2	2
No information obtainable	4	4	5	5

toward entering the administrative ranks. Through the efforts of Paddy Gordon, she was hired by a large Houston insurance company to work in their employee relations division in an administrative job with promising opportunities for promotion. "Mrs. Keller" was one of the 13 participants who were classified as "applied for one job, was hired for a better one."

The positive final outcomes (18% in job training, and 63% being hired for jobs at least as good as their occupational plan) are so strong that it seems very unlikely that a comparable group of women could have done as well without the benefits of the Career Options Program. However, without the full rigor of a study structure such as the Solomon four-groups design (which can assess simultaneously the possible effects of internal validity threats such as instrument reactivity as well as the direct effects of the program), we cannot be certain of this conclusion (Campbell & Stanley, 1963, p. 24).

Nature of the jobs taken. The 24 program participants who were found to have taken jobs by the end of the seventh month after the close of the program were classified into the following occupational categories: food service 4%, retail sales 4%, general office work 29%, administration, teaching, and paraprofessionals 33%, middle management and high-level sales 21%, and full professionals 8%. Comparison with the distribution of their previous jobs (some held many years ago) shows that the women made very striking gains in occupational status and economic level: while the proportion in clerical jobs and below greatly declined (down 42 percentage points), the proportion in the paraprofessional administrative ranks or higher greatly increased (from 21 to 62%), including an increase from 3 to 29% in the middle management or higher levels, which are still quite unusual attainments for women.

Socioeconomic status of the jobs entered. The scores on the Duncan SES index that were assigned to the occupations entered within 7 months of the end of the Career Options Program fell into a fair approximation of the normal curve, with a mean of 55.7, and a standard deviation of 15.1 points. When this "obtained job status" variable was entered into a multiple regression equation with the self-conception dimensions and the other important variables, it was found that the proportionate change in vigor (.132) and, especially, in autonomy (.345) stand in appreciable relation to the SES level of the job obtained, even when the powerful factors of social structural circumstance and interactive skill have been entered into the equation. (Alone, the self-conception dimensions produced a modest multiple correlation of .32.) Once again, the wisdom of breaking down self-conceptions into component elements rather than using only a global self-esteem measure is seen: the correlations with SES of the obtained job are -.23 for Time 1 self-esteem, -.15 for Time 2 self-esteem, and +.38 for self-esteem change. The association between enhanced self-conception and the SES level of the job obtained at the end of the program supports Hypothesis 4, yet the disaggregated analysis qualifies this finding by revealing that only changes in the vigor and autonomy dimensions showed strong relation to SES of the obtained job; changes in sociability and self-confidence did not.

Interesting patterns can be detected through examination of the beta weights associated with the social structural variables. The few Black participants had lower past SES scores and lower husbands' SES scores, but slightly higher SES ratings for their obtained jobs. Education (.349) and age (.158) are positive predictors, whereas the SES of the women's previous jobs stands in negative relation (-.281).

Change in socioeconomic status from previous circumstances to obtained job. Again we had two measures of starting point to use in considering status change to the ending point of the obtained job. When measuring change from the SES level of the women's previous jobs, we produced the change variable "difference between previous and present job status." The mean is 9.5 and the median is 16.0, indicating that many more of the participants obtained jobs higher in status than their previous jobs (77%) than obtained lower status jobs (18%).

Only the proportionate change in autonomy was at all strongly related to the difference between previous and present job status, echoing the pattern discovered in the change in SES from previous to planned job.[3] This unique predictive power of autonomy percentage change lends greater precision to the findings obtained for the overall dimension of self-esteem: correlations with the difference between previous and present job status were -.11 for Time 1 self-esteem, +.12 for Time 2 self-esteem, and +.23 for self-esteem change. As the women increased in their sense of personal autonomy, there was a tendency for them to set a higher goal and try harder to reach it.

The importance of an autonomous and assertive mental set in establishing and attaining occupational objectives was asserted long ago by Donald Super (1951), and is supported by our finding that the "mental set" factor surrogate (composed of decisiveness, motivation, and attitude rating by the staff) related very strongly to the difference between previous and present job status (partial correlation of .82). The two prior socioeconomic status scores showed the crisscross pattern noted in the previous analyses: husband's SES at -.13 and, especially, the woman's own previous job SES at -.74 indicate that the lower the starting point, the greater the resulting gain. The fact that education has a low positive (.15) relationship to the difference between previous and present job status is understandable when we remember that many of these women completed their education many years prior to entering the Career Options Program. The additional fact that education's partial correlation with the difference between previous and present job status (.15) is much lower than the parallel beta weight for education in the previous

---

[3] When the regression equation was set up regarding the difference between previous and present job status, the self-conception changes were found to stand in only small combined relation to this jump in SES level, but the social structural and personal style variables were so strongly related to "difference between previous and present job status" (and so complexly related to each other in the combination suggested by preliminary analysis) that the equation became overdetermined. For this reason, we have chosen to report the beta weight only for the self-conception factor of autonomy, and then to report the partial correlation coefficients for the variables not in that first equation.

prediction of planned occupation (.349) suggests that the actions of the program staff in assisting the women to actually get hired (often in jobs much higher in status than the women had planned) may have been effective in persuading employers to look beyond formal educational attainments in making their selections.

Change in socioeconomic status from husband's job to obtained job. A rather different indicator of change in socioeconomic status used husband's job as the reference point. The resulting variable, "difference between the husband's job status and the present job status," had a standard deviation of 20.6 points, a mean of -2.1, and a median of 0.0. Of the women reporting both a husband's occupation and an obtained job, 47% had negative values and another 47% had positive values. While these descriptive statistics do tell us that the women's obtained jobs are, on the average, slightly below those held by their current or former husbands, we must recall that the men have had many years to develop their current status level, after receiving higher levels of education and under an economic system that favors men. The fact that these "reentry" women could get jobs very near the socioeconomic status of their husbands after having been out of the work force so long is yet another valuable piece of evidence in support of the Career Options Program's claim to success.

Although the global self-esteem scores were negligibly correlated with the difference between the husband's job status and the present job status, three of the self-conception factor-surrogate dimensions had much stronger predictive relations, with two relating positively and one negatively.[4] Self-confidence percentage change was the strongest positive predictor (.329), indicating that women who improved in their sense of confident optimism were more likely to apply for and get jobs close to or even higher than the socioeconomic status of their husbands' jobs. The sociability percentage change measure also relates positively to this outcome (.247), indicating that the women who improved most in the capacity for outgoing, assertive, and adventurous action were also more likely to match or exceed the SES of their husbands' jobs. The vigor percentage change measure had only a small and negative relation to the difference between the husband's job status and the present job status, just as was the case with the difference between previous and present job status.

Particularly interesting is the negative relationship between autonomy percentage change and the difference between the husband's job status and the present job status (-.332). Autonomy percentage change had a moderate positive relation to the gap between previous experience and obtained job (.249), but the gap between husband's occupation and own obtained job is a movement away from present

[4] The same situation occurred with the difference between the husband's job status and the present job status as with the preceding analysis of the difference between previous and present job status: the predictive power of SES of the husband's job is so strong that the value of the multiple correlation became larger than 1.00, and we will thus again use partial correlation coefficients instead of beta weights in discussing these results.

status location. An examination of the regression results for the change in autonomy shows that those changing most were affluent white women with a higher than average mental set but also with more dependents. Although they had gained in the sense of autonomy and felt more free to enter the job market, their already high socioeconomic status (+.446 from husband's job status) made it very unlikely that they could rise much further. Inspection of the partial correlations support this interpretation: it is the women who had the least education (-.22) and whose husbands had lower status jobs (-.88) that made the largest status gains.

Change in socioeconomic status from planned job to obtained job. Yet another measure of the success of the program staff's efforts is the difference between the SES score of the job that the participant planned to enter as of the end of the program and the SES score of the job that she actually obtained as of the last available information, some 7 months later. This variable is an unusual one in that 14 of the 23 women who had obtained scorable occupations by the end of the data collection period had gotten and were still working in just the kind of job that they had planned, and thus had a score of 0 on the variable. In addition, almost as many women had obtained lower status jobs than they had planned as had achieved higher-status jobs by the seventh month; thus, the mean difference between planned and obtained job status was only -0.3.[5]

The four self-conception dimensions (all operating in the positive direction) explained a respectable proportion of the variance in the difference between planned and obtained job status variable ($MR = .49, MR^2 = .24$) but only sociability percentage change had even a moderate beta weight (.298). The more a woman had changed in the direction of conceiving herself as outgoing and assertive, etc., the more likely she was to have actually ended up in an occupation higher in status than the one she had planned at the close of the program. Other relevant factors in making such a shift were two of the staff ratings that reflect the "objective" side of this sociability: interactive style (+.287) and the mental set involving motivation, decisiveness, and attitude toward the program (+.226). Of course, these ratings do indicate a favorable staff response toward the women who scored highly on them, and it is likely that the staff members pushed harder to get good jobs for these women.

The two structural variables that emerged in this analysis are of special interest and importance. The older women were more likely to make a status jump from plan to final outcome (+.270), suggesting at least three possible interpretations:

[5] To illustrate the case of those four women who actually took lower status jobs than they had planned, one participant was offered (largely through the efforts of the program staff) a soon-to-be-opened position as manager of a new womens' department in a prestigious Houston store, and this high responsibility job was recorded as her plan. When it finally came time to take the job, however, she decided that it would involve too much pressure and too much time away from her family, and so she took a much lower status job as a geologist's assistant. But for each such case of lowered sights, there was one or more instance of increased aspiration in action: five women increased the SES score of the actually obtained job.

First, the staff may have worked harder to find especially good jobs for the older participants, feeling that they needed a special set of "breaks" through which to reenter the job market. Also, the older women may have tried harder to find a really good job, on the assumption that it would be much harder to change later on than it would be for younger women with many more years of potential employment before them in a job market that often does discriminate against hiring older women (cf. Freeman, 1979; M. Gordon, 1979; Seidman, 1978; Yankelovich, 1979). Finally, it is possible that some employers are happy to be able to find more mature women to fill positions that require judgment and discretion (Myers, 1979, pp. 185-191). Probably all three factors contributed to some degree.

The strongest predictor of the difference between planned and obtained job status was the status of the woman's previous job (-.428). This large negative beta indicated that the lower the status of the women's previous job, the greater was the chance that she would make a status jump from plan to final action. Our interpretation of this effect focuses on the fact that the women who had previously held only relatively low status jobs tended to plan for relatively modest jobs, but to take (after the efforts of the project staff) substantially higher status jobs than they had planned.

Change in rate of pay. A final measure of the success of the Career Options Program concerns the degree to which the women were able to improve their earning power as compared to their pay rates in their previous job, however long ago that job was held. As before, we were also interested in the degree to which any or all of the changes in the self-conception factors were associated with changes in the women's pay rates. Our general Hypothesis 4 asserts a positive relation: Those program participants who improve most in their self-conceptions will also be those who gain the greatest amounts in effective coping with their economic situations.

At the start of the program, the participants were asked to report the highest hourly earnings they had made in their previous jobs. At the end of the data collection period, the program staff attempted to learn (or to estimate) the current hourly pay rates for the 22 women who had by then taken a job. We can thus make a comparison of these two pay distributions, and then check against the national average hourly rates for working women, expressed in 1970 dollars for the past reference point and in 1980 dollars for the current situation (U.S. Department of Labor, 1980c, Table 48). In general, we found that the women who became employed were earning much more than they had in the past, with the median increasing from $2.00/hour to roughly $5.00/hour. It should be noted, however, that the women's median pay level roughly matched the average hourly pay for working women at both time periods.[6]

[6] It is sad to note that women have continued to earn only a little over 60% of what men earn, ever since 1967 when the ratio was 62%, up to 1980 when it was 63% (U.S. Department of Labor, 1980c, Table 48). A large disparity in earning power remains even after the effects of differential education have been removed: women with four years of college earned less in 1978 than did men with only an eighth

The frequency distribution of the variable "difference in salary between previous jobs and obtained jobs" (the number of steps of difference on the above-mentioned hourly rate scale) showed a wide range for the 21 women for whom both salary figures were available. This salary difference had a mean of +1.2 steps, with a standard deviation of 1.9 steps. In terms of directionality, 19% of the women reported declines in hourly pay rates from previous job to obtained job; another 19% reported staying in the same pay category, and 62% achieved at least a 1-step increase.

When the salary difference variable was entered into the final regression equation along with the four self-conception dimensions and the most important of the other variables, the combination of self-conception dimensions was found to produce a multiple correlation of .43, while the full set of variables produced a very high *MR* of .94. Only one of the self-conception variables (change in sense of autonomy) had a positive effect (.332), while the effects of the others were negative and smaller. Consideration of the beta weights suggests that those women who increased most in self-conceptions as vigorous and sociable and self-confident were *not* those who made the biggest gains in earning power. A "positive" interactive style also seems to work against this gain (-.206). Instead, the biggest pay rate gains were made by those who developed most along the autonomy dimension (independent, powerful, competent, and attractive), especially those who were therefore able to break away from lower-status previous jobs (-.634).

The positive mental set (decisiveness, motivation, and attitude) as rated by the program staff (+.364) supports this breakaway orientation, as does the self-reported motivation of seeking "identity" or personal fulfillment in the program (+.376). In addition, having a larger number of dependents to care for (but not the extremely large family typical of poverty groups) seems to have provided an additional motivation for seeking a job with the highest possible pay. Together, this combination of self-conception and action-set characteristics provides strong support not only for Hypothesis 4, but also for the recent analysis of the importance of earning power in establishing reciprocal relationships with self-esteem and general life-satisfaction (Rubenstein, 1981). In the present study, we have shown that an important aspect of self-conception (personal autonomy) can play an active role in shaping the person's actions directed toward securing increased earning power.

Antecedents of Change in the Self-Conception Dimensions

Although the focus of this chapter has been the effects of self-conception changes on a wide range of occupational plans, actions, and outcomes, we also have a strong interest in the antecedent factors associated with the self-conception changes them-

---

grade education (U.S. Department of Labor, 1980b, p. 2). Seniority in their jobs is one of the obvious factors accounting for this disparity of women's incomes, but sexism plays its part also. It is a pleasure for us to report that women who are well motivated and properly coached can in fact make large improvements in their earning power.

selves. Some of this information has been used in making interpretations of the findings in the immediately preceding section, but at this point we simply offer the regression results derived from equations using the most important variables, (selected in terms of their correlations with the self-conception changes; Table 9-5).

Consideration of these diverse patterns provides two further pieces of evidence for the assertion that the four self-conception changes are not simply different names for some overall evaluative dimension. First, the four differ greatly in the degree to which they are predictable from the given set of antecedent variables (from a low of 24% variance explained for sociability percentage change to 63% for autonomy percentage change). Second, particular predictors vary greatly in their unique and independent relation to each of the four self-conception changes. For example, husband's job SES score has the following beta weights: -.679 with vigor, .446 with autonomy, .144 with sociability, and a value too weak to even enter the self-confidence equation. Many important and independently measured factors show the same kind of variability in beta weights in predicting the different self-conceptions: for example, age, education, husband's SES score, and number of dependents.

Summary, Conclusions, and Implications

Hypothesis 1: Initial Negative Self-Conceptions

Our initial hypothesis asserted that women entering a program such as Career Options would feel negative about themselves along the *competence* and *self-determination* dimensions, rather than along the dimensions of *unity* and *moral worth*. These differential expectations were drawn from the literature on actual and potential displaced homemakers, together with Rosow's characterization of the general results of role loss.

The Time 1 mean self-ratings on the Self-Conception Profile revealed a different pattern of negative responses (see Figure 2 and accompanying text). As predicted, *self-determination* self-ratings (independent, dominant, adventurous, and powerful) were quite low relative to the general run of ratings. Opposite to prediction, however, the *unity* ("togetherness") self-ratings were also quite low (happy, confident, secure, and relaxed). As predicted, those ratings pertaining to *moral worth* were fairly high (friendly, good, healthy, and responsible). However, the second contradiction to Hypothesis 1 was the finding that ratings pertaining to *competence* were high rather than low (strong, active, creative, competent, healthy, and verbal).

Our interpretation of this pattern of partial support and partial refutation of Hypothesis 1 is that the women entering the Career Options Program were *not* really in a period of major crisis and severe emotional trauma that was battering their senses of competence and self-determination. The 14 women already divorced or separated may have gone through such a crisis previously, but by the time they arrived at the Career Options Program, they were fairly well composed and actually quite confident of their abilities (although quite *unconfident* regarding their chances for converting their capacities into good jobs). The 19 women who were

Table 9-5. Determination of Self-Conception Changes by Antecedent Variables

Self-conception	*MR*	MR^2	Predictor variables	Beta weight
Autonomy % change	.79	.63	Mental set rating	.478
			Physical presentation rating	−.472
			Husband's job SES score	.446
			Interactive skill rating	−.426
			Black	−.421
			Education	−.259
			Number of dependents	.236
			Mexican-American	−.232
			Identity as a goal for program	.191
			Age	.130
			Married	−.086
			Previous job SES score	.024
Vigor % change	.76	.58	Husband's job SES score	−.679
			Number of dependents	.673
			Interactive skill rating	.589
			Age	−.417
			Physical presentation rating	−.415
			Previous job SES score	.377
			Black	−.266
			Education	.259
			Mexican-American	−.197
			Mental set rating	.068
Self-Confidence % change	.61	.37	Mental set rating	.446
			Education	−.430
			Previous job SES score	.360
			Physical presentation rating	−.264
			Mexican-American	−.217
			Number of dependents	.172
			Identity as a goal for program	.131
			Interactive skill rating	.087
			Married	.035
Sociability % change	.48	.24	Black	−.313
			Mental set rating	.272
			Number of dependents	−.235
			Mexican-American	−.229
			Physical presentation rating	−.211
			Interactive style	−.178
			Married	−.168
			Husband's job SES score	.144
			Age	−.108
			Previous job SES score	.078

still living with their husbands were at least trying to establish a new work identity for themselves outside the home, and most were actively considering or anticipating divorce in the future. Thus, we conclude that most of the participants in the program were actually not in the direct circumstances depicted by Jacobs (1980) and Shields (1981), but rather were well past such a trauma (if it actually existed for them) or not yet fully into it (if it will ever hit them now that they have in fact gotten jobs).

We wish to point out, however, that although the different self-ratings clusters were not found to have the predicted starting points, they do differ among themselves rather than falling into a single pattern of low or high self-esteem. Further, our factor analyses of the self-ratings confirmed the theoretical perspective put forth in C. Gordon (1968a, 1968b) regarding unity or *self-confidence,* and that in C. Gordon (1968c) regarding *autonomy,* the combination of competence and self-determination.

Hypothesis 2: Confusion and Uncertainty About Occupational Futures

Consistent with Hypothesis 2, few of the women in the Career Options program had any well defined and actionable job or training plans; instead, they had only vague ideas about jobs that might be good. Their purpose in coming to the program was to discover what was available in the job market and what preparations were necessary for attaining the positions that were optimally appealing and attainable. Hypothesis 2 was fully supported, and this lack of clear plans established one baseline against which to measure the program's successes.

Hypothesis 3a: Changes in the Participants' Knowledge and Self-Conceptions

Self-conceptions improvement. The data of Figure 2 and the associated analyses demonstrate that the women's self-conceptions did improve, as measured in a wide variety of ways. At the level of individual self-ratings, 24 out of 30 dimensions in the profile showed change in the positive direction, including 14 changes that would have been deemed statistically significant if we had been using a true probability sample. When all 30 of the self-ratings were summed into a global self-esteem scale for each participant at Time 1 and again at Time 2, the average increase was quite substantial, larger than what would have been required for significance at the .001 level. When the factor-surrogate scores at the start and at the end of the program were contrasted and the differences expressed as percentage changes from the Time 1 starting point, it was found that while all four of the dimensions showed improvements, they did so differentially: sociability averaged +9%, autonomy +12%, vigor +14%, and self-confidence +17%.

As we stated in the previous discussion of results, we cannot know for certain that a similar group of women (who did *not* receive the concentrated training, coaching, role-modeling, and group experiences over the month of the Career Options Program) would *not* have shown similar increases along the four self-conception dimensions simply from such factors as maturation, external events, test reactivity, etc. Alternatively, since the advertising, intake procedures, discussion process, content, and continual feedback of the program dealt with just these dimensions (self-confidence, autonomy, and vigor), it is also possible that the improvements in scores on our measures were merely participants' responses to the demand characteristics of the training situation. In that case, we would not anticipate that the proportionate change measures would relate appreciably with the subsequently measured occupational progress outcomes. In fact, however, the self-conception proportionate change measures do relate in appreciable and theoretically interpretable ways even after removing the effects of other important variables. These patterns of robust relationships lend empirical support to the asserted validity of both the measurement procedures and the analysis procedures.

Market familiarity. In order to increase familiarity with the Houston job market, the 15 career areas that offered the greatest current employment potentials were discussed, with special emphasis on the jobs within those areas that would provide upward mobility and good benefits for women currently entering them. Due to a lack of funds for long-term educational programs, the women needed to know about apprenticeship programs and jobs providing on-site training so that they could enter the work world quickly. Thus, in addition to discussing the "traditional" women's occupations (clerical, nursing, teaching, retail sales, etc.), the program focused on higher status jobs that were unusual for women (such as in the computer field, real estate development leasing, industrial sales, word processing supervision, and other financial and management areas). Among the blue collar fields, much attention was given to construction, transportation, technical service, and industrial fabrication trades. Through a wide variety of methods (reading, discussions, lectures, site visits, and films), the participants got a broad but accurate and detailed picture of the Houston job market.

Values clarification. Use of a modification of Morris Rosenberg's procedure for ascertaining value priorities in relation to possible jobs showed that the participants' job values were grouped into three clusters of differing priority. Ranked most important were values dealing with application of skills in return for monetary and social rewards; of medium importance were values concerning the specific content of the job itself, such as nurturance, creativity, leadership, or freedom from supervision; of least importance were the "dramatic sizzle" values–adventure and glamor status. Once the participants' goals had been revealed by this procedure, the program staff then sought to help them get specific jobs tailored to the particular skills they wished to apply so as to get maximum monetary and social rewards.

Job skills development. Although the Career Options Program did provide some direct training in physical skills such as woodworking and basic machinists' operations, this training was really an attempt to introduce women who had never done such work to the nature of blue collar skills. It should be noted that this training was accompanied by factual information on the pay level that blue collar jobs now offer: typically much higher than any but the highest of the white collar jobs. More important for the women's later job-getting was program emphasis on the skills that are helpful in getting job interviews with desirable companies, and in getting successful employment results. Particularly valuable was the use of role-playing situations and videotape feedback sessions that allowed each participant to perceive very dramatically the mistakes being made by the others as they played out various applicant roles, and that also allowed each participant the opportunity to play out the "reverse" role of a personnel manager interviewing an applicant. Dress, grooming, punctuality, attitude, and interview strategy were all thoroughly discussed and enacted in the role-playing situations.

Hypothesis 3b: Changes in the Participants' Plans and Employment Status

Making plans. The first evidence concerning the success of the occupational aspects of the program were the facts that 63% of the women had developed a single, clear, and actionable plan by the end of their month of workshop sessions, and another 26% had developed somewhat more vague plans. Most of the women (68%) chose applying for some kind of job as their plan, with 47% aiming at least fairly clearly toward a traditional job in one of the "women's" fields, and 21% aiming to apply for either a blue collar job or one in a technical field in which women are rare. The remaining 32% chose to get some form of technical training. Those who planned to enter occupations chose administrative jobs most frequently, with general office work, high level sales, and retail sales following fairly closely. The SES scores of these planned jobs were, on the average, a full 15 points higher than the women's past jobs, and just 2 points lower than the jobs their husbands had been developing over many years. Thus, it is clear that the women in the Career Options Program had gone from no clear plans to a set of actionable plans that were much higher in status (and pay level) than their own past jobs, and that were almost as high as their husbands' jobs.

Getting hired. By the end of the first month following the end of the program, 58% of the participants had either gotten jobs or gotten into desired training programs. By 4 months, this figure had reached 74%, with a full 82% successfully placed by the end of the seventh month (18% entering job training, and 63% being hired for jobs). The jobs the women obtained (with substantial assistance from the program facilitators) were concentrated in the upper white collar range, with an SES mean that was only a fraction of a point lower than that of the planned occupations. The hourly pay rate of the obtained jobs was found to be approximately the national average for working women ($5.00), and they were almost as high in status level as the jobs of the husbands. These jobs probably could not have been attained without the Career Options Program.

Hypothesis 4: Self-Conception Change Related to Increased Coping

As a way of summarizing the relatively complex series of multiple regression analyses in which the four self-conception change dimensions were used in combination with the strongest other factors to predict the nine economic dependent variables that together operationalize "coping effectiveness," we present Table 9-6. The columns of Table 9-6 are in increasing order of the degree to which the four

Table 9-6. Summary of Predictive Patterns From the Self-Conception Proportionate Change Dimensions to the Nine Indicators of Economic Coping Effectiveness

	Dependent variables (SES scores or differences)									
Self-conception change dimension	Previous job to planned	Planned job SES	Husband's job to planned	Previous to obtained	Obtained job SES	Husband's job to obtained	Change in $/hr	Planned to obtained job	Clear plans	Frequency of substantial beta
Autonomy % change	+	+		+	+	–	+	+	+	8
Self-confidence % change	–	–	–			+	–	+	+	7
Sociability % change	+		+			+	–	+		5
Vigor % change				–	+				+	3
Value of MR^2, S-Cs only	.03	.04	.05	.06	.10	.14	.19	.24	.25	
Value of MR^2, all variables	.65	.20	.77	(over-determined)	.68	(over-determined)	.88	.53	.47	

Note. Out of the 36 relationships, 13 were too small to be shown (less than .100), 16 are positive, and 7 are negative.

self-conception proportionate change dimensions are able to predict the dependent variables (net of the effects of the other variables, which were chosen because of their strong correlations with that dependent variable). These increasing values of MR^2 attributable to the self-conceptions only are shown at the bottom of the table, as is the total MR^2 using all the variables. The rows are organized according to decreasing frequency of appreciable beta weights for the individual self-conceptions (as shown in the rightmost column of the table). "Appreciable" beta weights are here considered to be those equal to or greater than the .100 level. Only the signs of these beta weights are shown so as to emphasize the overall patterns.

Vigor percentage change was found to be appreciably related to only three of the dependent variables: negatively to the change from previous job to obtained job, and positively to the obtained job SES and to the presence of a clear plan at the end of the program. Only the .320 beta to presence of a clear plan was very strong, suggesting that developing an improved sense of strength and security of action may have made it easier for those women to enter into the process by which such plans were developed in the context of the Career Options Program, but inspection of Table 9-5 shows that the women who made the greatest gain in vigor were those who had low status husbands and a large number of dependents, thus dampening the range of further aspiration gaps.

Sociability percentage change was appreciably related to five of the dependent variables. Four of these were positive betas to difference or change measures involving the past job and the husband's job in relation to the planned job and obtained job. Our interpretation of these positive relationships is that the more a woman became (and sensed herself to be) outgoing, assertive, verbal, etc., the more actively involved she tended to be in the group experiences through which the strong moves away from past circumstances were developed. The single negative relationship, with change in rate of pay from past job to obtained job, suggests that improved sociability may not be a help in negotiating the tough dollars-and-cents issues of the new job, but rather make the applicant too eager to be "nice," and to please the new employer by settling for the first offer.

Self-confidence percentage change was found to relate positively to three dependent variables, the development of a clear plan and two gaps (husband's job and planned job to obtained job). These relations seem straightforward enough from self theory, but the four negative relationships take more explaining. The negative betas were found in predicting the SES of the planned job, the gap between previous job and planned job, the gap between husband's job and planned job, and change in pay rate. The gaps to the planned job may be negatively related to self-confidence percentage change because the women who made the greatest self-confidence gains were those who had relatively low educational backgrounds but fairly high previous jobs. Thus, those women making the largest improvements in self-confidence already had fairly high starting points from which to measure gaps to planned jobs and also may have felt educationally inadequate to aspire much higher. Examination of the relation to change in rate of pay supports this interpretation.

Autonomy percentage change can be seen to be appreciably related to eight of the economic variables, seven positively and one negatively. The positive relations permit a straightforward interpretation: the more a participant increased in the combination of sensed competence and sensed self-determination that we conceive of as autonomy, the higher the status of her occupational plans and obtained occupations and the greater the change from past job to future job. Autonomy percentage change was unrelated to the difference between the SES of the husbands' occupations and the wives' planned jobs, but showed a strong negative net relation (-.332) to the difference between the husband's job and the actually obtained job. We interpret this negative relation in terms of the fact that the women who moved up most in the sense of autonomy were the affluent Anglo women whose husbands' jobs (and their own derived status) were already quite high. These women thus were relatively unlikely to surpass the status of their husbands' jobs.

Implications for Future Research and Action

This study obviously has been very limited in both its research design and the number of participants. We therefore could not rule out the possibility that the very positive self-conception changes might have been caused by instrument reactivity, or the possibility that the positive occupational outcomes might have been caused by any number of factors other than the specific effects of the Career Options Program. Specifically, we could not use full causal modeling in a strong attempt to ascertain the direction of any possible causation between self-conception changes and occupational goal changes, although the timing of events and actions long after the program was completed does indicate that the self-conception changes came first.

We can conclude, however, that action programs such as Career Options can be successful in aiding women in making the transition from the homemaker role to the employee role, whether or not this role transition involves a woman being forced out on her own as was envisioned by Jacobs (1980) and Shields (1981), being engaged in a voluntary breakaway from her home as discussed by L. Rubin (1979), or being committed to building a two-career family with her husband (Hall & Hall, 1979; Harris, 1981). In any of these circumstances, a group process program that involves the combination of realistic clarification of goals and values, a realistic familiarization with the relevant job market, development of job-getting skills, full development of the relevant self-conceptions, and active assistance by a professionally qualified program staff can be dramatically successful in helping women obtain maximally fulfilling economic roles and maximally rewarding inner lives.

Acknowledgments. We wish to express our sincere appreciation to the Texas Education Agency and the Houston Community College System for supporting the Career Options Program, to the Women's Fund (of Houston, Texas) for partial support of the research, to Rice University and its Institute for Computer Services and Applications for support of the data analysis, and to the Career Options participants, who shared so much of their lives with us.

References

Berman, E. *Re-entering: Successful back-to-work strategies for women seeking a fresh start.* New York: Crown, 1980.

Bernard, J. *Women, wives, mothers: Values and options.* Chicago: Aldine, 1975.

Blau, P. M., & Duncan, O. D. *The American class structure.* New York: Wiley, 1967.

Blau, Z. Role exit: A theoretical essay. In Z. Blau, *Old age in a changing society.* New York: New Viewpoints, 1973.

Block, J. Some enduring and consequential structure of personality. In A. I. Rabin *et al.* (Eds.), *Further exploration in personality*. New York: Wiley Interscience, 1981.

Brim, O. G., Jr., & Kagan, J. (Eds.). *Constancy and change in human development*. Cambridge, Mass.: Harvard University Press, 1980.

Campbell, D. T., & Stanley, J. C. *Experimental and quasi-experimental designs for research.* Chicago: Rand McNally, 1963.

Costa, P. T., Jr., & McCrae, R. R. Still stable after all these years: Personality as a key to some issues in adulthood and old age. In P. B. Baltes & Brim, O. G., Jr. (Eds.), *Life-span development and behavior* (Vol. 3). New York: Academic Press, 1980.

Davis, J. A. *Great aspirations.* Chicago: Aldine, 1964.

Davis, J. A. *Undergraduate career decisions.* Chicago: Aldine, 1965.

Duncan, O. D., Featherman, D. L., & Duncan, B. *Socioeconomic background and achievement.* New York: Seminar Press, 1972.

Ekstrom, R. B. Evaluating women's homemaking and volunteer work experience for community college credit. In C. Elisaon (Ed.), *Equity counseling for community college women.* Washington, D. C.: American Association of Community and Junior Colleges, Center for Women's Opportunities, 1979.

Eliason, C. (Ed.). *Equity counseling for community college women.* Washington, D.C.: American Association of Community and Junior Colleges, Center for Women's Opportunities, 1979.

Erikson, E. *Childhood and society.* New York: Norton, 1950.

Erikson, E. Identity and the life cycle. In G. S. Klein (Ed.), *Psychological Issues.* New York: Norton, 1959.

Freeman, R. B. The work force of the future: An overview. In C. Kerr & J. M. Rosow (Eds.) *Work in America: The decade ahead.* New York: VanNostrand Reinhold, 1979.

George, L. K. *Role transitions in later life.* Monterey, Calif.: Brooks/Cole, 1980.

Glaser, B. & Strauss, A. L. *Status passage*. Chicago: Aldine, 1971.

Gordon, C. *Self-conceptions and social achievement.* (Doctoral dissertation, University of California at Los Angeles, 1963). Dissertation Abstracts International, 1963 (University Microfilms).

Gordon, C. Self-conceptions: Configurations of content. In C. Gordon & K. J. Gergen (Eds.), *The self in social interaction: Classic and contemporary perspectives.* New York: Wiley, 1968. (a)

Gordon, C. Systemic senses of self. *Sociological Inquiry,* 1968, *38*, 161-178. (b)

Gordon, C. On the sense of personal autonomy. Paper given at the meetings of the Eastern Sociological Society, Boston, Mass., 1968. (c)

Gordon, C. Self-conceptions methodologies. *Journal of Nervous and Mental Disease,* 1969, *148*, 328-364.

Gordon, C. Role and value development across the life cycle. In J. A. Jackson (Ed.), *Sociological studies IV: Role.* Cambridge, England: Cambridge University Press, 1971. (a)

Gordon, C. Social characteristics of early adolescence. *Daedalus*, 1971, *100*, 931-960. (Reprinted in J. Kagan & R. Coles (Eds.), *Twelve to sixteen: Early Adolescence.* New York: Norton, 1972.) (b)

Gordon, C. *Looking ahead: Self-conceptions, race and family as determinants of adolescent orientations to achievement.* Washington, D.C.: American Sociological Association's Rose Monograph Series, 1972.

Gordon, C. Development of evaluated role identies. In A. Inkeles (Ed.), *Annual Review of Sociology* (Vol. 2). Palo Alto, Calif.: Annual Reviews, 1976.

Gordon, C., Gaitz, C. M., & Scott, J. Self-evaluations of competence and worth in adulthood. In S. Arieti (Ed.), *American handbook of psychiatry* (2nd ed.), pp. 212-229. New York: Basic Books, 1975.

Gordon, C. & Gergen, K. J. (Eds.). *The self in social interaction: Classic and contemporary perspectives.* New York: Wiley, 1968.

Gordon, M. S. Women and work: Priorities for the future. In C. Kerr & J. M. Rosen (Eds.), *Work in America: The decade ahead.* New York: VanNostrand Reinhold, 1979.

Guilfoy, V. *Resource guide for vocational educators and planners: Helping displaced homemakers move from housework to paid work through vocational training.* Newton, Mass.: Educational Development Center, 1980.

Hall, F. S., & Hall, D. T. *The two-career couple.* Reading, Mass.: Addison-Wesley, 1979.

Harris, L. *Families at work: Strengths and weaknesses.* New York: Padilla & Speer, 1981.

Jacobs, R. H. Integrating displaced homemakers into the economy. Paper given at the meetings of the American Sociological Society, New York, August, 1980.

Kaplan, J. B. *Self-attitudes and deviant behavior.* Pacific Palisades, Calif.: Goodyear, 1979.

Levinson, D. J., et al. *The seasons of a man's life.* New York: Knopf, 1978.

Lopata, H. Z. Self-identity in marriage and widowhood. *Sociological Quarterly,* 1973, *14*, 407-418.

Manis, J. G., & Meltzer, B. N. (Eds). *Symbolic interaction: A reader in social psychology* (3rd ed.). Boston: Allyn & Bacon, 1978.

McCall, G. H., & Simmons, J. L. *Identities and interactions* (rev. ed.) New York: Free Press, 1978.

Myers, Henry (Ed.). *Women at work.* Princeton, N.J.: Dow Jones, 1979.

Reiss, A. J., Fr. (with O. D. Duncan, P. K. Hatt, & C. C. North). *Occupations and social status.* New York: The Free Press of Glencoe, 1961.

Rosenberg, M. *Occupations and values.* Glencoe, Ill.: The Free Press, 1957.

Rosenberg, M. *Conceiving the self.* New York: Basic Books, 1979.

Rosenberg, M. The self-concept: Social product and social force. Chap. 14 in M. Rosenberg & R. Turner (Eds.), *Social psychology: Sociological perspectives.* New York: Basic Books, 1981.

Rosenberg, M., & Simmons, R. G. *Black and white self-esteem.* Washington, D.C.: American Sociological Association's Rose Monograph Series, 1972.

Rosow, I. The social context of the aging self. *The Gerontologist,* 1973, *13*, 82-87.

Rosow, I. Status and role change through the life span. In R. H. Binstock & E. Shanas (Eds.), *Handbook of aging and the social sciences.* New York: VanNostrand Reinhold, 1976.

Rubin, L. B. *Women of a certain age: The midlife search for self.* New York: Harper & Row, 1979.

Rubin, Z. Does personality really change after 20? *Psychology Today*, May 1981, pp. 18-27.

Rubinstein, C. Money and self-esteem, relationships, secrecy, envy, satisfaction. *Psychology Today,* May 1981, pp. 29-44.

Sales, E. Women's adult development. In I. Friese *et al.* (Eds.), *Women and sex roles.* New York: Norton, 1978.

Saranson, S. *Work, aging and social change.* New York: Free Press, 1977.

Seidman, A. *Working women: A study of women in paid jobs.* Boulder, Colo.: Westview Press, 1978.

Shields, L. *Displaced homemakers: Organizing for a new life.* New York: McGraw-Hill, 1981.

Sontag, S. The double standard of aging. *Saturday Review,* September 23, 1972, pp. 29-38.

Super, D. E. Vocational adjustment: Implementing a self-concept. *Occupations*, 1951, *30*, 88-92.

Turner, R. Role-taking: Process versus conformity. A. Rose (Ed.), *Human behavior and social processes*. Boston: Houghton Mifflin, 1962.

Turner, R. Role: Sociological aspects. In D. Sills (Ed.), *International Encyclopedia of the Social Sciences* (Vol. 13). New York: Free Press, 1968.

Turner, R. The real self: From institution to impulse. *American Journal of Sociology*, 1976, *81*, 989-1016.

U.S. Department of Labor. *Employment and earnings.* (Vol. 27, No. 2, February), 1980. (a)

U.S. Department of Labor. *Twenty facts on women workers*. Washington, D.C.: D.O.L. Women's Bureau, 1980. (b)

U.S. Department of Labor. *Perspectives on working women: A databook*. Washington, D.C.: U.S. Superintendent of Documents, October, Bulletin 2080, 1980. (c)

Weiss, R. S. *Marital separation*. New York: Basic Books, 1975.

Yankelovich, D. Work, values and the new breed. In C. Derr & J. M. Rosow (Eds.), *Work in America: The decade ahead.* New York: VanNostrand Reinhold, 1979.

Chapter 10

Discretionary Justice: Influences of Social Role, Personality, and Social Situation

George J. McCall

One type of social behavior in which substantial efforts have been invested to isolate the influences of social role, personality, and social situation is discretionary decision making in the criminal justice system (Abt & Stuart, 1979; Shaver, Gilbert, & Williams, 1975). The first section of this chapter discusses the range and nature of criminal justice decision making. A conceptual framework for viewing the three types of influence as they operate in discretionary justice is developed in the second section. In the third section two major research paradigms for the study of these influences are examined and discussed. In a fourth section a number of empirical studies employing these paradigms are reviewed, and in the concluding section an attempt is made to resolve some of the conceptual and methodological difficulties confronting such efforts to identify the influences of role, personality, and social situation.

The Phenomenon of Discretionary Justice

One mode of comprehending the American criminal justice system is a flow chart of the passage of criminal offenders through the interconnected agencies of the police, prosecution, courts, and corrections. In Figure 10-1, each of the labeled white bands interrupting the flow (e.g., investigation, arrest, booking) represents a decision point at which some criminal justice agent elects either to continue or to discontinue the official processing of a case (note the numerous routes of exit of cases from the flow).

Decision makers throughout the criminal justice system are vested with considerable discretionary authority, as numerous commentators have been concerned to note (e.g., Davis, 1969; Reiss, 1974). A police officer, for example, may or may not choose to respond to a call to the scene of an allegedly criminal incident, determine that a crime did occur, arrest a suspect, etc. Similarly, a prosecuting attorney may or may not choose to seek a warrant or indictment, withdraw a criminal charge, oppose bail bond, accept a guilty plea to a lesser crime in lieu of trial, etc. A judge may or may not choose to issue a warrant, hold a suspect for trial, set a bail bond, accept a guilty plea, determine guilt (in certain types of cases), sentence convicted offenders (in certain cases), etc. A prison official has considerable discretionary authority in determining the type of confinement an inmate shall receive. And a probation or parole officer has substantial discretionary authority, for example, to recommend revocation of probation or parole.

It is such discretionary decision making that gives rise to the multiplicity of offender routes through the criminal justice system outlined in Figure 10-1. Consequently, a major focus of criminal justice research has been the attempt to discover the legal and extralegal influences on each of these many discretionary decisions of criminal justice agents (McCall, 1978). In much of this research, such extralegal influences on agents' decisions have been conceptualized as those of social role, personality, and social situation (cf. Abt & Stuart, 1979; Shaver et al., 1975).

A Framework for Understanding Discretionary Justice

Discretionary justice decisions are nearly always made in situational social encounters, for example, in a streetcorner conference among a policeman, complainant, and alleged offender; or in a courtroom proceeding. Although some research has focused on the subtle dynamics of the interaction process within such encounters, most studies of discretionary decision making have instead centered on the *outcomes* of these encounters, i.e., on the decisions reached by the criminal justice agents as resultants of such interaction. The research problem is then construed as one of statistical explanation of the variation in a set of outcomes as a function of the agents' roles, the agents' personalities, and/or situational influences on the agents.

Until rather recently, the methodology of much of this outcome research has not been highly sophisticated. Rather than striving to maximize variation explained, many studies appear instead to have reflected the conceptual commitments of the investigator to either a role framework, personality framework, or situational approach. That is to say, many such studies have sought to demonstrate some simple main effect of either role, personality, or situation on the outcomes of some type of decision rather than to sort out the independent and combined influence of all three elements. Although relatively few of these one-sided studies have simply ignored the possibility of influences by the other two elements, many seem to have assumed rather naively that the two nuisance elements (say, role and personality) could simply be held constant while allowing the element of interest (e.g., social situation) to vary. But such a simplistic strategy must founder on two major difficulties.

Fig. 10-1. Routes through the criminal justice system. Procedures and individual jurisdictions may vary from the pattern shown here. The differing weights of line indicate the relative volume of cases typically disposed of at various points in the system. (From the *Challenge of Crime in a Free Society*. By the President's Commission on Law Enforcement and Administration of Justice, Washington, D.C.: U.S. Government Printing Office, 1967, pp. 8-9.)

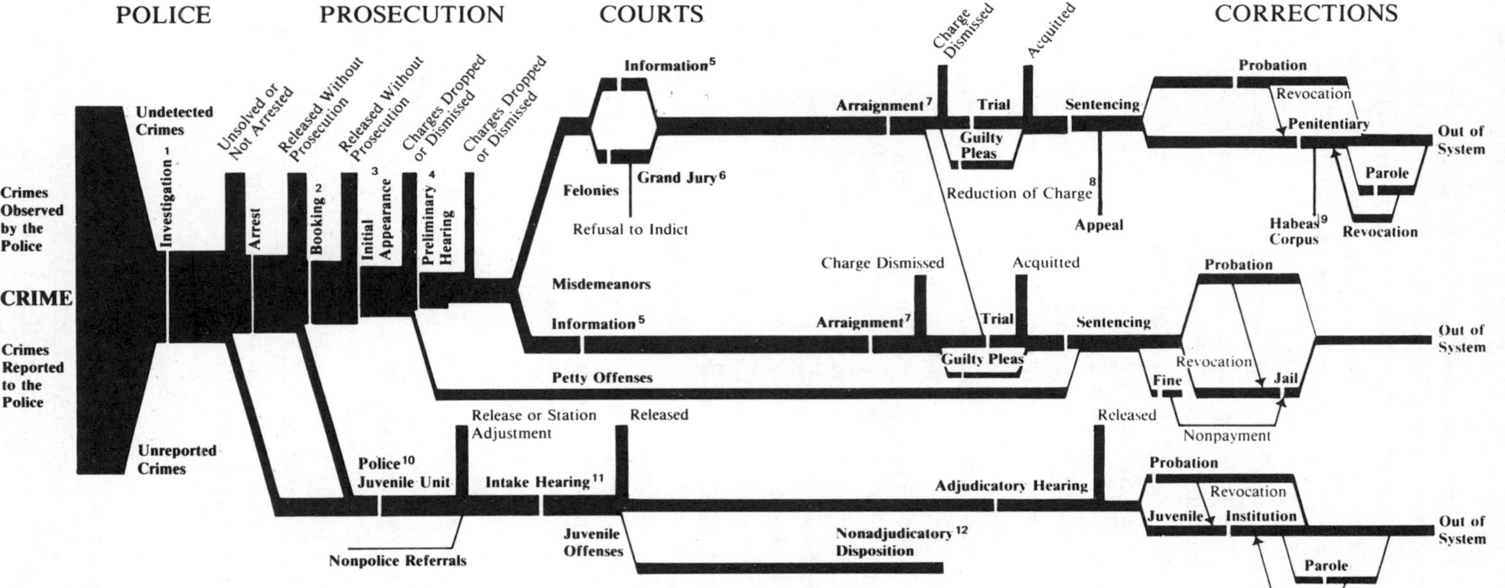

[1] May continue until trial.

[2] Administrative record of arrest. First step at which temporary release on bail may be available.

[3] Before magistrate, commissioner, or justice of peace. Formal notice of charge, advice of rights. Bail set. Summary trials for petty offenses usually conducted here without further processing.

[4] Preliminary testing of evidence against defendant. Charge may be reduced. No separate preliminary hearing for misdemeanors in some systems.

[5] Charge filed by prosecutor on bases of information submitted by police or citizens. Alternative to grand jury indictment; often used in felonies, almost always in misdemeanors.

[6] Reviews whether government evidence sufficient to justify trial. Some states have no grand jury system; others seldom use it.

[7] Appearance for plea; defendant elects trial by judge or jury (if available); counsel for indigent usually appointed here in felonies. Often not at all in other cases.

[8] Charge may be reduced at any time prior to trial in return for plea of guilty or for other reasons.

[9] Challenge on constitutional grounds to legality of detention. May be sought at any point in process.

[10] Police often hold informal hearings, dismiss or adjust many cases without further processing.

[11] Probation officer decides desirability of further court action.

[12] Welfare agency, social services, counseling, medical care, etc., for cases where adjudicatory handling not needed.

The first of these difficulties is that role, personality, and social situation are not mutually independent. To begin with, the social role selected by or ascribed to an individual has been shown to be related to the personality of that individual (Backman & Secord, 1968). Moreover, the social role that an individual plays has been shown to affect the individual's personality (Alexander & Knight, 1971). Similarly, one's social role is known to importantly condition the types of social situations one enters, and the role selected by or ascribed to an individual varies by situational characteristics (Jackson, 1971). The roles of policeman and of beautician, for example, tend to involve their occupants in very different ranges of situations, and different situations lead the military chaplain (Burchard, 1954) to perform primarily as a clergyman or as a military officer. Finally, personality features vary situationally (Endler & Magnusson, 1976), and which situations one enters is influenced by one's personality (e.g., Klausner, 1968). These intricate interdependencies among role, personality, and situation make it extremely difficult to hold constant any two of these elements while allowing a third to vary.

The second major difficulty is that none of these elements can truly be regarded as a discrete entity. A social role, for example, consists of the set of social expectations held by others toward the occupant of a specified social position. Some of these expectations may not be mutually compatible, and considerable disagreement about expectations may occur among persons regarding the occupant of a single position (Gross, Mason, & McEachern, 1958). And just as roles vary widely in clarity, compatibility, and consensus (Secord & Backman, 1974, pp. 420-460), personalities generally are not highly integrated or stable systems (Hartshorne, May, & Shuttleworth, 1930); furthermore, even the specific traits which enter into a personality may not prove to be situationally consistent (Endler & Magnusson, 1976). Finally, objectively similar social situations are often defined (or interpreted) quite differently by the various participants and therefore elicit dissimilar responses (Hastorf & Cantril, 1954). Consequently, even if the nominal identity of some role, personality, or situation is held constant across occasions, some proportion of its constituent aspects or features can be expected to vary.

Since for these reasons it is not fruitful to attempt to study role, personality, and situation as if they were discrete and independent entities, their influences are best conceptualized as the effects of clustered variables—role variables, personality variables, situational variables—in a multivariate space, as determined through an appropriately sophisticated statistical analysis. But, of course, not every study can afford to measure or manipulate directly all the many specific role variables, personality variables, and situational variables called for by such an approach. Many studies must simplify and economize by relying on comparatively crude measures of *overall differences* in role, in personality, or in situation.

Situational Variables

In the majority of discretionary justice decisions (i.e., those by police, prosecution, and courts), the influence of *two* distinct social situations may be seen as operative: the immediate social situation of the deliberation itself, and the initial social situation of the offense in question.

Most of the legally relevant considerations stem from the *initial situation.* Included here are the nature and circumstances of the offense, mitigating circumstances (including characteristics of the offender and of the offender-victim relationship), and consequences of the offense (taking into account certain characteristics of the victim). Criminal justice organizations evolve, and operate on the basis of, conceptions of "normal crimes" (Sudnow, 1965), i.e., conceptions of prevalent patterns of legally relevant and irrelevant characteristics of the immediate situations of various crimes. A "normal rape," for example, may be conceived as one taking place on the north side of the city, and involving a weapon, a white female victim and a young black perpetrator with a previous record of sex offenses, no prior relationship between the two parties, and some physical injury to the victim. Offense situations approximating the relevant conception of "normal crime" are responded to in a routinized fashion, whereas those departing significantly from such conceptions require more genuine deliberation in the criminal justice agent's decision making (Sudnow, 1965).

The central dynamics of the *immediate situation* of deliberation consist of attempts by the three parties—the presiding agent and functionaries, the victim and advocates, the offender and advocates—to control what information about features of the initial situation is introduced into the immediate situation of the deliberation. The victim's team largely controls informational inputs about the nature of the offense and its consequences (including information about the victim). The offender's team largely controls informational inputs about mitigating circumstances of the offense (including information about the offender and about the offender's relationship to the victim). However, the presiding agent typically exerts substantial control over what information either side will be allowed to introduce. In the end, it is the presiding agent's perception and interpretation of the body of information about the initial situation, and of the action recommendations made by the adversarial parties, that provide the basis for the decision.

The broad category of situational variables influencing discretionary justice outcomes must, therefore, include not only those legally relevant features of the initial situation (enumerated above) but also various features of the immediate situation of deliberation. Perhaps the most directly pertinent of these would be the respective action recommendations made by the adversarial parties (Black, 1970; Suffet, 1966). The weight given to such a recommendation might be expected to depend importantly on the adequacy of a party's case presentation (credibility, documentation, presentational strategy, etc.). One might also presume that more purely interpersonal aspects of an adversarial party's conduct (e.g., deference to the presiding agent, general demeanor) could also prove influential (Jaros & Mendelsohn, 1967; Mileski, 1971; Reiss, 1971). Immediate situational variables ideally also should include the nature and degree of the agent's control over informational inputs from the adversarial parties (Hood & Sparks, 1970), as well as the agent's perception and interpretation of the information that is in fact introduced into the deliberation by the two sides (Hogarth, 1971).

For reasons of economy, however, many studies fail to include direct measures of some of these specific situational variables, even important, legally relevant features of the initial situation of offense. Often the legally defined nature of the offense is employed as a simplistic proxy measure of overall differences in situation, an indicator readily obtainable from official records at every level within the criminal justice system.

Role Variables

The central feature of any social role is the specific pattern of interpersonal demands on and expectations of a person by virtue of the person's occupancy of a particular social position. Ideally, measured role variables would include the content and the clarity of each role expectation as well as the compatibility and the consensuality of role expectations within and between the various sectors of the role (Gross, Mason, & McEachern, 1958). Detailed role analysis of this type is a major undertaking in its own right; Preiss and Ehrlich's (1966) extensive analysis of the state policeman's role is a rare example in the study of criminal justice agents. The vast majority of studies of discretionary justice have instead relied on more economical proxy measures of *differences* in social role among agents.

Chief among these indicators of differences in social role is reference to the social position itself, on the reasonable assumption that persons occupying different positions in the criminal justice system confront differing social expectations (e.g., prosecuting attorney vs. defense attorney). Similarly, differences in rank (e.g., police sergeant vs. police captain) and differences in unit (e.g., patrol division vs. detective division) are not unreasonably assumed to index differences in the set of social expectations faced.

Aside from such structural types of proxy measure of differences in social role, contextual proxies may be employed, such as organizational characteristics of parallel agencies. For example, local police departments have been shown to vary substantially in the relative emphasis placed on the various police functions; Wilson (1968) describes a watchman style, a service style, and a legalistic style. Moreover, the style of a department has been shown to reflect the character of the local community (Banton, 1964; Cain, 1971, 1973). It is not unreasonable, therefore, to presume that the role of, say, police patrolman varies between departments of different styles or between communities differing in character.

Personality Variables

Perhaps the central core of personality variables is comprised of various personal dispositions: traits, attitudes, opinions, beliefs, values, habits, etc. As detailed in the next section, direct measures of many such dispositional variables have been employed in studies of discretionary justice. On the other hand, most contemporary concepts of personality (e.g., Carson, 1969; Mischel, 1973) now emphasize the importance of understanding the ways in which the expression of individuality is affected by situational and social organizational contexts. Since personal dispositions are difficult to distinguish from the influences of social roles and their situational prescriptions, a particularly strategic personality variable is the individual's degree of self-identification with his various social roles (Turner, 1978), i.e., the prominence, salience, and content of relevant role identities (McCall & Simmons, 1978). Although personality variables of these sorts have not yet been employed in discretionary justice research, rather elegant measurement techniques are now readily available (e.g., Burke, 1980).

Most often in studies of discretionary justice, more global and much less direct measures of overall *differences* in personality are employed. Such differences are often presumed to be indexed by the proxy variables of such simple personal attributes as age, sex, race, socioeconomic status, and marital status–a presumption loosely based on the psychology of group differences (Willerman, 1979). Still more crudely, presumed differences in personality are often simply indexed by the proxy of individual identity, i.e., subject variance. Criminal justice agent *A* is presumed to differ in overall personality from agent *B*, a presumption apparently based loosely on the psychology of individual differences.

Research Paradigms for Explaining Discretionary Justice

As noted above, relatively few studies of discretionary decision making in the criminal justice system have attempted evenhandedly to sort out the independent and combined influences of role variables, personality variables, and situational variables on the outcomes of decision making. Most research on this phenomenon has been much narrower in focus and implicitly policy oriented, concerned to investigate possible extralegal influences on either intraagent or interagent variation in decision outcomes. An earlier review of discretionary justice research (McCall, 1978) identified, and attempted to formalize, the implicit paradigms underlying these two principal lines of research.

Discretion Paradigm

A policeman on traffic patrol, for instance, may over a period of time observe several comparably speeding vehicles but may stop only some of these and let others go, may give warnings to some drivers but tickets to others, at his discretion. Issues of equality of treatment and of equity arise, and many citizens suspect that extralegal and prejudicial factors may underlie such intraagent variation. The discretion paradigm, accordingly, seeks to account for variation in the discretionary decisions of a single agent (intraagent variation in outcomes). This paradigm tacitly assumes that by examining only a single agent the influences of both social role and personality are necessarily held constant, so that variation in outcomes may be attributed solely to various situational variables.

A weaker version of this paradigm pools outcome data from several occupants of similar positions, effectively regarding them as so thoroughly interchangeable as to virtually represent one single agent. This version essentially stipulates by assumption that neither role variables nor personality variables exert appreciable influence on these outcomes.

As diagrammed in Figure 10-2, the discretion paradigm prescribes the collection of data (for each decision-making encounter studied) on a variety of features of

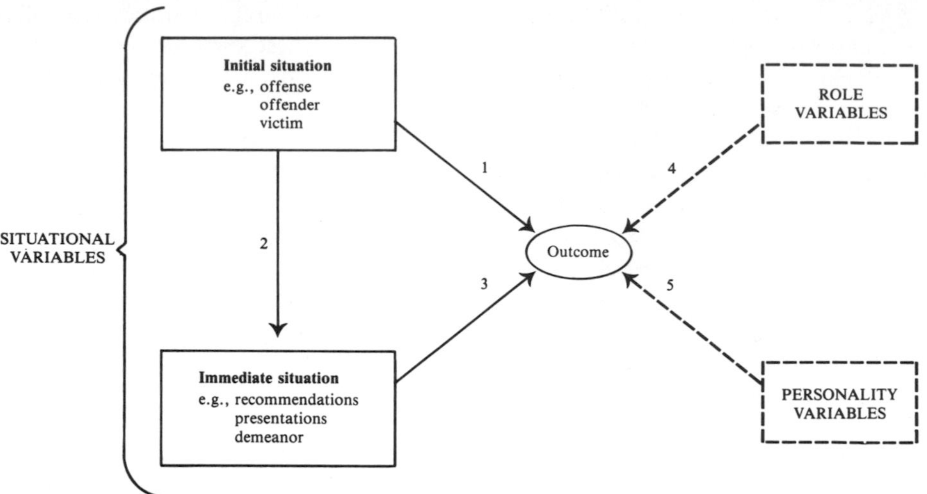

Fig. 10-2. Discretion paradigm.

both the initial and the immediate situations as well as on the outcome of the encounter. Through some appropriately multivariate procedure of statistical analysis (e.g., causal modelling, multiple regression, complex analysis of variance, partial correlation, or partial association), estimates of the independent effects corresponding to each of the three unbroken arrows in Figure 10-2 are to be obtained (i.e., controlling for the influences of other included variables).

In practice, however, many discretion studies only partially implement this paradigm. Some studies altogether omit the block of variables pertaining to either the initial situation or, more commonly, to the immediate situation (e.g., Chiricos & Waldo, 1975). Other studies include both blocks of situational variables but omit some of the prescribed variables within a block (e.g., Jaros & Mendelsohn, 1967) and/or omit one or more of the prescribed effect estimates (e.g., Kelley, 1976).

Disparity Paradigm

Many observers of the criminal justice system (e.g., Orland & Tyler, 1974) are disturbed by apparently serious disparities in, for example, sentences prescribed by different judges and jurisdictions for similar offenses. The second major paradigm may be called the disparity paradigm in that it seeks to account for interagent variation in outcomes among a number of agents dealing with similar cases. By emphasizing differences among agents, this paradigm shifts attention to the influences of social role and/or of personality and regards situational influences as nuisance variables.

In some few disparity studies, situational influences are controlled directly by having all agents deal with a single set of cases. In other studies, only selected situational variables are controlled or statistically adjusted (e.g., the nature of the offense). All too often, however, situational features are merely assumed to be equivalent or distributed randomly across the set of agents.

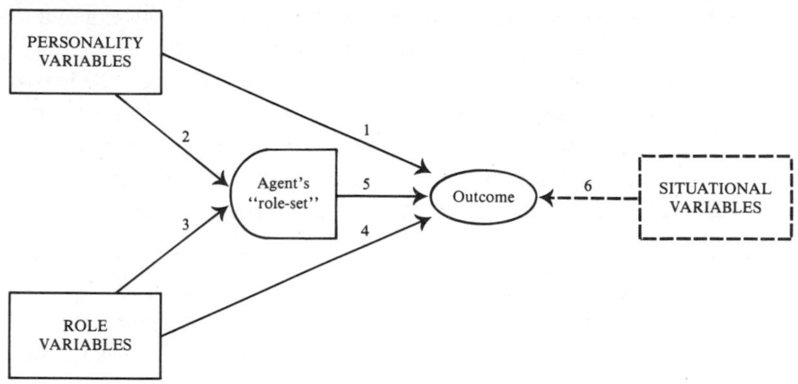

Fig. 10-3. Disparity paradigm.

As diagrammed in Figure 10-3, the disparity paradigm calls for the collection of data on a variety of personality and role variables and the multivariate estimation of several independent effects. Again, in practice, many disparity studies only partially implement this paradigm. In general, role variables are perhaps more often studied than personality variables, and the two sets of variables are seldom examined jointly. Role studies tend to assume that personality influences are comparable across roles, and personality studies tend to assume that role differences exert negligible effects.

However, many disparity studies do follow the schema of Figure 10-3 by devoting attention to the "role-set" of the criminal justice agent, i.e., to the mental set or action policy with which he approaches the decision making encounter. This "role-set," or characteristically distinctive perspective and purpose of an individual agent, is considered to arise through the confrontation between personal dispositions and the sociolegal constraints of the organizational role. To take just one example, Blumberg (1967) observed six principal "role-sets" among criminal court judges: "intellectual" scholar, routineer-hack, political adventurist-careerist, judicial pensioner, "hatchet man," and "tyrant"-"showboat"-"benevolent despot." Such personalized role orientations are viewed as being neither a personality nor a role variable quite, but as a joint resultant with a somewhat separate influence on the decision outcome. For example, the "intellectual" scholar and the routineer-hack tend to be lenient workhorses of the court, open to plea bargaining, whereas the "tyrant"-"showboat"-"benevolent despot" is generally harsh and intemperate, with occasional grandiose gestures of charity and forbearance.

Studies of Discretionary Justice

In this brief chapter it is not possible to present examples of studies of each of the many discretionary decision situations of the criminal justice system. Space permits only the review of discretion paradigm and disparity paradigm studies of a single such decision situation, namely, sentence hearings conducted by a criminal court judge.

In such studies, sentencing outcomes may be conceptualized in several ways. First, a study may focus on the relative frequencies of the use of suspended sentences, probation, fines, and imprisonment. Second, a study may examine the relative frequencies of specific types of imprisonment, e.g., jail vs. penitentiary. Third, a study may focus on the dollar amounts of fines imposed or on the length of imprisonment imposed. In any case, data on these dependent variables are ordinarily obtained from official records of the courts. These studies attempt to explain either intrajudge variation in sentencing outcomes (utilizing the discretion paradigm) or interjudge variation in sentencing outcomes (utilizing the disparity paradigm).

Discretion Paradigm Studies

The discretion paradigm, again, explains intrajudge variation in sentencing outcomes as a resultant of situational variables, controlling for the influences of the judge's social role and personality.

Initial situation. Among the situational variables employed in such studies, many derive from the initial situation of the criminal act. Legally relevant variables include the nature of the criminal offense, the severity of the offense, and the length and seriousness of the offender's previous criminal record. (Data on such variables are obtained from official court records.) So-called "extralegal" characteristics of the offender are also frequently studied (e.g., Burke & Turk, 1975; Pope, 1975a), including age, sex, race or ethnicity, social class, occupation, education, marital status, and rural or urban background. Occasionally, sentencing outcome studies (e.g., Green, 1964) take into account similar characteristics of the victim, at least in relation to those of the offender (i.e., as being of same or different race, sex, age, or class). (Data on extralegal characteristics of offender and victim are usually obtained from official presentence investigations conducted by a probation officer.)

Immediate situation. A few sentencing outcome studies (e.g., Hood, 1966) have examined the influence of sentencing recommendations made by the prosecuting or defense attorney or by the court's presentence investigation officer. A similar variable somewhat more often examined (e.g., Kelley, 1976) is the defendant's plea, i.e., guilty or innocent. (Data on either of these variables are ordinarily to be found in court records.) The effects of more subtle aspects of prosecution and defense strategies are only now beginning to come under study. The deference and demeanor of the defendant have been considered in several sentencing outcome studies (e.g., Kelley, 1976). (Measurement of either of these variables requires special on-site observation by the researcher.)

Referring again to Figure 10-2, the discretion paradigm optimally involves analysis of the effects of initial situational variables on both sentencing outcomes (Arrow 1) and immediate situational variables (Arrow 2) and of immediate situational variables on outcomes (Arrow 3). However, the majority of sentencing outcome studies have examined only Arrow 1. Early studies of this type examined only the effects on outcomes of extralegal characteristics of the offender, concluding that race, sex, and age significantly affected outcomes. Green (1961) showed, however, that when legally relevant variables are taken into account, the effects of age, sex, and race on sentence severity are negligible. Subsequently, Hagan (1974) reanalyzed the data from 20 of these early studies, controlling for legally relevant variables, and demonstrated that these data show only very small relationships between any extralegal offender characteristics and severity of sentence. Carefully controlled primary studies by Burke and Turk (1975), Chiricos and Waldo (1975), and Pope (1975a) similarly conclude that no single offender characteristic accounts for much variation in sentencing outcomes. Pope (1975b) and Hewitt (1976) did find evidence that certain *combinations* of offender characteristics (e.g., race and work history) may affect sentencing outcomes, but that such interaction effects were also generally negligible. Similarly, early studies of race of victim, in relation to race of offender, had suggested that interracial crime is punished more severely than intraracial crime. Again, however, subsequent studies (e.g., Green, 1964) and reanalyses (Hindelang, 1972) find very little support for this proposition when legally relevant variables are controlled for.

A few discretion paradigm studies have examined both Arrows 1 and 3, i.e., the effects of both initial situational and immediate situational variables. For example, Kelley (1976) found, controlling for offender's age, sex, marital status, rural/urban background, education, and prior criminal record, that type of plea (and type of defense counsel) was somewhat influential on sentencing for burglary but not for homicide, while race was not influential in either case. Jaros and Mendelsohn (1967) found that the defendant's courtroom dress and demeanor were more influential than the type of counsel or most offender characteristics, although less influential than legally relevant factors.

Even fewer studies have also incorporated examination of Arrow 2 (i.e., the effects of initial situational variables on immediate situational variables), thus exemplifying the full discretion paradigm of Figure 10-2. Hagan (1975b) presents data suggesting that extralegal characteristics of offenders may more significantly affect the sentencing recommendation of the court's presentence investigation officer than directly affect the sentencing dispositions of the judges themselves. Thus, any effects of extralegal characteristics on sentence received may be mediated by the presentence reports. Hewitt (1976) found, however, that such mediating effects through the sentencing recommendations of either the presentence investigation officer or the prosecutor were few (primarily relating to the sex of offender) and generally small.

Overall, then, discretion paradigm studies of sentencing outcomes rather consistently suggest that the legally relevant features of the initial situation are much more influential than any other situational variables.

Disparity Paradigm Studies

The disparity paradigm, again, explains interjudge variation in sentencing outcomes in terms of the social roles and the personalities of judges, controlling for any influences of the initial and immediate situations.

Personality variables. Sentencing outcome studies of this type (such as Hogarth, 1971) frequently utilize questionnaire or interview measures of various personal dispositions: traits (e.g., cognitive complexity), attitudes (e.g., liberalism, modernism, social defense, intolerance), opinions (e.g., regarding relative effectiveness of various treatment options), beliefs (e.g., views on the causes of crime), and habits (e.g., reading habits). More often (as in Bowen, 1965), interjudge differences in such personal dispositions are taken to be indexed by differences in such simple and publicly documented personal attributes as age, sex, race, socioeconomic background, education, religion, marital status, political affiliation, community ties, prior work experience, and length of judicial experience.

Role variables. Despite the enormous discretionary powers of criminal court judges, their work roles have received very little empirical study (Reiss, 1974). Detailed analysis of the specific patterns of interpersonal demands on and expectations of judges in particular court systems has been especially infrequent, although such analysis may begin to emerge from current research into variations in the social organization of various court systems (e.g., Eisenstein & Jacob, 1977; Mohr, 1976). In any case, specific role expectation profiles have rarely been employed in sentencing outcome studies. In fact, such studies seldom employ as an independent variable even interjudge differences in unit affiliation (e.g., lower, upper, and appellate court) or in rank (e.g., presiding judge or associate judge). Similarly, contextual proxy measures of differences in social role seldom appear in sentencing outcome studies, despite demonstrated differences in the organizational character of criminal courts in various communities (e.g., Jacob, 1973).

"Role-set" variables. As a joint resultant of his personality and social role, a judge approaches the sentence hearing with a characteristic mental "set" or action perspective. Ungs and Baas (1972) discriminated, through factor analysis of questionnaire items, five such sets: law interpreter, adjudicator, administrator, "the trial judge," and "peacekeeper." Although neither the Ungs-Baas nor the Blumberg (1967) typologies have yet been used in sentencing outcome research, similar measures have been employed as independent variables in such studies. For example, Hogarth (1971) employed penal philosophy scores (reflecting a judge's emphasis on reformation, general deterrence, individual deterrence, incapacitation, and punishment), and Hagan (1975a) used a law-and-order scale.

Referring again to Figure 10-3, the disparity paradigm optimally involves analysis of the effects on sentencing outcomes exerted by personality variables (Arrow 1), by role variables (Arrow 4), and by "role-set" variables (Arrow 5), as well as the effects of personality and role on "role-set" (Arrows 2 and 3, respectively), while controlling for any influences of situational variables (Arrow 6). However, a number of sentencing outcome studies have examined only the direct effects of personality variables (Arrow 1). For example, Nagel (1962) found that an attitude measure of liberalism and various personal attributes (e.g., political party affiliation, religious affiliation, American Bar Association membership, prior experience as a prosecuting attorney) were significantly related to judges' decision patterns. On the other hand, Bowen's (1965) replication study showed that, when analyzed through multiple regression techniques, none of the background variables explained more than a small fraction of the total variance among judges.

An occasional study examines only the effect on sentencing outcome of "role-set" variables (Arrow 5). Hagan (1975a), for example, found that judges scoring low on his law-and-order scale took more account of the extralegal characteristics of offenders than did judges scoring high on that scale.

Consistent with the above review of judicial role variables, there appear to have been no sentencing outcome studies that have solely, or even importantly, examined the effects of interjudge differences in role variables. However, measures of perceived legal and social constraints stemming from relationships with fellow judges, with probation officers, with prosecutors, with the Attorney General's office, and with the public at large were included in Hogarth's (1971) comprehensive study, which surely ranks as the outstanding example of the full-form disparity paradigm.

Not only did Hogarth's study consider the most nearly satisfactory set of role variables, it included the widest range of personality variables and a well-developed set of "role-set" variables. Explicit statistical controls were employed against the influence of both initial and immediate situational influences. The sample of judges was the entire population of major criminal magistrates in the province of Ontario, each of whom completed an attitude questionnaire and a personal interview, as well as a data form for every case of each of seven specified offenses. This form recorded the judge's perceptions of the initial and immediate situations of the case as well as his own purposes and the reasons for his actions. In addition to the more than 2000 select cases for which such forms were obtained, detailed court records were examined for *all* indictable cases dealt with by these judges during the study period. Fairly sophisticated procedures of multiple regression were employed in the analysis.

Perceived constraint variables included conformity to the law, conformity to other magistrates, attitude toward the sentencing practice of other magistrates, perceived accordance with other magistrates, satisfaction with probation officers, attitude toward the prosecuting attorney, the role of public opinion, perception of public opinion, and respectful relationships with particular other magistrates. The full ranges of both personal dispositions and personal attributes were measured. Personal dispositions included the trait of cognitive complexity, numerous judicial attitudes (such as tolerance, modernism, justice, punishment, deterrence), beliefs (e.g., regarding the causes of crime), opinions (e.g., regarding the effectiveness of various penal measures), and habits (such as criminological reading habits). Personal attributes included age, sex, marital status, religion, education, social class background and social mobility, birthplace, community ties, political affiliation, prior work experience, and length of experience as a magistrate. Statistical relationships within and between these two groups of personality variables were examined, finding, for example, that judicial attitudes correlated strongly with work experience variables but were unrelated to age or length of education.

For the 78 magistrates, some 21 different sentencing outcome scores, such as fines, jail sentences as a proportion of all institutionalization decisions, and mean length of penitentiary sentences, were regressed simultaneously on personality and role variables. For each type of outcome score, a different pattern of both personality and role variables was found to significantly influence outcomes (Arrows 1 and 4). For example, use of the suspended sentence without probation was best predicted by magistrates' low scores on attitude toward justice and on relationships with probation officers, whereas institutionalization was best predicted by high scores on attitude toward punishment and on relationships with prosecuting attorneys.

Central to Hogarth's study, however, were the "role-set" variables used to index the mental set (or sentencing policy) with which the various magistrates approached the sentencing decision. Penal philosophy scores were obtained through the magistrates' ratings of the importance and the applicability of each of the five classical purposes of sentencing: reformation, general deterrence, individual deterrence, punishment, and incapacitation. Self-imposed guidelines and rules of thumb in sentencing were assessed through the magistrates' designations of which situations they approach with presumptions for or against probation and for or against imprisonment. Several such "role-set" variables were regressed on both personality and role variables (Arrows 2 and 3). Magistrates' penal philosophies, for example, were found to depend on a complex interaction between community characteristics (such as size and ethnic composition), certain personal attributes (especially age and education), and certain judicial attitudes (particularly those toward justice and social defense).

In turn, the magistrates' "role-sets" were plausibly shown to determine their perceptions of the facts of individual criminal cases (as measured through the special data forms), supporting the view that "magistrates tend to interpret the 'facts' of the cases before them in such a way as to minimize inconsistency. In doing so, they rearrange the facts to fit the types of sentences they use habitually. It may be said that rather than 'seeking a punishment to fit the crime,' magistrates, through selective interpretation, 'seek an offender to fit the punishment.' " (Hogarth, 1971, p. 299). Regressing sentencing outcomes on these *perceptions* of fact, Hogarth found that approximately 50% of the variation is explained (as against about 9% explained by the objective facts of the initial situation as given in court records). Thus, Arrow 5, the effects of "role-set" variables on outcomes, appears to be more influential than the direct effects of either personality, role, or situational variables per se. In particular, Hogarth's findings suggest that the principal effects of personality and of role are indirect, mediated by the judge's "role-set," rather than direct.

Concluding Thoughts on Analyzing Discretionary Justice

Again, the sentencing outcome studies are only illustrative and not fully representative of the entire range of discretionary justice studies. For example, relative to studies of the policeman's decision whether to arrest, the sentencing studies more often employ direct measures of specific personality variables but less often directly measure variables pertaining to the immediate situation of deliberation. And certainly sentencing outcome studies tend to take less detailed account of role influences than do studies of decision making among police (Pepinsky, 1975), prosecutors (Neubauer, 1974), or parole officers (McCleary, 1975).

Considering the larger range of discretionary justice studies, a number of fairly common methodological flaws in the implementation of the discretion and disparity designs were noted above. First, these paradigms often are incompletely implemented. One or more blocks of variables may be omitted entirely, or too few of the variables within a block may actually be measured. But even when a study includes a proper set of variables, one or more of the major effect arrows may not be examined. Second, measurement of the included variables is often rather inadequate. Too often a proxy measure is used rather than an appropriate direct measure of role, personality, or situational variables. Third, the analysis of the data from such studies is often rather poorly controlled, resulting in biased estimates of effects. This is particularly true with respect to controlling the influences of variables excluded by a paradigm (e.g., situational variables in the disparity paradigm), but many studies fail to determine the *independent* effects of even the included variables.

Beyond these flaws in implementation, studies of discretionary justice face formidable methodological and conceptual obstacles in any attempt to sort out the influences of role, personality, and situation. The greatest methodological obstacle is posed by the absence of a single research paradigm that would simultaneously encompass all three influences. Since neither the discretion nor the disparity paradigm permits all three influences to operate at once, it is not possible through such studies to sort out the relative contributions of all three. Promising foundations for a more comprehensive paradigm may be found in the conceptualizations of Hood and Sparks (1970, pp. 141-170) and in the empirical study by Hogarth (1971) reviewed above. A more technical obstacle is the current reliance on linear, additive models of statistical analysis which, contrary to the argument of the section on "A Framework for Understanding Discretionary Justice," presupposes that role, personality, and situation are mutually independent influences. More complex statistical models may be necessary in order to properly identify the independent and combined effects of such variables.

But perhaps a still more fundamental obstacle lies in the choice of dependent variables. As previously noted, both the discretion and the disparity paradigms seek to locate the influences of role, personality, and situation in the study of the *outcomes* of decision making social interactions, rather than in the study of the *processes* of such episodes. This strategic choice is no doubt inspired by the political and practical desire to illuminate the many-branched flow of cases through the criminal justice system depicted in Figure 10-1, as well as by the wealth of readily available institutional data on outcomes and the relative absence of readymade data on process. Nevertheless, the comparative success of process models (in, e.g., small group interaction analysis and sociolinguistics) in analyzing the influences of role, personality, and situation might be taken to suggest considerable promise for similar investigations of discretionary justice encounters. Some support for this suggestion is already at hand. In an exemplary study of police-citizen interaction, Sykes and Clark (1975) employed a modified Interaction Process Analysis category system and portable digital encoding equipment to analyze such interaction as a sequential interchange of utterances and gestures. Although lacking specific personality data, this study did reveal substantial influences of situation and of role upon the interaction process.

Finally, some observations on laboratory experimental studies of discretionary justice may be in order. Most frequently, such studies have examined simulated jury decision making, a tradition dating at least to Marston (1924). Since laboratory experiments are typically conducted by academic social psychologists, one might have expected this tradition to devote considerable attention to the influences of role, personality, and situation. Remarkably, it has instead hewed closely to the discretion and disparity paradigms detailed above, investigating possible influences of situational variables (such as the nature and circumstances of the offense, characteristics of offender and/or victim, and lawyers' conduct of the case) and of agents' personal attributes (such as jury size, sex composition, and the social backgrounds of jurors).

Laboratory implementations of the two paradigms have been flawed in precisely the same ways noted for field studies, and have additionally suffered in both external and construct validity. Neither role variables nor situational variables lend themselves to realistic manipulation in the laboratory; most mock trials do not begin to resemble real trials or sentence hearings, and the act of role playing the sentencing of a rapist is far from having to perform that role in the real world.

The most promising possibility for the experimental study of discretionary justice outcomes would seem to require genuine field settings and/or genuine role-occupants who have well-developed "role-sets" sufficiently robust to evidence themselves even within somewhat contrived situations (see, e.g., McCall, 1978, pp. 125-126). Still greater promise for experimentation, one might suggest, would lie in the study of discretionary justice *process,* as noted above. Laboratory studies of general interpersonal processes have experienced considerable success in beginning to sort out influences of role, personality, and situation, and their paradigms might well be expected to point the way for subsequent field studies of discretionary decision making by criminal justice agents.

References

Abt, L. E., & Stuart, I. R. (Eds.). *Social psychology and discretionary law.* New York: Van Nostrand Reinhold, 1979.

Alexander, C. N., & Knight, G. W. Situated identities and social psychological experimentation. *Sociometry,* 1971, *34*, 65-82.

Backman, C. W., & Secord, P. F. The self and role selection. In C. Gordon & K. G. Gergen (Eds.), *The self and social interaction.* New York: Wiley, 1968.

Banton, M. *The policeman in the community.* London: Tavistock, 1964.

Black, D. J. Production of crime rates. *American Sociological Review,* 1970, *35*, 733-748.

Blumberg, A. S. *Criminal justice.* Chicago: Quadrangle, 1967.

Bowen, H. *The explanation of judicial voting behavior from sociological characteristics of judges.* Unpublished doctoral dissertation, Yale University, 1965.

Burchard, W. W. Role conflicts of military chaplains. *American Sociological Review,* 1954, *19*, 528-535.

Burke, P. J. The self: Measurement requirements from an interactionist perspective. *Social Psychology Quarterly,* 1980, *43*, 18-29.

Burke, P. J., & Turk, A. T. Factors affecting postarrest dispositions: A model for analysis. *Social Problems,* 1975, *22*, 313-332.

Cain, M. E. On the beat: Interactions and relations in urban and rural police forces. In S. Cohen (Ed.), *Images of deviance.* London: Penguin, 1971.

Cain, M. E. *Society and the policeman's role.* London: Routledge and Kegan Paul, 1973.

Carson, R. C. *Interaction concepts of personality.* Chicago: Aldine, 1969.

Chiricos, T. G., & Waldo, G. P. Socioeconomic status and criminal sentencing: An empirical assessment of a conflict proposition. *American Sociological Review,* 1975, *40*, 753-772.

Davis, K. C. *Discretionary justice.* Baton Rouge: Louisiana State University Press, 1969.

Eisenstein, J., & Jacob, H. *Felony justice: An organizational analysis of criminal courts.* Boston: Little, Brown, 1977.

Endler, N. S., & Magnusson, D. (Eds.). *Interactional psychology and personality.* Washington, D.C.: Hemisphere, 1976.

Green, E. *Judicial attitudes in sentencing.* London: Macmillan, 1961.

Green, E. Inter- and intra-racial crime relative to sentencing. *Journal of Criminal Law, Criminology and Police Science,* 1964, 55, 348-358.

Gross, N., Mason, W. S., & McEachern, A. W. *Explorations in role analysis.* New York: Wiley, 1958.

Hagan, J. Extra-legal attributes and criminal sentencing: An assessment of a sociological viewpoint. *Law and Society Review,* 1974, *8*, 357-383.

Hagan, J. Law, order, and sentencing: A study of attitude in action. *Sociometry,* 1975, *38*, 374-384. (a)

Hagan, J. The social and legal construction of criminal justice: A study of the presentencing process. *Social Problems,* 1975, *22*, 620-637. (b)

Hartshorne, H., May, M. A., & Shuttleworth, F. K. *Studies in the nature of character* (Vol. 3). *Studies in the organization of character.* New York: Macmillan, 1930.

Hastorf, A. H., & Cantril, H. They saw a game. *Journal of Abnormal and Social Psychology,* 1954, *49*, 129-134.

Hewitt, J. D. Individual resources, societal reaction, and sentencing disparity. *Western Sociological Review,* 1976, 7, 31-56.

Hindelang, M. Equality under the law. In C. E. Reasons & J. L. Kuykendall (Eds.), *Race, crime and justice.* Pacific Palisades, Calif.: Goodyear, 1972.

Hogarth, J. *Sentencing as a human process.* Toronto: University of Toronto Press, 1971.

Hood, R. A study of the effectiveness of pre-sentence investigations in reducing recidivism. *British Journal of Criminology,* 1966, *6*, 303-310.

Hood, R., & Sparks, R. *Key issues in criminology.* New York: McGraw-Hill, 1970.

Jackson, J. W. (Ed.). *Role.* London: Cambridge University Press, 1971.

Jacob, H. *Urban justice: Law and order in American cities.* Englewood Cliffs, N.J.: Prentice-Hall, 1973.

Jaros, D., & Mendelsohn, R. I. The judicial role and sentencing behavior. *Midwestern Journal of Political Science,* 1967, *11*, 471-488.

Kelley, H. E. A comparison of defense strategy and race as influences in differential sentencing. *Criminology,* 1976, *14*, 241-249.

Klausner, S. Z. (Ed.). *Why men take chances: Studies in stress-seeking.* Garden City, N.Y.: Doubleday Anchor, 1968.

Marston, W. M. Studies in testimony. *Journal of American Institute of Criminal Law and Criminology*, 1924, *15*, 5-31.

McCall, G. J. *Observing the law: Field methods in the study of crime and the criminal justice system.* New York: Free Press, 1978.

McCall, G. J., & Simmons, J. L. *Identities and interactions* (rev. ed.). New York: Free Press, 1978.

McCleary, R. How structural variables constrain the parole officer's use of discretionary powers. *Social Problems,* 1975, *23*, 209-225.

Mileski, M. Courtroom encounters: An observation study of a lower criminal court. *Law and Society Review,* 1971, *5*, 473-538.

Mischel, W. Toward a cognitive social learning reconceptualization of personality. *Psychological Review,* 1973, *80*, 252-283.

Mohr, L. B. Organizations, decisions, and courts. *Law and Society Review,* 1976, *10*, 621-642.

Nagel, S. S. Judicial backgrounds and criminal cases. *Journal of Criminal Law, Criminology and Police Science*, 1962, *53*, 333-339.

Neubauer, D. W. *Criminal justice in Middle America*. Morristown, N.J.: General Learning Press, 1974.

Orland, L., & Tyler, H. (Eds.). *Justice in sentencing.* Mineola, N.Y.: Foundation Press, 1974.

Pepinsky, H. E. Police decision-making. In D. M. Gottfredson (Ed.), *Decision-making in the criminal justice system: Reviews and essays.* Washington, D.C.: U.S. Government Printing Office, 1975.

Pope, C. E. *Sentencing of California felony offenders.* Washington, D.C.: U.S. Government Printing Office, 1975. (a)

Pope, C. E. *The judicial processing of assault and burglary offenders in selected California counties.* Washington, D.C.: U.S. Government Printing Office, 1975. (b)

Preiss, J., & Ehrlich, H. *An examination of role theory: The case of the state police.* Lincoln: University of Nebraska Press, 1966.

Reiss, A. J. *The police and the public.* New Haven, Conn.: Yale University Press, 1971.

Reiss, A. J. Discretionary justice. In D. Glaser (Ed.), *Handbook of criminology.* Chicago: Rand McNally, 1974.

Secord, P. F., & Backman, C. W. *Social psychology* (2nd ed.). New York: McGraw-Hill, 1974.

Shaver, K. G., Gilbert, M. A., & Williams, M. C. Social psychology, criminal justice and the principle of discretion: A selective review. *Personality and Social Psychological Bulletin,* 1975, *1*, 471-484.

Sudnow, D. Normal crimes: Sociological features of the criminal code. *Social Problems,* 1965, *12*, 255-276.

Suffet, F. Bail setting: A study of courtroom interaction. *Crime and Delinquency,* 1966, *12*, 318-331.

Sykes, R. E., & Clark, J. P. A theory of deference exchange in police-civilian encounters. *American Journal of Sociology,* 1975, *81*, 584-600.

Turner, R. H. The role and the person. *American Journal of Sociology,* 1978, *84*, 1-23.

Ungs, T., & Baas, L. R. Judicial role perceptions: A Q-technique study of Ohio judges. *Law and Society Review,* 1972, *6*, 343-366.

Willerman, L. *The psychology of individual and group differences*. San Francisco: Freeman, 1979.

Wilson, J. Q. *Varieties of police behavior: The management of law and order in eight communities*. Cambridge, Mass.: Harvard University Press, 1968.

Chapter 11

A Basic Paradigm for the Study of Personality, Roles, and Social Behavior

William Ickes

This is the story of a research paradigm: of its conception, "birth," and subsequent development. This story is particularly appropriate for the present volume because the paradigm it describes is, in many respects, ideally suited to the study of personality, roles, and social behavior.

Because the paradigm is somewhat unorthodox in conception and design, finding an appropriate name for it has proved to be a challenge. To better appreciate the problem, ask yourself what name you would use to describe a quasi-experimental observational method that permits the unobtrusive recording of social interactions as they occur spontaneously within a laboratory setting. You might choose to call it "an unusually eclectic empirical approach" or "a method with madness in it," but the nicknames my colleagues and I have used most frequently are "the unstructured interaction paradigm" and "the dyadic interaction paradigm." Both of these terms will be used throughout the paper, in most cases interchangeably.

As the principal architect and adherent of this admittedly unorthodox paradigm, I would like to give an account of its history. The account begins with a discussion of the conditions that led to the "birth" of the paradigm in the summer of 1975. It continues with a detailed description of the paradigm, makes note of some early critical reactions to it, and goes on to review the various empirical studies in which the paradigm has been applied. Following this review is a preliminary evaluation of the paradigm which assesses its strengths and weaknesses and responds to the initial criticisms raised. The account ends with a prospective look at other possible applications and extensions.

Birth of a Paradigm

The birth of the paradigm was preceded by a period of gestation that probably began about two or three years earlier. A number of events occurred during this interval that contributed greatly to the paradigm's latent development. These included my growing dissatisfaction with various aspects of the experimental method as it is typically applied to the study of human social behavior, my increasing interest in personality and some developing insights about why this field had fared so poorly over the years, and a fortuitous circumstance that had a pronounced impact on my professional identity and subsequent orientation to research.

Dissatisfaction with the Experimental Approach

Within a year after I completed my doctoral work in social psychology, I began to discover some problems with the experimental approach that I had not fully appreciated while in graduate school. One of the first things I discovered was how easy it is for a researcher to influence subjects' responses to paper-and-pencil dependent measures, even when the experimenter is kept "blind" to the subjects' condition. How? By building a "prompt"–an experimental demand characteristic–into the verbal or written instructions subjects receive about how to complete the self-report measure. Either the experimenter or the written instructions might say something like, "When you mark your response(s), think about your experience during the experiment to this point and then mark the response which best reflects your experience." Or, "Think about the context in which Person B's behavior occurred when you rate Person B." By using such "prompts" to direct subjects' attention to the relevant experimental manipulation(s) or independent variable(s), researchers can subtly bias subjects' behavior in a direction that is frequently consistent with the experimental hypotheses. Moreover, because most research journals do not require that authors report such instructions exactly (and may, because of space constraints, discourage authors from reporting them at all), many authors may feel justified in referring to these instructions in only the most abbreviated, nonincriminating manner.

After finding a number of fairly obvious instances of this practice in the published research literature, I was sufficiently concerned about it to begin citing it in lectures as a particularly insidious methodological offense. I was also motivated to formulate some rules of thumb designed to prevent its occurrence in my own and my students' research. These rules may be stated as follows:

Rule 1: If possible, use overt behavior(s) as the primary dependent variable measure(s), and collect self-report data only as secondary support.

Rule 2: For all dependent measures that take the form of a self-report, make sure that any instructions the subjects receive are nonbiasing with respect to the research hypotheses.

Rule 3: If possible, the procedure should be designed so that the experimenter is never present while the subject is completing a self-report measure.

Once I became aware of how subtly yet effectively researchers could "prompt" their subjects' responses, I was in a better position to appreciate the view of writers who have analyzed social psychological experiments from the role theory perspective provided by sociology (e.g., Alexander & Knight, 1971; Alexander & Lauderdale, 1977; Touhey, 1974). These authors have proposed that many, if not most, social psychological experiments present the subject with a well-defined, highly structured situation containing salient cues that indicate the most socially desirable and situationally appropriate mode of responding. The experiment is seen as resembling a theatrical production, having its own scenario, plot line, stage props, and actors. Of these actors (whose numbers at each session or "performance" may include one or more experimenters, confederates, and subjects), only the subjects' lines and actions are not scripted in advance; all other parts are prescripted and relatively inflexible. According to this view, the task of the subject is to infer what role he or she is expected to play in the experiment and then play it in the most appropriate and socially desirable manner possible. This task can be viewed either as one of selecting the most appropriate "situated identity" (Alexander & Knight, 1971; Alexander & Lauderdale, 1977) to display in the situation, or as one of deciding which of many possible "scripts" should be enacted (Abelson, 1976; Langer, 1978; Schank & Abelson, 1977).

In this view of the social psychological experiment, the act of "prompting" the subject's behavior takes on a new and expanded meaning. Prompting is no longer limited to giving the subject's attention a quick nudge just before a self-report measure is taken; it now becomes the motive underlying the construction of the entire experiment. The subject is prompted by the setting itself, by the various stage props employed, and not least by the plot line that is implacably defined by the prescripted lines and actions of the other participants (experimenters and confederates). There are, in effect, cue cards everywhere. And the researcher, the person responsible for putting them all there, is now seen as a highly creative and skillful *manipulator*—a combination writer-producer-director-stage manager whose job is to create a play so tightly constructed that the subjects in each condition are virtually compelled to play their parts "correctly."

Why does all this prompting occur? So that when the subject has reached what amounts to a choice point in the experimental script, the researcher can present a special "variable cue card" that constitutes the manipulation of the independent variable. This manipulation is strategically placed at the precise point in the script when the variable cue it provides can be expected to channel the subject's behavior in one direction or another. The fact that the placement of the variable cue must be strategic and nonarbitrary is important because it indicates that the independent variable derives part, if not most, of its meaning from the specific context established by the previous scripted events. In other words, the independent variable will not be interpreted in the same way or produce the same effects on subjects' behavior if it is presented in a different script or at a different point in the same script.

To the degree that the meaning of the independent variable depends on the particular scripted context in which it appears, the effects of that variable on subjects' behavior should be limited in their generalizability. Specifically, these effects should generalize only to situations in which the variable appears in the same (or a highly similar) scripted context, and should *not* generalize to situations in which the variable appears in a different scripted context. This scriptal constraint on generalizability is extremely important, and the magnitude of this constraint is typically unappreciated or underestimated by experimental social scientists. For this reason, its major implications should be summarized in another rule of thumb for research involving human subjects:

Rule 4: To produce findings having a high degree of external validity (i.e., generalizability), (1) study independent variables whose meaning is not dependent on the scripted context in which they appear, and/or (2) construct research paradigms with scripted contexts that provide the simplest, most prototypic analogues of the class of real-world situations to which one wants to generalize.

Clearly, the problem of low external validity can be further aggravated if the script used in the research paradigm is bizarre, unnatural, and not representative of the class of real-world situations to which the researcher wishes to generalize. This problem frequently occurs in experimental studies of ongoing dyadic interaction in which one participant is a confederate who has been preprogrammed to play a fixed role. When a subject attempts to converse freely with such a confederate, it is typically the case that the more closely the confederate adheres to the fixed role, the more likely the subject is to experience the resulting "interaction" as unnatural or even somewhat bizarre. A few years after I had decided that the costs of using "fixed confederate" paradigms far outweigh their gains, I read a similar judgment by Duncan and Fiske (1977). These authors not only questioned the external validity of such paradigms but also doubted whether even well-intentioned and highly trained confederates are really able to avoid changing their behavior in subtle yet meaningful ways in response to the unique characteristics and behavior of the subjects with whom they interact. Duncan and Fiske's (1977) conclusions coincided with my own rule of thumb:

Rule 5: Social interaction behavior should be studied in as naturalistic a manner as possible, and the use of "fixed confederate" paradigms should be avoided.

Developing Insights About Personality

At the same time that I was learning about the esoteric problems of social psychological experimentation, I was also learning about the fundamental problems of doing personality research. And there were definitely problems. In the late 1960s and early 1970s, the field of personality had begun to seem like a dead end. Major reviews of the research literature concluded that there was only weak and equivocal evidence that personality factors could be used to predict social behavior (Argyle, 1969; Mehrabian, 1972; Mischel, 1968, 1969; Shaw, 1971). Worse yet, influential critics like Walter Mischel proposed that since the correlations between personality measures and their behavioral criteria seldom ranged higher than .30, this value probably represented the true upper limit of prediction for most personality variables (Mischel, 1968, 1969). This view was widely publicized and helped contribute to a growing sense of disenchantment with personality research in general and with the trait approach in particular.

In essence, this pessimistic view was based on the assumption that if personality traits were consistently such poor predictors of behavior, the fault must lie in the specific personality traits or in the trait concept itself, and not in the methods used to measure these traits or test their validity. To believe otherwise was to assume that of the thousands of personality studies conducted over more than four decades of research, the overwhelming majority were methodologically deficient in some important respect(s). It is easy to see why the first of these assumptions would have been preferred over the second; however, the events of recent years suggest that the second assumption is probably the more correct. It now appears that personality research has been plagued throughout its history by fundamental methodological flaws that are only beginning to receive the attention they deserve.

As researchers and theorists sought reasons for the poor predictive validity of personality traits, it became evident that traits could not be used to predict the behavior of "all of the people, all of the time" (Bem & Allen, 1974). Instead, the predictive validity of traits was acknowledged to be limited such that accurate predictions could be made only some of the time–that is, for some people in some situations, and then only for some traits and some criterial behaviors. Subsequent theoretical and empirical efforts were therefore directed toward identifying the moderating variables that distinguish the instances in which traits do predict social behavior from those in which they do not.

In a review of these developments, Snyder and Ickes (in press) identified three classes of personality moderating variables: (1) those relating to the *predictor* (i.e., to the particular trait or disposition being studied); (2) those relating to the *criterion* (i.e., to the particular overt behavior(s) to which the predictor is being applied); and (3) those relating to the presence or absence of *a link between the predictor and the criterion* (i.e., to categories of individuals for whom and categories of situations in which such links are typically present or absent). Moderating variables in the first class answer the question "Which traits?" by specifying the types of traits and dispositions that will or will not be good predictors of behavior. Moderating variables in the second class answer the question "Which behaviors?" by specifying the types of behaviors that traits and dispositions are or are not likely to predict. Moderating variables in the third class answer the questions "Which people?" and "Which situations?" by specifying for which types of people and in which types of situations a given trait or disposition will or will not predict its criterial behavior(s).

Because a detailed review of the moderating variables in each of these three categories is available in the paper by Snyder and Ickes (in press), only two specific moderating variables will be considered here. These variables are of particular importance, not only because they account for much of the methodological inadequacy of previous personality research but also because they contributed most directly to the latent development of our unorthodox research paradigm. The first moderating variable concerns the question of "Which behaviors?" traits and dispositions are or are not likely to predict. The second concerns the question of "Which situations?" are or are not conducive to the trait-based prediction of social behavior.

Single-act versus multiple-act measures of behavior. Perhaps the most intense reaction to Mischel's (1968, 1969) conclusion has come from writers who have argued that the low "personality coefficients" of .30 are largely artifacts of unreliable measurement. According to this argument, because most of the studies on which Mischel's conclusion was based employed single-act measures of behavior for which the error of measurement is extreme, the indices of predictive validity in these studies were necessarily of low magnitude. However, when the error of measurement is reduced by using multiple-act measures of behavior (i.e., repeated measures that are summed or averaged to yield a single summary score), measures of predictive validity yield very high values, frequently in the .60 to .90 range. Prediction also can be substantially improved by combining the data from a number of different but conceptually related behavioral criteria, as Hartshorne and May (1928-1930) observed more than 50 years ago.

Unfortunately, Hartshorne and May's observation was generally overlooked during the next four decades, but by the early 1970s various researchers (e.g., Block, 1971; Fishbein & Azjen, 1974; Jaccard, 1974) were again advocating the use of multiple-act measures of criterial behaviors in personality research. The data reported by these investigators offered convincing evidence that improving the reliability of the behavioral measures could dramatically enhance trait-based prediction. Even more convincing evidence was later reported in a series of studies by Epstein (1979), whose data led him to conclude that a high level of measurement error was probably the greatest single methodological flaw in most of the previous personality research. Whether that particular conclusion is true or not, the fundamental implication of all of this work—apparent since the early 1970s—can be summarized in another rule of thumb:

> *Rule 6*: Because of their greater reliability (i.e., smaller error of measurement), multiple-act measures of behavior should be used instead of single-act measures whenever possible.

Psychologically "strong" versus "weak" situations. The most important phase in the latent development of the paradigm occurred when I realized that the "strong," highly structured test situations established in most research paradigms were frequently not well suited to the study of personality and other dispositional factors. This realization emerged as the product of insights derived from Duval and Wicklund's (1972) theory of objective self-awareness and Alexander and Knight's (1971) view of the social psychological experiment.

One of the first broad conclusions suggested by data relevant to self-awareness theory (Duval & Wicklund, 1972; Wicklund, 1975) was that the more attention an individual gives to a particular stimulus (i.e., source of information), the more likely it is that his or her subsequent behavior will be influenced by that stimulus. Thus, in situations in which the individual's attention is directed inward, onto the self, such "internal" sources of information as attitudes, traits, and role conceptions will tend to become salient and exert a primary influence on the individual's behavior. However, in situations in which the individual's attention is directed outward, onto aspects of the environment, the relative salience of these "external" stimuli will cause *them* to be used as the primary guides to the individual's behavior. This reasoning suggests that a given disposition may predict overt behavior quite strongly in conditions in which it is salient, but may predict the same behavior only weakly or not at all in conditions in which it is not salient (cf. Shaver, 1976).

Although the relative salience of dispositional ("internal") versus situational ("external") stimuli can be manipulated in a variety of ways (see Snyder & Ickes, in press, for a review), a simple and direct way to make dispositional factors salient is to *reduce* the salience of situational factors as much as possible. In operational terms, this would require creating a research paradigm quite unlike the highly structured, carefully scripted one that typifies most social psychological research (Alexander & Knight, 1971). This new paradigm would not expose subjects to a psychologically "strong" situation having a high degree of structure and many salient, scriptally converging cues to guide behavior. Instead, it would expose them to a psychologically "weak," relatively unstructured situation in which external cues to guide behavior are lacking. Theoretically, the influence of dispositional factors should be maximized in this new, unstructured situation because the absence of salient situational cues would force subjects to rely on the cues provided by their own internalized traits and dispositions.[1]

If this reasoning is correct, it suggests that another reason for the methodological inadequacy and poor predictive validity of previous personality research has been its inappropriate reliance on highly structured, "strong situation" paradigms. This reliance is understandable insofar as it reflects (1) the tradition of training graduate students in the "strong situation" experimental approach and (2) the historical lack of alternative operational models for studying personality processes in a laboratory setting. However, this reliance is ironic, and even tragic, in its implication that personality researchers throughout the last four decades have chronically employed "strong" test situations that tend to heighten the influence of situational factors while attenuating the influences of dispositional ones. It is no wonder that such studies have revealed personality traits to be weak predictors of social behavior!

Additional implications of this reasoning will be considered in subsequent sections of this chapter. For now, however, the following rule of thumb will suffice:

Rule 7: Because psychologically "strong" test situations typically attenuate individual differences in behavior, researchers studying the influences

[1] Mischel (1977) offers a similar conclusion, although he appears to have arrived at it by a different route and does not deal with its methodological implications:

> In sum, individual differences can determine behavior in a given situation most strongly when the situation is ambiguously structured (as in projective testing) so that people are uncertain about how to categorize it, have to structure it in their own terms, and have no clear expectations about the behaviors most likely to be appropriate (normative, reinforced) in that situation. To the degree that the situation is "unstructured" and each person expects that virtually any response is likely to be equally appropriate (i.e., will lead to similar consequences), the significance of individual differences will be the greatest. Conversely, when everyone expects that only one response is appropriate . . . and that no other responses are equally good, and all people are motivated and capable of making the appropriate response, then individual differences become minimal and situational effects prepotent. To the degree that people are exposed to powerful treatments, the role of the individual differences among them is minimized. Conversely, when treatments are weak, ambiguous, or trivial, individual differences in person variables should have the most significant effects. (p. 347)

of dispositional factors should use unstructured, psychologically "weak" test situations if they want to maximize such differences.

A Fortuitous Circumstance

In the summer of 1975, all the theoretical and methodological insights I have just described began to coalesce around a personality study that I and my graduate student, Richard Barnes, were planning to do in the fall. We wanted to study the influence of self-monitoring–a personality variable identified and operationally defined by Snyder (1974)–on subjects' interaction behavior, but I was unwilling to use a typical, "strong situation" paradigm for the reason just noted in Rule 7. As Rick and I took on the novel task of developing an appropriate "weak situation" paradigm to use in the study, the other six rules of thumb gradually came to mind (although not always in the explicit way that they have been stated here). One by one, these rules were incorporated into our plans in the form of methodological guidelines for the developing research paradigm.

The study's intended emphasis on interaction behavior made Rule 5 relevant, leading us to decide against a "fixed confederate" paradigm and in favor of one in which pairs of naive subjects could interact freely. Rule 4 encouraged us to use a simple, prototypic "waiting room" situation as the setting for the interaction. This decision was reinforced by the desirability of studying only pairs of strangers and thus avoiding the confounding effects due to previous interaction history. Rule 7 indicated that a minimal "script" should be used–one that allowed the subjects to interact or not, as they chose, with as few situational cues as possible. Rule 1 prescribed that the primary dependent measures should take the form of overt behaviors, and Rule 6 necessitated a means of acquiring reliable, multiple-act measures of these behaviors. Rules 1 and 2 guided our construction of a postinteraction questionnaire; Rule 3 helped determine the procedure for administering it. Other, more standard methodological considerations (those relating to the desirability of unobtrusive measurement, testing for suspicion, debriefing, etc.) were also brought to bear on our decisions.

As the paradigm took shape, I began to experience the anxiety of a prospective parent who fears that his child will be born with a socially stigmatizing deformity. (It already seemed likely that some of my more conservative colleagues would regard the paradigm as unorthodox, or worse.) About the time this anxiety had reached its peak, I took a scheduled trip to Lawrence, Kansas, with two of my colleagues, John Harvey and Robert Kidd. The primary purpose of the trip was to interview the eminent social psychologist, Fritz Heider, for a book the three of us were editing (Harvey, Ickes, & Kidd, 1976). An additional purpose of mine, however, was to take time to consider my apprehensions about the paradigm Rick Barnes and I were developing, and to try to decide if it was really worth all the resources (time, effort, money, etc.) we were planning to commit to it. I am not sure I was ready to abandon the entire enterprise at that point, but the idea had occurred to me more than once.

The trip was more rewarding than I could have anticipated. The reason was simple: our interview with Fritz Heider was a very positive experience that affected me greatly. At 80 years of age, Heider's intellectual powers were still formidable. His personal history closely paralleled the history of psychology as a science, and the insights he had achieved during his long and illustrious career were extraordinary. His wisdom and gentle humor were unique in my experience. In the course of our two-day visit, I learned many things from him—far more than I am able to recount here. But I left Lawrence, Kansas, with two very strong convictions: first, that the study of human relationships is the most important task in which social scientists can engage; and second, that there are times when even scientists must forgo established conventions and be guided by their deeper instincts. In retrospect, I realized that both were things I had needed to hear.

These two beliefs were not sufficient to dispel all the concerns I had about my research. But they did make it easier for me to live with these concerns, and they resulted in a sense of commitment to my profession more intense than any I had experienced before. I was ready to get back to work.

Toward the end of the summer, Rick and I prepared the laboratory setting and worked out the few remaining problems in our research paradigm. In its essential features, the paradigm is the same today as it was then, over six years ago. A complete description of it follows.

Description of the Paradigm

Our paradigm was independently developed, but we later discovered that it bore some resemblance to a paradigm used earlier by Mehrabian (Mehrabian, 1971; Mehrabian & Diamond, 1971). As in this earlier paradigm, the members of each of our dyads—two subjects who have not previously met—are led into a "waiting room" and left there together in the experimenter's absence. During this interval while the subjects are ostensibly waiting for the experiment to begin, certain of their verbal and nonverbal behaviors are audio- and videotaped over a 5-minute observation period. Any interaction that occurs during this period is essentially spontaneous since the subjects have not been introduced or instructed to get to know each other. If they do elect to engage in conversation (occasionally they *don't*), the resulting interaction is unconstrained by task demands and is naturalistic in its form and content.

Subjects and Design

The paradigm allows the researcher considerable flexibility in the choice of subjects and design. The accessibility of college students makes them the most convenient population for test purposes, but subjects potentially can be drawn from any population to which the researcher has access. Even preschool children's interaction behavior can be studied if the researcher is willing to forgo the use of sophisticated pre- and posttest questionnaires or to substitute appropriate interview techniques.

Within the general framework of the paradigm, the researcher can study the effects of independent variables that are manipulated or systematically varied at two levels of analysis: within dyads or between dyads. Often, effects occurring at both levels can be studied within a single design. Although the paradigm can be modified to assess the effects on social behavior of many situational, as well as dispositional, variables, it was especially designed for studying the impact of personality and internalized role influences on the initial interactions of strangers.

Consider, for example, a hypothetical study designed to test the impact of the personality variable of introversion-extraversion on the initial interaction behavior of dyads composed of two female strangers. The researcher decides to systematically vary introversion-extraversion at the between-dyads level, thus creating three different dyad types: I-I dyads composed of two introverts, E-E dyads composed of two extraverts, and I-E dyads composed of an introvert paired with an extravert. After a large sample of female subjects has been pretested with the Extraversion Scale of the Eysenck Personality Inventory (Eysenck & Eysenck, 1968), a research assistant selects introverts and extraverts from the resulting distribution of scores and contacts these individuals by telephone to solicit their participation in a laboratory study whose purpose is not specified. Within the constraints imposed by the three dyad types, the subjects who agree to participate are randomly assigned to one of the three conditions—or, more precisely, to one of the two types of interaction partners. Their interaction behavior is then studied in the manner described in the following sections.

The design of this hypothetical study permits the researcher to answer a very important question at the between-dyads level of analysis: Does the composition of the dyad make a difference when comparisons are made *between* dyad types? In other words, does the type of partner one has affect the interaction so that, for example, introverts who are randomly paired with other introverts have less involving interactions than introverts who are randomly paired with extraverts? A second important question might also be asked, however, at the within-dyads level of analysis: Does the composition of the dyad make a difference when comparisons are made *within* dyad types? For example, are there differences in the dyad members' behavior within the I-E dyads such that the extraverted members of these dyads talk, look, gesture, and smile more than their introverted partners? A major strength of the paradigm is its capacity to accommodate studies designed to answer either or both of these important questions.

Setting and Equipment

The observation room used as a setting for the paradigm is furnished so that it appears to be a storage area that has recently been controverted into a temporary waiting room (for schematics, see Figure 11-1). Boxes, printouts, old questionnaires, and various experimental paraphernalia are stacked in a disorderly fashion on a set of tables at one end of the room. These materials conceal an RCA VDT350 videocassette recorder and an RCA CC002 color videocamera fitted with an f2.0 6:1 zoom lens. The camera is positioned behind a jumble of boxes stacked on one of the tables and is hidden by a screen of translucent blue plastic placed directly in front of the lens. The videocassette recorder is concealed within a large box on an

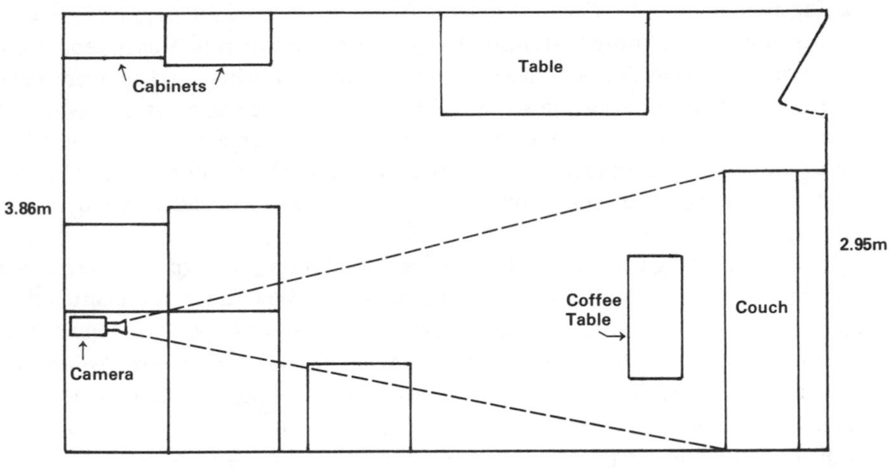

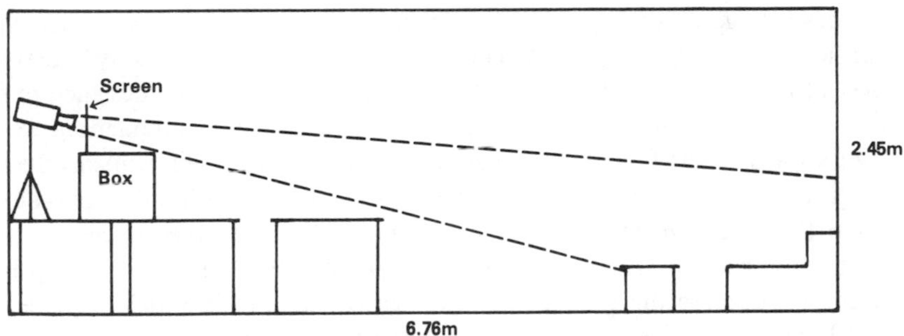

Fig. 11-1. Schematic views of the physical setting.

adjacent table. Directly across the room from the camera are a couch, approximately 245 cm in length, and a medium-sized coffee table.

Procedure

During the telephone solicitation, a research assistant (who feigns naiveté of what the study is about) instructs the subjects to report to specific areas in the psychology building. These areas are physically isolated from each other in order to ensure that the subjects will not meet and interact before their scheduled session begins. At the beginning of each session and prior to meeting each pair of subjects, the experimenter activates the video equipment and checks to see that it is well concealed and operating properly. The experimenter then turns off the lights in the room, closes and locks the door, and collects the two subjects from their respective waiting areas.

It is important to note that, insofar as possible, the experimenter is kept "blind" to the subjects' condition in terms of the independent variables that are manipulated or systematically varied in the study. Although there are some cases in which this cannot be done (e.g., when one of the variables is the subjects' race or gender), in the case of most personality or role-relevant variables the experimenter can be kept "blind" to the subjects' condition at both the between-dyad and within-dyad levels of analysis.

While conducting the subjects to the observation room, the experimenter explains that the first part of the study involves filling out copies of a questionnaire but that (s)he has just run out of these and will have to go to another part of the building to get some more. (S)he opens the door, leads the subjects into the observation room, and, turning on the lights, asks them to leave their belongings on a large table by the door and take a seat on the couch. Explaining that (s)he will return with some fresh copies of the questionnaire "in a minute or two," the experimenter then leaves the room, closing the door on the way out. In the same instant, (s)he consults a digital watch and begins timing a 5-minute interval in which the subjects are covertly audio- and videotaped.

When exactly 5 minutes have elapsed, the experimenter reenters the room and queries the subjects for possible suspicion about the videotaping before proceeding further. After this test for suspicion, (s)he explains that the study is actually half over at that point and that the first part of the study had been designed to examine the actual behavior of two strangers during their initial interaction. (S)he then shows the subjects how their interaction has been videotaped, explains the methodological importance of not telling them about the taping in advance, and informs them that their written permission is required for the tapes to be used as data.

The subjects are made aware at this point that no invasion of their privacy has occurred. Because the video equipment was activated before they entered the room and because there are no external monitors or outputs in use during the observation period, absolutely no one but the subjects themselves know what events transpired that are recorded on the tape. This means that if one or both subjects exercise the right to have the tape erased immediately, instead of releasing it for use as data, the content of the interaction will remain their own private concern. (This assurance, coupled with the usual assurance that the data will be used for statistical purposes only, appears to satisfy whatever concerns the subjects may have about the videotaping. Of the literally hundreds of subjects run in the paradigm to date, only *one* has exercised the option to have the tape of his interaction erased. The reason he gave was similarly exceptional: that he never let his image be recorded in a permanent form because he was wanted by the police!)

Following a complete debriefing regarding the first stage of the study, the experimenter continues by explaining that the second part involves assessing the subjects' perceptions of the interaction in which they have just engaged. Accordingly, both subjects are asked to fill out a posttest questionnaire designed to elicit perceptions of their own and their partners' behavior during the observation period. Before they complete the questionnaires, the subjects are seated at tables on opposite sides of the room, facing away from each other, and are explicitly instructed that their responses will not be seen by the other subject. The experimenter waits outside in the hall while the subjects complete the questionnaires and collects the forms from each of them as they leave the room. Each subject is asked not to discuss the study with others, is given the appropriate credit or payment for participating in the study, and then is thanked and released.

Dependent Measures

A variety of *behavioral* and *self-report* measures can be obtained from the data generated by this procedure. Some of these are *individual* measures that concern the behavior of the individual subjects within each dyad; others are *dyadic* measures that can be assessed only at the dyadic level of analysis. In general, the behavioral measures take the form of the coded or rated responses of two or more "blind," independent raters. The categories of behavior recorded by the raters can include: (1) objective measures of specific behaviors that are either "static" (i.e., relatively constant) or "dynamic" (i.e., relatively variable), (2) subjective or impressionistic ratings of specific aspects of the interaction, and (3) content and/or structural coding (either objective or subjective) of features of the verbal interaction. The self-report measures can address virtually any aspect of the interaction at either the between-dyad or within-dyad level of analysis. These measures are comprised by subjects' responses to the items on the posttest questionnaire and provide subjective views of the interaction that may complement the view emerging from the more objective behavioral data.

Examples of the dependent measures in each of these categories will be presented shortly, along with a review of the research my colleagues and I have conducted since the paradigm was developed. But now that the paradigm has been described in some detail, it may be informative to consider the initial reactions it engendered before proceeding further.

Initial Reactions to the Paradigm

The paradigm was now complete. And, having given form to this unorthodox construction, I found myself experiencing the curious mingling of triumph and unease that Baron von Frankenstein must have felt when the big hand on the operating table began to move. I felt that Richard Barnes and I had probably created something of significance, but at that point I had no clear idea how to react to it, what to expect from it, or what implications it would have for my career. As Rick and I began to talk about it between ourselves and with others, some initial reactions emerged.

Our reactions. Our own reactions were obviously mixed. Somewhere in the melange were a number of very positive feelings. A nice sense of accomplishment at having been able to develop a single paradigmatic solution to so many standard methodological problems. Satisfaction at having avoided the more obvious traps associated with demand characteristics, experimenter biases, and the use of "fixed" confederates. Excitement (and some relief) at being able to give up the manipulative writer-producer-director-stage manager role for one more closely resembling that of an intent, involved member of the audience—one who is ready to take in anything the actors have to show him. Above all, a heightened state of *curiosity.*

Somewhere else in the melange were other, not so positive feelings. Apprehension about taking such a large and potentially disastrous gamble. Concern about the possible permutations of a number of negative elements: wasted time, conspicuous failure, and public denunciations of heresy, unorthodoxy, or, worse yet, rank stupidity. (As the reader may have anticipated, the worst of these fears were not realized, but there was cause for the anxiety to continue a while longer.)

Others' reactions. The reactions of colleagues with whom I discussed the paradigm (in the absence of any data yet) were also mixed in the sense that I can recall at least one marginally encouraging comment. This was something along the lines of, "Well, it's an interesting idea, and I will probably be very impressed if you can make it work, but I really think you're wasting your time." Other reactions not only were less enthusiastic but were disturbingly consistent across respondents. Again and again, I heard the same two criticisms; and, because they evoked some of my own deep concerns, I eventually stopped soliciting them! In essence, these criticisms were:

1. There is no such thing as a "pure," unstructured situation. Such an entity exists only in theory, not in reality. Any attempt to define it in operational terms is doomed to fail, and is therefore foolish, misguided, and a waste of time.

2. The proposal to "just let subjects interact freely and observe what they do" requires a nearly total abdication of experimental control. How do you know they won't simply get up and leave? And even if they do stay and interact, all you can expect to observe is a lot of wildly idiosyncratic behavior. The only thing you will find in the source tables for your data analyses is a collection of gigantic error terms. There will probably be little, if any, systematic variance in your data, but even if there is, *the error variance will kill you.*

Back in the days when these criticisms were first raised, the little homunculus inside my head cringed each time I was subjected to them. The fact is, in those days I didn't have a convincing way of rebutting these arguments. All I had was a vague, persistent sense that the intuitions which guided the development of the paradigm were somehow correct, and that we should therefore follow through our plans to test it. So I was careful not to express too many misgivings to Richard Barnes, and he quite tactfully did not express too many to me, and we went on with the work. About two years later, after we had demonstrated the paradigm's success with the data from the two initial studies we ran together, I began to hear somewhat less of these two criticisms. By this time, however, a *third* criticism had emerged to which I was frequently being subjected. It went something like this:

3. Okay, your paradigm does seem to yield a fair number of statistically significant findings, and the convergence of the data within each study is reasonably good.

However, because you typically don't manipulate any variables in your personality studies, the data from these studies are *merely correlational* (i.e., are inherently "low-class" findings) and you can't draw any causal inferences from them. If you've been adequately trained in the experimental method, why would you want to waste your time collecting correlational data?

There is an end, and perhaps even a moral, to this little story. Eventually I developed answers to all three of the criticisms, and eventually I will tell you what they are (on pp. 331-335, in case you're curious and want to look them up now). But first I need to keep my promise of reviewing the specific applications of the paradigm, and, in doing so, either justify or qualify the grandiose claim I just made about how successful the paradigm turned out to be. I will, in fact, attempt to do all of these things.

Specific Applications

To date, the paradigm has been applied in over a dozen different studies. Although these have varied substantially in their designs, subject populations, and outcomes, they have all adhered closely to the basic paradigm and have employed essentially the same sets of dependent variable measures. After specifying the types of measures that have been obtained, I will briefly review the studies and attempt to summarize what we have learned from them.

Categories of Dependent Measures

Most of the behavioral measures we have studied are highly objective, easy to define operationally, easy to code from videotape data, and statistically reliable (interrater reliabilities are typically in the .80-.99 range). Below is a categorical listing of the behavioral measures, followed by a general summary of the kinds of self-report items employed in our research.

Behavioral measures. The paradigm permits a wide range of behavioral measures to be assessed, and my colleagues and I have only begun to explore the possibilities in our own research. The first category includes objective measures of specific behaviors that are coded directly from the videotapes by independent raters who are kept "blind" to each subject's condition. Of those static behaviors that either occur only once or are relatively invariant over the observation period, our raters have recorded dyadic measures of *who sat first, who talked first* (i.e., initiated conversation), and *interpersonal distance*; in addition, they have recorded individual measures of *body orientation* and *body posture*. Of those dynamic behaviors that occur more than once or are relatively variable over the interaction period, our raters have coded dyadic measures of the total frequency and duration of *mutual gazes* and individual measures of the total frequency and duration of *verbalizations, directed gazes, expressive gestures*, and expressions of *positive affect* (for details regarding measurement, see Ickes & Barnes, 1977a, 1978; Ickes, Schermer, & Steeno, 1979). These primary measures of interactional involvement can be supplemented with various contingency-based measures of reoccurring behavioral patterns, exchanges, etc. (see Gottman, 1979, for examples). To date, we have used such contingency-based measures in only one of our studies (Ickes & Barnes, 1977a), but because they appear to be particularly informative regarding interaction processes, we expect to use them increasingly in future research.

The second category of behavioral measures–raters' subjective impressions of specific aspects of the interaction–is illustrated not in our own data but in the data of a study by Lamke and Bell (1981) which employed the same basic paradigm. In addition to asking subjects to provide self-report ratings of the perceived quality of their interactions, Lamke and Bell asked "blind" raters to view the tapes of these interactions and then make independent ratings of their quality on the same dimensions the subjects had used. The results revealed that the raters' subjective impressions of interaction quality were highly reliable and corresponded closely to the subjects' own impressions. These findings suggest (1) that raters may be able to code reliably the qualitative as well as the quantitative features of interaction behavior, and (2) that data such as these may provide a valuable baseline against which to compare subjects' own self-reports.

The third category of behavioral measures–features of the verbal interaction–can be coded from the videotapes in terms of categories defined by various content (e.g., Bales, 1950, 1970; Gottman, 1979; Sillars, 1981) or structural (e.g., Ickes & Barnes, 1977b) coding schemes. The hierarchical categorization that Barnes and I developed permits the structural features of conversations (*verbal stimuli, verbal responses*, and *verbal reinforcers*) to be analyzed independent of their content (see Ickes & Barnes, 1978). More recently, I have developed a grammar-based classification of the personal pronouns that appear in conversation. In a current study, Susan Reidhead, Miles Patterson, and I are attempting to determine if this pronominal classification can be used to assess the focus and mode of individuals' attention during social interaction (for precedents, see Carver & Scheier, 1978; Davis & Brock, 1975; Stiles, 1978, 1980; Wegner & Giuliano, Chapter 6, this volume).

Self-report measures. The specific goals and purposes of a study will typically define the content of many of the items included on the posttest questionnaire. In addition to the items that are specific to a given study, our questionnaires generally include (1) a standard set of paired items tapping each dyad member's perception of some aspect of the interaction from the perspectives of self and other, and (2) an 18-item set of bipolar adjective dimensions (e.g., exciting-dull, sincere-insincere, cold-warm) on which the subjects within each dyad are asked to rate each other. The individual ratings on these 18 dimensions are later summed in order to compute a global index of liking for the other.

Review of Studies Employing the Paradigm

There are essentially two ways to organize a review of the studies in which the paradigm has been applied: either chronologically or categorically. Because a categorical review is more efficient (in terms of space requirements) and potentially more informative (in terms of theoretical development), the studies are grouped into seven categories. These include studies of (1) self-monitoring, (2) gender and sex-role orientation, (3) locus of control, (4) birth order, (5) interracial (black-white) interaction, (6) pronoun usage in conversation, and (7) preinteraction expectancies. The studies in the first six categories are either correlational or quasi-experimental in design, whereas the study in the seventh category is an experiment. Collectively, these studies illustrate the paradigm's flexibility and broad range of application.

Self-monitoring. The first study in which the paradigm was applied (Ickes & Barnes, 1977a) was conducted to determine how individual differences in self-monitoring were related to subjects' behavior during an initial interaction in same-sex (male-male or female-female) dyads. Self-monitoring is a personality construct that reflects the degree to which individuals employ the tactics of impression management in their relations with others (Snyder, 1974, 1979). Because of its construct validity and its demonstrated relevance to social behavior (e.g., Snyder, 1974; Snyder & Monson, 1975), the self-monitoring variable seemed particularly likely to influence behavior in the spontaneous interactions of two strangers. Accordingly, subjects at high (H), moderate (M), and low (L) levels of self-monitoring were drawn from a large population of students pretested with Snyder's (1974) Self-Monitoring Scale and were assigned to six different dyad types (HH, HL, LL, HM, MM, and ML).

The influences of self-monitoring (SM) were revealed by a converging pattern of behavioral and self-report data. At the within-dyad level, the higher-SM subjects (1) were perceived both by themselves and their partners as having a greater need to talk, (2) actually spoke first and tended to initiate conversation sequences more frequently, (3) perceived themselves as having been guided by the other's behavior to a greater degree, and (4) were perceived by their partners as having been more directive. Taken together, these data suggest that the higher-SM subjects felt particularly responsible for facilitating the interaction and maintaining a smooth flow of conversation during the observation period. Apparently, high-SM subjects deal with the awkwardness of an initial interaction by adopting the role of a social facilitator and applying their social skills to make the interaction "work."

A subsequent study by Barnes and Ickes (1979) explored the possibility that there are two major styles of self-monitoring: assimilative and accommodative. The assimilative self-monitor (As) is assumed to use impression management in a controlling, self-oriented way, to bring the behavior of others into line with his or her own goals, purposes, and expectations. In contrast, the accommodative self-monitor (Ac) is assumed to use impression management in an accommodating, other-directed way, to bring his or her behavior into line with the apparent goals, purposes, and expectations of others. Selected factors of the Self-Monitoring Scale were used to identify these two types of self-monitors, who were assigned to three different dyad types (As-As, Ac-As, Ac-Ac).

Results again emerged at the within-dyad level, revealing characteristic differences between the more assimilative dyad members and their relatively accommodative partners. The more assimilative dyad members exerted control over the flow and content of their interactions by talking longer, gesturing more often, and making more comments, whereas their more accommodative partners expressed acquiescence by providing more verbal reinforcers ("yeah," "uh-huh," "right," etc.). This characterization of the interaction was supported by postinteraction ratings indicating that the relatively assimilative subjects were perceived as more assertive than their partners but as less willing to take the other's viewpoint into account.

Gender and sex-role orientation. Gender differences have appeared in nearly all the studies in which the subjects' gender was systematically varied. Most of these differences have been found at the between-dyad level, in comparisons of male-male dyads with female-female dyads (Barnes & Ickes, 1979; Ickes, in preparation; Ickes & Anderson, unpublished data; Ickes & Barnes, 1977a; Ickes & Orlofsky, in preparation; Ickes et al., 1979; Reidhead, Ickes, & Patterson, in preparation). In general, the results indicate that the behavior observed in female-female dyads is more affiliative and socially expressive than that observed in male-male dyads. Relative to subjects in male-male dyads, subjects in female-female dyads have been found to sit closer together on the couch and orient their bodies more toward each other. They have also been found to talk more frequently and for longer durations, and to display more frequent and longer directed gazes, mutual gazes, expressive gestures, and expressions of positive affect (smiling and laughing). Only in the control of their arms and legs do females appear to be more inhibited than males, maintaining a more "closed" or compacted body posture and putting their feet upon the coffee table less often. Although some of these between-dyad gender differences are more robust and easier to replicate than others, nearly all these differences have now been replicated two or more times and appear to be real (i.e., nonartifactual) effects.

By contrast, relatively few gender differences have emerged at the within-dyad level, presumably because the behavior of the male and female dyad members is highly interdependent at this level of analysis. Females have been found to display more positive affect and to assume a more "closed" body posture than their male partners (Ickes & Barnes, 1978; Ickes & Turner, 1982), but they have not differed reliably from their male partners on other behavioral dimensions.

The "natural confounding" of subjects' gender with their sex-role orientations raises the question of what influences on social behavior are attributable to sex roles per se. This question has been addressed in studies by Ickes & Barnes (1978), Ickes and Orlofsky (in preparation), Ickes et al. (1979), LaFrance and Ickes (1981), and Lamke and Bell (1981). Most of the findings emerging from this research have been conceptually integrated in a recent theoretical model of sex-role influences in dyadic interaction (Ickes, 1981). Although space does not permit the presentation of even a simplified version of the theoretical model, some of the more well-replicated findings from this line of research should be noted.

In general, the studies by Ickes and Barnes (1978), Ickes et al. (1979), and Lamke and Bell (1981) reveal that an *androgynous* orientation—one that combines the agentic instrumentality of the masculine sex-role orientation with the communal expressivity of the feminine sex-role orientation (Bem, 1974)—is particularly conducive to a high level of interactional involvement. In these studies, the interactions of dyads composed of two androgynous individuals (A-A dyads) were found to be more intense and actively involving than the interactions of dyads composed of two stereotypically sex-typed individuals (ST-ST dayds). The members of the A-A dyads talked to, looked at, and gestured to each other more frequently and longer than did the members of the ST-ST dyads. In addition, the members of the A-A dyads rated both their partners and the interactions more positively than did the members of the ST-ST dyads. This pattern of differences was found in mixed-sex (male-female) interactions (Ickes & Barnes, 1978) as well as in same-sex (male-male and female-female) interactions (Ickes et al., 1979; Lamke & Bell, 1981).

The theoretical model I have proposed (Ickes, 1981) not only accounts for the data from the three studies just cited but also predicts a number of effects that have not yet been tested. In a study currently in progress (Ickes & Orlofsky, in preparation), one of my colleagues and I are attempting to test some of these novel theoretical derivations. A unique feature of this study is that it permits us to examine the behavior of subjects in successive interactions with two different partners. By comparing the changes in the behavior of androgynous and sex-typed individuals from one interaction to the next, we hope to determine if androgynous individuals are more flexible in their social behavior than sex-typed individuals, and, if so, exactly how this greater flexibility is manifested.

A final study relating sex-role orientations to interaction behavior (LaFrance & Ickes, 1981) was based on additional coding of the videotape data from the Ickes et al. (1979) study. "Blind" independent raters recoded the tapes and noted the degree of *posture mirroring*, i.e., the "mirror image"congruence of the interactants' body postures (Charney, 1966; LaFrance, 1979; LaFrance & Broadbent, 1976; Scheflen, 1964). The results revealed that posture mirroring tended to occur in the absence of verbal interaction and was associated with self-reports of self-consciousness and perceptions of the interaction as awkward and strained. The greatest degree of mirroring was observed in dyads composed either of two feminine females or two androgynous males, suggesting that these dyad types may be especially likely to adopt a relatively passive, communal, and nonverbal mode of relating instead of the more active, agentic, and verbal mode.

Locus of control. In a study designed to explore the influences on social behavior due to individual differences in locus of control (Nowicki & Strickland, 1973; Rotter, 1966), Rajecki, Ickes, and Tanford (1981) contrasted three different dyad types (I-I, I-E, and E-E). I-I dyads were composed of two males with internal locus of control orientations; I-E dyads were composed of one male with an internal orientation and one with an external orientation; and E-E dyads were composed of two males with external orientations. The results indicated that the members of the E-E dyads talked to and looked at each other more than did the members of the I-I dyads, with the I-E dyads intermediate to the other groups. These results were interpreted to mean that the externals were more socially dependent than the internals, and that their behavior represented an attempt to clarify an ambiguous social situation through interaction with their partners. The responses of the dyad members were found to be highly correlated, with the result that the effects for locus of control were evident at the between-dyad, but not the within-dyad, level of analysis.

Birth order. Do the relationships individuals have had with their siblings influence their subsequent relationships with nonsiblings? In an attempt to answer this question, Ickes and Turner (1982) studied mixed-sex dyads in which males who had either an older or a younger sister were systematically paired with females who had either an older or a younger brother. The design contrasted four dyad types: last-born males paired with last-born females, last-born males with first-born females, first-born males with last-born females, and first-born males with first-born females.

The results of the study were clear-cut and unequivocal. They revealed that interactions involving last-borns who had opposite-sex siblings were qualitatively better than those involving first-borns who had opposite-sex siblings. Moreover, the effects due to the males' birth order were more directly evident than those due to the females' birth order. Last-born males not only talked nearly twice as long as first-born males but also got a much better reception from their female partners, who looked at them longer, engaged them in more mutual gazes (eye contact), and expressed more liking for them than did the partners of the first-born males.

The influence of the females' last-born status was also positive but was evident in more subtle ways. Last-born females initiated the conversations in their dyads more frequently than first-born females, and were rated by their male partners as being significantly more likable.

Taken collectively, these data offer compelling evidence that individuals who have an older sibling of the opposite sex are particularly successful in their initial interactions with opposite-sex strangers. Because additional data rule out the possibilities that this advantage can be attributed to confounding differences in the subjects' age or sex-role orientation, the advantage appears to be due instead to the type of socialization and social skills training that individuals acquire through long-term interaction with an older, opposite-sex sibling.

Interracial (black-white) interaction. In a recently conducted study (Ickes, in preparation), I explored some of the factors affecting behavior in interracial (black-white) interactions. The independent variable of major interest was the premeasured disposition of the white subjects to either seek out (approach) or shun (avoid) social interaction with blacks. Other between-dyad factors were the race of the experimenter (black or white) and the sex composition of the same-sex dyads (male-male or female-female). It was expected that when whites who typically avoid interaction with blacks are put into a situation in which direct avoidance is impossible, their avoidance disposition would be manifested in an indirect manner, primarily through their nonverbal behavior.

Although all the data from the study have not yet been analyzed, the results obtained so far reveal some interesting patterns of effects. In general, the white dyad members displayed a higher level of interactional involvement by talking to, looking at, and smiling at their black partners more than their partners did in turn. These within-dyad "main effects" were qualified, however, by higher-order interactions with the between-dyad variables. Perhaps the best way to summarize these interactions is to note that although both dyad members displayed more smiles, directed gazes, and mutual gazes when the white member's disposition was to approach blacks for interaction rather than to avoid them, these differences were more evident in the behavior of the white than the black dyad members, particularly when the experimenter was black.

Pronoun usage in conversation. Studies by Davis and Brock (1975) and Carver and Scheier (1978) indicate that subjects who are self-aware or self-conscious are more likely to use self-reference pronouns (I, me, my, mine, myself) than subjects who are not self-aware or self-conscious. Stiles' (1978, 1980) work on conversation categories takes this observation an important step further by suggesting that a number of semantic and grammatical features of conversation can be used to assess the focus and mode of a speaker's attention during social interaction (for a related theoretical perspective, see Wegner & Giuliano, Chapter 6, this volume). The coding scheme Stiles developed for this purpose is highly creative and theoretically elegant, but it is also relatively complicated and difficult to use because of the subtle, three-dimensional judgments that raters are required to make.

Being familiar with the earlier work of Davis and Brock (1975) and Carver and Scheier (1978), it occurred to me that a simpler and more obvious alternative to Stiles' approach might be to code all the personal pronouns that are used in conversations in terms of the two-dimensional classification scheme available in any English grammar book. According to this scheme, personal pronouns are classified on one dimension as first person singular, first person plural, second person singular, etc., and on another dimension as nominative, objective, possessive, or reflexive (see Table 11-1). When this coding scheme is applied to the classification of personal pronouns used in a dyadic interaction context, the first dimension defines the focus of the speaker's remark (and, therefore, of his or her momentary attention), whereas the second dimension defines the mode or psychological orientation adopted by the speaker.

By summing the number of times personal pronouns in these various categories are used by interactants during a period of conversation, it is possible to compute frequency scores for each category as well as relative frequency scores (i.e., ratios of the raw frequencies to the total number of personal pronouns used). The use of a high percentage of first person singular pronouns may indicate that a speaker is self-focused, whereas the use of a high percentage of second person singular or third person plural pronouns may indicate a focus on the speaker's interaction partner or on parties outside the interaction. By the same token, a high percentage of nominative pronouns may indicate that the speaker has adopted an active, agentic orientation, whereas a high percentage of objective, possessive, or reflexive pronouns may indicate that the speaker has adopted a passive, possessive, or reflexive orientation. A study designed to test some of the implications of this reasoning is currently being conducted (Reidhead, Ickes, & Patterson, in preparation).

Preinteraction expectancies. To study the effects of subjects' preinteraction expectancies on their subsequent interaction behavior, Ickes, Patterson, Rajecki, and Tanford (in press, Experiment 1) used the paradigm in a completely experimental design. At the within-dyad level, one of the members of each dyad (the

Table 11-1. A Grammar-Based Classification of Personal Pronouns

	First person		Second person		Third person	
	Singular	Plural	Singular	Plural	Singular	Plural
Nominative	I	we	you	you	he, she, it	they
Objective	me	us	you	you	him, her, it	them
Possessive	my, mine	our, ours	your, yours	your, yours	his, her, hers, its	their, theirs
Reflexive	myself	ourselves	yourself	yourselves	himself, herself, itself	themselves

perceiver) was randomly assigned to receive preinteraction information about the other member (the *target*). At the between-dyad level, some perceivers were led to expect that their target partners would act very friendly, others were led to expect that their partners would act very unfriendly, and a third (control) group was given no expectancy information.

The results of the study converged to suggest that the perceivers with the "friendly" expectancy adopted a *reciprocal* interaction strategy (i.e., one designed to reciprocate the friendly behaviors they expected their partners to display). In contrast, the perceivers with the "unfriendly" expectancy adopted a *compensatory* interaction strategy (i.e., one designed to compensate for the unfriendly behaviors they expected their partners to display). In both cases, the perceivers' expectancies directly influenced their own interaction behavior and thereby indirectly influenced their partners' behavior as well. The perceivers' use of the reciprocal strategy in the friendly expectancy condition was evidenced by a high level of talking and looking and a high posttest level of interpersonal attraction. Although the perceivers' use of the compensatory strategy in the unfriendly expectancy condition also resulted in a high level of talking and looking, it was uniquely associated with an atypically high level of smiling, distrust of the target by the perceiver, and a low level of interpersonal attraction. Perhaps most interesting, however, was the finding that the perceivers' expectancies about their partners did not change regardless of which interaction strategy they employed. (For a discussion of the cognitive processes assumed to underlie these responses, see Ickes et al., in press).

General Conclusions Suggested by the Research

At least three general conclusions are suggested by the results of these studies. First, the data indicate that many of the dispositional influences on social behavior that we have studied are strong, internally consistent, and generally replicable, in contrast to the weak and often equivocal effects observed in much of the previous research. Although the strength and reliability of our results may be due in part to the selection of good dispositional predictors, it is likely that the quality of these data is also attributable to our use of the unstructured dyadic interaction paradigm.

Second, the pattern of results suggests that the majority of dispositional influences on social behavior will be found at the between-dyad, rather than the within-dyad, level of analysis. Although within-dyad effects may be especially likely to occur when the disposition itself reflects a tendency to respond differently to different interaction partners (e.g., self-monitoring), such effects have been relatively infrequent in our research—even when the research designs have permitted strong tests of them (cf. Ickes & Barnes, 1978; Rajecki et al., 1981). This asymmetrical distribution of results is mostly clearly revealed in the patterns of differences due to gender. Of the seven or eight gender differences reliably found in our between-dyad comparisons of male-male and female-female dyads, only two have been found in our within-dyad comparisons of male and female interaction partners. The implication for researchers appears to be clear: Do not neglect to study dispositional influences on social behavior at the between-dyad, as well as the within-dyad, level of analysis.

Third, the data suggest that the dispositional variables having the strongest and most pervasive influence on social behavior are also those most implicated in the individual's primary role identifications and role relationships. The variables of birth order, gender, sex-role orientation, racial and ethnic background, and self-monitoring are all closely related to the individual's past, present, or potential role relationships with others. In fact, the distinction between "personality" and "role" tends to break down in the case of variables like these. It is probably true, as many sociologists have argued, that much of the individual's personality is defined by the role-relevant behaviors that he or she habitually enacts. If it is also true that the best dispositional predictors of social behavior are the most role-relevant as well, it follows that personality and social psychologists should devote much more attention to the literature on roles than they have typically done in the past.

A Preliminary Evaluation

The studies I have just reviewed span a period of about 6 years, from the birth of the paradigm in the summer of 1975 to the summer of 1981. Conducting these studies has been a rewarding and enlightening experience. Each study has increased my appreciation of the strengths of the paradigm, and at the same time has apprised me of its limits. Although there is some risk in evaluating any research paradigm with so short a history, a preliminary appraisal may nonetheless be desirable. For this reason, I have compiled the following, separate lists of what I perceive to be the paradigm's major advantages and disadvantages.

Advantages

1. *Flexibility.* The paradigm is highly flexible in application. It can be used to conduct studies of dyadic interaction which are fully experimental, fully correlational, or which combine the two approaches. Although the paradigm can be modified to assess the effects on social behavior of a variety of situational factors, it has proved to be particularly useful for studying the impact of personality and internalized role influences on the initial interactions of strangers. The effects of virtually any dispositional variable and many, if not most, role-related variables can be studied by means of this approach.

2. *Levels of analysis.* Within the framework of the paradigm, the researcher can study the effects of independent variables that are manipulated or systematically varied at two levels of analysis: within dyads and between dyads. Frequently, effects occurring at both levels can be investigated within a single design. The primary advantage of this feature is its potential for revealing that main effects observed on one level of analysis are qualified by interactions that become apparent when both levels are considered.

3. *Controlled observation.* The spacial and temporal limits that the paradigm imposes on the subjects' interaction makes their behavior amenable to precise scientific measurement and analysis. The audio- and videorecording of the interactions not only facilitates objective, statistically reliable coding of the behavior but also

captures the behavior in a permanent form. After the initial data analyses are complete, the researcher may elect to preserve the videotapes as a data archive to be used for future inspection and analysis.

4. *Unobtrusive measurement.* The paradigm permits all the behavioral data of interest to be recorded unobtrusively, without the subjects knowing that their interaction is being studied.

5. *Naturalistic interaction.* The paradigm provides a context for the emergence of spontaneous, naturalistic interaction behavior that contrasts sharply with behavior observed in "fixed confederate" paradigms or in paradigms in which subjects are instructed to interact as part of an assigned task to be performed.

6. *Freedom from bias.* The paradigm is relatively free from the traditional sources of bias in laboratory research with human subjects. First, the possibility of subject bias is reduced through the use of the unobtrusive recording technique. Second, the possibility of experimenter bias or bias due to other demand characteristics can typically be reduced by (a) keeping the experimenter partially or totally "blind" to the subjects' conditions at both the within- and between-dyads levels of analysis; (b) holding the experimenter's interaction with the subjects to a minimum and providing the subjects with only minimal information until their behavior has been recorded; (c) employing a physical setting in which situational cues to guide the subjects' behavior can also be minimized; and (d) ensuring the experimenter's absence during those periods when the data are actually recorded.

7. *Internal and external validity.* Because it facilitates naturalistic interaction and is relatively free from traditional sources of bias, the paradigm should yield results that tend to be both internally and externally valid. In other words, the results obtained should be (a) relatively free from methodological artifact(s), and (b) relatively generalizable to "real-world" situations outside the laboratory setting.

8. *High data yield.* The paradigm allows the researcher to record and analyze a wide range of behavioral and self-report measures. The high potential data yield from studies employing the paradigm is important in two respects. First, through the application of analysis of variance techniques, the researcher can assess the generality or specificity of an independent variable's influence across a range of diverse behaviors. Second, through the application of correlational and factor- and sequential-analytic techniques, the researcher can assess how the various recorded behaviors are structurally and functionally interrelated.

9. *Objective, multiple-act measures.* The primary behavioral measures of interactional involvement used in the paradigm are objective and easy to score. Moreover, because they are aggregated over the entire observation period to create multiple-act measures of the behaviors' total frequency and total duration, the error of measurement associated with these summary measures is likely to be low.

10. *Behavioral and self-report data.* Because both behavioral and self-report data can readily be obtained, the subjects' social behavior and social cognitions can be studied within the same design. This enables the researcher to compare objective measures of actual behavior with subjective reports of perceived behavior and draw inferences about the processes giving rise to each. Both the convergences and the divergences of these two data sources are likely to be theoretically important and informative.

11. *Ethical considerations.* The paradigm is ethically defensible and affords protection to the researcher as well as the subjects. Although it requires the experimenter to defer obtaining the subjects' written consent until their overt behaviors have been videorecorded, it effectively safeguards the subjects' right to privacy through its provision that they can have the recording erased before anyone (including the experimenter) has seen it.

12. *Practical utility.* The greatest advantage of the paradigm appears to be its practical utility, as evidenced by the results of the studies I have reviewed above. The paradigm's "bottom line" can be stated simply: it works!

Disadvantages

1. *Limit on the observation period.* There is a practical limit on the length of time that subjects' behavior can be recorded during the observation period. Recording could probably continue up to 10 minutes without greatly arousing the subjects' suspicions, but recording for longer periods is likely to be infeasible unless it can be justified by substantial change(s) in the experimenter's cover story.

2. *Limit on situational manipulations.* In a similar vein, there is a practical limit on the kinds of situational manipulations which the paradigm can accommodate. In general, it would appear that researchers could establish only those treatment conditions that subjects would find credible in the context of a waiting room situation. Although this practical limitation still leaves researchers enough latitude to manipulate a considerable range of situational factors, there are some manipulations (e.g., having a dwarf in a Pilgrim costume enter the room and hand one of the subjects a dead turkey) that subjects would obviously find incredible.

3. *Carryover effects.* The paradigm is probably not well suited to the study of multiple interactions involving the same participant(s). If successive interactions of this type were scheduled for sessions held at different times, the subjects' experience and debriefing during the first session would clearly bias their behavior in the subsequent one(s). Although it is technically feasible to have the same subject interact with different partners during a single, longer session, it is still likely that "carryover effects" from the first interaction would be apparent in the later one(s) (e.g., Ickes & Orlofsky, in preparation). Obviously, the presence of such carryover effects would be a problem only for researchers who were not interested in them. When the exploration of such effects provides a major focus for the researcher's study, their probable occurrence within the paradigm should constitute an important advantage, rather than a disadvantage, of its use.

4. *"Candid Camera" syndrome.* Simply asking two subjects to wait together prior to their participation in a laboratory study may be sufficient to cause one or both to consider the possibility that their behavior is being covertly observed or recorded (i.e., the "Candid Camera" syndrome). In the studies my colleagues and I have conducted to date, this possibility has been verbally expressed by at least one member of about 20% of all the dyads run. Fortunately, the typical outcome in such cases is that the dyad members discuss this possibility for a few moments, scan the room quickly for any obvious evidence of secret windows or hidden

recording devices, and, finding no such evidence, simply drop the topic and begin discussing something else. About 3-5% of the dyads in our studies have evidenced a more active and persistent suspicion that their behavior has been covertly recorded, and the data from these dyads have routinely been excluded from the statistical analyses. This rate of subject loss due to suspicion is comparable to that reported in studies employing more traditional laboratory research paradigms.

5. *High cost factors.* The greatest disadvantage of the paradigm may be the relatively high costs incurred in conducting research of this type. In addition to the direct monetary costs of buying the necessary equipment, hiring research assistants, etc., there are substantial costs in (a) the number of subject hours required, (b) the sheer volume of behavioral and self-report data that must be coded, keypunched, and analyzed, and (c) the practical difficulties that tend to preclude running more than one study of this type each semester. Moreover, because each study may easily take from one to two years to complete (from the initial design phase to journal submission), the researcher who decides to use the paradigm may expect to publish less frequently than the researcher whose stock-in-trade is the paper-and-pencil questionnaire study. Although the data yield of studies employing the dyadic interaction paradigm can be considerably greater than that of studies employing more traditional paradigms, the costs of obtaining such data are undeniably proportional to the rewards.

It is possible that these lists of advantages and disadvantages are not as objective as they might be, but instead reflect some degree of positive bias toward the paradigm. Like the White House Press Secretary, I am willing neither to confirm nor deny this possibility. However, like the television editorialist, I welcome any responsible criticism of the views that have just been expressed (or, at the least, of the similes that have just been switched).

Responses to Initial Criticism

Speaking of responsible criticism, it can be argued that even this preliminary evaluation of the paradigm would not be complete without my responding to the three criticisms I earlier described as having given me some concern. As I continued to work with the paradigm, the answers to these criticisms gradually became clearer to me, and I was able to deal with each of them. Let's take another look at them now.

1. *There is no such thing as a "pure," unstructured situation. Such an entity exists only in theory, not in reality. Any attempt to define it operationally is a waste of time.*

Eventually it occurred to me that my difficulty in answering this criticism stemmed from the fact that its premise was absolutely correct; it was only the conclusion that was wrong. Except as a hypothetical entity, there really is no such thing as a "pure," unstructured situation. By the same token, except as theoretical ideals, there are no such things as perfect vacuums or frictionless planes either. But the nonoccurrence in reality of these latter entities has fortunately not discouraged physical scientists from attempting to *approximate* them as closely as possible in order to test important theoretical propositions. Similarly, the nonoccurrence in reality of the "pure," unstructured situation shouldn't discourage social scientists from attempting to approximate it for the same reason.

In other words, there is no need to operationalize a situation that is *absolutely* unstructured; for most test purposes, a situation that is only *relatively* unstructured will do. And that is exactly what the dyadic interaction paradigm seems to have captured—a situation that provides so relatively few external cues to guide subjects' behavior that they are forced to depend on their internalized roles and dispositions instead.

2. *By giving up nearly all of your experimental control, all you can expect to observe is wildly idiosyncratic behavior. If there is any systematic variance in your data, the error variance will overwhelm it.*

The simple aphoristic answer to this criticism is that one person's error variance may be another person's effect. Because experimental designs are typically used to reveal the influence of situational factors on behavior, they generally treat all other sources of variance in the data as "error variance." But not all of this variance is measurement error; in most cases, a sizable proportion of it is attributable to individual differences. It is easy to see how researchers who use experimental designs exclusively might forget that individual difference variance need not always be regarded as mere "error" or "noise," since in terms of their research that is all it is. However, for personality researchers and others who are interested in the behavioral influences of dispositional factors, the variance due to individual differences is *effect* variance, not error variance. Therefore, unlike the experimentalists, these researchers should prefer to use paradigms in which such variance is *not minimized* but *maximized* instead.[2]

As I have said elsewhere:

> Because the experiment historically evolved as a procedure for "isolating and measuring the effects" of situational variables, its application in psychology has typically been one in which "the independent variable (a situational manipulation) is designed and programmed to occur in a fixed and constant fashion, independently of the behavior of the subject" (Monson

[2] Occasionally, a more sophisticated version of this criticism is offered by a critic who assumes all that I've said to this point, but goes on to ask why I should expect the individual difference variance in social behavior to be *systematic* rather than *random*. In other words, given the multidimensional nature of personality and the complex interdependence of responses in social interaction, why should one expect the influence of personality variables to be manifested as simple, systematic "signal" rather than as complex, seemingly random "noise"? The quick and superficial answer to this more sophisticated question is that the data from our dyadic interaction studies have, to this point, consistently revealed systematic influences of personality on social behavior. (This is not to say, of course, that more-or-less random influences don't also occur.) In addition to this quick and superficial answer, I have a less superficial and more time-consuming one that does greater justice to the complexity of the question, but this footnote would go on for pages if I were to try to expound the more elaborate answer here.

> & Snyder, 1977, p. 97). This type of "strong situation" procedure makes sense when the researcher is attempting to study the impact of situational factors on behavior, since it ideally maximizes the variance in behavior due to the particular situational factor(s) under investigation while minimizing the "error" variance due to individual differences in personality.
>
> On the other hand, when the researcher is attempting to study the influences on behavior due to individual differences in personality, the "strong situation" procedure of the experiment may often be highly inappropriate (Ickes, 1978a, 1978b). Because the personality researcher presumably is interested in identifying the variance in behavior that is due to individual difference factors, he or she generally should be very reluctant to employ "strong situation" paradigms which treat such variance as experimental "error" and seek to minimize, if not eliminate, it. Ironically, however, the most cursory examination of the published literature in personality suggests that the overwhelming majority of personality studies are conducted in highly-structured, psychologically "strong" laboratory situations in which salient and relatively unambiguous cues are provided to guide behavior. Conversely, only a small minority of personality studies are conducted in psychologically "weak," unstructured situations in which individuals are forced to rely primarily on their own internal traits and dispositions to guide their behavior. The irony is that personality researchers, by carefully structuring their experimental situations, may thereby eliminate much of the same individual difference variance they are in fact purporting to study! (Snyder & Ickes, in press)

These remarks warrant an additional comment as well as a warning. The additional comment is my suspicion that, because of psychology's tradition of training graduate students in the experimental approach and because of the historical lack of alternative paradigms for the study of personality, even individuals who are explicitly trained to be personality researchers often turn out to be "strong situation" experimentalists in disguise. For this reason, they, too, are often susceptible to the experimentalist myopia that I have described.

The warning derives from my concern that the foregoing remarks may be *over*-interpreted as a blanket condemnation of any attempts to apply "strong situation" paradigms to the study of personality. In the article from which the above quotation was taken, I continue by stating the opinion that "strong situation" paradigms can be powerful tools for studying personality influences, providing that certain operational criteria are met (for discussion of these criteria, see Snyder & Ickes, in press). My point, then, is not that the highly structured, "strong situation" approach should never be used to study personality, but that it is often less well suited to this task than the relatively unstructured, "weak situation" approach with which the present chapter is concerned.

3. *Even if the paradigm works and much of what you've been proposing turns out to be correct, the data from your personality studies are still* merely correlational. *If you've been trained in the experimental method, collecting correlational data is a waste of time.*

Within the social sciences, this bias against the correlational approach may be peculiar to experimental psychologists, whose pride in their allegiance to the experimental method often takes the form of a curious elitism. Whatever the source of this bias, the criticism that our personality data are "merely correlational," in the most disparaging sense of that term, is considerably overstated.

First, the personality variables tested are always determined before the subjects' behaviors are recorded, thus reducing some of the ambiguity about the nature and direction of the causal relationships involved. For example, although a male's experience of having an older sister may be a cause of his having an engaging interaction style as an adult, his adult interaction style clearly cannot have been the cause of his having had an older sister. This constraint on the direction of causality is also evident in the case of personality variables such as sex-role orientation or locus of control. Because the patterns of social behavior associated with these dispositions are measured weeks after the dispositions themselves have been assessed, the previously measured disposition is a plausible cause of the present pattern of behavior, but not vice versa.

Second, although the assignment of subjects to conditions is not completely random in our paradigm, it approximates randomness at the between-dyads level of analysis. For example, if the behavior of masculine sex-typed males who are randomly paired with androgynous females is found to differ from that of masculine males who have been randomly paired with feminine females, the difference has to be attributed to the different types of female partners and not to self-selection-based differences in the personality dispositions of the males. In general, the random determination of the type of partners that subjects receive places an additional constraint on the possible causal relationships involved. This constraint frequently lends a quasi-experimental precision to the interpretation of effects occurring at the between-dyads level of analysis.

The critic may concede that the two features of the paradigm just cited can reduce the level of causal ambiguity in our data relative to that found in correlational studies which lack these features. But he or she may then retreat to the criticism that, even if the direction of causality can be specified, the degree of causal ambiguity is still high in any correlational paradigm because of the possibility that some unidentified third variable may be mediating the observed relationship between the personality variable and the behavioral variable. What the critic may not realize, however, is that the "third variable" problem and the intepretational ambiguity it creates is not unique to correlational research. It is, in fact, precisely analogous to the problem of the "confounded manipulation" in experimental research, and it yields to the same types of solutions. One can deal with the problem of a confounded manipulation in experimental research by a variety of methods, including the use of artifact control groups, yoked-control or matched-subjects designs, the triangulation of experimental results, and the application of the principle of theoretical parsimony. Similarly, one can deal with the problem of confounded assessment in personality research by the same methods or by analogous ones (e.g., conceptual refinement through factor analysis and the subsequent comparison of the data associated with each of the resulting factors).

Beyond these considerations, it should be noted that many individual difference variables simply cannot be studied experimentally. One can create experimental conditions designed to "manipulate" subjects' self-esteem (as a state, rather than a trait, variable), but how does one "manipulate" subjects' sex-role orientations? Effecting major alterations in the personalities of human subjects is generally viewed as scientifically unethical, as well as infeasible, so the researcher typically must be content to measure such variables rather than manipulate them. This necessitates the use of a correlational approach, of which the dyadic interaction paradigm is a relatively optimal variant.

In summary, collecting correlational data of the type associated with our dyadic interaction paradigm is not likely to be a waste of the researcher's time. Such data are less causally ambiguous than most correlational data to begin with, and their ambiguity can be further reduced through the use of the same types of methods employed in experimental research. Finally, there are many important dispositional variables that either cannot or should not be studied through experimentation; in such cases, the dyadic interaction paradigm may be the best correlational approach available.

Additional Applications and Extensions

As Duncan (1969; Duncan & Fiske, 1977) has noted, there are two distinct approaches to the study of ongoing interaction behavior: the structural study and the external variable study. The structural study seeks to analyze the structure of social interaction, accounting for the organization of behavior in terms of implicit, underlying "rules." In contrast, the more traditional external variable study seeks to relate indices of social behavior to such "external" variables as the personality traits of the participants, their role relationship(s), or features of their situation(s). Both types of studies can be conducted within the framework of the dyadic interaction paradigm.

Structural Studies

The paradigm is well suited to the structural study of social interaction that occurs during the first few minutes of an initial encounter. Although the previous applications of the paradigm were all designed as external variable studies, the data from many, if not all, of them could be reanalyzed to yield information about the structural features of the recorded interactions. Moreover, by modifying the procedure slightly, it may be possible to study not only the overt behavioral structure of the interaction but the underlying cognitive structure as well.

For example, in a current pilot study designed by Miles Patterson, dyad members are each given the opportunity to view the videotape of their initial encounter just after the interaction has taken place. They are instructed to stop the tape each time an event occurs to which they recall having had a distinct cognitive or affective response during the interaction itself. The dyad members are asked to list these thoughts and feelings according to the thought-listing technique proposed by Petty, Wells, and Brock (1976) in order to obtain a cognitive-emotional record of the "subjective" interaction that will later be coordinated with the behavioral events occurring on the videotape (cf. Harvey, Yarkin, Lightner, & Town, 1980). Structural analyses of these data will then be conducted to determine whether Patterson's (1976, 1981) functional model of nonverbal exchange can be used to predict the relationships between the dyad members' cognitive-emotional reactions to each other and their subsequent behavioral reactions.

External Variable Studies

The paradigm is also well suited to the external variable study of initial interactions. Personality, role, or situational variables can be systematically varied as external (independent) variables, and the interactants' behavior and cognitions can again be measured either separately or in conjunction.

Personality variables. There are essentially three types of personality studies to which the paradigm can be applied. First, it can be used inductively to determine the patterns of social behavior associated with various personality traits. For example, the behavioral concomitants of introversion-extraversion could be explored in a design similar to the hypothetical one described earlier in this chapter, with the line of research extended to include studies of both same-sex and mixed-sex dyads. The data resulting from these studies could then be used to formulate an empirically based theory of the influences of introversion-extraversion in dyadic interactions. This inductive approach, which has already been successfully applied in the development of a theory of sex-role influences (Ickes, 1981), can easily be extended to the study of other personality traits.

Second, the paradigm can be used deductively to test specific hypotheses derived from personality theories. Whether the theories tested are themselves derived from previous inductive applications of the paradigm or from some other source(s), the paradigm provides a good framework for testing specific hypotheses about the influence of personality traits on naturalistic, spontaneous interaction behavior.

Third, the paradigm can be used to conduct conceptual refinement studies in which the influences of two or more traits that have been confounded in previous research are now separated and compared. In some cases, conceptual refinement of the data from the original study can be performed simply by reanalyzing the data in terms of relevant factor scores. In other cases, conceptual refinement may require the collection of new data in studies whose designs or statistical analyses are unique in permitting the variances associated with each of the previously confounded traits to be segregated or partitioned.

Role variables. When applied to the study of role variables, the paradigm again can be used either inductively, deductively, or in the service of conceptual refinement. For example, the results of our inductive study of birth order influences in the interactions of mixed-sex dyads (Ickes & Turner, 1982) might lead us to develop a more general theory of birth order influences whose implications could be deductively tested in future research. Conceptual refinement studies might also be conducted to determine, for instance, whether the social skills associated with having an older, opposite-sex sibling are due primarily to interaction with the sibling or to extensive opportunities to interact with the sibling's same-sex friends.

As the birth order example indicates, researchers are not limited to studying the effects of role variables in their original context. They can also use the paradigm to study the influence of certain role variables in relationships other than those to which the variables themselves refer. It is possible, in other words, to determine whether the behaviors enacted in one role relationship are also enacted in later relationships with interaction partners who are at least superficially similar to the original one(s). Another intriguing use of the paradigm would be to determine whether role behaviors that individuals have merely observed closely in the past (e.g., those of a parent, a teacher, an employer) are also apparent in their own enactment of the roles.

Situational variables. Various aspects of the physical setting can be manipulated to create situations more or less conducive to certain types and degrees of interactional involvement. For example, changes in the furniture (e.g., Mehrabian & Diamond, 1971), the lighting (e.g., Gergen, Gergen, & Barton, 1973), or the temperature of the waiting room (e.g., Griffitt & Veitch, 1971) might all be expected to affect the nature and intensity of the participants' interaction.

Social cognition. The cognitive effects of information regarding the participants' personalities, role relationship(s), and their physical and psychological situation(s) can be studied either apart from or in conjunction with the behavioral effects. As the research by Ickes et al. (in press) indicates, the paradigm can be used to study the effects of an individual's preinteraction expectancies about the personality characteristics (e.g., friendly/unfriendly, similar/dissimilar) of his or her partner. By extension, researchers can also manipulate interactants' expectancies regarding the nature of their role relationship—defining it, for instance, as competitive versus cooperative (e.g., Jellison & Ickes, 1974) or as potentially a dating versus a nondating relationship (e.g., Berscheid, Graziano, Monson, & Dermer, 1976). Expectancies regarding other aspects of the interactants' situation can similarly be manipulated.

Unexpected Applications

It is quite possible that the potential applications of the paradigm are not exhausted by the categories of studies I have just described. Ideally, future research will reveal novel applications that neither I nor my colleagues have yet considered. The occurrence of such an outcome can only be desired. It would signal, in a way nothing else could, that the paradigm has become more than our creation—that it belongs, as we intended it should, to all investigators interested in the study of personality, roles, and social behavior.

Acknowledgments. The preparation of this chapter was facilitated by a National Science Foundation grant (BNS 79-21443) to the author, who would like to thank Eric Knowles and Dan Wegner for their detailed comments on an earlier draft.

References

Abelson, R. P. Script processing in attitude formation and decision making. In J. Carroll & T. Payne (Eds.), *Cognition and Social Behavior.* Hillsdale, N.J.: Erlbaum, 1976.

Alexander, C. N., Jr., & Knight, G. W. Situated identities and social psychological experimentation. *Sociometry,* 1971, *34,* 65-82.

Alexander, C. N., Jr., & Lauderdale, P. Situated identities and social influence. *Sociometry,* 1977, *40,* 225-233.

Argyle, M. *Social interaction.* Chicago: Aldine, 1969.

Bales, R. F. *Interaction process analysis: A method for the study of small groups.* Reading, Mass.: Addison-Wesyley, 1950.

Barnes, R. D., & Ickes, W. Styles of self-monitoring: Assimilative versus accommodative. Unpublished manuscript, 1979.

Bem, D. J., & Allen, A. On predicting some of the people some of the time: The search for cross-situational consistencies in behavior. *Psychological Review,* 1974, *81,* 506-520.

Bem, S. L. The measurement of psychological androgyny. *Journal of Consulting and Clinical Psychology,* 1974, *42,* 155-162.

Berscheid, E., Graziano, W., Monson, T. C., & Dermer, M. Outcome dependency: Attention, attribution, and attraction. *Journal of Personality and Social Psychology,* 1976, *34,* 978-989.

Block, J. *Lives through time.* Berkeley, Calif.: Bancroft Books, 1971.

Carver, C. S., & Scheier, M. F. Self-focusing effects of dispositional self-consciousness, mirror presence, and audience presence. *Journal of Personality and Social Psychology,* 1978, *36,* 324-332.

Charney, E. J. Psychosomatic manifestations of rapport in psychotherapy. *Psychosomatic Medicine,* 1966, *28,* 305-315.

Davis, D., & Brock, T. C. Use of first person pronouns as a function of increased objective self-awareness and performance feedback. *Journal of Experimental Social Psychology,* 1975, *11,* 381-388.

Duncan, S. D., Jr. Nonverbal communication. *Psychological Bulletin,* 1969, *72,* 118-137.

Duncan, S., Jr., & Fiske, D. W. *Face-to-face interaction: Research, methods, and theory.* Hillsdale, N.J.: Erlbaum, 1977.

Duval, S., & Wicklund, R. A. *A theory of objective self-awareness.* New York: Academic Press, 1972.

Epstein, S. The stability of behavior: I. On predicting most of the people much of the time. *Journal of Personality and Social Psychology,* 1979, *37,* 1097-1126.

Eysenck, H. J., & Eysenck, S. B. G. *Manual for the Eysenck Personality Inventory.* San Diego, Calif.: Educational and Industrial Testing Service, 1968.

Fishbein, M., & Azjen, I. Attitudes toward objects as predictors of single and multiple behavioral criteria. *Psychological Review,* 1974, *81,* 59-74.

Gergen, K. J., Gergen, M. M., & Barton, W. H. Deviance in the dark. *Psychology Today,* October 1973, pp. 129-130.

Gottman, J. M. *Marital interaction: Experimental investigations.* New York: Academic Press, 1979.

Griffitt, W., & Veitch, R. Hot and crowded: Influences of population density and temperature on interpersonal affective behavior. *Journal of Personality and Social Psychology,* 1971, *17*, 92-98.

Hartshorne, H., & May, M. A. *Studies in the nature of character* (Vol. 1). *Studies in deceit.* New York: Macmillan, 1928-1930.

Harvey, J. H., Ickes, W., & Kidd, R. F. (Eds.). *New directions in attribution research* (Vol. 1). Hillsdale, N.J.: Erlbaum, 1976.

Harvey, J. H., Yarkin, K. L., Lightner, J. M., & Town, J. P. Unsolicited interpretation and recall of interpersonal events. *Journal of Personality and Social Psychology,* 1980, *38*, 551-568.

Ickes, W. *The enactment of social roles in unstructured dyadic interaction.* Invited paper presented at the annual convention of the Midwestern Psychological Association, Chicago, 1978. (a)

Ickes, W. *The sound of one hand clapping: Isolating the influence of the individual personality in dyadic interacton.* Paper presented as part of the Symposium on the Self, annual meeting of the Society of Experimental Social Psychology, Princeton, N.J., 1978. (b)

Ickes, W. Sex role influences in dyadic interaction: A theoretical model. In C. Mayo & N. Henley (Eds.), *Gender and nonverbal behavior.* New York: Springer-Verlag, 1981.

Ickes, W. Compositions in black and white: Determinants of interaction in interracial dyads. Manuscript in preparation.

Ickes, W., & Barnes, R. D. The role of sex and self-monitoring in unstructured dyadic interactions. *Journal of Personality and Social Psychology,* 1977, *35*, 315-330. (a)

Ickes, W., & Barnes, R. D. Conversational structure categories. Unpublished manuscript, 1977. (b)

Ickes, W., & Barnes, R. D. Boys and girls together–and alienated: On enacting stereotyped sex roles in mixed-sex dyads. *Journal of Personality and Social Psychology,* 1978, *36*, 669-683.

Ickes, W., & Orlofsky, J. Reactions of androgynous and sex-typed individuals to different partners encountered in successive interactions. Manuscript in preparation.

Ickes, W., Patterson, M. L., Rajecki, D. W., & Tanford, S. Behavioral and cognitive consequences of reciprocal versus compensatory responses to preinteraction expectancies. *Social Cognition,* in press.

Ickes, W., Schermer, B., & Steeno, J. Sex and sex-role influences in same-sex dyads. *Social Psychology Quarterly,* 1979, *42*, 373-385.

Ickes, W., & Turner, M. On the social advantages of having an older, opposite-sex sibling: Birth order influences in mixed-sex dyads. Manuscript submitted for publication, 1982.

Jaccard, J. Predicting social behavior from personality traits. *Journal of Research in Personality*, 1974, *7*, 358-367.

Jellison, J., & Ickes, W. The power of the glance: Desire to see and be seen in cooperative and competitive situations. *Journal of Experimental Social Psychology*, 1974, *10*, 444-450.

LaFrance, M. Nonverbal synchrony and rapport: Analysis by the cross-lag panel technique. *Social Psychology Quarterly*, 1979, *42*, 66-70.

LaFrance, M., & Broadbent, M. Group rapport: Posture sharing as a nonverbal indicator. *Group and Organization Studies*, 1976, *1*, 328-333.

LaFrance, M., & Ickes, W. Postural mirroring and interactional involvement: Sex and sex-typing effects. *Journal of Nonverbal Behavior*, 1981, *5*, 139-154.

Lamke, L., & Bell, N. The influence of sex role orientation on initial interactions within same-sex dyads. Manuscript submitted for publication, 1981.

Langer, E. Rethinking the role of thought in social interaction. In J. H. Harvey, W. Ickes, & R. F. Kidd (Eds.), *New directions in attribution research* (Vol. 2). Hillsdale, N.J.: Erlbaum, 1978.

Mehrabian, A. Verbal and nonverbal interaction of strangers in a waiting situation. *Journal of Experimental Research in Personality*, 1971, *5*, 127-138.

Mehrabian, A. Nonverbal communication. In J. Cole (Ed.), *Nebraska Symposium on Motivation* (Vol. 19). Lincoln: University of Nebraska Press, 1972.

Mehrabian, A., & Diamond, S. G. The effects of furniture arrangement, props, and personality on social interaction. *Journal of Personality and Social Psychology*, 1971, *20*, 18-30.

Mischel, W. *Personality and assessment.* New York: Wiley, 1968.

Mischel, W. Continuity and change in personality. *American Psychologist*, 1969, *24*, 1012-1018.

Mischel, W. The interaction of person and situation. In D. Magnusson & N. S. Endler (Eds.), *Personality at the crossroads: Current issues in interactional psychology.* Hillsdale, N.J.: Erlbaum, 1977.

Monson, T. C., & Snyder, M. Actors, observers, and the attribution process: Toward a reconceptualization. *Journal of Experimental Social Psychology*, 1977, *13*, 89-111.

Nowicki, S., Jr., & Strickland, B. R. A locus of control scale for children. *Journal of Consulting and Clinical Psychology*, 1973, *40*, 148-154.

Patterson, M. L. An arousal model of interpersonal intimacy. *Psychological Review*, 1976, *83*, 235-245.

Patterson, M. L. A multi-stage functional model of nonverbal exchange. Manuscript submitted for publication, 1981.

Petty, R. E., Wells, G. L., & Brock, T. C. Distraction can enhance or reduce yielding to propaganda: Thought disruption versus effort justification. *Journal of Personality and Social Psychology*, 1976, *34*, 874-884.

Rajecki, D. W., Ickes, W., & Tanford, S. Locus of control and reactions to a stranger. *Personality and Social Psychology Bulletin*, 1981, 7, 282-289.

Reidhead, S., Ickes, W., & Patterson, M. L. You are what you say: Personal pronoun usage as an indicator of personality. Manuscript in preparation.

Rotter, J. B. Generalized expectancies for internal vs. external control of reinforcement. *Psychological Monographs,* 1966, *80,* 1-28.

Schank, R., & Abelson, R. P. *Scripts, plans, goals and understanding: An inquiry into human knowledge structures.* Hillsdale, N.J.: Erlbaum, 1977.

Scheflen, A. E. The significance of posture in communication systems. *Psychiatry,* 1964, *27,* 316-331.

Shaver, P. *Self-awareness theory: Problems and prospects.* Paper presented at a meeting of the New England Social Psychological Association, Dartmouth College, 1976.

Shaw, M. E. *Group dynamics: The psychology of small group behavior.* New York: McGraw-Hill, 1971.

Sillars, A. L. Attributions and interpersonal conflict resolution. In J. H. Harvey, W. Ickes, & R. F. Kidd (Eds.), *New directions in attribution research* (Vol. 3). Hillsdale, N.J.: Erlbaum, 1981.

Snyder, M. The self-monitoring of expressive behavior. *Journal of Personality and Social Psychology,* 1974, *30,* 526-537.

Snyder, M. Self-monitoring processes. In L. Berkowitz (Ed.), *Advances in experimental social psychology* (Vol. 12). New York: Academic Press, 1979.

Snyder, M., & Ickes, W. Personality and social behavior. In G. Lindzey & E. Aronson (Eds.), *Handbook of social psychology* (3rd ed., Vol. 2). Reading, Mass.: Addison-Wesley, in press.

Snyder, M., & Monson, T. C. Persons, situations, and the control of social behavior. *Journal of Personality and Social Psychology,* 1975, *32,* 637-644.

Stiles, W. B. Verbal response modes and dimensions of interpersonal roles: A method of discourse analysis. *Journal of Personality and Social Psychology,* 1978, *36,* 693-703.

Stiles, W. B. Comparison of dimensions derived from rating versus coding of dialogue. *Journal of Personality and Social Psychology,* 1980, *38,* 359-374.

Touhey, J. C. Situated identities, attitude similarity, and interpersonal attraction. *Sociometry,* 1974, *37,* 363-374.

Wicklund, R. A. Objective self-awareness. In L. Berkowitz (Ed.), *Advances in experimental social psychology* (Vol. 8). New York: Academic Press, 1975.

Author Index

Abelson, R. P., 67, 76, 82, 178, 186, 197, 307, 337, 340
Abrams, A. G., 103, 125
Abt, L. E., 285, 286, 300
Agee, J., 221, 237
Ainsworth, M. D., 220, 237
Alexander, C. N., Jr., 286, 300, 306, 307, 310, 311, 337
Allen, A., 14, 27, 309, 338
Allport, F. H., 16, 17, 22, 27
Allport, G. W., 10, 11, 12, 13, 14, 15, 16, 27
Alwin, D., 211, 218
Anderson, B. G., 221, 234, 237
Anderson, R. C., 173, 194, 197
Andreoli, V., 175, 198
Archer, D., 103, 104, 135
Archer, R. L., 90, 124
Ardener, E. W., 50, 52
Ardener, S. G., 50, 52
Argyle, M., 88, 95, 123, 125, 143, 145, 146, 150, 159, 160, 308, 338
Aries, P., 233, 237
Arkin, R. M., 157, 161
Asch, S., 108, 125
Athay, M., 68, 82
Atkinson, J. W., 14, 30
Averill, J. R., 221, 237
Azjen, I., 310, 338

Baas, L. R., 296, 303
Back, K., 20, 27, 29
Backman, C. W., 286, 288, 300, 303
Bahr, H. M., 221, 239
Baird, J. E., 123, 126
Bakeman, R., 143, 160
Bales, R. F., 19, 20, 27, 320, 338
Banton, M., 290, 300
Barker, R. G., 141, 160
Barnes, R. D., 97, 123, 131, 155, 157, 158, 159, 160, 175, 196, 312, 319, 320, 321, 322, 327, 338, 339
Barthel, J., 227, 237
Barton, W. H., 337, 338
Bassett, R. L., 24, 30
Baumeister, R., 104, 131
Beavin, J. H., 87, 138, 144, 162
Beck, A., 184, 194
Beck, F., 221, 224, 229, 237
Becker, G. S., 38, 52
Becker, H., 4, 27, 221, 237
Beckman, L., 112, 126
Bell, L. G., 109, 126
Bell, N., 320, 322, 340
Bell, P. A., 108, 126
Bem, D. J., 14, 17, 27, 32, 309, 322, 338
Bem, S. L., 14, 15, 27, 123, 126, 338
Bendann, E., 221, 237

Bennis, W. G., 20, 27
Benoliel, J. Q., 222, 237
Bercherer, R. C., 97, 126
Berg, J. H., 90, 124
Berger, P., 229, 230, 235, 238
Berkowitz, L., 82, 83, 92, 126, 181, 197
Berlyne, D. E., 93, 126
Berman, E., 245, 280
Bernard, J., 122, 123, 126, 244, 280
Bernstein, B., 227, 238
Berscheid, E., 94, 96, 109, 111, 112, 126, 128, 137, 182, 183, 194, 196, 337, 338
Bhaskar, R., 34, 35, 52
Bickman, L., 181, 197
Biddle, B. J., 6, 7, 27
Bieri, J., 183, 196
Billig, M., 21, 31
Birdwhistell, R. L., 141, 158
Birnbaum, M. H., 174, 195
Black, D. J., 289, 300
Blackman, S., 99, 109, 110, 130
Blau, P. M., 8, 27, 38, 52, 250, 281
Blau, Z., 245, 281
Blauner, R., 233, 238
Block, J., 245, 281, 310, 338
Blumberg, A. S., 293, 296, 301
Blumer, H., 6, 27
Borden, R., 183, 195
Borgatta, E. F., 20, 27, 82
Botkin, P., 70, 82, 170, 195
Bowen, H., 296, 297, 301
Bower, G. H., 110, 111, 116, 130, 174, 184, 195
Bowlby, J., 220, 238
Boyce, D., 112, 126
Bransford, J. D., 88, 102, 126
Braver, S. L., 112, 127
Breed, G., 147, 158
Breed, W., 222, 223, 238
Brenner, M. W., 96, 125, 126
Brett, G. S., 16, 27
Brewer, M. B., 172, 195
Bricker, P., 88, 132
Brickner, M. A., 24, 30
Brim, O. G., Jr., 245, 281
Broadbent, D. E., 91, 92, 95, 126
Broadbent, M., 323, 339
Brock, T. C., 180, 195, 320, 325, 336, 338, 340
Brockner, J., 97, 127, 184, 195
Brodey, L. R., 95, 125
Brothen, T., 182, 196
Bruner, J. S., 67, 82, 101, 127
Bryson, G., 201, 218
Bucher, C., 48, 52
Buck, R. W., 104, 105, 127, 145, 158
Bugenthal, D. B., 153, 158
Bundy, R., 21, 31
Burchard, W. W., 288, 301
Burke, P. J., 206, 218, 291, 294, 295, 301
Burnside, I. M., 222, 238
Burnstein, E., 17, 27
Buss, A. H., 95, 127, 129, 180, 195
Byrne, D., 108, 109, 110, 126, 127, 142, 161

Cain, M. E., 290, 301
Caine, L., 221, 225, 229, 238
Campbell, A., 154, 158
Campbell, D. T., 24, 27, 108, 132, 170, 195, 260, 267, 281
Campus, N., 14, 27
Cantor, N., 73, 82, 97, 136
Cantril, H., 288, 301
Cappella, J. N., 85, 127
Carlston, D. E., 116, 138
Carroll, J. S., 82
Carson, R. C., 290, 301
Cartwright, D., 17, 18, 27
Carver, C. S., 95, 127, 130, 136, 320, 325, 338
Cassirer, E., 18, 28
Caul, W. F., 104, 105, 127
Chaikin, A. L., 190, 195
Chance, M. R. A., 93, 127
Chapman, A. J., 147, 160
Chapple, E. D., 121, 122, 127

Charmaz, K. C., 221, 222, 238
Charney, E. J., 323, 338
Chein, L., 112, 132
Cherry, F., 109, 110, 127
Chester, P., 123, 127
Chiricos, T. G., 292, 295, 301
Chomsky, N., 8, 28
Christie, L. S., 103, 133
Christie, R., 10, 28
Chun, K., 11, 28
Cialdini, R. B., 112, 127, 183, 195
Cicourel, A. V., 8, 28
Cicourel, A. F., 8, 9, 28
Clark, H. H., 88, 127
Clark, J. P., 300, 303
Clark, M. S., 184, 185, 190, 195, 196
Clark, R. W., 14, 30
Clayton, P., 221, 222, 238
Clore, G., 154, 160
Cobb, S., 11, 28
Cohen, L. J., 220, 238
Collins, A. M., 116, 127
Cook, M., 88, 100, 123, 125, 131, 152, 154, 156, 160, 162
Cooley, C. H., 6, 28, 170, 191, 195, 202, 218, 226, 232
Coombs, C. H., 113, 128
Cooper, W. E., 21, 32, 172, 175, 181, 198
Costa, P. T., Jr., 245, 281
Costella, H., 96, 125
Cottrell, L. S., Jr., 108, 128
Coulson, M., 36, 52
Crocker, J., 88, 93, 102, 108, 137
Crosby, F., 122, 125

Dabbs, J. M., Jr., 143, 160
Daly, S., 154, 160
Danheiser, K., 97, 128
Daniell, R. F., 151, 160
Danziger, K., 104, 128
Darley, J. M., 68, 82, 108, 109, 112, 120, 126, 128
Dashiell, J. F., 16, 17, 28
Davey, R., 221, 238
Davis, D., 85, 87, 89, 91, 96, 98, 113, 117, 124, 125, 128, 180, 190, 195, 320, 325, 338
Davis, J. D., 113, 123, 128, 132
Davis, K. C., 7, 28, 285, 301
Davis, M. S., 195
Dean, J., 143, 146, 150, 159
Deaux, K., 109, 122, 128
De Four, D., 96, 104, 128
De Paulo, B. M., 104, 105, 122, 128, 135
Derlega, V. J., 190, 195
Dermer, M., 94, 96, 111, 112, 126, 337, 338
Desmarais, L., 221, 238
Deutsch, M., 20, 28, 188, 195
Devereux, G., 234, 238
Devoe, S., 144, 164
Dewey, J., 202, 218
Diamond, S. G., 154, 162, 313, 337, 340
Dickson, W. J., 19, 31
Diener, E., 96, 104, 128
Dillehay, R. C., 109, 132
DiMatteo, M. R., 103, 104, 105, 129, 135
Dion, K. K., 109, 128
Dittman, A. T., 122, 128
Donaldson, S. K., 119, 128
Droll, D., 96, 125
Duff, D. F., 152, 162
Duke, M. P., 155, 158, 160
Duncan, B. L., 109, 129, 250, 281
Duncan, O. D., 250, 281
Duncan, S. D., Jr., 85, 88, 129, 146, 160, 308, 335, 338
Durkheim, E., 16, 28, 57, 82, 236, 238
Duval, S., 95, 129, 169, 170, 179, 195, 310, 338
Dyk, R. B., 4, 14, 32

Eagly, A. H., 109, 131, 137
Eaton, W., 236, 242
Eckenrode, J., 97, 127
Ehrlich, H., 290, 302

Eifermann, R., 103, 129
Eisen, S. V., 176, 195
Eisenstein, J., 296, 301
Ekeh, P. P., 8, 28
Ekehammar, B., 13, 28
Ekman, P., 144, 145, 148, 160
Ekstrom, R. B., 245, 281
Eliason, C., 245, 281
Eliot, T. D., 221, 238
Elliott, G. C., 96, 129
Ellsworth, P. C., 142, 145–146, 154, 161, 164
Emerson, R., 38, 52
Endler, N. S., 13, 28, 151, 161, 288, 301
Entin, E., 123, 134
Enzle, M. E., 184, 195
Epstein, N. A., 182, 197
Epstein, S., 13, 28, 310, 338
Erber, R., 175, 197
Erdelyi, M. H., 111, 116, 129
Erickson, F., 88, 113, 114, 129
Erikson, E. H., 11, 28, 245, 281
Erikson, K. T., 236, 238
Ervin-Tripp, S. M., 102, 129
Etcoff, N. L., 176, 198
Exline, R. V., 154, 161
Eysenck, H. J., 99, 129, 158, 161, 314, 338
Eysenck, S. B. G., 99, 129, 314, 338

Faterson, H. F., 14, 32
Faules, D., 103, 129
Fazio, R. H., 97, 108, 109, 120, 128, 134, 138, 183, 197
Fearing, F., 109, 129
Featherman, D. L., 250, 281
Feffer, M., 103, 129
Feldstein, S., 85, 129, 131
Felipe, N. J., 142, 161
Fenigstein, A., 95, 129, 180, 182, 195
Ferris, S. R., 102, 103, 133
Festinger, L., 20, 28, 29
Fishbein, M., 310, 338
Fisher, J. D., 142, 147, 161, 164
Fiske, D. W., 85, 88, 129, 308, 335, 338
Fiske, S. T., 167, 170, 176, 179, 197, 198
Flament, C., 21, 31
Flavell, J. H., 70, 82, 83, 170, 195
Flax, R., 96, 104, 128
Fong, G., 121, 125
Forman, E., 156, 162
Fox, R., 45, 53
Franklin, M., 174, 196
Freeman, R. B., 271, 281
Freeman, S., 183, 195
French, J. R. P., Jr., 11, 28, 188, 196
Freud, S., 10, 11, 29
Friedman, H. S., 104, 105, 129
Friedman, R., 147, 162
Friesen, W. V., 144, 145, 148, 160
Froming, W. J., 95, 124, 125, 130
Fromm-Reichman, F., 222, 238
Fry, C. L., 70, 82, 170, 195
Fulton, R., 221, 238

Gabrenya, W. K., Jr., 157, 161
Gaitz, C. M., 245, 282
Gangestad, S., 97, 120, 125, 136
Garlock, L., 88, 132
Geen, R., 17, 29
Geis, F. L., 10, 28
Geizer, R. S., 97, 104, 130, 134
Geller, J., 144, 164
Geller, V., 104, 125
George, L. K., 245, 281
Gerard, H. B., 173, 198
Gergen, K. J., 245, 282, 337, 338
Gergen, M. M., 337, 338
Giddens, A., 33, 34, 35, 51, 52, 53
Gilbert, M. A., 285, 286, 303
Giuliano, T., 174, 176, 179, 180, 196, 198
Glaser, B., 245, 281
Glick, I. O., 221, 222, 238
Goffman, E., 7, 8, 29, 33, 53, 59–60, 73, 82, 95, 130, 141, 147, 149, 150, 161, 226, 238

Goldberg, B., 111, 116, 129
Goldscheider, C., 233, 239
Goldstein, K. M., 98, 99, 109, 110, 130
Gonos, G., 141, 161
Goodenough, D. R., 14, 32, 88, 98, 99, 119, 130, 138, 156, 159, 164
Goody, J., 221, 239
Gordon, C., 245, 247, 253, 257, 260, 261, 275, 281, 282
Gordon, M. S., 271, 282
Gottman, J. M., 320, 338
Graham, J. C., 100, 135
Graziano, W. G., 94, 96, 97, 111, 112, 126, 128, 182, 183, 194, 196, 337, 338
Green, E., 294, 295, 301
Green, L. R., 156, 161
Greenwald, A. G., 106, 130
Grice, H. P., 88, 130
Griffitt, W., 337, 338
Gross, N., 7, 29, 288, 290, 301
Guilfoy, V., 244, 245, 282
Gurnee, H. A., 17, 29
Guttentag, M., 37, 44–48, 53

Habenstein, R. W., 221, 239
Hagan, J., 295, 296, 297, 301
Hall, D. T., 280, 282
Hall, E. T., 143, 146, 149, 161
Hall, F. S., 280, 282
Hall, J. A., 102, 104, 130, 135
Hanks, M., 88, 135
Harms, L. S., 113, 130
Harper, R. G., 105, 122, 130
Harre, R., 35, 53
Harris, L., 280, 282
Hartshorne, H., 12, 14, 29, 288, 301, 310, 338
Harvey, C. D. H., 221, 239
Harvey, J. H., 21, 29, 94, 130, 312, 336, 339
Harvey, M. D., 184, 195
Hastorf, A. H., 288, 301
Hauser, R. M., 211, 218
Haviland, S. E., 88, 127
Hayden, T., 109, 130
Heckel, R. V., 155, 161
Hegel, G. W. F., 16, 29
Heider, F., 21, 29, 111, 130, 165, 170, 196
Heine, P. J., 9, 15, 29
Heise, D. R., 143, 161
Heise, G. A., 102, 103, 134
Helmreich, R. L., 15, 31
Henderson, S., 220, 239
Hendin, H., 114, 134
Henker, B., 155, 160
Henley, N. M., 122, 123, 130, 148, 161
Hensley, V., 179, 195
Heslin, R., 148, 161
Hewitt, J. D., 295, 301
Hiers, J. M., 155, 161
Hindelang, M., 297, 301
Hirschman, L., 122, 125
Hochschild, A. R., 221, 239
Hocking, W. E., 112, 130
Hoffman, C., 178, 196
Hogarth, J., 289, 296, 297, 298, 299, 301
Holley, M., 156, 161
Holmes, D. S., 154, 163
Holtgraves, T., 89, 124
Holzner, B., 170, 196
Homans, G. C., 8, 29, 38, 53
Hood, R., 289, 294, 299, 302
Hornstein, M., 115, 131
Horowitz, M. J., 19, 20, 29, 152, 162
Hoyt, M. F., 222, 239
Hubbard, M., 109, 135
Hull, J. G., 95, 131
Hunt, J. McV., 13, 28
Hurston, R. O., 221, 239
Hymes, D., 102, 131

Ickes, W. J., 21, 29, 97, 123, 131, 155, 157, 158, 162, 163, 175, 196, 300, 311, 312, 319, 320, 321, 322, 323, 324, 327, 330, 332, 333, 336, 337, 338, 339, 340, 341

Irwin, M., 183, 196
Isen, A. M., 184, 185, 195, 196

Jaccard, J. J., 13, 29, 310, 339
Jackson, C. O., 221, 233, 239
Jackson, D. A., 221, 241
Jackson, D. D., 87, 138
Jackson, D. N., 105, 131
Jackson, J. W., 288, 302
Jacob, H., 296, 301
Jacobs, R. H., 246, 247, 251, 274, 280, 282
Jaffe, J., 85, 123, 131, 134
James, W., 145, 162, 168, 169, 170, 196, 201, 206, 218
Janis, I. L., 222, 236, 239
Jaros, D., 289, 292, 295, 302
Jarris, P. E., 70, 82
Jarvis, P., 170, 195
Jefferson, G., 88, 135
Jellison, J., 337, 339
Jennings, H. H., 19, 29
Johnson, M. K., 88, 102, 126
Jolly, A., 97, 125
Jones, E. E., 60, 82, 104, 131, 170, 175, 177, 188, 196, 197
Jones, R. A., 108, 120, 131
Jourard, S. M., 147, 162
Justice, M. T., 156, 162

Kagan, J., 245, 281
Kahneman, D., 91, 92, 95, 116, 131, 137, 179, 198
Kalish, R. A., 221, 239
Kaplan, J. B., 245, 282
Karp, L., 184, 196
Karp, S. A., 14, 32, 98, 99, 131
Kasmer, J., 98, 125
Kelley, G. A., 108, 131
Kelley, H. E., 292, 294, 295, 302
Kelley, H. H., 21, 29, 38, 40, 42, 53, 111, 131, 177, 186, 197, 198
Kellner, H., 239, 230, 235, 238
Kelman, H. C., 109, 131
Kemper, T. D., 221, 239
Kendon, A., 85, 100, 131, 146, 152, 154, 156, 160, 162
Kendzierski, D., 97, 136
Kenney, D. A., 85, 137
Kenrick, D. T., 14, 29
Kent, G. G., 113, 132
Kidd, R. F., 21, 29, 312, 339
Kidder, K. L., 108, 132
Kihlstrom, J. F., 82, 105, 111, 116, 132
Kimble, C. E., 96, 125
Kinzel, A., 153, 162
Kirscht, J. P., 109, 132
Klausner, S. Z., 288, 302
Kleck, R. E., 108, 132
Klinger, E., 179, 196
Klugman, S. F., 17, 29
Knapp, R. J., 221, 240
Knight, G. W., 286, 300, 306, 307, 310, 311, 338
Knight, J. A., 112, 132
Knowles, E. S., 10, 24, 29, 30, 142, 162
Koffka, K., 179, 196
Kogan, N., 17, 32
Kohn, J. B., 221, 239
Kohn, W. K., 221, 239
Konstadt, N., 156, 162
Krauss, R. M., 88, 104, 125, 132
Kraut, R. E., 88, 124
Kriss, M., 179, 197
Kulik, J. A., 104, 132
Kutscher, A. H., 221, 239

LaFrance, M., 114, 123, 132, 322, 323, 339
Laird, J. D., 145, 162
Lalljee, M., 88, 123, 125
Lambert, W. W., 82
Lamers, W. M., 221, 239
Lamke, L., 320, 322, 340
Lamm, H., 17, 31
Langer, E. J., 142, 161, 167, 196, 307, 340
Langer, W. C., 11, 30

Lanzetta, J. T., 93, 132
Larkin, L., 109, 126
Lauderdale, P., 306, 307, 338
Layden, M. A., 97, 131, 175, 196
Lazarus, R. S., 222, 240
Le, B., 104, 137
Leavitt, H. J., 103, 132
Lehmann, H. C., 12, 30
Lemert, E. M., 226, 239
Lennard, H. L., 114, 134
Lepper, M. R., 109, 135
Leventhal, H., 145, 162
Levine, R., 112, 132
Levinger, G., 190, 196
Levinson, D. J., 245, 282
Levinson, H., 222, 239
Levi-Strauss, C., 8, 30
Levy, A. S., 95, 131
Levy, R. I., 221, 234, 239
Lewin, K., 16, 18, 19, 20, 22, 30
Lewis, C. S., 221, 224, 228, 229, 230, 235–236, 239
Lewis, H. B., 169, 174, 196
Lewis, P., 151, 160
Lewis, S. H., 88, 124
Lewis, S. K., 112, 127
Libby, W. L., 152, 160
Lichten, W., 102, 103, 134
Lifton, R. J., 221, 223, 226, 230, 236, 239
Lightner, J. M., 94, 130, 336, 339
Lindemann, E., 221, 222, 240
Linton, R., 6, 7, 30
Lippa, R., 97, 104, 125, 132, 157, 162
Lippitt, R., 19, 30
Lloyd, B. B., 83
Lofland, J., 226, 240
Lofland, L. H., 234, 240
Loftus, E. F., 116, 127
Lopata, H. Z., 221, 222, 223, 225, 227, 240, 245, 282
Lopyan, K. J., 95, 124
Lowell, E. L., 14, 30
Luce, R. D., 103, 133
Ludwig, L. M., 154, 161
Lusk, R., 96, 104, 128
Lykken, D. T., 105, 133
Lynch, J. J., 222, 240

McKay, D. M., 144, 162
McArthur, L. Z., 176, 195, 196
McCabe, C., 227, 240
McCall, G., 206, 218, 245, 282, 286, 291, 300, 302
McCleary, R., 298, 302
McClelland, D. C., 14, 30
McCrae, R. R., 245, 281
McDougall, W., 16, 30, 170, 197
McDowall, J. J., 85, 133
McEachern, A. W., 7, 29, 288, 290, 301
McElrea, C. E., 179, 197
McGhie, A., 104, 133
McGuire, W. J., 69, 82
McMahon, L., 88, 132
Macy, J., Jr., 103, 133
Magnusson, D., 13, 28, 151, 161, 288, 301
Maher, B. A., 104, 133
Mandelbaum, D. G., 221, 240
Malone, T. W., 85, 137
Malpass, R. S., 108, 133
Mandler, G., 11, 14, 30, 111, 116, 133
Manicas, P. T., 34, 53
Manis, J. G., 245, 282
Manko, G., 109, 126
Markus, H., 21, 30, 105, 106, 121, 125, 133
Marris, P., 221, 222, 240
Marshall, V. W., 233, 240
Marston, W. M., 300, 302
Martin, J. A., 85, 137
Marx, K., 57, 60, 82
Mash, M., 97, 132
Maslach, C., 95, 135
Mason, W. S., 7, 29, 288, 290, 301
Matarazzo, J. D., 105, 122, 130
Matter, C. F., 142, 162
May, M. A., 12, 14, 29, 288, 301, 310, 338

Mayo, C., 114, 123, 132
Mazze, K., 178, 196
Mead, G. H., 6, 30, 108, 133, 169, 170, 197, 201, 218, 226, 240
Meerloo, T. A. M., 113, 133
Mehrabian, A., 92, 101, 102, 103, 104, 112, 113, 122, 133, 141, 143, 146, 148, 154, 162, 182, 197, 308, 313, 337, 340
Meiselman, K. C., 104, 133
Meltzer, B., 200, 218, 245, 282
Mendelsohn, R. I., 289, 292, 295, 301
Menges, R. J., 113, 133
Merton, R. K., 6, 30, 55, 83
Michela, J. L., 177, 197
Middlemist, R. D., 142, 162
Mileski, M., 289, 302
Milgram, S., 181, 197
Miller, D. T., 112, 133
Miller, G. A., 102, 103, 133, 134
Miller, J. G., 101, 134
Miller, R. E., 104, 105, 127
Mills, J., 190, 195
Mischel, W., 12, 30, 69, 73, 82, 83, 109, 130, 151, 162, 178, 196, 290, 302, 308, 309, 311, 340
Mobbs, N. A., 100, 134, 154, 162
Mohr, L. B., 296, 302
Monat, A., 222, 240
Monson, T., 71, 83, 94, 96, 97, 111, 112, 126, 136, 321, 332, 337, 338, 340, 341
de Montmollin, G., 17, 31
Moos, R. H., 69, 83, 222, 240
Moreno, J. L., 19, 30
Morley, I. E., 100, 135
Morley, J., 221, 240
Morton, T. L., 190, 197
Moscovici, S., 17, 30, 114, 134
Mueller, R. A. H., 103, 132
Mullens, S., 142, 163
Mullins, N. C., 15, 20, 30
Murphy, G., 112, 132, 226, 240
Murray, E., 104, 134
Murray, H. A., 12, 31
Myers, D. G., 17, 31
Myers, H., 271, 282

Nagel, S. S., 297, 302
Natale, M., 123, 134
Neely, K. K., 102, 134
Neubauer, D. W., 298, 302
Nevill, D., 156, 163
Newman, R. C., 153, 163
Newtson, D., 106, 134
Nisbet, R. A., 236, 240
Nisbett, R. E., 177, 196
Norman, S. A., 112, 133
Nowicki, S., Jr., 155, 158, 160, 323, 340

Odbert, H. S., 10, 27
Olson, C., 104, 108, 125
Olson, J. M., 97, 138
Oltman, P. K., 99, 138
Orbach, C. E., 229, 240
Orland, L., 292, 302
Orlofsky, J., 322, 323, 330, 339
Osborne, A. F., 17, 31

Padgett, V. R., 113, 134
Palmore, E., 114, 134
Park, R. A., 203, 218
Parkes, C. M., 221, 222, 226, 230, 238, 240
Parsons, T., 4, 6, 7, 31, 33 ff., 53
Passer, M. W., 177, 197
Patterson, M. L., 142, 143, 147, 150, 151, 154, 158, 163, 320, 322, 327, 336, 337, 339, 340
Payne, J. W., 82
Pearce, W. B., 102, 112, 134
Pederson, D. M., 154, 163
Pennebaker, J. W., 167, 179, 197
Pepinsky, H. E., 298, 302
Pepitone, A., 18, 31, 112, 134
Peppers, L. G., 221, 240
Perkowitz, W. T., 85, 87, 89, 91, 98, 128
Perlmutter, H. V., 17, 31

Perrin, R. G., 236, 240
Petras, J. W., 200, 218
Petty, R. E., 336, 340
Pfeiffer, J. W., 110, 111, 134
Pichert, J. W., 173, 194, 197
Pine, V. R., 221, 240
Pittman, T. S., 111, 137
Planalp, S., 89, 134
Plath, D. W., 234, 240
Polanyi, M., 35, 53, 166, 167, 168, 197
Pollack, D., 153, 163
Pollack, I., 103, 137
Pomeroy, S. B., 43, 53
Pope, B., 100, 136
Pope, C. E., 294, 295, 302
Prados, M., 222, 241
Preiss, J., 290, 302
Pruitt, D. G., 17, 31
Pryor, J. B., 179, 197

Quarantelli, E. L., 236, 240
Quattrone, G. A., 175, 197

Rajecki, D. W., 155, 158, 163, 323, 327, 337, 339, 340
Rarick, D. L., 97, 104, 130, 134
Raven, B., 188, 196
Redfield, R., 4, 31
Reed, H., 92, 101, 103, 112, 113, 133
Regan, D. T., 109, 134, 183, 197
Reidhead, S., 320, 322, 327, 340
Reis, H. T., 97, 139
Reiss, A. J., Fr., 250, 282, 285, 289, 296, 302, 303
Reynolds, D. K., 221, 239
Reynolds, L. T., 200, 218
Richard, L. M., 97, 126
Riggio, R. E., 105, 129
Roethlisberger, F. J., 19, 31
Roger, D. B., 153, 163
Rogers, C. R., 107, 134
Rogers, P. L., 103, 104, 135
Rogers, T. B., 105, 106, 134
Rokeach, M., 108, 134
Romano, J., 142, 163
Rommetveit, R., 102, 112, 134
Rosch, E., 73, 83
Rosenberg, M., 253, 257, 282
Rosenblatt, P. C., 221, 241
Rosenfeld, H. M., 88, 89, 119, 135, 146, 163
Rosenthal, R., 102, 104, 105, 122, 128, 135
Rosow, I., 245, 246, 282, 283
Ross, L., 109, 121, 135
Rotter, J. B., 108, 135, 155, 163, 323, 340
Rubin, L. B., 244, 280, 283
Rubin, Z., 245, 283
Rubinow, S., 144, 164
Rubinstein, C., 273, 283
Ruderman, A. J., 176, 198
Runkel, P. J., 113, 135
Rushton, F. P., 154, 160
Rutter, D. R., 100, 135, 152, 153, 163, 164

Sacks, H., 88, 135
Salatas, H., 70, 83
Sales, E., 244, 283
Sampson, E. E., 97, 135
Sanders, C. M., 221, 241
Santee, R. T., 95, 135
Saranson, S., 244, 283
Sarason, S. B., 11, 14, 30
Schachter, S., 20, 29, 31, 147, 164, 180, 197
Schaefer, D., 179, 198
Schalekamp, E. E., 153, 163
Schank, R. C., 178, 186, 197, 307, 340
Schechter, E., 88, 124
Scheflen, A. E., 323, 340
Schegloff, E. A., 88, 135
Scheier, M. F., 95, 129, 135, 136, 180, 195, 320, 325, 338
Schermer, B., 123, 131, 319, 322, 323, 339
Schopler, J., 155, 164
Schmitt, E. P., 203, 218

Schoenberg, B., 221, 241
Schutz, A., 169, 170, 182, 197
Schutz, W. C., 121, 136
Scott, J., 245, 282
Secord, P. F., 35, 37, 44–48, 53, 286, 288, 300, 303
Segall, D. O., 105, 129
Seidman, A., 271, 283
Sennett, R., 235, 241
Sentis, K., 105, 106, 133
Shalker, T., 184, 196
Shapiro, D. A., 113, 132
Shaver, K. G., 285, 286, 304
Shaver, P., 310, 340
Shaw, M. E., 17, 31, 308, 340
Shennum, W. A., 156, 164
Shepard, H. A., 20, 27
Sherif, M., 19, 31
Sheskin, A., 221, 241
Shibuya, Y. A., 113, 136
Shields, L., 243, 244, 251, 275, 280, 283
Shils, E. A., 33, 53
Shuttleworth, F. K., 12, 29, 288, 301
Siegman, A. W., 100, 136, 154, 164
Sigal, J. J., 236, 242
Sillars, A. L., 320, 341
Simmel, G., 203, 218
Simmons, J., 206, 218, 245, 282, 291, 302
Simmons, R. G., 257, 282
Singer, J. E., 20, 31, 147, 164
Skelton, J. A., 179, 197
Smith, A. L., 113, 136
Smith, J., 105, 106, 133
Smith, R. E., 51, 53
Snyder, M., 14, 31, 71, 83, 96, 97, 104, 120, 121, 125, 136, 156, 158, 164, 309, 311, 312, 321, 332, 333, 340, 341
Soldow, G. F., 97, 104, 130, 134
Solomon, L. K., 176, 196
Sommer, R., 142, 152, 161, 164
Sontag, S., 244, 283
Sorokin, P. A., 4, 31
Sparks, R., 289, 299, 301
Spence, J. T., 15, 31
Springfield, D. O., 14, 29
Srull, T. K., 93, 102, 108, 138
Stanley, J. C., 260, 267, 281
Stannard, D. E., 221, 233, 241
Stark, W., 4, 31
Steeno, J., 123, 131, 319, 322, 323, 339
Stegner, S. G., 174, 195
Steiner, I. D., 15, 31
Steinmetz, J., 109, 135
Stephan, W., 112, 137
Stephenson, B., 111, 137, 193, 197
Stephenson, G. M., 152, 153, 164
Stern, K., 222, 241
Stiles, W. B., 320, 324, 341
Stoddart, R. M., 115, 125
Storms, M. D., 179, 197
Stotland, E., 170, 185, 197
Stoto, M., 85, 137
Strack, F., 109, 135, 175, 197
Stratton, L. O., 152, 162
Strauss, A. L., 245, 281
Strauss, E., 109, 134, 183, 197
Strauss, M. E., 154, 163
Strickland, B. R., 120, 137, 323, 340
Strodbeck, F. L., 19, 27
Stroebe, M., 109, 137
Stroebe, W., 109, 137
Stryker, S., 200, 203, 204, 205, 211, 212, 213, 218
Stuart, I. R., 285, 286, 300
Suchotliff, L., 103, 129
Sudnow, D., 289, 303
Suffet, F., 289, 303
Sullivan, H. S., 226, 241
Sumby, W. H., 103, 137
Super, D. E., 268, 283
Swann, W. B., Jr., 97, 111, 136, 137
Sykes, R. E., 300, 303

Tajfel, H., 21, 31
Tanford, S., 155, 156, 162, 323, 327, 328, 337, 339, 340

Tanke, E. D., 97, 136
Taranta, A., 104, 105, 129
Taylor, S. E., 88, 93, 102, 104, 108, 132, 137, 167, 170, 176, 179, 197, 198
Teddlie, C., 142, 164
Tesser, A., 167, 198
Thibaut, J. W., 20, 29, 31, 38, 40, 42, 53, 170, 186, 196, 198
Thomas, C., 221, 227, 241
Thomas, D. S., 203, 218
Thomas, E. A. C., 85, 137
Thomas, E. J., 10, 32
Thomas, W. I., 202, 203, 218
Thompson, A., 88, 124
Thorndike, R. L., 17, 32
Thorne, A., 183, 195
Thorne, B., 123, 130
Tiger, L., 45, 53
Timmons, W. M., 17, 32
Tinder, G., 235, 241
Tolman, E. C., 68
Tonnies, F., 1 ff, 32, 236, 241
Touhey, J. C., 306, 341
Tourangeau, R., 145–146, 164
Town, J. P., 94, 130, 336, 339
Tracy, K., 89, 134
Travis, L. E., 16, 32
Triandis, H. C., 112, 113, 114, 137
Triplett, N., 17, 32
Tripodi, T., 183, 196
Turk, A. T., 294, 295, 301
Turner, J., 104, 137
Turner, M., 322, 324, 337, 339
Turner, R. H., 7, 32, 33, 53, 226, 241, 245, 283, 290, 303
Tversky, A., 116, 137, 179, 198
Tyler, H., 292, 302

Ungs, T., 296, 303
U.S. Department of Labor, 244, 251, 263, 271, 272, 283

Vacchiano, R. B., 109, 110, 137
Valdez, E., 97, 125
Vallacher, R. R., 21, 32, 112, 132, 167, 175, 178, 182, 186, 198
Veitch, R., 337, 338
Vick, C. F., 113, 137
Vinokur, A., 17, 27
Volkart, E. H., 221, 234, 241

Waldo, G. P., 292, 295, 301
Walker, G. R., 95, 124
Walker, M., 183, 195
Wallace, A. F. C., 236, 241
Wallace, S. E., 221, 223, 225, 227, 230, 241
Wallach, M. A., 17, 32
Waller, W., 221, 241
Walsh, P., 221, 241
Walster, E., 109, 112, 128, 137
Walton, M., 155, 164
Warmington, W. A., 50, 52
Warner, R. M., 85, 137
Watson, G. B., 17, 32
Watzlawick, P., 87, 138, 144, 164
Waxer, P., 94, 138, 152, 164
Wedemeyer, D., 225, 241
Wegner, D. M., 21, 32, 166, 167, 168, 171, 174, 176, 178, 179, 180, 186, 187, 196, 198
Weiner, S. L., 88, 119, 138
Weinfeld, M., 236, 242
Weinheimer, S., 88, 132
Weiss, R. S., 220, 221, 222, 223, 225, 229, 234, 238, 245, 283
Welkowitz, J., 85, 129
Wells, G. L., 336, 340
West, L., 123, 139
Whalen, C. K., 155, 160
Wheaton, J., 108, 132
Whitcher, S. J., 147, 164
White, R. K., 11, 12, 19, 30, 32
Whorf, B. L., 113, 138
Wicklund, R. A., 95, 109, 126, 129, 138, 167, 169, 170, 175, 179, 184, 195, 197, 198, 310, 338, 341
Wiener, M., 102, 103, 133, 144, 164
Wiens, A. N., 105, 122, 130

Wilder, D. A., 21, 32, 172, 175, 181, 198
Willerman, L., 291, 303
Williams, E., 152, 164
Williams, G., 222, 241
Williams, J. R., 114, 138
Williams, M., 148, 162, 285, 286, 303
Wilson, G., 99, 138
Wilson, J. Q., 290, 303
Wilson, M., 190, 195
Winokur, G., 221, 238
Witkin, H. A., 14, 32, 98, 99, 138, 156, 159, 164
Wittig, B., 220, 237
Witty, P. A., 12, 30
Wolosin, R. J., 113, 134, 138
Wood, R. V., 113, 137
Worchel, S., 142, 164, 175, 198
Wright, E., 112, 133
Wright, J. W., 70, 82, 170, 195
Wrigley, E. A., 233, 242
Wundt, W., 16, 32
Wyer, R. S., Jr., 93, 102, 108, 116, 138

Yamamoto, J., 221, 234, 242
Yankelovich, D., 271, 283
Yarkin, K. L., 94, 130, 336, 339

Zadny, T., 173, 198
Zajonc, R. B., 17, 32, 112, 138, 182, 198
Zander, A. F., 15, 18, 20, 32
Zanna, M. P., 97, 108, 138
Zavalloni, M., 17, 30
Zehr, H. D., 96, 125
Zimmerman, D. H., 123, 139
Zuckerman, M., 97, 139
Zurcher, L. A., 226, 242

Subject Index

Acquaintance networks, 225–226
Affiliation, 120, 154–155, 155–156
Age-sex role, *see* Sex role
Androgyny, 14–15, 123, 322–323, *see also* Sex role
Attachment, social, 219 ff.
  evolutionary view, 220–221
  kinds of connections
    assistance, 224–225
    linkage to network, 225–226
    maintenance of future, 230–231
    maintenance of self, 226–228
    reality maintenance, 229–230
    role connections, 223–224
    support for myths, 228–229
  patterns of connections, 231–233
    cultural differences, 233–235
Attention
  communication accuracy and, 92, 101
  responsiveness and, 92–100
  selective, 92–93, 100, 108
  social awareness and, 179–182
Attitude
  communication accuracy and, 107–109
  judicial, 297–298
Attraction
  communication accuracy and, 109
  responsiveness and, 90–91
  social awareness and, 182–184
  social exchange and, 40–41
Attractiveness, 109
Attribution, 89, 111–112
  biased, self-serving, 111–112
  dispositional vs. situational, 175–178
  in interactions, 88–89, 94, 97
Authoritarianism
  communication accuracy and, 109–110

Back-channel response, 88, 114
Belief, and expectation, 120–121
Birth order, and social interaction, 323–324

Career Options Program
  description, 247–249
  evaluation, 250 ff.
Channel availability, and communication accuracy, 102–103
Cognition, social, *see* Social cognition
Cognitive complexity, 297–298
Commitment, 200, 207
  in relationships, 41–42
Commodity exchange, *see* Social exchange

Communication
  accuracy, 88–89, 92, 101–112
  channels, 92, 102–103
  content, 103
  encoding and decoding skill, 103–105, 116
  nonverbal aspects, 144–145
  responsiveness in, *see* Responsiveness
Compatability, 121
Compensation, in social interaction, 325–327
Complexity, cognitive, 297–298
Conflict, 4–5
Conformity, 71, 297
Contracts, in social relationships, 3, 61, *see also* Social exchange
Control
  in interaction, 87–88
  need for, 111–112, 120
  nonverbal aspects, 147–148
Conversation topic, 87, 115
Criminal justice system, 285–287, *see also* Discretionary justice
Cross-situational consistency, in behavior, 12–15, 308–312
Culture, variations in attachment, 233–237

Decision making
  group, 17 ff.
  legal, *see* Discretionary justice
Demand characteristics, in research, 306–308
Dependency, *see* attachment
  in groups, 22–25
  in social exchange, 40–42
Dialectics, 4 ff.
  in group theory, 16–21
  in personality theory, 13–15
  in role theory, 6–9
  in social theory, 5–6, 236–237
Discretionary justice
  definition, 185–186
  research, 287–300
    discretion paradigm, 291–292, 294–295
    disparity paradigm, 292–293, 295–298
    evaluation of, 287–288, 299–300
Displaced homemaker, 243 ff.
  definition, 243–244
  national scope, 244–245
  problems of, 245–247
  training for, 247 ff.
Disposition, *see* Personality trait
Dyadic interaction paradigm, 305 ff.
  applications, 335–337
    to personality variables, 336
    to role variables, 336–337
    to situational variables, 337
    to social cognition, 337
  description, 313–317
  evaluation, 317–319, 328–335
  illustrative research, 319–328
Dyadic power, *see* Power

Ecological psychology, 141
Emotion
  effect on communication accuracy, 110–111
  effect on social awareness, 182–184
Empathy, 170, 182, 185
Encoding and decoding skills, and communication accuracy, 103–105, 116
Ethnomethodology, 8–9, 56
Evaluation, of others, 167, 176–177
Exchange, *see* Social exchange
Expectation
  of others, 61–62, 74–75, 101–102, 117, 120–121, 325–327
  role, 74–75, 77*n* ff., 88, 288
Extraversion, *see* Introversion-extraversion
Experimenter, influence of, 306–308
External validity, of experiments, 307–308

Facial expressiveness, 145
Familiarity
  communication accuracy and, 114–115, 117
  social cognition and, 67–70
Family, 2, 323–324
  loss of, 219–237
Feedback, and communication accuracy, 102–103, 145
Femininity, *see* Sex role
Field dependence, *see* Psychological differentiation
Focus of attention, 179–182, 310, 324–325, *see also* Social awareness

Gaze, *see* Nonverbal behavior
Gemeinschaft and Gesellschaft, 1 ff., 236–237
Gender difference, *see* Sex difference
Grief, 220–222, 223 ff., *see also* Attachment
Group, 15 ff., 96
  awareness of, 169–171, 179–182, 188–190, 191–193
  history of research, 15 ff.
  ingroup-outgroup bias, 21, 175
  polarization of opinion, 17
  productivity, 16–17
  social cognition of, 21 ff., 181
Group dynamics movement, 18 ff.
  assumptions of, 18
Group mind, 16

Halo effect, 176
Help, loss of, 224–225

Identification, 183
Identity, 199–201, 205–208
  definition, 206
  effect of role loss, 246
  empirical issues, 205
  hypotheses, 207–208, 211–213
  religious, 202–213
  role, 36–37
Implicit situation theory, 178
Impression management, 14, 118–120, 147–148, 171
  sex differences in, 122
Influence
  in role relations, 61–67
  self-monitoring and, 97
  social awareness analysis, 187–190
Ingratiation, 60*n*, 189
Ingroup–outgroup bias, 21, 175
Interaction, *see* Social interaction
Interaction commodities, 62 ff., 75
  types of, 62–64
Interaction competencies, 69 ff., 80–82
  definition, 70
  production competency, 71–72
Interaction goals, 88
Interactionism
  personality theory, 13–15, 151–152
  role theory, 56 ff.
Interaction process analysis, 19, 300
Interaction rhythm, 121–122
Internal-external locus of control, *see* Locus of control
Interpersonal attraction, 40 ff., *see also* Attraction
Intersubjectivity, 63–64
Intimacy, 40, 120, 190–193
  development of, 190–192
  nonverbal aspects, 146–147
  problems with, 192–193
Intimacy exchange, 40, 147, 150–151, *see also* Social exchange
Introversion-extraversion, 99–100, 152–153, 155–156, 314
  attention to others and, 100
  communication accuracy and, 104–105
  nonverbal behavior and, 100, 153, 155–156
Involvement behavior, 150, 319–320, *see also* Nonverbal behavior

Justice, *see* Discretionary justice

Law-and-order scale, 296
Liking, 182–184, *see also* Attraction
Locus of control, 153
  nonverbal behavior and, 156
  social interaction and, 323
Loneliness, *see* Attachment
Loss, 219 ff., *see also* Attachment
  devastating, 235–236

Maintenance, of interaction, 86–87
Marital selection, 37 ff.
Masculinity, *see* Sex role
Memory
  interaction skill and, 115–117
  social awareness and, 174–175, 176–177
Moderator variables, in personality, 14–16, 69*n*, 309–312
Mood, 116, 184
Motivation, for interaction, *see also* Social interaction
  individual characteristics, 120–123
  influence of interaction partners, 119–120
  responsiveness and, 117–118
  situational influences, 118–119

Natural will vs. rational will, 4–5, *see also* Gemeinschaft and Gesellschaft
Need for approval, 90
Need for control, 111–112, 120
Nonverbal behavior, 102–103, 141 ff., 321–324
  abnormal populations, 152–154
  approach-avoidance, 152–153, 155–156
  functional analysis, 143–149
    evaluation of, 149–150
  gaze, 114, 152–153, 156
  involvement behavior, 150, 319–320
    definition, 150
    personality correlates, 151–157
  measures of, 142–143, 151–152, 319–320
  research, changes in, 141–143
  sex differences, 122–123
  spatial behavior, 142, 146, 151–156
Norm, 51, 56 ff., 65, 69, 78*n*
  social awareness and, 186–187

Objective self awareness, *see* Self awareness
Other awareness, 169–171, 179–182, 188–190, 191–193, *see also* Social awareness
Outcome dependency, 112

Penal philosophy scale, 296
Perception
  distortion in, 105–112, 298
  as instigator of social awareness, 179–182
  of persons, 175–177
Person perception, 175–177
Personality, 141, 290–291, 308–312, *see also* Personality trait
  correlational approach, 333–335
  criminal justice decisions and, 290–291, 295–298
  definition of, 10, 151
  interactionist approach, 13–15, 151–152
  interaction with role and situation, 287–288
  measurement of, 309–312
  moderator variables, 14–16, 69*n*, 309–312
  nonverbal correlates, 151–156
  research strategy, 332–333, *see also* Dyadic interaction paradigm
  situational influence, 310–312
  social behavior and, 327–328
  sociological approach, 15, 200, 207, 290–291
  trait approach, 10–15, 308–312, *see also* Personality trait

Personality development, effect of unresponsiveness, 90
Personality theory, dialectical processes, 10–15
Personality trait, 10–15, 308–312, *see also* Personality; specific trait
  criticism of, 12–13, 15, 308–312
  definition, 10
  generality vs. specificity, 12–13, 308–310
  individual vs. common, 11–12, 14
  research strategies, 310–312, *see also* Dyadic interaction paradigm
  single act vs. multiple act measures, 13–14, 309–310
Perspective taking, 64, 70–71, 173–174, *see also* Social awareness
  direct solicitation, 185–186
  in interaction, 65–66
  role effect on, 186–187
Posture mirroring, 323
Power, 38 ff.
  dyadic, 38–42, 45–48
  nonverbal aspects, 147–148, 159
  structural, 38, 42–45, 48–51
Predictability, and control, 87–88
Prejudice, 324
Private self consciousness, *see* Self consciousness
Proxemics, *see* Nonverbal behavior
Psychological differentiation, 14–15, 98–99, 156–157
  definition, 99, 156
  nonverbal behavior and, 99, 154–155, 157
  self disclosure and, 99
  social behavior and, 99
Psychopathology
  communication accuracy and, 104
  nonverbal behavior and, 152–154
Public self consciousness, *see* Self consciousness
Race, and social interaction, 324
Reciprocation, in social interaction, 325–327
Regulation of interaction, nonverbal aspects, 145–146
Relationships, 38 ff.
  intimate, 40, *see also* Intimacy
Religious role, 208–216
  identity theory analysis, 211–216
  measurement, 209–211
Representation, cognitive, 172–178, *see also* Schema; Social cognition
  opaque, 175–177
    definition, 175–176
  structure of, 177–178
  transparent, 173–175
    definition, 173–174
Repression, and communication accuracy, 110–114
Response elaboration, 86
Response relevance, 86
Response repertoire, and responsiveness, 115–117
Responsiveness, 85 ff.
  consequences of, 86–90
    attraction of, 90–91
    attribution, 89
    communication accuracy, 88–89
    facilitation of interaction goals, 88
    focus on conversation topic, 87
    maintenance of interaction, 86–87
    personality development, 90
    predictability, 87–88
  determinants of, 91–92
    attention to partner, 92–100
    communication accuracy, 101–115
    motivation, 117–123
    response repertoire, 115–117
  nature of, 85–86
Role, 6–9, 33–37, 51–52, 94, 199–200, 204, 205, *see also* Attachment; Identity; Sex role; Social position

Role [*cont.*]
asocialist position, 56–58, 72–77
change in, 34 ff.
commitment, 207
constructive aspects, 7–9, 56 ff., 101–102, 205
in criminal justice, 287–298
definition, 6–7, 34, 55, 73, 75–82
dialectic trends, 6–9
differentiation from self, 226*n*
discretion in, 285–291
displaced homemaker, 243–247
expectations, shared, 7, 36, 77*n*–79*n*, 288
as interaction competency, 77–82
interaction with personality and situation, 287–288
limits on behavior, 72–77
loss of, 245–247
network, 223–226, 231–237
nonverbal behavior and, 148–149
prototype, 74
religious, 208–216
social awareness and, 186–187
subject role, in experiment, 306–308
transformational model, 34–37
Role change, 34–37, 51–52
problems encountered, 245–247
Training for, 247–249
Role partner, 38, 51, 223–224
loss of, 223–224
Role playing, constructive aspects of, 7–9
Role relationships, 51
attention and, 94
responsiveness and, 119–120
Role-set variables
definition, 293
in discretionary justice, 287–298
Role taking, 14, 170, *see also* Other awareness

Schema, 93, 102, 105–109, 121, *see also* Representation; Social awareness
Script, 67–70, 76–77, 178, 307
social awareness and, 186–187
Selective attention, *see* Attention, selective
Self, 6, 105–107, 121, 199–200, 202–203
dependence on others, 226–228
development of, 202
identity theory analysis, 205–208
performed vs. phenomenal, 7
social aspects, 10
symbolic interactionist analysis, 201–205, 226*n*, *see also* Symbolic interactionism
Self awareness, 167, 169–171, 179–180, 183–184, 188–193, 310, 324–325
focal, 170–172, 179–180
tacit, 169–172
Self consciousness, 90, 114, 172, 180, *see also* Self awareness
definition, 95
effect on attention to others, 94–96
effect on communication accuracy, 104
responsiveness and, 96
Self disclosure
psychological differentiation and, 99
sex difference, 123
Self esteem, effect of role loss, 246
Self-monitoring, 14, 70–71, 90, 96–98, 312
definition, 157
effect on attention to others, 97–98
effect on communication accuracy, 104
nonverbal aspects, 157, 159
social interaction and, 321
Self presentation, 7–8, 66, 171
Self-schema, *see* Schema; Self
Sex difference, 37, 43 ff.
in communication accuracy, 104
in social interaction, 122–123, 321–323
Sex ratio, 45–51

Sex role, 14–15, 37–38, 43 ff., 122–123
effect of sex ratio, 45–51
homemaker role, 243–247
retraining of, 247–249
social interaction and, 321–323, 333–334
stereotypic belief, 44–45
Similarity, effect on communication accuracy, 112–114, 121
Situated identity, 307, *see also* Identity
Situation
communication accuracy and, 101–102
criminal justice decisions and, 288–290, 294–295
cues, in experiments, 306–308
effect on attention, 92–93
expectation of, 101–102
interaction with role and personality, 287–288
strong vs. weak, 310–312, 332–333
structured vs. unstructured, 311, 318, 331
Social anxiety, 154–155, 157–158
Social approach-avoidance, 152–155, 157–158, 325
Social awareness, 165 ff., 324–325, *see also* Group, awareness of; Other awareness; Self awareness
affective instigators, 182–184
evaluation, 182–184
mood, 184
attentional instigators, 179–182
cue target, 180–182
target salience, 179–180
focal, 166 ff.
definition, 166–167
primary forms, 169–171
symbolic instigators, 184–187
direct solicitation, 184–186
norms, roles and scripts, 186–187
tacit, 166 ff.
definition, 167–168
Social bond, *see* Attachment
Social change, 33–36, 205
Social cognition, 55–56, 65–74, 76 ff., 105 ff., 165–178, 337, *see also* Representation; Schema; Social awareness
contextualization, 67–70, 81–82
of groups, 21–25
of others, 172–178
of roles, 76–77
routinization, 67–70, 81–82
of self, 105–112, 166–172, *see also* Self awareness; Self consciousness
Social contract, *see* Contract
Social control, *see* Control
Social evaluation, 173–174
Social exchange, 3, 8, 38–43, 57 ff.
commitment, 41–42
criticism of, 39–40
interaction commodities, 62–64, 69, 75
interaction competencies, 70–72, 77–82
power and, 38
social structure and, 79–80
Social facilitation, 16–17
Social field, 22–25, *see also* Group
Social interaction, *see* Motivation, for interaction
conflict, 4–5
constructive aspects, 60 ff.
contextualization of, 67–70
dependence vs. independence, 16, 21, 22–25
effect of expectancy, 325–327
exchange features, 38–42, 58–62, *see also* Social exchange
external variable approach, 335–337
personality, 336
role, 336–337
situation, 337
instrumental orientation, 57 ff.
maintenance of, 86–87
market relations, 79–80
mastery of, 65–70

Social interaction [*cont.*]
measures of, 317, 319–320
perspective taking in, 65–66
regulation of, 145
responsiveness in, *see* Responsiveness
routinization of, 67–70
sequential properties, 85, 124
sex difference in, 122–123
structural approach, 335
Social norm, *see* Norm
Social position, 199–200, 204, 205, *see also* Status
Social power, *see* Power
Social role, *see* Role
Social self, 10, 170, *see also* Self
Social skills, interaction competencies, 70–72
Social status, *see* Status
Social structure, 1–9, 33–36, 56 ff., 79–82, 202, 204, 217
cognitive view, 22–25
influence of relationships, 42–45
mortality and, 233
Socialization, 34, 36
Socio-economic status, *see* Status
Status, 93, 148, 250, *see also* Social position
definition, 7
Stereotype, 108–109
Stress
role loss and, 245–246
unpredictability and, 87–88
Structural frame, 64 ff., 141, *see also* Social structure
Structural-functionalism, 6–7, 33–34
Structural power, *see* Power
Symbolic interactionism, 6–9, 13, 55–56, 199–205, 245
analysis of role change, 245–247
assumptions, 203–205
definition, 202–203
development of self, 202–203
historical development, 201–203, 206*n*
significant symbols, 202, 204

Tacit knowledge, 35, 166–172, 178 ff., *see also* Social awareness, tacit
Test anxiety, 11
Thought sampling, 179–180, 336
Topic of conversation, effect on response elaboration, 115
Training
as a determinant of communication accuracy, 105
for role change, 247–249
Trait, *see* Personality trait
Turn-taking, 146

Unresponsiveness, 90–91, *see also* Responsiveness
Unstructured interaction paradigm, *see* Dyadic interaction paradigm

Zeigarnik effect, 19, 174